Essential Readings in
Health Psychology

Essential Readings in Health Psychology

Edited by
Jane Ogden

Open University Press
Maidenhead

Open University Press
McGraw-Hill Education
McGraw-Hill House
Shoppenhangers Road
Maidenhead
Berkshire
England
SL6 2QL

email: enquiries@openup.co.uk
world wide web: www.openup.co.uk

and Two Penn Plaza, New York, NY 10121-2289, USA

First published 2008

A catalogue record of this book is available from the British Library

ISBN-13: 978 0 335 211388 (pb) 978 0 335 211395 (hb)
ISBN-10: 0 335 211380 (pb) 0 335 211399 (hb)

Library of Congress Cataloging-in-Publication Data
CIP data applied for

Typeset by Wearset Ltd, Boldon, Tyne and Wear
Printed and bound in Great Britain by Bell and Bain Ltd, Glasgow

Contents

Health Psychology: A Textbook

Also available: *Health Psychology: A Textbook,* 4th edition, **by Jane Ogden**
ISBN: 9780335222636 (Softback)   9780335222643 (Hardback)
Available from www.openup.co.uk

This Essential Readings follows the structure of the same author's *Health Psychology: A Textbook*, which has made a major contribution to the teaching and study of this rapidly expanding discipline. The market-leading textbook in the field, *Health Psychology* is essential reading for all students and researchers of health psychology. It will also be invaluable to students of medicine, nursing and allied health. Retaining the breadth of coverage, clarity and relevance that has made it a favourite with students and lecturers, the fourth edition has been thoroughly revised and updated.

Key features:

- new chapter on women's health issues, exploring recent research into pregnancy, miscarriage, birth, menopause and related areas
- new 'Problems' boxes analyse health psychology research and identify the shortcomings and limitations of research in the area
- updated 'Focus on Research' examples introduce you to contemporary topics and emerging areas for research in health psychology, including exercise, smoking and pain
- the new edition includes new data, graphs and further reading, plus suggestions about where you can access the most recent publications and other data
- revised end-of-chapter review questions
- Online Learning Centre which hosts web links and multiple-choice questions for students, plus supporting teaching resources for lecturers.

Below is a brief table of contents.

If you wish to use this reader as a supplementary text alongside the textbook, we have provided a list of readings from *Essential Readings in Health Psychology* alongside the related chapters in the textbook:

Reading in *Essential Readings in Health Psychology*	Corresponding chapters in *Health Psychology*
Mokdad, A.H., Marks, J.S., Stroup, D.F. and Gerberding, J.L. (2004) Actual causes of death in the United States, 2000	Chapter 1: An introduction to health psychology Chapter 2: Health beliefs
Kaplan, R.M. (1990) Behavior as the central outcome in health care	Chapter 1: An introduction to health psychology Chapter 2: Health beliefs
Sutton, S. (1998) Predicting and explaining intentions and behaviour: how well are we doing?	Chapter 2: Health beliefs Chapter 5: Smoking and alcohol use Chapter 6: Eating behaviour Chapter 7: Exercise Chapter 8: Sex Chapter 9: Screening
Ogden, J. (2003) Some problems with social cognition models: a pragmatic and conceptual analysis	Chapter 2: Health beliefs Chapter 5: Smoking and alcohol use Chapter 6: Eating behaviour Chapter 7: Exercise Chapter 8: Sex Chapter 9: Screening
West, R. (2005) Time for a change: putting the Transtheoretical (Stages of Change) Model to rest	Chapter 2: Health beliefs Chapter 5: Smoking and alcohol use Chapter 6: Eating behaviour Chapter 7: Exercise Chapter 8: Sex Chapter 9: Screening
Armitage, C.J. (2005) Can the theory of planned behaviour predict the maintenance of physical activity?	Chapter 2: Health beliefs Chapter 7: Exercise
Murgraff, V., White, D. and Phillips, K. (1999) An application of protection motivation theory to riskier single-occasion drinking	Chapter 2: Health beliefs Chapter 5: Smoking and alcohol use
DiClemente, C.C., Prochaska, J.O., Fairhurst, S.K. et al. (1991) The process of smoking cessation: an analysis of precontemplation, contemplation, and preparation stages of change	Chapter 2: Health beliefs Chapter 5: Smoking and alcohol use
Wardle, J. and Beales, S. (1988) Control and loss of control over eating: an experimental investigation	Chapter 2: Health beliefs Chapter 6: Eating behaviour
Woodcock, A.J., Stenner, K. and Ingham, R. (1992) Young people talking about HIV and AIDS: interpretations of personal risk of infection	Chapter 2: Health beliefs Chapter 8: Sex Chapter 14: HIV and cancer: psychology throughout the course of illness (1)
Aiken, L.S., West, S.G., Woodward, C.K. et al. (1994) Increasing screening mammography in asymptomatic women: evaluation of a second-generation, theory-based program	Chapter 2: Health beliefs Chapter 9: Screening

Reading in *Essential Readings in Health Psychology*	Corresponding chapters in *Health Psychology*
Gollwitzer, P.M. and Sheeran, P. (2006) Implementation intentions and goal achievement: a meta-analysis of effects and processes	Chapter 2: Health beliefs
Roter, D.L., Stewart, M., Putnam, S.M. et al. (1997) Communication pattern of primary care physicians	Chapter 4: Doctor–patient communication and the role of health professionals' health beliefs
Mead, N. and Bower, P. (2000) Patient-centredness: a conceptual framework and review of the empirical literature	Chapter 4: Doctor–patient communication and the role of health professionals' health beliefs
Marteau, T.M., Senior, V., Humphries, S.E. et al. (2004) Psychological impact of genetic testing for familial hypercholesterolemia within a previously aware population: a randomized controlled trial	Chapter 3: Illness cognitions Chapter 4: Doctor–patient communication and the role of health professionals' health beliefs Chapter 9: Screening
Horne, R. and Weinman. J. (2002) Self-regulation and self-management in asthma: exploring the role of illness perceptions and treatment beliefs in explaining non-adherence to preventer medication	Chapter 3: Illness cognitions Chapter 4: Doctor–patient communication and the role of health professionals' health beliefs
Simpson, S.H., Eurich, D.T., Majumdar, S.R. et al. (2006) A meta-analysis of the association between adherence to drug therapy and mortality	Chapter 2: Health beliefs Chapter 3: Illness cognitions Chapter 4: Doctor–patient communication and the role of health professionals' health beliefs Chapter 13: Placebos and the interrelationship between beliefs, behaviour and health
Everson, S.A., Lynch, J.W., Chesney, M.A. et al. (1997) Interaction of workplace demands and cardiovascular reactivity in progression of carotid atherosclerosis: population based study	Chapter 10: Stress Chapter 11: Stress and illness Chapter 15: Obesity and coronary heart disease: psychology throughout the course of illness (2)
Pereira, D.B., Antoni, M.H., Danielson, A. et al. (2003) Life stress and cervical squamous intraepithelial lesions in women with human papillomavirus and human immunodeficiency virus	Chapter 10: Stress Chapter 11: Stress and illness
Ebrecht, M., Hextall, J., Kirtley, L.G., et al. (2004) Perceived stress and cortisol levels predict speed of wound healing in healthy male adults	Chapter 10: Stress Chapter 11: Stress and illness
Pennebaker, J.W. (1997) Writing about emotional experiences as a therapeutic process	Chapter 3: Illness cognitions Chapter 10: Stress Chapter 11: Stress and illness
Petrie, K.J., Booth, R.J. and Pennebaker, J.W. (1998) The immunological effects of thought suppression	Chapter 10: Stress Chapter 11: Stress and illness Chapter 14: HIV and cancer: psychology throughout the course of illness (1)
Eccleston, C., Morley, S., Williams, A. et al. (2002) Systematic review of randomised controlled trials of psychological therapy for chronic pain in children and adolescents, with a subset meta-analysis of pain relief	Chapter 12: Pain
Smith, J.A. and Osborn, M. (2007) Pain as an assault on the self: an interpretative phenomenological analysis of the psychological impact of chronic benign low back pain	Chapter 12: Pain
Taylor, S.E. (1983) Adjustment to threatening events: a theory of cognitive adaptation	Chapter 3: Illness cognitions Chapter 13: Placebos and the interrelationship between beliefs, behaviour and health Chapter 14: HIV and cancer: psychology throughout the course of illness (1)

continued

Reading in *Essential Readings in Health Psychology*	Corresponding chapters in *Health Psychology*
Petrie, K.J., Cameron, L.D., Ellis, C.J. et al. (2002) Changing illness perceptions after myocardial infarction: an early intervention randomized controlled trial	Chapter 3: Illness cognitions Chapter 15: Obesity and coronary heart disease: psychology throughout the course of illness (2)
Antoni, M.H., Carrico, A.W., Duran, R.E. et al. (2006) Randomized clinical trial of cognitive behavioral stress management on human immunodeficiency virus viral load in gay men treated with highly active antiretroviral therapy	Chapter 3: Illness cognitions Chapter 10: Stress Chapter 11: Stress and illness Chapter 14: HIV and cancer: psychology throughout the course of illness (1)
Ogden, J., Clementi, C. and Aylwin, S. (2006) The impact of obesity surgery and the paradox of control: a qualitative study	Chapter 6: Eating behaviour Chapter 15: Obesity and coronary heart disease: psychology throughout the course of illness (2)
Rapkin, B.D. and Schwartz, C.E. (2004) Toward a theoretical model of quality-of-life appraisal: implications of findings from studies of response shift	Chapter 17: Measuring health status: from mortality rates to quality of life

Acknowledgements

This book has been a long time coming due to having children, life being busy, decisions about which papers to include and the administration that was originally going to be involved in putting the book together. However, given the support by McGraw-Hill to obtain permissions, this task was not as onerous as I expected. I am therefore grateful to the following: Katy Hamilton at McGraw-Hill for organising permissions for the different papers that are now included in the book; John Weinman for his comments on my list of papers, and for helping me to think through what should and should not be covered; Harry and Ellie for giving me that ever elusive work–life balance; the psychologists who invented sticker charts for getting children to bed on time; and to David Armstrong for looking after me (when I allow it) and for making life interesting.

Introduction and overview

Health psychology was first established as a formal part of psychology over 20 years ago. Nowadays, it remains increasingly popular for students at both the undergraduate and postgraduate level. New undergraduate modules and Masters courses are being set up each year and Stage 2 training has become a popular career move for many graduates. My textbook in health psychology was first published in 1996 and is now in its fourth edition. It provides a broad analysis and description of the main theories, methods and practices used within health psychology. This reader in health psychology aims to offer a selection of papers to promote a more in-depth understanding of the theories, methods and publication processes used within the discipline. To this end I have selected 29 papers that reflect the spread of health psychology research, which can be read by students and researchers alike who wish to supplement what they have been taught and read as part of their studies. Health psychology can be broadly broken down into five main areas. The papers in this reader reflect these areas as follows: the context of health psychology, health behaviours, health care, stress and health, and chronic illness.

Choosing the papers

I initially decided to compile this reader about ten years ago when my textbook was first published. I failed abysmally (as you can see by the date of publication!), in the main due to an inability to decide upon which papers to include (and exclude); choosing papers that I felt other people should read turned out to be a lot more complicated than I ever imagined. Here is an abbreviated version of how I finally decided upon the papers, and the framework I used. A more detailed justification and discussion of each paper can be found in the commentaries at the start of each part of the book.

- *The classics:* I originally assumed that I would select papers that were deemed 'classics' in health psychology and that I would identify those that every student '**should**' read. On going through the literature, however, I realised that health psychology doesn't really have many classic papers but reflects a more incremental approach to research and theory with each paper adding something to the existing literature but no one paper being absolutely core to that literature. In addition, I realised that the papers that probably are considered 'classics', such as those describing a theory, model or method for the first time, are often not that great upon reading them. The 'classic' part of the paper is often embedded within 'non-classic' parts and even the classic part is often unclear or not clearly articulated, probably due to this being the authors' first airing of their ideas which are better articulated in their later work. In addition, the new theory, model or method can be understood just as well (or better in some cases) by reading secondary sources which can synthesise it in a more focused and accessible way. This reader does not contain many 'classic' papers by the conventional meaning of the term.

- *Good examples:* Rather than including classic papers I have therefore opted to include 'good examples' of particular theories, models and methods. I have selected papers that provide a clear description of how the theories or models have been operationalised and provide 'best case' versions of how the different theories can be tested and applied. I have also included papers that reflect 'best case' versions of different methods.

- *Methodology:* Health psychology draws upon a range of methodologies, including quantitative methods such as cross-sectional surveys, experimental designs and prospective studies, and qualitative methods of data collection such as focus groups and interviews. It also uses approaches such as systematic reviews, meta-analyses, narrative reviews and critical analyses. The papers selected present a range of these different methodologies.

- *Area of study:* Health psychology studies a range of behaviours such as diet, smoking, alcohol intake and screening. It also explores the psychological factors involved in chronic illnesses such as cancer, coronary heart disease and diabetes. The papers have been selected to cover the span of these different areas of study.

- *Time frame:* There is often a tendency within research to prioritise recent publications over older ones. In part, this is aimed at making the reader believe that the book or paper being written is up to date. In part, it is due to a belief that research gets better over time. For this reader I have selected papers from the past few decades of health psychology. Where areas have been fast moving with new methodological developments I have selected recent publications, but where ideas have been best stated in the past I have included older papers.

- *Country of origin:* Researchers in health psychology are prolific and the journals are full of research that comes from all over the world. I have selected only papers in English and I have tried to select papers from a variety of countries.

- *Discipline:* Although this is a reader in health psychology a good health psychologist should be aware of research in other disciplines such as epidemiology, health service research, medicine and medical sociology. Although most of the papers chosen are directly within the umbrella of health psychology I have also included a few from other disciplines.

- *Interesting:* My final criterion for selecting papers was that they were interesting to read.

I have therefore identified 29 papers that employ different theories and methods and should offer a more in-depth approach to that covered in my textbook or at an undergraduate level. The selected papers are not a definitive list of good works and in some ways may be seen as idiosyncratic. But they are ones that I feel provide students and researchers alike with good case examples of health psychology work and by reading them people should have a better insight into what health psychology research can (and cannot) achieve.

The structure of this book

This book is divided into five parts which reflect five broad areas of health psychology research, each of which starts with a commentary on why I think the papers within that part make a useful contribution to the discipline. Part 1 refers to the **context of health psychology**, and highlights the importance of behaviour in understanding health and illness. Part 2 focuses on **health behaviours** and highlights the theoretical debates that have been held about the different theories. This part then provides good examples of empirical studies that have used the different theories. These have been chosen for their clarity and detail and because they provide a spread across the different health behaviours including diet, smoking, safer sex and alcohol use. This part ends with examples of interventions that have been developed to change behaviour. Part 3 highlights a range of **approaches to health care**, and provides papers on communication, illness cognitions, adherence, the self-regulatory model and screening. Part 4 focuses on **stress and health**, and emphasises the more biological aspects of health psychology. Papers within this part cover the link between stress and illness, and assess a range of mechanisms to explain this association including cardiovascular reactivity, immune function, behaviour and emotional expression. Finally, Part 5 focuses on **chronic illness** and provides papers on cancer, coronary heart disease obesity, pain and AIDS. In addition, this part contains a paper on the response shift which is an interesting addition to the literature on quality of life.

How to use this book

My textbook has provided the structure for choosing these papers. This reader could therefore be used as an adjunct to the textbook to provide more detail than that covered in a more general text. However, the structure of the reader also follows the key areas highlighted by the British Psychological Society as central to health psychology. The reader could therefore be used alongside any undergraduate or postgraduate course to provide good examples of key theories, models and methods. It could also provide the starting point for a reading list to accompany an undergraduate or postgraduate course, or the papers could be used to focus a seminar discussion or a journal club. In addition, the papers are published in their entirety, including their reference lists, which can be used to develop reading lists and recommend further reading.

PART 1

The context of health psychology

Part contents

Commentary

The traditional biomedical model emphasised biological factors such as viruses, lesions or bacterium as the main causes of illness, and its treatments focused on medication or surgery. From this perspective psychological factors were seen as possible consequences of illness but their role in its etiology was considered minor; having a heart attack may be distressing and being diagnosed as having cancer may make the person depressed but such psychological factors were conceptualised only as the result of the illness. Over the past century, however, such a perspective has been challenged and psychological variables are increasingly seen as relevant at all stages along the continuum from health to illness, and central to this shift has been the recognition that behaviour is at the core of any understanding of why someone becomes ill, how they manage their illness and how their illness progresses. Furthermore, as the main causes of death these days are chronic illness such as heart disease, cancer and diabetes, which are linked to behaviours such as eating, drinking, smoking and adherence to medication, behaviour is seen as central to both the onset of illness and its management. This focus on psychological factors, particularly behaviour and the cognitions and emotions that relate to behaviour, is the domain of health psychology. This part presents two papers that clearly highlight the importance of behaviour and provide the context to health psychology:

Mokdad, A.H., Marks, J.S., Stroup, D.F. and Gerberding, J.L. (2004) Actual causes of death in the United States, 2000. *Journal of the Amercan Medical Association*, 29 (10): 1238–45.

Kaplan, R.M. (1990) Behaviour as the central outcome in health care, *American Psychologist*, 45 (11): 1211–20. Reprinted with kind permission of the American Psychological Association.

Mokdad et al. (2004) present an analysis of the role that behaviours such as smoking, diet, activity, alcohol consumption, car crashes and sexual behaviour played in the deaths of the 2.4 million people who died in 2000 in the USA. Their analysis is based upon a search of papers that identified a link between risk behaviours and mortality to give them an estimate of how many of the disease-related deaths could be accounted for by a particular behaviour. They then multiplied this by the data on actual causes of deaths in the year 2000. For example, from the literature they estimated what proportion of deaths by cancer could be accounted for by diet. They then multiplied this estimate by the number of people who actually died from cancer in the year 2000. Then, by collating all these figures, they arrived at the total number of deaths (regardless of disease) attributable to each behaviour. This paper is interesting as it illustrates how to analyse secondary data and provides an insight into the language, statistics and methods of epidemiology and statistical modelling. It also illustrates how to answer a question that is central to much health psychology literature as the awareness of the link between behaviour and mortality forms the starting point for much research.

Mokdad et al. (2004) therefore emphasise behaviour as a predictor and cause of illness and mortality. In contrast, while still highlighting the importance of behaviour, the paper by Kaplan (1990) describes the importance of behaviour as an outcome variable. In particular, this theoretical piece describes how traditional research focuses on the impact of interventions on outcomes such as cell pathology, blood pressure, lesion size and cardiac output. Kaplan then argues that such outcomes are flawed in several ways and that behavioural outcomes are more useful. First, he suggests that biological outcomes often lack validity and reliability; second, he suggests that they rely on behavioural measures to give them their validity; third, he suggests that a focus on biological outcomes has sometimes led researchers down the wrong and occasionally dangerous path; and finally, he argues that even classic outcomes such as mortality and morbidity are essentially behavioural outcomes in disguise. In addition, he suggests that a behavioural conceptualisation of health does not negate a medical model but offers a broader perspective, and that medical interventions such as medicines and surgery should be seen as complementing those that aim to change behaviour. This paper is much earlier than that by Mokdad et al. (2004) and was published when health psychology was still in its early stages. In its time it was ground breaking as it presented a challenge to contemporary biomedical perspectives on health research. It remains highly relevant today, however, as many researchers, journal editors and clinicians still prioritise medical explanations and medical outcomes and see these as more 'real' than those that focus on behaviour. Furthermore, in a discipline such as health psychology which often sits on the edge of medicine, a researcher has to decide whether to 'go native' with medicine or fight the corner for psychological perspectives. This paper provides ammunition for a more fighting approach.

In summary, these two papers provide a context to health psychology, and illustrate why much of health psychology research is concerned with predicting, explaining or changing health-related behaviours.

Mokdad, A.H., Marks, J.S., Stroup, D.F. and Gerberding, J.L. (2004) Actual causes of death in the United States, 2000. *Journal of the American Medical Association*, 291 (10): 1238–45.

Actual causes of death in the United States, 2000

Ali H. Mokdad, PhD
James S. Marks, MD, MPH
Donna F. Stroup, PhD, MSc
Julie L. Gerberding, MD, MPH

Author Affiliations: *Division of Adult and Community Health (Dr Mokdad), Office of the Director (Drs Marks and Stroup), National Center for Chronic Disease Prevention and Health Promotion and Office of the Director (Dr Gerberding). Centers for Disease Control and Prevention, Atlanta, Ga.*

Abstract

Context: Modifiable behavioral risk factors are leading causes of mortality in the United States. Quantifying these will provide insight into the effects of recent trends and the implications of missed prevention opportunities.

Objectives: To identify and quantify the leading causes of mortality in the United States.

Design: Comprehensive MEDLINE search of English-language articles that identified epidemiological, clinical, and laboratory studies linking risk behaviors and mortality. The search was initially restricted to articles published during or after 1990, but we later included relevant articles published in 1980 to December 31, 2002. Prevalence and relative risk were identified during the literature search. We used 2000 mortality data reported to the Centers for Disease Control and Prevention to identify the causes and number of deaths. The estimates of cause of death were computed by multiplying estimates of the cause-attributable fraction of preventable deaths with the total mortality data.

Main Outcome Measures: Actual causes of death.

Results: The leading causes of death in 2000 were tobacco (435 000 deaths; 18.1% of total US deaths), poor diet and physical inactivity (400 000 deaths; 16.6%), and alcohol consumption (85 000 deaths; 3.5%). Other actual causes of death were microbial agents (75 000), toxic agents (55 000), motor vehicle crashes (43 000), incidents involving firearms (29 000), sexual behaviors (20 000), and illicit use of drugs (17 000).

Conclusions: These analyses show that smoking remains the leading cause of mortality. However, poor diet and physical inactivity may soon overtake tobacco as the leading cause of death. These findings, along with escalating health care costs and aging population, argue persuasively that the need to establish a more preventive orientation in the US health care and public health systems has become more urgent.

Corresponding Author: Ali H. Mokdad, PhD, Division of Adult and Community Health, 4770 Buford Hwy, NE, Mailstop K66, Atlanta, GA 30341 (amokdad@cdc.gov).

In a seminal 1993 article, McGinnis and Foege[1] described the major external (nongenetic) modifiable factors that contributed to death in the United States and labeled them the "actual causes of death." During the 1990s, substantial lifestyle pattern changes may have led to variations in actual causes of death. Mortality rates from heart disease, stroke, and cancer have declined.[2] At the same time, behavioral changes have led to an increased prevalence of obesity and diabetes.[3]

Most diseases and injuries have multiple potential causes and several factors and conditions may contribute to a single death. Therefore, it is a challenge to estimate the contribution of each factor to mortality. In this article, we used published causes of death reported to the Centers for Disease Control and Prevention (CDC) for 2000, relative risks (RRs), and prevalence estimates from published literature and governmental reports to update actual causes of death in the United States – a method similar to that used by McGinnis and Foege.

Methods

Our literature review used a MEDLINE database search of English-language articles that identified epidemiological, clinical, and laboratory studies linking risk behaviors and mortality. Our search criteria were to include all articles including the following key words: *mortality, smoking, physical activity, diet, obesity, alcohol, microbial agents, toxic agents, motor vehicle, firearms, sexual behavior, illicit drug use.* Our search allowed for words with similar meaning to be included (ie, exercise as well as physical activity). The search was initially restricted to articles published during or after 1990, but we later included relevant articles published in 1980 to December 31, 2002 (search strategies are available from the authors on request). For each risk factor, we used the prevalence and RR identified by the literature search. To identify the causes and number of deaths, we used mortality data reported in 2000 to the CDC.[4] We used no unpublished information or data.

We used the following formula to calculate attributable fractions for each disease: $[(P_0 + \Sigma P_i (RR_i)) - 1]/[P_0 + \Sigma P_i (RR_i)]$, in which P_0 is the percentage of individuals in the United States not engaging in the risk behavior, P_i is the percentage engaging in separate categories of the risk behavior, and RR_i is the RR of death for each separate category relative to none. For instance, in the case of smoking, P_0 is the percentage of persons who never smoked, P_i is the percentage of former smokers, P_2 is the percentage of current smokers, RR_i is the RR of a certain type of death for former smokers compared with those who never smoked, and RR_2 is the RR of death for current smokers compared with those who never smoked. We then multiplied estimates of the cause-attributable fraction of preventable deaths by total mortality data. Whenever possible, we used RRs of death and mortality data by other variables such as age, sex, and race.

We estimated ranges for our estimated number of deaths by using the smallest and highest RRs and their boundaries when available. When data were available, we used specific underlying causes of death in deriving some of our estimates (ie, firearms, motor vehicles, and illicit drug use). Further details of these methods may vary due to availability of data and are presented in each section below. We used SAS (version 8.2, SAS Institute Inc, Cary, NC) and SUDAAN (version 8.0, Research Triangle Institute, Research Triangle Park, NC) statistical software.

Results

The number of deaths in the United States in 2000 was 2.4 million, which is an increase of more than 250 000 deaths in comparison with the 1990 total, due largely to population growth and increasing age.[2,4] Leading causes of death were diseases of the heart (710 760), malignant neoplasms (553 091), and cerebrovascular diseases (167 661) (Table 1).

Table 1 Leading causes of death in the United States in 2000*

Cause of Death	No. of Deaths	Death Rate per 100 000 Population
Heart disease	710 760	258.2
Malignant neoplasm	553 091	200.9
Cerebrovascular disease	167 661	60.9
Chronic lower respiratory tract disease	122 009	44.3
Unintentional injuries	97 900	35.6
Diabetes mellitus	69 301	25.2
Influenza and pneumonia	65 313	23.7
Alzheimer disease	49 558	18.0
Nephritis, nephrotic syndrome, and nephrosis	37 251	13.5
Septicemia	31 224	11.3
Other	499 283	181.4
Total	**2 403 351**	**873.1**

* Data are from Minino et al.[4]

Tobacco

We used methods and software used in previous CDC reports to compute the annual smoking-attributable mortality for 2000.[5,6] As in previous reports, we used RRs for each cause of death from the American Cancer Society's Cancer Prevention Study II[7] and included deaths due to secondhand smoking.

We used data from the Behavioral Risk Factor Surveillance System (BRFSS), a cross-sectional telephone survey conducted by state health departments with the CDC's assistance, to determine changes in US smoking prevalence from 1995–1999 to 2000. A detailed description of survey methods is available elsewhere.[8] A slight decline in smoking was observed from 1995–1999 to 2000. The prevalence of smoking in 1995–1999 was 22.8% for current smokers (males: 25.1%; females: 20.6%), 24.1% for former smokers (males: 28.3%; females: 20.3%), and 53.1% for never-smokers (males: 46.5%; females: 59.2%). In 2000, these estimates were 22.2% for current smokers (males: 24.1%; females: 20.5%), 24.4% for former smokers (males: 28.3%; females: 20.7%), and 53.4% for never-smokers (males: 47.6%; females: 58.8%).

We estimate that approximately 435 000 deaths were attributable to smoking in 2000, which is an increase of 35 000 deaths from 1990 (Table 2). This increase is due to the inclusion of 35 000 deaths due to secondhand smoking and 1000 infant deaths due to maternal smoking, which were not included in the article by McGinnis and Foege.[1]

Poor diet and physical inactivity

To assess the impact of poor diet and physical inactivity on mortality, we computed annual deaths due to overweight.[9] Recent articles have reported that overweight increased in all segments of the US population.[10,11] To derive the attributable number of deaths due to overweight, we used estimates from the CDC's 1999 and 2000 National Health and Nutrition Examination Surveys.[12] We used the same procedure reported by Allison et al[13] to estimate annual over-weight-attributable deaths. We used the body mass index (BMI) range of 23 to 25 as our reference category to match the method used by Allison et al. Body mass index is calculated as weight in kilograms divided by the square of the height in meters. Using data from the 1999 and 2000 National Health and Nutrition Examination Surveys, the percentages for BMI cut points

Table 2 Actual causes of death in the United States in 1990 and 2000

Actual Cause	No. (%) in 1990*	No. (%) in 2000
Tobacco	400 000 (19)	435 000 (18.1)
Poor diet and physical inactivity	300 000 (14)	400 000 (16.6)
Alcohol consumption	100 000 (5)	85 000 (3.5)
Microbial agents	90 000 (4)	75 000 (3.1)
Toxic agents	60 000 (3)	55 000 (2.3)
Motor vehicle	25 000 (1)	43 000 (1.8)
Firearms	35 000 (2)	29 000 (1.2)
Sexual behavior	30 000 (1)	20 000 (0.8)
Illicit drug use	20 000 (<1)	17 000 (0.7)
Total	**1 060 000 (50)**	**1 159 000 (48.2)**

* Data are from McGinnis and Foege.[1] The percentages are for all deaths.

were less than 23 (22.3%), 23 to less than 25 (15.09%), 25 to less than 26 (7.49%), 26 to less than 27 (7.36%), 27 to less than 28 (6.23%), 28 to less than 29 (6.30%), 29 to less than 30 (5.94%), 30 to 35 (16.95%), and more than 35 (12.62%).

We used hazard ratios reported previously[13] to recompute annual deaths for 6 major population-based studies. The mean estimate of the total number of overweight-attributable deaths in 2000 was 494 921. For the Alameda County Health Study, the estimated number of overweight-attributable deaths in 2000 was 567 683; Framingham Heart Study, 543 981; Tecumseh Community Health Study, 462,005; American Cancer Society Cancer Prevention Study I, 451 708; Nurses Health Study, 504 602; and the National Health and Nutrition Examination Survey I Epidemiologic Follow-up Study, 439 548.[14–19]

As in the study by Allison et al, the estimate for the attributable number of deaths for non-smokers or never-smokers was higher than the estimate for the total because smoking is associated with both lower body weight and higher mortality. Also in 2000, the mean estimate of the total number of overweight-attributable deaths among nonsmokers or never-smokers was 543 797. For the Alameda County Health Study, the estimate of overweight-attributable deaths among nonsmokers or never-smokers was 639 026; Framingham Heart Study, 583 913; Tecumseh Community Health Study, 457 460; American Cancer Society Cancer Prevention Study I, 466 729; Nurses Health Study, 570 855; and the National Health and Nutrition Examination Survey I Epidemiologic Follow-up Study, 544 798. Our estimates indicate an increase of 76.6% over the 1991 estimate of overweight-attributable deaths, with more than 80% of excess deaths occurring among individuals with class 2 and 3 obesity.

The prevalence of overweight used in this study is based on data from 1999–2000. Because the effects of overweight on mortality may not appear until some years after a person becomes overweight, it is likely that the increase in prevalence of overweight in the 1990s overestimates the current actual number of deaths. However, the total number of deaths from the 1999–2000 data may well be the expected number of deaths in the next few years. Thus, we believe a more accurate and conservative estimate for overweight mortality in 2000 such as 385 000, which is the rounded average of 2000 and 1991 estimates (494 921 and 280 184).

Overweight would account for the major impact of poor diet and physical inactivity on mortality.[20] Diet may have a minor additional effect on mortality mainly from lack of certain essential nutrients.[21,22] Consumption of fruits and vegetables increased in the 1990s,[23] and fat intake as a percentage of calories declined.[24] Physical activity has increased slightly.[25] We estimate that poor diet and physical inactivity will cause an additional 15 000 deaths a year, although this too may be conservative. Nutritional deficiencies alone (*International Classification of Diseases, 10th Revision [ICD-10]* codes E40–E64) were reported as the causes of 4242 deaths in 2000.

We estimate that 400 000 deaths were attributable to poor diet and physical inactivity, an increase of one third from 300 000 deaths estimated by McGinnis and Foege,[1] and the largest increase among all actual causes of death. However, poor diet and physical inactivity could account for even more deaths (>500 000) when the 1999–2000 prevalence estimates of overweight have their full effect.

Alcohol consumption

We used 2 large nationally representative surveys to determine US alcohol consumption. The National Health Interview Survey, a household survey that measured alcohol intake in 1999 and 2000, and the BRFSS, a telephone survey that measured alcohol intake in 1999.[8,26]

We used RRs from the Australian National Drug and Safety Report that were based on mortality rates derived from pooled data of several studies.[27,28] The RR values were 1.33 for hazardous drinking (4.01–6.00 drinks/d for males and 2.01–4.00 for females) and 1.47 for harmful drinking (≥6.01 drinks/d for males and ≥4.01 for females) in contrast to low levels of drinking (0.26–4.00 drinks/d for males and 0.26–2.00 for females) and abstinence (0–0.25 drinks/d for both males and females).

We used BRFSS data to compute the number of alcohol-attributable deaths for the US population aged 18 years or older. The BRFSS also asked questions about binge drinking (ie, ≥5 drinks per occasion). To account for the effect that respondents appeared not to include binge drinking in their reported regular drinking, we reran our analyses, adding 5 drinks per binge occasion to average drinks per day. The total number of deaths attributable to alcohol was 103 350.

We also used 3 other recent studies to estimate alcohol-attributable mortality. Two studies were based on the National Health Interview Survey[29,30] and the National Alcohol Survey.[31] Using all-cause mortality and RRs from these studies, we estimated approximately 60 000 deaths per year. This difference in number of deaths is mainly due to the fact that BRFSS respondents report a higher percentage of heavy drinking than do respondents in a household survey such as the National Health Interview Survey.

In another approach, we aggregated alcohol-related deaths from specified *ICD* codes that were summed to provide an overall estimate of deaths. In 2000, 18 539 deaths were reported as alcohol-induced (*ICD-10* codes F10, G31.2, G62.1, 142.6, K29.2, K70, R78.0, X45, X65). In addition, 16 653 persons were killed in alcohol-related crashes.[32] We estimate another 34 797 deaths in 2000 using BRFSS alcohol consumption data and disease-specific RRs from the Australian study for oropharyngeal, esophageal, liver, laryngeal, and female breast cancers; stroke; hypertensive heart disease; and other chronic liver disease and cirrhosis (*ICD-10* code K73-74). This totals to 69 989 deaths in 2000 from these factors alone. In the Australian study, all-cause mortality was also higher than the summation of cause-specific mortality.

Total alcohol-attributable deaths would reach about 140 000 if mortality among previous alcohol drinkers were included. It is unclear whether excess mortality among former alcohol drinkers is due to damage or illness from past alcohol consumption.

Taking these various numbers into account, our best estimate for total alcohol attributable deaths in 2000 is approximately 85 000, based on the conservative estimate from cause-specific deaths and the high estimate using all-cause mortality. This is a reduction of 15 000 deaths from the 1990 estimates.

Microbial agents

We excluded human immunodeficiency virus (HIV) from this category and included it with sexual behaviors to be consistent with the analysis by McGinnis and Foege.[1] In the past, infectious agents were the leading cause of mortality.[33] These agents still present a major threat to the nation's health and are associated with high morbidity.[34] Several improvements in the health system have led to a decline in mortality from infectious diseases. The increase in US immunization rates led to a decline in mortality from many vaccine-preventable diseases.[33–37] Several laws ensure this high immunization rate for children by requiring vaccination for school and day-care enrollment.[38] There also have been substantial improvements in sanitation and hygiene, antibiotics and other antimicrobial medicines, and hospital-infection control.[35]

In 2000, influenza and pneumonia accounted for 65 313 deaths, septicemia for 31 224, and tuberculosis for 776.[4] In general, mortality from infectious and parasitic diseases has declined since 1990.[33] Because pneumonia and septicemia occur at higher rates among patients with cancer, heart disease, lung disease, or liver disease, some of these deaths really are attributable to smoking, poor diet, and alcohol consumption.[39–43] We estimate that approximately 75 000 deaths were attributable to microbial agents in 2000 from all *ICD-10* codes for infectious and parasitic mortality. The major cause of the decline was a decrease in deaths from influenza and pneumonia probably reflecting at least in part an increase in immunization in older adults against vaccine-preventable diseases. This contrasts with 90 000 deaths attributed to microbial agents in 1990 estimates.

Toxic agents

Estimating the number of deaths due to toxic agents is more challenging than any of the other risk factors due to limited published research and the challenges of measuring exposure and outcome. In the 1990s, many improvements were made in controlling and monitoring pollutants.[44] There is more systematic monitoring of pollutants at state and county levels, and exposure to asbestos, benzene, and lead have declined.[44] In fact, the US Environmental Protection Agency reported a decline of 25% from 1970 to 2001 in 6 principal air pollutants: carbon monoxide, lead, ozone, nitrogen dioxide, sulfur dioxide, and particulate matter.[45]

Toxic agents are associated with increased mortality from cancer, respiratory, and cardiovascular diseases.[46–49] We used the National Morbidity, Mortality, and Air Pollution Study to estimate mortality due to air pollution.[50] The study assessed the association between air pollution and mortality and morbidity in 90 cities in the United States. Only particulate matter (PM) was associated with a significant increase in mortality – an approximate 0.5% increase in total mortality for each 10-μ/m^3 increase in PM_{10}. Previous studies reported a range of 0.4% to 1% for that association.[51,52] We used 23.8 μ/m^3 as the daily average of PM_{10} concentration in 2000,[45] which results in an estimate of 24 000 deaths per year (range, 22 000–52 000 deaths) from air pollution alone.

The National Institute for Occupational Safety and Health (NIOSH) estimates that about 113 000 deaths are due to occupational exposure from 1968 to 1996.[53] The number of deaths caused by occupational exposure has declined during that period. In 1996, NIOSH estimated 3119 deaths from pneumoconiosis and 1176 from asbestosis. Although, particulate air pollution accounts for the majority (about 60%) of mortality related to toxic agents,[54] indoor air pollution, environmental tobacco smoke, radon, lead in drinking water, and food contamination are associated with increased mortality.[55,56] We estimate that toxic agents (excluding environmental tobacco exposure) were associated with 2% to 3.5% of total mortality in 2000. We estimate approximately 55 000 deaths attributable to toxic agents in 2000. This estimate is our least certain of the various causes.

Motor vehicles

Motor-vehicle crashes involving passengers and pedestrians resulted in 43 354 deaths in 2000.[4] This decline from 47 000 deaths in 1990 represents successful public health efforts in motor-vehicle safety.[57,58] Deaths from alcohol-related crashes declined from 22 084 in 1990 to 16 653 in 2000.[32] Major contributing factors include the use of child safety seats and safety belts,[59,60] decreases in alcohol-impaired driving,[61] changes in vehicle and highway design,[62,63] and national goals to reduce motor-vehicle-related mortality and injury.[64] We estimate that approximately 26 500 deaths in 2000 were attributable to motor-vehicle crashes in which alcohol was not a factor. This is an increase of 1500 from the 1990 report because both estimates were not adjusted for the number of registered vehicles, number of crashes, nor miles of travel. We included alcohol-related deaths to stress that efforts to educate the public and enforce laws against driving while intoxicated have accounted for most of the decline in deaths related to motor-vehicle crashes.

Firearms

Firearm-related incidents resulted in 28 663 deaths among individuals in the United States in 2000.[4] This is a decline from approximately 36 000 deaths in 1990. The largest declines were in deaths from homicides and unintentional discharge of firearms. In 2000, 16 586 deaths were due to intentional self-harm (suicide) by discharge of firearms (*ICD-10* codes X72–X74). Assault (homicide) by discharge of firearms (*ICD-10* codes X93–X95) resulted in 10 801 deaths. Unintentional discharge of firearms (*ICD-10* codes W32–W34) resulted in 776 deaths, while discharge of firearms, undetermined intent (*ICD-10* codes Y22–Y24), resulted in 230 deaths. The remaining 270 deaths were due to legal intervention (*ICD-10* code Y35). These numbers were ascertained from death certificate reports.

Sexual behavior

Sexual behavior is associated with an increased risk of preventable disease and disability.[65] An estimated 20 million persons are newly infected with sexually transmitted diseases each year in the United States.[66,67] Mortality from sexually transmitted diseases is declining due to the availability of earlier and better treatment, especially for HIV.[67,68] In 2000, HIV disease (*ICD-10* codes B20–B24) resulted in 14 578 deaths. In 1990, HIV was the cause of 27 695 deaths for persons older than 13 years, indicating about a 48% decline in HIV mortality during the decade. Based on the sexual behavior-attributable fraction from the literature,[69–71] we estimate that 20 000 deaths (range, 18 000–25 000 deaths) in 2000 were due to sexual behavior–mainly HIV; other contributors were hepatitis B and C viruses and cervical cancer. The decline of 10 000 deaths from the 1990 estimates[1] was due to the decline in HIV mortality.

Illicit use of drugs

Illicit drug use is associated with suicide, homicide, motor-vehicle injury, HIV infection, pneumonia, violence, mental illness, and hepatitis.[27,28,72–77] An estimated 3 million individuals in the United States have serious drug problems.[78,79] Several studies have reported an undercount of the number of deaths attributed to drugs by vital statistics;[80] however, improved medical treatments have reduced mortality from many diseases associated with illicit drug use. In keeping with the report by McGinnis and Foege,[1] we included deaths caused indirectly by illicit drug use in this category. We used attributable fractions to compute the number of deaths due to illicit drug use.[27,28,81] Overall, we estimate that illicit drug use resulted in approximately 17 000 deaths in 2000, a reduction of 3000 deaths from the 1990 report.

Other factors

Several other factors contribute to an increased rate of death. There are factors that we do not know of such as unknown pollutants or perhaps exposures that may cause a considerable number of deaths. Poverty and low education levels are associated with increased mortality from many causes,[82,83] partly due to differential exposure to the risks described above. However, controlling for differential exposure to risk factors is unlikely to explain the entire impact on mortality. Lack of access to proper medical care or preventive services is associated with increased mortality.[84] Biological characteristics and genetic factors also greatly affect risk of death.[85] In most studies we reviewed, low education levels and income were associated with increased risk of cardiovascular disease, cancer, diabetes, and injury. The Healthy People 2010 initiative has made the elimination of health disparities, especially racial and ethnic disparities, a primary goal.[86]

Comment

We found that about half of all deaths that occurred in the United States in 2000 could be attributed to a limited number of largely preventable behaviors and exposures. Overall, we found relatively minor changes from 1990 to 2000 in the estimated number of deaths due to actual causes. Our findings indicate that interventions to prevent and increase cessation of smoking, improve diet, and increase physical activity must become much higher priorities in the public health and health care systems.

The most striking finding was the substantial increase in the number of estimated deaths attributable to poor diet and physical inactivity. We estimate that roughly 400 000 deaths now occur annually due to poor diet and physical inactivity. The gap between deaths due to poor diet and physical inactivity and those due to smoking has narrowed substantially. Because rates of overweight increased rapidly during the 1990s, we used a conservative approach to make our estimates, accounting for the delayed effects of overweight on mortality. In addition, overweight lessens life expectancy.[87,88] However, it is clear that if the increasing trend of overweight is not reversed over the next few years, poor diet and physical inactivity will likely overtake tobacco as the leading preventable cause of mortality.

The most disappointing finding may be the slow progress in reducing tobacco-related mortality. A few states, notably California, have had major success in programs that led to reducing deaths from heart disease and cancer.[89] However, efforts in most other states are too recent or short-term to have a similar effect. In response to the increase in tobacco use among youth in the early 1990s, state and national tobacco-control efforts increased their focus on prevention of initiation and recognized the importance of cessation on reducing smoking-related deaths. Thus, most national and state efforts now address comprehensive program strategies.[90] Current tobacco-control efforts will also need strong cessation components to show a decline in tobacco deaths in a future assessment. Recent reports on the effects of telephone quit lines for smokers are encouraging.[91] On the other hand, large state budget shortfalls are leading to large cuts in public health, with a corresponding diversion of resources from tobacco taxes and settlement dollars to cover deficits instead of tobacco-control programs.

Despite the call to action on these risk factors a decade ago, there has been little progress in reducing the total number of deaths from these causes. The progress that has occurred primarily involves actual causes of death that are less prominent. With the shift in the age distribution of the population, more adults now are in the age group at highest risk because of the cumulative effects of their behavior. The net effect is that both total deaths and total burden due to the actual causes have increased.

Our analyses have several limitations. Our study reported actual causes of mortality in the United States. However, these causes are also associated with a large morbidity burden. In addition to premature death, years of lost life, diminished productivity, and high rates of disability, decreased quality of life is also strongly associated with these actual causes. A recent World Health Organization report finds these actual causes of death to be the leading causes of total disease burden, not just mortality, in the developed world.[92] Because we used self-reported estimates for some risk behaviors, (ie, prevalence of alcohol intake) they may have been underestimated. Finally, using all-cause mortality may result in overestimates of the number of deaths from specific causes. In addition, if the effect of the risk factor is age-dependent, then age- and sex-specific estimates are preferable.

Our analyses did not assess the effect of genetics. Genetic factors have been associated with several diseases discussed herein.[85] Much of the impact of genetics is likely mediated through increased physical susceptibility to these behavioral and other modifiable risks. However, increases in obesity and diabetes cannot be due to widespread changes in the human genome over the last 10 years. Nevertheless, genetics offers great potential for treating and ameliorating risk. Identifying individuals at higher risk for a disease through genetic testing may promote lifestyle changes that can help prevent the onset of that disease.[93]

In this study we also did not examine the effects of high blood pressure and cholesterol or lipid profile on mortality, although some of the effects of these factors are mediated through poor diet and physical inactivity. These risk factors are common among adults in the United States. More than 30% of US adults have high blood pressure or high cholesterol.[94 95] Monitoring and controlling blood pressure and cholesterol is crucial to preventing premature mortality and morbidity.

One of the most difficult aspects of this analysis is that the attribution of the actual cause that led to death varies depending on perspective. We used similar methods to those used by McGinnis and Foege[1] to allow comparisons. We tried when possible to use RRs that are fully adjusted for other risk factors in our analyses, but possibly not eliminating duplicate attribution of causes. We also explicitly included some deaths in more than 1 category (eg, alcohol and motor vehicle crashes) when choosing another category seemed as though it might artificially constrain interpretation for future prevention programs.

In summary, smoking and the deaths attributed to the constellation of poor diet and physical inactivity currently account for about one third of all deaths in the United States. The rapid increase in the prevalence of overweight means that this proportion is likely to increase substantially in the next few years. The burden of chronic diseases is compounded by the aging effects of the baby boomer generation and the concomitant increased cost of illness at a time when health care spending continues to outstrip growth in the gross domestic product of the United States. In ancient times, Hippocrates stated that "the function of protecting and developing health must rank even above that of restoring it when it is impaired." The findings in this study argue persuasively for the need to establish a more preventive orientation in health care and public health systems in the United States.

Notes

Author Contributions: Dr Mokdad had full access to the data in this study and takes full responsibility for the scientific integrity of the data and the accuracy of the analysis and content of the manuscript.

Study concept and design: Mokdad, Marks, Stroup, Gerberding.

Acquisition of data: Mokdad, Stroup, Gerberding.

Analysis and interpretation of data: Mokdad, Marks, Stroup, Gerberding.

Drafting of the manuscript: Mokdad, Marks, Stroup, Gerberding.

Critical revision of the manuscript for important intellectual content: Mokdad, Marks, Stroup, Gerberding.

Statistical expertise: Mokdad, Stroup.

Obtained funding: Marks, Gerberding.

Administrative, technical, or material support: Mokdad, Marks, Stroup, Gerberding.

Study supervision: Marks, Gerberding.

Funding/Support: There was no external funding for this work.

Acknowledgment: We acknowledge the valuable contributions of Barbara A. Bowman, PhD, Robert D. Brewer, MD, MSPH, Earl S. Ford, MD, MPH, Wayne H. Giles, MD, James M. Mendlein, PhD, Cheryl Pellerin, Susan Y. Chu, PhD, and Eduardo J. Simoes, MD, MPH.

Role of the Sponsor: The Centers for Disease Control and Prevention reviewed and approved this report before submission.

References

1 McGinnis JM, Foege WH. Actual causes of death in the United States. *JAMA.* 1993;270:2207–2212.

2 *Health, United States 2002.* Rockville, Md: Dept of Health and Human Services, Centers for Disease Control and Prevention; 2002. DHHS Publication No. 1232.

3 Koplan JP, Dietz WH. Caloric imbalance and public health policy. *JAMA.* 1999;282:1579–1581.

4 Minino AM, Arias E, Kochanek KD, Murphy SL, Smith BL. Deaths: final data for 2000. *Natl Vital Stat Rep.* 2002;50:1–120.

5 Annual smoking attributable mortality, years of potential life lost and economic costs: United States 1995–1999. *MMWR Morb Mortal Wkly Rep.* 2002;51:300–303.

6 Centers for Disease Control and Prevention. Smoking-attributable mortality, morbidity, and economic costs. Available at: http://www.cdc.gov/tobacco/sammec. Accessibility verified February 10, 2004.

7 Thun MJ, Day-Lally C, Myers DG, et al. Trends in tobacco smoking and mortality from cigarette use in Cancer Prevention Studies I (1959 through 1965) and II (1982 through 1988). In: *Changes in Cigarette-Related Disease Risks and Their Implication for Prevention and Control: Smoking and Tobacco Control Monograph 8.* Bethesda, Md: US Dept of Health and Human Services, Public Health Service, National Institutes of Health, National Cancer Institute; 1997: 305–382.

8 Mokdad AH, Stroup DF, Giles WH. Public health surveillance for behavioral risk factors in a changing environment: recommendations from the Behavioral Risk Factor Surveillance Team. *MMWR Recomm Rep.* 2003;52:(RR-9)1–12.

9 *Clinical Guidelines on the Identification, Evaluation, and Treatment of Overweight and Obesity in Adults: the Evidence Report.* Rockville, Md: National Institutes of Health, National Heart, Lung, and Blood Institute; 1998.

10 Mokdad AH, Bowman BA, Ford ES, Vinicor F, Marks JS, Koplan JP. The continuing epidemics of obesity and diabetes in the US. *JAMA.* 2001;286:1195–1200.

11 Flegal KM, Carroll MD, Ogden CL, Johnson CL. Prevalence and trends in obesity among US adults, 1999–2000. *JAMA.* 2002;288:1723–1727.

12 Centers for Disease Control and Prevention. Plan and operation of the Third National Health and Nutrition Examination Survey, 1988–94. *Vital Health Stat.* 1994;1:1–307.

13 Allison DB, Fontaine KR, Manson JE, Stevens J, Van Itallie TB. Annual deaths attributable to obesity in the United States. *JAMA.* 1999;282:1530–1538.

14 Berkham LF, Breslow L. *Health and Ways of Living: the Alameda County Studies.* New York, NY: Oxford University Press; 1983.

15 Dawber TR, Meadors GF, Moore FE. Epidemiological approaches to heart disease: the Framingham Study. *Am J Public Health.* 1951;41:279–286.

16 Epstein FH, Napier JA, Block WD, et al. The Tecumseh Study: design, progress and perspectives. *Arch Environ Health.* 1970;21:402–407.

17 Lew EA, Garfinkel L. Variations in mortality by weight among 750,000 men and women. *J Chronic Dis.* 1979;32:563–576.

18 Stampfer MJ, Willett WC, Colditz GA, Rosner B, Speizer FE, Hennekens CH. A prospective study of post-menopausal estrogen therapy and coronary heart disease. *N Engl J Med.* 1985;313:1044–1049.

19 Cox CS, Mussolino M, Rothwell ST, et al. Plan and operation of the NHANES I Epidemiologic Follow-up Study, 1992. *Vital Health Stat 1.* 1997;35:1–231.

20 Blair SN, Nichaman MZ. The public health problem of increasing prevalence rates of obesity and what should be done about it. *Mayo Clin Proc.* 2002;77:109–113.

21 Hu FB, Willet WC. Optimal diets for prevention of coronary heart disease. *JAMA.* 2002;288:2569–2578.

22 Peto J. Cancer epidemiology in the last century and the next decade. *Nature.* 2001;411:390–395.

23 Ruowei L, Serdula M, Bland S, Mokdad A, Bowman B, Nelson D. Trends in fruit and vegetable consumption among adults in 16 US states: Behavioral Risk Factor Surveillance System 1990–1996. *Am J Public Health.* 2000;90:777–781.

24 Ernst ND, Sempos CT, Briefel RR, Clark MB. Consistency between US dietary fat intake and serum cholesterol concentrations: the National Health and Nutrition Examination Surveys. *Am J Clin Nutr.* 1997;66:965S–972S.

25 Physical activity trends – United States, 1990–1998. *MMWR Morb Mortal Wkly Rep.* 2001;50:166–169.

26 Centers for Disease Control and Prevention, National Center for Health Statistics. National Health Interview Survey. Available at: http://www.cdc.gov/nchs. Accessibility verified February 10, 2004.

27 Stevenson RB. *The Quantification of Drug-Caused Mortality and Morbidity in Australia, 1998.* Canberra: Australian Institute of Health and Welfare, Commonwealth Department of Human Services and Health; 2001. Category No. PHE 29.

28 English DR, Holman CDJ, Milne E, et al. *The Quantification of Drug-Caused Morbidity and Mortality in Australia, 1995.* Canberra: Commonwealth Department of Human Services and Health; 1995.

29 Liao Y, McGee DL, Cao G, Cooper RS. Alcohol mortality: findings from the National Health Interview Survey (1988 and 1990). *Am J Epidemiol.* 2000;151:651–659.

30 Dawson DA. Alcohol consumption, alcohol dependence, and all-cause mortality. *Alcohol Clin Exp Res.* 2000;24:72–81.

31 Rehm J, Greenfield TK, Rogers JD. Average volume of alcohol consumption, patterns of drinking, and all-cause mortality: results from the US national alcohol survey. *Am J Epidemiol.* 2001;153:64–71.

32 National Highway Traffic Safety Administration. *Traffic Safety Fact, 2000.* Washington, DC: US Dept of Transportation; 2001.

33 Armstrong GL, Conn LA, Pinner RW. Trends in infectious disease mortality in the United States during the 20th century. *JAMA.* 1999;281:61–66.

34 Simonsen L, Conn LA, Winner RW, Teutsch S. Trends in infectious disease hospitalizations in the United States, 1980–1994. *Arch Intern Med.* 1998;158:1923–1928.

35 Control of infectious disease. *MMWR Morb Mortal Wkly Rep.* 1999;48:621–629.

36 Status report on Childhood Immunization Initiative: reported cases of selected vaccine-preventable diseases – United States, 1996. *MMWR Morb Mortal Wkly Rep.* 1997;46:665–671.

37 Influenza and pneumococcal vaccination levels among persons aged ≥ 65 years – United States, 2001 *MMWR Morb Mortal Wkly Rep.* 2002;51:1019–1024.

38 Vaccination coverage among children enrolled in Head Start programs and licensed child care centers and entering school – United States and selected reporting areas, 1999–2000 school year. *MMWR Morb Mortal Wkly Rep.* 2001;50:847–855.

39 Ortgvist A, Kalin M, Julander I, Mufson MA. Deaths in bacteremic pneumococcal pneumonia: a comparison of two populations – Huntington, WVA, and Stockholm, Sweden. *Chest.* 1993;103:710–16.

40 Valdez R, Narayam KM, Geiss L, Engelgau MM. Impact of diabetes mellitus on mortality associated with pneumonia and influenza among non-Hispanic black and white US adults. *Am J Public Health.* 1999;89:1715–1721.

41 Koziel H, Koziel MJ. Pulmonary complications of diabetes mellitus: pneumonia. *Infect Dis Clin North Am.* 1995;9:65–96.

42 Simonsen L, Clarke MJ, Williamson GD, Stroup DF, Arden NH, Schongerger LB. The impact of influenza epidemics on mortality: Introducing a severity index. *Am J Public Health.* 1997;87:1944–1950.

43 Simonsen L, Clarke MJ, Stroup DF, Williamson GD, Arden NH, Cox NJ. A method for timely assessment of influenza-associated mortality in the United States. *Epidemiology.* 1997;8:390–395.

44 *National Air Quality and Emissions Trends Report, 1999.* Research Triangle Park, NC: US Environmental Protection Agency, Office of Air Quality Planning and Standards; 2001.

45 US Environmental Protection Agency. Air trends – six principal pollutants. Available at: http://www.epa.gov/airtrends/sixpoll.html. Accessibility verified February 10, 2004.

46 Styper P, McMillan N, Gao F, Davis J, Sacks J. Effect of outdoor airborne particulate matter on daily death counts. *Environ Health Perspect.* 1995;103:490–497.

47 Burnett RT, Cakmak S, Brook JR. The effect of the urban air pollution mix on daily mortality rates in 11 Canadian cities. *Can J Public Health.* 1998;89:152–156.

48 Beckett WS. Current concepts: occupational respiratory diseases. *N Engl J Med.* 2000;342:406–413.

49 Peto J. Cancer epidemiology in the last century and the next decade. *Nature.* 2001;411:390–395.

50 Samet JM, Zeger SL, Dominici F, et al. *The National Morbidity, Mortality and Air Pollution Study, Part II: Morbidity and Mortality From Air Pollution in the United States.* Cambridge, Mass: Health Effects Institute; 2000. Research report 94.

51 Katsouyanni K, Touloumi G, Spix C, et al. Short-term effects of ambient sulphur dioxide and particulate matter on mortality in 12 European cities: results from time series data from the Air Pollution and Health: A European Approach project. *BMJ.* 1997;314:1658–1663.

52 Pope CA III, Dockery DW, Schwartz J. Review of epidemiological evidence of health and effects of particulate air pollution. *Inhal Toxicol.* 1995;7:1–18.

53 National Institute for Occupational Safety and Health. Worker health chartbook, 2000. Available at: http://www.cdc.gov/niosh/00-127pd.html. Accessibility verified February 10, 2004.

54 de Hollander AE, Melse JM, Lebret E, Kramers PG. An aggregate public health indicator to represent the impact of multiple environmental exposures. *Epidemiology.* 1999;10:606–617.

55 Khan AS, Swerdlow DL, Juranek DD. Precautions against biological and chemical terrorism directed at food and water supplies. *Public Health Rep.* 2001;116:3–14.

56 Smith KR, Corvalan CF, Kjellstrom T. How much global ill health is attributable to environmental factors? *Epidemiology.* 1999;10:573–584.

57 Motor vehicle safety: a 20th century public health achievement [published correction appears in *MMWR Morb Mortal Wkly Rep.* 1999;48:473]. *MMWR Morb Mortal Wkly Rep.* 1999;48:369–374.

58 Task Force on Community Prevention Services. Motor-vehicle occupant injury: strategies for increasing use of child safety seats, increasing use of safety belts, and reducing alcohol-impaired driving. *MMWR Recomm Rep.* 2001;50(RR-7):1–14.

59 *Traffic Safety Facts 1999: Occupant Protection.* Washington, DC: US Dept of Transportation, National Highway Traffic Safety Administration; 2000. Publication No. DOT HS 809090.

60 Zador PL, Krawchuk SA, Voas RB. Alcohol-related relative risk of driver fatalities and driver involvement in fatal crashes in relation to driver age and gender: an update using 1996 data. *J Stud Alcohol.* 2000;61:387–395.

61 Zaza S, Wright-De Agüero LK, Briss PA, et al. Data collection instrument and procedure for systematic reviews in the guide to community preventive services. *Am J Prev Med.* 2000;18:44–74.

62 Transportation Research Board. *Safety Research for a Changing Highway Environment* Washington, DC: National Research Council, Transportation Research Board; 1990. Special report No. 229.

63 Centers for Disease Control and Prevention and National Highway Traffic Safety Administration. *Position Papers From the Third National Injury Control Conference: Setting the National Agenda for Injury Control in the 1990s.* Washington, DC: US Dept of Health and Human Services, Public Health Service, Centers for Disease Control and Prevention; 1992.

64 US Department of Health and Human Services. *Healthy People 2010: Understanding and Improving Health and Objectives for Improving Health.* Washington, DC: US Government Printing Office; 2000.

65 Murry CJL, Lopez AD, eds. *Health Dimensions of Sex and Reproduction: the Global Burden of Sexually Transmitted Diseases, HIV, Maternal Conditions, Perinatal Disorders, and Congenital Anomalies.* Geneva, Switzerland: World Health Organization; 1998.

66 Michaud CM, Murray CJL, Bloom BR. Burden of diseases: Implications for future research. *JAMA.* 2001;285:535–539.

67 Centers for Disease Control and Prevention. *Sexually Transmitted Disease Surveillance 2000.* Atlanta, Ga: US Dept of Health and Human Services, Centers for Disease Control and Prevention; 2001.

68 Patella FJ, Delaney KM, Moorman AC, et al. Declining morbidity and mortality among patients with advanced human immunodeficiency virus infection. *N Engl J Med.* 1998;338:853–860.

69 Ebrahim SH, Peterman TA, Zaidi AA, Kamb ML. Mortality related to sexually transmitted diseases in US women, 1973 through 1992. *Am J Public Health.* 1997;87:938–944.

70 Cates W. Estimates of the incidence and prevalence of sexually transmitted diseases in the United States. *Sex Transm Dis.* 1999;26:52–57.

71 Recommendations for prevention and control of hepatitis C virus (HCV) infection and HCV-related chronic disease. *MMWR Morb Mortal Wkly Rep.* 1998;47:1–39.

72 Brook DW, Brook JS, Zhang C, Cohen P, Whiteman M. Drug use and the risk of major depressive disorder, alcohol dependence, and substance use disorders. *Arch Gen Psychiatry.* 2002;59:1039–1044.

73 Volkow ND. Drug abuse and mental illness: progress in understanding comorbidity. *Am J Psychiatry*. 2001;158:1181–1183.

74 Oyefeso A, Ghodse H, Clancy C, Corkery J, Goldfinch R. Drug abuse-related mortality: a study of teenage addicts over a 20-year period. *Soc Psychiatry Psychiatr Epidemiol*. 1999;34:437–441.

75 Phillips DP, Christenfeld N, Ryan NM. An increase in the number of deaths in the United States in the first week of the month – an association with substance abuse and other causes of death. *N Engl J Med*. 1999;341:93–98.

76 Rivara FP, Mueller BA, Somes G, Mendoza CT, Rushforth NB, Kellermann AL. Alcohol and illicit drug abuse and the risk of violent death in the home. *JAMA*. 1997;278:569–575.

77 Bruner AB, Fishman M. Adolescents and illicit drug use. *JAMA*. 1998;280:597–598.

78 Pope HG Jr, Ionescu-Pioggia M, Pope KW. Drug use and life style among college undergraduates: a 30-year longitudinal study. *Am J Psychiatry*. 2001;158:1519–1521.

79 Johnston LD, O'Malley PM, Bachman JG. *National Survey Results on Drug Use From the Monitoring the Future study, 1975–1999. Volume I: Secondary School Students*. Ann Arbor: University of Michigan; 2000.

80 Pollack DA, Holmgreen P, Lui K, Kirk ML. Discrepancies in the reported frequency of cocaine deaths, United States, 1983 through 1988. *JAMA*. 1991;266:2233–2237.

81 Single E, Rehm J, Robson L, Truong MV. The relative risks and etiologic fractions of different causes of death and disease attributable to alcohol, tobacco and illicit drug use in Canada. *CMAJ*. 2000;162:1669–1675.

82 Rogot E, Sorlie PD, Johnson NJ. Life expectancy by employment status, income, and education in the National Longitudinal Mortality Study. *Public Health Rep*. 1992;107:457–461.

83 Wong MD, Shapiro MF, Boscardin WJ, Ettner SL, Contribution of major diseases to disparities in mortality. *N Engl J Med*. 2002;347:1585–1592.

84 Franks P, Clancy CM, Gold MR. Health insurance and mortality: evidence from a national cohort. *JAMA*. 1993;270:737–741.

85 Khoury MJ, Beaty TH, Cohen BH. *Fundamentals of Genetic Epidemiology*. New York, NY: Oxford University Press; 1993.

86 Department of Health and Human Services. *Healthy People 2010: Understanding and Improving Health*. Washington, DC: Government Printing Office; 2000.

87 Fontaine KR, Redden DT, Wang C, Westfall AO, Allison DB. Years of life lost due to obesity. *JAMA*. 2003;289:187–193.

88 Peeters A, Barendregt JJ, Willekens F, et al, for the Netherlands Epidemiology and Demography Compression of Morbidity Research Group. Obesity in adulthood and its consequences for life expectancy: a life-table analysis. *Ann Intern Med*. 2003;138:24–32.

89 Centers for Disease Control and Prevention. Declines in lung cancer rates – California, 1988–1997. *MMWR Morb Mortal Wkly Rep*. 2000;49:1066–1069.

90 Reducing tobacco use: a report of the Surgeon General. *MMWR Recomm Rep*. 2000;49(RR-16):1–27.

91 Zhu SH, Anderson CM, Tedeschi GJ, et al. Evidence of real-world effectiveness of a telephone quitline for smokers. *N Engl J Med*. 2002;347:1087–1093.

92 Ezzati M, Lopez AD, Rodgers A, Vander Hoorn S, Murray Cl, and the Comparative Risk Assessment Collaborating Group. Selected major risk factors and global and regional burden of disease. *Lancet*. 2002;360:1347–1360.

93 Bruke W. Genetic testing. *N Engl J Med*. 2002;347:1867–1875.

94 Ford ES, Mokdad AH, Giles WH, Mensah GA. Serum total cholesterol concentrations and awareness, treatment, and control of hypercholesterolemia among US adults: findings from the National Health and Nutrition Examination Survey 1999–2000. *Circulation*. 2003;107: 2185–2189.

95 Hajjar I, Kotchen TA. Trends in prevalence, awareness, treatment, and control of hypertension in the United States, 1988–2000. *JAMA*. 2003;290:199–206.

96 Strum R. The effects of obesity, smoking, and problem drinking on chronic medical problems and health care costs. *Health Aff (Millwood)*. 2002;21:245–253.

97 Visscher TL, Seidell JC. The public health impact of obesity. *Annu Rev Public Health*. 2001;22:355–375.

Kaplan, R.M. (1990) Behavior as the central outcome in health care,
American Psychologist, 45 (11): 1211–20.

Behavior as the central outcome in health care

Robert M. Kaplan

Department of Community and Family Medicine, University of California, San Diego

Abstract

A predominant justification for health psychology and behavioral medicine is that behavior or environmental conditions affect a biological process. Thus, many investigators focus attention on the effects of behavior on cell pathology and blood chemistry. This article argues that behavioral outcomes are the most important consequences in studies of health care and medicine. These outcomes include longevity, health-related quality of life, and symptomatic complaints. Traditional measures in biomedical science often have limited reliability and validity. Their validity is demonstrated only through relationships with longevity, role performance, behavioral functioning, and symptomatic experience, and these correlations are often modest. A model is proposed to guide future investigations. Biological, environmental, and psychological variables are included in the model as predictors or mediators of behavioral health outcomes. Recognizing that health outcomes are behavioral directs intervention toward whatever method produces the most health benefit at the lowest cost.

Health psychology and behavioral medicine are among the most rapidly developing areas of psychological research and practice. Although no one model has dominated the field, the biomedical disease model has guided most thinking. According to this model, syndromes expressed as signs and symptoms are associated with lesions or some underlying pathology. This pathology is the focus of research and the target of treatment. Interventions are made to eradicate the lesion or prevent its pathogenesis. The lesion, however, is the central focus of examination.

Reviews of the emerging field of behavioral medicine and health psychology often emphasize the role of behavior in the onset, maintenance, and treatment of disease (Miller, 1983). Many of these reviews characterize the role of stress on bodily processes. Krantz, Grunberg, and Baum (1985) emphasized the links between behavior and health through basic physiological mechanisms. Their review concluded with an emphasis on new technologies for assessing physiologic, rather than behavioral, health outcomes. For example, they pointed to the availability of portable blood-withdrawal pumps, blood pressure monitors, and biochemical assessment tools. Rodin and Salovey (1989) underscored the importance of disease end points. They encouraged

An earlier version of this article was prepared for the American Psychological Association, Division 38 Symposium, New Orleans, Louisiana, August 1989.

Critical comments by Mark B. Andersen and Catherine J. Atkins, W. A. Hillix, Melbourne Hovell, and Thomas L. Patterson on an earlier version of this article are sincerely appreciated.

Correspondence concerning this article should be addressed to Robert M. Kaplan, Division of Health Care Sciences, M-022, School of Medicine, University of California, San Diego, La Jolla, CA 92093–0622.

health psychologists to focus on placement in specific disease categories such as cancer or coronary heart disease. These reviews characterize the field as emphasizing the impact of behavior on identified lesions or specific disease states.

Progressive versions of the medical model acknowledge that the cause of illness might be environmental or the lesion psychosocial. Even the biopsychosocial model (Engle, 1976), however, concentrates on sickness and its causes. Attention is directed toward the psychological or environmental etiology and the physiological lesion (White, 1988). These models have directed measurement toward assessment of disease categories, characteristics of lesions, and disease risk factors.

In their efforts to be in the mainstream, many behavioral research investigators also focus their studies on the health outcomes measured by physicians and other health care providers. Typically, these are measures of blood chemistry, physical characteristics, and blood or tissue sensitivity to medication. In this article I argue that the only important indicators of health and wellness are behavioral. Thus, outcome measures in health and medicine should be anchored in their relations with behavior. In this context the definition of behavior is general, as offered by Atkinson, Atkinson, Smith, and Hilgard (1987) in their widely used introductory psychology textbook. They define behavior as "those activities of an organism that can be observed by another organism or by an experimenter's instruments" (p. 657). Included in behavior are verbal reports about subjective conscious experiences. In this article, I refer to biological measures as measures of physiological state. Biological measures and disease classifications are important precisely because they are predictors or mediators of behavioral outcomes.

In the following sections, I argue that there has been too much concentration on purely biological measures and that the importance of behavioral health outcomes has been undervalued.

Behavioral health outcomes

The conceptualization and measurement of health status has interested scholars for many decades. After the Eisenhower administration, a report of the President's Commission on National Goals, (1960) identified health status measurement as an important objective. In his influential book, *The Affluent Society,* John Kenneth Galbraith (1958) described the need to measure the effect of the health care system on quality of life. In recent years there have been many attempts to define and measure health status.

The movement toward behavioral measures is an old one. When Sullivan (1966) reviewed the literature on health measurement nearly a quarter of a century ago, he emphasized the importance of behavioral outcomes. Bolstered by the accomplishments of behavioral scientists, Sullivan developed a convincing argument that behavioral indicators such as absenteeism, bed-disability days, and institutional confinement were the most important consequences of disease and disability. Ability to perform activities at different ages could be compared with societal standards for these behaviors. Restrictions in usual activity were seen as prima facie evidence of deviation from wellbeing. Health conditions affect behavior, and in this article behavioral health outcomes are conceptualized as observable behavioral consequences of a health state. Arthritis, for example, may be associated with difficulty in walking, observable limping, or problems in using the hands. Even a minor illness, such as the common cold, might result in disruptions in daily activities, alterations in activity patterns, and decreased work capacity.

Diseases and disabilities are important for two reasons. First, illness may cause a truncation of the life expectancy. In other words, those in specific disease categories may die prematurely. Death is a behavioral outcome. It can be defined as the point at which there is no observable behavior. Second, diseases and disabilities may cause behavioral dysfunctions as well as other symptoms. Biomedical studies typically refer to health outcomes in terms of mortality (death) and morbidity (dysfunction) and sometimes to symptoms.

Mortality remains the major outcome measure in most epidemiologic studies and clinical trials. In order to make informed decisions about the nation's health, Congress receives various reports of statistical indicators from the National Center for Health Statistics. These include the crude mortality rate, the infant mortality rate, and years of potential life lost. Although important, each of these measures ignores dysfunction while people are alive. The National Center for Health Statistics provides information on a variety of states of morbidity. For example, it considers disability, defined as a temporary or long-term reduction in a person's activity. Over the last 15 years, medical and health services researchers have developed new ways to assess health status quantitatively. These measures are often called *quality of life* measures. Because they are used exclusively to evaluate health status, the more descriptive *health-related quality of life* is preferred (Kaplan & Bush, 1982). Some approaches to the measurement of health-related quality of life combine measures of morbidity and mortality to express health outcomes in units analogous to years of life. The years-of-life figure, however, is adjusted for diminished quality of life associated with diseases or disabilities (Kaplan & Anderson, 1988).

Modern measures of health outcome consider future as well as current health status. Cancer, for example, may have very little impact on current functioning but may have a substantial impact on behavioral outcomes in the future. Today, a person with a malignant tumor in a leg may be functioning very much like a person with a leg muscle injury. However, the cancer patient is more likely to remain dysfunctional in the future. Comprehensive expressions of health status need to incorporate estimates of future behavioral dysfunction as well as to measure current status (Kaplan & Anderson, 1988).

The spectrum of medical care ranges from public health, preventive medicine, and environmental control through diagnosis to therapeutic intervention, convalescence, and rehabilitation. Many programs affect the probability of occurrence of future dysfunction rather than alter present functional status. In many aspects of preventive care, for example, the benefit of the treatment cannot be seen until many years after the intervention. A supportive family that instills proper health habits in its children, for example, may also promote better health in the future, even though the benefit may not be realized for years. The concept of health must consider not only the ability to function now but also the probability of future changes in function or probabilities of death. A person who is functional and asymptomatic today may harbor a disease with a poor prognosis. Thus, many individuals are at high risk of dying from heart disease even though they are perfectly functional today. Should we call them healthy? The term *severity of illness* should take into consideration both dysfunction and prognosis. Comprehensive models that combine morbidity, mortality, and prognosis have been described in the literature (Kaplan & Anderson, 1988). A behavioral conceptualization of health status can represent this prognosis by modeling disruptions in behavior that might occur in the future.

Many medical treatments may cause near-term dysfunction to prevent future dysfunction. For example, coronary artery bypass surgery causes severe dysfunction for a short period of time, yet the surgery is presumed to enhance function or decrease mortality at a later time. Patients may be incapacitated following myocardial infarction and restricted to coronary care units. Yet the treatment is designed to help them achieve better future outcomes. Pap smears and hysterectomies are performed in order to decrease the probability of future deaths due to cancer. Much of health care involves looking into the future to enhance behavioral outcomes over the life span. Therefore, it is essential to divide health into current and future components.

In appraising the importance of behavioral outcomes, we must ask why there is concern about diseases, injuries, and disabilities. The behavioral perspective suggests that the only reasons are the following: (a) Life expectancy may be shortened, (b) quality of life may be compromised either now or at some time prior to death, or (c) some combination of a and b. A disease that has no impact on either life expectancy or life quality would be unimportant. In fact, disease states gain their importance precisely to the degree to which they correlate with decreased longevity or impaired health-related quality of life.

The importance of behavioral outcomes has not been disregarded by the traditional medical community. In fact, recognition of the centrality of behavioral outcomes has been emphasized in several articles and editorials recently featured in *The New England Journal of Medicine* (Ellwood, 1988; Greenfield, 1989; Shortell & McNerney, 1990). Despite the growing recognition of the importance of behavioral outcomes by the medical community (Advances in Health Status Assessment, 1987; Bergner, 1989; Institutes of Medicine, 1989; Quality of Life Assessment, 1988a, 1988b; Shumaker, Furberg, Czajkowski, & Schron, in press; Walker & Rosser, 1988), behavioral scientists manifest a paradoxical reluctance to follow this trend. Instead, the trend has been to focus on measures of biological process.

Trend toward biological variables as opposed to behavioral indexes

We are witnessing a trend toward the biologicalization of both behavioral and biomedical sciences. Reviews of the health psychology literature criticize studies that do not focus on some aspect of blood chemistry or those that do not use disease categories (Baum, Grunberg, & Singer, 1982). Measures of biological process are seen to be more pure, more reliable, and more valid than are behavioral indicators. Thus, an increasing number of studies assess health status through measures of blood cholesterol, blood pressure, or characteristics of the immune response, including natural killer-cell and *t*-cell activity. W. T. Kelvin created the doctrine that measurement is the prerequisite to science. For most of this century, scientists and clinicians followed the doctrine and attempted to use measures, even when the validity of the measures was unknown. Feinstein (1967) suggested that modern trends represent the "curse of Kelvin." The fact that there is a measure for some variable does not always mean that the measure is useful. Clinicians have been more attracted to blood pressure and cardiac output than to headache and anxiety. Clearly, the former are easier to quantify, but are they more meaningful?

It is important to emphasize that not all biological variables are measures of health status or health outcome. They are, however, predictive of some health outcomes. Elevated blood pressure, for example, is important because it predicts premature mortality or behavioral dysfunction resulting from coronary heart disease and from stroke. If blood pressure were unrelated to these behavioral outcomes, it would be a matter of little concern. There are many aspects of blood chemistry that bear no relation to clinical outcomes. Even common clinical tests, such as urine analysis, serum phosphorus, and alkaline phosphatase, have only weak and inconsistent relations to outcomes in all but the most extreme cases. Amberg, Schneiderman, Berry, and Zettner (1982), for example, demonstrated empirically that the alkaline phosphatase screening test provides essentially no information relevant to health outcome. Elevated blood cholesterol may be predictive of future bad outcomes, including early mortality from heart disease. However, other lipids in blood such as very low-density lipoproteins or chylomicrons may bear little relation to health outcomes in all but the most extreme cases. Modest elevation in these fractions of blood lipids may be of little concern.

Recently there has been a significant growth of interest in the relation between stress and measurable aspects of immune function. Temoshok, Soloman, and Jenkins (1989) cautioned scientists against overinterpreting these immunologic measures. Normal oscillations in most immune parameters are still poorly understood. Immunologists are uncertain about whether absolute numbers or percentages of cell subtypes are most meaningful. Most important, the immune system is a genuine system in which various components adjust to changes in one another, and some important aspects of the system may remain to be identified. Our understanding of the relation between immune parameters and health is still very sketchy.

Biological measures are also assumed to be more reliable than behavioral tests. Often however, the reliability of these measures is not assessed. When data are available, the results can be discouraging. Many investigators, fascinated by blood pressure as an outcome measure, have criticized behavioral measures for being non-physiologic and unreliable. Yet the reliability of blood pressure is equally open to question because conventional sphygmomanometric measurements have poor test–retest coefficients. This leads to misclassification, incorrect diagnosis, and potentially damaging labeling (Hla, Vokaty, & Fuessner, 1986; Patterson, 1984). There are many sources of error in blood pressure measurement. These include misreading biases, time sampling problems (blood pressure changes minute to minute), and situational factors. For example, it has been demonstrated that some patients have specific arousal of blood pressure in the presence of physicians. The condition has now been given the diagnostic label *white coat hypertension* (Pickering et al., 1988). Low reliability is not limited to blood pressure. It also characterizes measures of blood cholesterol, glucose, and a large number of other biochemical assays.

One of the important appeals of biological measures is that they focus on objectively defined events. Behavioral outcomes are often not measured objectively. Observer bias common to behavioral measures may be less common with biological measures. However, at a conceptual level, behavioral outcomes can represent defined events such as exercise or role performance. Subjective events, such as pain or discomfort, are characterized in pain behaviors and through verbal behaviors. It is tempting to assume that biological measures are more valid and reliable because they have less observer bias. However, they may include several other sources of measurement error and they do not necessarily have evidence for validity.

To summarize, in order to avoid known problems with behavioral measures, researchers and clinicians have been attracted to outcomes that can be measured with biochemical assays, mechanical devices, or auto-analyzer machines. Although these measures are not subject to the same errors as behavioral tests, they have their own sources of error and often have low reliability and questionable validity. Establishing the validity of biological measures requires a model that relates them to health status.

Are medical measures more valid or meaningful?

It is often assumed that the relation between the biologic variables and health outcomes is nearly perfect. However, there is a remarkable variability in behavioral health outcomes within fixed levels of many biological variables. There are numerous examples, of which only three will be considered; biologic measures of arthritis, blood pressure, and blood cholesterol. The arthritis example emphasizes current behavioral health outcomes, whereas the latter two focus on future behavioral outcomes and mortality.

Arthritis

Clinical outcomes in studies of rheumatology have been difficult to evaluate (Deyo, 1988). Clinical measures often include joint tenderness, grip strength, and joint circumference. Some studies have shown that the reliability of these measures is often poor (Buchanan, 1982). Fries (1983) questioned the validity and reliability of a variety of traditional outcome measures, ranging from laboratory measures of erythrocyte sedimentation rate (ESR), latex fixation titer, and hemoglobin. It has been shown that rheumatoid arthritis patients may develop serological abnormalities that are poorly correlated with joint inflammation (McCarty, 1986). In addition, Fries suggested that traditional clinical measures such as grip strength, walking time, and patient global assessment are merely surrogates for the true outcomes in arthritis, which he argued are disability, physical discomfort, and financial loss. An elevated ESR means little to a patient who feels fine and can conduct his or her life without pain. The ESR characterizes current inflammation but does not give information about future dysfunction. Conversely, a patient with disabling arthritis pain is not well when the ESR is normal. Clinical tests are useful only when they identify treatment to remedy current dysfunction or predict future problems. Fries asserted that pain and functional outcomes are meaningful to the patients and that clinical measures are of less importance. As a result, a growing number of rheumatologists are focusing attention on behavioral or functional health outcomes (Anderson, Firschein, & Meenan, 1989).

Blood pressure

Elevated blood pressure is a serious problem in the United States and in most other developed countries. Following the Hypertension Detection and Follow-up Program (HDFP), elevated blood pressure came to be defined as systolic pressure exceeding 140 mmHg or diastolic pressure (DBP) exceeding 90 mmHg. Using these guidelines, it has been estimated that as many 58 million adults (about 30% of the adult population) have hypertension (Joint National Committee on Detection, Evaluation, and Treatment of High Blood Pressure, 1985). Investigators are concerned about elevated blood pressure because of its relation to future behavioral health outcomes. Several major epidemiologic studies have documented the relation between elevated blood pressure and both morbidity and mortality (National Heart, Lung and Blood Institute, 1984). In addition, evidence from the HDFP (1979) has demonstrated that reductions in blood pressure result in reductions in deaths due to heart disease. People are often not concerned about high blood pressure because it may produce no symptoms or current behavioral dysfunction. High blood pressure does have a bad prognosis, with affected individuals being at risk for behavioral dysfunction or death later in life. However, the relation between blood pressure and both mortality and morbidity are far from uniform. Severe elevated blood pressure is a severe risk for mortality, whereas blood pressure in the mild hypertension range (DBP = 90–104 mmHg) is a less significant risk (Rocella, Bowler, & Horan, 1987). Indeed, most of those with mild hypertension, even those untreated, have normal life expectancies with no complications.

Although high blood pressure is associated with risks, the treatment of high blood pressure may cause some problems. Significant numbers of patients experience dizziness, tiredness, and impotence when treated with medications (Breckenridge, 1988). Thus, the treatment of high blood pressure can cause undesirable health outcomes. Treatment, like hypertension, is a factor that may influence behavioral health outcomes, sometimes in the negative direction. Studies that measure only blood pressure and neglect these behavioral side effects will overestimate the net benefit. Conversely, too much focus on side effects might lead to an incorrect judgment that the treatment should be avoided. There may be considerable advantage in translating the side effects and benefits into common behavioral units and weighing them against one another in the treatment decision process (Kaplan & Atkins, 1989). The role of the clinician is to balance carefully the benefits and consequences of treatment (Aderman & Madhavan, 1981).

In summary, blood pressure is an important risk factor for heart disease and stroke. Systematic efforts to reduce blood pressure are advisable and effective. Yet, blood pressure is not a health outcome. It gains its importance through validity studies that demonstrate the association between blood pressure and behavioral outcomes including mortality, dysfunction, and symptomatic disturbances. Blood pressure is important because it provides probabilistic information about behavioral outcomes.

Cholesterol

The United States is currently experiencing a massive societal response to the presence of cholesterol in the diet. Numerous commercial products are promoted because they have no cholesterol. The term *hypercholesterolemia* suggests an increased concentration of cholesterol in blood. Total cholesterol values above 200 mg/dl are now considered to be diagnostic (Expert Panel on Detection, Evaluation, and Treatment of High Blood Cholesterol in Adults, 1988). Several epidemiologic studies have identified elevated blood cholesterol as a risk factor for cardiovascular disease mortality (Kannel, Castelli, Gordon, & McNamara, 1971). Yet the connection between dietary cholesterol and serum cholesterol has been less clearly established. Studies in metabolic wards and selected experimental studies do demonstrate that dietary manipulation can reduce serum cholesterol in the short run, although longer term changes have not been clearly documented. Furthermore, although there have been ecological correlations between estimated total fat consumption and total heart disease mortality across cultures, correlations within countries have not been systematically observed (Kaplan, 1985). A variety of explanations can be suggested for these "nonfindings." For example, measurement error in both dietary cholesterol and serum cholesterol may account for the null results (Jacobs, Anderson, & Blackburn, 1979). But the availability of an explanation for a nonfinding is not a demonstration that a significant association exists (Kaplan, 1988). Thus, the relation between dietary cholesterol and serum cholesterol is somewhat ambiguous.

Stallones (1983) criticized the diet–heart-disease connection, suggesting that there is no zero-order relation between diet and mortality. The problems with the cholesterol interventions have been reviewed in several earlier articles (Fries, Green, & Levine, 1989; Kaplan, 1984, 1985). These positions are regarded as controversial, but they are related to the current issue.

The reason that cholesterol is important is that elevated cholesterol is a risk factor for behavioral health outcomes. If it were not, why would one care? The important point is that the outcome itself must be considered. The role of the investigator is to determine the relation between modifiable habits (dietary patterns) and outcomes as mediated through the channel of serum cholesterol. Serum cholesterol can serve as a target for modification, but one must be assured that modifying serum cholesterol improves outcome and does not adversely affect health status.

Deaths in general versus deaths from specific causes

Some investigators, recognizing the problems with measures of disease process, turn their attention toward the ultimate medical outcome – death. As noted earlier in this review, vital status is considered to be a behavioral outcome. However, the behavioral approach differs from the traditional medical model in its emphasis on life–death status without reference to medical cause of death. The emphasis is on observable outcome rather than on disease category.

Many medical studies confuse outcome with placement in disease categories. Results from several recent clinical trials illustrate this point. In one widely cited study (Steering Committee of the Physicians' Health Study Research Group (1988, 1989)), physician subjects were assigned to take aspirin (325 mg/day) or placebo in order to prevent myocardial infarctions. The ultimate aim, of course, was to reduce the number of deaths associated with heart disease. Indeed, there was a significant reduction in deaths from myocardial infarctions over an eight-year follow-up period. This result was highly publicized and even earned aspirin the description of a "miracle drug" on the cover of *Newsweek* magazine (Clark, Gosnell, Hager, Carroll, & Gordon, 1988). Yet closer inspection of the data reveals that there was no advantage of aspirin for the crucial behavioral outcome – life or death. The left panel of Figure 1 shows deaths from all cardiovascular categories in the Physician's Health Study. This stacking histogram reveals that reductions in death from myocardial infarction were compensated for by increases in death from other cardiovascular causes. There was a trend toward more hemorrhagic strokes among those taking aspirin, and there was the suggestion that aspirin may cause these strokes because it reduces blood clotting. Overall, aspirin did not reduce the number of deaths but changed the distribution among categories (Kaplan, 1989b).

The center portion of Figure 1 shows a similar result for the Coronary Primary Prevention Trial (Lipid Research Clinics Coronary Prevention Trial Results, 1984). In this study, a group of about 1,900 men at risk for coronary heart disease was given cholestyramine, a resin that binds bial acids and lowers serum cholestrol, whereas another group of about 1,900 men was given a placebo. Among the 3,800 male participants, 38 (2%) in the control group and 30 (1.6%) in the experimental group died of heart disease. The study is widely cited as the crucial evidence for cholesterol reduction. In addition, data from the study have been used to argue that a 1% reduction in cholesterol results in a 2% reduction in mortality. This has come to be known in health promotion campaigns as the *1% to 2% rule*. The exact calculation of this 1% to 2% rule, so often cited in public statements, is difficult to follow. Forming a ratio of these small percentages of deaths and subtracting from 1.0 gives the estimate of about a 21% reduction in mortality $(1.0 - [0.0157/0.022])$. This combined with an observed 12% reduction in cholesterol yields the 1% to 2% rule.

This important study represents the scientific basis for the current campaign toward cholesterol reduction. The stacking histogram does suggest a significant reduction in heart disease deaths among those randomly assigned to cholestyramine. Yet the entire height of the bars in the stacking histogram shows that there was no advantage of treatment for total mortality. According to the behavioral conceptualization, the treatment had no benefit. Reductions in death from heart disease were compensated for by increases in death from other causes.

The right portion of Figure 1 shows similar results from the Helsinki Heart Study, which evaluated a similar drug called gemfibrozil (Frick et al., 1987). In the Helsinki study, 2,051 men were randomly assigned to take gemfibrozil twice daily, whereas another 2,030 men were given a placebo. After six years, 19 of the men in the placebo group had died of ischemic heart disease, whereas only 14 of those in the drug-treated group had died. This significant difference led the authors to conclude that gemfibrozil caused a 26% reduction in ischemic heart disease deaths. The 26% is calculated as follows: In the drug group, 0.68% (14/2,051) died, whereas in the placebo group 0.93% (19/2,030) died of ischemic heart disease. The actual difference is about one fourth of one percent. However, the ratio (0.0068/0.0093) subtracted from 1.0 yields about a 26% reduction. Furthermore, the total number of deaths in the Gemfibrozil group was actually higher than those in the placebo group (45 vs. 42).

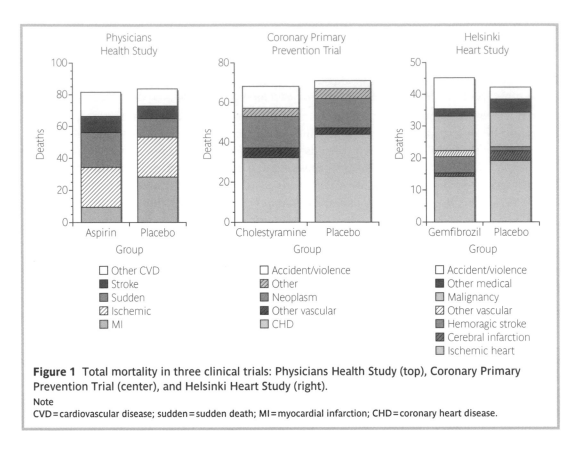

Figure 1 Total mortality in three clinical trials: Physicians Health Study (top), Coronary Primary Prevention Trial (center), and Helsinki Heart Study (right).

Note

CVD = cardiovascular disease; sudden = sudden death; MI = myocardial infarction; CHD = coronary heart disease.

Some argue that cholesterol-lowering drugs should still be regarded as efficacious because there is no biological model that would explain why decreased cholesterol should lead to increased deaths in nondisease categories. However, the finding that cholesterol lowering does not reduce total mortality has now been reported in several different studies (Fries et al., 1989). The burden of proving benefit rests with the treatment advocates. Those who adopt the traditional disease-specific view might be satisfied with reductions in cardiovascular deaths. However, the more comprehensive behavioral model requires a reduction in total mortality. Adoption of this model might stimulate new research designed to explain the increased deaths in nondisease categories.

In all three of these important clinical trials, there was a highly publicized benefit of treatment. However, the benefit only occurs for a specific disease category. There was no benefit of treatment with regard to the important life–death outcome (see total height of columns in each section of Figure 1). Investigators and the lay press often focus on improvements in a specific cause of death. Yet families of the deceased may be more concerned that the subject is dead than they are about the specific cause of demise. Focus on specific categories can obscure the most important behavioral outcomes. Research directed toward specific disease categories or aspects of a biological process may not capture global concerns about health. That task requires a comprehensive behavioral model.

Model of health outcomes

A model of behavioral health outcomes is presented in Figure 2. In the center of the figure is tissue or organ pathology, which makes up most of the study of medicine and results in most of the serious illnesses. These illnesses might be caused by multiple sources, including inherited birth problems, various diseases, the aging process, defects in the genetic program, and accidents. Each of these problems may be caused by biochemical or structural problems. The sources listed in Figure 2 are selected examples and are not intended to be exhaustive. Investigators are concerned about these biological problems because they may eventually affect behavior. If a disease or condition had an impact on a tissue or organ system but had no effect on life expectancy, no effect on function, no effect on appearance or symptoms, would it be of concern?

Most models in health psychology and behavioral medicine have a biological measure on the right side (implying that biology is the outcome). It is often emphasized that behavior is important because it can affect biological process. For example, diet can affect serum cholesterol and stress can affect natural killer cells. Figure 2 suggests a different focus. Both biological and environmental events gain their importance because they affect behavior.

Can a behavioral conceptualization influence research and practice?

Focus on biological rather than behavioral outcomes has led many investigators down the wrong path. For example, elevated levels of protein in urine suggest that the kidneys are misfiltering and removing some proteins that the body needs. Many years ago, when physicians measured high levels of protein in urine, they advised their patients to eat less protein. That advice led to poorer health outcomes because the body was already protein deprived. Ultimately, identifying the manipulations that led to better behavioral health outcomes led to more effective treatments. Another example involves the diagnosis and treatment of back pain. Legal definitions of disability sometimes require a physical diagnosis, and the medical evaluation often identifies a structural problem. This leads to the incorrect conclusion that the prognosis is poor. Thus, the medical model reinforces dysfunction, even though rehabilitation is common.

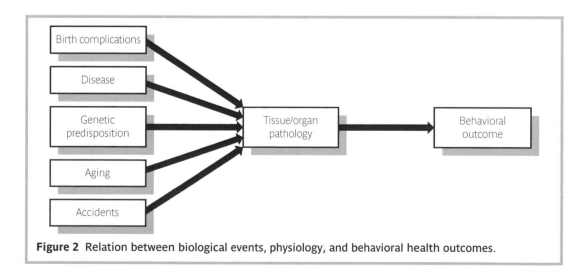

Figure 2 Relation between biological events, physiology, and behavioral health outcomes.

A comprehensive view of health can reveal when new treatment approaches are needed, whereas focus on specific processes might misdirect treatment.

The traditional approach leads to a focus on risk factors rather than on health outcomes. Yet, modification of risk factors may not necessarily improve health. For example, many epidemiologic studies have failed to find a relation between coffee consumption and death due to heart disease. Several very thorough evaluations have shown that those who drink coffee have the same life expectancies as those who abstain (Wilson, Garrison, Kannel, McGee, & Costelli, 1989). On the other hand, some investigators have reported that coffee increases low density lippoprotein cholesterol or blood pressure (Thelle, Heyden, & Fodor, 1987). Because cholesterol and blood pressure are risk factors for heart disease, people are advised to give up the coffee they enjoy. The logic behind this advice might be challenged, however, as coffee does not increase the risk of heart disease or other behavioral health outcomes.

Treatment of factors suspected of causing undesirable behavioral outcomes is usually advisable. Yet change in these risk factors does not assure that the behavioral goal will be achieved. One recent example is the treatment of cardiac arrhythmias. Research had demonstrated that adults who had suffered a heart attack were at risk for sudden death if they experienced asymptomatic cardiac arrhythmias (Bigger, Fleiss, Kleiger, Miller, & Rolnitzky, 1984). Drugs were available to suppress these cardiac arrhythmias, and these products were used often. In what many thought was a demonstration of the obvious, the National Institutes of Health initiated a major clinical study involving 1,455 post myocardial infarction patients in a variety of major medical centers (Cardiac Arrhythmia Suppression Trial [CAST] Investigators, 1989). The patients were randomly assigned to take anti-arrhythmic medication or placebos. All of the participants had been screened and demonstrated to experience suppression of their arrhythmia in response to the medication. Over an average of 10 months of follow-up, however, those assigned to the active drug had a significantly higher rate of death from arrhythmia than those assigned to the placebo. In addition, those in the active medication group had a higher overall death rate. If the investigators had only measured the response of the heart rhythm to anti-arrhythmic drugs, they would have concluded that the drug produced a benefit. Following the patients through the behavioral outcome (mortality) inspired them to stop the trial early and declare the medications unsafe.

The important point is that physiologic and biochemical measures do not necessarily have meaning. They gain their meaning through systematic correlations with health outcome. Attention directed at behavioral health outcomes can clarify the importance of biological processes.

Pathways to health outcomes

In this article I have argued that the only important outcomes in health and illness are behavioral. Clearly, these outcomes are deserving of one's attention. People expend tremendous resources in order to achieve better health status. In fact, in the United States, more is spent on health care than on food (Kaplan, 1989a). How might one realize the best return on one's investments in terms of health outcomes?

There are at least two ways to achieve better health outcomes. The first is through the modification of mediators of the behavioral outcomes. This is accomplished by identifying tissue pathology and seeking its remedy. Thus, those with diabetes experience poor health outcomes because of a problem in insulin production or insulin action. By supplying more insulin or by tuning up insulin receptors, better health outcomes may be achieved. Those with tumors may experience better health outcomes with the tumors excised. There is nothing wrong with the medical model. In fact, direct treatment of pathology (lesions) remains one of the best methods for improving health outcomes. The traditional practice of medicine and surgery should be viewed as a set of methods designed to improve behavioral outcomes.

Another pathway for improving health outcomes involves modification of behavior, independent of the disease pathway. For example, patients with chronic obstructive pulmonary disease may face a situation in which there are no known medical or surgical remedies. However, behavior modification programs may enhance functioning independent of improvement in disease state (Atkins, Kaplan, Reinsch, Lofback, & Timms, 1984; Kaplan & Atkins, 1988). Pain treatment may also benefit from this conceptualization. Substantial evidence now suggests that pain and suffering are distinct. Pain behavior can continue after the injury that initiated the pain has healed. Several studies have shown that behavior modification can alter behavioral health outcomes for those with back pain, even though it does not affect back physiology in measurable ways (Fordyce, 1988). Health outcomes are behavioral, and one way to improve them is to modify behavior.

The behavioral conceptualization does not disregard the traditional medical model. Indeed, medicines and surgeries are excellent methods for improving behavioral health outcomes. However, the behavioral model is broader. Medicines, surgeries, and behavioral interventions are complementary methods for enhancing behavioral health outcomes. Often one alternative is superior in terms of efficacy or efficiency. For example, hernias can be surgically repaired and it would be inappropriate to use behavioral treatment to modify outcomes related to these problems. On the other hand, several disabilities do not respond to medicines or surgeries. For these, behavioral interventions may be the best alternative for producing a health benefit. Using behavioral outcomes as the target of care allows different alternatives to compete. Ultimately, treatments should be favored if they produce the most benefit at the lowest cost.

Summary

Physicians have long recognized that disease categories provide minimal information about the impact of illness upon patient experiences (Ellwood, 1988). A diagnosis is important because it may identify a course of treatment. Yet within specific diagnoses, patients differ considerably in how they are affected. Multiple sclerosis, for example, may have essentially no impact on behavioral dysfunction or it could have devastating implications. The impact of the disease on the daily life of the patient may be more important than naming the condition. A recent editorial in the *Journal of the American Medical Association* concluded that physicians need to learn to "treat the patient, not the disease" (Riesenberg & Glass, 1989, p. 943).

There are only two health outcomes that are of importance. First, there is life expectancy. Second, there is function or quality of life during the years that people are alive. Biological and physical events are mediators of these behavioral outcomes. Individuals are concerned about cancer, high blood pressure, high cholesterol, or other problems because they may shorten the life expectancy or make life less desirable prior to death. There is a growing consensus that these behavioral outcomes are central in studies of health care and medicine. Yet refinement of these measures requires active participation of behavioral scientists. Although behavioral outcomes are gaining a stronger foothold in medical research, psychologists and behavioral scientists have shown minimal interest. A behavioral conceptualization of health outcomes may suggest important new directions for research and practice.

References

Aderman, M. H., & Madhavan, S. (1981). Management of the hypertensive patient: A continuing dilemma. *Hypertension, 3,* 192–197.

Advances in Health Status Assessment. (1987). Conference proceedings. *Journal of Chronic Disease, 40*(Suppl. 1).

Amberg, J., Schneiderman, L. J., Berry, C. C., & Zettner, A. (1982). The "abnormal" outpatient chemistry panel serum alkaline phosphatase: Analysis of physician response, outcome, cost and health effectiveness. *Journal of Chronic Disease, 35,* 81–88.

Anderson, J. J., Firschein, H. E., & Meenan, R. F. (1989). Sensitivity of a health status measure to short-term clinical changes in arthritis. *Arthritis and Rheumatism, 32,* 844–850.

Atkins, C. J., Kaplan, R. M., Reinsch, S., Lofback, K., & Timms, R. M. (1984). Behavioral exercise programs in the management of patients with chronic obstructive pulmonary disease. *Journal of Consulting and Clinical Psychology, 52,* 591–603.

Atkinson, R. L., Atkinson, R. C., Smith, E. E., & Hilgard, E. R. (1987). *Introduction to psychology* (9th ed.). San Diego, CA: Harcourt Brace Jovanovich.

Baum, A., Grunberg, N. E., & Singer, J. E. (1982). The use of psychological and neuroendocrinological measurements in the study of stress. *Health Psychology, 1,* 217–236.

Bergner, M. (1989). Health status as a measure of health promotion and disease prevention: Unresolved issues and the agenda for the 1990's. *Proceedings of the 1989 Public Health Conference on Records and Statistics.* Rockville, MD: National Center for Health Statistics.

Bigger, J. T., Fleiss, J. L., Kleiger, R., Miller, J. P., & Rolnitzky, L. M. (1984). Multicenter post-infarction research group: The relationships among ventricular arrhythmias, left ventricular dysfunction and mortality in the two years after myocardial infarction. *Circulation, 69,* 250–258.

Breckenridge, A. (1988). Current controversies in the treatment of hypertension. *American Medicine, 84*(Suppl. 1B), 36–46.

Buchanan, W. W. (1982). Assessment of joint tenderness, grip strength, digital joint circumference and morning stiffness in rheumatoid arthritis. *Journal of Rheumatology, 9,* 763–766.

Cardiac Arrhythmia Suppression Trial (CAST) Investigators. (1989). Preliminary report: The effect of encanide and flecainide on mortality in a randomized trial of arrhythmia suppression after myocardial infarction. *The New England Journal of Medicine, 321,* 406–412.

Clark, M., Gosnell, M., Hager, M., Carroll, G., & Gordon, J. (1988, February 8). What you should know about heart attacks. *Newsweek,* pp. 50–54.

Deyo, R. A. (1988). Measuring the quality of life of patients with rheumatoid arthritis. In S. R. Walker & R. M. Rosser (Eds.), *Quality of life: Assessment and application* (pp. 205–222). London: MTP Press.

Ellwood, P. M. (1988). Outcomes management: A technology of patient experience. *The New England Journal of Medicine, 318,* 1549–1556.

Engle, G. L. (1976). The need for a new medical model: A challenge for biomedicine. *Science, 196,* 129–136.

Expert Panel on Detection, Evaluation, and Treatment of High Blood Cholesterol in Adults (1988). Report on the national cholesterol education program. *Archives of Internal Medicine, 148,* 36–69.

Feinstein, A. R. (1967). *Clinical judgment.* Huntington, NY: Kreiger.

Fordyce, W. E. (1988). Pain and suffering: A reappraisal. *American Psychologist, 43,* 276–283.

Frick, M. K., Elo, O., Haapa, K., Heinonen, O. P., Heinsalmi, P., Helo, P., Huttunen, J. K., Kaitaniemi, R., Koskinen, P., & Manninen, V. (1987). Helsinki Heart Study: Primary prevention trial with gemfibrozil in middle-aged men with dyslipidemia. *The New England Journal of Medicine, 317,* 1237–1245.

Fries, J. F. (1983). Toward an understanding of patient outcome measurement. *Arthritis & Rheumatism, 26,* 697–704.

Fries, J. F., Green, L. W., & Levine, S. (1989). Health promotion and the compression of morbidity. *Lancet, I,* 481–483.

Galbraith, J. K. (1958). *The affluent society.* Boston: Houghton Mifflin.

Greenfield, S. (1989). The state of outcome research: Are we on target? *The New England Journal of Medicine, 320,* 17,1142–1143.

Hypertension Detection and Follow-up Program Cooperative Group (HDFP). (1979). Five-year findings of the hypertension, detection, and follow-up program: 1. Reduction in mortality of persons with high blood pressure, including mild hypertension. *Journal of the American Medical Association, 242,* 2562–2576.

Hla, K. M., Vokaty, K. A., & Feussner, J. (1986). Observer error in systolic blood pressure measurement in the elderly: A case for automatic requarters. *Archives of Internal Medicine, 146,* 2373–2376.

Institutes of Medicine. (1989). Advances in health status assessment: Conference proceedings. *Medical Care, 27*(Suppl.), S1–S293.

Jacobs, D. R., Anderson, J. T., & Blackburn, H. (1979). Diet and serum cholesterol: Do zero correlations negate the relationship? *American Journal of Epidemiology, 110,* 77–87.

Joint National Committee on Detection, Evaluation, and Treatment of High Blood Pressure. (1985). Hypertension prevalence and the status of awareness, treatment, and control in the United States. *Hypertension, 7,* 457–468.

Kannel, W. B., Castelli, W. P., Gordon, T., & McNamara, P. M. (1971). Serum cholesterol, lipoproteins and the risk of coronary heart disease. *Annals of Internal Medicine, 74,* 1.

Kaplan, R. M. (1984). The connection between clinical health promotion and health status: A critical review. *American Psychologist, 39,* 755–765.

Kaplan, R. M. (1985). Behavioral epidemiology, health promotion, and health services. *Medical Care, 23,* 564–583.

Kaplan, R. M. (1988). The value dimension in studies of health promotion. In S. Spacapan & S. Oskamp (Eds.), *The social psychology of health* (pp. 207–236). Beverly Hills, CA: Sage.

Kaplan, R. M. (1989a). Health outcome models for policy analysis. *Health Psychology, 8,* 723–735.

Kaplan, R. M. (1989b). Physicians' health study: Aspirin and primary prevention of heart disease. *The New England Journal of Medicine, 321,* 1826–1827.

Kaplan, R. M., & Anderson, J. P. (1988). The general health policy model: Update and application. *Health Services Research, 23,* 203–235.

Kaplan, R. M., & Atkins, C. J. (1988). Behavioral interventions for patients with COPD. In J. McSweeney & I. Grant (Eds.), *Chronic obstructive pulmonary disease: A behavioral perspective* (pp. 701–740). New York: Marcel Dekker.

Kaplan, R. M., & Atkins, C. J. (1989). The well-year of life as a basis for patient-decision making. *Patient and Education Counseling, 13,* 281–295.

Kaplan, R. M., & Bush, J. W. (1982). Health-related quality of life measurement for evaluation research and policy analysis. *Health Psychology, 1,* 621–680.

Krantz, D. S., Grunberg, N. E., & Baum, A. (1985). Health psychology. *Annual Review of Psychology, 36,* 349–383.

Lipid Research Clinics Coronary Prevention Trial Results. (1984). 1. Reduction in incidence in coronary heart disease. *Journal of the American Medical Association, 251,* 351–364.

McCarty, D. J. (1986). Clinical assessment of arthritis. In D. J. McCarty (Ed.), *Arthritis and allied conditions* (9th ed., pp. 131–147). Philadelphia, PA: Lea & Febiger.

Miller, N. E. (1983). Behavioral medicine: Symbiosis between laboratory and clinic. *Annual Review of Psychology, 34,* 1–31.

National Heart, Lung and Blood Institute. (1984). Tenth report of the director: Vol. 1. Progress and promise (NIH Publication No. 84–2356). Bethesda, MD: National Institutes of Health.

Patterson, H. R. (1984). Sources of error in recording blood pressure of patients with hypertension in general practice. *British Medical Journal, 289,* 1661–1664.

Pickering, T. G., James, G. D., Boddie, C., Harshfield, G. A., Blank, S., & Laragh, J. H. (1988). How common is white coat hypertension? *Journal of the American Medical Association, 259,* 225–228.

President's Commission on National Goals. (1960). Report. (Available from Robert Kaplan, Division of Health Care Sciences, M-022, School of Medicine, University of California, San Diego, La Jolla, CA 92093-0622)

Quality of life assessment. (1988a, Fall). *Quality of Life in Cardiovascular Care, 4*(3).

Quality of life assessment. (1988b, Winter). *Quality of Life in Cardiovascular Care, 4*(4).

Riesenberg, D., & Glass, R. M. (1989). The medical outcomes study. *Journal of the American Medical Association, 262,* 943.

Rocella, E. J., Bowler, A. E., & Horan, N. (1987). Epidemiologic considerations in defining hypertension. *Medical Clinics of North America, 71,* 785–801.

Rodin, J., & Salovey, P. (1989). Health psychology. *Annual Review of Psychology, 40,* 533–579.

Shortell, S. M., & McNerney, W. J. (1990). Criteria and guidelines for reforming the U.S. Health Care System. *The New England Journal of Medicine, 322,* 463–467.

Shumaker, S., Furberg, C., Czajkowski, S., & Schron, E. (in press). Quality of life in cardiovascular disease. New York: Wiley.

Stallones, R. A. (1983). Ischemic heart disease and lipids in blood and diet. *Annual Review of Nutrition, 3,* 155–185.

Steering Committee of the Physicians' Health Study Research Group. (1988). Preliminary report: Findings from the aspirin component of the ongoing Physicians' Health Study. *The New England Journal of Medicine, 318,* 262–264.

Steering Committee of the Physicians' Health Study Research Group. (1989). Final report on the aspirin component of the ongoing Physicians' Health Study. *The New England Journal of Medicine, 321,* 129–135.

Sullivan, D. F. (1966). *Conceptual problems in developing an index of health* (Monograph Series II, No. 17). Washington, DC: Office of Health Statistics, National Center for Health Statistics.

Temoshok, L., Soloman, G. F., & Jenkins, S. (1989, August). *Methodological issues in research on psychoneuroimmunology.* Paper presented at the 97th Annual Convention of the American Psychological Association, New Orleans, LA.

Thelle, D. S., Heyden, S., & Fodor, J. G. (1987). Coffee and cholesterol in epidemiological and experimental studies. *Atherosclerosis, 67,* 97–103.

Walker, S., & Rosser, R. (Eds.). (1988). *Quality of life: Assessment and applications.* London: MTP Press.

White, N. F. (1988). Medical and graduate education in behavioral medicine and the evolution of health care. *Annals of Behavioral Medicine, 10,* 23–29.

Wilson, P. W., Garrison, R. J., Kannel, W. B., McGee, D. L., & Castelli, W. P. (1989). Is coffee consumption a contributor to cardiovascular disease? Insights from the Framingham study. *Archives of Internal Medicine, 149,* 1169–1172.

PART 2

Health behaviours

Part contents

Commentary

Health psychology research explores the predictors of a range of health behaviours. These include eating, smoking, exercise, alcohol, screening, adherence to medication, condom use and contraception use. Researchers even study blood donation, speeding, cycle helmet wearing and tooth flossing. In addition, interventions have been developed as a means to change these behaviours and promote healthier lifestyles. To achieve these ends a number of constructs, theories and models have been developed which form the frameworks for much of the research. Core constructs include attributions, risk perception, self-efficacy, cost–benefit analysis, attitudes and affect. Parts of these constructs have been incorporated into several models which include the stages of change (SOC), the health belief model (HBM), the protection motivation theory (PMT), the theory of reasoned action (TRA) and the theory of planned behaviour (TPB). Such models have been applied across a range of behaviours. In addition, behaviour-specific theories have been developed, such as restraint theory which was developed to understand eating behaviour and the impact of dieting, which also have implications for understanding other behaviours. Further, some research has used qualitative methods to try to understand why people behave in the ways that they do. This part focuses on health behaviours and is divided into three sections. First, the theoretical debates around the theories are considered; second, good examples of research using different models for different behaviours are presented; and finally, papers relating to behaviour change are included.

Theoretical debates

The most frequently used models in health behaviour research are the social cognition models and the stages-of-change model. This section includes three papers that have analysed and critically assessed these models:

Sutton, S. (1998) Predicting and explaining intentions and behavior: how well are we doing? *Journal of Applied Social Psychology*, 28 (15): 1317–38. Reprinted with kind permission of Blackwell Publishing Ltd.

Ogden, J. (2003) Some problems with social cognition models: a pragmatic and conceptual analysis, *Health Psychology*, 22 (4): 424–8. Reprinted with kind permission of the American Psychological Association.

West, R. (2005) Time for a change: putting the Transtheoretical (Stages of Change) Model to rest, *Addiction*, 100: 1036–9. Reprinted with kind permission of Blackwell Publishing Ltd.

Most of the main models used in health psychology research include a measure of behavioural intentions and a measure of actual behaviour. From this perspective a range of cognitions are seen as predicting intentions which in turn predict behaviour. Some research projects include a measure of both these variables whereas some (particularly older studies) only include a measure of intentions. Sutton (1998) provided an early and challenging critique of the main models and assessed the extent to which the models were able to predict both intentions and behaviour. This paper is important as it explores the usefulness of models that are used throughout health psychology. It also clearly illustrates how the results from different studies can be synthesised to produce a better idea of effectiveness and highlights how research is an incremental process.

In contrast, Ogden (2003) and West (2005) provide a more conceptual critique of social cognitions models and the SOC model respectively. Ogden (2003) carried out analysis of papers published in four health psychology journals that had used the TRA, TPB, HBM and PMT, and assessed their pragmatic and conceptual basis. She concluded from her analysis that they cannot be tested as their constructs are often unspecific, they focus on analytic truths and therefore their conclusions are often true by definition rather than by observation, and suggested that the use of such models may create and change cognitions rather than actually assess them. West (2005) carried a similarly conceptual analysis of the SOC model and argued that the model is flawed for a range of reasons, including its focus on stages which are only arbitrarily differentiated from each other, that it assumes people make coherent and stable plans, that each stage confounds a range of construct, that it neglects many factors that are known to influence motivation, such as reward and associative learning, and that it is no better at predicting behaviour than simply asking 'Do you want to . . .?' West concludes from his analysis that the model should be abandoned and replaced by a more comprehensive model of behaviour change. These papers are interesting as they provide fairly forceful critiques of models that are often taken for granted by researchers and used in uncritical ways to guide their research studies. Students are commonly told to be critical in order to gain higher marks but often do not really know what being critical means. These papers help to make the reader think about the basic conceptual groundings of any model and encourage them to believe that it is acceptable to think 'Actually, that doesn't make sense to me' or 'So what?' Because of this, the papers make a good starting point for a discussion about theory and what constitutes a theory worth adopting. Predictably both these papers have been met with their own critiques, particularly by the authors being criticised, and can be read alongside the responses made by these authors who present a defence of their perspectives.

Sutton, S. (1998) Predicting and explaining intentions and behavior: how well are we doing?
Journal of Applied Social Psychology, 28 (15): 1317–38.

Predicting and explaining intentions and behavior

How well are we doing?

Stephen Sutton[1]

Health Behavior Unit, University College London, London, United Kingdom

Abstract

Meta-analyses of research using the theory of reasoned action (TRA) and the theory of planned behavior (TPB) show that these models explain on average between 40% and 50% of the variance in intention, and between 19% and 38% of the variance in behavior. This paper evaluates the performance of these models in predicting and explaining intentions and behavior. It discusses the distinction between prediction and explanation, the different standards of comparison against which predictive performance can be judged, the use of percentage of variance explained as a measure of effect size, and presents 9 reasons why the models do not always predict as well as we would like them to do.

Consider this assessment by Marks (1996) of the contribution of the theory of reasoned action (TRA) to health psychology: "The theory failed as an explanatory account of health behaviour or health status, and the dependent variable preferred for its convenience by almost all investigators – behavioural intention – proved to be a notoriously poor predictor of health-protective action" (p. 8). Researchers who use attitude–behavior models such as the TRA are usually more positive about their utility in predicting and explaining intentions and behavior. Nevertheless, even the proponents of such models believe that there is room for improvement, and there are frequent theoretical and empirical attempts to extend existing models by incorporating additional explanatory variables with the aim of accounting for more of the variance.

This paper attempts to evaluate the performance of the TRA (Ajzen & Fishbein, 1980; Fishbein & Ajzen, 1975) and the closely related theory of planned behavior (TPB; Ajzen, 1988, 1991) in predicting and explaining intentions and behavior. These particular models were chosen because they are widely used, tightly specified, and several meta-analyses have been conducted. The paper briefly discusses the distinction between prediction and explanation, summarizes the results of meta-analyses of the TRA/TPB, discusses the different standards of comparison against which predictive performance can be judged, discusses the use of percent variance explained as a measure of effect size, and, with particular reference to the intention–behavior relationship, presents nine reasons why the models do not always predict as well as we would like them to do. Both hypothetical and real data (the latter from studies of breast screening and smoking cessation) are used to illustrate the main points.

---

1 Correspondence concerning this article should be addressed to Stephen Sutton, Health Behavior Unit, University College London, Brook House, 2–16 Torrington Place, London WCIE 6BT, United Kingdom, e-mail: s.sutton@ucl.ac.uk.

The theories of reasoned action and planned behavior

Since both the TRA and the TPB are well known, only a brief exposition of the models is given here. According to the TRA, most behaviors of social relevance are under volitional control and, hence, behavioral intention is both the immediate determinant and the single best predictor of behavior. The theory specifies two determinants of intention to perform a given behavior: attitude toward the behavior (AB; the person's overall evaluation of the performing the behavior) and subjective norm (SN; the person's perceived expectations of important others with regard to his or her performing the behavior in question). In an attempt to extend the TRA to behaviors that are not entirely under volitional control, the TPB added a third determinant of intention, known as perceived behavioral control (PBC; the extent to which the individual feels he or she has control over performing the behavior, or the perceived ease of performing the behavior). According to the TPB, people will have strong intentions to perform a given action if they evaluate it positively, believe that important others would want them to perform it, and think that it is easy to perform. The TPB also specifies that, for behaviors that are not completely under volitional control, PBC will add to the prediction of behavior over and above the effect of behavioral intention. (For recent critical commentaries on the TPB, see Conner & Armitage, 1998; Eagly & Chaiken, 1993; Manstead & Parker, 1995; and Sutton, 1997.)

Prediction and explanation

Prediction and explanation are not the same thing. Explanation means identifying the determinants of intentions and behavior and specifying how these factors combine. The models we use to help us achieve this aim are causal models which can be represented graphically in the form of path diagrams or mathematically as sets of equations. Both the TRA and the TPB can be regarded as causal models, in this sense.[2] If the main aim is to develop a causal model, we need to carefully specify the causal paths (which variables influence which other variables) and the process by which two or more variables may act in combination to influence another variable. If the main aim is to develop a predictive model, we do not need to concern ourselves with identifying the determinants of a given construct or with specifying causal processes (although a causal model may suggest suitable predictor variables). We are free to choose convenient predictors and weights. For example, if we were concerned only about maximizing predictive power, there would be a strong argument for including past behavior as well as intention and PBC in a predictive model, since it often adds substantially to the prediction of both intentions and behavior (Conner & Armitage, 1998; Ouellette & Wood, 1998; Sutton, 1994).

Prediction can be useful without explanation. Even if the underlying causal processes are not well understood, it is useful to be able to predict tomorrow's weather, who is at high risk for becoming a problem drinker, or who is likely to be a successful doctoral student. In the case of problem drinking, for example, identification of high-risk individuals may enable an early intervention to be made. Prediction enables interventions to be targeted. However, an understanding of the factors that lead some people but not others to develop a drinking problem (explanation) would be even more useful because it would have implications for the nature and content of the intervention program; it would not only tell us who to target but also what to do to them. An explanatory model should also have wider implications and greater strategic value

---

2 In relation to behavior, perceived behavioral control has both a causal and a purely predictive role (Ajzen, 1991). Overall, then, its causal status is ambiguous.

than a purely predictive model. Although prediction and explanation are not the same, the first is necessary for the second; models that do not enable us to predict behavior are unlikely to be useful as explanatory models.

Meta-analyses of the theories of reasoned action and planned behavior

Table 1 summarizes the findings from a number of meta-analyses and quantitative reviews of the TRA/TPB. These reviews vary greatly in terms of the number and type of studies included and the sophistication of the meta-analytic methods used. Table 1 displays the findings in terms of widely used effect size measures: for the bivariate case (the intention–behavior relationship), the product-moment correlation (r) and its square; and, for the multivariate case (e.g., predicting intention from AB and SN; predicting behavior from intention and PBC), the multiple correlation (R) and its square. Both the squared simple correlation and the squared multiple correlation can be interpreted as the proportion of variance explained. For power analysis, where the statistical test involves testing multiple correlations, Cohen (1988, 1992) recommends an effect size index called f^2, which is a simple nonlinear function of R^2: $f^2 = R^2/(1-R^2)$.

Although this effect size index has not been used in studies of the TRA/TPB to date, it is also shown in Table 1.

The findings for behavioral intention show reasonable consistency, with multiple correlations ranging between 0.63 to 0.71 (between 40% and 50% of variance explained). For intention, the value of f^2 ranges from 0.67 to 1.00 – well above Cohen's (1988, 1992) definition of a "large" effect size. Prediction of behavior was lower, as expected, and more variable. When behavior was predicted from intention only, the product-moment correlation ranged between 0.44 and 0.62 (equivalent to explaining between 19% and 38% of the variance). In Cohen's (1988, 1992) terms, these would all be described as "medium" or "large" effects. Three of the

Table 1 Summary of findings from quantitative reviews and meta-analyses of the theories of reasoned action and planned behavior

Review	Effect size[a]							
	Predicting intention (BI) from AB+SN or from AB+SN+PBC			Predicting behavior				
				from BI only		from BI+PBC		
	R	R^2	f^2	r	r^2	R	R^2	f^2
Farley et al. (1981)	0.71	0.50	1.00	–	–	–	–	–
Sheppard et al. (1988)	0.66	0.44	0.79	0.53	0.28	–	–	–
Sutton (1989)[b]	0.63	0.40	0.67	–	–	–	–	–
Ajzen (1991)	0.71	0.50	1.00	0.45	0.20	0.51	0.26	0.35
van den Putte (1993)	0.68	0.46	0.85	0.62	0.38	–	–	–
Randall & Wolff (1994)	–	–	–	0.45	0.20	–	–	–
Godin & Kok (1996)[c]	0.64	0.41	0.69	0.46	0.21	0.58	0.34	0.52
Conner & Armitage (1998)	0.63	0.40	0.67	0.47	0.22	0.48	0.23	0.30
Sheeran & Orbell (in press)[d]	–	–	–	0.44	0.19	–	–	–

[a] Small, medium, and large effect sizes are defined by Cohen (1988, 1992) as follows: Product-moment $r = 0.10, 0.30, 0.50$. Multiple correlation R: Effect size index is $f^2 = R^2/(1 - R^2)$: 0.02, 0.15, 0.35. [b] Restricted to studies of smoking. [c] Restricted to studies of health-related behaviors. [d] Restricted to studies of condom use.

reviews examined the prediction of behavior from intention and PBC in accordance with the TPB (Ajzen, 1991; Conner & Armitage, 1998; Godin & Kok, 1996). The findings fell within the range of those for the intention–behavior relationship. The f^2 values were medium or large.

Should we be impressed or disappointed by the figures in Table 1? On first reaction, it might be judged that we are doing pretty well for intention, but less well for behavior. However, even for intention, we are typically explaining no more than 50% of the variance. This seems disappointing in view of the fact that in the vast majority of studies, intention and its predictors are measured at the same time on the same questionnaire using similar items – conditions that should maximize predictive power.

There are a number of different standards of comparison that can be used in evaluating the percentage of variance explained. One possible standard is the ideal maximum of 100%. Neither the TRA nor the TPB fares well by this standard. In practice, however, the maximum percentage of variance that can be explained in a real application is often substantially less than 100; reasons for this are discussed at length later in this paper.

Another possible benchmark is provided by the effect sizes that are typically found in the behavioral sciences using a diverse range of outcomes and predictors. The simplest way of making such a comparison is to use Cohen's (1988, 1992) operational definitions. Cohen (1992, p. 156) explains that the values for medium effect sizes were chosen to "represent an effect likely to be visible to the naked eye of a careful observer," small effect size values were set to be "noticeably smaller than medium but not so small as to be trivial," and values for large effect sizes were set to be "the same distance above medium as small was below it." Although Cohen acknowledges that the definitions were made subjectively, he also notes that the values chosen to represent medium effect sizes approximate the average size of observed effects in various fields. As mentioned above, using Cohen's definitions, the effect sizes in Table 1 are large for intention and medium or large for behavior.

A third possible standard of comparison is the percentage of variance in intention and behavior explained by other theoretical models. Here the question is the extent to which one model does better or worse than another model that purports to explain the same dependent variable. The meta-analysis reported by Conner and Armitage (1998) directly compared the TRA and the TPB. PBC added, on average, 5% to the variance explained in intention, over and above attitude and subjective norm, and 1% to the variance explained in behavior, over and above intention. In Cohen's (1988, 1992) terms, the improvement afforded by the TPB was between small and medium for intention, but less than small for behavior.

A fourth standard by which the predictive performance of the TRA/TPB can be judged is in terms of practical utility. This will be briefly considered in relation to the examples discussed in the next section.

In evaluating the predictive performance of a model, the number of predictors should be taken into account. At least in terms of their global constructs, the TRA and the TPB are highly parsimonious. The TPB, for example, specifies two proximal causes of behavior and three proximal determinants of intention. Other things being equal, we would be more impressed by a model that accounted for 50% of the variance in intentions using two or three predictors than by a model that explained the same amount of variance but required eight or nine predictors to do so.

Percentage of variance explained is a pessimistic measure of effect size

Percentage of variance explained is a widely used measure of effect size. However, several authors have pointed out that it tends to give a rather pessimistic impression (e.g., Abelson, 1985; Rosenthal & Rubin, 1979). This is not the fault of the effect size measure itself; it is more the case that researchers are not always very good at interpreting what the values mean. Different measures of effect size can give a very different impression, as the simple example in Table 2 shows. Suppose we have a new treatment for smoking and we decide to test its effectiveness in a randomized controlled trial in which 200 smokers are randomly assigned to either intervention or control conditions with 100 in each group. Seventy out of 100 smokers in the intervention condition succeed in quitting smoking, compared with 30 out of 100 in the control condition.

Table 2 gives six effect size measures. The difference measure shows that the intervention improved the success rate by 40 percentage points. The odds of successfully quitting smoking were over five times higher in the intervention condition, compared with the control condition. The relative success rate shows that the intervention more than doubled the chances of successfully quitting. All of these measures suggest that the new treatment had a substantial and clinically useful effect. However, the percentage of variance explained in the dichotomous outcome measure by the dichotomous independent variable (intervention vs. control) was 16%, which seems unimpressive. (Also shown in Table 2 is the value of the effect size measure known as h which is used in power analysis when the significance test to be employed is the normal curve test for the difference between two independent proportions; Cohen, 1988, 1992. In this example, h has a value of 0.82, which is large in Cohen's terms.)

Figure 1 illustrates two real examples. The first is taken from a study of breast screening uptake (part of an ongoing research program on the uptake and psychological impact of mammographic screening; Sutton, Bickler, Sancho-Aldridge, & Saidi, 1994; Sutton, Saidi, Bickler, & Hunter, 1995). The upper curve is based on previously unpublished data from 1,033 women aged between 50 and 64 who responded to a postal questionnaire prior to being sent their first invitation to attend for screening in the U.K. National Breast Screening Program. In the questionnaire, they were asked "If you are invited to go for breast screening, do you think you will attend?" The response categories were *Definitely not; Probably not; Not sure; Yes, probably;* and *Yes, definitely.* Strictly speaking, this is a measure of behavioral expectation, rather than behavioral intention (Warshaw & Davis, 1985). Several months later, information on attendance was obtained from the computer database maintained by the breast screening center.

The relationship is approximately linear. Of those women who said that they definitely would not accept an invitation for screening, 30% subsequently attended for screening, compared with almost 90% of those who said "Yes, definitely." The 5-point intention measure explained 10% of the variance in the dichotomous measure of behavior. Although only 10% of

Table 2 Example showing how different measures of effect size can give a different impression

Randomized controlled trial of a new treatment for smoking			
Condition	N	Succeed	Fail
Intervention	100	70	30
Control	100	30	70

Note. Difference in success rates = 70 − 30 = 40. Odds ratio = $(70 \times 70)/(30 \times 30)$ = 5.4. Relative success rate = 70/30 = 2.3. Product-moment r (phi coefficient) = 0.40. Percentage of variance explained = 16. Cohen's (1988, 1992) h = 0.82.

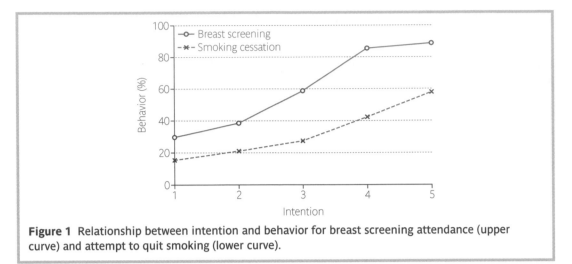

Figure 1 Relationship between intention and behavior for breast screening attendance (upper curve) and attempt to quit smoking (lower curve).

variance was explained, inspection of Figure 1 suggests that the relationship was actually quite substantial. If it were possible to produce differences in attendance rate of this magnitude, we would surely consider our intervention to be quite powerful. This example shows that it is possible to have an effect size that is worthwhile from a practical viewpoint without explaining a large proportion of the variance.

In this data set, the distribution of the intention measure was highly skewed, with 90% of women saying "Yes, probably" or "Yes, definitely." However, even with a uniform distribution on the intention measure (equal numbers of women in each of the five intention categories), the relationship depicted in Figure 1 would still represent no more than 25% of variance explained. Indeed, even if there was a perfect linear relationship between intention and attendance rate, running from 0% attendance among the "Definitely not"s to 100% attendance among the "Yes, definitely"s, still only about 50% of the variance in behavior would be explained. The problem here is the lack of correspondence between the intention scale, which has 5 points, and the behavior measure, which has 2 points. With unequal numbers of scale categories, it is simply not possible to have a linear relationship, even a perfect one, and explain 100% of the variance. The same applies in any situation in which the number of the categories used to measure intention does not equal the number of categories used to measure behavior.

Figure 1 shows a second example, from a study of natural smoking cessation among a sample of 966 smokers in the United Kingdom (Sutton, Marsh, & Matheson, 1987). The lower curve shows the relationship between intention to try to quit smoking (assessed at baseline) and whether or not an attempt was made (based on self-reports obtained 6 months later). Again, the relationship is approximately linear, running from a 16% attempt rate among those smokers with very low intention scores to 58% among those with strong intentions to try to quit. About 11% of the variance was explained in this case.

The second curve is shifted downward relative to the first. Forty-two percent of smokers who expressed very strong intentions to quit failed to translate their intentions into an actual attempt to quit. By contrast, only 11.5% of women who said they would definitely go for breast screening subsequently did not go. Their self-predictions were more accurate. On the other hand, 30% of women in the first study who said that they would definitely not go for screening apparently changed their minds when they received the invitation, compared with 16% of the smokers who reported having tried to quit in spite of having low intentions at baseline. In this case, it was the smokers who made more accurate judgments about their future behavior. However, this comparison is based on much smaller sample sizes than the first.

A full discussion of the reasons for these differences is beyond the scope of this paper. Two general points can be made, however. First, although the intention–behavior correlation provides an appropriate test of the TRA prediction that intention determines behavior (assuming that there is no other factor that influences both intention and behavior), a more fine-grained analysis provides information on how accurately individuals can predict their own behavior. I am aware of only a few studies that have examined the intention–behavior relationship in this way (e.g., Davidson & Beach, 1981; Orbell & Sheeran, 1998; Piliavin, 1991). Second, given appropriate measures, studies of the intention–behavior relationship can be used to investigate optimistic (or pessimistic) biases in people's judgments of probability. Most work to date has studied such biases in relation to perceptions of the risk of experiencing future hazards or health problems (for a review, see Hoorens, 1994). Few studies have examined the intention–behavior relationship from this perspective.

Nine reasons for poor prediction

In this section, I discuss nine reasons why our models, in particular the TRA/TPB, often have lower predictive power than we would like. I use as the example the simple case of predicting behavior (measured at Time 2) from intention (measured at Time 1). Many of these reasons are well known. Nevertheless, it seems a useful exercise to collate them. In discussing reasons why the intention–behavior correlation and the percentage of variance explained may sometimes be lower than we might wish or expect, I am not necessarily endorsing the use of linear correlation and regression methods. In some cases, other methods of analysis and other measures of effect size might be considered more appropriate. For example, when the behavior measure is dichotomous, as in the smoking and breast screening examples outlined above, it can be argued that nonlinear regression methods such as logistic regression would be more appropriate (e.g., Menard, 1995). The rationale for limiting the present discussion to linear correlation and regression is that almost all studies of the TRA/TPB use these methods; in fact, all of the quantitative reviews listed in Table 1 used the correlation coefficient or its square as the measure of effect size. The reasons listed below may be regarded as possible explanations for the heterogeneity in the intention–behavior correlation across studies.

1. Intentions may change

Fishbein and Ajzen repeatedly make the point that, for maximal prediction, the measurement of the intention should be as close as possible in time to the observation of the behavior (e.g., Ajzen & Fishbein, 1980). They also note that sometimes it may not be feasible to do this (e.g., if the aim is to predict the behavior of soldiers in battle or people caught up in a natural disaster) or even desirable to do so (if the aim is long-range prediction). In most studies that apply the TRA/TPB, however, intentions are measured several days, weeks or months prior to the measurement of behavior; there is literally a "gap" between intentions and behavior. If intentions change over time and this change is differential (i.e., different individuals change by different amounts), a distal measure of intention (i.e., distal with respect to the behavior) will be a poorer predictor of behavior than will a proximal measure of intention.

The longer the interval between the measurement of intention and behavior, the greater the likelihood that unforeseen events will occur that lead to changes in intention. Generally speaking, then, the longer the time gap, the lower the correlation between intention and behavior. In their meta-analysis, Randall and Wolff (1994) present evidence to suggest that the strength of the intention–behavior relationship does not vary as a function of the time interval between the measurement of intention and behavior ($r=-0.06$, *ns*). Sheeran and Orbell (in press), however, have argued that the data used by Randall and Wolff were too sparse to draw this conclusion, and that time interval and behavior type were confounded in their analysis. They report the results of their own meta-analysis of studies of condom use which showed, as predicted, that shorter time intervals were associated with significantly stronger intention–behavior correlations.

A point not mentioned by Fishbein and Ajzen is that, in general, longer time intervals allow more opportunities for a behavior to be performed and would thus tend to increase the intention–behavior correlation, other things being equal. For example, consider the intention to go for an eye test. Assuming that intentions remain stable, we are likely to obtain a higher intention–behavior correlation if we allow 4 weeks for the behavior to be performed than if we allow only 24 hr.

2. Intentions may be provisional

Many participants in applications of the TRA/TPB are not engaging in real decision making while they are filling out the questionnaire. Some may have already formed relevant intentions prior to taking part in the study, but for other participants, intentions as expressed on the questionnaire are merely hypothetical or provisional. If intentions are measured after they are actually formed, in the context of a real decision, one would expect to find a stronger relationship between intention and behavior. One way of doing this would be to present participants with a real decision that had significant personal consequences and to measure their intentions in that situation. This is rarely done, however.

This point relates to the preceding point. Intentions measured proximally are less likely to be provisional than intentions measured distally.

3. Violation of the principle of compatibility

The *principle of correspondence* (Ajzen & Fishbein, 1977; Fishbein & Ajzen, 1975) or *compatibility* (as it was renamed by Ajzen, 1988) states that in order to maximize predictive power, the predictor (intention) and the criterion (behavior) should be measured at the same level of specificity or generality. The measures should be matched with respect to four components: action, target, time, and context. In practice, since most studies rely on self-report measures of behavior, this means using the same form of wording for the measures of intention and behavior. For example, if the aim is to predict which smokers try to quit smoking in the New Year, it might be appropriate to use the following two questions: "Do you intend to try to quit smoking in the New Year?" (intention); "Did you try to quit smoking in the New Year?" (behavior). There is substantial empirical support for this idea (Ajzen, 1988; van den Putte, 1993). For example, Ajzen (1996) reports data from Ajzen and Driver (1992) showing that the amount of money respondents were willing to pay for different leisure activities (e.g., mountain climbing, boating) was largely unrelated to their intention to engage in these activities, but was strongly predicted by their intention to pay a user fee for doing so.

Most researchers who use the TRA/TPB recognize the importance of using compatible measures, though the principle is frequently violated in empirical applications of the models. Researchers who use other models (e.g., the health belief model, stage models) seem largely unaware of the principle. The theoretical rationale for the principle of compatibility is presumably that by measuring intention and behavior at the same level of specificity, we are matching cause and effect. In other words, according to the TRA, trying (or not trying) to quit smoking in the New Year is directly caused by the intention to try (or not to try) to quit smoking in the New Year; it is not caused by the intention to try to quit smoking in the next 5 years or by any other intention.

Matching the wording of self-report measures of intention and behavior, in accordance with the principle, has the potential drawback that the two measures may be correlated partly because of shared method variance; that is, a person may answer the questions in a similar way, in part, because they have the same wording. In some cases, it is possible to get around this by using alternatives to behavioral self-reports, as in the breast screening example discussed above.

4. Violation of scale correspondence

Courneya (1994; Courneya & McAuley, 1993) has noted a related problem that arises when the TRA/TPB is applied to repeated behaviors, such as engaging in regular physical activity. A lack of scale correspondence occurs when different magnitudes, frequencies, or response formats are used for the assessment of intention and behavior. Consider the following measures of intention and behavior: "I intend to engage in vigorous physical activity at least 15 times during the month of October" (measured on a 7-point scale ranging from *definitely* to *definitely not*); "I engaged in vigorous physical activity_____times during the month of October." Courneya (1994) points out that the variation obtained by these the two measures is not congruent:

> The former variation is in the degree of certainty or commitment with respect to a set amount or frequency of behavior (e.g., exercise 15 times in a given month or not), whereas the latter variation is in the actual amount or frequency of a behavior (e.g., number of times exercised in a given month).
>
> (p. 584)

Courneya presents data to show that violating scale correspondence results in attenuated correlations.

According to Courneya, the most satisfactory solution to the scale correspondence problem is to use either continuous-open or continuous-closed numerical scales for both intention and behavior. Examples of the two formats are: "I intend to engage [I engaged] in vigorous physical activity _____ times during the month of October" (continuous-open); "I intend to engage [I engaged] in vigorous physical activity during the month of October the following number of times: 0–4/5–9/10–14/15–19/20–24/25–29/30+" (continuous-closed numerical). Courneya also notes that the adoption of these scales may present problems for the TRA/TPB since these models treat each different frequency of engaging in exercise as a different behavior toward which an individual may have different attitudes, subjective norms, and intentions. Thus, although the implications for prediction seem clear (to maximize prediction, always use correspondent measures), the theoretical issues remain unresolved.

5. Unequal number of response categories for intention and behavior

Although Courneya (1994) focused on repeated behaviors, it should be noted that incompatible or noncorrespondent response formats are used routinely in applications of the TRA/TPB to traditional single-act criteria (e.g., attending or not attending for breast screening; voting or not voting for a particular candidate). Indeed, in this case, incompatible response formats are implied by the theory. Thus, intention is conceptualized as a subjective probability continuum running from 0 to 1 (though Fishbein and Ajzen recommend that it be measured on a 7-point likelihood scale), whereas behavior is regarded as a dichotomous Yes/No response. As I pointed out in discussing the breast screening example, if the numbers of categories used to assess intention and behavior are not equal, then it is not possible to obtain a correlation of 1.0, even if the probability of performing the behavior increases linearly across the intention scale.

Although this can be regarded as a purely methodological point, it also makes theoretical sense. The TRA assumes that intention (conceptualized as a continuum but measured on a multipoint scale) is somehow transformed into a dichotomous behavior. Exactly how this transformation occurs is not explained. Attempting to represent the relationship as a straight line (the greater the intention, the greater the probability of performing the behavior) inevitably leads to a lack of fit. Treating the relationship as a step function would potentially allow a better fit. It would be possible to amend the model so that it specified that only if intention reached a particular threshold value (e.g., subjective probability equal to 0.80 or "likely") would the behavior be performed. Alternatively, one could treat intention as an all-or-none phenomenon; either a person has an intention to perform a given behavior or he does not. Treating both intention and behavior as genuine dichotomies would allow the possibility of a perfect relationship between the two (but see Point 8 below).

6. Random measurement error in the measures of intention and/or behavior

If the measures of intention or behavior are not perfectly reliable, the observed correlation will be attenuated relative to that between the true scores (e.g., Schmidt & Hunter, 1996). There is a standard formula that can be used for disattenuating the correlation coefficient if estimates of the reliabilities of the two variables are available: The observed correlation is divided by the square root of the product of the two reliability estimates. For example, if the reliabilities of the intention and behavior measures are 0.80 and 0.90, respectively, the observed correlation is disattenuated by dividing it by $(= \sqrt{(0.80 \times 0.90)})$. Thus, an observed correlation of 0.50 would become 0.59. None of the quantitative reviews listed in Table 1 were based on disattenuated correlations. Thus, the intention–behavior correlations in Table 1 may be regarded as underestimates of the true correlation. The main barrier to routinely correcting observed correlations is lack of good information on reliability. Most studies of the TRA/TPB still use single-item measures of intention and behavior.

Using multiple indicators of intention and behavior would be expected to improve reliability and lead to higher observed correlations. It would also enable reliabilities to be estimated (using Cronbach's alpha) and would allow the use of structural equation modeling, which adjusts for random measurement error in the observed variables. However, the multiple indicator approach is problematic in the case of highly specific behaviors. It is difficult to think of six different ways of asking people whether they intend to buy a particular brand of toothpaste the next time they go to the local supermarket.

In the bivariate case (e.g., the correlation between intention and behavior), the direction of the bias is predictable; the correlation is biased downward. In the multivariate case, the consequences of random measurement error in one or more of the predictors are difficult to predict.

Reliability and validity are usually discussed together. How does lack of validity affect the intention–behavior correlation? Fife-Shaw (1997) notes that use of invalid measures may lower the predictive power of attitude–behavior models. Suppose that behavioral intention does directly cause behavior, as the TRA claims, but our measure of intention is largely tapping the construct of behavioral expectation which, let us assume, is only moderately correlated with intention and does not have any causal impact on behavior. In this situation, we may underestimate the intention–behavior correlation. Other sources of invalidity may inflate the intention–behavior correlation. For example, if people's responses to the Time 2 behavior measure are based in part on recalling and repeating their responses to the Time 1 intention measure, the true intention–behavior correlation will be overestimated.

7. Restriction of range/variance in intention or behavior

Suppose there exists a strong linear relationship between a particular intention and behavior in the population (using the term in its statistical sense), but only those people with fairly or very strong intentions to perform the behavior volunteer for our study. The observed correlation (and percentage of variance explained) in the sample will be lower than that in the population because of the restriction of range or variance; we will underestimate the true size of the relationship (Cohen & Cohen, 1983). The same will be true if the range or variance of the behavior measure is restricted. If, on the other hand, the study attracts people with extreme intention scores (either very high or very low), then the sample correlation will tend to overestimate the population correlation.

Restriction of range arising from sample selection bias should be distinguished from the situation in which, in a given population, there is little variance in intention assessed at Time 1 but substantial variance in behavior assessed at Time 2 (or, conversely, restricted variance in Time 2 behavior but not in Time 1 intention). Here the variance restriction is not the result of biased sampling. It exists in the population; it is a fact of life. If our study sample is unbiased, the same situation should obtain in our sample, subject to sampling variability. In this case, the low correlation can be interpreted substantively.

8. Marginal distributions of the measures do not match

A necessary condition for obtaining a correlation of 1.0 (or explaining 100% of the variance) is that the marginal distributions of the measures of intention and behavior are equal. Even if the number of categories is equal, if the distributions do not match, then the correlation must be less than perfect (Cohen & Cohen, 1983). Table 3 shows a simple example in which both intention and behavior are dichotomous. There is an 80/20 split on intention but a 50/50 split on behavior. The cross-tabulation shows the cell frequencies that yield the largest possible correlation between intention and behavior, given these marginal distributions. The correlation (which in this 2×2 situation is known as the phi coefficient or the fourfold point correlation) is 0.50; thus 25% of the variance is explained. It should be stressed that this is the maximum possible proportion of variance that can be explained, given the marginal frequencies shown. The problem is not that we have dichotomous measures, but that the distributions do not match. (Note that even with dichotomous measures of intention and behavior, if the marginal distributions are equal, it is possible to obtain a correlation of 1.0.)

If intention and behavior can be regarded as genuine dichotomies and intention is assumed to cause behavior (such that those who say "I intend to do X" do it and those who say "I don't intend to do X" do not), then finding unequal distributions is itself inconsistent with the hypothesis (since the distribution on behavior should be a function of the distribution on intention and the causal effect of intention on behavior). If, on the other hand, one (or both) of the measures is not a genuine dichotomy but has been created by collapsing a measure that had more than two categories, the marginal frequencies shown in Table 3 may reflect a less than optimal choice of cut point. Although this example used a 2×2 table for simplicity, the same argument applies to multicategory measures of intention and behavior.

9. Intention may not be the sufficient cause of behavior

For behaviors that are completely under volitional control, it follows by definition that proximal intention is the sufficient cause of behavior. (For *volitional control,* read *intentional control.*) Assuming optimal measurement (perfectly reliable, valid, and compatible measures with equal numbers of categories), a proximal measure of intention should correlate perfectly with the measure of behavior; there is no room for other factors to influence behavior independently of intention. This is the assumption made by the TRA. The TPB, on the other hand, allows behavior to be influenced by control factors in addition to intention; for example, lack of skills, resources, opportunity, or cooperation of other people. Thus, according to the TPB, although intention remains an important cause of behavior, it is not the sufficient cause, except where the behavior is entirely under volitional control, in which case the TPB reduces to the TRA.

In the context of the TRA/TPB, a number of other factors have been proposed as additional determinants of behavior; that is, as factors whose effects on behavior are not entirely mediated by intention. These include past behavior, habit, attitude toward the behavior, and self-identity (see Conner & Armitage, 1998, for a review). Although such factors may have an independent influence on behavior, the possibility remains that the findings simply reflect inadequacies in the measurement of intention. If intentions were measured proximally using highly reliable measures, the effects of factors such as past behavior may be shown to be mediated entirely through intentions.

If other factors in addition to intention independently influence behavior, even with optimal measurement of intentions and behavior, then this would seem to imply that the relationship between intention and behavior, as measured by the product-moment correlation, will be less than perfect. However, it is important to appreciate that this will be the case only when these other factors are uncorrelated with intention. If behavior is influenced solely by intention and a second factor X (and we assume for simplicity that the effects are linear and additive) and if X is correlated zero with intention in the population, then the expected value of the correlation between intention and behavior must be less than 1.0. However, if intention and factor X are correlated, it is possible in principle to obtain a perfect correlation between intention and behavior. This is because the intention–behavior correlation is made up of a component due to the causal effect of intention on behavior and a spurious component due to the fact that X is correlated with intention and has an independent effect on behavior.

Table 3 Example showing unequal marginal distributions

Intention	Behavior		Total
	Yes	No	
Yes	50	30	80
No	0	20	20
Total	50	50	100

Note. r = 0.50; *r*^{2} = 0.25.

The last point relates to the distinction made earlier between prediction and explanation. If the aim is simply to predict behavior, there can be no theoretical objection to using intention on its own as a predictor and the correlation coefficient as one possible measure of predictive power. If, on the other hand, the aim is to estimate the size of the causal effect of intention on behavior, then it is essential to control for the effects of variables that, according to theory, influence both intention and behavior.

Conclusions and recommendations

Meta-analyses of the TRA and the TPB show that these models explain, on average, between 40% and 50% of the variance in intention and between 19% and 38% of the variance in behavior. It is important to compare these reviews in detail and to analyze the reasons for the variability in the findings, particularly for behavior. It is also important to examine the variability in findings across studies within a single review to address the question of why the models perform better in some studies than in others. Whether the overall level of predictive power afforded by the TRA/TPB is judged as impressive or disappointing depends on the standard of comparison used. For instance, the models fare poorly by comparison with the ideal maximum of 100% variance explained, but perform well when judged in relation to typical effect sizes in the behavioral sciences.

Percentage of variance explained may give a rather pessimistic impression. An effect size equivalent to explaining 10% of the variance may be extremely worthwhile from a practical viewpoint. This is not to suggest that we should abandon percentage of variance explained as a measure of effect size, but rather that we should learn not to be dismissive of models that explain only 10% of the variance, particularly if they do so with a small number of predictors. Different measures of effect size can give a very different impression. Researchers should therefore compute a variety of effect size measures. In addition, rather than simply reporting the correlation or the proportion of variance explained, investigators should consider reporting the intention–behavior relationship in more detail, for example by presenting a full cross-tabulation or using a graphical representation such as that used in Figure 1. This would enable prediction accuracy to be analyzed.

The discussion of reasons for poor prediction makes it clear that explaining 100% of the variance is unlikely to be achievable in practice. It also has a number of implications for maximizing the intention–behavior correlation. Generally speaking, intentions should be measured proximally, after rather than before people have made a real decision, and using compatible measures of intention and behavior based on multiple indicators for high reliability. (These are generalizations; I have noted several exceptions and provisos.) Where it is not possible to use multi-item scales, researchers should at least explore the possible effects of different degrees of reliability on their findings. This is particularly important in multivariate analysis where the consequences of unreliability are difficult to predict.

The principle of compatibility should be extended to include not simply the wording of the question, but also the response format and the number of response categories. For instance, if the behavioral measure is dichotomous, investigators might consider including a dichotomous measure of intention, as well as the conventional 7-point likelihood rating scale. I have suggested elsewhere (Sutton, 1994) that behavioral intentions (strictly speaking, behavioral expectations) could be measured by showing respondents the measure of behavior that will be used in the follow-up questionnaire and asking them to predict how they will answer the question. This method guarantees perfect compatibility. I am not aware of any studies that have used this approach to date.

Where unequal numbers of response categories are used, researchers should be encouraged to compute the correlation and percentage of variance explained under different assumptions (e.g., linear relationships vs. step functions, different distributions) to explore the effects of such factors on effect size. This can easily be done using standard software.

Where categories of a variable (e.g., a measure of intention) are collapsed for analysis, one consideration that should influence the choice of cut point is the extent to which it produces a distribution that approximates the distribution of the behavior measure. Put simply, infrequent behaviors should be predicted infrequently.

The distinction between prediction and explanation is an important one. It should be emphasized that explanation is not simply a matter of maximizing the intention–behavior correlation. Rather, the aim is to obtain an accurate estimate of the causal effect of intention on behavior (which is one component of the intention–behavior correlation). Validity issues are therefore particularly pertinent. If the main aim is to predict behavior, then lack of validity in the measure of the predictor(s) is not a problem. It matters little if a scale that is designed to measure construct X in fact measures construct Y, so long as it is a good predictor of behavior. However, it is crucial that the criterion is measured validly, otherwise we may not be predicting what we thought we were predicting. If the aim is to explain behavior, we need to be concerned about the validity of the measures of both the predictors and the criterion.

Finally, a number of additional suggestions may be made for future research on the intention–behavior relationship. Where possible, studies should include proximal as well as distal measures of intention so that change can be measured and the impact on the intention–behavior relationship assessed. This would enable a fairer test of the TRA's sufficiency assumption (i.e., the assumption that all influences on behavior act through proximal intention). Even the effect of past behavior, a variable that often strongly predicts future behavior over and above a distal measure of intention, may be shown to be entirely mediated by a reliable and valid proximal measure of intention. Although Fishbein and Ajzen say little about the role of memory processes, these would seem to be crucial in understanding the relationship between intention and behavior. In order to influence behavior, a distally formed intention has to be retrieved or re-formed when an opportunity to perform the behavior arises. More attention also needs to be paid to situational factors. Intentions may change because the context changes (Ajzen, 1996; Sutton, 1996). For example, when forming an intention to use a condom, a person may fail to accurately predict the circumstances of the next sexual encounter. There are a number of ways in which the TRA/TPB can accommodate situational influences. Indeed, the emphasis on salient beliefs in these models implies a potentially important role for situational factors in influencing behavior. Finally, method effects should be investigated in future studies by measuring intentions and behavior using more than one method.

References

Abelson, R. P. (1985). A variance explanation paradox: When a little is a lot. *Psychological Bulletin*, **97**, 129–133.

Ajzen, I. (1988). *Attitudes, personality, and behavior*. Milton Keynes, UK: Open University Press.

Ajzen, I. (1991). The theory of planned behavior. *Organizational Behavior and Human Decision Processes*, **50**, 179–211.

Ajzen, I. (1996). The directive influence of attitudes on behavior. In P. M. Gollwitzer & J. A. Bargh (Eds.), *The psychology of action: Linking cognition and motivation to behavior* (pp. 385–403). New York, NY: Guilford.

Ajzen, I., & Driver, B. L. (1992). Contingent value measurement: On the nature and meaning of willingness to pay. *Journal of Consumer Psychology, 1,* 297–316.

Ajzen, I., & Fishbein, M. (1977). Attitude–behavior relations: A theoretical analysis and review of empirical research. *Psychological Bulletin, 84,* 888–918.

Ajzen, I., & Fishbein, M. (1980). *Understanding attitudes and predicting social behavior.* Englewood Cliffs, NJ: Prentice-Hall.

Cohen, J. (1988). *Statistical power analysis for the behavioral sciences* (2nd ed.). Hillsdale, NJ: Lawrence Erlbaum.

Cohen, J. (1992). A power primer. *Psychological Bulletin, 112,* 155–159.

Cohen, J., & Cohen, P. (1983). *Applied multiple regression/correlation analysis for the behavioral sciences.* Hillsdale, NJ: Lawrence Erlbaum.

Conner, M., & Armitage, C. J. (1998). Extending the theory of planned behavior: A review and avenues for further research. *Journal of Applied Social Psychology, 28,* 1429–1464.

Courneya, K. S. (1994). Predicting repeated behavior from intention: The issue of scale correspondence. *Journal of Applied Social Psychology, 24,* 580–594.

Courneya, K. S., & McAuley, E. (1993). Predicting physical activity from intention: Conceptual and methodological issues. *Journal of Sport and Exercise Psychology, 15,* 50–62.

Davidson, A. R., & Beach, L. R. (1981). Error patterns in the prediction of fertility behavior. *Journal of Applied Social Psychology, 11,* 475–488.

Eagly, A. H., & Chaiken, S. (1993). *The psychology of attitudes.* Fort Worth, TX: Harcourt Brace Jovanovich.

Farley, J. U., Lehmann, D. R., & Ryan, M. J. (1981). Generalizing from "imperfect" replication. *Journal of Business, 54,* 597–610.

Fife-Shaw, C. (1997). Commentary on Joffe (1996) AIDS research and prevention: A social representation approach. *British Journal of Medical Psychology, 70,* 65–73.

Fishbein, M., & Ajzen, I. (1975). *Belief, attitude, intention, and behavior: An introduction to theory and research.* Reading, MA: Addison-Wesley.

Godin, G., & Kok, G. (1996). The theory of planned behavior: A review of its applications to health-related behaviors. *American Journal of Health Promotion, 11,* 87–98.

Hoorens, V. (1994). Unrealistic optimism in health and safety risks. In D. R. Rutter & L. Quine (Eds.), *Social psychology and health: European perspectives* (pp. 153–174). Aldershot, UK: Avebury.

Manstead, A. S. R., & Parker, D. (1995). Evaluating and extending the theory of planned behavior. In W. Stroebe & M. Hewstone (Eds.), *European Review of Social Psychology* (Vol. 6, pp. 69–95). Chichester, UK: John Wiley & Son.

Marks, D. F. (1996). Health psychology in context. *Journal of Health Psychology, 1,* 7–21.

Menard, S. (1995). *Applied logistic regression analysis.* Thousand Oaks, CA: Sage.

Orbell, S., & Sheeran, P. (1998). *"Inclined abstainers": A problem for predicting health-related behaviour.* Manuscript submitted for publication.

Ouellette, J. A., & Wood, W. (1998). *Habit and intention in everyday life: The multiple processes by which past behavior predicts future behavior.* Manuscript submitted for publication.

Piliavin, J. A. (1991). Is the road to helping paved with good intentions? Or inertia? In J. A. Howard & P. L. Callero (Eds.), *The self-society dynamic: Cognition, emotion, and action* (pp. 259–279). Cambridge, UK: Cambridge University Press.

Randall, D. M., & Wolff, J. A. (1994). The time interval in the intention–behaviour relationship: Meta-analysis. *British Journal of Social Psychology, 33,* 405–418.

Rosenthal, R., & Rubin, D. B. (1979). A note on percent variance explained *Journal of Applied Social Psychology, 9,* 395–396.

Schmidt, F. L., & Hunter, J. E. (1996). Measurement error in psychological research: Lessons from 26 research scenarios. *Psychological Methods*, **1,** 199–223.

Sheeran, P., & Orbell, S. (in press). Do intentions predict condom use? Meta-analysis and examination of six moderator variables. *British Journal of Social Psychology*.

Sheppard, B. H., Hartwick, J., & Warshaw, P. R. (1988). The theory of reasoned action: A meta-analysis of past research with recommendations for modifications and future research. *Journal of Consumer Research*, **15,** 325–343.

Sutton, S. R. (1989). Smoking attitudes and behavior: Applications of Fishbein and Ajzen's theory of reasoned action to predicting and understanding smoking decisions. In T. Ney & A. Gale (Eds.), *Smoking and human behavior* (pp. 289–312). Chichester, UK: John Wiley & Sons.

Sutton, S. R. (1994). The past predicts the future: Interpreting behaviour–behaviour relationships in social psychological models of health behaviour. In D. R. Rutter & L. Quine (Eds.), *Social psychology and health: European perspectives* (pp. 71–88). Aldershot, UK: Avebury.

Sutton, S. R. (1996). Some suggestions for studying situational factors within the framework of attitude–behaviour models. *Psychology and Health*, **11,** 635–639.

Sutton, S. R. (1997). Theory of planned behaviour. In A. Baum, S. Newman, J. Weinman, R. West, & C. McManus (Eds.), *Cambridge handbook of psychology, health and medicine* (pp. 177–180). Cambridge, UK: Cambridge University Press.

Sutton, S. R., Bickler, G., Sancho-Aldridge, J., & Saidi, G. (1994). Prospective study of predictors of attendance for breast screening in inner London. *Journal of Epidemiology and Community Health*, **48,** 65–73.

Sutton, S. R., Marsh, A., & Matheson, J. (1987). Explaining smokers' decisions to stop: Test of an expectancy-value approach. *Social Behaviour*, **2,** 35–49.

Sutton, S. R., Saidi, G., Bickler, G., & Hunter, J. (1995). Does routine screening for breast cancer raise anxiety? Results from a three wave prospective study in England. *Journal of Epidemiology and Community Health*, **49,** 413–418.

van den Putte, B. (1993). *On the theory of reasoned action.* Unpublished doctoral dissertation, University of Amsterdam, The Netherlands.

Warshaw, P. R., & Davis, F. D. (1985). Disentangling behavioral intention and behavioral expectation. *Journal of Experimental Social Psychology*, **21,** 213–228.

Ogden, J. (2003) Some problems with social cognition models: a pragmatic and conceptual analysis, *Health Psychology*, 22 (4): 424–8.

Some problems with social cognition models

A pragmatic and conceptual analysis

Jane Ogden
University of London

Abstract

Empirical articles published between 1997 and 2001 from 4 health psychology journals that tested or applied 1 or more social cognition models (theory of reasoned action, theory of planned behavior, health belief model, and protection motivation theory; $N=$ 47) were scrutinized for their pragmatic and conceptual basis. In terms of their pragmatic basis, these 4 models were useful for guiding research. The analysis of their conceptual basis was less positive. First, these models do not enable the generation of hypotheses because their constructs are unspecific; they therefore cannot be tested. Second, they focus on analytic truths rather than synthetic ones, and the conclusions resulting from their application are often true by definition rather than by observation. Finally, they may create and change both cognitions and behavior rather than describe them.

Keywords: social cognition models, critique, problems, health cognitions

Despite the widespread use in health psychology of social cognition models, there have been some critiques. Conner and Norman (1996) described an overlap in the variables between the different models, Sutton (1998) concluded that although such models are designed to predict behavior they leave much of the variance in behavior unexplained, and Smedlund (2000) criticized them for their logical construction. This article highlights further problems with the health belief model (HBM; Becker & Rosenstock, 1987), the theory of reasoned action (TRA; Fishbein & Ajzen, 1975), the protection motivation theory (PMT; Rogers, 1975), and the theory of planned behavior (TPB; Ajzen, 1985) in terms of their pragmatic and conceptual basis and asks whether they can be considered good theories. Specifically it addresses the questions: Are the theories useful? Can the theory be tested? Does the theory use analytic or synthetic truths? and Does the theory access or create cognitions?

Method

The main journal outlets for health psychology work for researchers in the United States, the United Kingdom, and across other European countries are *Health Psychology,* published by the

Correspondence concerning this article should be addressed to Jane Ogden, Reader in Health Psychology, Department of General Practice, Guy's, King's and St Thomas' School of Medicine, King's College London, University of London, 5 Lambeth Walk, London SE11 6SP, United Kingdom. E-mail: Jane.Ogden@kcl.ac.uk

American Psychological Association; the *British Journal of Health Psychology*, published by the British Psychological Society; *Psychology and Health*, the official journal of the European Health Psychology Society and published by Brunner Routledge; and the *Journal of Health Psychology*, published by Sage. All articles published in these journals between 1997 and 2001 (inclusive) excluding commentaries, introductions to special issues, and letters to the editor that focused on the most common structured models (HBM, TRA, TPB, and PMT) were scrutinized for their pragmatic and conceptual basis. Exemplar articles were noted and illustrative quotes were recorded.

Results

The articles

During the 5-year period from 1997 to 2001, 923 articles were published in these four journals. Of these, 727 did not focus on health-related cognitions. The remaining 196 articles (21%) contained a substantial focus on health-related cognitions. Twenty-two of these were nonempirical reviews or discussion pieces. A total of 47 empirical articles focusing on structured models form the basis of the present article: HBM ($n=9$), PMT ($n=5$), TRA ($n=5$), and TPB ($n=33$). (Note that 5 articles focused on two models simultaneously.)

Pragmatic basis to a theory: are the theories useful?

In the sample of articles examined, the behaviors covered were condom use, exercise, sugar restriction, sun cream use, health screening, exercise, low-fat diet, dental flossing, breast self-examination, safety helmet use, providing care for parents, donating bone marrow, hormone replacement therapy use, ecstasy use, the request for hospital autopsies, smoking, antibiotic prescribing, and voting. These articles constituted 5.1% of the total number of articles published in the four journals over the 5-year period. The journal offering most of its space to research relating to health cognitions was *Psychology and Health* (33.2%, $n=82$), then *Health Psychology* (19.5%, $n=63$), then the *British Journal of Health Psychology* (18.5%, $n=25$), with the *Journal of Health Psychology* showing the least commitment to this perspective (11.9%, $n=26$). Of these articles, the journal publishing the largest proportion of research relating to the four structured models (HBM, PMT, TRA, and TPB) was the *British Journal of Health Psychology* (40%, $n=10$), then *Psychology and Health* (33%, $n=27$), then the *Journal of Health Psychology* (19.2%, $n=5$), and the least was published in *Health Psychology* (7%, $n=5$). From the perspective of researchers, these models are therefore useful. The models are also used to inform service development and the development of health-related interventions to promote health behaviors. This sample of articles contained five theory-based interventions. These aimed to reduce sun tanning based on the PMT (McClenden & Prentice-Dunn, 2001), to explore the relationship between alcohol use and the intention to use condoms (Conner, Graham, & Moore, 1999), to increase sun cream use using the HBM (Castle, Skinner, & Hampson, 1999), to encourage safety helmet use using the TPB (Quine, Rutter, & Arnold, 2001), and to promote cervical cancer screening using the TPB and implementation intentions (Sheeran & Orbell, 2000).

Conceptual basis to a theory: can the theory be tested?

A good theory should consist of constructs that are sufficiently specific so as to generate hypotheses. Such hypotheses should be testable, and, in principle at least, a good theory should be able to be rejected. Of the articles examined, almost all indicated that they were "testing" a theory, and nearly three quarters concluded that their data provided support for their particular model. For example, Povey, Conner, Sparks, James, and Shepherd (2000) concluded that "the results from this study suggest that the TPB is generally a useful framework to predict health eating intentions and behaviour" (p. 1004), Steen, Peay, and Owen (1998) concluded from their study of intentions to minimize sun exposure that "our findings generally supported the theory of reasoned action" (p. 116), and Flynn et al (1997) concluded from their study of voting behavior using the TPB that "legislator surveys that use this conceptual model can provide results relevant to understanding tobacco policy development" (p. 401). But what do such statements of support really mean? What results would indicate that the models being used were not a useful framework? Could data be collected that would lead to the model being rejected?

Within the present sample, two thirds reported that at least one of the variables within the given model did not predict the outcome variable being studied. For example, many studies using the TPB reported no role for subjective norms (e.g., Bozionelos & Bennett, 1999; De Wit, Stroebe, De Vroome, Sandfort, & Van Griensen, 2000; Jamner, Wolitski, Corby, & Fishbein, 1998), some showed no predictive role for perceived behavioral control (e.g., Flynn et al., 1997; Sutton, McVey, & Glanz, 1999), and some showed no role for attitudes (e.g., Yzer, Siero, & Buunk, 2001). Similarly, some studies using the HBM reported no role for susceptibility (e.g., Castle et al., 1999; Pakenham, Pruss, & Clutton, 2000), and those using the PMT found no role for a range of variables (e.g., Murgraff, White, & Phillips, 1999; Plotnikoff & Higginbotham, 1998). Further, all of the articles examined left much of the variance unexplained, with explained variance ranging from 1% to 65% for behavior and 14% to 92% for behavioral intentions.

The variables described by the models may not be predictive and the variance explained is low, but, instead of rejecting the models, several explanations are offered. The first explanation argues that the model should be accepted but that the variables were not operationalized properly. For example, Murgraff et al. (1999) suggested from their study of the PMT that their results may be due to the "wording of the intention measure" (p. 348); similarly Castle et al. (1999) suggested that "the operationalisation of constructs of the Health Belief Model may not have been optimal" (p. 526). The second explanation suggests that the model should be accepted but that sample characteristics may explain their results. For example, Hagger, Chatzisarantis, Biddle, and Orbell (2001) argued that the usefulness of the TPB depends on the type of population used and that the young people in their study may have different cognitive predictors of their behavior than an older sample. Similarly, De Wit et al. (2000) suggested that the type of population being considered by those answering the questionnaire may also influence the way the cognitions relate to behavior and differentiate between casual and primary sexual partners in their study using the TPB. Other studies explain the failure of the model in terms of the type of behavior studied. For example, Sheeran, Conner, and Norman (2001) argued that the low variance found in their study using the TPB is "probably because the health screening was a novel behaviour for participants" (p. 17), and Murgraff et al. (1999) suggested that the performance of the PMT in their study of single-occasion drinking was due to participants being "exposed to a new, previously unknown threat to their health" (p. 347). Sutton et al. (1999) also explained the failure of the TPB in their study assessing intentions to use condoms in terms of the characteristics of the behavior in question. Finally, several articles argued that the model being studied should be accepted but only if it is extended. For example, Sparks, Conner, James, Shepherd, and Povey (2001) argued for the addition of ambivalence, and Trafimow (2000) argued for the addition of habit to the TPB.

The majority of the articles did not strongly support the models being used either in terms of the expected associations between variables or in terms of the models' ability to predict the designated outcome variable. But such data are not used to reject the model in question. Instead, explanations are offered that function as caveats perpetuating the belief that the models have been verified. All data can be used to indicate the strength of a social cognition model, but it would appear that no data can be collected to show that it is wrong. They therefore cannot be tested.

Are the models testing analytic or synthetic truths?

Philosophy of science differentiates between two types of truth: synthetic truth that can be known through exploration and testing and analytic truth that is true by definition. A good theory should generate synthetic rather than analytic truths to avoid being tautological. Almost all articles correlated cognitions such as *perceived behavioral control, attitudes, severity, susceptibility,* and the *costs and benefits of a behavior* with the cognition *behavioral intention.* At times the operationalization of these different cognitions appeared very similar. For example, Lugoe and Rise (1999) correlated perceived behavioral control measured by the statement, "How certain are you that you would be able to use a condom at the next intercourse?" with intentions that were operationalized as "I intend to use a condom at the next sexual intercourse." Similarly, the same two cognitions were operationalized by Masalu and Astrom (2001) as "How easy or difficult will it be for you to avoid between-meal intake of sugared snacks and drinks in future?" (p. 439) and "How likely or unlikely is it that you will avoid between-meal intake of sugared snacks and drinks in future?" (p. 438) and by Rapaport and Orbell (2000) as "Even if I wanted, I might not be able to provide practical assistance/emotional support for a parent of mine in need of care within the next twenty years" (p. 314) and "If a parent of mine were in need of care within the next twenty years, I intend to personally provide practical assistance/emotional support" (p. 315). If they are significantly correlated, then is it really surprising? Such cognitions are defined as different and yet operationalized in similar ways. The majority of studies explored analytic truths that were true by definition rather than by exploration.

Over two thirds of these articles also correlated these same cognitions with a measure of behavior. For example, Plotnikoff and Higginbotham (1998) assessed diet and exercise, Yzer et al. (2001) assessed condom use, and Conner, Sherlock, and Orbell (1998) assessed ecstasy use. These could be considered to be assessing synthetic truths as the cognition is operationalized differently to the behavior. However, although one article (Jones, Abraham, Harris, Schulz, & Chrispin, 2001) assessed the reliability of their self-reported behavior, only a quarter of articles used an objective measure of behavior that was not reliant on self-report (e.g., Flynn et al., 1997; McClendon & Prentice-Dunn, 2001; Pakenham et al., 2000; Sheeran et al., 2001; Sheeran & Orbell, 2000). Such self-reported behavior could also be contaminated by the self-reported cognitions, and any association found between the two could also reflect a truth by definition rather than one that requires an empirical test.

Are they accessing or creating cognitions?

All of the articles asked participants to complete a questionnaire to describe their cognitions. This procedure is based on the assumption that the answers given will reveal preexisting states of mind rather than ones that have been generated by the questionnaire. It is possible, however, that cognitions may be created simply by completing a questionnaire. This finds reflection in the use of questions to manipulate affect and cognition in both the cognitive and clinical literatures (e.g., Wenzlaff & Wegner, 2000). This might be particularly the case if the behavior being considered is novel and unfamiliar and is illustrated by several articles in the present sample. For example, Cecil, Pinkerton, and Bogart (1999) used the HBM in the context of the female condom. However, 93% of their sample had never used a female condom and yet were asked to provide details of their attitudes toward them. Questionnaire statements such as "the appearance of the female condom turns me off" (p. 170) and "female condom decreases sexual pleasure for a man" (p. 170) might not be accessing such cognitions but creating them in this novice sample. Likewise Bagozzi, Lee, and Van Loo (2001) explored decisions to donate bone marrow using the framework of the TRA. As a means of gaining informed consent, all of the participants were given a brief description "of the need for bone marrow donation" that was introduced as follows: "Because most people are unfamiliar with bone marrow donation, we have prepared a short summary of the reasons for collecting bone marrow" (p. 38). Information was then provided "compiled from a variety of sources including publications from the National Marrow Donor Program" (p. 38). For many participants, these may be novel areas for consideration, and their cognitions may easily be manipulated. Such questionnaire items could create feelings of guilt and a sense of duty in the participants, shifting their cognitions toward that which might seem more socially desirable. It may not, however, only be novelty that can create a shift in cognitions. In line with the cognitive and clinical literatures (e.g., Wenzlaff & Wegner, 2000), even focusing on a familiar behavior could create a shift in cognitive set. Accordingly, completing questions about an individual's cognitions may change and create rather than access the way in which they think.

Completing a questionnaire may also change a participant's subsequent behavior. About half of the articles assessed behavior at a follow-up time point. This methodological approach is considered appropriate if synthetic rather than analytic truths are being assessed. The process of completing a baseline measure of cognitions may, however, determine rather than simply predict subsequent behavior. For example, Morrison, Baker, and Gillmore (1998) asked teenagers to complete a range of cognitive measures based on the TRA at baseline and then assessed their behavior 3 months later. Although the teenagers' subsequent behavior was predicted by the earlier cognitions, completing items relating to their intentions to use condoms, their attitudes toward them, and their perceptions of what their significant others thought about condoms may have raised the salience of condom use, created a sense that this behavior was socially desirable, and therefore changed their subsequent behavior. Similarly, Masalu and Astrom (2001) asked a large sample of students to record their cognitions about consuming sugared snacks and drinks in line with the TPB. Items rated included "How likely or unlikely is it that you will avoid between meal intake of sugared snacks and drinks in future?" (p. 438) and "Most people important to me think that I should avoid between meal intake of sugared snacks and drinks in the future" (p. 438). They then assessed self-reported consumption 4 weeks later. Baseline beliefs predicted behavior at follow-up. But they may also have raised the issue of between-meal snacks and drinks and changed the participants' behavior.

Discussion

This article explored the pragmatic and conceptual basis to a series of articles based on four social cognition models. This analysis showed these models are useful and fruitful and provide a framework for the development of interventions designed to change health-related behaviors. The models pass the present article's criteria to assess their pragmatic basis.

The results from the analysis of their conceptual basis are less positive. Most articles using the social cognition models purport to "test," "apply," or "assess the utility" of the model in question. In line with this, the majority of studies reported results that were not consistent with the predicted associations between constructs and left much of the variance in the outcome variable unexplained. However, rather than using the data to challenge the models, a range of explanations were offered relating to the wording used, the population studied, the behavior of concern, or the need for additional variables. All data are used to support the models, but it is not clear what data would enable the models to be rejected. Therefore they cannot be tested. Further, most studies using the social cognition models assessed associations between constructs that were true by definition rather than by observation. This focus on analytic truths was illustrated by the multiple correlations between cognitions such as perceived behavioral control and behavioral intention but was also implicit within those associations between cognitions and self-reported behavior. Finally, although intended to measure an individual's cognitions, the use of questionnaires based on social cognition models may change rather than access the way a person thinks. Such a methodological approach may also change any subsequent behavior. This problem seems particularly pertinent to the more recent interest in the relationship between intentions and behavior and the intention behavior gap (e.g., Bagozzi, 1993; Gollwitzer, 1993). Researchers studying this area ask participants to rate their intentions to perform a particular behavior such as taking vitamins, performing breast self-examination, and doing exercise (e.g., Orbell, Hodgkins, & Sheeran, 1997; Sheeran & Orbell, 1998). These data are regarded as illustrating and describing the respondents' views. Some researchers then ask respondents to describe when and where this behavior will be performed in line with "action plans" or "implementation intentions" (e.g., Orbell et al., 1997; Sheeran & Orbell, 1998). This second set of data is considered an intervention as it has been shown to change subsequent behavior. The first process of questioning is conceptualized as descriptive and as a method of data collection that elicits views. In direct contrast, the second process is conceptualized as manipulative and considered to change views. The process of making a participant construct an implementation intention is now promoted as one of the simplest and more powerful mechanisms for bringing about change (Sheeran & Orbell, 1998, 2000). This must also indicate that all question asking can also bring about change. It seems unlikely that the same process of question asking can be descriptive and passive for some of the time and interventional and active at others.

In conclusion, the present analysis indicates that social cognition models such as the HBM, PMT, TPB, and TRA can be considered pragmatic tools for health psychologists and researchers from allied research areas to draw upon. But in using them for this purpose, one should recognize the essential flaws in their conceptual basis. These models cannot be tested, they focus on analytic truths rather than synthetic ones, and they may create and change both cognitions and behavior rather than describe them and as such do not pass the criteria set for a good theory. If they are to be given the status of theories, then it is recommended that the critical eye that psychologists place on other areas of research also be cast on this one.

References

Ajzen, I. (1985). From intention to actions: A theory of planned behavior. In J. Kuhl & J. Beckman (Eds.), *Action-control: From cognition to behavior* (pp. 11–39). Heidelberg, Germany: Springer.

Bagozzi, R. P. (1993). On the neglect of volition in consumer research: A critique and proposal. *Psychology and Marketing, 10,* 215–237.

Bagozzi, R. P., Lee K.-H., & Van Loo, M. F. (2001). Decisions to donate bone marrow: The role of attitudes and subjective norms across cultures. *Psychology and Health, 16,* 29–56.

Becker, M. H., & Rosenstock, I. M. (1987). Comparing social learning theory and the health belief model. In W. B. Ward (Ed.), *Advances in health education and promotion* (pp. 245–249). Greenwich, CT: JAI Press.

Bozionelos, G., & Bennett, P. (1999). The theory of planned behaviour as predictor of exercise. *Journal of Health Psychology, 4,* 517–529.

Castle, C. M., Skinner, T. C., & Hampson, S. E. (1999). Young women and suntanning: An evaluation of a health education leaflet. *Psychology and Health, 14,* 517–527.

Cecil, H., Pinkerton, S. D., & Bogart, L. M. (1999). Perceived benefits and barriers associated with the female condom among African-American adults. *Journal of Health Psychology, 4,* 165–175.

Conner, M., Graham, S., & Moore, B. (1999). Alcohol and intentions to use condoms: Applying the theory of planned behaviour. *Psychology and Health, 14,* 795–812.

Conner, M., & Norman, P. (Eds.). (1996). *Predicting health behaviour.* Buckingham, England: Open University Press.

Conner, M., Sherlock, K., & Orbell, S. (1998). Psychosocial determinants of ecstasy use in young people in the UK. *British Journal of Health Psychology, 3,* 295–317.

De Wit, J. B. F., Stroebe, W., De Vroome, E. M. M., Sandfort, T. G. M., & Van Griensven, G. J. P. (2000). Understanding AIDS preventive behaviour with casual and primary partners in homosexual men: The theory of planned behaviour and the information-motivation-behavioural-skills model. *Psychology and Health, 15,* 325–340.

Fishbein, M., & Ajzen, I. (1975). *Belief, attitude, intention, and behavior: An introduction to theory and research.* Reading, MA: Addison-Wesley.

Flynn, B. S., Dana, G. S., Goldstein, A. O., Bauman, K. E., Cohen, J. E., Gottlieb, N. H., & Solomon, L. J. (1997). State legislators' intentions to vote and subsequent votes on tobacco control legislation. *Health Psychology, 16,* 401–404.

Gollwitzer, P. M. (1993). Goal achievement: The role of intentions. *European Review of Social Psychology, 4,* 141–185.

Hagger, M. S., Chatzisarantis, N., Biddle, S. J. H., & Orbell, S. (2001). Antecedents of children's physical activity intentions and behaviour: Predictive validity and longitudinal effects. *Psychology and Health, 16,* 391–407.

Jamner, M. S., Wolitski, R. J., Corby, N. H., & Fishbein, M. (1998). Using the theory of planned behaviour to predict intention to use condoms among female sex workers. *Psychology and Health, 13,* 187–205.

Jones, F., Abraham, C., Harris, P., Schulz, J., & Chrispin, C. (2001). From knowledge to action regulation: Modeling the cognitive prerequisites of sun screen use in Australian and UK samples. *Psychology and Health, 16,* 191–206.

Lugoe, W., & Rise, J. (1999). Predicting intended condom use among Tanzanian students using the theory of planned behaviour. *Journal of Health Psychology, 4,* 497–506.

Masalu, J. R., & Astrom, A. N. (2001). Predicting intended and self-perceived sugar restriction among Tanzanian students using the theory of planned behaviour. *Journal of Health Psychology, 6,* 435–445.

McClendon, B. T., & Prentice-Dunn, S. (2001). Reducing skin cancer risk: An intervention based on protection motivation theory. *Journal of Health Psychology, 6,* 321–328.

Morrison, D. M., Baker, S. A., & Gillmore, M. R. (1998). Condom use among high-risk heterosexual teens: A longitudinal analysis using the theory of reasoned action. *Psychology and Health, 13,* 207–222.

Murgraff, V., White, D., & Phillips, K. (1999). An application of protection motivation theory to riskier single-occasion drinking. *Psychology and Health, 14,* 339–350.

Orbell, S., Hodgkins, S., & Sheeran, P. (1997). Implementation intentions and the theory of planned behavior. *Personality and Social Psychology Bulletin, 23,* 945–554.

Pakenham, K. I., Pruss, M., & Clutton, S. (2000). The utility of sociodemographics, knowledge and health belief model variables in predicting reattendance for mammography screening: A brief report. *Psychology and Health, 15,* 585–591.

Plotnikoff, R. C., & Higginbotham, N. (1998). Protection motivation theory and the prediction of exercise and low-fat diet behaviours among Australia cardiac patients. *Psychology and Health, 13,* 411–429.

Povey, R., Conner, M., Sparks, P., James, R., & Shepherd, R. (2000). The theory of planned behaviour and healthy eating: Examining additive and moderating effects of social influence variables. *Psychology and Health, 14,* 991–1006.

Quine, L., Rutter, D. R., & Arnold, L. (2001). Persuading school-age cyclists to use safety helmets: Effectiveness of an intervention based on the theory of planned behaviour. *British Journal of Health Psychology, 6,* 327–345.

Rapaport, P., & Orbell, S. (2000). Augmenting the theory of planned behaviour: Motivation to provide practice assistance and emotional support to parents. *Psychology and Health, 15,* 309–324.

Rogers, R. W. (1975). A protection motivation theory of fear appeals and attitude change. *Journal of Psychology, 91,* 93–114.

Sheeran, P., Conner, M., & Norman, P. (2001). Can the theory of planned behavior explain patterns of health behavior change? *Health Psychology, 20,* 12–19.

Sheeran, P., & Orbell, S. (1998). Implementation intentions and repeated behaviour: Augmenting the predictive validity of the theory of planned behaviour. *European Journal of Social Psychology, 28,* 1–21.

Sheeran, P., & Orbell, S. (2000). Using implementation intentions to increase attendance for cervical cancer screening. *Health Psychology, 19,* 283–289.

Smedlund, G. (2000). A pragmatic basis for judging models and theories in health psychology: The axiomatic method. *Journal of Health Psychology, 5,* 133–258.

Sparks, P., Conner, M., James, R., Shepherd, R., & Povey, R. (2001). Ambivalence about health-related behaviours: An exploration in the domain of food choice. *British Journal of Health Psychology, 6,* 53–68.

Steen, D. M., Peay, M. Y., & Owen, N. (1998). Predicting Australian adolescents' intentions to minimize sun exposure. *Psychology and Health, 13,* 111–119.

Sutton, S. (1998). Predicting and explaining intentions and behaviour: How well are we doing? *Journal of Applied Social Psychology, 28,* 1317–1338.

Sutton, S., McVey, D., & Glanz, A. (1999). A comparative test of the theory of reasoned action and the theory of planned behavior in the prediction of condom use intentions in a national sample of English young people. *Health Psychology, 18,* 72–81.

Trafimow, D. (2000). Habit as both a direct cause of intention to use a condom and as a moderator of the attitude-intention and subjective norm-intention relations. *Psychology and Health, 15,* 383–393.

Wenzlaff., R. M., & Wegner, D. M. (2000). Thought suppression. *Annual Review of Psychology, 51,* 59–91.

Yzer, M. C., Siero, F. W., & Buunk, B. P. (2001). Bringing up condom use and using condoms with new sexual partners: Intentional or habitual? *Psychology and Health, 16,* 409–421.

West, R. (2005) Time for a change: putting the Transtheoretical (Stages of Change) Model to rest, *Addiction*, 100: 1036–9.

Time for a change

Putting the Transtheoretical (Stages of Change) Model to rest

Robert West

Health Behaviour Unit, Department of Epidemiology, Brook House,
University College London
2–16 Torrington Place, London WCIE 6BT
E-mail: robert.west@ucl.ac.uk

Introduction

The Transtheoretical Model of behaviour change, known to many as the Stages of Change (SOC) model, states that with regard to chronic behaviour patterns such as smoking, individuals can be characterized as belonging to one of five or six 'stages' (Prochaska *et al.* 1985; Prochaska & Goldstein 1991; Prochaska & Velicer 1997). Stage definitions vary from behaviour to behaviour and across different versions of the model but in the case of smoking: 'precontemplation' involves an individual not thinking about stopping for at least 6 months; 'contemplation' involves an individual planning to stop between 31 days and 6 months, or less than 31 days if they have not tried to quit for 24 hours in the past year; 'preparation' involves the individual having tried to stop for 24 hours in the past year and planning to stop within 30 days (it has been accepted by the proponents of the model that having tried to stop should perhaps be dropped from this stage definition); 'action' involves the individual having stopped for between 0 and 6 months; 'maintenance' involves the individual having stopped for more than 6 months. In some versions of the model there is also a 'termination' stage in which the individual has permanently adopted the new behaviour pattern.

The model further proposes that individuals progress through stages sequentially but usually revert to prior stages before achieving maintenance and then termination (Prochaska & Velicer 1997). The model also proposes that different self-change strategies (the so-called 'processes of change') are involved in moving between different stages (Prochaska & Velicer 1997) and that the different stages are associated with different beliefs (assessment of the 'pros' and 'cons' of the behaviour and self-confidence in ability to change the behaviour). It argues that interventions to promote change should be designed so that they are appropriate to an individual's current stage (Prochaska & Goldstein 1991). Moving an individual from one stage to another is purported to be a worthwhile goal because it will increase the likelihood that this person will subsequently achieve the termination stage (Prochaska & Goldstein 1991). Proponents of the model have argued that the model has revolutionized health promotion, claiming that interventions that are tailored to the particular stage of the individual improve their effectiveness (Prochaska & Velicer 1997) (for a readily accessible outline of the model and the assessment tools that accompany it see: http://www.uri.edu/research/cprc/transtheoretical.htm).

There are serious problems with the model, many of which have been well articulated (Etter & Perneger 1999; Bunton *et al.* 2000; Whitelaw *et al.* 2000; Sutton 2001; Etter & Sutton 2002; Littell & Girvin 2002). However, its popularity continues largely unabated. This editorial does not seek to revisit the plethora of empirical evidence and conceptual analysis that has been ranged against the model. It simply argues that the problems with the model are so serious that it has held back advances in the field of health promotion and, despite its intuitive appeal to many practitioners, it should be discarded. It is now time for a change. A replacement is needed that more accurately reflects observations about behaviour change, is internally consistent, and generates useful ideas and predictions. It needs to provide a way of describing how people can change with apparent suddenness, even in response to small triggers. It needs to be a stimulus to research that will go beyond a simplistic decision-making model of behaviour and produce genuinely novel insights. However, even in the absence of a new theory, simply reverting to the common sense approach that was used prior to the Transtheoretical Model would better than staying with the model. In that approach people were asked simply about desire to change and ability to change and it was recognized that these were affected by a range of personal and situational factors including addiction.

This editorial draws primarily from research in smoking. It is in this area that the model was first developed and where much of the research relating to it has been carried out. To give some idea of the extent of the dominance of smoking, of 540 articles found in PubMed using the search phrase 'stages of change', 174 also had 'smoking' in the abstract or title, 60 had 'alcohol', seven had cocaine, two had 'heroin' or 'opiate' and one had 'gambling'.

What is wrong with the Transtheoretical Model

First of all the model is flawed even in its most basic tenet, the concept of the 'stage'. It has to draw arbitrary dividing lines in order to differentiate between the stages. This has to mean that these are not genuine stages. For example, an individual who is planning to stop smoking is in the preparation stage if this is within the next 30 days (provided that the smoker has made a quit attempt that lasted 24 hours in the past 12 months) but only the contemplation stage if it is in 31 days' time (Sutton 2001). Boundaries between so-called 'stages' are therefore simply arbitrary lines in the sand and statements of the kind 'xx per cent of smokers are in the "contemplation stage"' have little useful meaning. They should not be taken to mean, as they so often are, that 'xx per cent of smokers are thinking about stopping smoking'.

Secondly, this approach to classifying individuals assumes that individuals typically make coherent and stable plans. People responding to multiple-choice questionnaires are compliant and will generally try to choose an answer, but this does not mean that they think about things in the terms set by the response options. Apart from those individuals that set a specific occasion or date for change (e.g. in a New Year's resolution), intentions about change appear to be much less clearly formulated. In what appears to be the first study of its kind, Larabie (in press) found that more than half of reported quit attempts in a general practice sample involved no planning or preparation at all – not even going so far as to finish the current packet of cigarettes. Another recent study found considerable instability in intentions to stop smoking over short periods (Hughes *et al.* in press). A high level of instability in stages has also been found in other domains (De Nooijer *et al.* 2005).

Thirdly, it has been pointed out by others that the stage definitions represent a mixture of different types of construct that do not fit together coherently (e.g. time since quit, past quit attempts and intention) (Etter & Sutton 2002). It is not, as some of those using the model would like it to be, a statement of 'readiness' to change. Readiness or even preparedness is not actually assessed.

Fourthly, the model focuses on conscious decision-making and planning processes and draws attention away from what are known to be important underpinnings of human motivation. It neglects the role of reward and punishment, and associative learning in developing habits that are hard to break (Baumeister *et al.* 1994; Mook 1996; Salamone *et al.* 2003). Much of the problem of behaviour change arises from the fact that unhealthy habit patterns become entrenched and semi-automated through repeated reward and punishment (Robinson & Berridge 2003). These processes operate outside conscious awareness and do not follow decision-making rules such as weighing up costs and benefits. There is little or no consideration of the concept of addiction which is clearly a crucial consideration when it comes to behaviours such as smoking.

Where the model makes predictions beyond those that could be made from common sense it has been found to be incorrect or worse than competing theories (Farkas *et al.* 1996; Herzog *et al.* 1999; Abrams *et al.* 2000). Strong claims have been made for the model (Prochaska & Velicer 1997) but the main body of evidence given in support of the theory is that individuals who are closer to maintenance at any one time are more likely to have changed their behaviour when followed up (e.g. Reed *et al.* 2005). The relationship is often not strong, and by no means all studies find it (Hernandez-Avila *et al.* 1998; Littell & Girvin 2002) but the fact that it is present is given as evidence for the model. However, this says no more than that individuals who are thinking of changing their behaviour are more likely to try to do so than those who are not, or that individuals who are in the process of trying to change are more likely to change than those who are just thinking about it. Put that way, it is simply a statement of the obvious: people who want or plan to do something are obviously more likely to try to do it; and people who try to do something are more likely to succeed than those who do not.

Surprisingly, the proponents of the model appear not to report findings showing that the model is better at predicting behaviour than a simple question such as 'Do you have any plans to try to...?' or even 'Do you want to...?'. However, where others have made the comparison (e.g. SOC versus a simple contemplation latter that preceded it), little difference has been found (Abrams *et al.* 2000), or a simple rating of desire has been found to be better (Pisinger *et al.* 2005). There have also been problems in the reliability of the assignment to categorical stages, as one might expect given that these are designated arbitrarily (Hodgins 2001). One might imagine that a scientific model would need to show an improvement at least on this kind of simple assessment.

Proponents of the model may point to the fact that at least it has drawn attention to the fact that many people are not ready for interventions and progress can be made by moving them in the direction of changing their behaviour. However, in the years that the model has been in use there appears to be no convincing evidence that moving an individual closer to action actually results in a sustained change in behaviour at a later date. In fact, the history of behaviour change research is littered with studies that have succeeded in changing attitudes without accompanying changes in behaviour. Where interventions have been developed that are based on the model these have not proved more effective than interventions which are based on traditional concepts. A recent review comparing stop smoking interventions designed using the SOC approach with non-tailored treatments found no benefit for those based on the model (Riemsma *et al.* 2003). Another review of the effects of applying the model to primary care behaviour change interventions has similarly found no evidence for a benefit (van Sluijs *et al.* 2004) and nor has there been found to be a benefit of applying the model in promotion of physical activity (Adams & White 2005). By contrast, there is good evidence that tailoring interventions in other ways, including triggers and motives are more effective than untailored approaches (Lancaster & Stead 2002).

Why the model should be abandoned

The model has been little more than a security blanket for researchers and clinicians. First, the seemingly scientific style of the assessment tool gives the impression that some form of diagnosis is being made from which a treatment plan can be devised. It gives the appearance of rigour. Secondly, the model also gives permission to go for 'soft' outcomes such as moving an individual from 'precontemplation' to 'contemplation' which is of no proven value. Thirdly, it provides scientific labels to categorise people who would otherwise have to be described using phrases that any non-expert would understand: an individual is a 'precontemplator' not 'someone who is not planning on changing'. Appealing as this may be, it is not founded on evidence and arguably has been damaging to progress.

The model tends to promote the wrong intervention strategy. For example, precontemplators tend to be provided with interventions aimed at 'moving them along' the stages, for example by attempting to persuade them about the benefits of changing. However, if their apparent lack of interest in changing arises from their addiction, these individuals may respond favourably to the offer of a new and promising treatment as appears to have happened when the drug Zyban was launched as a smoking cessation aid (e.g. Zwar & Richmond 2002).

The model is likely to lead to effective interventions not being offered to people who would have responded. There is now evidence in the case of smoking cessation that help should be offered to as wide a group as possible (Pisinger *et al.* 2005a; b), but the SOC model can be taken as giving permission to those attempting to promote behaviour change to give weak interventions or no intervention to 'precontemplators'. This approach fails to take account of the strong situational determinants of behaviour. Behaviour change can arise from a response to a trigger even in apparently unmotivated individuals.

It is common in the case of psychological theories for which there is accumulating evidence that they are not proving helpful, to argue that better measurement is needed or that the theory has not been applied properly. This particular model is no exception (e.g. DiClemente *et al.* 2004). In the end one is often forced to acceptance that fundamental precepts of the theory are misplaced and arguably that is the case here.

What to do now?

A better model of behaviour change is clearly needed. There are of course many other decision-making models, such as the Health Belief Model (Garcia & Mann 2003) and the Theory of Planned Behaviour (Garcia & Mann 2003). What is needed is one that operates at the same level of generality as the SOC model and encompasses decision-making processes and motivational processes that are not necessarily accessible to conscious awareness. The model needs to take account of the fact that the behaviours concerned reflect the moment-to-moment balance of motives. At a given time an individual may 'want' to do one thing (e.g. smoke a cigarette) but feel they 'ought' to do something else (e.g. not smoke it) – but these feelings and beliefs are not present most of the time – they arise under specific circumstances. A model of change needs to describe what these circumstances are and how an individual's desires and values are shaped and changed. The model needs to consider the difference between desire and value attaching to a specific behaviour (smoking a cigarette) vs. a label (being a smoker). Lasting behaviour change relies on the balance of motivational forces regarding the specific behaviour consistently favouring the alternative whenever the opportunity to engage in it arises. The model of change needs to describe and explain how this occurs. It is apparent that self-labelling plays an important role in generating this consistency (Kearney & O'Sullivan 2003). An individual who is committed to being a 'non-smoker' is motivated to exercise restraint when temptation to smoke arises. A 'state of change' model is needed which provides a coherent account of the balance of motivational forces that operate on habitual behaviours, and how these need to change for a different pattern of behaviour to emerge. It needs to consider 'state', not as an outcome but as a measurable characteristic (possibly a self-label) that can help to stabilize a new behaviour pattern. It is worth noting, finally, that many practitioners already regard the SOC model as a state of change model in that they informally consider it to represent the state of readiness to change.

In the course of researching this editorial, I have been forced to think about the kind of comprehensive model that is required and have proposed a draft of a model (West in press). It remains to be seen how far this can form a more scientifically sound basis for analysis of behaviour change. In the meantime, when it comes to intervening to promote behaviour change, health professionals should adopt the approach that worked well in Russell *et al.*'s seminal study of GP advice (Russell *et al.* 1979) and has been found to be effective more recently as well (Pisinger *et al.* 2005), which is to encourage change in, and offer help to, all-comers (except those who are clearly resistant). They should do this respectfully but firmly and with the offer of support and assistance. When it comes to assessing motivation to change, it would be better to revert to simple questions about desire to change that were in place before the SOC model was developed.

References

Abrams, D. B., Herzog, T. A., Emmons, K. M. & Linnan, L. (2000) Stages of change versus addiction: a replication and extension. *Nicotine and Tobacco Research,* **2,** 223–229.

Adams, J. & White, M. (2005) Why don't stage-based activity promotion interventions work?' *Health Education Research,* **20,** 237–243.

Baumeister, R. F., Heatherton, T. F. & Tice, D. (1994) *Losing Control: How and Why People Fail at Self-Regulation.* San Diego: Academic Press.

Bunton, R., Baldwin, S., Flynn, D. & Whitelaw, J. (2000) The 'stages of change' model in health promotion: science and ideology. *Critical Public Health,* **10,** 55–70.

De Nooijer, J., Van Assema, P., De Vet, E. & Brug, J. (2005) How stable are stages of change for nutrition behaviors in the Netherlands? *Health Promotion International,* **20,** 27–32.

DiClemente, C. C., Schlundt, D. & Gemmell, L. (2004) Readiness and stages of change in addiction treatment. *American Journal of Addiction,* **13,** 103–119.

Etter, J. F. & Perneger, T. V. (1999) A comparison of two measures of stage of change for smoking cessation. *Addiction,* **94,** 1881–1889.

Etter, J. F. & Sutton, S. (2002) Assessing 'stage of change' in current and former smokers. *Addiction,* **97,** 1171–1182.

Farkas, A. J., Pierce, J. P., Zhu, S.-H., Rosbrook, B., Gilpin, E. A., Berry, C. & Kaplan, R. M. (1996) Addiction versus stages of change models in predicting smoking cessation. *Addiction,* **91,** 1271–1280; discussion 1281–1292.

Garcia, K. & Mann, T. (2003) From 'I Wish' to 'I Will'; social-cognitive predictors of behavioral intentions. *Journal of Health Psychology,* **8,** 347–360.

Hernandez-Avila, C. A., Burleson, J. A. & Kranzler, H. R. (1998) Stage of Change as a predictor of abstinence among alcohol-dependent subjects in pharmacotherapy trials. *Substance Abuse,* **19,** 81–91.

Herzog, T. A., Abrams, D. B., Emmons, K. M., Linnan, L. A. & Shadel, W. G. (1999) Do processes of change predict smoking stage movements? A prospective analysis of the transtheoretical model. *Health Psychology,* **18,** 369–375.

Hodgins, D. C. (2001) Stages of Change assessments in alcohol problems: agreement across self- and clinician-reports. *Substance Abuse,* **22,** 87–96.

Hughes, J., Keeley, J., Fagerstrom, K. O. & Callas, P. W. (2005) Intentions to quit smoking change over short periods of time. *Addictive Behaviors,* **30,** 653–662.

Kearney, M. H. & O'Sullivan, J. (2003) Identity shifts as turning points in health behavior change. *Western Journal of Nursing Research,* **25,** 134–152.

Lancaster, T. & Stead, L. F. (2002) Self-help interventions for smoking cessation. *Cochrane Database Systematic Reviews,* CD001118.

Larabie, L. (in press) To what extent do smokers plan quit attempts? *Tobacco Control.*

Littell, J. H. & Girvin, H. (2002) Stages of change. A critique. *Behavior Modification,* **26,** 223–273.

Mook, D. G. (1996) *Motivation: the Organization of Action.* New York: W. W. Norton.

Pisinger, C., Vestbo, J., Borch-Johnsen, K. & Jørgensen, T. (2005a) It is possible to help smokers in early motivational stages to quit. The Inter99 study. *Preventive Medicine,* **40,** 278–284.

Pisinger, C., Vestbo, J., Borch-Johnsen, K. & Jørgensen, T. (2005b) Smoking cessation intervention in a large randomised population-based study. The Inter99 study. *Preventive Medicine,* **40,** 285–292.

Prochaska, J. O., DiClemente, C. C., Velicer, W. F., Ginpil, S. & Norcross, J. C. (1985) Predicting change in smoking status for self-changers. *Addictive Behaviors,* **10,** 395–406.

Prochaska, J. O. & Goldstein, M. G. (1991) Process of smoking cessation. Implications for clinicians. *Clinical Chest Medicine,* **12,** 727–735.

Prochaska, J. O. & Velicer, W. F. (1997) The transtheoretical model of health behavior change. *American Journal of Health Promotion,* **12,** 38–48.

Reed, D. N., Wolf, B. Jr, Barber, K. R., Kotlowski, R., Montanez, M., Saxe, A., *et al.* (2005) The stages of change questionnaire as a predictor of trauma patients most likely to decrease alcohol use. *Journal of the American College of Surgeons,* **200,** 179–185.

Riemsma, R. P., Pattenden, J., Bridle, C., Sowden, A. J., Mather, L., Watt, I. S. & Walker, A. (2003) Systematic review of the effectiveness of stage based interventions to promote smoking cessation. *BMJ,* **326,** 1175–1177.

Robinson, T. E. & Berridge, K. C. (2003) Addiction. *Annual Review of Psychology,* **54,** 25–53.

Russell, M. A., Wilson, C., Taylor, C. & Baker, C. (1979) Effect of general practitioners' advice against smoking. *BMJ,* **2,** 231–235.

Salamone, J. D., Correa, M., Mingote, S. & Weber, S. M. (2003) Nucleus accumbens dopamine and the regulation of effort in food-seeking behavior: implications for studies of natural motivation, psychiatry, and drug abuse. *Journal of Pharmacology and Experimental Therapeutics,* **305,** 1–8.

van Sluijs, E. M., van Poppel, M. N. & Van Mechelen, W. (2004) Stage-based lifestyle interventions in primary care: are they effective? *American Journal of Preventive Medicine,* **26,** 330–343.

Sutton, S. (2001) Back to the drawing board? A review of applications of the transtheoretical model to substance use. *Addiction,* **96,** 175–186.

West, R. (in press) *Theory of Addiction.* Oxford: Blackwells Publishing Ltd.

Whitelaw, S., Baldwin, S., Bunton, R. & Flynn, D. (2000) The status of evidence and outcomes in Stages of Change research. *Health Education Research,* **15,** 707–718.

Zwar, N. & Richmond, R. (2002) Bupropion sustained release. A therapeutic review of Zyban. *Australian Family Physician,* **31,** 443–447.

Explaining behaviour

There are a vast number of studies designed to explain health behaviours. Some of these use the social cognition models, others use behaviour-specific models or qualitative methods. Further, those that use quantitative methods employ different research designs such as cross-sectional, case control, prospective or experimental. In this section I have selected papers that I believe are good examples of health behaviour research, and I have attempted to cover the variability of research in terms of behaviour being studied and method or model being used.

Armitage, C.J. (2005) Can the theory of planned behaviour predict the maintenance of physical activity? *Health Psychology*, 24 (3): 235–45. Reprinted with kind permission of the American Psychological Association.

Murgraff, V., White, D. and Phillips, K. (1999) An application of protection motivation theory to riskier single-occasion drinking. *Psychology and Health*, 14: 339–50. Reprinted with kind permission of the Taylor & Francis Group.

DiClemente, C.C., Prochaska, J.O., Fairhurst, S.K. et al. (1991) The process of smoking cessation: an analysis of precontemplation, contemplation, and preparation stages of change, *Journal of Consulting and Clinical Psychology*, 59 (2): 295–304. Reprinted with kind permission of the American Psychological Association.

Wardle, J. and Beales, S. (1988) Control and loss of control over eating: an experimental investigation. *Journal of Abnormal Psychology*, 97 (1): 35–40. Reprinted with kind permission of the American Psychological Association.

Woodcock, A.J., Stenner, K. and Ingham, R. (1992) Young people talking about HIV and AIDS: interpretations of personal risk of infection, *Health Education Research: Theory and Practice*, 7 (2): 229–47. Reprinted with kind permission of Oxford University Press.

Armitage (2005) is an excellent example of a study using the TPB to predict behaviour, in this case physical activity, and includes many of the elements of high standard research. It uses a prospective design with measures taken at baseline and follow-up, and includes an objective measure of behaviour in the form of data from the participants' card swipes as they entered the gym. Further, It uses 'real people' rather than students. The measures are clearly described and the analysis, though complicated, can be followed quite easily. It also provides an interesting insight into how the development of habits can be studied. This paper therefore provides a good example of TPB research and could be used as a template for future research. The paper by Murgraff, White and Phillips (1999) also provides a good example of research but uses the PMT as its framework and focuses on drinking. This also uses a prospective design and provides clear descriptions of the measures use. In contrast to Armitage (2005), this paper uses students as its sample but provides an example for when students are appropriate as a study population – if the behaviour is particular to students then there is a good justification for a having a study based upon their views and behaviours. The paper by DiClemente et al. (1991) is also a good example of research, this time using the SOC approach and in the area of smoking, but it is included as it was one of the first papers to test the SOC empirically and is written by its authors. It uses a prospective design and followed smokers up from baseline to six months to see who had stopped smoking. It includes many of the standard measures of tolerance, perceived stress and stage of change and has a large sample size. The paper is also interesting as it was based around a smoking cessation programme and illustrates how it is possible to add research onto an existing intervention. Together, these three papers provide excellent case illustrations of quantitative research using best-case research designs within the framework of models.

Within the field of eating behaviour researchers have tended to use theories and models that are specific to eating rather than simply draw upon existing models of behaviour and behaviour change. One such perspective is restraint theory, which was developed in the 1970s and has provided a framework for a vast number of studies focusing on dieting, food intake and over- and undereating. Research from this perspective has explored the extent to which trying not to eat actually results in overeating and studies have been carried out to explore the role of cognitions and affect in explaining the dieting – overeating relationship. Wardle and Beales (1988) were early researchers in this field and this paper set the scene for much subsequent research by experimentally illustrating that trying to eat less could actually result in eating more. The study uses an experimental design, which is increasingly rare in health behaviour research and as such enabled conclusions about causality to be made. The paper illustrates how small-scale experimental studies can be effective and also shows how experiments can be carried out in a naturalistic setting rather than just in the laboratory. This paper has therefore been included as a good example of the experimental method and one that established a firm footing for subsequent research studies. The paper has also been included because while restraint theory has only been applied to eating behaviour and is therefore only read or known by those focusing on what we eat, the theory also has relevance to all other health-related behaviours. Much health psychology research aims to explain and subsequently change behaviour. In line with more recent theories such as the ironic processes of mental control and studies of automaticity, restraint theory argues that if one tries to change a behaviour by putting oneself into denial then ultimately this fails and can lead to over- rather than underconsumption. Such a premise is as relevant to giving up smoking and cutting down alcohol intake as it is to trying to eat less.

Woodcock et al. (1992) is the final paper in this section and provides an excellent qualitative analysis of how people perceive their risk about HIV. The study involved interviewing 16 – 25 year olds about their perceptions of personal risk, and produced some interesting insights into how young people interpret safe sex messages and justify their own behaviour. The interviews were analysed for their themes and categories which are illustrated by exemplar quotes. In addition, the authors provide a quantitative description of the numbers of categories according to whether the respondent was male or female. This paper is very easy and interesting to read and provides a good example of how to present qualitative data. It also illustrates how some of the constructs used within social cognition models, in this case risk perception, may be more complex than assumed when measured using quantitative scales. Furthermore, it illustrates the ways in which health promotion information can be managed, interpreted and dismissed when juxtaposed against a person's existing beliefs and behaviour. Finally, this paper uses qualitative quotes and provides some quantification of these quotes. This dual process of analysis is often favoured by the more medical journals, and is sometimes recommended by their editors (as in this case) and raises questions about the usefulness of such an approach and whether the quotes benefits from being quantified.

Overall, these five papers provide examples of clear and thorough studies that use a range of methods and cover the span of health-related behaviours.

Armitage, C.J. (2005) Can the theory of planned behavior predict the maintenance of physical activity? *Health Psychology*, 24 (3): 235 – 45.

Can the theory of planned behavior predict the maintenance of physical activity?

Christopher J. Armitage
University of Sheffield

Abstract

This study tested the ability of the theory of planned behavior to predict actual participation in physical activity and explored the development of activity habits in a 12-week longitudinal study. People enrolling in a gymnasium ($N = 94$) completed standard theory of planned behavior measures at baseline and follow-up; behavior was monitored objectively in the intervening period. The data were analyzed by using both standard and repeatable events survival analysis. Results showed that (a) perceived behavioral control was significantly predictive of intentions and actual behavior, (b) stable exercise habits developed in the first 5 weeks of the study, and (c) successful prior performance enhanced perceptions of behavioral control. The implications for developing theory-based interventions that promote the maintenance of health behavior are discussed.

Keywords: maintenance, exercise, theory of planned behavior, habit, past behavior

Participation in regular physical activity protects against numerous serious medical conditions, most notably coronary heart disease and cancer (Byers et al., 2002; Erikssen, 2001). In spite of this, national surveys typically demonstrate low levels of participation in physical activity (e.g., Martinez-Gonzalez et al., 2001). One approach to better understanding low uptake and maintenance of physical activity has been to investigate the psychosocial antecedents of exercise with a view to developing effective theory-driven campaigns (e.g., Marcus et al., 2000). Research on the theory of planned behavior (Ajzen, 1991) has dominated this field, as evidenced by the large number of reviews and meta-analyses, which consistently report strong relationships between theory of planned behavior variables and physical activity (e.g., Blue, 1995; Godin, 1993, 1994; Godin & Kok, 1996; Hagger, Chatzisarantis, & Biddle, 2002; Hausenblas, Carron, & Mack, 1997). However, in spite of these important theoretical advances in understanding people's motivation to initiate participation in physical activity, relatively little research has addressed the question of how participation in physical activity is sustained (Marcus et al., 2000). The

I thank Stuart Parke for his help with collecting and entering the data.

Correspondence concerning this article should be addressed to Christopher J. Armitage, Centre for Research in Social Attitudes, Department of Psychology, University of Sheffield, Western Bank, Sheffield S10 2TP, United Kingdom. E-mail: c.j.armitage@sheffield.ac.uk focus on initiation – as opposed to maintenance – of behavior has resulted in a literature that is characterized by cross-sectional and short-term prospective designs and that relies on self-reported measures of behavior. The present article reports a longitudinal study with 12 objective measures of behavior, which was designed to address some of the limitations associated with research in this area.

Central to the theory of planned behavior (Ajzen, 1991) is the idea that the performance of any behavior is codetermined by behavioral intention and perceived behavioral control. Behavioral intentions are representations of people's plans of action and summarize people's motivation to engage in a behavior; thus, the more motivated people are to engage in the behavior, the more likely will be its successful performance. Perceived behavioral control reflects people's confidence in their ability to carry out a particular behavior and is regarded as being synonymous with Bandura's (1997) self-efficacy construct (e.g., Ajzen, 1991, 1998). Perceived behavioral control is held to determine behavior to the extent that it reflects people's actual control over the behavior (Sheeran, Trafimow, & Armitage, 2003). In turn, behavioral intentions are determined by three independent constructs: perceived behavioral control, subjective norm (perceived social pressure to perform the behavior), and attitude (positive–negative evaluations of behavior). Thus, people are more likely to intend to participate in physical activity if they are positively disposed toward it (attitude), if they perceive social pressure to do so (subjective norm), and if they believe they will be successful (perceived behavioral control).

Although the theory of planned behavior (Ajzen, 1991) is regarded as a universal model of social behavior, it has been applied extensively in the domain of exercise. For example, Courneya (1995) examined the theory of planned behavior in the context of physical activity in older individuals and found that attitude, subjective norm, and perceived behavioral control were all significantly correlated with the intention to exercise ($rs = 0.51$, 0.47, 0.48, respectively; $ps < 0.05$), together accounting for 38% of the variance. In terms of predicting behavior, Rosen's (2000a) study of sedentary college students found that behavioral intention was the dominant predictor of subsequent exercise behavior, accounting for 5% of the unique variance, and Baker, Little, and Brownell (2003) reported intention–behavior correlations in excess of $r = 0.40$. Hagger et al.'s (2002) meta-analysis of 72 studies applying the theory of planned behavior in the domain of exercise confirmed this pattern of findings and reported substantial correlations between each of the key components and with behavior (cf. Godin & Kok, 1996; Hausenblas et al., 1997).

In spite of this impressive body of evidence attesting to the importance of the theory of planned behavior for predicting exercise behavior, research in this area has been characterized by a number of conceptual and empirical limitations. The present study was designed to address four limitations in particular. First, there is a dearth of research on the maintenance of behavior. The problem was highlighted by Wing (2000) in a special issue of *Health Psychology*: "To date, researchers have considered behavior change as a process, with maintenance as the last step. However, throughout this meeting [the U.S. National Heart, Lung, and Blood Institute Maintenance of Behavior Change in Cardiorespiratory Risk Reduction conference in July 1998], there was the recognition that maintenance is itself a process" (Wing, 2000, p. 84).[1]

---

1 Wing (2000) was alluding to the transtheoretical model of change. The transtheoretical model of change explicitly includes a maintenance stage, which is defined as "the period beginning 6 months after action has started and...involves continued change" (Prochaska et al., 1994, p. 40). Wing (2000) went on to note that in research using the transtheoretical model to understand the maintenance of physical activity, it is common practice for "researchers [to] ask only about the last 7 days or past 2 weeks" (Wing, 2000, p. 84; see also Marcus et al., 2000). Even when adhering to the 6-month time period, researchers in the exercise domain

In the domain of physical activity in particular, Marcus et al.'s (2000) review reported that adherence research has typically focused on prescribed exercise in at-risk populations (e.g., King et al., 1997), which limits the ability to generalize beyond these contexts and populations. When research has examined maintenance of physical activity in general populations, retrospective designs have typically been used to identify correlates of relapse (e.g., Cardinal, 1998; Sallis et al., 1990). There are still fewer studies that have used the theory of planned behavior as a theoretical framework; as a result, a great deal is known about the ability of the theory of planned behavior to predict the initiation of behavior, but very little research has examined the factors important in maintaining behavior.

In preparing the present article, I located just one study that tested the ability of the theory of planned behavior to predict the maintenance of health behavior. Sheeran, Conner, and Norman (2001) examined patterns of health behavior change in relation to attendance at screening. Dividing people into *consistent, initial, delayed,* and *refused* attendance groups, Sheeran et al. (2001) showed that theory of planned behavior variables could discriminate between attenders and nonattenders (i.e., the consistent, initial, and delayed groups versus the refused group) but that the variables were unable to discriminate between people who had attended just once (the initial and delayed groups) and those who maintained their behavior (the consistent group). The latter finding is potentially problematic because it implies that the theory of planned behavior is unable to account for the maintenance of behavior. However, it should be acknowledged that Sheeran et al.'s target behavior (health screening) was an annual event, whereas a common theme of maintenance behavior is that it involves frequent repeated performance of the behavior (e.g., Prochaska et al., 1994), which in the context of annual health screening would require a study spanning several years. The implication is that repeated opportunities for recurrence of the behavior in question are important in understanding the maintenance of behavior.

The second potential limitation concerns the accumulated research showing that past behavior is often the best predictor of future behavior, even controlling for the effects of theory of planned behavior variables (e.g., Conner & Armitage, 1998; Ouellette & Wood, 1998), a finding that has been replicated in studies of participation in physical activity (see Hagger et al., 2002). Ouellette and Wood (1998) argued that behaviors performed frequently (i.e., on a daily or weekly basis) in stable predictable contexts become habitual and are therefore less likely to be guided by variables found in the theory of planned behavior. However, despite the fact that the independent effects of past behavior on future behavior are well established, past behavior has rarely been conceptualized as an index of maintenance. More important, relatively little is known about the effects of repeated past behavior on future behavior. In other words, do repeated experiences exert cumulative effects on subsequent behavior? To date, all that is known about the development of habits is that they occur following repeated experience in stable predictable environments. Presumably, though, there is a critical period after which continued performance of the health behavior exerts a diminishing effect on future behavior and the behavior in question may be regarded as habitual. The present study examines this issue by evaluating the cumulative effects of past behavior on future behavior.

---

have found it difficult to discriminate between the action and maintenance stages, and in his meta-analysis of this literature, Rosen (2000b) concluded, "it may be more appropriate to think of exercise readiness as a continuous variable rather than as discrete stages" (p. 602). On the basis of these and related studies, I decided to focus the present research on a continuum model (i.e., the theory of planned behavior) rather than a stage model of physical activity (cf. Rosen, 2000a).

Past behavior also exerts powerful effects on cognition, and Bandura's (1997) concept of personal mastery experiences is important in understanding potential past behavior–cognition relationships. Personal mastery experiences are regarded as a key means by which perceived behavioral control (or *self-efficacy,* to use Bandura's, 1997, terminology) is enhanced. The key to personal mastery experiences is the idea that successful performance of a behavior increases perceived behavioral control, which in turn increases the likelihood of successful performance in the future. Bandura's work suggested that perceived behavioral control will both predict and be enhanced by successful repeated performance of the behavior. Indirect evidence supports Bandura's position: Both Sallis et al. (1990) and Miller, Ogletree, and Welshimer (2002) found positive correlations between reported prior physical activity and perceived behavioral control, implying that successful adherence may enhance perceptions of control. However, Sallis et al.'s (1990) and Miller et al.'s (2002) studies utilized retrospective designs, and it would be valuable to replicate these effects longitudinally and to use objective measures of behavior. Moreover, given that the theory of planned behavior posits perceived behavioral control as antecedent to intention, it seems likely that intention would also be enhanced by successful performance of behavior.

The third limitation associated with previous research is methodological: Armitage and Conner (2001) reported that of all theory of planned behavior studies published before the end of 1997, only 41% included a prospective measure of behavior, and likewise a large proportion of studies in the physical activity domain use cross-sectional designs. Cross-sectional designs represent a significant limitation because consistency bias is likely to inflate the correspondence between, for example, behavioral intention and behavior when they are measured contemporaneously. A related concern is that even where prospective designs are used, the interval between initial assessment of theory of planned behavior variables and the subsequent measure of behavior is often short. For example, in their meta-analysis of studies examining the intention–behavior relationship, Randall and Wolff (1994) reported that more than one half of all time intervals were less than 1 month and that more than one third were less than 1 week. In terms of physical activity, relatively few studies use intervening periods that exceed 1 month (but for notable exceptions, see Courneya, Nigg, & Estabrooks, 1998; Courneya, Plotnikoff, Hotz, & Birkett, 2001; Rosen, 2000a). Given that the health benefits associated with physical activity take some time to accrue, additional prospective studies that span several months are required.

The fourth limitation of past research is that exercise behavior has typically been measured with self-reports, and it would be valuable to extend this research by using a more objective measure of behavior. Single-occasion self-report measures are potentially problematic because they are susceptible to memory biases, most notably the primacy and recency effects that are typically found in free recall (e.g., Murdock, 1962). Primacy and recency effects mean that single-occasion self-report measures of behavior are likely to elicit responses that focus on earlier episodes of exercise (e.g., at the time of the original questionnaire) and on more recent physical activity, rather than providing an accurate representation of participation in physical activity over the course of the preceding weeks or months. An objective measure of behavior would also provide a more exacting test of the predictive validity of the theory of planned behavior.

The present study

On the basis of the research reviewed above, the present study used an objective measure of participation in physical activity and a longitudinal repeated measures design. It was predicted that (a) the predictive validity of the theory of planned behavior would be further supported in the physical activity domain by using an objective measure of behavior; (b) the theory of planned behavior would be predictive of both initiation and maintenance of behavior; (c) the effects of past behavior on future behavior would accrue to a critical point after which the behavior in question becomes habitual and further performance of behavior decreases in impact; and (d) continued performance of a behavior would represent personal mastery experiences that enhance perceived behavioral control over time.

Method
Participants and procedure

Ninety-four participants were recruited from a private gymnasium in the south of England. The sample consisted of 53 women and 41 men between 16 and 65 years of age ($M = 37.57$, $SD = 10.13$). The gymnasium had been closed for several months for refurbishment, and all participants reported never having attended this particular gymnasium prior to the study. Participation in the study was on an unpaid, voluntary basis.

All participants received a baseline questionnaire as part of their induction pack and were asked to complete it in situ. The measures used are described in the following section. Three months later, participants completed an identical follow-up questionnaire.

Measures

Variables derived from the theory of planned behavior were measured with standard items (Ajzen, 1991) at baseline and follow-up. Attitude, subjective norm, perceived behavioral control, and behavioral intention were all measured on 7-point scales. For the measure of attitude, participants were presented with the stem "For me, participating in regular physical activity would be...," which they were asked to rate on six bipolar (-3 to $+3$) semantic differential scales, anchored by the adjectives *dull–interesting, unpleasant–pleasant, boring–stimulating, unhealthy–healthy, bad–good,* and *useless–useful.* Cronbach's alpha indicated that the attitude scale possessed good internal reliability ($\alpha s = 0.90$ at baseline, 0.81 at follow-up), and so the mean of these six items was used as a measure of attitude. Subjective norm was operationalized by using three items: "People close to me think I should participate in regular physical activity, *disagree/agree*"; "People who are important to me would... *disapprove of my participating in regular physical activity/approve of my participating in regular physical activity*"; and "People close to me think I... *should not participate in regular physical activity/should participate in regular physical activity.*" Responses to the subjective norm items were made on unipolar ($+1$ to $+7$) scales; Cronbach's alpha showed that the scale possessed good internal reliability ($\alpha s = 0.85$ at baseline, 0.96 at follow-up). The mean of the three subjective norm items was used in subsequent analyses.

Perceived behavioral control was measured by averaging (using the mean) responses to four items: "To what extent do you see yourself as being capable of participating in regular physical activity? *incapable–capable*"; "How confident are you that you will be able to participate in regular physical activity? *not very confident–very confident*"; "I believe I have the ability to participate in regular physical activity. *definitely do not–definitely do*"; and "How much personal control do you feel you have over participating in regular physical activity? *no control–complete control.*" All were measured on unipolar (+1 to +7) scales. Cronbach's alpha for the perceived behavioral control scale was 0.85 at baseline and 0.95 at follow-up.[2] Behavioral intention was measured on two bipolar (−3 to +3) scales with the following items: "How often do you intend to take part in regular physical activity? *never–frequently*," and "I want to exercise regularly. *definitely do not–definitely do.*" The internal reliability of the scale was good (Cronbach's αs = 0.72 at baseline, 0.76 at follow-up), and so the mean of the items was used as a measure of behavioral intention.[3]

Self-reported behavior was measured at follow-up by asking participants, "How often have you participated in regular physical activity in the last 3 months? *never–frequently.*" Actual attendance at the gymnasium was monitored on a weekly basis in the intervening time period by using the computer records of membership card swipes at the turnstile entrance of the gymnasium (scored 1 = *did not attend this week*, 2 = *did attend this week*).

Analyses

The data were analyzed by using a variety of univariate and multivariate techniques, most of which are common in theory of planned behavior research and multiple regression analysis in particular. However, multiple regression is regarded as potentially unsuitable for analyzing repeated measures data over a sustained period of time because biases are likely to arise from missing data.[4] The present study therefore used *survival analysis.* In its simplest form, survival analysis requires just two variables – the presence or absence of a particular event and the time it took for the event to occur – and has typically been used to predict terminal events, such as death and systems failures (e.g., Allison, 1984; Greenhouse, Stangl, & Bromberg, 1989; Luke, 1993; Luke & Homan, 1998). The main advantage of survival analysis over more traditional regression analyses is that it can produce unbiased estimates of survival time associated with the dependent variable and thereby minimize bias and reduce the number of missing cases (e.g.,

---

2 There is a growing body of research showing that whereas the first three reported perceived behavioral control items tap self-efficacy, the fourth item taps perceived control over behavior (see Armitage & Arden, 2002; Armitage, Conner, Loach, & Willetts, 1999). This body of research stems from the observation that when scaled together, items designed to tap perceived behavioral control often do not produce Cronbach's alpha values greater than 0.70, indicating a lack of internal reliability and possibly a multidimensional underpinning to perceived behavioral control. This was not the case in the present study: Not only did Cronbach's alpha far exceed 0.80, but the corrected item-total correlations for the fourth item were in excess of 0.65 at both baseline and follow-up. Given that the individuals in the present sample were already highly motivated and were tested inside a gymnasium, it is plausible that they felt simultaneously confident and in control of the behavior, thereby undermining the distinction between self-efficacy and perceived control over behavior.

3 Several authors have proposed a distinction between desires (i.e., I want to exercise regularly) and intentions (see Bagozzi, 1992) that is comparable to the proposed distinction between self-efficacy and perceived control over behavior. To date, however, meta-analysis has revealed few differences between desires and intentions (Armitage & Conner, 2001), and a reanalysis of the present data by using desire and intention as separate constructs revealed no substantive differences.

4 For example, for anyone who attended every week within the 12-week study period, the value of the dependent variable is actually unknown: Individuals may lapse in the week following the end of the study or maintain their exercise behavior for another 12 weeks. Similarly, although multiple regression would treat people who missed the last 6 weeks and those who missed alternate weeks as the same (i.e., overall attendance = 6 weeks), it seems likely that these two groups will differ in some important respects. In either case, multiple regression analysis would produce large biases in the data (Allison, 1984). The technical term for this scenario is *censoring;* this form of censoring is known as *right censoring* and is the only form of censoring that is relevant to the present study. In *left censoring,* events occur before the start of the observation period, which is therefore rarely relevant to experimental work. The potential effects of left censoring were removed from the present study by ensuring that participants had not previously attended this particular gymnasium.

Allison, 1984; Greenhouse et al., 1989). More complex versions of survival analysis are able to incorporate the factors that predict the timing of events by using Cox's (1972) proportional hazards model. In the context of the present study, Cox's proportional hazards model will use theory of planned behavior variables to predict lapses in exercise.

As implied by its label, one limitation of traditional survival analysis is that it was designed to predict terminal events, whereas many of the events of interest to health psychologists are repeatable. Once events have been censored in standard survival analysis, it is assumed they cannot be observed again, yet even the most committed exerciser might experience one insurmountable barrier to exercising over a 3-month period (e.g., through illness or vacation). This means that using a *time to first lapse* criterion could bias the analyses in much the same way as assuming that participants either continue or discontinue exercising in Week 13 (i.e., after the study has finished), and so an adapted form of survival analysis, namely, *repeatable events survival analysis,* was used in addition to the traditional survival analysis. This adaptation involves pooling observations and includes "as an observation each period of time between events for any individual as a separate observation" (Luke, 1993, p. 236; see also Allison, 1984). Thus, every individual has exactly one censored interval but may also have none, one, or more uncensored intervals. The advantage of this technique is that, as with standard survival analysis, theory of planned behavior variables can be used to predict overall survival by using Cox's (1972) proportional hazards model.

A related goal of the present research was to assess the impact of past behavior on future behavior, and so two further approaches not typically found in research on the theory of planned behavior were adopted. First, Heckman and Borjas (1980) recommended – couched in terms of the present study – calculating the total number of people who missed each week and then testing the distribution of attendance–nonattendance over the study period.[5] If weekly attendance at the gymnasium is independent of attendance during the preceding weeks, one would expect that patterns of attendance would be uniformly distributed across the weeks. Alternatively, if (as predicted) attendance–nonattendance at the gymnasium affects subsequent attendance, there should be a nonuniform pattern of attendance. The uniformity of the distribution is determined by using the Kolmogorov–Smirnov (K-S) statistic, which compares the distribution of attendance–nonattendance against a flat (uniform) distribution, where all possible outcomes are equally probable. A statistically significant K-S value indicates that the pattern deviates from uniformity. Heckman and Borjas also recommended testing the robustness of this analysis by examining the number of lapses not immediately preceded by a lapse, as well as the number of lapses that are immediately preceded by a lapse (see Table 1).

Second, I used repeated measures analysis of variance with Helmert contrasts. Helmert contrasts test the effect of each variable compared with the mean effect of subsequent variables. In the context of the present research, the Helmert contrasts test the effects of current attendance against subsequent attendance. For example, physical activity participation at Week 2 is compared with physical activity participation in Weeks 3–12, and physical activity participation in Week 5 is compared with physical activity participation in Weeks 6–12. The Helmert contrast analyses should therefore corroborate the Heckman and Borjas (1980) econometric analyses and enhance confidence in the conclusions drawn. In addition, Helmert contrasts provide univariate *F* tests, which means it is possible to identify patterns in the data and, more specifically, whether there is a critical period by which the cumulative effects of past behavior no longer exert significant influence on future behavior.

5 Note that Heckman and Borjas's (1980) article actually referred to periods of employment–unemployment. The present research extrapolates these techniques to the analysis of attendance–nonattendance.

Table 1 Testing the effects of past behavior on future behavior

Week	Total lapses	Lapses with no immediate prior lapses	Lapses following one immediate prior lapse	$F(1, 90)^a$
1	29	–	–	–
2	30	7	23	6.08*
3	29	10	19	4.82*
4	26	7	19	6.70*
5	41	18	23	15.20**
6	43	10	33	0.01
7	37	4	33	0.45
8	42	10	32	1.13
9	42	6	36	0.23
10	41	5	36	0.43
11	38	4	34	0.23
12	41	5	36	1.29
K-S test	1.32*	2.05**	1.64**	–

Note. K-S test = Kolmogorov – Smirnov test testing the distribution against uniformity.
[a] Helmert contrasts are based on a within-subjects analysis of variance of attendance data; these test for differences between one week and subsequent weeks and control for the effects of behavioral intention and perceived behavioral control.
*$p < 0.05$. **$p < 0.01$.

Results
Predictive validity of the theory of planned behavior

The means, standard deviations, and intercorrelations between the key variables are presented in Table 2. As one would anticipate, scores on all theory of planned behavior variables were extremely positive, with participants reporting positive attitudes and intentions toward engaging in regular exercise. Despite these positive attitudes and intentions, however, the mean level of subsequent attendance reliably obtained from records was only 1.60 ($SD = 0.37$; maximum = 2.00), which differed significantly from full attendance, $t(91) = -10.38$, $p < 0.01$, even in this sample of highly motivated people. The zero-order correlations revealed strong positive correlations between each of the theory of planned behavior components, as well as a strong correlation between self-reported and actual behavior ($r = 0.63$, $p < 0.01$).

The predictive validity of the theory of planned behavior was initially tested with two multiple regression analyses (see Table 3). First, behavioral intention was regressed on attitude, subjective norm, and perceived behavioral control. Comparable to relevant meta-analyses, the

Table 2 Zero-order correlations, means, and standard deviations of measured variables

Variable	1	2	3	4	5	6	M	SD
1. Attitude	–	0.21*	0.37**	0.37**	0.36**	0.39**	2.06	0.99
2. Subjective norm	–	–	0.28**	0.35**	0.14	0.02	5.97	1.20
3. Perceived behavioral control	–	–	–	0.65**	0.51**	0.40**	6.02	1.05
4. Behavioral intention	–	–	–	–	0.42**	0.51**	2.49	0.80
5. Actual behavior	–	–	–	–	–	0.63**	1.60[a]	0.37
6. Self-reported behavior	–	–	–	–	–	– –	5.78	1.71

[a] This value refers to mean attendance per individual over 12 weeks.
*$p < 0.05$. **$p < 0.01$.

three independent variables accounted for 49% of the variance in behavioral intention, and subjective norm and perceived behavioral control were independent predictors. The second multiple regression analysis involved actual behavior as the dependent variable (calculated as mean attendance) and behavioral intention and perceived behavioral control as independent variables. The two proximal determinants of behavior accounted for 22% of the variance in actual behavior; perceived behavioral control was the only significant independent predictor. Thus, Table 3 demonstrates that the theory of planned behavior is a significant predictor of exercise intentions and – for the first time – actual behavior.

These data were further explored by using standard survival analysis. First, a Kaplan–Meier survival curve was computed, where vertical lines represent the proportion of lapses and the horizontal lines represent the passage of time (see Figure 1). These data revealed that 29 people failed to attend during Week 1, meaning that there was a cumulative survival rate of 68.48% by the end of Week 1. Overall, the mean survival time was 5.62 (95% CI = 4.68, 6.56), meaning that, on average, participants maintained at least weekly attendance over the first 5 weeks. After Week 5, the survival curve shows a marked decrease in gradient: The survival rate dropped from 47.83% in Week 4 to 39.13% in Week 5 but dropped only a further 3.26% between Weeks 5 and 6 (Week 6 survival rate = 35.87%). In fact, the survival rate dropped 29.35% between Weeks 1 and 5 but dropped just 9.78% between Weeks 6 and 12. This means that the rate of lapse decreased over time. Moreover, there was a significant minority of people ($n = 27$) whose data were censored, meaning that 29.35% of the sample maintained full attendance over the 12-week study period (see Figure 1).

Second, I used Cox's (1972) proportional hazard technique to examine whether variables from the theory of planned behavior could predict survival (see Table 4). These data showed that, consistent with the prior analyses, perceived behavioral control was significantly related to

Table 3 Multiple regression analysis predicting behavioral intention and behavior

Variable	R^2	F	β
Predicting behavioral intention	0.49	26.74**	–
Attitude	–	–	0.12
Subjective norm	–	–	0.19*
Perceived behavioral control	–	–	0.57**
Predicting behavior	0.22	9.08**	–
Behavioral intention	–	–	0.11
Perceived behavioral control	–	–	0.38*

*$p < 0.05$. **$p < 0.01$.

Table 4 Proportional hazards models: using theory of planned behavior variables to predict time to lapse

Predictor variable	B	SE	B/SE = Z	RR
Predicting time to first lapse	–	–	–	–
Behavioral intention	−0.10	0.19	−0.53	0.90
Perceived behavioral control	−0.38	0.14	−2.71**	0.68
Predicting time to pooled lapse	–	–	–	–
Behavioral intention	−0.06	0.16	−0.37	0.94
Perceived behavioral control	−0.35	0.11	−3.18**	0.71

Note. RR = relative risk.
**$p < 0.01$.

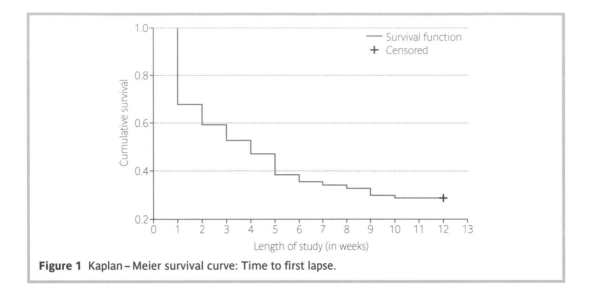

Figure 1 Kaplan–Meier survival curve: Time to first lapse.

the hazard rate such that greater perceived behavioral control was associated with a shift down the hazard curve. The relative risk of relapsing was 0.68, meaning that for every unit increase in perceived behavioral control, the hazard rate was reduced by 32% ($p<0.01$). It is interesting to note that although behavioral intention was not significantly related to survival, a unit increase in behavioral intention would reduce the hazard rate by 10%, which would lead to beneficial maintenance of physical activity if extrapolated to a larger population.

I then pooled the data by treating each period of time between events as a separate observation (Allison, 1984). Thus, the pooled data set consisted of 440 observations with 94 censored cases (i.e., one for each participant), which means that participants missed 4.68 weeks (i.e., $440 \div 94$) on average. A Kaplan–Meier survival curve was computed, revealing a 1-week cumulative survival rate of 38.68% (see Figure 2); in other words, a relapse occurred in the week immediately after a prior lapse in 61.32% of cases. There was a marked decline in the gradient of the survival curve around 5 weeks: This means that the proportion of people surviving

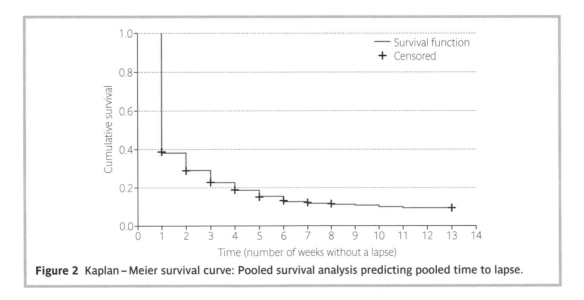

Figure 2 Kaplan–Meier survival curve: Pooled survival analysis predicting pooled time to lapse.

5 weeks without a lapse was 18.73%. The proportion of people surviving 6 or 12 weeks ranged between 15.35% and 9.81%, meaning that maintaining behavior over 5 weeks increased the likelihood that the behavior would persist. This issue is dealt with further in depth in the following section. Overall, these data revealed a mean survival time of 3.02 (95% CI = 2.68, 3.37), meaning that, on average, participants sustained weekly attendance over a period of 3 weeks.

Consistent with the traditional survival analysis, Cox's (1972) proportional hazard model was used to examine whether variables from the theory of planned behavior could predict cumulative survival (see Table 4). These data showed that perceived behavioral control was significantly related to the hazard rate such that greater perceived behavioral control was associated with a shift down the hazard curve. The relative risk of relapsing was 0.71, meaning that for every unit increase in perceived behavioral control, the hazard rate was reduced by 29% ($p < 0.01$). Although behavioral intention was not significantly related to survival, a unit increase in behavioral intention would reduce the hazard rate by 6%, which if extrapolated to a larger population would accrue significant health benefits. The pooled survival analysis therefore replicated the effects found by using traditional survival analysis (see Table 4).

Effects of past behavior on future behavior

I used the techniques described by Heckman and Borjas (1980) to examine the effects of past behavior on future behavior. Thus, rather than simply using actual behavior as a dependent variable, these analyses examined the cumulative effects of past behavior on future behavior. The effects of attendance were first analyzed by calculating the total number of people who missed each week (see Table 1). The distribution of total lapses differed significantly from uniformity (K-S = 1.32, $p < 0.05$), meaning that attendance in later weeks was dependent on attendance in earlier weeks. The second analyses reported in Table 1 aggregated the number of nonattendances that were not directly preceded by a week of nonattendance. Again, the distribution differed significantly from uniformity (K-S = 2.05, $p < 0.01$). Analysis of the distribution of nonattendance that was immediately preceded by a nonattendance event also differed significantly from uniformity (K-S = 1.64, $p < 0.01$). Together, these analyses suggest that accumulated past behavior exerts a significant effect on future behavior.

The question then arises as to whether there is a critical period for attendance – in other words, whether it takes a certain length of time to form a habit. I tested this by using Helmert contrasts, which test the effect of each variable compared with the mean effect of subsequent variables. In other words, the Helmert contrasts test the effects of current (i.e., week-by-week) attendance against mean subsequent attendance. First, a repeated measures analysis of variance with 12 levels (i.e., weekly attendance) was computed: Consistent with the K-S tests, there was a significant effect of time on attendance, $F(11, 81) = 2.54$, $p < 0.01$. Second, Helmert contrasts were computed; the univariate F tests associated with these contrasts indicated that attendance during the first 5 weeks exerted significant effects on subsequent attendance, $Fs(1, 91) = 4.82–15.18$, $ps < 0.05$, but that from Week 6 on, attendance–nonattendance failed to exert significant effects on subsequent weeks, $Fs(1, 91) = 0.01–1.29$, $ps > 0.25$ (see Table 1). These effects corroborate the first Kaplan–Meier survival curve (see Figure 1) and suggest that behavior up to Week 5 was crucial in determining subsequent behavior. The implication is that it may take 5 weeks to develop a habit with respect to participating in physical activity. It is important to note that these effects remained when theory of planned behavior variables were entered as covariates. Consistent with the prior analyses, perceived behavioral control was the only significant covariate ($\beta = 0.41$, $p < 0.01$).

Effects of past behavior on subsequent cognition

The final set of analyses was designed to examine whether past behavior affected future cognition. It was reasoned that the best predictor of subsequent cognition would be prior cognition and that the most rigorous test of effects of past behavior on subsequent cognition would therefore control for the baseline theory of planned behavior measures. Four independent hierarchical multiple regression analyses (one for each theory of planned behavior variable) were used to test this hypothesis (see Table 5). Each theory of planned behavior variable measured at follow-up was first regressed on the corresponding baseline measure. In each case, the baseline measure was a significant predictor of the follow-up measure, meaning that each variable was stable across the 12 weeks ($rs = 0.68–0.73$, $ps < 0.01$; see Table 5). To test the influence of actual behavior on cognition, mean attendance was computed and added into the regression equation on Step 2 of the analysis. In only two cases did actual behavior explain significant additional variance: behavioral intention and perceived behavioral control (see Table 5). The direction of the effects means that successful performance of the behavior increased intention and perceived behavioral control, whereas unsuccessful performance of the behavior undermined these constructs. Consistent with predictions, the effect of past behavior on the follow-up measure of perceived behavioral control was stronger than the baseline measure of perceived behavioral control ($\beta s = 0.49$ and 0.46, respectively; $ps < 0.01$).

Table 5 Testing the effects of past behavior on future cognition: hierarchical multiple regression analyses

Predictor	ΔR^2	F_{change}	$\beta_{at\ step}$
Predicting attitude at follow-up			
Step 1	0.51	71.50**	
Attitude at baseline			0.71**
Step 2	0.02	2.38	
Attitude at baseline			0.65**
Actual behavior			0.14
Predicting subjective norm at follow-up			
Step 1	0.53	78.32**	
Subjective norm at baseline			0.73**
Step 2	0.01	0.60	
Subjective norm at baseline			0.71**
Actual behavior			0.06
Predicting perceived behavioral control at follow-up			
Step 1	0.48	63.85**	
Perceived behavioral control at baseline			0.69**
Step 2	0.19	40.59**	
Perceived behavioral control at baseline			0.46**
Actual behavior			0.49**
Predicting behavioral intention at follow-up			
Step 1	0.47	62.31**	
Behavioral intention at baseline			0.68**
Step 2	0.12	19.70**	
Behavioral intention at baseline			0.54**
Actual behavior			0.37**

**p < 0.01.

Discussion

This is the first study to examine actual behavior by using a within-participants longitudinal design in the area of exercise and the theory of planned behavior. Findings provide some support for the predictive validity of the theory of planned behavior (the perceived behavioral control component in particular) and for the ideas that past behavior exerts cumulative but diminishing effects on subsequent behavior and that perceived behavioral control is enhanced by personal mastery experiences. The following discussion considers the theoretical and practical implications of this research.

Although the present study incorporated several novel features in both its design and execution, it is important to note its consistency with prior research. For example, Simkin and Gross (1994) conducted a 14-week study of new members at a health club and found that 66% ($n=$ 19) of all participants experienced a lapse at some point during the study period. This is strikingly similar to the 70.65% of participants who lapsed at some point during the present study and suggests that the present findings may generalize beyond the current context. The present findings also provide further support for the predictive validity of the theory of planned behavior, which was shown to be predictive of actual behavior across a 3-month time period. In fact, the effect sizes are remarkably similar to those reported in meta-analyses of applications of the theory of planned behavior to exercise (e.g., Hagger et al., 2002). This is important because studies of physical activity typically use time intervals measured in days rather than weeks and because earlier research has not used objective measures of behavior. Moreover, in contrast with Sheeran et al. (2001), the present study supports the idea that the theory of planned behavior can account for the maintenance of health behavior. However, it should be noted that the present findings are also consistent with Bandura's (1997) social-cognitive theory, from which the present measure of perceived behavioral control was taken. The issue of maintenance is discussed in depth below.

On a methodological level, the present study is one of the first to use repeatable events survival analysis and econometric techniques to analyze health psychology data. The use of these techniques is likely to increase as greater research attention is focused on understanding the maintenance – as well as the initiation – of health behavior and as it is recognized that single-occasion reports of behavior are not optimal (cf. Marcus et al., 2000; Murdock, 1962). In particular, the use of Cox's (1972) proportional hazard technique to predict multiple cases of lapse, reinitiation, and relapse demonstrated that the perceived behavioral control component of the theory of planned behavior could account for the maintenance of behavior. In addition, the use of econometric techniques showed that the effects of past behavior on future behavior declined after 5 weeks. Given that habits develop in stable, predictable contexts, it seems plausible that this 5-week period maps the shift from initial voluntary control to repeated habitual behavior (e.g., Dickinson, 1985). Although research into maintenance as a process is in its infancy (Wing, 2000; but see Prochaska & DiClemente, 1983, and below), one potential application of research into maintenance would be to prescribe not just the content of an intervention but also its duration. On a theoretical level, it would be interesting to compare the present findings to see whether other health habits form in comparable time intervals.

Prochaska and DiClemente's (1983) transtheoretical model is one of the few models that explicitly includes a maintenance stage. Maintenance is distinguished from the preceding action stage by specifying not just that the health behavior in question has been achieved, but that the health behavior has been performed consistently for a period of 6 months or more.[6] However, the present research suggests that the distinction between the action and maintenance stages might actually be shorter than 6 months and may even be as short as 5 weeks (e.g., Marcus et al., 2000). This would explain why researchers have often struggled to discriminate between the action and maintenance stages in research on exercise behavior. For example, Courneya (1995) found that it was possible to discriminate participants in the precontemplation, contemplation, and preparation stages from one another (and from action and maintenance) but found no differences between action and maintenance on any of the six dependent variables used. Similarly, Marcus, Rossi, Selby, Niaura, and Abrams (1992) conducted 10 separate analyses and found only three significant differences between action and maintenance, all of which were in the opposite direction to that predicted, showing decreases in the use of the processes of change between the action and maintenance stages. Moreover, in the conclusion to his meta-analysis of stages and processes of change, Rosen (2000b) argued, "it may be more appropriate to think of exercise readiness as a continuous variable rather than as discrete stages" (p. 602). The present research supports this assertion, although further research is required to identify the "time to maintenance" of other health behaviors. This would seem to support research focusing on continuum models, rather than stage models (see Rosen, 2000a).

Consistent with prior retrospective studies, the present research demonstrated that perceived behavioral control was the dominant predictor of exercise maintenance across all the analyses (cf. Miller et al., 2002; Sallis et al., 1990). The question then arises as to whether perceived behavioral control can be targeted to change behavior. In fact, Bandura (1986) provided four different approaches to the way in which perceived behavioral control (synonymous with self-efficacy, see Ajzen, 1991, 1998) can be changed. First, persuasive techniques can be used to persuade people they have sufficient control over the behavior. For example, one might target the control beliefs that Ajzen (1991) regarded as underpinning perceived behavioral control to enhance perceived behavioral control. The second approach is *personal mastery,* which involves the accomplishment of subgoals; in other words, rather than trying to persuade a nonexerciser to start attending the gymnasium on a weekly basis, it might be advisable to encourage something easier, such as walking part of the way to work. As the present study shows, successful performance of the behavior further enhances perceived behavioral control. The third approach advocated by Bandura (1986) is modeling, or observing other people and learning about their success. The fourth approach is learning to use relaxation techniques in order to control feelings of arousal or anxiety, which has also been used successfully to enhance perceived behavioral control. The present study demonstrated that personal mastery experiences successfully enhanced perceived behavioral control across the period of the research. Future research that experimentally manipulates perceived behavioral control is therefore likely to change actual behavior and, more important, to sustain behavior change.

There are three possible limitations that should be addressed in future research. First, because the primary goal of the research was to study maintenance behavior in a naturalistic environment rather than the effects of cardiovascular training, participants did not record the duration and intensity of each exercise session, and the analyses focused on frequency of attendance because it was most theoretically relevant and could be assessed objectively. In spite of

---

6 It is interesting to note that the theory of planned behavior has been shown to be predictive of transitions between transtheoretical model stages of change: In a study of healthy food choice, Armitage, Sheeran, Conner, and Arden (2004) showed that perceived behavioral control predicted the progression from action to maintenance and that behavioral intention predicted regression from the maintenance stage.

this, confidence in the validity of the findings can be drawn from the strong correlation between attendance and the self-report measure of actual exercise behavior ($r = 0.63$, $p < 0.01$), which in turn has been validated against biological markers (e.g., Sallis, Buono, Roby, Micale, & Nelson, 1993). That said, it would be valuable to replicate the effects with objective tests of fitness.

A related concern is that it was not possible to distinguish between those people who exercised five times per week from those who exercised once a week. This is potentially problematic because most recommendations center around exercising three times per week. However, any criterion more frequent than attending at least once per week would mean that the data would have to be analyzed at the level of days, rather than the level of weeks. This would be problematic in the context of the present study because even if all participants exercised three times per week, by definition there would be four lapses per week at the daily level of analysis (and maybe more if people exercised more than once per day). Depending on the pattern of daily attendance, this could seriously bias the findings despite the fact that people might be adhering to the recommendations. In other words, daily level analyses were inappropriate for the present purposes because recommended levels of exercise are phrased in terms of weekly, not daily, exercise. Similarly, gym attendance is typically not specified in the recommendations to exercise three times per week, and it seems likely that a lot of people attending a gym would do so as part of a more general exercise regimen. In other words, attending a gym is probably one of a range of physical activities, and under such circumstances, a criterion of attending the gym at least once a week seems reasonable. This is borne out by the fact that in the present study gym attendance accounted for 39.69% of the variance in general participation in physical activity, showing that although gym attendance was an important part of people's overall physical activity participation, it was not tapping all of their exercise behavior.

A second possible limitation is that theory of planned behavior variables were measured only at baseline and follow-up, meaning that week-by-week changes in perceived behavioral control were not assessed. However, this feature of the design meant that the burden on participants was minimized and ensured that the effects of past behavior could not be attributed to repeated expression effects, which have been shown to increase the strength and extremity of social-cognitive variables (e.g., Judd & Brauer, 1995). A related concern is that past behavior (other than prior nonattendance at the gymnasium in question) was not measured at baseline, meaning that the maintenance effects reported in the present study are therefore limited to attendance at the gymnasium only.

The third potential limitation is that the sample consisted of people attending a private gymnasium. It is therefore highly likely that the present participants were of a higher socioeconomic status than a random sample of the general population would have been, and so caution must be adopted before generalizing the findings to other samples. Future research might replicate the present effects in a broader sample of the population; however, some level of confidence can be gleaned from the fact that the present findings corroborate earlier studies (e.g., Sallis et al., 1990; Simkin & Gross, 1994).

In conclusion, the present study demonstrates that the perceived behavioral control component of the theory of planned behavior is predictive of both initiation and maintenance of actual exercise attendance, which seems to reflect general exercise behavior, and sheds light on the likely genesis of exercise habits. Further research that examines multiple health behaviors over longer periods of time is required.

References

Ajzen, I. (1991). The theory of planned behavior. *Organizational Behavior and Human Decision Processes, 50,* 179–211.

Ajzen, I. (1998). Models of human social behavior and their application to health psychology. *Psychology and Health, 13,* 735–739.

Allison, P. D. (1984). *Event history analysis: Regression for longitudinal event data.* Newbury Park, CA: Sage.

Armitage, C. J., & Arden, M. A. (2002). Exploring discontinuity patterns in the transtheoretical model: An application of the theory of planned behaviour. *British Journal of Health Psychology, 7,* 89–103.

Armitage, C. J., & Conner, M. (2001). Efficacy of the theory of planned behaviour: A meta-analytic review. *British Journal of Social Psychology, 40,* 471–499.

Armitage, C. J., Conner, M., Loach, J., & Willetts, D. (1999). Different perceptions of control: Applying an extended theory of planned behavior to legal and illegal drug use. *Basic and Applied Social Psychology, 21,* 301–316.

Armitage, C. J., Sheeran, P., Conner, M., & Arden, M. A. (2004). Stages of change or changes of stage? Predicting transitions in transtheoretical model stages in relation to healthy food choice. *Journal of Consulting and Clinical Psychology, 72,* 491–499.

Bagozzi, R. P. (1992). The self-regulation of attitudes, intentions, and behavior. *Social Psychology Quarterly, 55,* 178–204.

Baker, C. W., Little, T. D., & Brownell, K. D. (2003). Predicting adolescent eating and activity behaviors: The role of social norms and personal agency. *Health Psychology, 22,* 189–198.

Bandura, A. (1986). *Social foundations of thought and action.* Englewood Cliffs, NJ: Prentice Hall.

Bandura, A. (1997). *Self-efficacy: The exercise of control.* New York: Freeman.

Blue, C. L. (1995). The predictive capacity of the theory of reasoned action and the theory of planned behavior in exercise research: An integrated literature review. *Research in Nursing and Health, 18,* 105–121.

Byers, T., Nestle, M., McTiernan, A., Doyle, C., Currie-Williams, A., Gansler, T., & Thun, M. (2002). American Cancer Society guidelines on nutrition and physical activity for cancer prevention: Reducing the risk of cancer with healthy food choices and physical activity. *CA: A Cancer Journal for Clinicians, 52,* 92–119.

Cardinal, B. J. (1998). Interaction between stage of exercise and history of exercise relapse. *Journal of Human Movement Studies, 34,* 175–185.

Conner, M., & Armitage, C. J. (1998). Extending the theory of planned behavior: A review and avenues for further research. *Journal of Applied Social Psychology, 28,* 1429–1464.

Courneya, K. S. (1995). Understanding readiness for regular physical activity in older individuals: An application of the theory of planned behavior. *Health Psychology, 14,* 80–87.

Courneya, K. S., Nigg, C. R., & Estabrooks, P. A. (1998). Relationships among theory of planned behavior, stages of change, and exercise behavior in older persons over a three year period. *Psychology and Health, 13,* 355–367.

Courneya, K. S., Plotnikoff, R. C., Hotz, S. B., & Birkett, N. J. (2001). Predicting exercise stage transitions over two consecutive 6-month periods: A test of the theory of planned behaviour in a population-based sample. *British Journal of Health Psychology, 6,* 135–150.

Cox, D. R. (1972). Regression models and life tables. *Journal of the Royal Statistical Society, Series B, 34,* 187–202.

Dickinson, A. (1985). Actions and habits: The development of behavioural autonomy. *Philosophical Transactions of the Royal Society of London. Series B, Biological Sciences, 308,* 67–78.

Erikssen, G. (2001). Physical fitness and changes in mortality: The survival of the fittest. *Sports Medicine, 31,* 571–576.

Godin, G. (1993). The theories of reasoned action and planned behavior: Overview of findings, emerging research problems and usefulness for exercise promotion. *Journal of Applied Sport Psychology, 5,* 141–157.

Godin, G. (1994). Theories of reasoned action and planned behavior: Usefulness for exercise promotion. *Medicine and Science in Sport and Exercise, 26,* 1391–1394.

Godin, G., & Kok, G. (1996). The theory of planned behavior: A review of its applications to health-related behaviors. *American Journal of Health Promotion, 11,* 87–98.

Greenhouse, J. B., Stangl, D., & Bromberg, J. (1989). An introduction to survival analysis: Statistical methods for analysis of clinical trial data. *Journal of Consulting and Clinical Psychology, 57,* 536–544.

Hagger, M. S., Chatzisarantis, N. L. D., & Biddle, S. J. H. (2002). Meta-analysis of the theories of reasoned action and planned behavior in physical activity: An examination of predictive validity and the contribution of additional variables. *Journal of Sport and Exercise Psychology, 24,* 3–32.

Hausenblas, H. A., Carron, A. V., & Mack, D. E. (1997). Application of the theories of reasoned action and planned behavior to exercise behavior: A meta-analysis. *Journal of Sport and Exercise Psychology, 19,* 36–51.

Heckman, J. J., & Borjas, G. J. (1980). Does unemployment cause future unemployment? Definitions, questions and answers from a continuous time model of heterogeneity and state dependence. *Economica, 47,* 247–283.

Judd, C. M., & Brauer, M. (1995). Repetition and evaluative extremity. In R. E. Petty & J. A. Krosnick (Eds.), *Attitude strength: Antecedents and consequences* (pp. 43–71). Mahwah, NJ: Erlbaum.

King, A. C., Kiernan, M., Oman, R. F., Kraemer, H. C., Hull, M., & Ahn, D. (1997). Can we identify who will adhere to long-term physical activity? Signal detection methodology as a potential aid to clinical decision making. *Health Psychology, 16,* 380–389.

Luke, D. A. (1993). Charting the process of change: A primer on survival analysis. *American Journal of Community Psychology, 21,* 203–246.

Luke, D. A., & Homan, S. M. (1998). Time and change: Using survival analysis in clinical assessment and treatment evaluation. *Psychological Assessment, 10,* 360–378.

Marcus, B. H., Dubbert, P. M., Forsyth, L. H., McKenzie, T. L., Stone, E. J., Dunn, A. L., & Blair, S. N. (2000). Physical activity behavior change: Issues in adoption and maintenance. *Health Psychology, 19*(Suppl. 1), 32–41.

Marcus, B. H., Rossi, J. S., Selby, V. C., Niaura, R. S., & Abrams, D. B. (1992). The stages and processes of exercise adoption and maintenance in a worksite sample. *Health Psychology, 11,* 386–395.

Martinez-Gonzalez, M. A., Varo, J. J., Santos, J. L., De Irala, J., Gibney, M., Kearney, J., & Martinez, J. A. (2001). Prevalence of physical activity during leisure time in the European Union. *Medicine and Science in Sports and Exercise, 33,* 1142–1146.

Miller, K. H., Ogletree, R. J., & Welshimer, K. (2002). Impact of activity behaviors on physical activity identity and self-efficacy. *American Journal of Health Behavior, 26,* 323–330.

Murdock, B. (1962). The serial position effect of free recall. *Journal of Experimental Psychology, 64,* 482–488.

Ouellette, J. A., & Wood, W. (1998). Habit and intention in everyday life: The multiple processes by which past behavior predicts future behavior. *Psychological Bulletin, 124,* 54–74.

Prochaska, J. O., & DiClemente, C. C. (1983). Stages and processes of self-change in smoking: Toward an integrative model of change. *Journal of Consulting and Clinical Psychology, 51,* 390–395.

Prochaska, J. O., Velicer, W. F., Rossi, J. S., Goldstein, M. G., Marcus, B. H., Rakowski, W., et al. (1994). Stages of change and decisional balance for 12 problem behaviors. *Health Psychology, 13,* 39–46.

Randall, D. M., & Wolff, J. A. (1994). The time interval in the intention–behaviour relationship: Meta-analysis. *British Journal of Social Psychology, 33,* 405–418.

Rosen, C. S. (2000a). Integrating stage and continuum models to explain processing of exercise messages and exercise initiation among sedentary college students. *Health Psychology, 19,* 172–180.

Rosen, C. S. (2000b). Is the sequencing of change processes by stage consistent across health problems? A meta-analysis. *Health Psychology, 19,* 593–604.

Sallis, J. F., Buono, M. J., Roby, J. J., Micale, F. G., & Nelson, J. A. (1993). Seven-day recall and other physical activity self-reports in children and adolescents. *Medicine and Science in Sports and Exercise, 25,* 99–108.

Sallis, J. F., Hovell, M. F., Hofstetter, C. R., Elder, J. P., Faucher, P., Spry, V. M., et al. (1990). Lifetime history of relapse from exercise. *Addictive Behaviors, 15,* 573–579.

Sheeran, P., Conner, M., & Norman, P. (2001). Can the theory of planned behavior explain patterns of health behavior change? *Health Psychology, 20,* 12–19.

Sheeran, P., Trafimow, D., & Armitage, C. J. (2003). Predicting behaviour from perceived behavioural control: Tests of the accuracy assumption of the theory of planned behaviour. *British Journal of Social Psychology, 42,* 393–410.

Simkin, L. R., & Gross, A. M. (1994). Assessment of coping with high-risk situations for exercise relapse among healthy women. *Health Psychology, 13,* 274–277.

Wing, R. R. (2000). Cross-cutting themes in maintenance of behavior change. *Health Psychology, 19*(Suppl. 1), 84–88.

Murgraff, V., White, D. and Phillips, K. (1999) An application of protection motivation theory to riskier single-occasion drinking, *Psychology and Health*, 14: 339–50.

An application of protection motivation theory to riskier single-occasion drinking

Vered Murgraff[1], David White[2],* and Keith Phillips[3]
[1]*Department of Psychology, University of East London, Romford Road, London, E15 4LZ, UK*
[2]*School of Social Sciences, Staffordshire University, College Road, Stoke-on-Trent, ST4 2DE, UK*
[3]*School of Social Policy Sciences, University of Westminster, 309 Regent Street, London, W1R 8AL, UK*

Abstract

Cognitions in relation to drinking alcohol on a single occasion were explored within the framework of Protection Motivation Theory (PMT). One hundred and twenty three students provided information about their current weekend drinking, beliefs about drinking, and intentions to drink at safer limits. Data on self reported weekend drinking were gathered two weeks later from the same respondents. Analyses showed PMT components to be predictive of intentions but not of later behaviour. Perceived severity and self-efficacy related significantly to intentions for drinking at safer limits. No PMT measure differentiated between those who engaged in riskier single-occasion drinking at follow up and those whose drinking was less risky. Past behaviour was the only significant predictor of riskier single-occasion drinking at follow up. Implications for the current utility of PMT are discussed particularly in relation to respondents' reactions to newly identified health threats.

Keywords: Protection motivation, single-occasion drinking, intentions, behaviour, behaviour change, past behaviour.

Introduction

Increasingly, concern about the harm caused by alcohol consumption is focusing upon moderate as well as heavy drinking. The changing emphasis follows reports of studies showing that harm may be associated with single occasion drinking at lower levels of consumption than previously thought harmful (e.g. Midanik, Tam, Greenfield and Caetano, 1996). There is a significant correlation between the number of alcohol units consumed on a single drinking occasion and alcohol-related harm such as traffic accidents, crime, unwanted pregnancies, contracting sexual transmitted diseases such as HIV/AIDS, and mild damage to the heart, liver, brain and immune system (e.g. Department of Transport, 1992; Goddard and Ikin, 1988; HEA, 1996; Morgan, Plant and Plant, 1990; Tuck, 1989). To date attempts to promote sensible drinking habits have had limited success (Foxcroft, Lister-Sharp and Lowe, 1997). One reason for the limited success may be the incomplete understanding of the cognitive mediators of alcohol use (Coggans and Watson, 1995). Identification of such mediators could enhance the effectiveness of preventive programmes (Donaldson, Sussman, MacKinnon, Severson, Glynn, Murray and Stone, 1996).

Protection Motivation Theory (PMT) is a theoretical account of the cognitive antecedents of behaviour which has been applied to other health issues (Rogers, 1983) and may also be relevant to an understanding of single occasion drinking. PMT focuses on an individual's judgements of the probability of a harmful event happening to them (vulnerability), the severity of that event should it happen, the efficacy of a preventive response (response efficacy), their perceived ability to execute coping behaviours successfully (self-efficacy), the costs associated with the execution of the response, and the intrinsic and extrinsic rewards associated with any maladaptive (i.e. alternative) responses.

The strength of protection motivation is estimated by assessing intentions to adopt the recommended behaviour. Thus, PMT components are assumed to have significant associations with the intention to perform a desired behaviour. PMT therefore, has been tested most frequently as a model accounting for the formation and maintenance of intentions to perform desired health behaviours. Support for the mediating role of PMT cognitions has been provided for a range of health behaviours including intentions to enhance diagnostic health behaviours such as breast self examination (Rippetoe and Rogers, 1987) and intentions to adopt a healthy lifestyle, for example, in relation to exercise (Wurtele and Maddux, 1987; Fruin, Pratt and Owen, 1991) and safer sexual behaviour (e.g. Abraham and Sheeran, 1994). A small number of studies have also explored the ability of PMT to predict future behaviour (Aspinwall, Kenemy, Taylor, Schneider and Dudley, 1991; Plotnikoff and Higginbotham, 1995; Seydel, Taal and Wiegman, 1990; Stanley and Maddux, 1986; Wurtele and Maddux, 1987). These studies provide only modest support for the ability of PMT to predict future behaviour. However, the small number of studies and the limited numbers of health behaviours explored restrict the conclusions that can be drawn.

Despite this limited support, there are reasons for thinking that PMT may provide a suitable framework for understanding alcohol consumption. PMT components such as vulnerability, severity and cost–benefit analysis, were found to be predictive of entry into treatment (Bardsley and Beckman, 1988) and adherence to treatment programmes among problem drinkers (Rees, 1985). Furthermore, school based alcohol reduction interventions and other substance prevention programmes which emphasised these same features were successful in producing positive attitude and behaviour changes over the period of the intervention (e.g. Gonzalez, 1988). The present study, therefore, examined the contribution of PMT cognitive mediating variables to the prediction of single-occasion drinking intentions and behaviour.

In the USA and in other countries such as Canada and Australia previous investigations of single occasion drinking have taken drinking in excess of 6 units for both men and women as constituting increased risk of alcohol-related problems (frequently referred to as binge drinking) (Marlatt, Baer and Larimer, 1995; Smart and Walsh, 1993; Wechsler and Isaac, 1992). However, this limit has not been adopted uniformly. For example, one UK study favoured a more generous limit of 10 units for men and 7 units for women (Bennett, Smith and Nugent, 1991). The current British advice is to restrict drinking to 3 units per day for men and 2 units per day for women (BMA, 1995; HEA, 1996). However, as yet there is no evidence favouring one cut-off point over another (Catarino, 1992; HEA, 1995) so that single occasion risky-drinking research focuses on relative rather than absolute risk. In the present study, then, participants were informed that the risk of harm increases at the levels of six units for women and eight units for men.

A recent study reported that riskier single occasion drinking was common among College/University students (Wechsler, Dowdall, Davenport and Castillo, 1995) and that weekends were the occasions when such drinking occurred most frequently (Moore, Smith and Catford, 1994). The present study therefore measured riskier single-occasion drinking on weekends using students as the sample population. Following the practice of other researchers in the area (e.g. Wechsler and Isaac, 1992) this study focuses upon specific recent drinking occasions to minimise errors in the recollection of consumption.

Method
Study design

The items included in this study for measuring PMT cognitions were developed in a pilot study of undergraduates. Subsequently, a longitudinal questionnaire study was conducted on a different undergraduate sample with data collected at two time points separated by two weeks. The Time 1 questionnaire included 3 parts: (1) collection of demographic data and data about previous alcohol consumption; (2) presentation of written information about recommended safer limits for single-occasion drinking and the possible adverse consequences of exceeding these limits, and (3) collection of data relating to PMT cognitions, including intentions for future single occasion drinking. The questionnaire completed at Time 2 assessed single-occasion drinking riskiness two weeks following the completion of the first questionnaire.

The pilot study

A pilot study was conducted to develop appropriate PMT measures. Items corresponding to those used in other PMT research (e.g. Seydel et al., 1990) were tested. All items were formulated as Likert scale items in which statements were followed by seven response options anchored "strongly agree" and "strongly disagree". As costs and rewards have not been measured frequently in previous PMT research, items were selected following interviews with 20 self identified heavy drinkers. A large number of items were selected to represent the broad range of beliefs expressed by these drinkers. A 68 item questionnaire was completed by a sample of 196 students.

Items were designed to measure each of the cognitions specified by PMT as follows: perceived severity of the threat (10 items); vulnerability to the threat (9 items); perceived efficacy of the recommended response (7 items); perceived capability of performing the advised behaviour (7 items); the costs involved in performing the recommended behaviour (6 items); the rewards associated with the threat (23 items); and behavioural intentions to perform the advised behaviour (6 items). These measures were tested for their psychometric properties and subsequently reduced to a 36 item questionnaire for use in the longitudinal study.

Data reduction. The mean and standard deviation of each item was scrutinised revealing that each had an adequate spread of responses. Cronbachs' alpha was calculated for each of the PMT scales. For each scale, items with poor correlations to the scale total were excluded sequentially in order to maximise the coefficient. This resulted in a 5 item severity scale (Cronbach alpha 0.72), a 5 item vulnerability scale (0.83), a 2 item response efficacy scale (0.63), a 7 item self-efficacy scale (0.89), an 8 item intrinsic rewards scale (0.87), a 9 item extrinsic rewards scale (0.90), a 3 item costs scale (0.76) and a 2-item intention scale (0.83). To confirm the scale structure of this reduced set of 41 items responses were subjected to a principal components analysis with varimax rotation. Only those items loading onto a factor with a loading of 0.55 or more were considered to have sufficient overlapping variance to be included in scales (Comrey and Lee, 1992). Thirty eight of the 41 items loaded onto ten factors with factor loadings ranging from 0.86 to 0.55 accounting for 71% of the total variance. Two reward items and one cost item were dropped as they did not load onto any factor (Tabachnick and Fidell, 1996). The results of the principal components analysis are presented in Table 1.

It can be seen from Table 1 that two rewards scales emerged, one relating to stress management with seven items (e.g. "I sometimes drink beyond safe daily limits as a relaxation strategy"), and one relating to conforming with six items (e.g. "I sometimes drink beyond the safe daily limits because of pressure from friends and workmates"). As the two rewards scales correlated together above 0.7 they were combined into one scale (Tabachnick and Fidell, 1996).

A number of the scales identified were made up of only two items. Tabachnick and Fidell (1996) argue that the interpretation of scales in these cases is hazardous and they should be included only if their reliability is demonstrated by showing the items to be highly inter-correlated and relatively uncorrelated with other items. The two response efficacy items did not correlate highly with other measures, but they were not highly correlated ($r = 0.46$) and so were treated as two single item measures. In the case of both costs (0.8) and intentions (0.8) the two items correlated highly together and were retained as scales. However, the rewards (depressant/stimulant) items related only weakly to each other (0.6) and related strongly to other factors and so were omitted from the analysis. Thirty six items were therefore used to construct the main study questionnaire.

The longitudinal study

Respondents, procedure and design. A sample of 166 psychology undergraduate students were recruited during lectures. Although given the opportunity to refuse to participate, no respondent did so. Of these, 123 completed both phases of the study and their data are presented here. The Time 2 sample ($N = 123$) did not differ significantly from the initial sample ($N = 166$) on any of the measures. The Time 2 sample comprised 32 males and 91 females (74% females), their mean age was 22 years with a range of 18 to 46 years.

At recruitment (Time 1) respondents received two questionnaires: one was for immediate completion and the second for completion two weeks later (Time 2). To allow matching of Time 1 and Time 2 questionnaires, while maintaining anonymity, respondents identified themselves with a personally generated code. At Time 1 respondents completed the study questionnaire, providing demographic data and data about previous single occasion drinking before

Table 1 Factor analysis of PMT measures

Measure	No. of items	Range of factor loading	Eigen values
Vulnerability	5	0.55 – 0.73	1.98
Severity (general)	3	0.72 – 0.85	1.75
Severity (specific)	2	0.83, 0.86	1.28
Self-efficacy	7	0.58 – 0.77	12.77
Response efficacy	2	0.65, 0.80	10.07
Costs	2	0.82, 0.86	1.44
Rewards (stress management)	7	0.59 – 0.80	3.43
Rewards (conforming)	6	0.59 – 0.74	2.56
Rewards (depressant/stimulant)	2	0.64, 0.74	1.15
Intention	2	0.74, 0.85	1.60

being presented with written information on safer single occasion drinking. They then completed the PMT items. Two weeks later they provided information about their single-occasion drinking during the intervening period.

The PMT measures collected at Time 1 were considered as possible determinants of behavioural intentions. These together with behavioural intentions were considered as possible determinants of single occasion riskier drinking at follow up.

Information on safer single occasion drinking limits. Subjects received written information about recommendations for limiting single-occasion drinking, informing them that healthy alcohol drinking recommendations apply not only to the number of drinks consumed per week but also to the number of drinks consumed on any drinking occasion and that consuming 8 or more units of alcohol for men and 6 or more units of alcohol for women is associated with increased risk of harm. They also received information about the possible direct and indirect health consequences of exceeding these limits. They were informed about possible health threats from drinking above the safer limits in terms of increases in the risk of: hepatitis and cirrhosis (inflammation and permanent scarring of the liver); stomach disorders (gastritis, bleeding, and ulcers); cancer of the mouth, throat and gullet; brain damage; sexual difficulties; high blood pressure; muscle disease; problems with the nervous system (especially pains in the legs and arms); and vitamin deficiency. They were also informed of the indirect health risks of excessive single occasion drinking including its association with reckless driving, road traffic deaths and injuries and with unsafe sexual practices.

The questionnaire[1]

Demographics. Sex, age, and marital status were recorded but as 90.4% were single, marital status was excluded from the analysis.

Previous weekend drinking. Respondents recorded the number of units of alcohol consumed on the previous Saturday and Sunday separately (respondents were provided with a table converting measures of various alcoholic drinks to units of alcohol to assist them in calculating their consumption). The combined total of units consumed on the two days gave the Past Drinking measure.

Threat appraisal was measured by four scales: Two perceived severity scales, one relating to specific threat with two items (e.g. "high blood pressure and muscle disease are very damaging health conditions"), and one relating to generalised threat with three items (e.g. "binge drinking severely damages health"); one perceived vulnerability scale with five items (e.g. "considering my present and past behaviour my chances of getting health problems from binge drinking are very high"); and one rewards scale with 13 items, (e.g. "I sometimes drink beyond safe daily limits as a relaxation strategy").

Coping appraisal was measured by four scales: Two single item response efficacy measures: Response efficacy (health related problems) "sticking to safe daily drinking limits will ensure that I avoid the health problems associated with binge drinking"; and Response efficacy (general) "avoiding drinking beyond daily safe levels is the most effective way of preventing binge drinking related problems"; one self-efficacy scale with seven items (e.g. "I am capable of starting and continuing drinking at safe levels"), and one response costs scale with two items (e.g. "one of the difficulties in restricting drinking to safe daily levels is the inconvenience in having to explain to others why I restrict my drinking").

---

1 A list of items is available on request.

Behavioural intention was measured by a two item scale (e.g. "from now on I intend to drink within safe levels as a regular habit").

Self reported drinking behaviour at two-week follow up was identical to the past drinking measure. Any male who reported drinking 8 units or more and any female who reported drinking 6 units or more on either of these two days was classified as a riskier drinker (the outcome measure was dichotomous (riskier/non riskier)).

Cronbach's alpha coefficients, scale means and standard deviations were computed for the longitudinal sample of 123 respondents and are shown in Table 2.

Results

At follow up 98 respondents were identified as safer single occasion drinkers and 25 as riskier drinkers. There were no age ($F = 1.72$, df = 1,120) or gender differences (Chi square = 0.24, df = 1) between the two groups.

Thirteen measures were included in the study. To limit the number of measures actively explored and to ensure adequate subjects to variable ratios, only those showing significant zero order correlations with intention or future behaviour were included in further analyses. Correlations ranged between 0.00 and 0.62 (see Table 3).

Predictors of behavioural intentions. A direct entry multiple regression analysis was performed with intentions for future single occasion drinking as the dependent variable and severity, vulnerability, self-efficacy, rewards, and past drinking behaviour (number of weekend units consumed) as independent variables.[2] Table 4 displays the unstandardised regression coefficients and intercept, the standardised regression coefficients (beta), the semi partial correlations (providing an estimate of the variance uniquely attributable to the variable) and R and R^2. Table 4 also shows confidence intervals for the correlation coefficients. R for regression was significantly different from zero, $F(5, 113) = 10.39$, $P < 0.000$. Severity and self-efficacy contributed significantly to the prediction of intentions for single occasion drinking ($Sr^2 = 0.05$ and $Sr^2 = 0.02$ respectively). Altogether, 31% (28% adjusted) of the variability in intentions for single occasion drinking was predicted by these five independent variables.

Table 2 Cognitive measures, Cronbach's alphas, means and standard deviations

Measure	No. of items	Alpha	Min – Max	Mean	SD
Threat:					
Severity (general)	3	0.72	8 – 21	18.21	3.15
Severity (specific)	2	0.75	3 – 14	12.01	2.43
Vulnerability	5	0.76	5 – 35	14.44	6.97
Rewards	13	0.90	13 – 81	38.25	17.79
Coping appraisal:					
Response efficacy (health)	1	–	1 – 7	4.97	1.86
Response efficacy (general)	1	–	1 – 7	5.45	1.56
Self-efficacy	7	0.80	11 – 49	40.29	9.84
Response costs	2	0.80	2 – 12	4.43	3.12
Intention	2	0.90	2 – 14	8.61	3.82

2 The data on past behaviour were transformed to normalise the distribution.

Table 3 Zero order correlations between PMT factors, intentions, past drinking, crinking at follow up, and demographics

Variable name	(1)	(2)	(3)	(4)	(5)	(6)	(7)	(8)	(9)	(10)	(11)	(12)	(13)
(1) Severity (general)	1.00	0.28*	-0.01	0.23*	0.24*	0.16	-0.01	-0.19	0.30**	-0.19	-0.15	-0.14	-0.07
(2) Severity (specific)	-	1.00	-0.01	0.19	0.13	0.16	-0.01	-0.18	0.13	-0.04	-0.07	-0.16	0.05
(3) Vulnerability	-	-	1.00	-0.06	0.04	-0.49**	0.03	0.42**	-0.32**	0.46**	0.23*	-0.11	0.03
(4) Response efficacy (health)	-	-	-	1.00	0.46**	0.17	-0.11	-0.09	0.09	-0.08	-0.14	-0.00	-0.01
(5) Response efficacy (specific)	-	-	-	-	1.00	0.06	-0.11	-0.08	0.02	-0.07	0.00	-0.05	0.13
(6) Self-efficacy	-	-	-	-	-	1.00	-0.25*	-0.62**	0.44**	-0.44**	-0.28**	0.19	-0.06
(7) Costs	-	-	-	-	-	-	1.00	0.32**	-0.01	0.12	0.02	-0.04	-0.01
(8) Rewards	-	-	-	-	-	-	-	1.00	-0.46**	0.39	0.28*	-0.05	-0.03
(9) Intention	-	-	-	-	-	-	-	-	1.00	-0.42**	-0.31**	0.19	0.17
(10) Past drinking	-	-	-	-	-	-	-	-	-	1.00	0.45**	-0.18	-0.06
(11) Drinking at follow-up	-	-	-	-	-	-	-	-	-	-	1.00	-0.06	v0.10
(12) Sex	-	-	-	-	-	-	-	-	-	-	-	1.00	0.01
(13) Age	-	-	-	-	-	-	-	-	-	-	-	-	1.00

$*p < 0.01$ $**p < 0.001$.

Table 4 Direct multiple regression of severity, vulnerability, self-efficacy, rewards, and past drinking (units) on intentions to drink at safe limits on single drinking occasion

Variables	B	Beta	Sr² unique	95% confidence intervals for B	
				Lower	Upper
Severity (general)	−0.27***	0.23	0.05	0.09	0.46
Vulnerability[a]	−0.04	−0.08	0.01	−0.14	0.06
Self-efficacy	0.08**	−0.04	0.02	0.01	0.16
Rewards (conformity/reduce stress)[a]	−0.04*	−0.18	0.02	−0.08	−3.11
Past drinking (units)[b]	1.51*	0.16	0.02	−0.08	0.01
Intercept	1.78	–	–	–	–
$R^2 = 0.31$	–	–	–	–	–
$R = 0.56$	–	–	–	–	–

$*p < 0.1$ $**p < 0.05$ $***p < 0.01$.
[a] Higher vulnerability and rewards are associated with lower intentions resulting in a negative regression coefficient.
[b] Higher levels of past drinking were associated with lower levels of intentions (the valence is not negative as transformation of past behaviour changed the direction of the variable).

Predictors of behaviour at follow up. A direct Logistic regression was performed on levels of single occasion drinking at follow up (riskier = 1, safer = 0), with vulnerability, rewards, self-efficacy, intention and past behaviour as independent variables.

Table 5 shows the regression coefficients for each variable (B), Wald statistics which uses the Chi square distribution to test whether a regression coefficient is zero; the odds ratio for each variable with its 95% confidence intervals; and an overall Chi square test of the relationship between all of the variables and single occasion drinking status. According to the Wald criterion, only past drinking behaviour predicted drinking behaviour at follow up. Past drinking levels predict the likelihood of riskier future drinking with an odds ratio per unit increase in past drinking of 1.11. Higher levels of past drinking increase the chances of a respondent being a riskier future weekend drinker, independent of the intention, self-efficacy, perceived vulnerability and reward measures.

A test of the full model including the constant plus all 5 predictors against a constant only model was statistically reliable (Chi square = 24.38, df = 4, $N = 113$, $p < 0.001$) indicating that the predictors, as a set, reliably distinguished between respondents who were riskier drinkers and

Table 5 Logistic regression analysis of higher-risk drinking as a function of vulnerability, self-efficacy, rewards, intentions, and past behaviour (units)

Variables	B	Wald test (Z-ratio)	Odds ratio	95% confidence intervals for odds ratio	
				Lower	Upper
Vulnerability	0.00	0.00	1.00	0.94	1.09
Self-efficacy	−0.02[a]	0.11	0.99	0.95	1.03
Rewards (conforming/reduce tension)	0.00	0.11	0.99	0.95	1.03
Intention	−0.12[a]	2.37	0.88	0.76	1.03
Past behaviour (units)	0.11	6.68*	1.11	1.03	1.21

$*p < 0.01$.
[a] Negative scores on self-efficacy and intention are expected as high levels on these variables are associated with lower likelihood of being classified as binge drinker.

those who were not at follow up. Prediction success was 93.6% for the safer drinkers but only 32% for the riskier drinkers. The overall success rate was 80.7%. By chance 67.6% of the cases would be correctly classified.

Discussion

PMT components were found to predict a substantial proportion of behavioural intentions to drink at safer limits on single drinking occasions but no support was found for PMT as a model of health behaviour.

PMT accounted for 31% of the variance on intentions for future single occasion drinking. The strength of this relationship is similar to those found when exploring other health behaviours (e.g. Boer and Seydel, 1996; Maddux and Rogers, 1983). The present findings extend the range of health behaviours where PMT may be usefully applied. Intentions for the riskiness of future single occasion drinking do relate to the cognitive components identified by PMT. Partial support was found for the associations between threat appraisal (severity, vulnerability and rewards) and intentions with severity having the only significant effect. Partial support was also found for associations between coping appraisal (self-efficacy, response efficacy, and response costs) and intentions with self-efficacy having the only significant effect.

Evidence for the effects of severity on intentions in previous PMT research is inconsistent. Research in the areas of smoking, exercise, and risky sexual behaviours (e.g. Maddux and Rogers, 1983; Van der Velde and Van der Pligt, 1991; Wurtele and Maddux, 1987) found no significant associations, leading some to suggest that severity should be dropped from analyses (e.g. Wurtele and Maddux, 1987), or that severity may be a more distal antecedent of intention (e.g. Schwarzer, 1992). Other studies, however, have found significant effects of severity on intention in the areas of cancer related preventive behaviours (Boer and Seydel, 1996; Rippetoe and Rogers, 1987; Seydel et al., 1990). A resolution of this discrepancy has been suggested, "the picture emerges that only in those cases where the subject learns about a new, previously unknown, threat does threat appraisal play a role in the adoption of preventive health behaviours" (Boer and Seydel, 1996). The present findings are consistent with this observation. Very few drinkers are aware of the possible harm associated with single occasion drinking other than the risk of a "hangover" (Moore et al., 1994; Posavac, 1993). Participants in this study were for the most part, exposed to a new, previously unknown threat to their health. Their response to this threat then depended in part on their judgements of the severity of that threat. Severity became salient for them and was associated with their motivation for change. However, it is probable that in situations where new health threats are identified (as with single occasion drinking and cancer preventive behaviours) the motivation to protect health will be weakly formed and will rapidly dissipate unless reinforced.

In the present study vulnerability was not a significant predictor of intentions although jointly with the other cognitions it did contribute. The significant correlation between perceived vulnerability and past drinking levels shows that heavier drinkers recognise their increased personal risk. Further, as the significant high correlation between vulnerability and self-efficacy showed, they may perceive their ability to adopt the required behaviour change to be low. Enhancing vulnerability alone is unlikely to be productive unless coupled with the enhancement of self-efficacy and skills required for behaviour change.

The significant effects for self-efficacy found in this study are consistent with the majority of previous PMT research in supporting the role of perceived self-efficacy in intention formation (e.g. Plotnikoff and Higginbotham, 1995; Rippetoe and Rogers, 1987; Stanley and Madden, 1986).

In this study no support was found for the other two coping components, costs and response efficacy. None of the small number of studies which have included costs measures have found an association between costs and intention (Campis, Prentice-Dunn, and Lyman, 1989; Flynn, Lyman and Prentice-Dunn, 1995; Peterson, Farmer and Kashani, 1990). Previous research of the association between response efficacy and intention has yielded inconsistent findings. Whereas several researchers report significant findings (e.g. Stanley and Maddux, 1986; Rippetoe and Rogers, 1987; Van der Velde and Van der Pligt, 1991) others do not (e.g. Beck and Lund, 1989; Fruin *et al.,* 1991; Wurtele and Maddux, 1987). No consistent pattern is found for identifying the behaviours or conditions for which response efficacy is salient.

The intentions formed did correlate significantly with later behaviour ($r=0.31$). In this regard the present findings are similar to those of other PMT studies (Plotnikoff and Higginbotham, 1995; Wurtele and Maddux, 1987). However, when previous drinking behaviour was also considered as a predictor of future behaviour, the association with intentions disappeared and none of the PMT components were found to significantly predict future behaviour. Thus, intentions formed on the basis of the discovering of a new threat are unlikely to be sufficiently robust to persist into sustained behaviour change without further consolidation. Such consolidation could include manipulation of perceived social norms around riskier single-occasion drinking. In support of the latter Donaldson *et al.* (1996), in a review of the alcohol misuse prevention literature, reported that manipulating social norms can be effective in reducing alcohol misuse and alcohol-related harm.

The pattern of results found in this study have been interpreted as resulting from the nature of the health threat characterised as being "new". However, it is also possible that the pattern of results reflect methodological features. One factor which may have attenuated this relationship concerns the wording of the intention measure which lacked specificity, referring to safer drinking without specifying the number of units per occasion or time equal to the follow up period. A more precisely specified intention measure (e.g. "I intend to drink no more that 7 units on the Saturday or Sunday in two weeks time") may have differentiated more between riskier and non riskier drinkers at follow up and thus enhanced the utility of the PMT beyond intentions. Likewise, several of the PMT measures specifically severity and vulnerability did not specify time equal to the follow up period. Sutton (1996) discusses the importance of giving detailed context in all questionnaire items. He points out, for example, that people are likely to have different intentions in different contexts and therefore questionnaire items which do not specify a detailed context are quite reasonably answered by a typical 'it depends' response. Whether one would engage in riskier single occasion drinking when going to a club may depend on whether or not one drives, works the next day, and so forth. Sutton argues that the less respondents are left to generate the appropriate context for themselves, the stronger the relationship between measures and behaviour. The utility of PMT in predicting single occasion drinking behaviour could perhaps be improved in future studies if measurement specificity were improved.

Acknowledgements

We would like to thank Dr. Charles Abraham and two anonymous reviewers for their comments on earlier drafts of the manuscript. We would also like to thank Dr. Stephen Sutton for comments made on the final version of the manuscript.

References

Abraham, C.S. and Sheeran, P. (1994) Exploring teenagers' adaptive and maladaptive thinking in relation to the threat of HIV infection. *Psychology and Health,* **9,** 253–272.

Aspinwall, L.G., Kenemy, M.E., Taylor, S.E., Schneider, S.G. and Dudley, J.P. (1991) Psychosocial predictors of gay men's AIDS risk-reduction behaviour. *Health Psychology,* **10,** 432–444.

Bardsley, P.E. and Beckman, L.J. (1988) The health belief model and entry into alcoholism treatment. *International Journal of the Addictions,* **23,** 19–28.

Beck, K.H. and Lund, A.K. (1981) The effects of health threat seriousness and personal efficacy upon intentions and behaviour. *Journal of Applied Social Psychology,* **11,** 401–415.

Bennett, P., Smith, C. and Nugent, Z. (1991) Patterns of drinking in Wales. *Alcohol and Alcoholism,* **26,** 367–374.

Boer, H. and Seydel, E. (1996) Protection motivation theory. In: M. Conner and P. Norman (Eds), *Predicting Health Behaviour* (pp. 95–120). Open University Press.

BMA. (1995) *Alcohol: Guidelines on Sensible Drinking.* British Medical Association, London.

Campis, L.K., Prentice-Dunn, S. and Lyman, R.D. (1989) Coping appraisal and parents' intentions to inform their children about sexual abuse: a protection motivation theory analysis. *Journal of Social and Clinical Psychology,* **8,** 304–316.

Catarino, P.A. (1992) Is there a safe level of drinking?: a student's view. *Alcohol and Alcoholism,* **27,** 465–470.

Coggans, N. and Watson, J. (1995) Drug education: approaches, effectiveness and delivery. Drugs Education, *Prevention and Policy,* **2,** 211–223.

Comrey, A.L. and Lee, H.B. (1992) *A First Course in Factor Analysis* 2nd ed. Hillsdale, N.J.: Erlbaum.

Department of Transport (1992) *Road Accidents Great Britain 1991: The Casualty Report.* London: HMSO.

Donaldson, S.I., Sussman, S., MacKinnon D.P., Severson, H.H., Glynn, T., Murray, D. and Stone, E. (1996) Drug abuse prevention programming: do we know what content works? *American Behavioural Scientist,* **39,** 868–883.

Flynn, M.F., Lyman, R.D. and Prentice-Dunn, S. (1995) Protection motivation theory and adherence to medical treatment regimens for muscular dystrophy. *Journal of Social and Clinical Psychology,* **14,** 61–75.

Foxcroft, D.R., Lister-Sharp, D. and Lowe, J. (1997) Alcohol misuse prevention for young people: a systematic review reveals methodological concerns and lack of reliable evidence for effectiveness. *Addiction,* **92,** 531–537.

Fruin, D.J., Pratt, C. and Owen, N. (1991) Protection motivation theory and adolescents' perceptions of exercise. *Journal of Applied Social Psychology,* **22,** 55–69.

Goddard, E. and Ikin, C. (1988) *Drinking in England and Wales in 1987.* London, HMSO.

Gonzalez, G.M. (1988) Theory and applications of alcohol and drug education as a means for primary prevention on the college campus. Special issue: alcoholism/chemical dependency and the college student. *Journal of College Student Psychotherapy,* **2,** 89–113.

HEA. (1995) *Sensible drinking: the report of the inter-departmental working group.* Health Education Authority, Department of Health, Wetherby.

HEA. (1996) *Think about drink: There's more to a drink than you think.* Health Education Authority, London.

Maddux, J.E. and Rogers, R.W. (1983) Protection motivation and self-efficacy; a revised theory of fear appeals and attitude change. *Journal of Experimental and Social Psychology,* **19,** 469–479.

Marlatt, G.A., Baer, J.S. and Larimer, M. (1995) Preventing alcohol abuse in college students: a harm reduction approach. In: *Alcohol Problems Among Adolescents,* Northvale, N.J.: Lawrence Erlbaum.

Midanik, L.T., Tam, W.T., Greenfield, T.K. and Caetano, R. (1996) Risk functions for alcohol-related problems in a 1988 US national sample. *Addiction,* **91,** 1427–1437.

Moore, L., Smith, C. and Catford, J. (1994) Binge drinking: prevalence, patterns, and policy. *Health Education Research,* **9,** 497–505.

Morgan, R., Plant, M.A. and Plant, M.L. (1990) Alcohol, AIDS risks and sex industry clients: results from a Scottish study. *Drug and Alcohol Dependence,* **26,** 265–269.

Peterson, L., Farmer, J. and Kashani, J.H. (1990) Parental injury prevention endeavours: a function of health beliefs? *Health Psychology,* **9,** 177–191.

Plotnikoff, R.C. and Higginbotham, N. (1995) Predicting low-fat diet intentions and behaviours for the prevention of coronary heart disease: an application of protection motivation theory among Australian population. *Psychology and Health,* **10,** 397–408.

Posavac, E.J. (1993) College students' views of excessive drinking and the university's role. *Journal of Drug Education,* **23,** 237–245.

Rees, D.W. (1985) Health beliefs and compliance with alcoholism treatment. *Journal of Studies on Alcohol,* **46,** 517–524.

Rippetoe, P.A. and Rogers, R.W. (1987) Effects of components of protection motivation theory on adaptive and maladaptive coping with a health threat. *Journal of Personality and Social Psychology,* **52,** 596–604.

Rogers, R.W. (1983) Cognitive and physiological processes in fear appeals and attitude change; a revised theory of protection motivation. In: J.T. Capcioppo and R.E. Petty (Eds). *Social Psychophysiology; A Source Book.* New York: Guilford Press.

Schwarzer, R. (1992) Self-efficacy in the adoption and maintenance of health behaviours: theoretical approaches and a new model. In R. Schwarzer (Ed). *Self-efficacy: Thought Control of Action.* Washington DC: Hemisphere.

Seydel, E., Taal, E. and Wiegman, O. (1990) Risk appraisal, outcome and self-efficacy expectancies: cognitive factors in preventive behaviour related to cancer. *Psychology and Health,* **4,** 99–109.

Smart, R.G. and Walsh, G.W. (1993) Do some types of alcoholic beverages lead to more problems for adolescents? *Journal of Studies on Alcohol,* **56,** 35–38.

Stanley, M.A. and Maddux, J.E. (1986) Cognitive processes in health enhancement: investigation of a combined protection motivation and self-efficacy model. *Basic and Applied Social Psychology,* **7,** 101–113.

Sutton, S. (1996) Some suggestions for studying situational factors within the framework of attitude-behaviour models. *Psychology and Health,* **11,** 635–639.

Tabachnick, B.G. and Fidell, L.S. (1996) *Using Multivariate Statistics.* New York: Harper Collins College Publishers.

Tuck, M. (1989) *Drinking and Disorder: A Study of Non-Metropolitan Violence.* Home Office Research Study No. 10. HMSO, London.

Van der Velde, F.W. and Van der Pligt, J. (1991) AIDS-related health behaviour: coping, protection motivation and previous behaviour. *Journal of Behavioural Medicine,* **14,** 429–451.

Wechsler, H., Dowdall, G.W., Davenport, A. and Castillo, S. (1995) Correlates of College Student Binge Drinking. *American Journal of Public Health,* **85,** 921–926.

Wechsler, H. and Isaac, N. (1992) "Binge" drinkers at Massachusetts colleges. *Journal of the American Medical Association,* **267,** 2929–2931.

Wurtele, S.K. and Maddux, J.E. (1987). Relative contributions of protection motivation theory components in predicting exercise intentions and behaviour. *Health Psychology,* **6,** 453–466.

DiClemente, C.C., Prochaska, J.O., Fairhurst, S.K. et al. (1991) The process of smoking cessation: an analysis of precontemplation, contemplation, and preparation stages of change, *Journal of Consulting and Clinical Psychology*, 59 (2): 295–304.

The process of smoking cessation

An analysis of precontemplation, contemplation, and preparation stages of change

Carlo C. DiClemente
University of Houston

James O. Prochaska
Cancer Prevention Research Center, University of Rhode Island

Scott K. Fairhurst
University of Houston

Wayne F. Velicer
Cancer Prevention Research Center, University of Rhode Island

Mary M. Velasquez
University of Houston

Joseph S. Rossi
Cancer Prevention Research Center, University of Rhode Island

Abstract

Traditionally smoking cessation studies use smoker and nonsmoker categories almost exclusively to represent individuals quitting smoking. This study tested the transtheoretical model of change that posits a series of stages through which smokers move as they successfully change the smoking habit. Subjects in precontemplation ($n = 166$), contemplation ($n = 794$), and preparation ($n = 506$) stages of change were compared on smoking history, 10 processes of change, pretest self-efficacy, and decisional balance, as well as 1-month and 6-month cessation activity. Results strongly support the stages of change model. All groups were similar on smoking history but differed dramatically on current cessation activity. Stage differences predicted attempts to quit smoking and cessation success at 1- and 6-month follow-up. Implications for recruitment, intervention, and research are discussed.

This research was supported by Grant CA 27821 from the National Cancer Institute.

The gathering of such a large data set involved many staff and volunteers at both the Self-Change Laboratory at the University of Rhode Island and the Change Assessment Research Program at the University of Houston. We are grateful to all who assisted in the project.

Correspondence concerning this article should be addressed to Carlo C. DiClemente, Psychology Department, University of Houston, Houston, Texas 77204–5341.

Traditionally smoking cessation outcome has been viewed as a dichotomy. Smoker and non-smoker categories have been used almost exclusively to represent the population of individuals quitting smoking. As smoking modification researchers began to confront the issues of resistance and recidivism (Bernstein, 1970; Hunt & Bespalec, 1974; Lichtenstein & Danaher, 1976), cessation came to be understood more as a process than as a dichotomous product (DiClemente & Prochaska, 1982; Pechacek & Danaher, 1979; Prochaska & DiClemente, 1983).

Understanding and examining this process of change for smoking cessation as well as other problematic behaviors has been the central focus of the transtheoretical framework or model developed by Prochaska and DiClemente (1984). They propose that two interrelated dimensions are needed to adequately assess behavior modification of smoking. The first dimension is labeled the *stages of change*. These four stages represent the temporal, motivational, and constancy aspects of change (DiClemente & Prochaska, 1985). The second dimension, called *processes of change*, focuses on activities and events that create successful modification of a problem behavior. These 10 processes of change represent coping activities used to modify smoking behavior (Prochaska, Velicer, DiClemente, & Fava, 1988).

Precontemplation, contemplation, action, and maintenance are the four stages enumerated in the transtheoretical model (Prochaska & DiClemente, 1986). Relapse is an event that terminates the action or maintenance phase prompting a cyclical movement back through the initial stages of precontemplation or contemplation. Particularly for addictive behaviors like cigarette smoking, movement through the stages involves a cycling and recycling process (DiClemente & Prochaska, 1985; Prochaska, Velicer, DiClemente, Guadagnoli & Rossi, 1990).

Stages of change have been identified in a variety of settings with a wide range of problems or target behaviors. A stages of change scale (URICA; McConnaughy, Prochaska, & Velicer, 1983) measures subjects' attitudes toward change on 32 items that represent precontemplation, contemplation, action, or maintenance statements and yields stage scores and profiles. Stage of change profiles confirming the stage model have been found with outpatient psychotherapy clients (McConnaughy, DiClemente, Prochaska, & Velicer, 1989); outpatient alcoholism treatment patients (DiClemente & Hughes, 1990); weight control program participants (O'Connell & Velicer, 1988); and head injury rehabilitation patients (Lam, McMahon, Priddy, & Gehred-Schultz, 1988). In addition, stages have been assessed using a classification schema based on attitudes and behaviors regarding change of a target behavior. Using the classification schema, we have identified groups of subjects in various stages of change for smoking cessation (Prochaska & DiClemente, 1984; 1985). Evidence for the validity of the stage classification is strong (DiClemente & Prochaska, 1985). Stage classifications for smoking cessation are consistently related to self-efficacy (DiClemente, 1986; DiClemente, Prochaska, & Gibertini, 1985), to a decision-making construct (Velicer, DiClemente, Prochaska & Brandenburg, 1985), and to the processes of change for smoking cessation (DiClemente & Prochaska, 1985; Prochaska, Velicer, DiClemente, & Fava, 1988) in a consistent and theoretically compatible manner. An analysis of stage profiles of subjects over time (longitudinal typologies) demonstrated that processes of change vary in use across the stages of change with experiential processes peaking in the contemplation stage and behavioral processes in the action and maintenance stages (Prochaska et al., in press). In addition to these empirical studies, stages have been used as a useful framework to examine the population of smokers in the United States (U.S. Department of Health and Human Services; USDHHS, 1988) and to conceptualize treatment of addictive behaviors (Marlatt, Baer, Donovan, & Kivlahan, 1988). There is substantial support for the construct validity of the stages model and growing support for predictive validity (Lam et al., 1988; Biener, Abrams, & Follick, 1988).

This study will provide the most extensive test to date of the stages of change model with a large sample of smokers volunteering for a minimal intervention smoking cessation research program. Using the classification schema, subjects will be placed in precontemplation and contemplation stages of change. In this study the contemplation stage has been subdivided to create a preparation stage, as was proposed in an early formulation of the stages model. Comparisons among smokers in the precontemplation, contemplation, and preparation stages will be analyzed for process and outcome differences on relevant smoking history dimensions as well as on prospective cessation activities. On the basis of previous studies, smokers in these three stages will demonstrate a clear developmental sequence of movement toward smoking cessation. Significant differences across stages are hypothesized for smoking cessation change process activity and for the mediating variables of self-efficacy and decisional balance, as well as for the standard cessation outcome measures over 6 months. We will analyze extensively the process of cessation from a stage of change perspective.

Method

Subjects

Subjects volunteered for a research project on minimal interventions for smoking cessation and were recruited to represent four groups: precontemplators, contemplators, subjects who were prepared or ready for action, and action subjects. Subjects were randomly assigned to interventions stratified by stage. For the purposes of this article, only those subjects still smoking (precontemplators, contemplators, and subjects prepared for action) will be included, and only stage effects will be analyzed. Because subjects were recruited at two sites (Texas and Rhode Island), volunteer groups from each site will be described first; then the breakdown of subjects by stage will be given, combining subjects from both sites.

Texas subjects were 691 volunteers who responded to newspaper, radio, and other media advertisements seeking participants to test materials developed for smokers in various stages of change. Subjects had a mean age of 40 ($SD=11$), started smoking at age 17, and were smoking an average of 27 cigarettes per day. Sixty-four percent of the subjects were female. Eighty-six percent were White, 9.5% Black, 3% Hispanic, and 1% other. The majority of subjects had a high school or greater education level (93%) and were married (52%). Average income for this group of subjects was in the $15–$25 thousand per year range.

Rhode Island subjects were 775 volunteers who responded to advertisements similar to those in Texas. Subjects had a mean age of 43 ($SD=12$), started smoking at 16 years of age, and were smoking an average of 27 cigarettes per day. Sixty-two percent of the subjects were female, and 98% were White. The majority of subjects had a high school or greater education level (94%) and were married (64%). Average income for this group of subjects was in the $15–$25 thousand per year range.

Combining subjects from both sites yielded the following groups of subjects in each of the stages of change. Justification for combining sites is presented in the Results section.

Precontemplation stage. These 166 subjects were smoking and were not seriously considering quitting within the next 6 months, the defining characteristics for precontemplation (PC). They represented 11.3% of the total sample of smokers, were 66% female, and averaged 41 years of age. These subjects averaged 29 cigarettes per day, began smoking at age 17, and had smoked for an average of 24 years.

Contemplation stage. These 794 subjects were smoking and seriously considering quitting within the next 6 months; however, they were not considering quitting within the next 30 days, had not made a quit attempt of 24 hr in the past year, or both. They represented 54.2% of the total sample of smokers, were 66% female, and averaged 41 years of age. These contemplation (C) subjects averaged 29 cigarettes per day, began smoking at age 17, and had smoked for an average of 23 years.

Preparation stage. These 506 subjects were seriously considering quitting in the next 6 months and were planning to quit within the next 30 days. In addition they had made a 24-hr quit attempt in the past year. These prepared for action (PA) subjects represented 34.5% of the total sample of smokers, were 58% female, and averaged 42 years of age. They averaged 24 cigarettes per day, began smoking at age 17, and had smoked for an average of 23 years.

The stage classification algorithm was mutually exclusive so that all smoking subjects were classified in only one stage. Intention to quit in the next 6 months was used to identify precontemplators. Then both intention to quit in the next 30 days and quit attempt in the past year were used to subdivide contemplators from prepared subjects. All subjects who were smoking at screening were classified in this manner. Both sites used the same classification algorithm.

Measures

Smoking Abstinence Self-Efficacy (SASE; DiClemente, Prochaska, & Gibertini, 1985). The SASE measure assessed the smoker's level of confidence that he or she would not smoke in 20 challenging situations. Level of confidence was indicated on a 5-point Likert scale from (1) *not at all* to (5) *extremely confident.* This measure has been revised since its original 12-item format (DiClemente, 1981) and was expanded to 31 items (DiClemente, Prochaska, & Gibertini, 1985) and then pared down to the current 20-item format. The various forms of this self-efficacy scale for smoking have demonstrated good internal consistency (Cronbach alpha = 0.88–0.92) and both construct and predictive validity. This scale has predicted maintenance for both therapy changers and self-changers (DiClemente, 1981) and movement from contemplation into action and maintenance (Prochaska, DiClemente, Velicer, Ginpil, & Norcross, 1985). In a cross-sectional analysis, self-efficacy scores discriminated between subjects representing each of the four stages of change. Included in this self-efficacy assessment is a Temptation scale that assesses the level of temptation on a similar 1–5 Likert scale in the same 20 situations. The Temptation scale has psychometric properties comparable to the Self-Efficacy scale and correlates – 0.68 with efficacy scores (DiClemente, Prochaska, & Gibertini, 1985).

Perceived Stress Scale (PSS; Cohen, Kamarck, & Mermelstein, 1983). The PSS is designed to tap how unpredictable, uncontrollable, and overloaded respondents find their lives. It is considered a global measure of how much perceived stress subjects have experienced within the past month. The original scale contained 14 items. For this study a shorter 4-item version (Cohen & Williamson, 1987) was used. This short version is made up of the items that correlated most highly with the original scale and has been judged to be a useful measure of perceived stress for situations requiring a short scale.

Fagerstrom Tolerance Questionnaire (FTQ; Fagerstrom, 1978). The FTQ is an 8-item scale designed to measure physical dependence on nicotine. The questionnaire combines responses about the smoking habit (number of cigarettes smoked, minutes to first morning cigarette, smoking while ill, etc.) to create a measure of addiction. The FTQ has been used to discriminate level of addiction, withdrawal responses, heart rate, and past smoking behavior. It focuses on observable behavior of the smoker instead of less clear judgments, such as emotions. In this study, one item of the FTQ, brand type, was not used to calculate the total score.

Smoking Decisional Balance scale (SDB; Velicer, DiClemente, Prochaska, & Brandenburg, 1985). This 20-item questionnaire assesses 10 pros and 10 cons of smoking. Subjects rate agreement with each item on a 5-point Likert scale from (1) *not at all* to (5) *very much*. Both Pros and Cons scales of the SDB have been found to have high internal consistency (alpha = 0.88 and 0.89, respectively). The Pros and Cons scales reveal highly significant differences for different stages of change in cross-sectional analyses. In longitudinal analyses, the pros and cons have been salient variables in predicting movement from precontemplation to action.

Smoking Processes of Change scale (SPC; DiClemente & Prochaska, 1985; Prochaska et al., 1988). This 40-item questionnaire measures the 10 processes of change from the transtheoretical model with 4 items each. Subjects indicate the frequency of these 40 activities or events within the last month on a 5-point Likert scale from (1) *never* to (5) *repeatedly*. This instrument has demonstrated high reliability, internal validity, discriminative validity, and predictive validity.

Demographic questionnaire. Demographic data including age, gender, education, and income were collected on a separate assessment sheet.

Smoking history questionnaire. Smoking history data collected include age of acquisition, parent and peer smoking patterns, number of previous quit attempts, as well as current level of smoking, confidence to be able to quit or maintain nonsmoking, current concerns about smoking cessation, and the Fagerstrom assessment questions. The 18-item Reasons for Smoking scale (Horn, 1969), which assesses types of smokers, was also included.

Procedures

Subjects were recruited in both Texas and Rhode Island through media advertisements and were offered $5 for completing questionnaires as well as an opportunity for 10 bonus prizes amounting to $2,000 at each round of data collection. Subjects called in to volunteer and were screened by telephone for initial stage data. Subjects were randomly assigned, stratified by stage, to one of four minimal intervention conditions: (a) American Cancer Society/American Lung Association materials and manuals; (b) transtheoretical manuals; (c) transtheoretical manuals and individualized written feedback based on pretest, posttest, and 6-month questionnaires; and (d) transtheoretical manuals and individualized written feedback plus a series of four personalized counselor calls at pretest, posttest, 3 months, and 6 months. All interventions were done by mail or phone contact or both.

Subjects who were smoking at telephone screening were mailed pretests and told they would be sent materials when they returned the questionnaires. When questionnaires were returned, subjects were randomized and sent materials. The recruitment phase of the project lasted approximately 2–3 months. Subjects in the precontemplation, contemplation, and preparation groups were equally represented in each intervention group.

At each assessment, subjects were asked to provide names of significant others who could validate their smoking patterns. In the initial stages of data collection, this procedure acted as a bogus pipeline because significant others were not contacted. Approximately 1 and 6 months after pretest, subjects were sent follow-up questionnaires similar to the posttest battery. Follow-up assessments continued every 6 months for the next 2 years. Only 6-month follow-up data were used in the current analysis, inasmuch as pretest stage was most relevant to the first 6 months after assessment, and interventions continued through this time period.

Results

A preliminary analysis compared Texas and Rhode Island subjects to assess whether there were significant demographic or smoking history differences. There were no significant differences for number of cigarettes smoked per day, age began smoking, proportion of subjects in each stage, duration of the smoking habit, and the Fagerstrom measure of addiction. There were small but significant differences in number of quit attempts in the past year (Texas $M = 2$; Rhode Island $M = 1.8$, $p < 0.05$) and in length of most current quit attempt (Texas $M = 31.6$ days; Rhode Island $M = 44.8$ days, $p < 0.05$). When we examined Site $\times$ Demographic variables, there were no significant differences in sex distribution, education levels, mean age, and average income range. Texas had a greater distribution of ethnicity, with 87% White, 9% Black, and 3% Hispanic, than did Rhode Island, which was 98% White, reflecting the ethnic differences in state populations.

Although there were a few differences between sites, the majority of smoking history and demographic variables were quite similar. Thus, subsequent analyses combined the samples in order to maximize number of subjects in the various stages. In this study comparisons were made across groups of precontemplators, contemplators, and prepared subjects on a number of smoking history and change variables, using regression and logistic regression procedures. Whenever there was a conceptually similar group of measures, a multivariate analysis of variance (MANOVA) was used in a preliminary analysis. Because of the large number of comparisons being made, an alpha level for significant differences of < 0.01 was chosen to reduce experiment-wise error rate, and a more conservative Tukey procedure was used for post hoc analyses.

Demographic and smoking history comparisons

There were no significant differences among precontemplator (PC), contemplator (C), and prepared subjects (PA) on age, education levels, and sex distribution, using analysis of variance (ANOVA) and chi-square analyses. There was a tendency for a greater percentage of women to be found in PC (66.1%) and C (65.6%) groups than in the PA (57.7%) group. However this difference did not reach our predetermined level of significance.

Table 1 indicates significant differences among groups on certain smoking variables. We examined smoking history, current smoking habit patterns, and cessation history. No stage differences emerged on smoking history. Current stage or status with respect to change had little to do with historical events such as years of smoking and age of initiation. When current smoking patterns were examined, however, many differences emerged. Prepared subjects (PA) were smoking fewer cigarettes per day and were less addicted as measured by the Fagerstrom scale. Precontemplator (PC) and Contemplator (C) subjects appeared similar on these variables with both being significantly different from PA stage subjects. The PA group had the lowest scores on all current smoking habit variables. Historically, the PA subjects' habit appeared nondistinct from the other groups with the sole exception that they did report slightly fewer maximum number of cigarettes smoked lifetime. However, 33 cigarettes per day reported by PA subjects was a substantial number and certainly not indicative of light smoking. In contrast to the PC and C groups, the PA group members appeared to be successfully modifying or in the process of modifying their current smoking habit. They obtained less pleasure from smoking, were less addicted, and were smoking less. These differences did not appear to be due to chance but to movement through the cycle of change.

Cessation history variables supported this interpretation. Prepared smokers were significantly more active in the process of changing their smoking behavior. They had the greatest number of lifetime quit attempts (5.0) and in the past year had been much more active in making 24-hr quit attempts. In fact, almost 6% of this group reported being in a current 24-hr quit attempt at the time they completed the pretest, possibly using the pretest as a cue to make another quit attempt. Preparation stage smokers were clearly prepared and ready for action.

Table 1 Pretest comparisons of smoking habit variables across stages of change

Variable	Precontemplation (n=166)		Contemplation (n=794)		Preparation (n=506)		Tukey comparisons
	M	SD	M	SD	M	SD	
Smoking history							
Age of initiation	17.3	5.2	16.7	4.4	16.9	4.3	–
Total years smoking	23.9	12.3	22.9	12.2	22.8	12.9	–
Years smoking before first quit attempt	14.8	15.8	15.0	13.5	15.5	12.9	–
% spouse current smoker	36.7	–	40.2	–	40.4	–	–
% father current smoker	50.6	–	51.3	–	51.0	–	–
% mother current smoker	33.1	–	34.5	–	27.7	–	–
Current smoking							
No. cigarettes/day*	29.1	15.2	28.7	15.4	24.0	16.3	PA<PC, C
Life maximum	–	–	–	–	–	–	–
No. cigarettes/day*	34.8	15.7	36.3	15.6	32.7	15.6	PA<C, PC
Addiction level (Fagerstrom)*	6.5	1.9	6.6	1.8	5.8	2.0	PA<PC, C
Time to first morning cigarette (minutes)*	30.5	38.9	36.8	77.6	62.1	100.6	PC, C<PA
Horn's typology							
Stimulation	7.6	3.6	7.8	3.1	7.3	3.2	–
Handling	6.5	2.8	6.4	2.5	6.3	2.5	–
Relaxation*	11.6	2.0	10.6	2.3	10.1	2.5	PA<C<PC
Crutch: tension reduction	11.6	2.6	11.6	2.6	11.2	2.6	–
Craving and addiction*	11.3	2.2	11.3	2.3	10.6	2.5	PA<PC, C
Habit	7.5	2.4	7.7	2.6	7.2	2.6	PA<C

Note. All comparisons were made using regression procedures. Post hoc comparisons were made using the Tukey procedure. Tukey comparisons that were significant are shown using a < symbol. If differences were not significant, a comma was used. Dash = no significant differences. Fagerstrom = Fagerstrom Tolerance Scale.
* $p < 0.01$.

Current smoking habit and cessation variables supported the model of movement through the stages of change (see Table 2). Prepared smokers appeared quite different from those in other stages in their cessation activity, although contemplator and precontemplator subjects appeared similar along most of these dimensions. The one dimension where PC differed significantly from the C subjects was previous quitting. Precontemplators had significantly fewer lifetime quit attempts than C or PA subjects, which confirmed their reluctance or resistance to cessation and supported their early status in the cycle of change. Although differences were most noteworthy, it is quite important to underscore the fact that stage differences were unrelated to smoking history. Smokers in different stages of change did not represent different types of smokers by history; they differed by change activity.

Self-efficacy comparisons

Stage comparisons were performed using standardized scores with MANOVA, regression, and post hoc procedures for the measure of temptation to smoke and self-efficacy. These comparisons demonstrated significant differences among all three stage groups (see Table 3). PA subjects had significantly higher levels of confidence to stop or maintain nonsmoking and efficacy to abstain from smoking across various cues to smoke. Contemplator (C) subjects were

Table 2 Pretest comparisons of smoking change history variables across stages of change

Change history	Precontemplation (n=166)		Contemplation (n=794)		Preparation (n=506)		Tukey comparisons
	M	SD	M	SD	M	SD	
No. of prior quit attempts*	2.2	2.3	3.5	2.8	5.0	2.9	PC<C<PA
Quit attempts past year*	0.9	1.8	1.1	1.9	3.3	2.6	PC, C<PA
Length of prior quit (days)	33.9	130	38.9	137	22.9	89	–
% reporting not currently smoking at pretest*	0.0	–	0.3	–	5.7	–	PC, C<PA
Concerns about quitting*	29.4	13.5	34.9	13.2	36.6	12.0	PC<C, PA
Time since first quit attempt (years)	9.5	12.8	9.7	10.8	9.1	8.8	–
Frequency of quit attempts over time* (Time since first quit/no. of prior quits)	5.7	6.5	3.9	6.2	2.3	2.9	PA<C<PC

Note. All comparisons were made using regression procedures. Post hoc comparisons were made using the Tukey procedure. Tukey comparisons that were significant are shown using a<symbol. If differences were not significant, a comma was used. Dash=no significant differences.
* $p<0.01$.

significantly different from both PC and PA groups on these dimensions. Exactly the opposite pattern of differences emerged for levels of temptation to smoke. PC subjects were the most tempted, followed in numerical sequence by C and PA subjects. A simple arithmetical calculation subtracting efficacy from temptation scores for the groups indicates that the gap between confidence to abstain and overall temptation significantly narrowed and shifted across the stages. Inasmuch as this relationship between efficacy and temptation levels has been related to cessation of smoking (DiClemente, Prochaska, et al., 1985), this pattern dramatically confirmed stage differences among current smokers.

Decision-making comparisons

Decision making, particularly an individual's evaluation of the pros and cons of a particular behavior, has been identified by Janis and Mann (1977) as a critical component in the modification of a behavior. Again significant differences among all three stages emerged on standardized score comparisons (see Table 3). Importance of the positive aspects of the smoking habit decreased significantly across groups with PC subjects holding smoking pros most important and PA subjects holding pros least important. As expected, the reverse pattern emerged for the importance of the negative aspects of the smoking habit. The arithmetical difference between pros and cons across groups demonstrated a significantly increasing shift in decisional balance against smoking among PA subjects compared with PC subjects. Decisional considerations supported the stages of change classification schema.

Processes of change comparisons

Specific activities related to smoking cessation have been summarized in the 10 processes of change. Comparisons among stage of change groups for the processes of change are enumerated in Table 4. Precontemplators were the least active and the prepared subjects the most active on almost every process. Although significant differences among all three stage groups were plentiful and the pattern of differences across all processes were very similar, actual scores

Table 3 Standardized score comparisons for self-efficacy and decisional balance measures across stages of change

Variable	Precontemplation (n=166)		Contemplation (n=794)		Preparation (n=506)		Tukey comparisons[a]
	M	SD	M	SD	M	SD	
Efficacy[b]							
Temptation*	53.0	9.2	51.0	10.0	47.5	9.7	PA<C<PC
Self-efficacy (SE)*	44.4	9.0	48.8	9.3	53.8	10.1	PC<C<PA
Tempt-SE difference*	8.7	16.6	2.1	17.1	−6.3	17.6	PA<C<PC
Decisional balance							
Pros of smoking*	53.6	10.4	50.5	9.9	48.0	9.7	PA<C<PC
Cons of smoking*	42.4	10.6	50.3	9.5	52.0	9.4	PC<C<PA
Pro−con difference*	11.1	14.1	0.3	12.7	−4.0	12.8	PA<C<PC

Note. All comparisons were made using regression procedures on standardized T scores ($M=50$; $SD=10$).

[a] The standardization sample consisted of all 1,466 smokers in the study. Post hoc comparisons were made using the Tukey procedure. Tukey comparisons that were significant are shown using a < symbol. If differences were not significant, a comma was used.

[b] A preliminary multivariate analysis of variance was significant ($p<0.01$) for temptation and self-efficacy scores by group and for Pro and Con scores by group.

*$p<0.01$.

Table 4 Standardized score comparisons for processes of change across stages of change

Processes of change[a]	Precontemplation (n=166)		Contemplation (n=794)		Preparation (n=506)		Tukey comparisons
	M	SD	M	SD	M	SD	
Helping relationships*	47.7	10.2	50.5	9.9	50.0	10.0	PC<C, PA
Consciousness-raising*	44.3	9.8	49.9	9.7	52.1	9.7	PC<C<PA
Self-liberation*	41.9	8.7	48.5	9.1	55.0	9.2	PC<C<PA
Environmental reevaluation*	44.8	8.6	49.8	9.8	52.1	10.0	PC<C<PA
Self reevaluation*	40.6	10.1	50.3	9.4	52.5	9.1	PC<C<PA
Counterconditioning*	46.1	9.0	48.7	9.4	53.3	10.4	PC<C<PA
Reinforcement management*	45.8	8.5	49.3	9.7	52.4	10.3	PC<C<PA
Social liberation	48.6	10.9	50.1	10.1	50.2	9.6	–
Stimulus control*	45.8	6.6	48.8	9.0	53.3	11.3	PC<C<PA
Dramatic relief*	44.7	8.9	50.0	9.7	51.7	10.2	PC<C<PA

Note. All comparisons were made using regression procedures on standardized T scores ($M=50$; $SD=10$).

[a] The 10 processes by group were analyzed first for overall differences using a multivariate analysis of variance (MANOVA) procedure ($p<0.01$).

[b] The standardization sample consisted of all 1,466 smokers in the study. Post hoc comparisons were made using the Tukey procedure. Tukey comparisons that were significant are shown by using a < symbol. If differences were not significant, a comma was used.

* $p<0.01$.

varied in interesting ways. On the more cognitive/affective processes like consciousness-raising, dramatic relief, and self-reevaluation, C and PA subjects were more similar and differed more from PC subjects. On the self-liberation process, which is a measure of commitment, there was a graded pattern of differences. On the more behavioral processes of stimulus control and counterconditioning, C and PC subjects were more similar. Processes of change patterns support the interpretation that PA subjects were more actively modifying their smoking habit,

C subjects were gathering information and evaluating their smoking habit, and PC subjects were doing the least across all change processes.

One-month posttest comparisons

Stage assignment at pretest should be predictive of participation in the intervention as well as cessation activity with individuals closer to the action stage engaging in more of these activities. At 1 month, stage of change groups differed in predicted fashion on use of self-help manuals during the previous month. PA subjects reported greater use and thus more exposure to the treatment. In turn, C subjects used the manuals more than did PC subjects (see Table 5).

Dramatic differences emerged in the proportion of subjects making a 24-hr quit attempt in the past month. A majority of the PA group (56%) made a quit attempt, whereas only 8% of the PC group attempted cessation. Some larger number of C stage subjects made an attempt (24%). Average number of quit attempts also significantly differed among stage groups and was greatest for PA subjects. This cessation activity was reflected in the percentage of point prevalence abstinence reported. At 1 month, only a small percentage (1.9%) of the PC group were currently not smoking. That percentage more than doubled by stage, increasing to 5.4% for the C and 13.3% for the PA subjects. The current nonsmoking prevalence rate represented a quarter of each quit attempt percentage. The same pattern of significant differences emerged when we used the more conservative procedure of counting missing subjects as smokers. One-month point prevalence rates with this adjustment were as follows: PC=1.8%, C=4.8%, and PA=11.9%. This 1-month posttest data clearly supports the stage of change classification of these smokers. Hypothesized predictive validity of the stage model both for cessation attempts and cessation success are strongly supported.

Six-month follow-up

Six months is the time frame encompassed by our categorization of the stages. Precontemplators were not considering quitting in the next 6 months. Contemplators were, on the other hand. The 6-month follow-up should provide a clear confirmation or disconfirmation of the utility of stage classifications. The results illustrated in Table 5 strongly confirm the stage model.

Although level of manual use reported at 6 months did not significantly differ among the stages, cessation activity and success again supported stage classifications. The PA group made significantly more quit attempts than did the other stage groups and had a larger number of individuals reporting point prevalence abstinence (21%). In addition, almost 80% of the prepared or ready-for-action smokers reported having made a 24-hr quit attempt over the 6 months since recruitment. This is a nonduplicated count of subjects reporting quit attempts at 1 month and 6 months. Contemplators had lower levels of cessation attempts (48%) and point prevalence abstinence (12%). Although these subjects stated at pretest that they were seriously considering quitting smoking in the next 6 months, less than 50% actually made a 24-hr quit attempt, supporting our contention that contemplators can become fixed in place in the contemplation stage, becoming "chronic contemplators." Abstinence at 6 months follows the pattern of cessation. Once again the same pattern of significant differences emerged when outcome was analyzed using the more conservative procedure of counting missing subjects as smokers. These 6-month point prevalence adjusted rates were as follows: PC=6.0%, C=9.1%, and PA=16.2%.

Cessation activity among the groups is more graphically demonstrated in Figures 1 & 2, which plot the percentage of subjects in each group who made a 24-hr quit attempt at 1 and 6

Table 5 One-month and 6-month outcome variable comparisons across the stages of change

Outcome variables	Precontemplation (PC)	Contemplation (C)	Preparation (PA)	Tukey comparisons
One-month posttest				
n	155	702	444	–
Level of manual use (1–5)*				
M	2.8	3.0	3.3	PC<C<PA
SD	1.0	0.9	0.9	–
No. quit attempts since contact*				
M	0.2	0.7	1.9	PC<C<PA
SD	1.0	1.6	2.4	–
% making quit attempt in last month*	7.7	23.8	55.5	PC<C<PA
% currently not smoking (point prevalence)*	1.9	5.4	13.3	PC, C<PA
% reporting no cigarettes per day average past 7 days	1.3	4.6	8.6	PC, C<PA
Six-month follow-up				
n	127	612	395	–
Level of manual use (1–5)				
M	3.1	3.3	3.3	–
SD	0.9	0.8	0.9	–
No. quit attempts since last contact*				
M	0.5	1.1	2.6	PC<C<PA
SD	1.2	2.1	2.8	–
% currently not smoking (point prevalence)*	7.9	11.8	20.8	PC, C<PA
% making quit attempt over 6 months*	25.6	47.5	79.9	PC<C<PA
% reporting no cigarettes per day average past 7 days*	8.7	10.2	18.0	PC, C<PA

Note. Comparisons were made using regression and post hoc Tukey procedures on continuous data and categorical modeling on dichotomous data. Tukey comparisons that were significant are shown by using a<symbol; if differences were not significant, a comma was used. Sample size for 1-month and 6-month comparisons reflect subjects missing at each follow-up. Linear regression analyses of missing subjects by stage were nonsignificant at both 1 and 6 months. Dash=No significant differences.
* $p < 0.01$.

months or reported point prevalence abstinence at pretest, 1 month, and 6 months. Although this report of the study does not focus on treatment effects, we can report that there were no significant interaction effects between interventions and stage at 1 and 6 months. At 6 months, interventions were continuing, so 12- and 18-month follow-ups are more appropriate measures of treatment outcome. An extensive examination of these results is under way and will be reported in a subsequent publication. Stage effects, however, were dramatic both at 1 month and 6 months. Over the period from 1 month to 6 months, there was a gradual increase in reported cessation activity for each of the three stage groups, with PC, C, and PA groups increasing in the proportion of subjects who stopped smoking in sequential fashion as predicted by the model.

Discussion

This analysis of the stages of change model as applied to these volunteer intervention subjects provides the most comprehensive set of data to test the stage conceptualization of smoking cessation. The results overwhelmingly support the stage categories, Stage × Processes of Change interactions, Stage × Self-Efficacy and Decisional Balance differences, and stage-specific predictions of 1- and 6-month cessation activity. All subjects were smoking as they volunteered for the study and were classified into stages according to intention to quit and previous cessation activity. Stage classifications (PC, C, PA) provided robust subgroups of smokers who clearly were at different points in the process of changing their smoking behavior.

The magnitude and consistency of the results of this study are quite impressive. There was not one instance in which the ordering of the effects was contrary to prediction and previous research. Smokers in different stages of change represented distinct subgroups. At 1 month, 3 times as many contemplators and 7 times as many preparation stage smokers made a 24-hr quit attempt when compared with precontemplators. Point prevalence cessation at 1 month doubled from precontemplation to contemplation and doubled again for preparation stage smokers. These differences continued at 6 months.

Stage effects support our previous research on self-changers (DiClemente & Prochaska, 1985; Prochaska et al., 1988; Prochaska et al., 1990). Stage of change differences allow us to examine microanalytically the process of change with relevance for outcome and process considerations. Our study confirmed and extended these findings to intervention populations. In addition, this study subdivided the contemplation phase into two very different groups of smokers. From previous studies we learned that a recent quit attempt that resulted in relapse could prime the pump for a future quit. In addition, we discovered that there were a group of chronic contemplators who had great difficulty making the actual quit attempt. This study teased these groups apart by subdividing subjects who stated they were seriously considering quitting in the next 6 months by using a more proximal intention to quit and a recent quit attempt. As demonstrated in this study, the distinction is clearly relevant and supports reinstating a preparation stage of change between contemplation and action stages. In previous versions this stage was labeled determination or decision making. However, preparation seems better able to capture the readiness for action of these subjects regarding smoking cessation.

This study demonstrated that movement into the action stage of smoking cessation is not impossible for individuals in each stage of change. A few precontemplators and a significantly greater number of contemplators were able to move ahead and take action to break the smoking habit over the 6-month posttest period. However, PA subjects were closest to action and entered that stage with greater frequency and success. The implications for subject recruitment and selection are enormously important. Studies that use a broad net for recruitment or attempt to treat whole populations could be expected to recruit large numbers of PC and C subjects. Surveys of worksite populations have found large numbers of subjects in PC and C stages (Biener et al., 1988). Outcome effects would vary greatly depending on the various stages of subjects recruited. Studies that recruited subjects from the PA stage would be able to demonstrate a greater effect size than studies that had subjects from all these stages or predominantly from C or PC stages.

Reported 6-month quit rates for various types of smoking cessation programs can vary dramatically (USDHHS, 1989). In this report the median 6-month quit rate for 11 self-help trials was 17% and for 15 group therapy trials was 24%. Cohen and colleagues (1989) reported quit rates from a number of self-change and minimal intervention studies. The median 6-month point prevalence abstinence rate was 13.2%. Point prevalence rates in this study were quite comparable. Collapsing across groups, 6-month point prevalence abstinence for all subjects in this study counting missing subjects as smoking was 11.2%. Because we recruited early stage smokers, had a heavy-smoking group ($M = 27$ cigarettes per day), and offered minimal interventions, these figures appear comparable to other studies. However, the dramatic stage differences in rates supports the contention that variation in cessation rates among programs and studies may have more to do with differences in smoker selection than in treatment methods themselves (Cohen et al., 1989).

The stages of change provide a substantial challenge for intervention development. Intensity, duration and type of intervention should be responsive to the stage of change of the client. Later stage subjects may benefit from more intense, shorter, action-oriented types of interventions. Subjects earlier in the process of change may need less intense and more extensive types of programs to be able to follow them through a quitting cycle and move them to successful action. It is clear that once into action, all subjects need strategies to sustain cessation long term. Population-based interventions could profitably take these differences into account in order to develop carefully orchestrated and conceptually sound packages of techniques, messages, and channels of delivery. Some of our current population-based projects involve more proactive strategies to reach precontemplators, serial interventions, stepped care types of programs, and targeted interventions attempting to maximize special cessation opportunities. At the level of the individual, cessation interventions may be able to increase success rates by being sensitive to stage and by shifting strategies depending on stage of change. For early stage smokers, repeated contacts seem essential. Feedback that focuses on stage-specific goals and strategies holds great promise. However, maintaining contact with individuals as they move through the cycle of change over time can be the greatest challenge. Paying attention to the stages of change dimension should help increase the effectiveness and efficiency of our interventions.

The interrelationship of the stages and the processes of change provide avenues for significant new research. Programs can be examined not only for the outcomes they produce but for the processes they engender. Significant differences among stage subgroups on most processes of change coincide with previous findings of process fluctuation across the stages of change (Prochaska et al., 1990). Programs need to be designed and evaluated on the basis of these Process × Stage patterns.

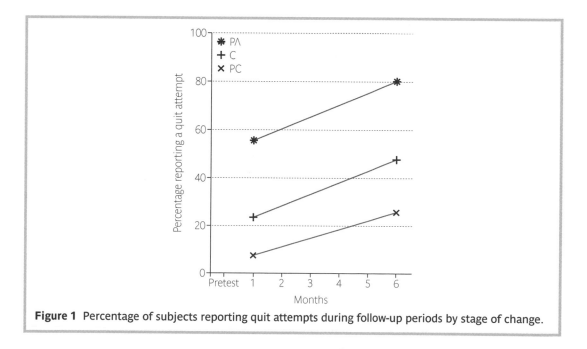

Figure 1 Percentage of subjects reporting quit attempts during follow-up periods by stage of change.

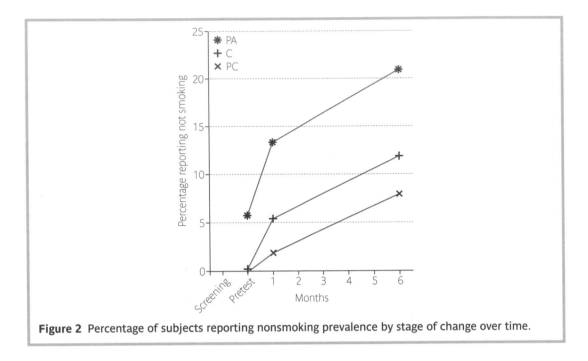

Figure 2 Percentage of subjects reporting nonsmoking prevalence by stage of change over time.

Several cautions are needed regarding this study and the results reported. Cessation figures noted were self-reported ones and not biochemically validated. A minimal bogus pipeline effect was used and could be expected to increase validity. In addition, cessation activity results are certainly in line with other studies. Subjects were specifically recruited from all stages for this study. Thus results may not be comparable to studies that make entry into a study more arduous or that specifically recruit preparation subjects. Our intention was to attract even subjects who were not currently wanting to quit. Even so, we expect that we recruited precontemplators who may have been more amenable to hearing nonsmoking messages. Precontemplators who are completely resistant to any cessation related activity (USDHHS, 1988) were not represented in this study.

We have limited the results of this study to the first 6 months after recruitment. This was done intentionally. We focused on short-term cessation activity, not long-term abstinence. As such, this was an action not a maintenance study. Inasmuch as the stage classification schema used a 6-month framework, the 6-month period seemed most appropriate to assess the outcome for pretest stage categories. Once assessments go beyond 6 months, outcome becomes moderated by shifts in stage. Because this is a dynamic model, stage movement can occur at any time. Even for our study, shifts in stage (e.g., from PC to C) were occurring for these subjects. Extending a pretest stage categorization analysis beyond the 6-month outcome seemed unreasonable without adding stage movement. This would complicate the present report. Measuring movement through the stages will be the focus of another analysis from our study.

The stages of change model provides a valuable and intriguing view of the process of change for smoking cessation. The current research strongly supports the contention of the transtheoretical model that stages and processes of change are the basic building blocks of the process of change. Implications for assessment, recruitment, intervention, and research are only beginning to be understood.

References

Bernstein, D. A. (1970). The modification of smoking behavior: A search for effective variables. *Behavior Research and Therapy, 8,* 133–146.

Biener, L., Abrams, D. B., & Follick, M. W. (1988, November). Maximizing the impact of self-help smoking cessation programs at the worksite: The recruitment problem. In G. M. Boyd (Chair), *Self-help smoking cessation programs.* Symposium conducted at the 116th Annual Meeting of the American Public Health Association; Boston, MA.

Cohen, S., Kamarck, T., & Mermelstein, R. (1983). A global measure of perceived stress. *Journal of Health and Social Behavior, 24,* 385–396.

Cohen, S., & Williamson, G. M. (1987). Perceived stress in a probability sample of the United States. In S. Spacapan & S. Oskamp (Eds.), *Psychology and Health* (pp. 31–67). Newbury Park, CA: Sage.

Cohen, S., Lichtenstein, E., Prochaska, J. O., Rossi, J. S., Gritz, E. R., Carr, C. R., Orleans, C. T., Shoenbach, V. J., Biener, L., Abrams, D., DiClemente, C. C., Curry, S., Marlatt, G. A., Cummings, K. M., Emont, S. L., Giovino, G., & Ossip-Klein, D. (1989). Debunking myths about self-quitting. *American Psychologist, 44,* 1355–1365.

DiClemente, C. C. (1981). Self-efficacy and smoking cessation maintenance: A preliminary report. *Cognitive Therapy and Research, 9,* 181–200.

DiClemente, C. C. (1986). Self-efficacy and the addictive behaviors. *Journal of Social and Clinical Psychology, 4,* 302–315.

DiClemente, C. C., & Hughes, S. O. (1990). Stages of change profiles in outpatient alcoholism treatment. *Journal of Substance Abuse, 2,* 217–235.

DiClemente, C. C., & Prochaska, J. O. (1982). Self-change and therapy change of smoking behavior: A comparison of processes of change in cessation and maintenance. *Addictive Behaviors, 7,* 133–142.

DiClemente, C. C., & Prochaska, J. O. (1985). Processes and stages of change: Coping and competence in smoking behavior change. In S. Shiffman & T. A. Wills (Eds.), *Coping and substance abuse* (pp. 319–343). New York: Academic Press.

DiClemente, C. C., Prochaska, J. O., & Gibertini, M. (1985). Self-efficacy and the stages of self-change of smoking. *Cognitive Therapy and Research, 9,* 181–200.

Fagerstrom, K. (1978). Measuring degree of physical dependence to tobacco smoking with reference to individualization of treatment. *Addictive Behaviors, 3,* 235–241.

Horn, D. (1969). *Why do you smoke?* (Public Health Service Publication No. 2013). Washington, DC: U.S. Department of Health, Education and Welfare.

Hunt, W. A., & Bespalec, D. A. (1974). An evaluation of current methods of modifying smoking behavior. *Journal of Clinical Psychology, 30,* 431–438.

Janis, I. L., & Mann, L. (1977). *Decision making: A psychological analysis of conflict, choice and commitment.* New York: Free Press.

Lam, C. S., McMahon, B. T., Priddy, D. A., & Gehred-Schultz, A. (1988). Deficit awareness and treatment performance among traumatic head injury adults. *Brain Injury, 2,* 235–242.

Lichtenstein, E., & Danaher, B. G. (1976). Modification of smoking behavior: A critical analysis of theory, research and practice. In P. M. Mullen & M. Hersen (Eds.), *Advances in behavior modification* (pp. 79–132). New York: Academic Press.

Marlatt, G. A., Baer, J. S., Donovan, D. M., & Kivlahan, D. R. (1988). Addictive behavior: Etiology and treatment. *Annual Review of Psychology, 39,* 223–252.

McConnaughy, E. A., DiClemente, C. C., Prochaska, J. O., & Velicer, W. F. (1989). Stages of change in psychotherapy: A follow-up report. *Psychotherapy: Theory, Research and Practice, 26,* 494–503.

McConnaughy, E. A., Prochaska, J. O., & Velicer, W. F. (1983). Stages of change in psychotherapy: Measurement and sample profiles. *Psychotherapy: Theory, Research and Practice, 20,* 368–375.

O'Connell, D. O., & Velicer, W. F. (1988). A decisional balance measure and the stages of change model for weight loss. *International Journal of the Addictions, 23*, 729–750.

Pechacek, T. F., & Danaher, B. G. (1979). How and why people quit smoking: A cognitive-behavioral analysis. In P. C. Kendall & S. D. Hollon (Eds.), *Cognitive-behavioral intervention: Theory, research and procedures* (pp. 389–416). New York: Academic Press.

Prochaska, J. O., & DiClemente, C. C. (1983). Stages and processes of self-change of smoking: Toward an integrative model of change. *Journal of Consulting and Clinical Psychology, 51*, 390–395.

Prochaska, J. O., & DiClemente, C. C. (1984). *The transtheoretical approach: Crossing traditional boundaries of therapy.* Homewood, IL: Dow Jones Irwin.

Prochaska, J. O., & DiClemente, C. C. (1985). Common processes of change in smoking, weight control and psychological distress. In S. Shiffman & T. A. Wills (Eds.), *Coping and substance abuse* (pp. 345–363). New York: Academic Press.

Prochaska, J. O., & DiClemente, C. C. (1986). The transtheoretical approach: Towards a systematic eclectic framework. In J. C. Norcross (Ed.), *Handbook of eclectic psychotherapy* (pp. 163–200). New York: Brunner/Mazel.

Prochaska, J. O., DiClemente, C. C., Velicer, W. F., Ginpil, S. E., & Norcross, J. C. (1985). Predicting change in smoking status for self-changers. *Addictive Behaviors, 10*, 395–406.

Prochaska, J. O., Velicer, W. F., DiClemente, C. C., & Fava, J. (1988). Measuring processes of change: Application to the cessation of smoking. *Journal of Consulting and Clinical Psychology, 56*, 520–528.

Prochaska, J. O., Velicer, W. F., DiClemente, C. C., Guadagnoli, E., & Rossi, J. S. (1990). Patterns of change: Dynamic typology applied to smoking cessation. *Multivariate Behavioral Research, 25*, 587–611.

U.S. Department of Health and Human Services. (1988). *The health consequences of smoking: Nicotine addiction. A Report of the Surgeon General* (DHHS Publication No. [CDC] 88–8406). Washington, DC: U.S. Dept. of Health and Human Services, Public Health Services.

U.S. Department of Health and Human Services. (1989). *Reducing health consequences of smoking: 25 years of progress. A report of the Surgeon General* (DHHS Publication No. [CDC] 89–8411). Washington, DC: U.S. Government Printing Office.

Velicer, W. F., DiClemente, C. C., Prochaska, J. O., & Brandenburg, N. (1985). A decisional balance measure for assessing and predicting smoking status. *Journal of Personality and Social Psychology, 48*, 1279–1289.

Wardle, J. and Beales, S. (1988) Control and loss of control over eating: an experimental investigation, *Journal of Abnormal Psychology*, 97 (1): 35–40.

Control and loss of control over eating

An experimental investigation

Jane Wardle and Sally Beales

Institute of Psychiatry and King's College, University of London

Abstract

The present study provides experimental evidence for the restraint theory's proposition of a causal link between restraint and disturbances in food-intake control. Twenty-seven obese women were randomly assigned to a diet group (high restraint), an exercise group (low restraint), or a control group for a 7-week group treatment program. On Weeks 4 and 6, all subjects participated individually in two laboratory sessions designed to investigate the regulation of food intake. In Session 1, food intake and appetite for food were assessed before and after a preload. In Session 2, food intake was assessed under stressful conditions. The results showed that the dieters ate more than either of the other two groups in all conditions. The possible mechanisms linking conscious regulation of eating with disturbances in control are discussed.

Dieting, or the conscious restriction of food intake, is a common feature of the eating behavior of women who are concerned about their weight. Although restriction is often successful, restraint theory (Herman & Polivy, 1980) proposes that the eating behavior of dieters can be disinhibited by a variety of conditions. These include emotional states, such as anxiety or depression, alcohol consumption, or dietary violations (preloads). Under these conditions restrained eaters have been shown to abandon their habitual restraint and even to eat more than unrestrained eaters (Herman & Polivy, 1975; Hibscher & Herman, 1977; Polivy & Herman, 1976; Ruderman, 1985). In a number of other studies, however, restrained eaters have shown some degree of overeating across all experimental conditions (Kirschenbaum & Tomarken, 1982; Lowe, 1982; Ruderman & Christensen, 1983; Ruderman & Wilson, 1979; Tomarken & Kirschenbaum, 1984; Wardle & Beales, 1987), prompting the suggestion that "some degree of loss of control may be the reaction of restrained eaters to many situations" (Ruderman, Belzer, & Halperin, 1985, p. 555). Disinhibition on such a broad scale can probably be attributed to the features of the experimental situations (e.g., the highly palatable food in the taste tests), but it emphasizes the instability of cognitive regulation of eating (Wardle, 1987a).

The research published on restraint has mainly been carried out on college students. Its relevance to the eating behavior of patients with eating and weight disorders has therefore not been fully investigated. Also, it has mainly been correlational in design: Subjects are classified

We gratefully acknowledge the assistance of a grant from the Health Promotion Research Trust.

Correspondence concerning this article should be addressed to Jane Wardle, Psychology Department, Institute of Psychiatry, De Crespigny Park, London SE5 8AF, United Kingdom.

on the basis of their scores on the Restraint Scale and then tested on tasks or questionnaires involving the control of eating (Hibscher & Herman, 1977; Ruderman et al., 1985; Spencer & Fremouw, 1979; Wardle, 1980). This means that it is impossible to be entirely certain whether dieting causes control problems or, alternatively, that an inclination toward overeating causes someone to begin dieting. Conclusive evidence that dieting itself sets the stage for loss of control over eating requires that restraint be manipulated experimentally and the impact on eating behavior then be assessed.

Going on a diet to reduce weight represents a situation in which restraint would be increased (Polivy & Herman, 1983). Dieters can be assumed to be making some kind of commitment to reduce energy intake, but restraint theory predicts that they would also experience a paradoxical increase in food-intake control problems. The only experimental work to examine the control of food intake after dieting is the series of studies by Rodin, Slochower, and Fleming (1977). Their principal interest was to find evidence of alterations in "externality," not to study food intake per se, but the results of the two experiments in which they specifically measured food intake revealed substantial changes in the amount of food consumed. In the first experiment, subjects ate more in a second test meal, after having participated in a diet group for 10 weeks, than they ate at the first testing. In a second experiment, women attending a weight-reduction group were compared with nondieting controls, first just after the obese subjects had joined the weight group and then after they had lost 15 to 20% of their initial body weight (an average of 22 weeks). No statistics were quoted for the groups' change in intake, but comparisons of the means showed that on average, the obese dieters increased their intake in the second test meal by 32 g, whereas the normal-weight controls decreased their intake by 16 g. This study confounds dieting and weight status but nevertheless supports the idea that dieting may provoke paradoxical overeating.

The present study was specifically designed to investigate dieting's effect on food-intake regulation. It consisted of a brief obesity treatment program with three experimental conditions: (a) a dieting group (Group D), (b) a nondieting exercise group (Group E), and (c) a nondieting control group (Group C). Group D was designed to be a high-restraint group, whereas both the others were to be low-restraint groups. Our rationale for including an exercise group was to attempt to provide a control for the energy imbalance in the diet group by increasing in energy expenditure. Food-intake regulation was assessed in two laboratory tests conducted during the treatment period. One of the tests was an investigation of appetite and food intake before and after a preload, and the other was a study of food intake during stress.

The overall aim of the study was to replicate, in the setting of an experimental manipulation of restraint, the cross-sectional results showing that restrained eaters are prone to paradoxical overeating. The specific hypotheses concerning the laboratory studies are described after the effectiveness of the treatment manipulations has been discussed.

Study design

Method

Subjects

To gain entry in the study, subjects had to be overweight women who wanted to lose weight, for we assumed that normal-weight women would have less motivation to persist with dieting. Subjects were recruited from a newspaper advertisement asking for overweight subjects to participate in a weight-control study run by psychologists. A lengthy screening questionnaire, which was a modification of the Research Questionnaire for Obese Patients (Agras et al., 1976) was mailed, and 120 women returned it. Subjects were selected for further assessment if they had a body mass index (BMI) between 25 and 40, as BMI has been shown to be a valid index of obesity (Keys, Fidanza, Karvonen, Kimura, & Taylor, 1972). We excluded very fat women because of the difficulties they might have had in complying with the exercise requirement. Women with physical health problems were excluded for the same reason. Women taking medication that might affect their weight (principally appetite suppressants and antidepressants), women planning to become pregnant, and women who had very recently had a baby were excluded because of the chance of weight loss for reasons unrelated to the treatment. From the remainder, 35 women attended individual assessment sessions. After the assessment 4 more subjects were excluded on the basis of the criteria already described, and 4 others were excluded because they found the times inconvenient. Subjects were randomly assigned to the three groups according to their age, BMI, and initial restraint score. Two subjects switched groups because of time problems. Twenty-seven subjects therefore started the program, but 1 subject came to only one session. Data are included on the remaining 26 subjects who took part in the whole treatment. Their mean age was 40 years ($SD=9.9$), their mean weight was 169 lb (76.6 kg; $SD=8.9$), and they had a BMI of 30.4 ($SD=3.1$), representing an average of 35% overweight. There were no significant group differences on any of the demographic variables.

Procedure

Three groups of women ($ns=8$, 8, and 10) took part in a 7-week treatment program for weight loss. One group was placed on a fairly strict diet that was intended both to increase restraint level and to generate a negative energy balance (Group D). A second group was discouraged from dieting but participated in an intensive exercise program (Group E). This group was intended to match Group D with respect to caloric deficit without the restraint component. Both of these groups were expected to lose body fat over the course of the program. The third, or control, group (Group C) neither dieted nor exercised but took part in a discussion group and monitored their food intake. After 3 weeks on the program, when treatment differences should have been well established, all subjects took part individually in a laboratory experiment involving food-intake regulation before and after a preload. Restraint levels and weight changes were assessed to validate the experimental manipulation. The laboratory session was run by someone other than the therapist. Two weeks later, after returning to the program, all subjects took part in a second laboratory test assessing incidental food intake while they watched a stressful film. Weight changes and restraint levels were again assessed. After a final week of treatment all subjects were reassessed.

Treatments

All three treatments were conducted on a group basis, with five treatment sessions held on Weeks 1, 2, 3, 5, and 7 of the treatment period. Treatment sessions were run by Jane Wardle, an experienced therapist.

Diet group

The emphasis in the diet group was on increasing restraint and achieving a negative energy balance. Subjects were asked to reduce their normal intake by 500 kilocalories (kcal). We predicted that in trying to achieve that, they would increase their levels of restraint. Insofar as they succeeded in reducing their calorie intake they should be in negative energy balance. The treatment sessions were organized around teaching behavior-modification skills to improve adherence to a diet, including self-monitoring, stimulus control, and self-reinforcement. All subjects kept food-intake diaries, which were discussed in the sessions. They were also asked not to start a new exercise program during the study.

Exercise group

The target for the exercise group was a negative energy balance, comparable to the diet group but achieved through increasing energy expenditure. Three kinds of increase in activity were suggested: (a) a daily session of at least half an hour of vigorous exercise to increase pulse rate to the range 120 to 160 beats per minute, (b) increased walking as part of the daily routine, and (c) reduced time spent in sedentary activity. Subjects were encouraged to avoid or reduce dieting and to aim for "a normal healthy amount of food" for the duration of the experiment. Treatment sessions were organized around giving behavior-modification advice, similar to that given to the diet group, for increasing activity level, such as self-monitoring, stimulus control, and self-reinforcement. All subjects kept activity records, which were discussed during the sessions.

Control group

The aim for the control group was avoidance or reduction of restraint or weight loss via an attention-control placebo treatment. The sessions comprised a series of discussions of the development of weight problems, the role that food and eating played in their early family life, and the relation between mood states and the urge to eat. Subjects were encouraged to eat "a normal healthy amount of food" for the duration of the experiment and to avoid dieting. The rationale given for this was that they would come to a better appreciation of their own needs for food and difficulties in controlling eating that would enable them to control their food intake better in the future. The same food-intake records as in the diet group were kept and discussed in the sessions.

Effectiveness of the treatment manipulation
Compliance with treatment

Attendance at meetings was never 100%, but all subjects attended at least three of the five treatment sessions, and most attended four or five. Any subject who missed a session was spoken to on the telephone within a few days and had a brief consultation along similar lines to the group meeting. All subjects in the diet group reported consistent efforts to adhere to the diet, as was evidenced by their weight loss of around 1.1 lb (0.5 kg) per week over the treatment period (see the Results section). This compares well with weight-loss rates reported from general treatment research (Jeffrey, Wing, & Stunkard, 1978). A crude calculation of the caloric cost of losing 3.06 kg of fat (the mean loss of the diet group at 6 weeks) is 23,562 kcal, which divided across the 6 weeks of the treatment study gives an average daily energy deficit of 558 kcal, which is very close to the intended caloric deficit.

In the exercise group it rapidly became clear that none of the subjects was able (or willing) to exercise at a level even close to an additional expenditure of 500 kcal over their usual level. Their fitness levels were very low, and therefore they became exhausted after only a few minutes of exercise. They also had very little free time in which to exercise. All except one subject said that they took part in vigorous physical exercise intermittently over a 20- to 30-min period on most days each week, and all reported that they walked more. Subjects' reports of increasing activity level were confirmed by the results of a 3-min step test (Katch & McArdle, 1983). The exercise group showed a significantly greater increase in cardiovascular fitness (i.e., lower heart rates on completing the step test) than did the other two groups, $F(1, 17) = 7.10$, $p < 0.01$.

However, a rough estimate of the excess energy expenditure for 15 min of walking instead of sitting and 15 min of vigorous exercise versus standing suggested that the extra caloric expenditure was in the order of 150 kcal per day, which was substantially lower than the energy imbalance in the dieting group. The subjects in the exercise condition also reported that their food intake increased as a result of abandoning their usual dieting, although they felt that the exercise prevented them from putting on as much weight as they would have done otherwise.

In the control group all subjects found giving up dieting very difficult. All were convinced (and indeed most were right) that unless they dieted they would gain weight. After the second session, however, a spirit of enthusiasm for the endeavour of not dieting, and learning to become more sensitive to bodily needs, was established. In some ways this proved to be the most popular group, and a number of subjects described their experiences in it as a revelation.

Restraint changes

The effectiveness of the diet program in increasing restraint was assessed with the Restrained Eating scale of the Dutch Eating Behavior Questionnaire (Van Strien, Frijters, Bergers, & Defares, 1986). We chose this scale over the Restraint Scale because it focuses specifically on restraint and includes no items relating to weight fluctuation (Wardle, 1986, 1987b). It therefore allowed restraint to be assessed independently of weight change. We assessed restraint levels before treatment and twice during the treatment period (Weeks 4 and 6), that is, at the times of the laboratory tests.

The restraint scores at the initial assessment had a mean of 3.04, with no significant differences between the groups. These scores were higher than those of normal-weight women but lower than those of obese women attending Weightwatchers (Wardle, 1987). Over the treatment period, we had predicted that Group D would become more restrained than Groups C and E, and so the data were analyzed with a planned contrast between Group D and the other two groups combined. They were significantly different both at Week 4, $F(1, 24) = 14.4$, $p < 0.001$, and at Week 6, $F(1, 24) = 5.71$, $p < 0.05$. The mean restraint score of Group D increased to 4.01 ($SD = 0.51$), whereas the restraint score of the other two groups decreased to 2.65 ($SD = 0.54$). These results confirmed that the dieters became more restrained.

Weight changes

The weights of the three groups initially did not differ significantly, but the amounts of weight lost over the treatment period did differ significantly, $F(2, 23) = 10.36$, $p < 0.005$. Only the diet group lost weight (mean weight loss = 6.75 lb, or 3.06 kg). Groups C and E gained, respectively, 1.5 lb (0.68 kg) and 3.02 lb (1.37 kg). These results suggest that the manipulation of energy balance was successful in the diet group but not in the exercise group.

Discussion of the treatment manipulation

The effectiveness of the treatment manipulation was demonstrated both by the weight loss in the diet group and by the changes in the restrained eating scores. This allowed us to test, as planned, the predictions of restraint theory by comparing aspects of food-intake control in subjects in the diet group, who became high restrainers, with subjects in the exercise and control groups, who became (relatively) low restrainers.

Unfortunately the results of the exercise manipulation were largely unsuccessful, for although the exercisers increased their activity level, there was no evidence for an overall energy imbalance comparable to the diet group. In fact, they gained a small amount of weight, suggesting that the increase in energy expenditure from exercise was more than offset by the increase in food intake resulting from giving up dieting. Accordingly, no predictions based on comparing restraint effects with deprivation effects could be tested.

Laboratory experiment 1: food intake and counterregulation

The principal aim of this experiment was to test the proposition that subjects whose restraint levels have been increased will show a paradoxical increase in food intake during a laboratory taste test. Food intake was assessed by an independent assessor, Sally Beales, using a repeated measures design in which all subjects ate two test meals, one before and one after a preload.[1] In this way it was possible to see whether dieters simply ate more overall when exposed to the highly palatable food used in the test meals, as some studies have shown (Lowe, 1982; Ruderman & Wilson, 1979; Tomarken & Kirschenbaum, 1984), or whether they overate only after the preload, that is, showed a classic "counterregulatory" response (Hibscher & Herman, 1977). The present design had the drawback that the order of the two test meals was not balanced, because the whole experiment took place in a single session. However, it had the advantage of allowing an accurate assessment of the regulatory capacities of the subjects without the need to draw inferences from group differences.

Another aspect of the eating behavior of dieters that was investigated was appetite for food. This has been studied predominantly by using a physiological measure of appetite, namely salivation to food stimuli (Wooley & Wooley, 1981). However, as the literature on salivation has yielded such inconclusive results (Sahakian, 1981), appetite was assessed from ratings of photographs of foods. Food preferences and desire to eat have been found to be sensitive to a variety of manipulations of hunger (Blundell & Rogers, 1980; Hill, Magson, & Blundell, 1984). We predicted that appetite for food should be less affected by food intake in restrained than in unrestrained eaters, so the dieting group was expected to show a smaller diminution in appetite ratings as a consequence of food intake than were the other two groups.

Method
Procedure

All subjects attended the session individually, between 10:00 a.m. and 5:00 p.m. in the fourth week of the treatment program. They were informed that the session was designed to assess how the treatment was affecting them. They were told that they would be given pictures of food to rate and would be asked to taste some ice cream. The preload was not mentioned until after the first taste test. A hunger rating and the food-picture ratings were completed first. The taste test procedure followed. It was based on the method of Hibscher and Herman (1977) and amended to be acceptable to the present subjects. They were given three 2-l containers of ice cream and were left alone for 5 min to taste and rate it. All subjects then had a preload consisting of one 150-ml milk shake containing 250 kcal. (A single milk shake was used for the experiment because it was deemed too difficult to persuade subjects to drink two milk shakes, given that they were in the middle of a weight-loss program. In practice it proved hard to persuade some subjects – predominantly the dieters – even to drink one, but eventually all subjects cooper-

---

1 We use the term *preload* to refer to the caloric load given to induce satiety because it is widely used in the literature on eating. It is not entirely appropriate in this context, however, because the "preload" came between the two test meals.

ated.) They then repeated the taste test and the food-picture ratings. Finally, subjects completed the Restrained Eating Questionnaire and were weighed.

Measures

Food intake. This was calculated from preweighing and reweighing the ice-cream containers on an Avery electronic balance, recorded to an accuracy of 1 g.

Hunger rating. A visual analogue scale (VAS) was used to rate hunger.

Food-picture ratings. Subjects were asked "How much would you like to eat the food now?" and "How appetizing does the food look to you?" They responded on 10-cm VASs anchored by *not at all* and *extremely*. Subjects were shown six food pictures taken from cookery books and judged in an informal pilot study to be extremely appetizing. The same six pictures were used in the second presentation. The mean rating across the six pictures was used in the analyses.

Results

Food intake

The data analysis was designed around two sets of a priori (planned) contrasts: one to test the effect of restraint levels in predicting food intake (Group D vs. Groups C and E) and one to test the effect of weight loss (Groups D and E vs. Group C) (Rosenthal & Rosnow, 1985). As the outcome of the exercise condition was unsuccessful in terms of weight loss, the second contrast was rendered invalid, so only the contrast testing the difference between Group D and the other two groups was used in the analyses. The results of the repeated measures analysis of variance indicated a significant main effect for occasion, $F(1, 24) = 5.04$, $p < 0.05$, with a lower intake in the second taste test. There was also a significant main effect for group, $F(1, 24) = 4.53$, $p < 0.05$, with the dieters eating more than twice as much as the other two groups. Mean food intake in each of the two taste tests is shown in Table 1.

As is apparent from these results, there was no overall counterregulation in any of the groups because the average intake fell by around 15 to 20 g. The data from individual subjects showed that 6 out of 8 dieters, 6 out of 8 exercisers, and 9 out of 10 controls ate less after the preload. Of those who actually did counterregulate, only 1 (a dieter) ate substantially more on the second occasion (90 g vs. 20 g).

For comparability with other results, the relation between restraint and food intake was also assessed across all three groups using a correlation coefficient. This revealed modest positive correlations between restraint and food intake in each taste test (before the preload: $r = 0.24$, $p = 0.11$; after the preload: $r = 0.31$, $p = 0.06$), although they failed to reach significance.

Hunger ratings

There were no significant differences between the groups in the pretest hunger ratings. Group D had an average rating of 28.7, Group C a rating of 31.8, and Group E a rating of 28.5.

Table 1 Food intake before and after the preload (in grams)

Group	n	Before the preload		After the preload	
		M	SD	M	SD
D	8	77.8	84.4	55.1	66.2
C	10	37.3	27.3	22.6	12.4
E	8	33.4	18.6	19.2	7.0

Appetite ratings

There were no significant initial differences in appetite rating between the groups. Overall means for "like-to-eat" ratings fell from 33.9 before eating to 24.7 after eating, and the "appetizing" ratings fell from 52.3 to 44.2, but there were no significant group differences.

Laboratory experiment 2: food intake during stress

The aim of this experiment was to replicate the finding that restrained eaters eat more than unrestrained eaters under stress. Because of the limitation to the number of test sessions that could be interposed into the treatment program, we did not include a control condition. However, in the context of the present study there was independent evidence for the preservation of restraint in everyday life (i.e., weight loss), so the inclusion of a condition in which the restrained subjects were predicted to restrain was not crucial.

Method

All subjects (except one who was on holiday) attended this session individually during Week 6 of the treatment program. The rationale given was that it was an assessment of stress levels, which would be measured during the session.

The State version of the Spielberger State–Trait Anxiety Inventory (STAI; Spielberger, Gorsuch, & Lushene, 1970) was completed at the start of the session to check for baseline differences in anxiety. Stress was then induced by showing the subjects part of a frightening video (*The Shining*, Stanley Kubrick, 1980), which they watched alone in a semidarkened room. Electrodes were attached to their hands to add to the strangeness of the situation. Anxiety during the film was assessed using rating scales. While the subjects watched the film, two bowls of sweets and nuts, which had been preweighed, were left beside them on a table, and they were told that they were free to eat any food if they wished. This procedure was similar to some other stress and food-intake studies in that food intake was incidental rather than the main focus, and eating was optional (e.g., Frost, Goolkasian, Ely, & Blanchard, 1982). The amount of food eaten was the dependent variable.

Results

Preexperimental anxiety

The three groups differed slightly with respect to anxiety level at the start of the experiment, with the STAI State scores of the exercise group being lower ($M=29.7$) than those of the diet group ($M=36.8$) or the control group ($M=38.3$), $F(2, 20)=3.26$, $p=0.06$. However, in the relevant comparison between the diet group and the other two groups, the difference was not significant, $F(1, 23)=0.71$.

Ratings for the film

The ratings of how frightening the film was, and how anxious the subjects felt during the experiment (on a 100-mm scale), suggested that they found the film frightening ($M=44.1$, $SD=25.6$) and that the whole procedure made them fairly anxious ($M=44.3$, $SD=21.4$). There were no significant group differences for either rating.

Table 2 Food intake during the stress experiment

Group	n	Food intake (in grams)	
		M	SD
D	8	58.75	47.41
C	10	10.00	15.45
E	7	19.29	28.64

Food intake

The planned comparison showed that the diet group ate significantly more than the other two groups, $F(1, 23) = 10.01$, $p < 0.005$. Means are given in Table 2, where it can be seen that dieters ate 3 times as much as subjects in the other two groups.

The positive correlation across all three groups between restraint and intake was significant and similar to those found in the first laboratory experiment ($r = .40$, $p < 0.02$).

General discussion

The principal aim of these experiments was to show that the paradoxical overeating that can characterize dieters is an effect, as much as a cause, of dieting. Accordingly, dieting was manipulated experimentally, and eating was assessed in settings chosen to represent those in which dieters have been found to overeat. Because there was a practical limit on the number of possible testing sessions that could be included in a 6-week treatment period, control sessions could not be included. Therefore, from the present data it was possible only to find out if paradoxical overeating occurred and not to identify the particular factors that might precipitate it.

A second aim, which was unsuccessful, was to compare the predictive power of restraint levels and weight loss in accounting for the pattern of laboratory results. In view of the exercise condition's failure to generate weight loss, it was not possible to test the effect of restraint changes independently of weight changes, as the diet group was both restrained and lost weight.

The results of the two laboratory experiments broadly supported the idea that dieting causes disturbances of food intake in the (unusual) circumstances of the study. Against a background of generally successful restraint (as indexed by the weight loss), subjects in the diet group ate substantially more, both in the taste tests and while watching the film, than subjects in the two low-restraint groups.

The specific phenomenon of counterregulation (i.e., eating more after a preload than before) was not demonstrated in the first experiment, and only one subject showed this pattern. It is possible that the failure to find counterregulation was a function of the repeat testing, in that the subjects had already eaten too much. However, the combination of one milk shake and the food intake in the first preload was no larger than the two milk shakes used in some other experiments (e.g., Hibscher & Herman, 1977) and should not have surpassed any upper satiety boundary. Ruderman (1986), reviewing the literature on restraint and obesity, also concluded that the counterregulatory pattern was less evident in restrained obese subjects than restrained normal-weight subjects, which she attributed to the properties of the Restraint Scale. The present results certainly give little support to the idea that dieters become less sensitive to sensations of satiety, because their intake was reduced to the same extent as that of the nondieters. The dieters therefore appeared to regulate appropriately, but at an altogether higher level than the nondieters.

The mechanisms whereby restraint generates paradoxical disturbances of eating behavior have been discussed by several authors (Herman & Polivy, 1984; Polivy & Herman 1984;

Ruderman, 1986; Wardle, 1987a). The emphasis has been predominantly on cognitive mechanisms because the factors that precipitate disinhibition have been found to lie in the cognitive and emotional domains. However, successful restraint should also influence the availability of energy stores in the body, which in turn may activate behavioral and physiological mechanisms tending to restore energy supplies. So although the triggers for abandonment of restraint may lie mainly in the psychological domain, a range of psychological and biological factors probably determine the size of the subsequent food intake.

Surprisingly, in the present studies there was no evidence that the dieters felt hungrier, nor did they give higher ratings on the appetite scales. However, these results should be interpreted cautiously in view of the scope for dissimulation or self-deception in rating scales.

To investigate the mechanisms underlying control and loss of control over eating fully, weight loss and restraint must be varied independently. Unfortunately in the present study the exercise manipulation was not sufficiently powerful to match the weight loss of the dieters and so could not offer an experimental control for the weight-loss component of restraint. Further work is therefore needed to disentangle the contribution of the psychological aspects of restraint itself as opposed to the food deprivation that usually accompanies restraint.

References

Agras, W. S., Ferguson, J. M., Greaves, C., Qualls, B., Rand, C., Ruby, J., Stunkard, A., Taylor, C., Werne, J., & Wright, C. (1976). A clinical and research questionnaire for obese patients. In B. J. Williams, S. Martin, & J. P. Foreyt, (Eds.), *Obesity: Behavioural approaches to treatment.* New York: Brunner/Mazel.

Blundell, J. E., & Rogers, P. J. (1980). Effects of anorexic drugs on food selection and preferences and hunger motivation and subjective experiences. *Appetite, 1,* 151–165.

Frost, R., Goolkasian, G., Ely, R., & Blanchard, F. (1982). Depression, restraint and eating behavior. *Behaviour Research and Therapy, 20,* 113–121.

Herman, C. P., & Polivy, J. (1975). Anxiety, restraint, and eating behavior. *Journal of Abnormal Psychology, 84,* 666–672.

Herman, C. P., & Polivy, J. (1980). Restrained eating. In A. J. Stunkard (Ed.), *Obesity* (pp. 208–225). Philadelphia: Saunders.

Herman, C. P., & Polivy, J. (1984). A boundary model for the regulation of eating. In A. J. Stunkard & E. Stellar (Eds.), *Eating and its disorders* (pp. 141–156), New York: Raven Press.

Hibscher, J. A., & Herman, P. C. (1977). Obesity, dieting, and the expression of "obese" characteristics. *Journal of Comparative and Physiological Psychology, 91,* 374–380.

Hill, A. J., Magson, L. D., & Blundell, J. E. (1984). Hunger and palatability: Tracking ratings of subjective experience before, during and after the consumption of preferred and less preferred food. *Appetite, 5,* 361–371.

Jeffrey, R. W., Wing, R. R., & Stunkard, A. J. (1978). Behavioral treatment of obesity: The state of the art. *Behavior Therapy, 9,* 189–199.

Katch, F. I., & McArdle, W. D. (1983). *Nutrition, weight control and exercise.* Philadelphia: Lea and Febiger.

Keys, A., Fidanza, F., Karvonen, M. J., Kimura, N., & Taylor, H. L. (1972). Indices of relative weight and obesity, *Journal of Chronic Diseases, 25,* 329–343.

Kirschenbaum, D. S., & Tomarken, A. J. (1982). Some antecedents of regulatory eating by restrained and unrestrained eaters. *Journal of Abnormal Psychology, 5,* 326–336.

Lowe, M. G. (1982). The role of anticipated deprivation in overeating. *Addictive Behaviors, 7,* 103–112.

Polivy, J., & Herman, P. (1976). The effect of alcohol on eating behaviour: Disinhibition or sedation. *Addictive Behaviors 1*, 121–125.

Polivy, J., & Herman, P. (1983). *Breaking the diet habit.* New York: Basic Books.

Polivy, J., & Herman, P. (1984). Binge eating: A causal analysis. *American Psychologist, 40*, 193–201.

Rodin, J., Slochower, J., & Fleming, B. (1977). Effects of degree of obesity, age of onset, and weight loss on responsiveness to sensory and external stimuli. *Journal of Comparative and Physiological Psychology, 91*, 586–597.

Rosenthal, R., & Rosnow, R. L., (1985). *Contrast analysis: Focussed comparisons in the analysis of variance.* Cambridge, England: Cambridge University Press.

Ruderman, A. J. (1985). Dysphoric mood and overeating: A test of restraint theory's disinhibition hypothesis. *Journal of Abnormal Psychology, 94*, 78–85.

Ruderman, A. J. (1986). Dietary restraint: A theoretical and empirical review. *Psychological Bulletin, 99*, 247–262.

Ruderman, A. J., Belzer, L. J., & Halperin, A. (1985). Restraint, anticipated consumption, and overeating. *Journal of Abnormal Psychology, 94*, 547–555.

Ruderman, A. J., & Christensen, H. (1983). Restraint theory and its applicability to overweight individuals. *Journal of Abnormal Psychology, 92*, 210–215.

Ruderman, A. J., & Wilson, G. T. (1979). Weight, restraint, cognitions and counter-regulation. *Behaviour Research and Therapy, 17*, 581–590.

Sahakian, B. (1981). Salivation and appetite: Commentary on the forum. *Appetite, 2*, 386–389.

Spencer, J. A., & Fremouw, W. J. (1979). Binge eating as a function of restraint and weight classification. *Journal of Abnormal Psychology, 88*, 262–267.

Spielberger, C. D., Gorsuch, R. L., & Lushene, R. E. (1970). *Manual for the State–Trait Anxiety Inventory.* Consulting Palo Alto, CA. Psychologists Press.

Tomarken, A. J., & Kirschenbaum, D. S. (1984). Effects of plans for future meals on counterregulatory eating in restrained and unrestrained eaters. *Journal of Abnormal Psychology, 93*, 458–472.

Van Strien, T., Frijters, J. E. R., Bergers, G. P. A., & Defares, P. B. (1986). The Dutch Eating Behaviour Questionnaire (DEBQ) for assessment of restrained, emotional, and external eating behaviour. *International Journal of Eating Disorders, 5*, 295–315.

Wardle, J. (1980). Dietary restraint and binge eating. *Behavioural Analysis and Modification, 4*, 201–209.

Wardle, J. (1986). The assessment of restrained eating. *Behaviour Research and Therapy, 24*, 213–215.

Wardle, J. (1987a). Compulsive eating and dietary restraint. *British Journal of Clinical Psychology, 26*, 47–56.

Wardle, J. (1987b). Eating style: A validation study of the Dutch Eating Behaviour Questionnaire in normal subjects and women with eating disorders. *Journal of Psychosomatic Research, 31*, 161–169.

Wardle, J., & Beales, S. (1987). Restraint and food intake: An experimental study of eating patterns in the laboratory and in everyday life. *Behaviour Research and Therapy, 25*, 179–185.

Wooley, O. W., & Wooley, S. C. (1981). Relationship of salivation in humans to deprivation, inhibition and the encephalization of hunger. *Appetite, 2*, 331–350.

Woodcock, A.J., Stenner, K. and Ingham, R. (1992) Young people talking about HIV and AIDS:
interpretations of personal risk of infection, *Health Education Research:
Theory and Practice*, 7 (2): 229 – 47.

Young people talking about HIV and AIDS

Interpretations of personal risk of infection

A.J. Woodcock, K. Stenner and R. Ingham

*Department of Psychology, University of Southampton, Salisbury Road,
Southampton SO9 5NH, UK*

Abstract

Although young people in Britain are quite knowledgeable about the major routes of transmission of HIV, questionnaire studies have revealed widespread perceived invulnerability to infection. In this study, in-depth interviews with 16 – 25 year olds explored perceptions of personal risk of infection, in relation to sexual careers. Reasons for acknowledging or denying risk were examined and categorized on the basis of detailed examination of transcribed interviews. Some acknowledged that their behaviour had put them at risk, but this was often followed by a dismissal of risk because such behaviour was in the past. Denial of personal risk was more common among the respondents and their justifications for this position are categorized into: dismissal of HIV messages generally; general comments about not applying HIV risk to oneself; comments made about partners; and comments made about oneself. Subcategories are illustrated with quotations from individuals. There was a tendency for respondents to interpret their own behaviour and that of sexual partners in relation to only part of the safer sex message and considerable emphasis was placed upon promiscuity. Some basic misconceptions underlying reasons for denial of risk are considered and the implications for health education discussed.

Introduction

There have been several questionnaire studies in Britain in recent years investigating young people's knowledge, attitudes and beliefs about AIDS. It is becoming evident that the large majority of people sampled in schools and colleges since the first mass health education intervention in 1986 are quite knowledgeable about the major routes of transmission. Most are aware that the Human Immunodeficiency Virus (HIV) can be passed on through heterosexual intercourse without a condom (e.g. Clift *et al.*, 1989, data collected in 1988; Pocock *et al.*, 1989, data collected in 1987; Memon, 1990, review).

Abrams *et al.* (1990a), however, reported the results of a questionnaire administered in 1987 and concluded that young people "have a strong sense of AIDS invulnerability which seems to involve a perception that they have control over the risk at which they place themselves." (p. 49). They suggested that the young people may have "cognitive structures which credit the self with more responsibility and control over oneself than others have over themselves. Thus, while others are irresponsible and hence dangerous, the self is safe." (p. 44). This *perceived invulnerability* appeared illogical, given the extent of knowledge about AIDS. More recently, Fazal *et al.* (1990) found that very few young people in the West Midlands in their 1989 survey perceived themselves as being at risk either presently or in the future, with only 8% seeing themselves as being at either 'high' or 'moderate' risk at present (the first two of five levels of possible response).

Such findings indicate that a change to safer sex will be unlikely, at least for some people, since one of the four basic prerequisites for behaviour change, according to models of preventive health behaviour, such as the Health Belief Model (HBM) (Rosenstock, 1986; Kirscht and Joseph, 1989) is that one should see oneself as susceptible or vulnerable to the health threat. In the case of the HBM, the other components are the perceived severity of the condition, the value of adopting a particular line of behaviour and, conversely, the perceived barriers to this action.

Further, MacDonald and Smith (1990) found that between 1988 and 1989, young people in Wales seemed to become *more,* rather than less complacent about HIV and AIDS, with more people agreeing that "AIDS is something that most people do not need to do anything about".

Such questionnaire studies do not, however, investigate the reasons behind young people's complacency and perceived vulnerability, though Frankham and Stronach (1990) have given an indication of the variety of reasons that may be given. Lawrence and Kelly (1989) have expressed concern about incomplete understanding of personalization of health risk as a problem in HIV/AIDS interventions in the USA. The teaching methods of "classroom teaching, whole-class discussion, showing a video and 'question and answer' exchanges", which were found to be most common in school HIV and AIDS education in the South-East of England (Clift and Stears, 1991, p. 3), were unlikely to include personal involvement by the pupils, so that they might be able to apply the facts given about HIV to themselves.

Clift *et al.* (1989) found, from their questionnaire study of young people, that perception of personal vulnerability to *future* infection with HIV was related to a positive attitude to condom use, a non-blaming and sympathetic attitude to people infected with HIV, and not believing that sex should be restricted to marriage. They emphasized, however, the limitations of a questionnaire asking questions out of context, when decision-making "will also be influenced strongly by social and contextual factors" (p. 242).

Hastings *et al.* (1987, in Scotland) and Frankham and Stronach (1990, in Norfolk) found that young people did not see themselves as promiscuous, and thus did not consider themselves to be at risk. Abrams *et al.* (1990b) reported that, since young people believe themselves to be less promiscuous than average, they also tend to perceive themselves as being less at risk. Indeed, the young people studied by Pocock *et al.* (1988) most commonly gave 'sleeping around' as one of the behaviours carrying a risk of HIV infection and those who claimed to have changed their behaviour in response to AIDS risk mostly said that they had become less promiscuous or were more careful in choosing partners. Only 33% of these people claimed to use condoms in response to the threat of AIDS. Thus, it appears that *non*-promiscuity and careful choice of partners may be considered by at least some young people to be adequate reasons for assuming that they are not at risk of becoming infected.

Area of habitation has also been suggested as being related to perceived vulnerability (Wight, 1990). His work in Glasgow gave some indication that the reputation of Edinburgh meant that those on the West Coast felt unthreatened. Also, Frankham and Stronach (1990) observed that perceived concentration of HIV in cities (in this case Norwich and London) allowed people in rural areas to feel less vulnerable. In contrast, Ford and Bowie (1989) found no significant differences in AIDS-related knowledge of 16–21 year olds in urban, semi-urban and rural areas of Somerset, but there was some indication that the safer sex message had been taken on board more by the rural young people, in terms of their reported sexual behaviour and behavioural intentions. Generally, however, it seems that there is a gap between perception of risk and *intention* to behave safely on the one hand, and any actual change in heterosexual behaviour, on the other (e.g. see the review by Wight, 1990).

In order to explore in greater detail the ways in which young people justify their opinion that they are not at risk, this subject was raised during in-depth interviews with young people between the ages of 16 and 25. We were interested in discovering *on what basis* people made judgements about themselves and others as risky or non-risky, because as long as young people perceive the threat of HIV infection as being inapplicable to themselves, the measures advocated to reduce risk, such as use of condoms, will be ignored. It was considered important to allow young people to explain in their own words their perception of AIDS risk, without the constraints of a questionnaire format, so that their view of their own situation might be useful to health educators in bridging the gap between knowledge about AIDS and in encouraging a change to safer sex.

Respondents

Between Summer 1989 and February 1990, volunteers aged between 16 and 25 years were contacted through colleges and training establishments, hostels for single young people, youth centres and sports clubs in Hampshire and Berkshire. Schools were not included in this study, partly because school pupils are already over-represented in the research literature and partly because the school environment might not seem appropriate for many young people for the honest discussion of personal sexual behaviour.

The project was explained to the young people in small groups, or sometimes individually, and a private appointment made with those who volunteered. Respondents were assured of the confidentiality and anonymity of the interviews.

Unlike questionnaire studies, it was not possible to calculate a percentage response rate, since initial contacts with individuals were made in different ways according to the particular establishment. Thus, in a youth club, several visits could be made and the project could be explained to a small gathering around a coffee bar table. Should the researchers then include in the percentage calculation the group around the pool table, who did not gather round the coffee table and the two people who left the table before the explanation of the project began? In contrast, at a college or training establishment, the project was usually explained at the beginning of a class, in which case there was a group response either of enthusiasm for, or rejection of, the invitation to participate. Depending on when the interview was arranged (in course time or private time, and how long in advance), the volunteer might either arrive or fail to attend the appointment. If a volunteer did not attend, two more efforts were made to make an appointment, and if she/he did not attend, the person was considered not to wish to take part.

The majority of the 125 interviews were conducted by the two female authors (A.W. and K.S.), whilst the remaining 21 were carried out by two medical students: one male and one female.

Throughout this paper, the terms 'virgin' and 'non-virgin' are used. Alternative terms, such as 'sexually active', whilst sounding more scientific, are far more confusing, since 'sexual activity' can include the whole range of behaviours from holding hands to any form of penetrative intercourse with either gender of partner. The term also implies that the young person was currently sexually active, which might not be the case. Since, without exception, all the non-virgins interviewed reported a heterosexual experience as their first occasion of sexual intercourse, 'virginity' is in terms of whether the person had experienced vaginal penetration with or without ejaculation. These were the criteria used by the young people for 'losing their virginity', and for this reason had meaning for them in terms of their sexual careers and for the study in terms of possible HIV infection. All but one among the respondents remained heterosexual in preference. One female had become a lesbian, following several heterosexual relationships.

The respondents were

Males (N=58):

Occupation:	Youth training 28; further education 8; higher education 3; employed 15; unemployed 4.
Living with:	Both original parents 35; adoptive parents 2; one original parent 11; hostel, hall or rented 7; grandparents 1; friend's family 1.
Ethnic origin:	Asian 1; Afro-Carribean 0; white European 57.
Virginity status:	Virgins ($n=18$, mean age, 16.9 years, range 16–21); non-virgins ($n=40$, mean age 18.3 years, range 16–25, mean age first intercourse 15.1 years).

Females (N=67):

Occupation:	Youth training 17; further education 26, sixth form college 1; higher education 2; employed 16; unemployed 4; mother 1.
Living with:	Both original parents 26; one original parent 20; hostel, hall or rented 17; male partner 3; husband 1.
Ethnic origin:	Asian 0; Afro-Carribean 3; white European 64.
Virginity status:	Virgins ($n=10$, mean age 17.4 years, range 16–19); non-virgins ($n=57$, mean age 17.8 years, range 16–24, mean age first intercourse 15.3 years).

Due to the nature of the particular issue addressed here, the investigation will be limited to the non-virgins in the sample.

Since they were volunteers, there is no reason to suppose that they represented the views or behaviour of non-volunteers.

Method

At the start of the session, the respondent was thanked for participating and reassured again of confidentiality. This was confirmed by writing a code number on the cassette tape to be used and emphasizing that the comments made would be stored under this code rather than by name. It was emphasized, however, that the respondent was at liberty to refuse to answer any particular question. A friendly and unthreatening tone was established by the interviewer, who made a point of not appearing official. S/he would arrange the room as informally as possible, and chat about general matters while sorting out paperwork and unwrapping cassettes. The actual interview began with general topics such as home, school, work and interests, then moved on to friendships and then relationships with any sexual component, from kissing and holding hands, to more intimate acts. Each relationship was followed through from meeting the partner to the termination of the relationship and as much information as possible was gained about the relationship in terms of not only sexual activities, protection and contraception, but also how much they talked to each other about sex, love, and their pasts, including sexual histories. The interview was conversational, and every effort was made to help the respondent to feel at ease, by using their language to refer to sexual acts, for example, and by demonstrating an interest in their point of view. Respondents were free to joke, tell anecdotes about themselves, their friends and relatives, as well as to share their feelings about sex, their emotions concerning particular partners and so on, since all these gave some insight into influences upon and the expression of their sexuality. The personality of the respondents dictated to a considerable extent the directions taken within the interview. Two pieces of paper were sometimes used to draw the interview back to matters of specific interest. These were a grid showing a chronological perspective of the respondent's life and a list of sexual acts, to be completed for each partner as part of the discussion. Sources of information on sexual matters and HIV/AIDS were explored in most of the interviews, as well as perceived risk of infection, though the order in which these subjects were covered depended to some extent on the individual.

All of those interviewed were asked at some point in the interview to relate HIV and AIDS to their own behaviour. Depending upon how the subject arose, they could be asked whether they worried about AIDS at all, whether AIDS had affected them in any way or whether they felt that they had put themselves at risk. Some mentioned the subject spontaneously. This part of the interview usually took place after the full sexual history had been recalled by the respondent, unless the respondent raised the subject earlier in the interview, in which case the flow of the conversation was allowed to continue in that direction. In a much shorter and more structured 'interview' procedure adopted by Pocock *et al.* (1988) some respondents acknowledged more risk towards the end of the interview than the beginning. By introducing the topic towards the end of our interviews, it was hoped that a considered response would be given, rather than a glib response without any reference to personal sexual lifestyle. We believe that this hope was fulfilled, in that most respondents *argued* their particular point of view. At the end of the interview, the respondent was encouraged to ask questions. Any points of uncertainty or misunderstanding regarding HIV and AIDS were clarified or corrected. The issue of personal risk of infection was not addressed in two interviews with females, due to time constraints.

The interviews were tape recorded and transcribed. Each lasted between 1 and 3.5 hours, depending upon time available, extent of sexual experience and ability to verbalize views on sexual matters. The typewritten transcripts were examined for the parameters used by respondents to estimate their personal risk. The categories of explanation were discussed at length and cross-checked by two of the researchers (A.W. and K.S.) and categories were combined until there was no disagreement between the researchers in allocating any comments to the categories, though a single person could make a statement and then use several different arguments to explane it.

Results

This section will outline the explanations given by respondents that they had or had not been risky. In each case, where a young person is quoted (*shown in italics*), any names have been changed, and the gender and age of the respondent is given in brackets. It should be emphasized here that being a non-virgin could have involved as little as one episode of vaginal intercourse with a condom, or maybe without ejaculation, or as great as "so many sexual partners that they couldn't possibly remember them all". So there is an enormous range of sexual activity, which had been brought to the attention of the respondent whilst describing it during the interview. When confronted with the problem of assessing their own behaviour in terms of risk of HIV infection they responded in a variety of ways (summarized in Table I). Individuals could use several of the types of response, including contradictions, so that risk could be acknow-

Table 1 Categories of interpretations of personal risk of infection with HIV: number of respondents giving each category of reasons (40 males and 55 females)

	Males	Females
Acknowledgement of risk:		
General admission that one's own behaviour has been risky	5	3
Worry dismissed on the grounds it would show by now	1	5
Worry dismissed on the grounds that riskiness was in the past	6	13
Denying risk:		
Dismissal of HIV message generally		
1. It's been blown out of proportion	4	5
2. AIDS is a risk you take in living	7	4
3. Part of the advice is impossible to put into action	7	4
General comments about not applying HIV risk to oneself		
1. It doesn't affect me	9	14
2. It's never going to happen to me	2	5
3. Pregnancy was a greater worry	4	5
4. Not knowing anyone who was infected/low incidence in one's neighbourhood	3	2
Comments made about partners		
1. Partners were (or are) not promiscuous	25	25
2. My partner is faithful	3	7
3. Partner(s) only had long and/or serious relationships before me	5	7
4. Partner gave the impression of being safe (appearance, general impression, family, job, etc.)	9	16
5. Partner has been tested	2	3
6. I knew all my partners	14	15
7. If my partner had AIDS, he or she would have told me	2	4
Comments made about oneself		
1. I am not in a high risk group	11	8
2. I am not promiscuous/I don't go in for one-night stands	14	22
3. I always use condoms/I always use condoms when I think it's necessary	19	15
4. I have been tested	3	8
5. I do not have sex in risky geographical areas	5	3

Note 1: Each person could give several reasons, including contradictions.

Note 2: Topic was raised in different contexts during the interview, therefore direct comparisons between the genders are not necessarily valid.

Note 3: Future intentions are not included.

ledged and denied at different points in the interview. Thus, people could not simply be categorized as 'acknowledgers' or 'deniers' of risk. Acknowledgement was often followed by one or more reasons for denying risk. Where reasons for denial were clearly at odds with sexual history already described, this was pursued by the interviewer for clarification, but, sometimes, the contradictions were not evident until the transcript was analysed in detail. Some such contradictions have been pointed out following the quotations given in the text, but it is not the aim of the paper to examine these in detail. It was clear, however, that some people were not as honest with themselves in assessing their personal risk as they had been in describing their sexual histories to us.

Acknowledgement of risk

Firstly, some people did indeed acknowledge that they had at some time put themselves at risk. The ways they did this and the reasons behind their conclusions are given in the following sections.

General admission that one's own behaviour is or has been risky

Only one person, the male quoted below, gave an outright acknowledgement of risk without any mitigating factors, or subsequent reasons for believing that he had not put himself at risk:

> *I'm a chancer and I know I'm a chancer and I know I should really take care, you know, but – well, you know, with the AIDS thing, I know that I should use a condom.*
> (Male, 25, with eight sexual partners to intercourse, none of whom was a virgin.)

Usually, an acknowledgement of risk was qualified by several reasons from categories A and B for denying that they could have been infected.

Some respondents had a frequently recurring doubt that they may have come into contact with HIV through their sexual relationships, but were anxious about confirming this doubt by having an antibody test:

> *Scared in case I have, you know. I don't want to know if I have. It's a case of that, you know. It's better to be scared of the unknown than to be scared of what you do know.*
> (Female, 17.)

The next two areas describe reasons for dismissing a past worry of HIV infection, and are really variations on the same theme, concerning past rather than present behaviour:

Worry dismissed on the grounds it would show by now

> *I did (worry) but I sort of like over the years, I thought well, if I've got it, then it would show by now, or it will do soon, sort of thing.*
> (Female, 17.)

> *Afterwards, when I've sobered up, cause when I'm drunk, I just don't worry. Well, you've got it there somewhere in your subconscious but the alcohol has blotted it out. There is only one thing you are thinking of at the time. A couple of days later I think 'Oh, no. I might have caught something. Think I'll go to the clinic' and 'No, I'll leave it for a little while' and then no symptoms. I don't really bother going.*
> (Male, 23.)

The lack of symptoms of HIV infection is something that several young people had not genuinely come to terms with. Although, on the whole, they realized that partners could not be *seen* to be infected, many failed to examine their own or partner's past behaviour in the long term.

Worry dismissed on the grounds that riskiness was in the past

This time in the past was often seen as a time when the respondent had not heard about AIDS or 'it was not around':

AIDS wasn't around in those days. You might catch something but you could go down the clinic and be cleared up but now AIDS is a lot more serious.

(Female, 21.)

I trusted him. I knew him. I knew he had other girlfriends and everything but that was all sort of before I'd sort of become aware of all this AIDS stuff.

(Female, 21.)

The risky experiences described above, as with other examples, actually took place since 1986. Thus, although some claimed now to be more concerned about their sexual behaviour in relation to AIDS, they had put previous risky events behind them.

Denying risk

Many people argued that they had not put themselves at risk, and did not worry about AIDS in terms of their own behaviour. They talked about this in various ways, with at least five individuals having given a reason within each of the following sub-categories. There were some additional explanations mentioned by fewer people. Only the main themes are outlined here.

Dismissal of HIV message generally

HIV advice was dismissed for the following three reasons:

1 It's been blown out of proportion

> *I think it's been blown up. I don't think it's worth bothering about.*

(Female, 17.)

The claim that the risk of HIV infection had been overstated was made by some respondents, and the media was implicated in some cases either by over-coverage or by over-coverage followed by neglect:

> *AIDS was around before the publicity stunt. Maybe it has increased but so has many other things increased, but there was this big publicity stunt about AIDS all of a sudden. Then it just went! Gone!*

(Female, 17.)

2 AIDS is a risk you take in living
The risk of AIDS was described in the context of other risks taken in living. Whilst such reasons might at first appear to be an acknowledgement of risk, they were used as reasons for not worrying about AIDS, or for not treating the risk personally, which has implications for making individual decisions about protection:

> *... like sometimes, like if I'm on the bus back (home) or something and sort of think (sigh) 'I wonder if I have got AIDS' and I think about it, then I think 'No, no,' and I push it, but I do think about it. 'What if I get it' and all that. But then I think 'Yeah, you know, it's the same like I could get cancer from smoking. I could get kidney disorders from drinking, I could get some sort of disease from food, I could get run over by a bus. It's a risk you take in living.'*

(Female, 17.)

The claim that there is a saturation with health messages, with the result that a decision has been made to ignore all of them was frequently made. The theme of being run over, particularly by buses, was also quite common among our respondents. Chance events were sometimes emphasized when considering personal risk of coming into contact with HIV and this could be linked to a fatalistic approach to HIV infection:

> *And another thing about AIDS. I could go out and get raped tomorrow. No-one would rape me, but if you go out and get raped and that person's got AIDS I mean there's nothing you can do about it is there.*
>
> (Female, 17.)

3 Part of the advice is impossible to put into action
Thinking about HIV and AIDS is not compatible with the idea that sex should be spontaneous and enjoyable. This could be used as a reason for not worrying about it. Some saw this as their own personal view, whereas the following female claimed that her attitude conformed to a consensus among young people:

> *Yeah, but you can't sort of say – can't have sex because of the risk of getting AIDS, can you?... They sort of say don't sleep around and have casual sex but no-one cares, do they? Not a lot of people, young people especially.*
>
> (Female, 16.)

Even though, for some people, HIV and AIDS is a serious issue outside the sexual situation, it is considered to be inappropriate to put the advice into practice in context:

> *Well, in cold blood and sitting here with all my clothes on, it's very sensible and it's perfect and it's the thing you should do and obtain a full sexual history of your prospective partner, but you get in a dimly lighted room, wearing not quite so many clothes, with somebody you find very attractive, you sort of feel a bit awkward.*
>
> (Male, 19.)

General comments about not applying HIV risk to oneself

1 It doesn't affect me
Many such comments came from people within relationships that they thought would last:

> *Oh, I think about it but it doesn't affect me, not where sex is concerned anyway...I don't know, don't think about it. Doesn't concern me.*
>
> (Female, 22.)

Others were not in a sexual relationship at the time:

> *... I try not to let it worry me from the point of view that I don't intend to get myself into any situations where it is likely to affect me. Until such time as I do, then I don't think I'm going to consider it a hazard to me.*
>
> (Male, 21, intercourse once only, without condom: his partner's past was, in his assessment, *not angelic*.)

All comments that HIV did not affect them were included in this category, whether or not relationship status was mentioned as support for the argument.

2 It's never going to happen to me
Variations upon this phrase were used by several respondents.

> *I mean it doesn't bother me at all. I goes 'No. I won't get it, no. You know, not me – everyone else, not me. I won't get it.'...OK, I think of VD and thrush and all that stuff, but AIDS, no way, that won't get to me. I shouldn't think that way, but that's the way I think.*
>
> (Female, 17.)

The following male, considered this 'can't happen to me' argument to be one *commonly held*, especially among his friends. He bolstered his argument with evidence from his perceived risk of another illness, thus describing it as a strategy he employs to deny risk of illnesses generally:

> *I mean as far as I know, everybody, all my friends seem to say 'It's going to happen to someone else' and I'm carried away in that relation, where I suppose – I will never admit that it might happen to me or could happen to me. I don't know – three people have died from cancer in the past 2 years, just over in the building across the road from me and I still don't think I'm going to get cancer.*
>
> (Male, 18.)

The fact that our respondents almost placed this phrase in inverted commas as they spoke indicated that they knew they were using a well-worn and perhaps illogical argument to avoid thinking of the risk. Some explained that ignoring AIDS had the function of self-protection from infection itself or from the fear that acknowledgement of risk might bring, as the following two examples illustrate:

> *No, I think Oh Christ sometimes you think it could be up here (points to his head), do you know what I mean – mind over matter. You think I ain't going to get it, like some girls getting pregnant, know what I mean, but if you're going to get it, you're going to get it ...*
>
> (Male, 18.)

> *'Cause you know, you take it too seriously, you think you're paranoid and you start thinking you've got HIV, like.*
>
> (Female, 17.)

3 Pregnancy was a greater worry
Many people emphasized pregnancy risk above AIDS risk in their decisions to either avoid certain partners or to use a condom. When asked about personal risk of AIDS, however, nine reflected in retrospect that they *had* been safe from AIDS in behaving this way:

> *(worry about AIDS was) only very minute. The main thing that worried me was getting pregnant–it wasn't really catching any virus.*
>
> (Female, 17.)

The fact that many females were on the pill, and that most males did not use condoms when they believed a female partner to be on the pill, however, indicates that for many more of our respondents, protection against HIV was not the issue when a choice about contraception was made.

4 Not knowing anyone who was infected/low incidence in one's neighbourhood
The lack of personal experience of AIDS was frequently endorsed as a reason not to think about AIDS in relation to oneself:

> *Well maybe if I found that one of my past girlfriends carries HIV or maybe one of my mates has got it, or, I don't know, maybe just someone I know suffers from it or catches it or dies from it or whatever. Someone that I know about. I don't know, you see a lot about it in the papers, on the telly, but ...*
>
> (Male, 17.)

In the South of England at the time of the interviews, young heterosexuals were mostly rather removed from AIDS and any knowledge of people who were HIV positive was either remote or non-existent, with only one having had a close friend who had committed suicide when he tested positive as a result of intravenous drug use. She, incidentally did not use condoms and had several partners to intercourse, indicating that there is not necessarily a change in behaviour when one does indeed have personal contact in this way.

Comments made about partners

In considering the likelihood that they may have come into contact with HIV, some made detailed assessments of one or more of their partners. Below are the types of assessment that were made, though an individual respondent might make such comments about certain partners, whilst either pointing out or ignoring more risky aspects of another partner or partners.

1 Partners were (or are) not promiscuous
This was a very common reason, given for believing one had not become infected. It was used by 25 of each gender:

> *I don't worry about it because I don't go with people who go around a lot.*
>
> (Female, 20.)

> *I don't think any of them would have anything like that. No real reason, just hoping. . . . Not the type of girl that would get around. It didn't really bother me.*
>
> (Male, 16.)

In both the examples, there is a belief that one is able to judge whether someone 'goes around, but perhaps more subtle is the suggestion by the female that *she* is not the sort of person who goes around. The male, on the other hand is making judgements about the female herself. The following quote illustrates this point more clearly:

> *Well, I thought if he had been sleeping around with anything, with anybody, you know, then I suppose I would have thought about it.*
>
> (Female, 22.)

The term 'anything' referring to the past girls has the effect of sounding judgemental upon the girls rather than on the boyfriend himself. Many females judged their male partners in terms of the reputations of their previous female partners.

Where there was some knowledge of the partner's sexual history, based either upon actual discussion or more often upon hearsay, reputation or upon guesswork arising from a general impression, two issues became apparent regarding perceived promiscuity of the partner. The first was that the person was either a virgin beforehand, or had had sexual intercourse with relatively few partners. The problem of whether a partner tells the truth is one that several respondents mentioned. When assessing risk for AIDS during the interview, however, it was the *least* risky scenario that was usually favoured. Often, the account of why they were safe did not conform to the facts already given. One male (23), for example thought he was safe because all his partners had been virgins, but he had already told the interviewer that one was not. There are many examples of this sort. The second issue concerned age. Since the majority of our female sample tended to favour male partners older than themselves, there was likely to be some expectation that males were more experienced and had already had intercourse with more females. This was considered to be neither promiscuous nor risky. One, for example, knew from the grapevine that he had had intercourse with many previous partners. She gave the explanation:

> *Well, he is nearly 20.... But it didn't matter.*
>
> (Female, 17.)

Another thought it was quite acceptable within her understanding of male sexuality that her current partner had had four casual sexual partners early in his sexual career:

> *Oh, yeah, but they were the sort of thing when he was 16, what most boys wanted, you know, to get their leg over, it seems, but that girl, he was absolutely besotted, really.*
>
> (Female, 16.)

Apparently, some women thought that a male was not promiscuous if he had several sexual partners to intercourse over a number of years. The emotional significance of those relationships, rather than their potential for disease transmission, was of paramount consideration.

2 My partner is faithful

Some people interviewed appeared to have a block to thinking about riskiness in terms of a partner's previous sexual history, emphasizing their faithfulness within the current relationship:

> *He said I've only slept with you in the last 6 months and I said I've only slept with you, so AIDS doesn't really bother me at the moment.*
>
> (Female, 17, whose partner had nine previous partners to intercourse.)

Underlying this argument, is the basic misunderstanding that, in a long-term serious relationship, one is safe. Both one's own past and that of the partner are forgotten. Some in steady relationships said that, considering some of the people that they had been with before, they had had 'a lucky escape'. The fundamental fact about HIV, that it can be in one's system for many years before symptoms of AIDS occurred, had not been taken in and used *logically* to apply to the importance of learning about sexual histories.

3 Partner(s) only had long and/or serious relationships before me

As already described, emotional involvement with previous partners was more important for some people than the sexual activities in which they engaged. The length of previous relationships was described by this male:

> ... *if the girl said she goes out with boys for a year or a year and a half or something and made love in that time, then that's fair enough.*
>
> (Male, 18.)

4 Partner gave the impression of being safe (appearance, general impression, family, job, etc.)

> *I don't seriously think he's the sort of person that's going to sleep with someone who's high risk or whatever.*
>
> (Female, 17.)

> *I think (boyfriend) was very careful – said he was always – has been very careful and found out about people first.*
>
> (Female, 21, who had sex herself with this partner for the first time on their first date, yet apparently believed that he had never done this before.)

Some males claimed to have steered clear of females they considered may be risky and described ways in which they would recognize the stereotype of a promiscuous girl who would be likely to be infected with HIV:

> *Well, just generally being with her – with a girl, if they are really sort of like putting it out a lot, then I think well, you know, you're best off steering clear of that, because if she's doing it with me, she could be doing it with God knows, anyone.*
>
> (Male, 19.)

The ability to assess riskiness and avoid partners judged likely to be promiscuous contrasts with the stereotyped male attitude of the pre-AIDS era, to which some other males interviewed still adhered, by seeking out female partners who appeared to be likely to agree to early intercourse.

Apart from a general impression, some people looked at family background and employment factors when assessing riskiness of partners:

> *She didn't come across as the sort of person like that – she came from a nice family and stuff and I just didn't think there was that much risk attached. I certainly didn't have the right attitude. I was basing everything on the wrong criteria, but nothing bad came out of it. That's the trouble – have a lucky escape and you think Oh, I'll get away with it again and again, perhaps.*
>
> (Male, 19.)

The following female used a range of impressions about a boyfriend and his family to come to her conclusion;

It's silly really, I don't know a lot about him, you know. I don't know much about his background. I mean, he's like well brought up and comes from a good family and everything and his Dad's like a (jobtitle) and his sister's a (jobtitle) and he like works in a laboratory. He's really intelligent, so someone who's like intelligent like that, I expect him to, you know ... You know, I trust him, cause he's a sensible bloke, so obviously, you know, he's sensible THAT way.

(Female, 18.)

The reputation of riskiness attached to certain professions could be said to bear no resemblance to the real risk. Two females said they used condoms with a particular partner because he was in the Army, both believing that 'squaddies' were likely to have a different girl every week, though in both cases it was the soldier who produced the condom.

Two females used impressions to judge the *partners* of their boyfriends, and these two have been included in this category, e.g.:

They lived in the New Forest.... I don't think from the way he describes them to me, they don't seem the sort to sleep around and get it. I've met one of them and she certainly doesn't seem the sort of person to be on drugs or, I don't know. I just don't think they come across as being that sort of person to me.

(Female, 19, who had earlier in the interview explained that her boyfriend was surprised and pleased she was a virgin *because all the girls he had been out with had always slept with quite a few nippers.*) ('Nipper' is a local term for a young man.)

Implicit in these sorts of arguments is the notion that AIDS affects certain sorts of people, and some respondents truly believed that both they and all their previous partners had been able to detect and avoid such people, while actually knowing little of their sexual histories.

5 Partner has been tested

Five of our respondents said that a certain partner had been 'tested for AIDS'. For example, one young woman insisted that her current partner should be tested because she had been tested herself. Another said her current partner had had one amongst many tests when he was ill *because they tested him for everything.* We do not know whether these partners actually had tests for HIV antibodies, but the respondents believed they had.

More worrying is a woman, one of whose past boyfriends had a test after they had finished. His negative result led her to believe that she was not HIV positive. The thought that she might be the infected one was not considered. She continued, as before, her habit of not using condoms.

Some of the problems of 'the test' will be addressed under (4) (I have been tested) in the next subsection.

6 I knew all my partners

It never entered my head at all. 'Cause I knew most of them, so there was only one which was a one-night stand. I knew nothing of him, that's it. All the rest, I knew them 6, 7 years or whatever, so it was alright.

(Female, 19, who had earlier described herself as having been 'a slag' in the past:
Anyone who wanted to get a bit, I'd let 'em. It was that bad.)

Some pointed out at some stage of the interview:

> *You'd never think anybody you know's got it.*
>
> (Female, 17.)

which emphasizes one of the problems with this issue. The notion of 'knowing' one's partner is in fact extremely problematic. Some of the AIDS health information leaflets advocate 'getting to know partners' so that it is possible to negotiate condom use and discuss sexual histories.

'Knowing' a partner could be used as a substitute for discussing sexual histories and condom use, rather than as a prerequisite for doing so. Most people knew very little about their partner's sexual histories, even though they may have, for example, *known him from Infants*. Moreover, even when they knew that the partner had had many previous partners, they would make excuses for them, on the basis of age, as already described, or because they believed it was fair to give people a chance to reform. Such comments were all made by females with reference to their current partner.

7 If my partner had AIDS, he or she would have told me

> *Er, really, it's up to her if she's gone with loads and loads of boys, then – if she did have it then I think she would have told me straight away … She's not one to lie.*
>
> (Male, 17.)

> *It's just not worth worrying (about using condoms). You might just as well ask them if they've got any venereal diseases, and if they say they've got AIDS, say 'bugger off then', sort of thing.*
>
> (Female, 16.)

This is further evidence of a lack of understanding by some people of the latency between infection and symptoms.

Comments made about oneself

Whilst the comments included in previous sections were general comments about non-application of risk to oneself, those in this section are comments in which the individual makes reference to her or his own behaviour. Implicit in all the statements made under the previous section about partners was the statement about oneself that one was indeed careful in choosing partners and not the sort of person to sleep with anyone who was available. In addition to this claim, there were several other ways in which people justified their own perceived safety:

1 I am not in a high risk group
   At the simplest level, excluding oneself from risk took the form of referring to 'high risk groups':

> *I know that I'm not ever going to start taking drugs or swapping needles with nobody and I know (boyfriend) wouldn't so I don't really think I've got anything to worry about.*
>
> (Female, 19.)

> *I only have sex with girls. I know that doesn't stop – women can carry it but it hasn't really sunk into me as a major worry.*
>
> (Male, 17.)

Among those who used such arguments were four males and two females who said they *used to* believe that HIV only affected such groups, but they now realized that heterosexuals could be infected too, whereas the remainder all in some way emphasized the *relative* safety of heterosexuals compared with the high risk groups.

2 I am not promiscuous/I don't go in for one-night stands

This was a very common reason for feeling safe. Fourteen males and 22 females claimed not to sleep around or consider 'one-night stands'. In some cases, evidence from their sexual histories indicated that they had, for example, had intercourse on the first night of meeting a partner, but that this had marked the beginning of a relationship:

> *'Cause I'm not like someone who sleeps around all the time. I mean, yeah, there's always a chance, but I like pick my partners carefully, you know what I mean.*
> (Male, 17.)

> *Whereas lots of people meet someone and sleep with them that night, but I won't.*
> (Female, 17.)

3 I always use condoms/I always use condoms when I think it's necessary

Whilst some did say they always used a condom and this conformed to what had already been said in the interview, there were very few (only two of each gender) for whom that was the case, so this category included a range of statements emphasizing how good the person's record was in using condoms. Most had had one or two lapses and had not used a condom on at least one occasion with a certain partner, even if they were otherwise quite conscientious in this way. The rules that individuals had for condom use regarding when they thought it necessary were varied. Some people, for example, used a condom only for first intercourse with a new partner and others for one particular partner who was thought to have a risky background. Often, the female would move onto the pill in a steady relationship and stay on it thereafter, with subsequent partners, abandoning the condom as unnecessary.

4 I have been tested

Eleven people told us that they had been tested and were sure that they were not infected. The interviewers became concerned about this and began to ask for more detail about what the testing entailed. The interviewers thought that at least *some* of them were mistaken in thinking they had been tested for HIV antibodies, e.g.:

> *I have to have a blood test done every week – and they automatically test it for AIDS nowadays anyway, so I know I'm fine – cause I have a blood test done every week and I know damn well that I haven't got AIDS.... Yeah, they do. Every blood test is done automatically for AIDS now.*
> (Female, 16.)

Another woman explained her reason for believing she was not infected:

> *… as far as the tests have proven, I haven't had anything wrong with me at all.*
> (Int: You were tested for HIV were you?)

I'm not sure. They took so many tests. I don't know what they were. – I had blood tests, urine tests, they take swabs of everything, of the cervix, the womb, took quite a lot of tests – they took a cancer test as well, but nothing really showed up on any of them.

(Female, 17.)

Clearly, the concept of random anonymous testing as described in the media some time ago had been misinterpreted by a significant few. They thought they would be given a result. Secondly, either some GPs and genito-urinary clinics had not been following pre- and post-testing procedures for HIV antibody tests or, perhaps more likely, people thought they had been tested for HIV antibodies, when in fact they had not. When people visited the doctor or genito-urinary clinic about sexual matters, particularly sexually transmitted diseases, and particularly following an instance of rape, they were often so embarrassed and frightened that they did not know what was happening. Under such circumstances, they may not have been able to recall what they had been tested for or whether they had given written consent for a particular test. There were certainly some who assumed that a blood test *meant* an AIDS test and were mistaken, since the reported medical reasons for having a blood test included pregnancy, a bad back and diabetes, as well as mysterious illnesses for which *they tested me for everything.*

4 I do not have sex in risky geographical areas
Some individuals had their own personal views on the riskiness of certain geographical areas and avoiding sex in these areas was a personal reassurance of safety.
One male, for example, avoided sex at London raves, because he had seen the *addicts* up there:

London is the capital: has to be more AIDS.

(Male, 17.)

Another male (17) said he did not have sex with the girls in London that his friend set up for him. (He told his friend, however, that he had.) A young woman interviewed who had had many partners in her home town without using a condom did in fact take condoms with her to London. She explained:

He was Irish, they were all Irish and I had it with him but I wouldn't do it without a condom with him, cause, I don't know, I just don't trust people from London. I don't know why.

(Female, 17.)

One male (19) slept with a woman in Amsterdam but avoided sex in the USA because of AIDS. Another, since he had realized that AIDS was in his home town restricted his sexual activity to his *particular area* of that town. He considered:

Glasgow and Edinburgh – the capital of AIDS. They all Jack up there.

(Male, 22.)

He said he would also avoid sex in Spain because he had heard the tabloid newspaper story of a Spanish waiter who gave a girl a parting gift of a coffin containing the message 'welcome to the AIDS club', a story which was often quoted elsewhere in interviews as a source of information about AIDS. One female (16) said she had avoided sex with a Spanish waiter because of this story. Another female (17), whose brother told her about prostitutes on Tenerife, concluded that you could 'catch it on holiday'. Examples of individual perception of risky areas are many, but it is worthy of note that Africa was not mentioned, although the heterosexual risk in Africa had been mentioned in the tabloid press around that time (*Daily Mail*, 17.11.89; *The Sun*, 24.11.89).

There were several who felt safe in their own home area, among people they had known from school, but not outside that area. Nonetheless, there was evidence from some interviews of a belief that holidays were a legitimate time to have sexual intercourse with comparative strangers, without loss of reputation at home. Thus, the belief that one could judge a person's riskiness on the basis of their reputation *must* be called into question, if only upon this evidence.

Discussion

Models of preventive health behaviour, of which the HBM (Rosenstock, 1974) is perhaps the most familiar, have been described as having several drawbacks in application to education for safer sex in the light of the threat of HIV infection (e.g. Kirscht and Joseph, 1989). Not least is the assertion that people do not behave rationally where sexual behaviour is concerned (e.g. Ingham *et al.*, 1991b). In this paper, various personal reasons have been described which may explain why for some people, knowledge of HIV and AIDS is not followed through into behaviour change because of a failure to see oneself as susceptible to the threat of AIDS, a crucial component of the HBM.

Objectively, some ways of organizing sexual relationships make them relatively safe, such as wearing condoms for penetrative vaginal intercourse, or staying in the first sexual relationship with someone who had also been a virgin. Of course, apart from the non-virgins, described here, 22% of our total sample had not engaged in penetrative vaginal intercourse at the time of the interview. Many other reasons for asserting personal safety are far less easy to assess objectively, and it is quite possible that an apparently flawed argument could actually be quite effective within one individual's social and sexual lifestyle, but not within another's.

In the context of the interview, in which attention had been drawn to sexual history, some people did acknowledge that their behaviour had put them at risk of coming into contact with HIV. The reasons centred upon not using condoms and not knowing the sexual history of one or more earlier partners. Acknowledgement of risk, however, was often followed by a dismissal of the risk on the grounds that there were no symptoms, there had been a lucky escape or that there was little one could do about the past. To someone with an understanding of the latency between infections and symptoms, this would be a false belief.

The four main types of reason for not worrying about the risk of AIDS or for feeling that they had been safe are in some cases related to earlier findings and to the notion of perceived invulnerability (e.g. Abrams *et al.*, 1990a,b). It is one thing to believe that one is working within the advice given and behaving more safely than others, which is how Abrams and his colleagues explained perceived invulnerability, but it is quite another to know the facts and dismiss them. In our first category of dismissal of HIV messages generally, the comments indicated that some people believed risk to be overstated and so they went on without worrying. Others called upon the discourse that there are too many health messages already which restrict behaviour and

AIDS was dismissed with the rest. For some there was a tendency to dwell upon chance events that could result in AIDS, so that there was no point in taking precautions.

The idea that it is a matter of luck or chance events whether you get AIDS was a theme that emerged in our interviews. Blaxter (1989) has referred to the 'fatalistic bias', in which the threat of AIDS is so great that it is ignored or distorted. The 'serendipitous' lay explanation of the causation of AIDS reported by Aggleton *et al.* (1988) is relevant in this context, but in the interviews reported here the same sort of reasoning is used as a 'logical' explanation or justification for not worrying about it. For someone who does not wish to take responsibility for sexual activities, e.g. not wanting to wear a condom, perhaps because of a dislike of them, it is easier to adopt discourses which exaggerate chance events. This is functional in that helplessness in the face of the chance nature of infection involves making no effort to change one's behaviour or protect oneself and one's partner in sexual encounters. This proposition is worthy of investigation in a larger sample.

It is possible that, since the early interviews by Aggleton *et al.*, health education initiatives have made considerable headway in replacing lay understandings with factual information about routes of transmission, as the 'miasmatic' and 'endogenous' explanations for AIDS were not evident in the interpretations of risk described in our study. Nonetheless, the fact that some media reporting has drawn attention to incidences of infection, which were beyond the control of the individual, particularly blood transfusions, may be related to the finding that some young people dwell upon these as a justification for not taking precautions against sexual transmission.

There was some evidence for a gulf between intentions and behaviour, voiced in terms of the inappropriateness of being sensible and putting known HIV protection advice into practice in context. This position had been given credence around the time of our interviews by Lord Kilbracken in *The Sun* (24.11.89): "You would hardly be likely to enquire, By the way, have you been to Africa lately? or Do you go with prostitutes!" With newspapers and peers of the realm 'giving permission' to ignore official advice to learn a partner's sexual history, it is hardly surprising that some of our respondents also dismissed such advice as unlikely to be followed in a sexual context. The idea that sexual activity is spontaneous and that it should be unplanned acts as a reason for not putting safer sex advice into practice (see also Holland *et al.* 1991; Wilton and Aggleton, 1991) and some of our respondents indicated that they indeed had better intentions when not carried away in the heat of the moment.

Some young people interviewed dismissed AIDS as being inapplicable to themselves, distancing themselves from the risk, whilst apparently *realizing* that this was not logical. Comments such as "It doesn't affect me" and "It's never going to happen to me" reflect strategies for denial of personal risk of many types of illness and misfortune (e.g.: Weinstein, 1980, 1984, 1989: Perloff and Fetzer, 1986). Some actually voiced the anxiety-reduction, 'ego-defensive' function of the denial of personal risk of HIV (see also Memon, 1991). The re-telling of one's sexual history in such a way that it conformed more closely to the safer sex message (e.g. forgetting that a partner was not a virgin and believing the best of partners where there was any doubt) may also be seen in this way.

The theme of personal knowledge of people with AIDS has been one often referred to in the context of behaviour change among gay men (e.g. McKusick *et al.*, 1985). Especially in areas of the US where there is a high incidence of AIDS, there are few gay men who have not been affected in a personal way. The effect of proximity to such areas has been explored in relation to young people's knowledge about AIDS (e.g. Price *et al.*, 1985; DiClemente *et al.*, 1986). The lack of contact with HIV infected individuals made it hard for some of our respondents to perceive that it was a risk to them.

Some young people, however, did not reject the health messages they had heard about HIV, but expressed a belief that they were behaving in a safe manner, as in Abram *et al.*'s (1990a,b) explanation of perceived invulnerability. Respondents interpreted advice to fit in with their own attitudes and behaviour, or they interpreted their own behaviour in such a way that it adhered to only *part* of the recipe for being safe, as they understood it. Thus, for example, someone who did not like and did not use condoms for vaginal intercourse could focus upon another aspect of safer sex advice, such as knowing one's partner (see also Ingham *et al.*, 1991a) or selecting partners carefully, neither of which involve change in behaviour within a sexual encounter.

Some still subscribed to the idea of risk groups (homosexuals and people who inject drugs) but all knew that heterosexuals can be at risk and many have added a new risk group: 'slags' or 'people who sleep around'. Not only did they consider themselves *not* to be in that risk category, but many people credited themselves with the ability to be able to recognize the sort of person who would sleep around in such a way as to get infected. They based their judgements on various factors, some of which may appear to be irrational to an outsider, but have considerable salience for that individual and were argued logically within that person's understanding of AIDS and sexual behaviour. There were some common means of judging partners, such as the way people dressed, the way they acted and talked, how sensible they were in other matters, their family and their reputation within the social group, and their intelligence. Our respondents sometimes preceded these descriptions with such phrases as "I know you can't tell by looking at them, but ...", as if acknowledging that such simplifications did not bear scrutiny. The reduction of characteristics of potentially risky people into stereotypes helped people to make decisions about others and, in the context of the interview, bolstered feelings of safety.

There was, however, an overriding belief by many people that the *number* of previous partners was an important factor, so that those judged to have had fewer sexual partners would be safer. This was sometimes backed by reference to the seriousness of their previous relationships. Such beliefs were in some cases at odds with the evidence from behaviour with the individual interviewed, in that a partner was believed to have had only serious (long-term rather than casual) relationships *before* the one with the respondent and yet had penetrative sex with the respondent very early in the relationship. There was considerable evidence from some respondents that they preferred to believe the best of their previous partners and particularly the current partner when it came to assessing risk of HIV infection. This, along with the tendency, particularly for females, to make excuses for the history of the current partner means that it is unlikely that potential partners will be rejected on the basis of sexual history.

The finding that some females tended to judge the safety of their male partners on the basis of the appearance or reputation of previous female partners is related to the female collusion with male denigration of women on the basis of sexual activity or reputation described also by Lees (1986). Descriptions of 'prostitutes', 'slags' and girls who were 'easy lays' made by both males and females in our sample reflected the tendency by some to judge females in this way. It has been pointed out by Cochran (1989) that women are often viewed as potential 'infection vectors' of men and children. Thus they are seen as being to blame for infecting others, rather than as individuals who may themselves suffer. A woman labelled as a prostitute is perceived as even more to blame (Plant, 1989), just as she has been blamed historically for the spread of a range of sexually transmitted diseases. It has to be said, however, that some female respondents also said they would avoid, or had avoided, 'Jack the lads' or 'male slags', though for others, the fact that they had tamed such a young man into faithfulness was a matter of pride.

Many respondents claimed to *know* their partners, but knew precious little about their sexual histories (see also Ingham *et al.*, 1991a). 'Knowing' can be used as a substitute for condom use and asking about sexual histories, rather than a prerequisite. The sort of 'knowing' described by some of them would not be compatible with knowing each other's sexual histories since it was often only a matter of seeing someone around or having been to the same school. Thus, respondents could dwell on their *knowledge* of the partner either before the boyfriend–girlfriend relationship began or the *trust* that had developed since it had begun as a reason for believing it was safe not to use a condom.

The lack of understanding of the implications of the latency period between HIV infection to the detection of antibodies by blood test and finally to the symptoms of HIV-related illnesses including AIDS runs through many justifications of personal safety. Such implications include the importance of learning about sexual histories and previous condom use rather than reliance upon reputation, general personality characteristics, trust, faithfulness and the number of previous partners. The *ordinariness* of HIV positive individuals portrayed in the 1990–91 television campaign may have gone some way to destroy the image of the easily recognized caricature of promiscuity as the only type of person to harbour HIV and to reduce the emphasis upon the number of partners, but this has been counterbalanced by conflicting messages (e.g. from Sir Donald Acheson), emphasizing the importance of condom use in the context only of unknown partners (e.g. *The Daily Telegraph*, 16.10.90). Uncertainty about the length of time between infection with HIV and first symptoms was expressed by many respondents, and was evident in arguments put forward for feeling sure that they themselves and their previous partners were not infected.

Stockdale *et al.* (1989) reported that people judged to be at risk of HIV are 'not like me' and the comments made by many young people interviewed in the present study were in this vein. Their reasons, however, went beyond the simple categories of gay/not gay and other assertions that they were 'not in a high risk group'. Most respondents were keen to portray themselves as being selective of partners, not promiscuous themselves, and not the sort of person who goes in for one-night stands. Some individuals had their own rules which they believed rendered them safe, and the use of statements such as 'I'm not like the people who pick someone up and sleep with them on the first night' implied that others were seen as less safe and hence more vulnerable, as in the studies by Abrams *et al.* (1990a,b).

The misconceptions about testing for HIV as described in the section 'I have been tested' is a further area which needs addressing. In this case, it seems important that people who are given blood tests for other reasons should be told that their blood will *not* be tested for HIV antibodies, or that if it is tested for HIV as part of the anonymous testing procedure, that they will *not* be told the results. It seems that mass campaigns attempting to describe and clarify the testing procedure have not dispelled the belief by some individuals that a blood sample is always tested for HIV, thus convincing them that if they have not heard anything, they are not infected.

Apart from the rather common reasons for believing that one is safe and uninfected, there were many other reasons which were specific to particular individuals, such as various geographical considerations, but have been grouped into types of justification for the purpose of this paper. Since these beliefs are in some cases so individual, it is hard to see how they can be addressed through mass campaigns.

Educational implications

It could be the very reasons described above that stop individuals from picking up AIDS leaflets in the chemist's or tuning into a discussion programme on television. It simply does not concern them. Mass campaigns thus have considerable limitations. It seems that the only way that such mistaken reasonings can be exposed to the individual is through either a group discussion or an individual session with each person concerned. In our experience of listening to young people, it appears that a sympathetic and non-judgmental outsider who made her- or himself available for individual confidential discussions after leading a small group session with a high level of participation (e.g. role play) might be the most effective method for broaching the subject of individual perceptions of invulnerability. This should, however, be in the context of a full programme of personal, social and health education. Whilst an HIV/AIDS 'expert' from the local Health Education Service, for example, may be considered by teachers to be the best person to provide this input in certain schools and colleges, a teacher may be the one to whom the young person turns, perhaps some time later, to discuss problems individually. This could be one of a number of teachers who are involved in sex and HIV/AIDS education, in those schools favouring a more integrated approach to this work. Thus, it is crucial that insider(s) and outsider work in partnership to prepare and deliver this type of input. It is important that the right person addresses the seemingly illogical misconceptions such as those described here, since 'illogical' may easily be reinterpreted as 'wrong' or 'stupid'.

Ideally, young people should be allowed to explore their beliefs about risk in an environment which enables them to see for themselves the inconsistencies between their knowledge about HIV transmission and their perceptions of personal risk of infection, as well as the influences of emotions and trust within relationships upon rational judgements of risk. In the area of sexual activity, where so much is to be lost and gained in terms of reputation among one's peers, however, it is unrealistic to suppose that participants in a group discussion in most educational establishments would divulge the truth about their behaviour. Hopefully, the misconceptions and flawed arguments that are described above may be of use to teachers, and others involved in personal education to provide material for role-plays and discussions, following a session sharing information about routes of transmission. Personal misconceptions and doubts may then be the topic of individual or friendship group/pair sessions with the teacher or other facilitator on a more voluntary basis.

Of course, this may be more easy to organize within the more enlightened schools, colleges and training establishments than when people have begun their working career. Moreover, there is no reason to believe that the beliefs described here are exclusive to people between the ages of 16 and 25. Workers may be reluctant to attend sessions in their spare time, especially when they feel that AIDS does not concern them, and employers are reluctant to give paid time to employees to discuss a topic related to their private lives. They are, however, willing to release people to hear experts talk about their occupational risks of coming into contact with HIV. Some people we interviewed had quite rightly been trained by their employers to take care at work, e.g. when cleaning behind toilets in a pub, in case used needles were deposited there, but their knowledge of occupational risks in these cases tended to be counterbalanced by a dismissal of personal risk within their sexual relationships. It seems important therefore that such in-service training provides an opportunity for discussion also of sexual transmission.

Due to the small sample size (125 respondents interviewed in depth, of whom only those who had at some time had penetrative vaginal intercourse are considered here), generalizations according to factors such as age, gender, experience, sexual preference, ethnicity, living arrangements, marital status and social class have not been made. The role of qualitative research such as this is, however, to describe explanations and beliefs that may exist and not necessarily the prevalence of each category of explanation. The diversity of reasons described in this paper points to the importance of an *individual* approach to safer sex awareness training. As Warwick and Aggleton (1990) have pointed out, young people are by no means a homogenous group. They are neither universally ignorant about AIDS, nor are they universally irresponsible nor at high risk of coming into contact with HIV. Nonetheless, it is important to challenge the feelings of safety described by some individual young people and dispel some of the myths that are used to bolster such feelings. If these measures are not taken, it is likely that, as many of our respondents explained, people will not take notice until their friends and relations start to die.

Acknowledgements

Our thanks go to Belinda Bateman and Jeremy Braybrooke for conducting some of the interviews, and to Brenda Colwell for typing the interview transcripts. Thanks also to Professor Roy Davis for the use of interview rooms at Reading University, and to Dr Amina Memon and three anonymous reviewers for their comments on the manuscript. Particular thanks to all the respondents who shared so much of their lives and views with the interviewers, and to the people who helped us to contact those respondents in various organizations. The work was supported by the Economic and Social Research Council (grant no. XA44250012 to R.I.).

References

Abrams, D., Abraham, C., Spears, R. and Marks, D. (1990a) AIDS invulnerability: relationships, sexual behaviour and attitudes among 16–19-year-olds. In Aggleton, P., Davies, P. and Hart, G. (eds), *Aids: Individual, Cultural and Policy Dimensions.* Falmer Press, Basingstoke, pp. 35–52.

Abrams, D., Sheeran, P. and Abraham, C. (1990b) Social identity, normative context and vulnerability to HIV. Paper presented at *British Psychological Society Conference*, Swansea, UK, April 1990.

Aggleton, P., Homans, H. and Warwick, I. (1988) Young people, sexuality education and AIDS. *Youth and Policy*, **23**, 5–13.

Blaxter, M. (1989) Behaviour change in the context of HIV/AIDS. Paper prepared for ESRC steering group, unpublished.

Clift, S. and Stears, D. (1991) AIDS education in secondary schools. *Education and Health*, **9**, 1–4.

Clift, S., Stears, D. Legg, S., Memon, A. and Ryan, L. (1989) *Report on Phase One of the HIV/AIDS Education and Young People Project.* Christchurch College, Canterbury.

Cochran, S.D. (1989) Women and HIV infection. Issues in prevention and behaviour change. In Mays, V.M., Albee, G.W. and Schneider, S.F. (eds), *Primary Prevention of AIDS. Psychological Approaches.* Sage, London, pp. 309–327.

DiClemente, R.J., Zorn, J. and Temoshok, L. (1986) Adolescents and AIDS: A survey of knowledge, attitudes and beliefs about AIDS in San Francisco. *American Journal of Public Health: Public Health Briefs*, **76**, 1443–1445.

Fazal, N., Geall, J. and Pocock, R. (1990) *Do Young People Perceive Themselves Vulnerable to HIV Infection – and Have they Changed their Behaviour?* Report 90/04, Midland Environment Ltd, Birmingham.

Ford, N. and Bowie, C. (1989) Urban–rural variations in the level of heterosexual activity of young people. *Area*, **21**, 237–248.

Frankham, J. and Stronach, I. (1990) *Making a Drama out of a Crisis: An Evaluation of the Norfolk Action Against AIDS Health Education Play.* Centre for Applied Research in Education, University of East Anglia, Norwich.

Hastings, G.B., Leather, D.S. and Scott, A.C. (1987) AIDS publicity; some experiences from Scotland. *British Medical Journal*, **294**, 48–49.

Holland, J., Ramazanoglu, C., Scott, S., Sharpe, S. and Thomson, R. (1991) Between embarrassment and trust: Young women and the diversity of condom use. In Aggleton, P., Hart, G. and Davies, P. (eds), *AIDS: Responses, Interventions and Care.* Falmer Press, London, pp. 127–148.

Ingham, R., Woodcock, A. and Stenner, K. (1991a) Getting to know you.... Young people's knowledge of their partners at first intercourse. *Journal of Community and Applied Social Psychology,* **1,** 117–132.

Ingham, R., Woodcock, A. and Stenner, K. (1991b) The limitations of rational decision-making models as applied to young people's sexual behaviour. Paper presented at *5th Social Aspects of AIDS Conference,* South Bank Polytechnic, London.

Kirscht, J.P. and Joseph, J.G. (1989) The Health Belief Model: Some implications for behaviour change with reference to homosexual males. In Mays, V.M., Albee, G.W. and Schneider, S.F. (eds), *Primary Prevention of AIDS. Psychological Approaches,* Sage, London, pp. 111–127.

Lawrence, St, J.S. and Kelly, J.A. (1989) AIDS prevention: community and behavioural interventions. In Hersen, M., Eisler, R. and Miller, P. (eds), *Progress in Behaviour Modification.* Sage, London, vol. 24.

Lees, S. (1986) *Losing Out: Sexuality and Adolescent Girls.* London, Hutchinson.

MacDonald, G. and Smith, C. (1990) Complacency, risk perception and the problem of HIV education. *AIDS Care,* **2,** 63–68.

McKusick, L., Horstman, W. and Coates, T. (1985) AIDS and the sexual behaviour reported by gay men in San Francisco. *American Journal of Public Health,* **75,** 493–496.

Memon, A. (1990) Young people's knowledge, beliefs and attitudes about AIDS: a review of research. *Health Education Research: Theory and Practice,* **5,** 327–335.

Memon, A. (1991) Perceptions of AIDS vulnerability. The role of attributions and social context. In Aggleton, P., Hart, G. and Davies, P. (eds), *AIDS: Responses, Interventions and Care.* Falmer Press, London, pp. 157–168.

Perloff, L.S. and Fetzer, B. (1986) Self–other judgements and perceived vulnerability to victimisation. *Journal of Personality and Social Psychology,* **50,** 502–510.

Plant, M. (1990) Sex work, alcohol, drugs and AIDS. In Plant, M. (ed.), *AIDS, Drugs and Prostitution.* Routledge, London, pp. 1–17.

Price, J.H., Desmond, S. and Kukulka, G. (1985) High school students' perceptions and misperceptions of AIDS. *Journal of School Health,* **55,** 107–109.

Pocock, R., Simmons, S., Cross, G., Fazal, N. and Toolan, M. (1988) *AIDS and Young People: A Report to the West Midlands Regional Health Authority.* Midland Environment Ltd, Birmingham.

Rosenstock, I.M. (1974) The Health Belief Model and Preventive health behaviour. *Health Education Monographs,* **2,** 354–386.

Stockdale, J.E., Dockrell, J.F. and Wells, A.J. (1989) The self in relation to mass media representatives of HIV and AIDS – match or mismatch. *Health Education Journal,* **48,** 121–130.

Warwick, I. and Aggleton, P. (1990) 'Adolescents', young people and AIDS research. In Aggleton, P., Davies, P. and Hart, G. (eds), *AIDS: Individual, Cultural and Policy Dimensions.* Falmer Press, Basingstoke, pp. 89–102.

Weinstein, N.D. (1980) Unrealistic optimism about future life events. *Journal of Personality and Social Psychology,* **89,** 808–820.

Weinstein, N.D. (1984) Why it won't happen to me: perception of risk factors and susceptibility. *Health Psychology,* **3,** 431–457.

Weinstein, N.D. (1989) Perceptions of personal susceptibility to harm. In Mays, V.M., Albee, G.W. and Schneider, S.F. (eds), *Primary Prevention of AIDS. Psychological Approaches.* Sage, London, pp. 142–167.

Wight, D. (1990) *The Impact of HIV/AIDS on Young People's Heterosexual Behaviour in Britain: A Literature Review.* Working paper No. 20. MRC Medical Sociology Unit, Glasgow.

Wilton, T. and Aggleton, P. (1991) Condoms, coercion and control: Heterosexuality and the limits to HIV/AIDS education. In Aggleton, P., Hart, G. and Davies, P. (eds), *AIDS: Responses, Interventions and Care.* Falmer Press, London, pp. 149–156.

Changing behaviour

Health psychologists not only describe and explain behaviour, they also develop and inform interventions designed to change behaviour. To this end they take either individual constructs or complete models as a means to develop the intervention and evaluate its effectiveness. This section includes two papers concerned with changing behaviour:

Aiken, L.S., West, S.G., Woodward, C.K. et al. (1994) Increasing screening mammography in asymptomatic women: evaluation of a second-generation, theory-based program, *Health Psychology*, 13 (16): 526–38. Reprinted with kind permission of the American Psychological Association.

Gollwitzer, P.M. and Sheeran, P. (2006) Implementation intentions and goal achievement: a meta-analysis of effects and processes, *Advances in Experimental Social Psychology*, 38: 69–119. Reprinted with kind permission of Elsevier.

Aiken et al. (1994) carried out an evaluation of two programmes designed to increase mammography screening rates among women without any breast cancer-related symptoms. The first was based upon the health belief model (HBM) and was designed to increase women's perceptions of their susceptibility to breast cancer, the severity of breast cancer and their perceptions of the benefits of the screening programmes, while decreasing their perceptions of the costs of the programme. The programme was essentially an educational programme and included information about factors such as the prevalence of breast cancer, the risk factors for breast cancer, how it can be detected and the benefits of early detection in terms of survival rates. The second programme was essentially the same as the first but included exercises focused upon compliance such as role playing, asking a doctor for a mammogram, describing and rehearsing the steps required to get a mammogram and writing down a personal commitment to telephone and organise a mammogram. The effectiveness of these theory-based interventions was evaluated against a control group. The results showed that both interventions improved screening uptake rates compared to the control group. This paper includes many of the features of a good randomised control trial as the sample is large and the outcome data are based upon actual attendance. It also presents a good example of how theory can be used to inform an intervention in a clinical setting. The paper describes the intervention well and highlights the different components of the HBM. There is much debate within current health psychology about the importance of theory in developing interventions. It is argued, however, that many interventions are either theory free, or that the theoretical framework is implicit and unclear. This paper provides a good template for how theory can be turned into practice.

Aiken et al. (1994) is therefore a single study that makes an incremental contribution to the literature. At times, however, different research studies need to be synthesised so that overall effects can be explored. Gollwitzer and Sheeran (2006) provide a meta-analysis of the impact of implementation intentions on goal achievement as a means to see the extent to which implementation can be considered effective. Implementation intentions involve a brief intervention whereby the participant spells out the 'when', 'where' and 'how' of a particular behaviour. They have been used to promote a range of health behaviours including snacking, smoking, binge drinking and exercise, as well as other behaviours unrelated to health such as study, performance tasks and returning a postcard. This meta-analysis involved an analysis of 94 independent tests and concluded that implementation intentions have a positive effect on goal attainment. This paper provides an answer to a question currently central to much of health (and social) psychology and illustrates how behaviours can be changed. The paper also provides a clear example of the process of meta-analysis in terms of how the studies were identified, how the effect sizes were calculated and how these were synthesised to produce the final effect size. This paper also offers an excellent and comprehensive review of the implementations intentions literature. Therefore, though detailed and long, this paper is worth reading as a good example of a methodological approach which has up until recently existed mainly within medicine but is becoming increasingly relevant for health psychology.

Papers within this section should therefore provide insights into the theoretical debates surrounding health behaviours, and are excellent examples of good research designed to predict, explain and change behaviour.

Aiken, L.S., West, S.G., Woodward, C.K. et al. (1994) Increasing screening mammography in asymptomatic women: evaluation of a second-generation, theory-based program, *Health Psychology*, 13 (6): 526–38.

Increasing screening mammography in asymptomatic women

Evaluation of a second-generation, theory-based program

Leona S. Aiken, Stephen G. West, Claudia K. Woodward, Raymond R. Reno, and Kim D. Reynolds

Leona S. Aiken and Stephen G. West, Arizona State University; Claudia K. Woodward, University of Miami; Raymond R. Reno, University of Notre Dame; Kim D. Reynolds, University of Alabama, Birmingham.

Abstract

Two theory-based programs to increase mammography screening rates among asymptomatic women were implemented and evaluated in the community. One program (E) was based on the Health Belief Model (HBM); the second program (EP) added exercises adapted from the social psychology of compliance. Program impact on screening among 295 primarily Caucasian, middle-class women was evaluated against untreated controls (C) over a 6-month period. Both programs led to increases in HBM components (Perceived Susceptibility, and Perceived Benefits) and Intentions to obtain a mammogram. Screening rates 2 to 3 times higher were observed in the EP and E over C conditions; EP and E did not differ. A mediational model of compliance illustrated the interplay of HBM components in the compliance process.

Keywords: mammography screening intervention, health belief model, mediation of intervention effects

This article reports the results of an evaluation of the second generation of two theory-based interventions conducted to increase mammography screening rates in a community sample of asymptomatic women. The interventions were carried out in a large metropolitan area during 1987–1989, a time when relatively few eligible women received regular screening mammograms. One intervention was based on the Health Belief Model (HBM; Becker & Maiman, 1975); the second intervention added exercises adapted from the social psychology of

This research was supported by National Cancer Institute Grant R03 CA46736 to Leona S. Aiken, Steven G. West, and Kim D. Reynolds. We also acknowledge the support of the Office of the Dean, College of Liberal Arts and Sciences, Arizona State University. Consultation by Robert B. Cialdini, Darwyn E. Linder, and Carol D. Silver on program design is gratefully acknowledged.

Correspondence concerning this article should be addressed to Leona S. Aiken, Department of Psychology, Arizona State University, Box 871104, Tempe, Arizona 85287-1104.

compliance (Cialdini, 1984). The focus of these community-based programs was to induce women to obtain mammography screening in accordance with the guidelines of the American Cancer Society (ACS) and the National Cancer Institute (NCI) at that time: (a) a baseline mammogram between ages 35 and 39, (b) a mammogram every year or two according to physician recommendation between ages 40 and 49, and (c) a yearly mammogram beginning at age 50 (American Cancer Society, 1988).

The low levels of mammography screening at the time presented a serious health compliance problem. The National Health Interview Survey Supplement on Cancer Control gathered in early 1987 showed that 31% of women 40 years of age and older had ever had a mammogram; only 17% had had a screening mammogram within the past year ("Provisional Estimates," 1988). Although screening rates increased over the 1987–1990 period, only 31% of women aged 40 and older in 1990 were in compliance with ACS guidelines ("Use of Mammography," 1990). Only 25% to 42% of women 50 years of age and older had had more than one mammogram (National Cancer Institute Breast Screening Consortium, 1990), falling far short of the NCI's goals for screening by the year 2000 (Greenwald & Sondik, 1986).

Correlates of mammography screening suggested two possible targets for an intervention: physicians and women themselves. The strongest single correlate of whether women have had mammograms is whether their physicians have recommended mammograms (e.g., Fox, Murata, & Stein, 1991; Lerman, Rimer, Trock, Balshem, & Engstrom, 1990). However, not all physicians recommend mammography screening according to current guidelines (Turner et al., 1992), and even when physicians refer women for screening, not all women follow these recommendations. For example, Fox et al. (1991) reported that 48% of women aged 50–64 and 56% of women aged 65 and older whose physicians had encouraged mammography were not in compliance with ACS guidelines. Bastani, Marcus, and Hollatz-Brown (1991) pointed out that women who have never had a mammogram were less likely to agree that they would get a mammogram in accordance with their physician's recommendation than women who have had a mammogram. Physician input, although a powerful factor in inducing compliance, by no means guarantees that women will obtain screening.

Women's health beliefs about breast cancer and mammography are associated with compliance with screening recommendations (Aiken, West, Woodward, & Reno, 1994; Champion, 1992; Rutledge, Hartmann, Kinman, & Winfield, 1988; Stein, Fox, Murata, & Morisky, 1992), lending credence to the potential effectiveness of health-belief-oriented interventions with women themselves. According to the HBM (Janz & Becker, 1984), a woman will undertake mammography screening if she perceives herself to be susceptible to breast cancer (Perceived Susceptibility), perceives the consequences of breast cancer to be severe (Perceived Severity), perceives that there are strong benefits of mammography screening for lessening the threat or impact of breast cancer (Perceived Benefits), and perceives the barriers to obtaining a mammogram as relatively low (Perceived Barriers; Becker & Maiman, 1975). Aiken et al. (1994) found that the HBM accounted for 16% of the variance in current compliance with ACS screening guidelines in a community sample of 615 women. Even when physicians' recommendations, demographics, objective risk for breast cancer, and knowledge of breast cancer and mammography were all statistically controlled, the HBM still accounted for an additional 7% of the variance in current compliance.

Reynolds, West, and Aiken (1990) developed and evaluated two pilot programs targeted at women to increase mammography screening. In contrast to most previous interventions (see review by Vernon, Laville, & Jackson, 1990), the interventions by Reynolds et al. (1990) targeted women in existing community groups rather than through their workplace or HMO. In addition, they directed women to obtain mammograms through their physicians or through a relatively low-cost screening program available in the metropolitan area rather than providing them with free mammograms at the program site. These differences presented women with substantially greater barriers of cost and effort in obtaining a mammogram than in previous research, yet these barriers are ones that realistically exist for many women. The pilot interventions by Reynolds et al. (1990) led to increased knowledge of breast cancer and mammography, greater perceived benefits of mammography, and greater intention to obtain a mammogram. However, there was no increase in mammography screening during a 3-month follow-up period.

Program design

The present, second-generation programs are a revision of the original Reynolds et al. (1990) interventions; they are based on the results of the process and outcome evaluations of the pilot study, as well as theory and research in both health psychology and social psychology. We developed two programs that were targeted at changing health beliefs in service of increasing screening. Specifically, we designed these programs to increase women's perceptions of their Susceptibility to breast cancer, the Severity of breast cancer, and the Benefits of mammography screening while decreasing perceived Barriers to screening. The Educational Program (E) contained components that specifically targeted the four constructs of the HBM. The second program, the Educational Plus Psychological Program (EP), contained the complete E program. We supplemented this information with a series of compliance exercises drawn from the social psychological literature. Several reviews have suggested that educational programs often produce changes in knowledge but no corresponding changes in health behavior unless additional steps are taken to link changes in beliefs to behavior (Flay, 1985; Leventhal, Meyer, & Guttman, 1980; West, Reich, McCall, & Dantchik, 1989).

Mediation of program effects

Because the educational content of the two programs was identical[1] and was based on the four components of the HBM, we were able to probe the contribution of these components to screening outcomes in a mediational analysis (Baron & Kenny, 1986; West, Aiken, & Todd, 1993). Most research involving the HBM treats the four components as equal predictors of health behavior (Rosenstock, 1990). In contrast, Ronis (1992) proposed a model in which the HBM components follow a specific causal sequence: Perceived Susceptibility and Perceived Severity lead to Perceived Benefits; Perceived Benefits and Perceived Barriers, in turn, lead to health behavior. Ronis found support for this model, with Perceived Benefits providing partial mediation of the relation between Perceived Susceptibility and Perceived Severity and behavior. We tested this hypothesized mediational structure here. In addition, the HBM as typically stated does not include Intentions to perform a behavior as a mediational link between health beliefs and health behavior. Drawing on the theory of reasoned action (Ajzen & Fishbein, 1980), we included Intentions to obtain a mammogram as a link between health beliefs and compliance in the months following the program, and explored whether Perceived Barriers had a direct effect on compliance or had an indirect effect through Intentions to comply.

---

1 A content analysis of the two programs showed that the compliance exercises of the EP program did not provide any mammography-related information beyond that contained in the E program.

Method

Subjects and recruitment

The targets of the intervention were women's community groups in the Phoenix metropolitan area, identified through lists of community organizations and through networking among women's organizations. During the recruitment process we explained our intent to gather data and to present a program on breast cancer and mammography. Invitations to participate in the study were proffered to 253 women's groups, of which 44 participated. The participating groups included 12 (27%) religious, 11 (25%) business and professional, 12 (27%) social, and 9 (20%) educational-political-service organizations. Nonparticipating groups were 27% religious, 20% business and professional, 29% social, 20% educational-political-service, and 4% other (e.g., hobby), indicating fairly even responsiveness to our solicitation across categories of women's groups. In all, 19 of the 44 participating groups were chapters of organizations of which other chapters in the metropolitan area had declined our invitation to participate, reflecting similarity of mission between groups that did and did not participate. The most frequently given reason for nonparticipation was that program schedules were filled for the data-collection period; several groups indicated that their highly specialized mission (e.g., gardening) or their format (e.g., both genders as members) did not permit participation.

Across the 44 participating groups there were 615 women aged 35 and above; these are the same women described by Aiken et al. (1994). Of these women, 348, or 56%, were not in compliance with the ACS guidelines for mammography screening at the point of the pretest and had never been diagnosed as having breast cancer. Of these 348 women, the 295 women between the ages of 35 and 74 are represented in the outcome evaluation reported here. They were on average 52.8 years of age ($SD=11.5$), Caucasian (97%), and married (64%). In all, 30% had completed some college, and another 40% had at least a bachelor's degree. Their median total family income fell between $30,000 and $40,000 (see also Aiken et al., 1994).

Design

Two intervention groups were defined by the presentation of the EP versus the E program; participants completed the pretest, viewed one of the programs, and then received an immediate posttest. They were interviewed 3 months later and then again 6 months following program presentation. In the control condition (C), participants completed the same pretest questionnaire as in the EP and E conditions but received neither a program nor the immediate posttest questionnaire, and they were re-interviewed on the same schedule as were the two intervention groups. Data collection from groups in the three conditions was equally spread over the 20-month enrollment and data collection period.

Assignment of community groups to conditions

Assignment to condition was by community group in a trickle flow process. During recruitment we explained to all groups that we were using two schedules for gathering data and presenting the program: Schedule 1 was all data collection and program presentation in one session, and Schedule 2 was brief data collection followed by a delayed program presentation 6 months after the initial data collection. We used Schedule 1 in fact for the EP and E conditions, whereas we used Schedule 2 for the C condition (allowing presentation of a delayed payback program following collection of the 6-month follow-up data). Those 11 groups that agreed to accept either schedule were randomly assigned to condition (EP, E, or C). The remaining 33 groups had scheduling constraints that precluded their accepting either schedule and thereby being fully randomly assigned. For these 33 groups, we used a modified quasi-experimental assignment method in which we randomly assigned groups opting for Schedule 1 to either the E or EP conditions, whereas those opting for Schedule 2 served as quasi-experimental controls. Note that all groups recruited had agreed both to provide data and to receive a program presentation. They were also unaware that there was more than one intervention program and that their selection of schedule would partially determine their assignment to conditions within the design. This assignment method eliminated any possible selection bias associated with differential attractiveness of the programs.

We assigned 16, 13, and 15 groups to the EP, E, and C conditions respectively; out of these, 4 groups in the EP condition, 3 groups in the E condition, and 4 groups in the C condition were completely randomly assigned. There were 101, 81, and 113 women in EP, E, and C, respectively. The distribution of type of group (e.g., social or business and professional) was approximately even across the three conditions.

Sociodemographics of women in the three conditions are reported in Table 1. Women in the three conditions did not differ in annual family income, educational level, ethnicity, or marital status. However, those in the E condition were older than those in the C condition, $F(2, 292) = 3.89$, $p < 0.05$, $\eta 2 = 0.03$. Finally, 27%, 32%, and 39% of women in EP, E, and C had ever had a previous mammogram, $\chi^2(2, N = 295) = 3.63$, $p > 0.10$.

Program interventions

Educational Program (E). Several studies have suggested that women misperceive risk factors related to susceptibility to breast cancer (Burg, Lane, & Polednak, 1990; Johnson, Aiken, & Luckett, 1993; Payne, 1990) and the benefits of mammography screening (Rimer, Keintz, Kessler, Engstrom, & Rosan, 1989; Zapka, Stoddard, Costanza, & Greene, 1989). To increase Perceived Susceptibility, we provided information about the prevalence rates and risk factors

Table 1 Sociodemographics of the three conditions

Variable	EP	E	C	Test of difference
n	101	81	113	–
Age	–	–	–	$F(2, 294) = 3.89*$
M	52.34	55.68	51.15	–
SD	11.37	11.61	11.13	–
Income category[a]	–	–	–	$F(2, 257) = 2.14$
M	4.53	4.78	4.07	–
SD	2.43	2.35	2.06	–
Highest education category[b]	–	–	–	$F(2, 287) = 1.03$
M	5.13	5.20	5.41	–
SD	1.55	1.56	1.35	–
% Caucasian	97	100	94	$\chi^2(2, N = 292) = 5.50$
% married	69	70	56	$\chi^2(2, N = 289) = 5.27$
% ever had mammogram	27	32	39	$\chi^2(2, N = 295) = 3.63$

EP = Educational Plus Psychological Program; E = Educational Program; C = control condition.
[a] Income categories: (1) ≤ $10,000; (2) $10,001 – $20,000; (3) $30,001 – $40,000; (4) $40,001 – $50,000; (5) $50,001 – $60,000; (6) $60,001 – $70,000; (7) $70,001 – $80,000; (8) > $80,000.
[b] Education categories: (1) grade school; (2) some high school; (3) high school graduate; (4) technical school; (5) some college, AA degree; (6) college graduate (bachelor's degree); (7) some graduate school or graduate degree.
*$p < 0.05$.

for breast cancer, including increasing age and family or personal history of breast cancer. In line with the HBM, we attempted to increase Perceived Severity of late-detected breast cancer by describing the pathological course of breast cancer and distinguishing between early-detected localized versus late-detected, metastatic breast cancer. We also gave survival rates for early- versus late-detected breast cancer. To increase Perceived Benefits of mammography screening, we explained the advantages of early detection for treatment of breast cancer, including having the option of lumpectomy as an alternative to more radical surgery and, most importantly, reduction in breast cancer mortality. We emphasized the effectiveness of mammography screening for early detection, particularly the decrease in breast cancer mortality associated with regular screening. To decrease Perceived Barriers, we reviewed the minimal nature of radiation risks associated with mammography screening, pointed out the availability of low-cost mammograms ($50), and provided a slide presentation of a woman getting a mammogram. We outlined options for obtaining a mammogram. A slide presentation of the important facts accompanied the program presentation.

Educational Plus Psychological Program (EP). The EP program added five compliance manipulations drawn from the social psychological literature to the E program. The compliance exercises were as follows:

1 The program presenter gave counterarguments or refutations of arguments against mammography screening (McGuire, 1985). We included this exercise to help immunize newly acquired pro-mammography beliefs against negative information that might be presented by other sources.

2 The program presenter and an assistant modeled the desired behavior of the woman telling her physician she wanted to be referred for a mammogram (Bandura, 1977).

3 The women enumerated in writing the steps they would take to obtain a mammogram, increasing the cognitive availability of these steps and hence the probability of the occurrence of the behavior (Tversky & Kahneman, 1973; see also Gregory, Cialdini, & Carpenter, 1982; Leventhal, 1970).

4 Women wrote a personal commitment to telephone within the next 2 weeks to make an appointment to obtain a mammogram. Theoretically, people behave in accordance with a consistency principle in which they modify their behavior so it is consistent with their public expressions of intent to behave in a particular fashion (Cialdini, 1984; Kiesler, 1969; Sensenig & Cialdini, 1984).

5 A cue to action (e.g., a symptom or a reminder notice) theoretically will trigger a person to take a health action, given that health beliefs are favorable to that action[2] (Larsen, Olsen, & Cole, 1979). Women had written their enumeration of steps and personal commitments on special paper with second carbon sheets. Three weeks following the program, we mailed the carbon sheets to participants, along with a letter reminding them of their commitment to inquire about obtaining a mammogram and a pack of Post-it notes on which was printed "Stick to your commitment, get a mammogram."

---

2 Cues to action is one of the constructs proposed in the original statements of the HBM (e.g., Becker & Maiman, 1975). However, this construct has received little research attention relative to other constructs of the HBM.

Process evaluation

We used a process evaluation to monitor how well the programs were implemented in the field. A trained observer monitored every program, evaluating the extent to which the presenter stated each of 38 critical facts identified in a content analysis of the educational portion of the program and the extent to which the presenter adequately implemented each of the psychological compliance exercises.

Questionnaires

Pretest. The pretest questionnaire, administered to all participants, was described in detail by Aiken et al. (1994). All scales were developed based on psychometric examination and revision of items previously used by Reynolds et al. (1990). The questionnaire covered demographics, mammography screening history, breast-related medical history, and family history of breast cancer. An eight-item scale assessed knowledge of breast cancer and mammography. We assessed each of the four components of the HBM with a set of 6-point Likert scale items; there were four items per component except Perceived Severity, with five items. Four 6-point Likert scale items assessed Intentions to obtain a mammogram within the next 3 months.

Confirmatory factor analysis, applied to the 17 HBM items plus 4 Intentions items confirmed an adequately fitting, five-construct measurement model of the four HBM components plus Intentions, $\chi^2(179, N=280)=401.6$, Bentler-Bonett normed fit index$=0.91$ (fit indices above 0.90 reflect acceptable fit, Bentler & Bonett, 1980). Loadings of all items on their respective constructs were significant ($p<0.001$ in all cases). Internal consistency reliabilities (coefficient α) of the five scales over the 295 women in the intervention were as follows: Susceptibility, 0.93; Severity, 0.92; Benefits, 0.88; Barriers, 0.23; and Intentions, 0.90. The low internal consistency of the Barriers scale resulted from the diverse set of barriers, including cost, fear of radiation, inconvenience, and ability to talk to one's physician about mammography.

Posttest. The posttest questionnaire, given to the EP and E groups immediately following the program, reassessed knowledge, the four HBM components, and Intentions to obtain a mammogram, with scales identical to corresponding pretest scales. Tracing information was also gathered so that women could be re-interviewed. Because we could not feasibly collect an immediate posttest measure in the C condition, we functionally treated the pretest measure in this condition as the posttest measure in the outcome analyses.

Three-month follow-up. The 3-month questionnaire assessed a series of graded Steps to Compliance, that is, steps toward obtaining a mammogram: (0) taking no action whatever, (1) contacting a physician or health organization about mammography, (2) discussing having a mammogram with a health provider, (3) making an appointment for a mammogram, and (4) obtaining a mammogram. A binary measure of compliance, whether or not the woman had obtained a mammogram, was also derived from the 3-month follow-up.

Six-month follow-up. Once again, the graded series of Steps to Compliance was assessed.

Procedure

We conducted all data collection and program presentation at regular meetings of the community groups. Intervention sessions (EP and E) were administered by trained health educators, who first invited all women to participate in the pretest. We assured confidentiality and obtained written informed consent; local and NCI internal review groups had reviewed all forms and procedures. Following the pretest, we administered the program and then asked women to provide the posttest measure plus tracing information for a telephone follow-up. Pretest data collection in the C group followed the same procedures as in the E and EP groups.

Follow-up interviews were administered by telephone. Women who obtained a mammogram during the 3-month period following the initial data collection were not re-interviewed at 6 months. Of the 295 women, 221 were re-interviewed at 3 months (75% completion rate). Of these 221 women, 174 had not obtained mammograms; 155 were eligible for re-interview at 6 months[3]; 76% completed 6-month interviews. Reasons for attrition are provided below.

Verification of mammography self-reports

A central service that referred women to major hospitals and mammography facilities throughout the metropolitan area for mammography screening provided verification of self-reported mammography screening. Eleven women reported using this organization to obtain mammograms; all these self-reported mammograms were corroborated by facility records. This represented 16% of all mammograms obtained during the study. There was no correlation between the use of this referral service versus other mammography facilities and age, income, education, ethnic identity, or marital status.

Scale creation and dependent measures

We created scale scores for each pretest HBM component and pretest intentions to obtain a mammogram by converting each item of the scale to z scores and taking the mean of the z scores. We standardized posttest scores on these scales by applying the pretest mean and standard deviation to the posttest data, yielding pretest and posttest standardized scores calculated on the same basis and permitting the detection of any change between the two measurement points. We allowed one missing response per scale. Knowledge scores were the proportion correct of the eight knowledge items. Dependent variables derived from the 3-month follow-up included Steps to Compliance and the binary Compliance measure. The four Steps to Compliance (Steps 1 to 4 described above) were shown to follow a Guttman scale (Torgerson, 1958), with 93% of women's response patterns to the graded steps following the order assumed for the scale. We computed analogous compliance measures from the 6-month interview; these measures reflected mammography-related behavior over the entire 6-month follow-up period.

Results
Process evaluation

The process evaluation showed that the E portion of the program was well implemented, with an average of 98.9% of the 38 critical program facts being presented. The process evaluator rated the P program exercises as being generally well implemented: On a 7-point scale where 7 represented *very well implemented,* the modeling segment received the highest mean rating (6.6), and the commitment exercise received the lowest mean rating (5.4). The actual written exercise sheets of EP participants were coded for compliance with instructions. In the exercise requiring participants to enumerate the steps involved in calling a doctor for a mammogram, 82% complied with the instruction to list a day during the next 2 weeks when they would telephone, and 61% followed the instruction to indicate the name of the physician, facility, or

---

3 Some control subjects received the delayed program presentation prior to completion of their 6-month interview, eliminating 19 women from eligibility for re-interview as control subjects at the 6-month follow-up point.

HMO they would call. However, participants were far less willing to write a personal commitment to themselves to make an appointment for a mammogram within the next 2 weeks. Only a third wrote a definite commitment, another 13% promised to take some action about mammography, 8% to contact their doctor, and 9% to call a physician sometime in the future.

Analysis of individuals versus groups

Because data had been gathered from intact community groups, significant clustering of outcomes within groups could potentially lead to positive bias in tests of significance based on individual cases (Barcikowski, 1981). We examined these potential clustering effects for each continuous outcome variable. Within each condition, we computed a series of one-way analyses of variance (ANOVAs) with community group as the independent variable and continuous outcome variables (Knowledge, four HBM scales, Intentions to comply, and Steps to Compliance) as the dependent variables. In only 1 of the 21 comparisons (7 scales within each of 3 conditions) did we detect a tendency to differences among community groups within an experimental condition at $p < 0.10$; this was for Knowledge across groups within the EP condition at posttest, $F(15, 82) = 1.59$, $p = 0.09$. We also examined compliance at 3-month follow-up for clustering effects associated with community-group membership. There was no association between group membership and compliance within any of the three conditions, $\chi^2(15, N=78) = 8.87$, $p = 0.88$; $\chi^2(12, N=58) = 15.88$, $p = 0.20$; $\chi^2(14, N=85) = 7.11$, $p = 0.93$, for EP, E, and C, respectively. Because we wished the unit of generalization to be the individual woman, and because we had found no clustering effects, analyses carried out with the individual as unit of analysis are reported here. We performed all analyses again with the 44 groups as units of analysis with the same results.

Pretest measures

Means of pretest measures for the three conditions are given in Table 2. The three conditions did not differ in Knowledge, or any of the four HBM components at pretest. However, the C condition reported significantly lower Intentions to obtain a mammogram at pretest, $F(2, 272) = 5.36$, $p < 0.01$, $\eta2 = 0.04$. Sociodemographic comparisons of the three conditions were previously presented in Table 1.

Immediate posttest measures

One-way ANOVAs comparing EP, E, and C. We performed a series of one-way ANOVAs, followed by Tukey tests to probe the source of significant overall effects of Condition. We carried out the analysis on the immediate Posttest scores of EP and E versus the Pretest scores of C because only the pretest measure had been gathered on the C group. Posttest means are given in Table 2. Posttest means of both E and EP were significantly higher than the pretest mean of C on Knowledge, $F(2, 279) = 119.60$, $p < 0.001$, $\eta2 = 0.46$; Susceptibility, $F(2, 284) = 12.91$, $p < 0.001$, $\eta2 = 0.08$; and Benefits, $F(2, 281) = 11.97$, $p < 0.001$, $\eta2 = 0.08$. There was no difference among Conditions in Perceived Barriers, $F < 1$. Although the overall test of differences among Conditions on Severity (posttest EP and E versus pretest C) reached significance, $F(2, 278) = 3.00$, $p = 0.05$, no pair of groups differed by Tukey test. Finally, both E and EP had higher posttest means than pretest C on Intention to obtain a mammogram, $F(2, 264) = 35.85$, $p < 0.001$. The difference between EP and E versus C in Intentions was substantially larger at posttest, $\eta2 = 0.21$, than it had been at pretest, $\eta2 = 0.04$. We also repeated all analyses as analyses of covariance (ANCOVAs), controlling for age, income, education, and marital status. The results remained

Table 2 Pretest and posttest means on knowledge, health belief components, and intentions to comply and analysis of outcomes in the EP and E conditions

Scale		Cell means by condition				F tests in two-factor analysis[c]			
		EP (n=101)	E (n=81)	C (n=113)		df[d]	Condition (EP, E)	Time (Pretest – Posttest)	Interaction (Condition × Time)
Knowledge[a]	Pre	0.58	0.59	0.57	ANOVA	1,166	0.01	340.51***	1.11
	Post	0.87	0.85	–	ANCOVA	1,143	1.90	318.00***	2.14
Health belief components									
Susceptibility[b]	Pre	2.37	2.69	2.35	ANOVA	1,172	4.93*	63.46***	0.13
	Post	2.83	3.24	–	ANCOVA	1,144	3.69	53.75***	0.08
Severity[b]	Pre	4.04	3.76	4.22	ANOVA	1,168	2.74	1.55	3.68
	Post	4.20	3.75	–	ANCOVA	1,144	2.00	1.00	3.56
Benefits[b]	Pre	4.86	4.66	4.63	ANOVA	1,170	1.84	52.87***	0.21
	Post	5.33	5.19	–	ANCOVA	1,144	2.15	48.91***	0.39
Barriers[b]	Pre	2.21	2.14	2.11	ANOVA	1,169	0.18	6.67*	0.35
	Post	2.03	2.02	–	ANCOVA	1,148	0.00	8.23**	0.12
Intentions[b]	Pre	3.48	3.45	2.88	ANOVA	1,154	1.46	96.87***	5.29*
	Post	4.51	4.04	–	ANCOVA	1,131	1.88	80.47***	5.37*

Note. Percentage of missing data was on average 3.7% for pretest scales and 4.7% for posttest scales. EP=Educational Plus Psychological Program; E=Educational Program; C=control condition; ANOVA=analysis of variance; ANCOVA=analysis of covariance.
[a]Score is proportion correct of eight items. [b]Score is mean on 6-point Likert scale. [c]F values in ANOVA and ANCOVA of Condition (EP, E) by Time (Pretest – Posttest). [d]Degrees of freedom for the three tests of each ANOVA are constant for each dependent variable. The decreased degrees of freedom for the ANCOVAs is due to missing demographic information, typically income.
*$p \le 0.05$. **$p \le 0.01$. ***$p \le 0.001$.

the same: $F(2, 241) = 126.01$, $F(2, 244) = 9.42$, $F(2, 244) = 9.80$, $F(2, 229) = 30.46$, for Knowledge, Susceptibility, Benefits, and Intentions, respectively ($p < 0.001$ in all cases).

Two-way repeated measures ANOVAs comparing EP and E. To provide a more powerful comparison of the changes over time in the E and EP conditions, we conducted a series of two-factor repeated measures ANOVAs of Condition (EP and E) × Time (pretest and posttest). Results of these ANOVAs are given in Table 2. Both Conditions showed a significant increase from pretest to posttest in Knowledge, in the perception of Susceptibility to breast cancer, in the Benefits of mammography screening, and in Intentions to obtain a mammogram, with a significant decline in Barriers to screening. For Intentions, the significant Condition × Time interaction reflected greater gain in Intentions to comply in the EP than the E condition. The significant decline in the Barriers scale was obtained on two of the four Barriers items: inconvenience versus convenience of obtaining a mammogram, $F(1, 167) = 4.73$, $p < 0.05$, and ineffectiveness versus effectiveness of speaking to a health care provider about mammography screening, $F(1, 167) = 7.38$, $p < 0.01$. ANCOVAs with age, income, education, and marital status controlled once again did not alter the results (see Table 2).

Compliance rates

Three-month follow-up. Table 3 shows compliance rates for the 221 women aged 35 to 74 who were re-interviewed at 3 months and for the subset of 180 women in the sample between the ages of 40 and 74. Of all women 35 to 74 years of age, 29% and 28% of women in the EP and E conditions respectively, versus 9% of women in C had obtained mammograms ($p < 0.01$).

Table 3 Analysis of compliance rates by condition at 3-month follow-up

Age (years)	EP	E	C	Chi-square
35 – 74 (n = 221)				
%	29.5	27.6	9.4	$\chi^2(2, N = 221) = 11.67$
n	78	58	85	(p < 0.01)
40 – 74 (n = 180)				
%	33.8	29.8	10.3	$\chi^2(2, N = 180) = 11.36$
n	65	47	68	(p < 0.01)

Note. For women 35 – 74 years of age, for EP versus C and E versus C, $\chi^2(1, n = 163) = 10.64$, p < 0.01, and $\chi^2(1, n = 143) = 8.15$, p < 0.01, respectively. For women 40 – 74 years of age, for EP versus C and E versus C, $\chi^2(1, n = 133) = 10.81$, p < 0.01, and $\chi^2(1, n = 115) = 7.06$, p < 0.01, respectively. EP = Educational Plus Psychological Program; E = Educational Program; C = control condition.

Each of the intervention conditions – which did not themselves differ – had higher compliance rates than did controls (ps < 0.01). We obtained similar results when we considered women 40 to 74, with compliance rates being 34%, 30%, and 10%, for EP, E, and C, respectively. Compliance rates differed significantly among Conditions (p < 0.01), specifically between each intervention condition and controls (ps < 0.01).

The continuous measure of Steps to Compliance showed similar results at the three-month follow-up. The mean number of Steps to Compliance was 1.53, 1.55, and 0.66 in the E, EP, and C conditions, respectively, $F(2, 218) = 7.90$, p > 0.001.

Six-month follow-up. We computed cumulative compliance rates by the 6-month interview using two different assumptions about the nature of attrition between 3 and 6 months. First, we computed compliance rates making the conservative assumption that none of the participants who had been lost between the 3 and 6-month interviews had obtained a mammogram, (Compliance – Conservative Estimate). Second, we computed compliance rates based only on women who were retained in the study, (Compliance – MAR Estimate). This latter method assumes that participants who were lost at follow-up were screened at the same rate as those who remained in the program, that is, were missing at random (MAR; Rubin, 1976). These compliance rates are given in Table 4 for women 35–74 and for women 40–74. For women aged 35–74 years, the Compliance – Conservative Estimate was 35%, 39%, and 18% in EP, E, and C, respectively (p < 0.01), with both intervention groups exceeding controls (p < 0.05). The corresponding Compliance – MAR Estimate was 42%, 49%, and 21% in EP, E, and C, respectively (p < 0.01), with both EP and E exceeding C (p < 0.01). For women 40–74, the Compliance – Conservative Estimate was 41%, 42%, and 17%, respectively (p < 0.01). The Compliance – MAR Estimate was 49%, 49%, and 20% (p < 0.01). Regardless of the assumptions made about attrition, rates in both intervention groups exceeded those of controls, as reported in Table 4.

Compliance controlling for pretest differences

The design of the present study was quasi-experimental because only one fourth of the community groups could be completely randomly assigned to treatment conditions. Following Cook and Campbell (1979) and Higginbotham, West, and Forsyth (1988), we probed whether treatment effects remained significant after controlling for possible pretest differences among the treatment conditions. We carried out logistic regression analyses predicting compliance from the intervention condition, while controlling for pretest measures (Hosmer & Lemeshow, 1989). We used two a priori contrasts, each with one degree of freedom, to represent the differences among treatment conditions: (a) Intervention contrasted the two intervention conditions (each coded + 1) with controls (coded –2); (b) EP vs. E contrasted the two experimental groups

Table 4 Analysis of cumulative compliance rates by condition at 6-month follow-up

Age (years)	EP	E	C	
Compliance – Conservative Estimate				
35 – 74 (*n* = 204)				
%	35.1	39.0	17.6	$\chi^2(2, N=204)=8.07$
n	77	59	68	($p<0.05$)
40 – 74 (*n* = 166)				
%	40.6	41.7	16.7	$\chi^2(2, N=166)=9.81$
n	64	48	54	(p<0.01)
Compliance – MAR Estimate				
35 – 74 (*n* = 168)				
%	42.2	48.9	21.1	$\chi^2(2, N=168)=9.84$
n	64	47	57	($p<0.01$)
40 – 74 (*n* = 139)				
%	49.1	48.8	20.0	$\chi^2(2, N=139)=10.66$
n	53	41	45	($p<0.01$)

Note. For conservative estimates for women 35 – 74 years of age, for EP versus C and E versus C, χ^2 (1, $N=145$)=5.57, $p<0.05$, and $\chi^2(1, N=127)=7.20$, $p<0.01$, respectively.

For missing at random (MAR) estimates for women 35 – 74 years of age, for EP versus C and E versus C, $\chi^2(1, N=121)=6.17$, $p<0.05$, and $\chi^2(1, N=104)=8.97$, $p<0.01$, respectively.

For conservative estimates for women 40 – 74 years of age, for EP versus C and E versus C, $\chi^2(1, N=118)=8.06$, $p<0.01$, and $\chi^2(1, N=102)=7.81$, $p<0.01$, respectively.

For MAR estimates for women 40 – 74 years of age, for EP versus C and E versus C, $\chi^2(1, 98)=8.95$, $p<0.01$, and $\chi^2(1, N=86)$ =7.95, $p<0.01$, respectively. EP = Educational Plus Psychological Program; E = Educational Program; C = control condition.

with each other (coded + 1, −1, and 0 for EP, E, and C, respectively). We carried out analyses at 3 months and 6 months with the MAR estimates of compliance as the dependent measures.

In logistic regression the contribution of a predictor can be characterized by an odds ratio, the ratio of the likelihood that any participant complied versus did not comply as a function of values on the predictor. Considering first the prediction of compliance at 3 months using only the two contrasts between treatment conditions, we obtained an overall significant effect, $\chi^2(2, N=221)=12.76$, $p<0.01$. The odds of complying versus not complying were significantly greater than 1.0 for the contrast between the two intervention groups and the control group, (Intervention odds ratio = 1.57, $p<0.01$, confidence interval (CI): 1.19–1.94), but did not differ as a function of which program had been seen (EP vs. E odds ratio = 1.05, CI: .72–1.53). In a logistic regression equation containing all demographics, the four pretest HBM measures, and pretest Intentions, the Intervention odds ratio remained significantly greater than 1 (odds ratio = 1.46, $p<0.05$, CI: 1.04–2.04), with 11% of the variance accounted for by the set of predictors.[4] That the Intervention odds ratio exceeded unity indicated that intervention subjects who had seen either program were more likely to have obtained a mammogram within 3 months than were control subjects, even when all demographic and pretest differences among the groups were controlled. For the MAR estimate of compliance at 6 months, the Intervention contrast was again significant when only the two experimental contrasts were included as predictors (overall $\chi^2(2, N=168)=10.28$, $p<0.01$; Intervention odds ratio = 1.46, $p<0.01$, CI: 1.14–1.87; EP vs. E odds ratio = 0.87, CI: 0.68–1.13). With all demographic and pretest predictors added to the equation, 13% of the variance was accounted for, and the Intervention contrast remained significant (odds ratio = 1.41, $p<0.05$, CI: 1.03–1.93).

4 The percentage of variance accounted for in the logistic regression was computed as the ratio of the model chi-square including the predictors to the deviance (−2 log likelihood) in a model containing only the intercept.

Compliance among women ever versus never screened

In all, 27%, 32%, and 39% of women in EP, E, and C, respectively, had ever had a mammogram prior to enrollment in the study. At the 3-month follow-up, among women 35–74 years of age, compliance rates for those who never versus ever had a mammogram were 26%, 24%, and 9% and 40%, 35%, and 10% in EP, E, and C, respectively. Compliance rates for the pooled EP and E groups were higher than those for controls among both women who had never had, $\chi^2(1, N = 150) = 7.08$, $p < 0.01$, and women who had ever had, $\chi^2(1, N = 71) = 8.88$, $p < 0.01$, a mammogram. The interventions were effective both for inducing initial mammograms and repeated mammograms, though slightly but not significantly higher for inducing repeated mammograms (38% vs. 27% for ever versus never, respectively).

Reactance among wealthy women

The process evaluation suggested that wealthier women may have reacted negatively to the compliance exercises of the EP program. For the 30 women who reported family incomes of at least $60,000, the 6-month MAR estimates of compliance were 22%, 67%, and 11% for EP, E, and C, respectively, $\chi^2(2, N = 30) = 4.99$, $p < 0.10$. For the remaining women, corresponding rates were 44%, 43%, and 21%, $\chi^2(2, N = 122) = 6.63$, $p < 0.05$.

Reasons for noncompliance

Women who had not obtained mammograms responded to 11 questions concerning their reasons for not having done so. The most frequently endorsed reason (59%) was not having any symptoms of breast cancer, such as a lump, although endorsement rates were higher among controls (72%) than among the two experimental groups (41% and 58% for EP and E, respectively), $\chi^2(2, N = 161) = 11.92$, $p < 0.01$. The next most frequently endorsed reasons were not needing a mammogram (35%), expense (34%), and the trouble involved in obtaining a mammogram (26%).

Attrition and demographic characteristics of the final sample

We explored causes of attrition and effects of attrition on the demographic characteristics of the sample by the 6-month follow-up. Of the original 295 cases, 57% were traced and re-inter-

Table 5 Correlation matrix of scales in the mediational analysis

Scale	1	2	3	4	5	6	7
1. Intervention[a]	–	0.260***	–0.075	0.275***	–0.045	0.448***	0.260***
2. Susceptibility	–	–	0.131*	0.281***	0.018	0.232***	0.051
3. Severity	–	–	–	0.142*	0.099	–0.009	0.004
4. Benefits	–	–	–	–	–0.327***	0.494***	0.115
5. Barriers	–	–	–	–	–	–0.190**	–0.199**
6. Intentions	–	–	–	–	–	–	0.303***
7. Steps	–	–	–	–	–	–	–

Note. Health belief model scales and intentions were taken at immediate posttest. Steps to Compliance was measured at the 3-month follow-up.

[a] Contrast of the two intervention conditions with the control condition: Intervention conditions (Educational Plus Psychological and Educational Programs) are coded +1; control (C) is coded –2.

*$p < 0.05$. **$p < 0.01$. ***$p < 0.001$.

viewed at 6 months following pretest or had obtained mammograms by 3 months and did not require follow-up. Another 13% provided no follow-up information, 16% could not be reached despite repeated callbacks, 6% were from control groups that received the intervention prior to the 6-month follow-up and were thus ineligible for re-interview, 5% refused further participation, 1% were mistakenly never assigned for interviewing, and 1% could not respond due to serious illness.

The sociodemographic characteristics of cases retained at 6 months versus initially enrolled into the study were examined in a series of ANOVAs of Condition (EP, E, and C) × Follow-Up Status (followed and not followed), as described by Jurs and Glass (1971).[5] No association of Follow-Up Status or the Follow-Up Status × Condition interaction with age, income level, or educational level was found. Similar chi-square tests of difference in ethnic identity and marital status of those followed versus not followed yielded no difference within each condition. The baseline characteristics had not been altered by attrition.

Mediation of program effects

The mediational linkages of the intervention through health beliefs to intention and actual compliance were estimated with path analysis. We used the regression-based procedure for testing path models outlined by Pedhazur (1982) that results in a just identified model. We combined and contrasted the EP and E interventions with the C condition, using the Intervention contrast described above. The continuous measure of Steps to Compliance at 3 months served as the behavioral outcome. Correlations among all measures used in the mediational analysis are given in Table 5.

Three mediational questions of central interest were examined in the analysis. The first two questions tested portions of the model of the relationships between HBM components proposed by Ronis (1992). The third question examined the role of Perceived Barriers in compliance versus Intentions to comply. Table 6 outlines the regression analyses used to answer each of these questions and gives the percentage of the total effect that was mediated. Figure 1 presents the final mediational model of program effects.

1 Do Susceptibility and Severity mediate the relation of the Intervention to Benefits? The relation between the Intervention and Perceived Benefits was accounted for by both a significant direct path and a significant indirect (mediated) path through Perceived Susceptibility (see Figure 1). The indirect path through Perceived Severity was not significant.

Table 6 Regression analyses for mediational analysis and percentage mediation at each stage

Mediation question	Dependent variable	Independent variables	Putative mediators	Multiple correlations			Mediation (%)
				$r^2_{Y,I}$	$r^2_{Y,MI}$	$r^2_{Y,M}$	
1	Benefits	Intervention	Sus, Sev, Ben, Bar	0.076	0.140	0.090	34
2	Intention	Sus, Sev	Ben	0.244	0.261	0.055	69
3	Steps	Intervention, Sus, Sev, Ben, Bar	Intention	0.092	0.146	0.105	55

Note. $r^2_{Y,I}$ is the squared multiple correlation based on the independent variable alone, $r^2_{Y,MI}$ is based on the independent variable plus mediators, and $r^2_{Y,M}$ is based on the mediators alone. Percentage mediation $= .\{[r^2_{Y,I} - (r^2_{Y,MI} - r^2_{Y,M})]/r^2_{Y,I}\} \times 100$.
Sus = Susceptibility; Sev = Severity, Ben = Benefit, Bar = Barrier.

5 The Jurs and Glass (1971) analysis assumes random assignment to condition.

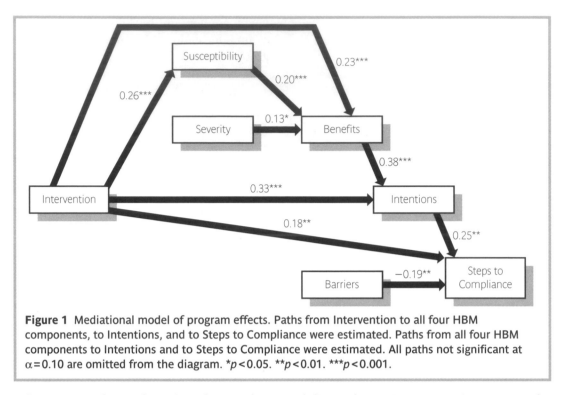

Figure 1 Mediational model of program effects. Paths from Intervention to all four HBM components, to Intentions, and to Steps to Compliance were estimated. Paths from all four HBM components to Intentions and to Steps to Compliance were estimated. All paths not significant at $\alpha = 0.10$ are omitted from the diagram. *$p < 0.05$. **$p < 0.01$. ***$p < 0.001$.

2 Does Benefits mediate the relation of Susceptibility and Severity to Intentions to comply? The relation between Perceived Susceptibility and Perceived Severity and Intentions to comply was largely accounted for by the significant indirect paths through Perceived Benefits. The direct paths from Perceived Susceptibility and Perceived Severity to Perceived Intentions were not significant.

3 Do Perceived Barriers act on Steps to Compliance, indirectly through Intentions, along with the other HBM components, or does Perceived Barriers have a separate direct influence on Steps to Compliance, in a manner similar to that for perceived behavioral control in the theory of planned behavior (Ajzen, 1991)? The relation between Perceived Susceptibility, Perceived Severity, and Perceived Benefits and Steps to Compliance was largely mediated by Perceived Intentions.[6] None of the direct paths from these three HBM components to Steps to Compliance were significant, which, taken in conjunction with the analyses of Question 2, indicated that the indirect effects of Perceived Susceptibility and Perceived Severity on Steps to Compliance were through both Perceived Benefits and Perceived Intentions. In contrast, perceived Barriers had a significant negative direct effect on Steps to Compliance, but the indirect effect through Perceived Intentions was not significant.

In summary, consistent with Ronis' (1992) model, Perceived Susceptibility and Severity led to increased perception of Benefits of mammography screening, which, in turn, led to increased Intention to obtain a mammogram. In addition, Perceived Barriers to screening appeared to act independently of this sequence, with a direct negative effect on compliance.

6 Guttman scaling of Steps to Compliance had supported an ordinal scale; yet we treated Steps as an interval-scale level dependent variable in the ordinary-least-squares (OLS) based path analysis. However, when Steps was predicted in an ordinal logistic regression, which does not assume an equal interval scale (McCullagh & Nelder, 1989), results remained the same. We retained the OLS equation for Steps to Compliance in the path analysis for comparability with other equations in the analysis.

Discussion

The two programs produced substantial increases in screening mammograms, with women in the E and EP programs obtaining mammograms at 2 to 3 times the rate of women in the control condition. These findings are particularly impressive because the population we targeted may have been resistant to mammography screening – 71% of women in EP and E conditions had never had a mammogram at the beginning of the study. Such women are less responsive to interventions to increase screening than are women who have had prior mammograms (Rimer et al., 1992; Rothman, Salovey, Turvey, & Fishkin, 1993). In addition, women had to overcome the barriers typically associated with the medical system to obtain a mammogram: getting a referral from a physician, going to a separate site for the screening, and paying for the procedure. That these barriers were overcome with a potentially resistant population is encouraging for both the E and EP programs.

The EP program is more difficult and costly to implement than the E program. Yet in no comparison did the EP program produce a higher rate of screening than did the E program, and there was some evidence that it was less successful than the E program with high-income women. The present educational program, based on the HBM, made an explicit and strong attempt to link the women's changed health beliefs with their actually following the ACS guidelines for mammography screening. Apparently, the compliance exercises of the present psychological component did not lead to further strengthening of this link.

One likely reason for the failure of the EP program to produce higher screening rates than the E program was that the E program itself produced surprisingly high screening rates among a group of women selected because they were not in compliance. Among the original cohort of 615 women from which our study sample was drawn, fully 44% were in compliance at the beginning of the study and were not included in the analyses. Among the 56% of the women not in compliance, between 40% and 50% complied within 6-months if they had seen the E program, adding another 22% to 28% to those in compliance. If we make the optimistic assumption that most of the original 44% remained in compliance, then approximately 70% of the original cohort would then be in compliance by the end of the follow-up period. Even under the pessimistic assumption that 25% of those originally in compliance would fall out of compliance during the 6-month period, approximately 60% of the original cohort would be in compliance at the end of the follow-up period. This accumulated compliance rate is approximately double the compliance rates in the general population reported during the period 1987–1989. For the EP program to have exceeded the E program in producing compliance, it would have had to produce compliance in the most resistant third of the original cohort.

Another potential reason for the failure of EP to produce additional compliance was lack of full participation in the compliance exercises. Of the five psychological compliance exercises, three were designed to be passively received by the women: counterarguments made by the presenter against failing to be screened, modeling by the presenter and an assistant of telephoning a physician for a mammogram, and receiving the reminder letter as a cue to action. Women themselves were asked to enumerate the steps involved in calling a doctor for a mammogram, and a substantial majority followed the instructions. However, only a third made a definite personal commitment to themselves to make an appointment for a mammogram.

A third reason for the failure of EP to produce higher compliance was the negative response of wealthy women to the strong manipulations of the EP program. Similar negative reactions have been noted to strong health-oriented manipulations among women high in internal health locus of control (Quadrel & Lau, 1989). It is possible that higher income women felt sufficient control over their own ability to act on the program message and reacted negatively to what Quadrel and Lau referred to as the "hand-holding" character of the stronger EP manipulation, leading to decreased compliance relative to the E condition. However, among women with total family incomes less than $60,000, response to EP and E was equivalent (44% versus 43%, MAR estimate, 6-month follow-up). While income was related to responsiveness to the EP program, it likely served as a proxy for internal health locus of control beliefs, which we did not measure, with only those women low in internal health locus of control responding positively to the pressure of the program[7] (Wallston, Wallston, Kaplan, & Maides, 1976).

Both interventions produced most of the more proximal changes expected from the HBM. The two programs produced substantial increases in knowledge of breast cancer and mammography, Perceived Susceptibility and Benefits, and Intentions to comply with screening guidelines. That Perceived Severity was not affected may be because of the perception of breast cancer under any conditions as a severe and life-threatening disease. Alternatively, our program emphasized that early-detected breast cancer is much less deleterious than late-detected breast cancer for survival, for extensiveness of breast surgery, and for psychological outcomes. Because we did not distinguish in our measurement between the severity of early- and late-detected breast cancer, we may have failed to detect this more differentiated effect (see Ronis & Harel, 1989).

Our interventions failed to produce an overall effect on Perceived Barriers. Following Melnyk (1988), it is useful to distinguish between medical system barriers and psychological barriers. Our program objectively did not change the medical system barrier of cost (i.e., we did not provide free mammograms). Cost, identified as a barrier by 34% of noncompliant women, was clearly a factor in failures to comply. Although the cohort studied was on average middle class, 22% had total annual family incomes of less than $20,000, with lower incomes among elderly women. At the time of the intervention, neither Medicare ("Rules and Regulations," 1990) nor Arizona's alternative to Medicaid (Arizona Health Care Cost Containment System, AHCCCS) provided coverage for screening mammography. Also, the trouble involved in getting mammograms was a frequently reported barrier. Rimer et al. (1992) have shown that for older women, lack of transportation to a mammography facility is a significant impediment to screening. These two system barriers of cost and access may well have precluded higher screening rates that might approach the year 2000 goals set by the National Cancer Institute; they cannot be addressed by educational programs. Such system barriers are even more formidable for less well-insured women of lower socioeconomic status, who are often of minority ethnicity (see, e.g., Fletcher et al., 1993; Wells & Horm, 1992; Zapka, Stoddard, Barth, Costanza, & Mas, 1989).

In contrast, two of the psychological barriers, inconvenience and ineffectiveness of communication with health providers, did show evidence of change from pretest to posttest in the E and EP conditions. However, the program failed to convey the message to all women of the importance of being screened if one is asymptomatic. The programs reduced the perception that screening is unnecessary if one has no breast cancer symptoms; however, they did not fully eliminate this perception. Program redesing should focus on this issue.

For women with sufficient resources to overcome medical-system-access barriers, other psychological barriers to screening not measured in this study may have existed. These include fear of pain associated with the procedure (Rimer et al., 1989) and anxiety about a potential positive

---

7 We appreciate the insight of Angela Bryan into the potential relationship of health locus of control to responsiveness to the EP program.

diagnosis (Mootz, Glazer-Waldman, Evans, Peters, & Kirk, 1991), particularly among higher risk women (Lerman & Schwartz, 1993; Polednak, Lane, & Burg, 1991). Such barriers might be less likely to operate among women who do not have sufficient financial resources even to contemplate screening.

In the final prediction equation in the model, 15% of the variance in Steps to Compliance was accounted for by Intervention, the four HBM components, and Intentions. Factors missing from this model included demographics, which had accounted for only 2% of the variance in compliance in the parallel logistic regression analysis. Also missing from the analysis were separate indicators of the system barriers of expense (though cost was a single item on the barriers scale) and access to screening facilities, and the perception of whether screening is necessary if one is asymptomatic. Finally, there was no measure of when or if a physician had recommended a mammogram. The medical-system barriers plus physician recommendation are powerful determinants of screening and would likely increase overall predictability.

The mediational analysis provided insight into how the HBM components concatenate to produce compliance, supporting Ronis's (1992) model. All four components of the HBM were shown to play a role in the process of instituting a health behavior. In contrast, simple inspection of correlations of the four HBM components with Steps to Compliance would have suggested that only Barriers impacted on screening behavior. Consideration of only Intentions to comply would have failed to surface the role of Perceived Severity in inducing the important perception of Benefits of screening. The mediational analysis in conjunction with the strong quasi-experimental design provided clear support for Ronis's (1992) prediction that Perceived Susceptibility and Severity lead to the perception of Benefits.

The HBM, in its early formulations, did not address the important issue of self efficacy or behavioral control with regard to health behavior (Bandura, 1982). More recently, Rosenstock, Stretcher, and Becker (1988) and Rosenstock (1990) have advocated the integration of self-efficacy into the HBM. Ajzen (1991) in the theory of planned behavior, expanded the theory of reasoned action (Ajzen & Fishbein, 1980) to include perceived behavioral control as a second force that operates on behavior, along with intentions. Two of our four measures of Barriers (efficacy in speaking to a health provider about screening, and the inconvenience of obtaining a mammogram) reflect perceived behavioral control. We found that perceived barriers here correlated negatively with both intentions and behavior, and were the sole HBM correlate of actual compliance, supporting the theory of planned behavior under the condition set forth by Ajzen (1991) – that the behavior in question is not completely under volitional control. The mediational analysis provided support for both an elaboration of the relationships among HBM components and of the role of perceived behavioral control in the intention-behavior link.

In summary, this study illustrates the utility of a theory of health behavior, the HBM, as a heuristic for designing an effective intervention to increase mammography screening. Perhaps less obvious at the outset was the ability of applied theory-based interventions to inform basic theories of health behavior. The mediational analyses provided support for Ronis's (1992) recent elaboration of the interrelationships among HBM components and clarified the role of psychological barriers in the sequence from health beliefs to a complex screening behavior. Such careful probing of the effects of theory-based interventions provides an important opportunity to inform basic theories of health behavior (Coie et al., 1993; West, Aiken, & Todd, 1993).

References

Aiken, L. S., West, S. G., Woodward, C. K., & Reno, R. R. (1994). Health beliefs and compliance with mammography screening recommendations in asymptomatic women. *Health Psychology, 13,* 122–129.

Ajzen, I. (1991). The theory of planned behavior. *Organizational Behavior and Human Decision Processes, 50,* 179–201.

Ajzen, I., & Fishbein, M. (1980). *Understanding attitudes and predicting social behavior.* Englewood Cliffs, NJ: Prentice-Hall.

American Cancer Society (1988). *Summary of current guidelines for the cancer-related checkup: Recommendations.* New York: Author.

Bandura, A. (1977). *Social learning theory.* Englewood Cliffs, NJ: Prentice-Hall.

Bandura, A. (1982). Self-efficacy mechanism in human agency. *American Psychologist, 37,* 122–147.

Barcikowski, R. S. (1981). Statistical power with group mean as the unit of analysis. *Journal of Educational Statistics, 6,* 267–285.

Baron, R. M., & Kenny, D. A. (1986). The moderator–mediator variable distinction in social psychological research: Conceptual, strategic, and statistical considerations. *Journal of Personality and Social Psychology, 51,* 1173–1182.

Bastani, R., Marcus, A. C., & Hollatz-Brown, A. (1991). Screening mammography rates and barriers to use: A Los Angeles County survey. *Preventive Medicine, 20,* 350–363.

Becker, M. H., & Maiman, L. A. (1975). Sociobehavioral determinants of compliance with health and medical care recommendations. *Medical Care, 13,* 10–24.

Bentler, P. M., & Bonett, D. G. (1980). Significance tests and goodness of fit in the analysis of covariance structures. *Psychological Bulletin, 88,* 588–606.

Burg, M. A., Lane, D. S., & Polednak, A. P. (1990). Age group differences in the use of breast cancer screening tests. *Journal of Aging and Health, 2,* 514–530.

Champion, V. L. (1992). Compliance with guidelines for mammography screening. *Cancer Detection and Prevention, 16,* 253–258.

Cialdini, R. B. (1984). *Influence: How and why people agree to do things.* New York: William Morrow.

Coie, J. D., Watt, N., West, S. G., Hawkins, D., Asarnow, J., Markman, H., Ramey, S., Shure, M., & Long, B. (1993). The science of prevention: A conceptual framework and some directions for a national research program. *American Psychologist, 48,* 1013–1022.

Cook, T. C., & Campbell, D. T. (1979). *Quasi-experimentation: Design and analysis issues for field settings.* Chicago: Rand McNally.

Flay, B. R. (1985). Psychosocial approaches to smoking prevention: A review of findings. *Health Psychology, 4,* 449–488.

Fletcher, S. W., Harris, R. P., Gonzalez, J. J., Degnan, D., Lannin, D. R., Strecher, V. J., Pilgrim, C., Quade, D., Earp, J. A., & Clark, R. L. (1993). Increasing mammography utilization: A controlled study. *Journal of the National Cancer Institute, 85,* 112–120.

Fox, S. A., Murata, P. J., & Stein, J. A. (1991). The impact of physician compliance for older women. *Archives of Internal Medicine, 151,* 50–56.

Greenwald, P., & Sondik, E. (Eds). (1986). *Cancer control objectives for the nation: 1985–2000* (NCI Monograph 2, PHS 86–2580, pp. 27–32). Bethesda, MD: National Cancer Institute.

Gregory, W. L., Cialdini, R. B., & Carpenter, K. M. (1982). Self-relevant scenarios as mediators of likelihood estimates and compliance: Does imagining make it so? *Journal of Personality and Social Psychology, 43,* 89–99.

Higginbotham, H. N., West., S. G., & Forsyth, D. R. (1988). *Psychotherapy and behavior change: Social, cultural, and methodological perspectives.* Elmsford, NY: Pergamon.

Hosmer, D. W, & Lemeshow, S. (1989). *Applied logistic regression.* New York: Wiley.

Janz, N. K., & Becker, M. H. (1984). The health belief model: A decade later. *Health Education Quarterly, 11,* 1–47.

Johnson, J. J., Aiken, L. S., & Luckett, T. L. (1993, April). *Breast cancer: Risk estimates and risk perceptions in asymptomatic women.* Paper presented at the meeting of the Western Psychological Association, Phoenix, AZ.

Jurs, S. G., & Glass, G. V. (1971). The effect of experimental mortality on the internal and external validity of the randomized comparative experiment. *Journal of Experimental Education, 40,* 62–66.

Kiesler, C. A. (1969). *The psychology of commitment.* New York: Academic.

Larsen, E. B., Olsen, E., & Cole, W. (1979). The relationship of health beliefs and a postcard reminder to influenza vaccination. *Journal of Family Practice, 8,* 1207–1211.

Lerman, C., Rimer, B., Trock, B., Balshem, A. A., & Engstrom, P. (1990). Factors associated with repeat adherence to breast cancer screening. *Preventive Medicine, 19,* 279–290.

Lerman, C., & Schwartz, M. (1993). Adherence and psychological adjustment among women at high risk for breast cancer. *Breast Cancer Research and Treatment, 28,* 145–155.

Leventhal, H. (1970). Findings and theory in the study of fear communication. In L. Berkowitz (Ed.), *Advances in experimental social psychology* (Vol. 5, pp. 140–208). New York: Academic.

Leventhal, H., Meyer, D., & Guttman, M. (1980). The role of theory in the study of compliance to high blood pressure regimens. In R. B. Haynes, M. E. Mattson, & T. O. Engebretson (Eds.), *Patient compliance to prescribed antihypertensive medication regimens: A report to the National Heart, Lung, and Blood Institute* (No. 1–21–2). Washington, DC: National Institutes of Health.

McCullagh, P., & Nelder, J. A. (1989). *Generalized linear models* (2nd ed.). London: Chapman & Hall.

McGuire, W. J. (1985). Attitudes and attitude change. In G. Lindzey & E. Aronson (Eds.), *Handbook of social psychology* (Vol. 1, pp. 233–346). New York: Random House.

Melnyk, K. A. M. (1988). Barriers: A critical review of recent literature. *Nursing Research, 37,* 196–201.

Mootz, A. R., Glazer-Waldman, H., Evans, W. P., Peters, G. N., & Kirk, L. M. (1991). Mammography in a mobile setting: Remaining barriers. *Radiology, 180,* 151–165.

National Cancer Institute Breast Screening Consortium. (1990). Screening mammography: A missed clinical opportunity? Results of the NCI Breast Cancer Screening Consortium and National Health Interview Survey Studies. *Journal of the American Medical Association, 264,* 54–58.

Payne, S. (1990). Lay representations of breast cancer. *Psychology and Health, 5,* 1–11.

Pedhazur, E. J. (1982). *Multiple regression in behavioral research.* New York: Holt, Rinehart, & Winston.

Polednak, A., Lane, D., & Burg, M. (1991). Risk perception, family history, and use of breast cancer screening tests. *Cancer Detection and Prevention, 15,* 257–263.

Provisional estimates from the National Health Interview Survey Supplement of cancer control–United States, January–March, 1987. (1988, July 15). *Mortality and Morbidity Weekly, 37,* 417–425.

Quadrel, M. J., & Lau, R. R. (1989). Health promotion, health locus of control, and health behavior: Two field experiments. *Journal of Applied Social Psychology, 19,* 1497–1521.

Reynolds, K. R., West, S. G., & Aiken, L. S. (1990). Increasing the use of mammography screening: A pilot intervention. *Health Education Quarterly, 17,* 429–441.

Rimer, B. K., Keintz, M. K., Kessler, H. B., Engstrom, P. F., & Rosan, J. R. (1989). Why women resist screening mammography: Patient related barriers. *Radiology, 172,* 243–246.

Rimer, B. K., Resch, N., King, E., Ross, E., Lerman, C., Boyce, A., Kessler, H., & Engstrom,

P. F. (1992). Multistrategy health education program to increase mammography use among women ages 65 and older. *Public Health Reports, 107,* 369–380.

Ronis, D. L. (1992). Conditional health threats: Health beliefs, decisions, and behaviors among adults. *Health Psychology, 11,* 127–134.

Ronis, D. L., & Harel, Y. (1989). Health beliefs and breast examination behaviors: An analysis of linear structural relations. *Psychology and Health, 3,* 259–285.

Rosenstock, I. M. (1990). The health belief model. In K. Glanz, F. Lewis, & B. Rimer (Eds.), *Health behavior and health education: Theory, research, and practice* (pp. 39–62). San Francisco: Jossey-Bass.

Rosenstock, I. M., Stretcher, V. J., & Becker, M. H. (1988). Social learning theory and the Health Belief Model. *Health Education Quarterly, 15,* 175–183.

Rothman, A. J., Salovey, P., Turvey, C., & Fishkin, S. A. (1993). Attributions of responsibility and persuasion: Increasing mammography utilization among women over 40 with an internally oriented message. *Health Psychology, 12,* 39–47.

Rubin, D. B. (1976). Inference and missing data. *Biometrika, 63,* 581–592.

Rules and regulations. (1990, December 31). *Federal Register, 55*(251), p.53513.

Rutledge, R. N., Hartmann, W. H., Kinman, P. O., Winfield, A. C. (1988). Exploration of factors affecting mammography behaviors. *Preventive Medicine, 17,* 412–422.

Sensenig, P. E., & Cialdini, R. B. (1984). Social psychological influences on the compliance process: Implications for behavioral health. In J. Matarazzo, N. E. Miller, S. M. Weiss, J. A. Herd, & S. M. Weiss (Eds.), *Behavioral health: A handbook of health enhancement and disease prevention* (pp. 384–392). New York: Wiley.

Stein, J. A., Fox, S. A., Murata, P. J., & Morisky, D. B. (1992). Mammography usage and the Health Belief Model. *Health Education Quarterly, 19,* 447–462.

Torgerson, W. S. (1958). *Theory and methods of scaling.* New York: Wiley.

Turner, B. J., Amsel, Z., Lustbader, E., Schwartz, J. S., Balshem, A., & Grisso, J. A. (1992). Breast cancer screening: Effect of physician specialty, practice setting, year of medical school graduation, and sex. *American Journal of Preventive Medicine, 8,* 78–85.

Tversky, A., & Kahneman, D. (1973). Availability: A heuristic for judging frequency and probability. *Cognitive Psychology, 5,* 207–232.

Use of mammography – United States, 1990. (1990, September 14). *Mortality and Morbidity Weekly, 39,* 621–630.

Vernon, S. W., Laville, E. A., & Jackson, G. L. (1990). Participation in breast screening programs: A review. *Social Science and Medicine, 30,* 1107–1118.

Wallston, B. S., Wallston, K. A., Kaplan, G. D., & Maides, S. A. (1976). Development and validation of the health locus of control scale. *Journal of Consulting and Clinical Psychology, 44,* 580–585.

Wells, B. L., & Horm, J. W. (1992). Stage at diagnosis in breast cancer: Race and socioeconomic factors. *American Journal of Public Health, 82,* 1383–1385.

West, S. G., Aiken, L. S., & Todd, M. (1993). Probing the effects of individual components in multiple component prevention programs. *American Journal of Community Psychology, 21,* 571–605.

West, S. G., Reich, J. W., McCall, M. A., & Dantchik, A. (1989). Applied social psychology. In W. L. Gregory & W. J. Burroughs (Eds.), *Introduction to applied psychology* (pp. 301–326). Glenview, IL: Scott, Foresman.

Zapka, J. G., Stoddard, A., Barth, R., Costanza, M. E., & Mas, E. (1989). Breast cancer screening utilization by Latina community health center clients. *Health Education Research, 4,* 461–468.

Zapka, J. G., Stoddard, A. M., Costanza, M. E., & Greene, H. L. (1989). Breast cancer screening by mammography: Utilization and associated factors. *American Journal of Public Health, 79,* 1499–1502.

Gollwitzer, P.M. and Sheeran, P. (2006) Implementation intentions and goal achievement: a meta-analysis of effects and processes, *Advances in Experimental Social Psychology*, 38: 69–119.

Implementation intentions and goal achievement

A meta-analysis of effects and processes

Peter M. Gollwitzer
Paschal Sheeran

Holding a strong goal intention ("I intend to reach Z!") does not guarantee goal achievement, because people may fail to deal effectively with self-regulatory problems during goal striving. This review analyzes whether realization of goal intentions is facilitated by forming an implementation intention that spells out the when, where, and how of goal striving in advance ("If situation Y is encountered, then I will initiate goal-directed behavior X!"). Findings from 94 independent tests showed that implementation intentions had a positive effect of medium-to-large magnitude ($d = 0.65$) on goal attainment. Implementation intentions were effective in promoting the initiation of goal striving, the shielding of ongoing goal pursuit from unwanted influences, disengagement from failing courses of action, and conservation of capability for future goal striving. There was also strong support for postulated component processes: Implementation intention formation both enhanced the accessibility of specified opportunities and automated respective goal-directed responses. Several directions for future research are outlined.

I. Introduction

Understanding what factors determine whether people succeed or fail in achieving desired outcomes is a fundamental concern in both basic and applied psychology. Most theories of motivation and self-regulation converge on the idea that setting a behavioral or outcome goal is the key act of willing that promotes goal attainment (e.g., Ajzen, 1991; Atkinson, 1957; Bandura, 1991; Carver & Scheier, 1998; Gollwitzer, 1990; Locke & Latham, 1990). The basic assumption is that the strength of a person's intention determines respective accomplishments (Austin & Vancouver, 1996; Gollwitzer & Moskowitz, 1996; Oettingen & Gollwitzer, 2001; Sheeran, 2002). Although accumulated research supports this idea (e.g., Armitage & Conner, 2001; Sheeran, 2002; Sutton, 1998), there is also contrary evidence that gives credence to the proverb that "the road to hell is paved with good intentions" (Orbell & Sheeran, 1998; Sheeran, 2002). To address this issue, Gollwitzer (1993, 1996, 1999) proposed that successful goal achievement is facilitated by a second act of willing that furnishes the goal intention with an if–then plan specifying when, where, and how the person will instigate responses that promote goal realization. These plans are termed *implementation intentions*.

Implementation intentions appear to be effective at enhancing the likelihood of goal achievement. However, the effectiveness of if–then planning has been reviewed only in narrative (e.g., Gollwitzer, 1999; Gollwitzer, Bayer, & McCulloch, 2005) and small-scale quantitative (e.g., Koestner, Lekes, Powers, & Chicoine, 2002b; Sheeran, 2002) reports to date, and a comprehensive evaluation of implementation intention effects and processes is overdue. The aim of this review is to quantify the overall impact of implementation intention formation on goal achievement using meta-analytic techniques. In addition, this chapter tests the effectiveness of implementation intentions in relation to different self-regulatory problems and goal domains and assesses potential moderators of implementation intention effects. Finally, the impact of implementation intentions on theoretically specified component processes is examined to understand why implementation intentions may help people obtain outcomes that they desire.

II. Goal intention strength and goal achievement

Goal intentions are self-instructions to attain certain outcomes or perform particular behaviors and typically take the format of "I intend to reach Z!" They are derived from beliefs about the feasibility and desirability of actions and end states (e.g., Ajzen, 1991; Atkinson, 1957; Bandura, 1991, 1997; Brehm & Self, 1989; Carver & Scheier, 1998; Heckhausen, 1991; Locke & Latham, 1990; Vroom, 1964) and represent the culmination of the decision making process (Gollwitzer, 1990). Goal intentions signal the end of deliberation about what actions to perform or outcomes to reach; they imply a commitment to act that may vary in strength (Ajzen, 1991; Gollwitzer, 1990; Sheeran, 2002; Webb & Sheeran, 2005a).

In traditional theories of goal pursuit, goal intentions are construed as the most immediate and important predictor of attainment. For instance, pre-eminent accounts of goal-directed behavior, such as control theory (Carver & Scheier, 1982, 1998), social cognitive theory (Bandura, 1991, 1997), and goal setting theory (Locke & Latham, 1990), models of attitude–behavior relations, such as the theories of reasoned action (Fishbein, 1980; Fishbein & Ajzen, 1975) and planned behavior (Ajzen, 1991), and the model of interpersonal behavior (Triandis, 1980), as well as theories of health-related behavior, such as protection motivation theory (Rogers, 1983) and the prototype/willingness model (Gibbons, Gerrard, Blanton, & Russell, 1998), each accord goal intentions a central role in their theorizing about action. Accordingly, research has been concerned for several decades with the factors that determine strong intentions – the assumption being that intention strength is a good predictor of intention realization.

This assumption seems to be supported by meta-analyses of correlational studies in which participants' goal intentions (e.g., "I intend to perform behavior W!" or "I intend to achieve outcome Z!") are measured at one time-point and behavior is measured at a later time-point. For example, reviews of the theory of reasoned action (Kim & Hunter, 1993; Sheppard, Hardwick, & Warshaw, 1988; van den Putte, 1993), the theory of planned behavior (Armitage & Conner, 2001; Godin & Kok, 1996; Hausenblas, Carron, & Mack, 1997), and protection motivation theory (Floyd, Prentice-Dunn, & Rogers, 2000; Milne, Sheeran, & Orbell, 2000), as well as meta-analyses of particular behaviors (e.g., condom use, Sheeran & Orbell, 1998; physical activity, Hagger, Chatzisarantis, & Biddle, 2002), indicate that strength of intention typically explains 20–35% of the variance in goal achievement. To gain insight into the overall strength of intention–behavior consistency in this type of research, Sheeran (2002) conducted a meta-analysis of 10 meta-analyses of the intention–behavior relation. Findings showed that intentions accounted for 28% of the variance in behavior, on average, across 422 studies involving 82,107 participants. According to Cohen's (1992) power primer, $R^2 = 0.28$, constitutes a "large" effect size, which suggests that intentions are "good" predictors of behavior – as traditional theories of goal pursuit have supposed.

However, bivariate correlations between goal intentions and future behavior may overestimate the strength of intention–behavior relations because it is possible that future behavior and goal intentions are both determined by self-perceptions of past behavior (Bem, 1972). The implication is that analyses should control for previous performance in order to determine to what extent goal intentions are associated with behavior *change*. Sutton and Sheeran (2003) conducted a meta-analysis along these lines. Sampled-weighted average correlations between past behavior, goal intentions, and future behavior were computed from 51 studies involving 8166 participants and then used as inputs for a hierarchical regression analysis. Findings indicated that, not surprisingly, past behavior was a good predictor of future behavior on the first step of the equation and accounted for 26% of the variance. Entering goal intentions on the second step was associated with a significant increment in the variance explained in future behavior ($R^2_{change} = 0.07$). These findings suggest that goal intentions have significant associations with future behavior even when previous performance is taken into account. However, the effect size for goal intentions is small-to-medium rather than large.

Even correlational analyses that statistically control for past behavior in estimating the goal intention–goal achievement relation are problematic, however, because it is always possible that a third variable is responsible for the observed associations. To eliminate this alternative explanation of intention–behavior consistency, it is necessary to experimentally manipulate goal intentions and then determine whether this manipulation produces a significant difference in subsequent goal attainment. Webb and Sheeran (in press a) tested this idea in a recent meta-analysis. They identified 47 studies ($N = 8802$) that (1) were successful at inducing statistically significant differences in goal intentions between experimental versus control participants and (2) followed up participants in order to measure differences in subsequent goal attainment. Findings showed that the mean difference in goal intention strength produced by the experimental manipulations had an effect size of medium-to-large magnitude ($d = 0.66$). Findings also indicated that manipulating goal intention strength engendered a significant difference in goal achievement. However, the effect size was small-to-medium only; d was 0.36 that equates to $R^2 = 0.03$. Thus, producing significant changes in goal intention strength only generates a modest change in goal achievement. This finding indicates that there is a substantial "gap" between people's goal intentions and their subsequent attainment.

A converging line of research has decomposed the intention–behavior relation in terms of a 2 (goal intention: to act vs. not to act) × 2 (goal achievement: acted vs. did not act) matrix (McBroom & Reid, 1992; Orbell & Sheeran, 1998; Sheeran, 2002). This decomposition provides insight into the sources of consistency and discrepancy between intentions and action. Consistency is attributable to participants who intend to act and subsequently act (termed "inclined actors") and to participants who do not intend to act and do not act ("disinclined abstainers"). Discrepancies between intentions and action, on the other hand, can be attributed to participants who intend to act but do not act ("inclined abstainers") and to participants who do not intend to act but end up acting ("disinclined actors"). A review by Sheeran (2002) found that inclined abstainers, rather than disinclined actors, were principally responsible for the intention–behavior "gap." The median proportion of participants who intended to but did not act was 47%, whereas the median proportion of participants who did not intend to act but subsequently acted was only 7%. These findings would seem to confirm that the proverbial road to hell is paved with good intentions – barely more than one-half of people who intended to act were successful at translating those intentions into action.

In sum, it appears that the single act of willing involved in forming a goal intention is not sufficient to ensure goal achievement. The implicit assumption in traditional models of goal pursuit – that goal intentions fashioned from appropriate evaluation of feasibility and desirability considerations satisfactorily account for the intensity of goal striving – is not strongly supported by the evidence. Clearly, some additional psychological concepts are needed (1) to understand why people often become inclined abstainers rather than inclined actors and (2) to develop self-regulatory strategies to help people "bridge" the gap between their intentions and their behavior.

III. Self-regulation of goal striving

Recent research on goals has demonstrated that variables other than strength of goal intention affect the intensity of goal striving and rate of goal attainment (Gollwitzer & Moskowitz, 1996; Oettingen & Gollwitzer, 2001). Some goal theories focus on the implications of particular goal contents and structural features. For instance, people who set themselves learning goals rather than performance goals are better at dealing with failure experiences and, consequently, show more persistent and successful goal pursuit (Dweck, 2000). Higgins (2000) demonstrates that people who pursue their goals using means that have a natural fit to the content of the goal have a better chance of goal attainment. For example, people with promotion goals (that focus on gain and achievement) are more likely to realize those goals using eagerness means whereas prevention goals (that focus on safety and security) are more likely to be realized by vigilance means. Other important distinctions between types of goals have been drawn by Locke and Latham (1990) (e.g., specific vs. "do your best" goals), Bandura (1991) (e.g., proximal vs. distal goals), and Deci and Ryan (1991) (e.g., goals based on needs for autonomy, competence, and social integration vs. goals based on other needs). All of these theories construe features related to the content and structure of set goals as critical in determining the likelihood of goal achievement.

Other goal theories assume that setting a goal (of whatever kind) is only a first step *en route* to goal realization. A key impetus for self-regulation research on goals is the model of action phases (Gollwitzer, 1990; Heckhausen, 1991; Heckhausen & Gollwitzer, 1987) that construes goal attainment in terms of solving a number of consecutive tasks. Goal setting is viewed as merely the first of these tasks – with planning how to achieve the goal, getting started, and successfully completing goal striving as equally important subsequent tasks.

The model of action phases seeks to provide a comprehensive temporal account of goal pursuit. Four different consecutive action phases are postulated by the model. The first, *predecisional*, phase starts from the assumption that people have many more wishes and desires than they can possibly realize. Here people's task is to deliberate about the desirability and feasibility of their various wishes in order to choose which ones will be turned into binding goals. The model agrees with classic motivational notions (e.g., Atkinson, 1957; Fishbein & Ajzen, 1975; Lewin, 1926) that people commit to those goals in which attainment is perceived as both highly desirable and feasible. However, the model of action phases also states that goal attainment is not yet secured by the act of goal setting (i.e., by having formed strong goal intentions). Rather, goal accomplishment requires in addition that the individual effectively regulates the actual striving for the goal (i.e., engages in effective goal implementation).

Once a person has committed to a goal, she makes the transition to the second action phase, *preactional*. Here the goal-relevant task is to initiate goal-directed behaviors successfully. This may be straightforward when the respective actions have become routinized through frequent and consistent performance in stable situational contexts. However, matters are likely to be more complex when people are unfamiliar with, or imprecise about, the respective goal-directed actions and contexts of performance. In these circumstances, people are likely to benefit from fashioning plans that spell out when, where, and how to implement goal-directed behaviors.

The initiation of actual performance of the respective goal-directed behaviors marks the transition to the third, *actional*, phase. The task to be accomplished during this phase pertains to responding flexibly and adaptively to contextual threats to goal progress so that goal striving is not derailed prematurely. In other words, the key actional task is to bring the respective goal-directed activity to a successful conclusion by shielding it from distractions and temptations that could potentially disrupt goal striving.

In the final action phase, *postactional*, the task is to evaluate goal achievement both in terms of degree of attainment ("Did I do as well as I had hoped?") and quality of attainment outcomes ("Was it worth doing?"). This process involves comparing what has been achieved with one's original wishes and desires, and it may at times imply effortful disengagement from the goal (if further striving is inappropriate). Thus, goal completion is likely to provide valuable information that can feed back into evaluations of the feasibility and desirability of future courses of action; people return to the position of deliberating about their various wishes and desires from which they started.

A. Problems *en route* to goal completion

The foregoing discussion suggests that merely forming a goal intention does not guarantee goal achievement as people often face problems en route to goal completion. So what are these challenges, and how can people tackle them successfully by using self-regulatory strategies? We propose that the following four problems may prevent people from reaching their goals.

1. Failing to get started

The first problem that can undermine goal attainment is failing to get started with goal striving. A number of factors militate against getting started on one's goals. The first has to do with remembering to act. When a behavior is not part of one's routine, or when one has to postpone acting until a suitable opportunity presents itself, one can easily forget to perform the intended behavior. This is because situational demands on attention and memorial resources may serve to reduce the activation level of a focal goal intention compared to other intentions (Einstein & McDaniel, 1996). Dealing with many things at once or becoming preoccupied by a particular task can make it difficult to remember to act on one's goals, especially when the intended behavior is new or unfamiliar. Empirical support for this explanation of intention–behavior discrepancies comes from retrospective reports by inclined abstainers. For example, 70% of participants who had intended to perform a breast self-examination but failed to do so, offered "forgetting" as their reason for nonperformance (Milne, Orbell, & Sheeran, 2002; Orbell, Hodgkins, & Sheeran, 1997). Similarly, meta-analysis has shown that the longer the time interval between measures of goal intentions and goal achievement, the less likely it is that intentions are realized (Sheeran & Orbell, 1998). These findings speak to the idea that remembering to act can be a vital but difficult task.

Even if one remembers what one intends to achieve, there is a second problem that may need to be resolved, namely, seizing the opportunity to act. This problem is especially acute when there is a deadline for performing the behavior or when the opportunity to act is presented only briefly. In these circumstances, people may fail to initiate goal-directed responses either because they fail to notice that a good time to get started has arrived or they are unsure how they should act when the moment presents itself. For instance, Oettingen. Hönig, and Gollwitzer (2000, Study 3) showed that considerable slippage can occur even when people have formed strong goal intentions to perform a certain behavior at a particular time. In one of their experimental conditions, participants were provided with diskettes containing four arithmetic tasks and formed goal intentions to perform these tasks on their computers at a particular time each Wednesday morning for the next 4 weeks. The program on the diskette recorded the time that participants started to work on the task from the clock on participants' computers. Findings indicated that the mean deviation from the intended start time was 8 hours, that is, a discrepancy of 2 hours on average for each specified opportunity. Similar findings were obtained by Dholakia and Bagozzi (2003, Study 2) using a "short fuse behavior" paradigm in which participants' task was to evaluate a website that could be accessed only during a short time window. Here, only 37% of participants who formed goal intentions were successful at accomplishing the task (see also Gollwitzer & Brandstätter, 1997). In sum, people may not get started with goal striving because they fail to seize suitable opportunities to act.

Third, there are also many instances in which people remember their "good" intention (e.g., to order a low fat meal) and recognize that an opportune moment is upon them (e.g., it is lunchtime at one's usual restaurant) but, nonetheless, they fail to initiate action (e.g., because "I just didn't fancy the low fat meal!"). This problem has to do with overcoming an initial reluctance to act. Initial reluctance is likely to arise when people have decided to initiate a behavior that involves a trade-off between attractive long-term consequences versus less attractive short-term consequences. For example, a strong goal intention to order the low fat meal might have been formed on the basis of longer-term cognitive considerations (e.g., the low fat meal is perceived as "healthy" or "beneficial"); however, one might not have anticipated how the short-term affective considerations would occupy attention at the moment of action (e.g., the low fat meal is perceived as "unsatisfying" or "tasteless" at the critical juncture). Such dilemmas between the head and the heart are commonplace (e.g., Loewenstein, Weber, Hsee, & Welch, 2001; Metcalfe & Mischel, 1999; Trafimow & Sheeran, 2004). Evidence for this explanation of intention–behavior discrepancies comes, for instance, from the field of sexual health in which findings show that young people may, in "the heat of the moment" of a sexual encounter, have problems overcoming reluctance to practice safer sex (e.g., Abraham et al., 1999; Sheeran, White, & Phillips, 1991; Wight, 1992). Overcoming initial reluctance is also a significant problem in several other domains (e.g., environmental, consumer, and academic goals).

2. Getting derailed

The goals of interest to social and health psychologists are not usually discrete one-shot actions but sequences of action that require continuous striving and repeated behavioral performance to be accomplished. The problem with such striving is that many situational contexts or self-states are not conducive to intention realization but instead hold the potential to derail an ongoing goal pursuit. Thus, the person's self-regulatory task is to shield goal striving from unwanted influences.

Shielding one's goal striving is necessary under the following circumstances. First, shielding is called for when conflicting attention and behavioral responses could make people stray off course. For example, despite making good initial progress with one's goal intention to finish a report, one may find one's attention wandering and feel compelled to join colleagues whom one hears gathering around the water cooler. In these instances, spontaneous attention to distracting stimuli may have to be suppressed in order to complete the goal. Such suppression may not be easy when the distractions are vivid, arousing, or highly valenced because, as the literature on cravings has shown (Kavanagh, May, & Andrade, 2005), people are liable to elaborate desirable stimuli through mental imagery. However, failing to control the attention paid to enticing stimuli (opportunities related to competing goal pursuits) can greatly undermine achievement of the focal (task) goal – as was demonstrated by Mischel and Patterson's (1978; Patterson & Mischel, 1976) classic studies on resistance to temptation (see also Gollwitzer & Schaal, 1998).

Of course, it may not be enough to suppress unwanted attention responses to appealing distractions in order to reach one's goal. Often, it will be necessary to suppress behavioral responses. For example, the person who succeeded in enacting her goal intention to order the low fat meal at lunchtime still has to forego the chocolate dessert after dinner if the superordinate goal intention is to lose weight. If an unwanted behavior possesses features of automaticity, it should be especially difficult to control (Aarts & Dijksterhuis, 2000a,b; Sheeran et al., 2005a; Verplanken & Aarts, 1999; Wood, Quinn, & Kashy, 2002). Keeping such behavioral responses in check merely by forming the respective goal intention may not be sufficient, as research on weight loss and smoking cessation has shown (e.g., COMMIT Research Group, 1995; Garner & Wooley, 1991). Findings from a recent meta-analysis (Ouellette & Wood, 1998) are also consistent with this idea. Goal intentions emerged as much poorer predictors of future action when antagonistic behaviors had been performed frequently and consistently in relevant contexts (see also Verplanken, Aarts, van Knippenberg, & Moonen, 1998). In sum, controlling interfering unwanted attention and behavioral responses makes an important difference to whether one's goal-directed efforts warrant the designation "inclined actor" versus "inclined abstainer."

There is a second circumstance in which shielding an ongoing goal pursuit becomes crucial (Gollwitzer et al., 2005). So far, our discussion of controlling unwanted attention and behavioral responses has assumed that people have some knowledge and awareness of what sorts of obstacles (distractions, temptations, barriers) the environmental context is likely to present, when those obstacles are likely to arise, and what kind of unwanted responses those obstacles typically generate. Knowing what might happen, when it might happen, and how it might affect us thus appears to be a prerequisite for the successful use of any strategy of suppression. However, there is a route to effectively shielding an ongoing goal pursuit that does not require the anticipation of a situational threat or its impact on goal striving. The existence of such an alternative strategy is crucial as, more often than not, we are not in a position to consciously anticipate the occurrence of obstacles and the working of habits, or in what form and intensity these will threaten ongoing goal pursuits. The following three social psychological phenomena exemplify what we have in mind when we speak of obstacles to an ongoing goal pursuit that are not anticipated by the individual: deindividuation effects on social loafing, the impact of loss frames on negotiation outcomes, and nonconscious priming of antagonistic goals.

Social loafing effects occur when people are asked to work in groups in which performance outcomes cannot be checked at an individual level (Karau & Williams, 1993; Latané, Williams, & Harkin, 1979). Under these circumstances, people show reduced effort and performance compared to situations in which individual outcomes can be identified. The problem is that people are unlikely to have insight into the negative impact of the group setting and task instructions on their performance. Not surprisingly, therefore, having the goal intention to perform well is not sufficient to overcome social loafing (Gollwitzer & Bayer, 2000).

A similar issue arises in relation to the impact of loss versus gain frames on negotiation outcomes (De Dreu, Carnevale, Emans, & van de Vliert, 1995; Neale & Bazerman, 1985). In a typical experiment, pairs of participants are asked to negotiate the distribution of some finite resource (e.g., land on an island). The framing of the negotiation is manipulated by either providing participants with information about how many points they lose by giving up elements of the resource (loss frame) or by telling participants how many points they gain by receiving these elements (gain frame). Findings indicate that cognitive loss frames lead to comparatively unfair agreements about resources and also hinder integrative solutions. Participants are not aware of the negative impact of loss frames on their negotiation behavior. Again, merely forming a goal intention to engage in fair and cooperative negotiation with one's partner fails to be sufficient to overcome the negative impact of loss framing (Trötschel & Gollwitzer, 2004).

Finally, people are unaware of the fact that their behavior is often guided by goals that have become activated directly by the situational context at hand. Auto-motive theory (Bargh, 1990; Bargh & Gollwitzer, 1994) proposes that goals that have a history of being acted upon in a particular situation have the potential to become directly activated by this critical situation without the need for conscious intent. Studies have used priming techniques to show that activated chronic goals have predictable effects on the intensity of goal striving. For example, participants who completed scrambled sentences designed to prime achievement goals performed better on a word puzzle task as compared to controls (Bargh, Gollwitzer, Lee-Chai, Barndollar, & Trötschel, 2001). Moreover, extensive debriefing indicated that participants had no awareness of either the activation of the goal or its impact on respective performance. Direct goal activation has serious implications for realizing one's goal intentions when the situational context activates a goal that is antagonistic to the focal goal. Consistent with this idea, Gollwitzer, Sheeran, Trötschel, and Webb (2004d) found that participants who had formed a goal intention to drive carefully in a driving simulator exhibited greater speed and more errors when they had been primed with the auto-motive of "moving fast" compared to when the primed automotive was to "move slow." Clearly, therefore, blocking the adverse contextual threat posed by situationally activated antagonistic goals constitutes an important challenge in shielding an ongoing goal pursuit.

The discussion so far only refers to derailments of goal striving by unanticipated unwanted influences that originate in the environment. But such unanticipated unwanted influences can also originate within the person (Gollwitzer et al., 2005). This is the third circumstance in which the shielding of an ongoing goal pursuit is needed – when detrimental self-states threaten goal attainment. The negative consequences of the following three self-states on goal striving may serve as examples: the effects of mood on stereotyping, the influence of self-definitional incompleteness on social sensitivity, and the impact of ego-depletion on subsequent task performance.

Being in a good mood signals to the self that one's current situation is unproblematic, and thus information processing is less elaborate or systematic as compared to being in a bad mood (Schwarz, 1990; Schwarz, Bless, & Bohner, 1991). Consequently, people are more liable to stereotyping when they are in a good mood than when they are in a bad mood (Bless, 1997; Bless & Fiedler, 1995). The impact of positive mood on stereotyping target persons is difficult to anticipate by the layperson and, thus, should be difficult to control. Indeed, Gollwitzer and Bayer (2000) found that merely having the goal intention to form nonstereotypical impressions did not attenuate the good-mood-effect on increased stereotyping.

Symbolic self-completion theory (Wicklund & Gollwitzer, 1982) proposes that when people who are highly committed to an identity goal (e.g., becoming a lawyer) obtain negative feedback about their accomplishments in the respective domain, they experience a sense of self-definitional incompleteness. This is a highly aversive self-evaluative state that is associated with compensatory efforts to show off alternative symbols or indicators of the aspired to identity in front of other people (e.g., by wanting to talk about one's achievements). Consequently, incomplete individuals tend to become absorbed in self-symbolizing activities and thus neglect the thoughts and feelings of an audience; their interactions with others exhibit social insensitivity (Gollwitzer & Wicklund, 1985). Gollwitzer and Bayer (2000) observed that this effect cannot be ameliorated by explicitly assigning participants the goal of taking the perspective of their interaction partners.

Finally, ego-depletion refers to the phenomenon that exerting self-control on an initial task produces a temporary reduction in people's capacity for self-control that is reflected in poor performance on a subsequent task (Baumeister, Bratlavsky, & Muraven, 1998; Muraven & Baumeister, 2000). For example, Baumeister et al. (1998, Experiment 1) showed that participants who had to eat radishes instead of tempting chocolate during an initial task, persisted for less time on a subsequent unsolvable puzzles task than did participants who were allowed to eat the chocolate during the initial task (these participants did not have to exert self-control). Apparently, ego-depletion can undermine task performance even when people have strong goal intentions to perform well. Consistent with this idea, Webb and Sheeran (2003) found that ego-depleted participants and nondepleted controls exhibited substantive differences in puzzle task performance. However, both groups reported devoting equivalent effort to the puzzle task and had equivalent desire to quit. Thus, ego-depletion would seem to be an important factor in reducing the intensity of goal striving and one in which appropriate goal intentions are not necessarily an effective defense.

3. Not calling a halt

Initiating and shielding goal striving from unwanted influences are crucial for successfully reaching goal completion. However, there is a third problem that needs to be resolved, namely, disengaging from goal striving that has become unproductive (Wrosch, Scheier, Carver, & Schulz, 2003). Disengagement may be straightforward when goal monitoring indicates satisfactory progress, or attainment of desired outcomes. However, a good deal of research indicates that it is very difficult to disengage from an ongoing goal pursuit when self-defensive concerns are activated. Researchers have studied such failure to disengage under varying labels, such as sunk costs (e.g., Arkes & Blumer, 1985), entrapment (e.g., Brockner, Rubin, & Lang, 1981), and escalation of commitment (e.g., Tan & Yates, 2002). However, the basic conceptualization of the phenomenon is similar (Bragger, Hantula, Bragger, Kirnan, & Kutcher, 2003). Again, mere goal intentions to halt a failing course of action are often insufficient as has been shown by work using standard escalation paradigms (Henderson, Gollwitzer, & Oettingen, 2004).

4. Overextending oneself

There is a fourth problem in goal striving that has to do with the fact that people have to pursue multiple goals (e.g., Austin & Vancouver, 1996; Carver & Scheier, 1998; Gollwitzer & Moskowitz, 1996). Thus, overextending oneself in an ongoing goal pursuit is likely to jeopardize the achievement of subsequent important goals. Accordingly, effective self-regulation of goal striving needs to conserve the person's capability to successfully engage in subsequent goal pursuit once striving for the initial goal has ended. However, action control by goal intentions makes people vulnerable to overextension.

A good example is the phenomenon of ego-depletion in which assigning participants goal intentions to perform well on an initial task that requires self-control is associated with reduced self-regulatory capability (and diminished performance) on a subsequent task (Baumeister et al., 1998). The well-known ironic effects of mental control (Wegner, 1994) constitute another instance in which goal intentions can produce overextension on an initial task and thereby diminish future capability. For example, Macrae, Bodenhausen, Milne, and Jetten (1994) assigned participants the goal intention of forming a nonstereotypical impression of a homeless person (or not) and asked them to provide a written statement of their impression. After a 5-minute filler task, participants were asked to evaluate homeless people in general on semantic differential scales that included five stereotypical adjective pairs (e.g., drunk–sober, busy–lazy).

Findings indicated that goal intentions were successful in producing less stereotypical impressions of the person on the initial task compared to controls. However, on the subsequent rating task, goal intention participants gave *more* stereotypical evaluations of homeless people in general. That is, goal intentions to suppress stereotypes produced a rebound effect. In sum, achieving desired outcomes on the basis of mere goal intentions has costs in terms of undermining the success of subsequent goal pursuits.

B. Forming implementation intentions: a strategy for effective self-regulation of goal striving

The idea tested in the present meta-analysis is that implementation intentions (i.e., if–then plans) facilitate effective self-regulation of goal striving. Implementation intentions should enhance people's ability to initiate, maintain, disengage from, and undertake further goal striving and thereby increase the likelihood that strong goal intentions are realized successfully. In other words, this form of planning is expected to bridge the intention–behavior gap.

Implementation intentions are if–then plans that connect good opportunities to act with cognitive or behavioral responses that are effective in accomplishing one's goals. Whereas goal intentions specify what one wants to achieve (i.e., "I intend to reach Z!"), implementation intentions specify both the behavior that one will perform in the service of goal achievement and the situational context in which one will enact it (i.e., "If situation Y occurs, then I will initiate goal-directed behavior X!"). Thus, goal intentions and implementation intentions can easily be distinguished on the basis of their content and structure; a goal intention refers to *what* one intends to achieve, whereas an implementation intention specifies *when, where,* and *how* one intends to achieve it.

To form an implementation intention, the person must (1) identify a response that will promote goal attainment and (2) anticipate a suitable occasion to initiate that response. For instance, a possible implementation intention in the service of the goal intention to do more exercise would link an appropriate behavior (e.g., take the stairway instead of the elevator) to a suitable situational context (e.g., standing in front of the entrance to the elevator at work). As a consequence, a strong mental link is created between the critical situation of waiting for the elevator and the goal-directed response of walking upstairs.

Selecting suitable opportunities to enact goal-directed responses entails that people anticipate situations in which it would be fitting to execute goal-directed responses. The critical situation specified in one's plan can involve an internal cue (e.g., a strong feeling) or an external cue (e.g., a particular place, object, person, or point in time). The cues can either be related to good opportunities to act (i.e., it is easy to perform actions that are instrumental for reaching the goal) or to anticipated obstacles to goal striving. Thus, cue selection can focus on initiating and stabilizing the goal striving at hand or on shielding it from particular anticipated obstacles.

Forming an implementation intention also involves the selection of an effective goal-directed behavior. In line with the theory of goal systems (Kruglanksi et al., 2002; Shah, Kruglanksi, & Friedman, 2003), it is assumed that for any given goal, various routes to goal attainment are available. Accordingly, the specification of the then-component of an implementation intention can take many different forms. For instance, not only can an implementation intention specify one of the many behaviors that lead to goal attainment, it can also specify the suppression of one of the many responses that prevent goal attainment. In addition, the specification of the goal-directed responses can either focus on the initiation or the maintenance of goal striving. Finally, the then-component of an implementation intention may specify ignoring those stimuli that have the potential to instigate unwanted attention or behavior responses that could derail an ongoing goal pursuit (see Appendix 1 for sample implementation intentions).

C. Component processes of implementation intentions

The mental links created by implementation intentions are expected to facilitate goal attainment on the basis of psychological processes that relate both to the anticipated situation (specified in the if-component of the plan) and the specified response (the plan's then-component). As forming implementation intentions implies the selection of a critical future situation, it is assumed that the mental representation of this situation becomes highly activated (Gollwitzer, 1999). The person who forms an implementation intention selects a situation that is ripe for action to achieve the goal; the person is therefore perceptually ready to encounter this critical situation. This idea implies that processing information about the critical situation is highly proficient (Gollwitzer, 1993; Gollwitzer, Bayer, Steller, & Bargh, 2004a; Webb & Sheeran, 2004). That is, compared to those who merely form a respective goal intention, people who form implementation intentions should exhibit increased accessibility of the critical cue, and thus should be better able to detect the cue and discriminate the cue from other similar stimuli. For instance, Webb and Sheeran (2004) used a classic illusion paradigm from the psychology of language to investigate cue detection by goal intentions as compared to implementation intentions. Participants were asked to form the goal intention to count the instances of the letter *f* in the following piece of text: "Finished files are the/result of years of scientific/study combined with the/experience of years." (Line breaks are marked by back slashes.) The illusion resides in the fact that most people count only three *f*s because they miss the *f* in the three instances of the word "of." However, when participants furnished the goal intention with a respective implementation intention (i.e., "And as soon as I see the letter *f*, then I'll add one more to my count!") their detection of the difficult-to-identify *f*s improved. Additional experiments showed that this improved detection of critical cues did not have costs in terms of false alarms or reduced performance on identifying noncritical stimuli, even when these stimuli were quite similar to the critical cue (i.e., ambiguous cues).

Increased accessibility of the specified situation should also facilitate spontaneous attention to the cue and engender better recall of the cue (Gollwitzer et al., 2004a). Spontaneous attention was demonstrated in a dichotic listening experiment. When the critical cues specified in implementation intentions were presented in the nonattended channel, participants' shadowing performance (i.e., repeating the words presented in the attended channel) declined. Gollwitzer et al. (2004a) also showed in a cued recall experiment that the situations specified in if–then plans are better remembered compared to alternative good opportunities to act. In sum, forming an implementation intention should induce heightened sensitivity to the critical situation at each stage of information processing such that people are better able to detect, attend to, and remember specified cues when these cues are encountered later.

Specifying that one will perform a particular goal-directed response in the then-component of a plan, at the critical moment stipulated in the if-component of the plan, involves a strategic abdication of effortful action control. This is because forming an implementation intention delegates control of behavior from the self to specified situational cues that directly elicit action (i.e., implementation intentions create "instant habits") (Gollwitzer, 1999). Forming an if–then plan means that the person commits herself in advance to acting as soon as certain contextual constraints are satisfied. Once that situation is encountered, action initiation should proceed swiftly and effortlessly and without requiring the person's conscious intent. Accordingly, the execution of a behavior specified in an implementation intention should exhibit features of automaticity as identified by Bargh (1992, 1994).

Automaticity commonly characterizes highly overlearned activities (e.g., driving a car, typing) including the operation of habits (Aarts & Dijksterhuis, 2000a,b; Sheeran et al., 2005a; Wood et al., 2002). Action control by implementation intentions seems to exhibit three features of automatic processes: immediacy, efficiency, and lack of conscious intent. Immediacy has been tested by means of response latencies (e.g., Webb & Sheeran, 2004) and the temporal proximity of actual performance to the time of performance specified in the implementation intention (e.g., Gollwitzer & Brandstätter, 1997; Oettingen et al., 2000, Experiment 3). For instance, Gollwitzer and Brandstätter had research participants watch a video presentation of a presumed Nazi who expressed racial slurs and mark good opportunities to speak up. Participants all formed the goal intention to counterargue at opportune moments when watching the video a second time. A subset of participants also formed implementation intentions by mentally linking these critical situations with respective counter-arguments. Only having marked critical opportunities (mere goal intention condition) was less effective in promoting the immediate initiation of counter-arguments compared to having also formed implementation intentions (i.e., if–then plan participants were much faster in using the marked opportunities).

The efficiency of implementation intention effects is supported by studies that varied cognitive load either through selection of the sample (e.g., schizophrenic patients, heroin addicts under withdrawal) or by experimental manipulations using dual task paradigms (e.g., Brandstätter, Lengfelder, & Gollwitzer, 2001; Lengfelder & Gollwitzer, 2000). For instance, Brandstätter et al. (2001) assigned heroin addiction patients the task of writing a curriculum vitae within a set time period. Forming implementation intentions that specified exactly when and where to get started with this task helped not only control participants (i.e., heroin users who were no longer experiencing withdrawal symptoms) to meet this task but also those participants who still showed withdrawal symptoms. Apparently, the effect of implementation intentions on task achievement did not interact with the cognitive load (drug urge) experienced by the participants. Evidence for efficiency of action control by implementation intentions was also observed in experiments in which participants had to perform two tasks at the same time. The secondary task in these studies was always a Go/No Go task, whereas the primary task was either a memorization task or a tracking task (Brandstätter et al., 2001, Studies 3 and 4; Lengfelder & Gollwitzer, 2001, Study 2). The implementation intention was linked to performing the Go/No Go task and the difficulty of the primary task was varied (easy vs. difficult). The beneficial effects of implementation intentions on performance in the secondary task were not qualified by an interaction with the primary task indicating that the operation of implementation intentions is efficient (i.e., independent of cognitive load). Moreover, better performance was observed in the primary task during those phases of the secondary task that were guided by implementation intentions (i.e., a transfer of freed resources).

Finally, there is evidence that the effective operation of implementation intentions does not require that people be consciously aware of either the anticipated critical situation or the respective goal intention (e.g., Bayer, Moskowitz, & Gollwitzer, 2004; Sheeran, Webb, & Gollwitzer, 2005c). Bayer et al. (2004) demonstrated that conscious awareness of the specified situation was redundant in two experiments that used subliminal priming of respective cues. In one study, participants were asked to classify a series of geometric figures (e.g., circles, ellipses, squares) as rounded or angular objects by left- or right-button–press responses. All participants formed the goal intention to classify the objects as fast and accurately as possible. Implementation intention participants were in addition asked to make the following plan: "And if I see a triangle, then I will press the respective button immediately!" This implementation intention led to faster classification responses for triangles. Importantly, classification performance on all angular figures was facilitated when these figures were preceded by a subliminal triangle prime compared to a control prime (the percentage symbol, %). No such effects were observed for goal intention participants.

Moreover, Sheeran et al. (2005c) showed that people need not be consciously aware of the underlying goal intention for implementation intention effects to occur. All participants formed the conscious goal intention to solve puzzles from the Wechsler Adult Intelligence Scale (WAIS III) as accurately as possible. Half of the participants also formed an implementation intention in relation to another dimension of performance, namely, to solve the puzzles as quickly as possible. This implementation intention manipulation was then crossed with a priming procedure that activated the goal of responding quickly outside of awareness. Speed and accuracy of responses to the puzzles was then measured. Even though participants reported no awareness of the primed goal during debriefing, findings indicated that responses were fastest when participants were primed to respond quickly and had formed respective implementation intentions. This study shows that conscious intent is not required to observe implementation intention effects on performance.

In sum, the evidence on component processes suggests that people can enhance rates of goal completion obtained by conscious and effortful guidance of behavior (action control by goal intentions) by strategically switching to automated self-regulation of goal striving (action control by implementation intentions).

IV. Present review

Accumulated research indicates that there is a substantial gap between people's goal intentions and their goal achievement. This is because forming a goal intention does not prepare people sufficiently for dealing with self-regulatory problems in initiating, maintaining, disengaging from, or overextending oneself in goal striving. Forming an implementation intention, on the other hand, spells out the when, where, and how of goal striving in advance. If–then plans are therefore thought to enhance the accessibility of the specified critical situation and induce automatic execution of the specified response. The consequence is that people should remember to act, seize good opportunities, overcome initial reluctance, suppress unwanted responses, block detrimental self-states and adverse contextual influences, and successfully disengage from goals without costs to self-regulatory capability. Goal striving should be regulated effectively, and goal achievement should thereby be facilitated.

The present review tests these ideas using meta-analysis. First, we assess the overall impact of implementation intention formation on goal achievement. We evaluate potential moderators of implementation intention effects and test whether implementation intentions are effective in promoting performance in different domains of attainment. Second, we test the effectiveness of implementation intentions in overcoming self-regulatory problems that have to do with initiating goal striving, shielding goals from unwanted influences, disengaging from failing goals, and conserving self-regulatory capability. Finally, we calibrate the effect sizes for the component (if–then) processes of implementation intentions.

A. Method

1. Sample of studies

Several methods were used to generate the sample of studies: (1) computerized searches were conducted on social scientific and medical databases (PsychINFO, Social Science Citation Index and Conference Papers Index [Web of Knowledge], Medline, Index Medicus, and Dissertation Abstracts International Online) from January 1990 to December 2003 using the keywords *implementation intention(s)* and *plan(s)*, (2) references in each article identified above were evaluated for inclusion, and (3) authors were contacted and requests were made for unpublished studies and studies in press.

Studies were included in the review if (a) the implementation intention formed by participants specified the performance of a goal-directed response upon encountering an internal or external critical cue and (b) a statistical association between the formation of an implementation intention and an outcome variable could be retrieved (or obtained). Using these criteria, 94 tests of the relationship between implementation intentions and goal achievement could be included in the meta-analysis. The focal goal and effect size for each test are presented in Table I. The 94 independent tests come from 63 reports (these reports are preceded by an asterisk in the reference list).

2. Meta-analytic strategy

The effect size estimate used here was d, which is the difference between the means for two groups divided by a pooled standard deviation and corrected for small sample bias (Hedges & Olkin, 1985). We subtracted the control group mean from the mean for the implementation intention group so that a positive d value indicates the benefit in performance conferred by forming an implementation intention. The average effect size was computed by averaging the d values with each d weighted by the reciprocal of its variance. As a test of significance, 95% confidence intervals were computed around each mean. Where studies reported r, t, F, χ^2, or contingency tables, we transformed values into ds using the formulas supplied by Hedges and Olkin (1985) and Hunter (1990). Homogeneity of effect sizes was tested by means of the Q statistic that has an approximate chi-square distribution with k-1 degrees of freedom, k being the number of effect sizes. When Q is significant ($p < 0.05$), effect sizes are heterogeneous.

3. Multiple measures and multiple tests

Several papers contained data from more than one sample or reported effect sizes for multiple measures of an independent variable or multiple measures of the dependent variable. We tried to take advantage of the richness of these data without violating the assumption of independence that underlies the validity of meta-analysis. Data from independent samples were, therefore, treated as separate units. In the case of multiple measures of independent or dependent variables, the average d within each study was the unit of analysis. Where studies contained multiple nonindependent samples, we used the conservative strategy of computing the weighted average effect size and using the smallest N in the analysis in order to determine the overall effect size for that study (Sheeran, Abraham, & Orbell, 1999). For example, Holland, Aarts, and Langendam (in press) examined the impact of forming implementation intentions on objective measures of recycling old paper ($N = 54$, $d = 1.32$) and recycling plastic cups ($N = 109$, $d = 1.50$). The effect size used to represent this study is the weighted average of the two effects ($d = 1.42$), and the sample size is 54.

Table I Studies of the impact of implementation intention formation on goal achievement

Author(s)	Goal	N	d
Aarts, Dijksterhuis, and Midden (1999)	Collect a coupon/latencies to cues	40	0.80
Ajzen, Czasch, and Flood (2002)	Rate TV newscasts	102	0.47
Armitage (2004)	Eat a low-fat diet	126	0.30
Bagozzi, Dholakia, and Basuroy (2003)	Personal goals	153	0.68
Bamberg (2000)	Public transport use	90	0.45
Bamberg (2002)	Organic food purchase	160	0.32
Bayer, Jaudas, and Gollwitzer (2002)	Task switch	40	0.85
Bayer, Moskowitz, and Gollwitzer (2004) Study 1	Retaliation behavior	61	0.98
Bayer et al. (2004) Study 2	Classification of geometric shapes	61	0.49
Brandstätter et al. (2003)	Initiation of vocational retraining	126	0.72
Brandstätter, Lengfelder, and Gollwitzer (2001) Study 1	Write a curriculum vitae	41	1.32
Brandstätter et al. (2001) Study 2	Go/No Go task	61	0.93
Brandstätter et al. (2001) Study 3	Go/No Go task	68	0.63
Brandstätter et al. (2001) Study 4	Go/No Go task	33	1.10
Brüwer, Bayer, and Gollwitzer (2002)	Simon effect task	34	2.20
Bulgarella, Oettingen, and Gollwitzer (2003)	Numerical judgment dilemma	34	0.80
Chasteen, Park, and Schwarz (2001) Study 1	Prospective memory task	68	0.82
Dewitte, Verguts, and Lens (2003) Study 1	Ten personal goals	15	0.10
Dewitte et al. (2003) Study 2	Ten personal goals	14	0.10
Dewitte et al. (2003) Study 3	Ten personal goals	16	0.18
Dholakia and Bagozzi (2003) Study 1	Reading assignment	102	0.56
Dholakia and Bagozzi (2003) Study 2	Visit website	138	0.43
Dholakia and Bagozzi (2003) Study 3	Visit website	179	0.82
Dholakia and Bagozzi (2002) Study 1	Product/service purchase	131	0.49
Dholakia and Bagozzi (2002) Study 2	Personal goals	169	0.41
Dieffendorf and Lord (2003)	Human resource task	170	0.41
Einstein, McDaniel, Williford, Pagan, and Dismukes (2003)	Prospective memory task	48	−0.24
Gillholm, Ettema, Sellart, and Garling (2004a) Study 1	Mundane activities	28	1.01
Gillholm et al. (1999) Study 2	Mail response forms	48	0.02
Gollwitzer and Bayer (2004a) Study 1	Degree of perspective taking	34	1.16
Gollwitzer and Bayer (2004a) Study 2	Social loafing task	42	0.75
Gollwitzer and Bayer (2004a) Study 3	Mood-induced gender stereotyping	54	0.80
Gollwitzer, Bayer, Steller, and Bargh (2002) Study 1	Cue detection	46	0.82
Gollwitzer et al. (2002) Study 2	Dichotic listening task	55	0.72
Gollwitzer et al. (2002) Study 3	Recall of specified cues	79	0.87
Gollwitzer and Brandstätter (1997) Study 1	Personal goals	70	0.43
Gollwitzer and Brandstätter (1997) Study 2	Complete a written report	36	0.90
Gollwitzer and Brandstätter (1997) Study 3	Counter arguments to racist remarks	60	0.52
Gollwitzer, Sheeran, and Seifert (2004c) Study 3	Solving law cases	55	1.10
Gollwitzer, Sheeran, Trötschel, and Webb (2004d) Study 1	Driving simulation dilemma	69	0.98

continued

Table I Continued

Author(s)	Goal	N	d
Gollwitzer et al. (2004d) Study 2	Accessibility of drinking behavior	72	0.49
Gollwitzer et al. (2004d) Study 3	Helping behavior dilemma	60	1.25
Gollwitzer et al. (2004d) Study 4	Cooperation in resource dilemma	60	0.90
Gollwitzer, Trötschel, Bayer, and Sumner (2004e) Study 1	Stereotype rebound task	30	1.81
Gollwitzer et al. (2004e) Study 2	Anagram performance	31	1.12
Henderson, Gollwitzer, and Oettingen (2004) Study 1	Escalation of commitment task	87	0.52
Henderson et al. (2004) Study 2	Escalation of commitment task	96	0.54
Henderson et al. (2004) Study 3	Escalation of commitment task	187	0.43
Holland, Aarts, and Langendam (in press)	Recycling behaviors	54	1.42
Koestner, Downie, Horberg, and Hata (2002a)	Personal goals	106	0.39
Koestner, Lekes, Powers, and Chicoine (2002b) Study 1	Personal goals	106	0.39
Koestner et al. (2002b) Study 2	New Year resolutions	38	−0.32
Koole and Van't Spijjker (2000)	Write a report	80	0.75
Lengfelder and Gollwitzer (2001) Study 2	Go/No Go task	67	0.80
Lippke and Ziegelmann (2002)	Exercise	88	0.18
Milne, Orbell, and Sheeran (2002)	Exercise	248	1.25
Milne and Sheeran (2002a)	Testicular self-examination	432	0.43
Milne and Sheeran (2002b)	Persistence with boring task	66	1.35
Milne and Sheeran (2002c)	Visit study skills website	183	0.87
Murgraff, White, and Phillips (1996)	Binge drinking	102	0.68
Oettingen, Hönig, and Gollwitzer (2000) Study 2	Compose a CV	20	1.25
Oettingen et al. (2000) Study 3	Complete a project	25	0.80
Orbell, Hodgkins, and Sheeran (1997)	Breast self-examination	155	1.22
Orbell and Sheeran (1999) Study 3	Reduce snack food consumption	111	0.61
Orbell and Sheeran (1999) Study 4	Reduce snack food consumption	93	0.45
Orbell and Sheeran (2000)	Recovery of functional activities	64	0.70
Prestwich, Lawton, and Conner (2003a)	Personal goals	79	0.54
Prestwich, Lawton, and Conner (2003b)	Exercise	58	0.68
Rise, Thompson, and Verplanken (2003)	Exercise and recycling	112	1.58
Schaal (1993)	Arithmetic task	40	0.93
Sheeran and Milne (2003)	Reduce snack good consumption	129	0.49
Sheeran and Orbell (1999) Study 1	Vitamin supplement use	78	0.35
Sheeran and Orbell (1999) Study 2	Vitamin supplement use	37	0.59
Sheeran and Orbell (2000)	Cervical cancer screening	104	0.58
Sheeran and Silverman (2003)	Attendance at workplace safety training	271	0.52
Sheeran and Webb (2003)	Stroop performance	48	1.62
Sheeran, Webb, and Gollwitzer (2005c) Study 1	Independent study	85	0.35
Sheeran et al. (2005c) Study 2	Performance on puzzle task	40	0.70
Sniehotta, Scholtz, and Schwarzer (2002a)	Cardiac rehabilitation exercise/training	74	0.61
Sniehotta, Scholtz, and Schwarzer (2002b)	Physical activity	65	0.70
Steadman and Quine (2000)	Vitamin supplement use	174	0.32
Steadman and Quine (in press)	Testicular self-examination	75	0.54

Table I Continued

Author(s)	Goal	N	d
Stephens and Conner (1999)	Resist taking up smoking	124	0.37
Trötschel and Gollwitzer (2004) Study 1	Framing effects in negotiation	43	0.82
Trötschel and Gollwitzer (2004) Study 2	Framing effects in negotiation	57	0.87
Verplanken and Faes (1999)	Healthy eating	102	0.47
Webb and Sheeran (2003) Study 1	Persistence with unsolvable puzzles	32	0.87
Webb and Sheeran (2003) Study 2	Stroop performance	57	0.87
Webb and Sheeran (2004) Study 1	Letter identification	54	0.63
Webb and Sheeran (2004) Study 2	Number identification	42	0.75
Webb and Sheeran (2004) Study 3	Number identification	53	0.82
Webb and Sheeran (in press, b) Study 1	Personal goals	646	0.75
Webb and Sheeran (in press, b) Study 2	Academic performance	129	0.56
Williams (2003)	Return postcard	60	0.56

B. Results

1. Overall effect size

The overall impact of forming implementation intentions on goal achievement was $d = 0.65$ based on $k = 94$ tests that involved 8461 participants. This effect had a 95% confidence interval from 0.60 to 0.70. According to Cohen's (1992) power primer, $d = 0.20$ is a "small" effect, $d = 0.50$ is a "medium" -sized effect, whereas $d = 0.80$ is a "large" effect. Thus, the effect size that characterizes the impact of if–then planning on goal achievement is of medium-to-large magnitude.

a. Moderators of Implementation Intentions Effects. We examined methodological moderators of the relationship between implementation intentions and goal achievement in order to ensure that the effect sizes for if–then plans were not exaggerated by weaker methods (e.g., correlational rather than experimental designs). The homogeneity test encouraged a search for moderators as there was significant variability in the effect sizes obtained in individual studies, $Q(93) = 173.46$, $p < 0.001$. Moderator analyses were conducted for three methodological factors: type of sample, study design (correlational vs. experimental), and measurement of goal attainment (self-report vs. objective).

Table II shows that most tests of implementation intention effects were conducted among university students ($k = 79$) though eight tests sampled members of the public and there were two tests of children/young people. Four tests were conducted with physically ill people, and there were three tests among people with psychological problems (schizophrenic patients, frontal lobe patients, and heroin addicts). Findings showed that, excluding people with psychological problems, effect sizes were of medium size and equivalent magnitude across samples, $Q(3) = 4.01$, $p > 0.25$. Implementation intentions appeared to have stronger effects for people with psychological problems compared to the other groups; this difference proved significant when subgroup comparisons were conducted ($ds = 1.10$ and 0.66, respectively), $Q(1) = 4.54$, $p < 0.04$. This finding suggests that forming implementation intentions is especially beneficial to goal attainment among people who have difficulties with regulating their behavior.

Findings indicated that implementation intentions were similarly effective whether the study design was correlational or experimental ($ds = 0.70$ and 0.65, respectively), $Q(1) = 1.93$, $p > 0.16$. Moreover, the impact of implementation intentions on goal achievement was not exaggerated by overreliance on self-report measures of behavior. Implementation intentions had similar

Table II Impact of methodological factors on effect sizes for implementation intentions

Factor	N	k	d	95% CI	Q
Sample					
General public	1076	8	0.58	[0.45, 0.70]	14.09*
Children/young adults	144	2	0.47	[0.14, 0.85]	2.38
People with physical illness	291	4	0.52	[0.28, 0.77]	3.66
People with psychological problems					
Schizophrenic patients	20	1	1.01	–	–
Brain-injured patients	34	1	0.87	–	–
Heroin addicts	41	1	1.32	–	–
University students	6855	79	0.65	[0.61, 0.70]	147.93***
Design					
Correlational	1688	11	0.70	[0.61, 0.82]	20.23*
Experimental	6773	83	0.65	[0.61, 0.70]	151.59***
Measurement					
Self-report	4488	36	0.63	[0.58, 0.70]	80.96***
Objective	3973	58	0.67	[0.61, 0.74]	92.32**
Publication status					
Unpublished	3759	46	0.67	[0.61, 0.72]	75.13***
Published	4702	48	0.65	[0.59, 70]	98.23***

$*p < 0.05$, $**p < 0.01$, $***p < 0.001$.

Note: The sum of k equals 96 because data from two different samples were disaggregated in two studies (Lengfelder & Gollwitzer, 2001, Study 2; Brandstätter et al., 2001, Study 2). N=sample size; k=number of independent effects; d=effect size; CI=confidence interval; Q=homogeneity statistic.

effects whether or not the outcome was measured objectively ($d=0.67$) or by self-report ($d=0.63$), $Q(1)=2.18$, $p=0.14$.

We also examined whether publication status was associated with the strength of observed implementation intention effects. Forty-nine percent of the effects that could be included in the review were unpublished ($k=46$), and it is possible that unpublished tests may be of poorer methodological quality than are published tests (Rosenthal, 1984). This could mean that the overall estimate of effect size is inflated. However, there was no difference in effect sizes from published versus unpublished tests ($ds=0.65$ and 0.67, respectively), $Q(1)=1.53$, $p=0.22$.

b. Effect Sizes for Different Goal Domains. To test the generality of implementation intention effects, values of d were computed for different goal domains. We drew on the classification of domains used in Kim and Hunter's (1993) comprehensive meta-analysis of the impact of topic on attitude-behavior relations in order to categorize the goals (Canary & Seibold, 1984). Effects were available for seven of the domains identified by Kim and Hunter (health, academic, consumer, environmental, prosocial, antiracist, and laboratory tasks). An eighth category was personal goals because several studies asked participants to nominate their own desired outcomes that were then furnished with implementation intentions (or not).

Findings indicated that implementation intentions had medium or large effects for all domains (Table III). The goals examined most frequently related to laboratory tasks ($k=38$) and health ($k=23$). There were large effects for antiracist, prosocial, and environmental behaviors ($ds=0.87$, 1.01, and 1.12, respectively). There were medium-to-large effects for laboratory tasks and academic achievement ($ds=0.70$ and 0.72, respectively) and medium-sized effects for consumer behaviors, health behaviors, and personal goals. Overall, Table III indicates that implementation intentions have reliable effects for a wide range of goal domains.

Table III Meta-analysis of implementation intention effects for different goal domains

Goal domain	N	k	d	95% CI	χ^2
Consumer	291	2	0.41	[0.16, 0.65]	0.50
Environmental	256	3	1.12	[0.85, 1.42]	17.07***
Antiracist	144	3	0.87	[0.52, 1.25]	5.30
Prosocial	254	5	1.01	[0.72, 1.28]	1.91
Academic	836	9	0.72	[0.56, 0.87]	7.42
Personal	1391	11	0.58	[0.47, 0.70]	14.11
Health	2861	23	0.59	[0.52, 0.67]	47.92***
Laboratory	2428	38	0.70	[0.61, 0.79]	59.90*

$*p < 0.05$, $**p < 0.01$, $***p < 0.001$.

Note: N = sample size; k = number of independent effects; d = effect size; CI = confidence interval; Q = homogeneity statistic.

2. Effect sizes for different self-regulatory problems

Table IV presents the effect sizes for implementation intentions for self-regulatory problems associated with initiating goal striving, shielding goals from unwanted influences, disengaging from failing goals, and conserving self-regulatory capability. Three problems that militate against action initiation are remembering to act, seizing opportunities, and overcoming initial reluctance. There were $k = 11$, 20, and 21 tests of these problems, respectively. For all three problems, effect sizes for implementation intentions were of medium-to-large magnitude ($ds = 0.54$, 0.61, and 0.65, respectively). These findings indicate that implementation intentions help to ensure that people (1) do not forget to perform intended actions, (2) do not miss good opportunities to initiate action, and (3) do not fail to act because they are swayed by short-term considerations. The overall effect size was $d = 0.61$ indicating that implementation intention formation makes an important difference to whether or not people initiate goal striving successfully.

We identified three self-regulatory tasks in relation to shielding goals from unwanted influences, namely, suppressing unwanted responses, blocking detrimental self-states, and blocking

Table IV Meta-analysis of implementation intention effects for different self-regulatory tasks in goal striving

Self-regulatory tasks	N	k	d	95% CI	Q
Initiating goal striving					
Remembering to act	983	11	0.54	[0.45, 0.72]	16.79
Seizing opportunities	2270	20	0.61	[0.52, 0.70]	23.75
Overcoming initial reluctance	2588	21	0.65	[0.56, 0.72]	72.82***
Overall	5841	52	0.61	[0.56, 0.67]	114.21***
Shielding goal striving from unwanted influences					
Suppressing unwanted responses					
Attention responses	184	3	0.90	[0.61, 1.25]	5.75
Behavioral responses	559	5	0.54	[0.35, 0.70]	1.59
Blocking detrimental self-states	248	5	1.10	[0.80, 1.39]	4.40
Blocking adverse contextual influences	405	8	0.93	[0.70, 1.16]	2.22
Overall	1396	21	0.77	[0.67, 0.87]	27.60
Disengaging from futile goal striving	370	3	0.47	[0.26, 0.70]	0.22
Conserving self-regulatory capability	93	3	1.28	[0.77, 1.76]	3.08

$*p < 0.05$, $**p < 0.01$, $***p < 0.001$.

Note: N = sample size; k = number of independent effects; d = effect size; CI = confidence interval; Q = homogeneity statistic.

adverse contextual influences. Implementation intentions proved beneficial for all three tasks. First, implementation intentions had a large effect on suppressing unwanted attention responses ($d=0.90$) and had a medium effect on suppressing unwanted behavioral responses ($d=0.54$). Second, implementation intentions had a large effect on goal achievement even when participants were in a detrimental self-state ($d=1.10$). Implementation intentions promoted performance when participants had incomplete self-definitions ($d=1.12$, $k=2$), were ego-depleted ($d=1.22$, $k=2$), or were in a good mood and therefore liable to stereotyping ($d=0.80$, $k=1$). Third, a large effect was obtained for implementation intentions when goal achievement was blocked by adverse contextual influences ($d=0.93$). Forming an implementation intention meant that participants were able to overcome the characteristic impacts of deindividuation on social loafing ($d=0.80$, $k=1$), loss frames on negotiation ($d=0.85$, $k=2$), and situational activation of goals that were antagonistic to the focal goal striving ($d=0.98$, $k=5$). In sum, implementation intentions are effective in blocking adverse contextual influences.

As well as initiating goal striving and shielding ongoing goal pursuits from unwanted influences, people must also disengage from goal striving when such striving is no longer productive. Three studies tested the efficacy of implementation intentions in helping people disengage from failing goals. Findings indicated that implementation intention effects were of approximately medium size ($d=0.47$).

The final self-regulatory problem is whether implementation intention formation conserves people's capability for future goal striving. Findings showed that, even when the experimental settings involved two phases and the initial task was known to engender performance deficits on the subsequent task, implementation intentions still had a large effect on performance ($d=1.28$). Participants who formed implementation intentions to control initial performance did not exhibit ego-depletion or stereotype rebound. In both cases, effect sizes for implementation intentions were positive and large ($ds=0.87$, and 1.81, respectively).

3. Component processes of implementation intentions

Forming implementation intentions should activate the mental representation of the specified cues (if-component) and automate responding to these cues (as specified in the then-component). Table V shows that implementation intentions had large effects on the detection, discrimination, and accessibility of critical cues ($ds=0.72$, 0.82, and 0.95, respectively) and on the

Table V Meta-analysis of component processes of implementation intentions

Component process	N	k	d	95% CI	Q
If-component					
Cue detection	100	2	0.72	[0.30, 1.16]	0.23
Cue discrimination	53	1	0.82	–	–
Cue accessibility	40	1	0.95	–	–
Attention to cue	55	1	0.72	–	–
Memory for cue	79	1	0.87	–	–
Overall	327	6	0.80	[0.56, 1.04]	0.89
Then-component					
Immediacy	363	7	0.77	[0.49, 0.98]	2.09
Efficiency	278	7	0.85	[0.58, 1.12]	26.45
Lack of intent	122	3	0.72	[0.39, 1.07]	1.62

*$p<0.05$, **$p<0.01$, ***$p<0.001$.

Note: $N=$ sample size; $k=$ number of independent effects; $d=$ effect size; $CI=$ confidence interval; $Q=$ homogeneity statistic.

attention paid to, and memory for, those cues ($ds = 0.72$ and 0.87, respectively). The overall effect size for processes related to the if-component of the plan was large ($d = 0.80$) indicating that implementation intentions are associated with highly proficient processing of critical cues.

There were 7, 7, and 3 tests, respectively, of the immediacy and efficiency of, and redundancy of conscious intent for action control by implementation intentions. Implementation intentions showed large effects for each of these three key features of automaticity. If–then plans produced more immediate responding ($d = 0.77$), were efficient with respect to cognitive resources ($d = 0.85$), and proceeded without the need for conscious intent ($d = 0.72$). These findings provide strong support for the postulated automaticity of action control induced by implementation intentions.

C. Discussion

Findings from 94 studies involving more than 8000 participants indicated that the effect size associated with the impact of implementation intention formation on goal attainment is $d = 0.65$, an effect of medium-to-large magnitude (Cohen, 1992). This effect size is impressive because $d = 0.65$ represents the difference in goal achievement engendered by furnishing a goal intention with a respective implementation intention compared to the formation of a goal intention on its own. The implication is that if–then planning substantially increases the likelihood of attaining one's goals.

Several features of the meta-analysis serve to underline the effectiveness of implementation intentions in promoting goal achievement. First, it is unlikely that the review suffers from the "file drawer problem" (e.g., Rosenthal, 1984) as 49% of the included tests were unpublished. Moreover, publication status had no impact on the effect size obtained for implementation intentions. Second, 88% of tests involved experimental designs (i.e., random assignment of participants to implementation intention formation) that increase confidence in the findings. It was also the case that the effect sizes obtained for experimental versus correlational studies were equivalent (unlike meta-analyses of the impact of goal intentions on goal achievement in which experimental tests show much weaker effects compared to correlational tests; Webb & Sheeran, in press a). Third, the composition of the sample generally did not moderate implementation intention effects. If–then plans were similarly effective in promoting goal achievement among students, members of the general public, and people with physical illness. Fourth, when we used Kim and Hunter's (1993) system to classify domains of attainment, implementation intentions were shown to have medium or large effects for a wide variety of goals. Finally, the effectiveness of implementation intentions was not exaggerated by overreliance on self-report measures of behavior. The effect size for implementation intentions was of equivalent magnitude in studies in which objective measures of performance were used. In sum, implementation intentions seem to have benefited goal achievement no matter how one looks at the data.

1. Implementation intentions and self-regulatory tasks in goal striving

Whereas traditional theories of goal pursuit assumed that strong goal intentions are a sufficient determinant of goal achievement (e.g., Ajzen, 1991; Atkinson, 1957; Fishbein, 1980; Locke & Latham, 1990; Rogers, 1983), the present research started from the position that there is a substantial gap between intentions and action as there are numerous problems of goal striving that need to be solved even if people hold strong binding goals (Gollwitzer, 1990, 1993, 1996, 1999; Heckhausen & Gollwitzer, 1987; Gollwitzer et al., 2005; Orbell & Sheeran, 1998; Sheeran, 2002). We analyzed the intention–behavior gap in terms of four key self-regulatory tasks: initiating goal striving, shielding ongoing goal pursuit from unwanted influences, disengaging from unproductive goal striving, and conserving self-regulatory capability. Findings indicated that if–then planning facilitated initiation of goal striving no matter whether getting started was an issue of remembering to act, seizing good opportunities, or overcoming initial reluctance.

Although fewer studies were conducted on the issue of shielding goal striving, the beneficial effects of implementation intentions were also strong. Forming if–then plans helped with different problems of maintaining an ongoing wanted (focal) goal pursuit. The implementation intentions used were geared either at suppressing unwanted attention and behavioral responses, or toward spelling out the focal goal striving and thereby blocking detrimental self-states and adverse contextual influences. It is worth noting that various detrimental self-states and adverse contextual influences have been scrutinized and the awareness of their presence varied between studies, as did the awareness of their potential negative impact on the person's goal striving.

Three studies investigated disengagement from failing courses of action (Henderson et al., 2004) using standard escalation of commitment paradigms (i.e., escalation of commitment was induced by instigating the justification motive; e.g., Bobocel & Meyer, 1994). Even though it is well established that it is very difficult to overcome strong self-justification concerns and thus halt escalation of commitment, implementation intention formation was effective in doing so and produced an effect of approximately medium size. Thus, implementation intentions provide a useful means for successfully bringing futile goal striving to a close.

The final self-regulatory task in goal striving is conserving capability for pursuing subsequent goals once an initial goal has been completed. Whereas action control by goal intentions has been shown to generate ironic rebound and ego-depletion effects for subsequent task performance, action control by implementation intentions did not produce such costs. In other words, controlling goal striving with implementation intentions allows people to move on to subsequent goal striving without these self-regulatory handicaps; compared to self-regulation by goal intentions, self-regulation by implementation intentions conserves rather than diminishes capability for further goal striving.

2. *Psychological processes underlying implementation intention effects*

Several studies explored the if- and then-component processes of implementation intentions. Findings strongly support the postulated mechanisms (Gollwitzer, 1999). Apparently, specifying a situational cue in the if-component of an implementation intention creates a heightened activation of the respective mental representation of the situation. The implied ease of accessibility could be observed in respective lexical decision, perceptual detection, cue discrimination, and memory performances. Moreover, implementation intention participants attended to specified critical cues even when the cues were presented on the nonattended channel in a dichotic listening task. Although studies used different paradigms to assess heightened activation, the effect sizes obtained were uniformly large. These findings strongly suggest that having selected a situational cue for acting toward one's goal, it is hard for the person to overlook this opportunity. This contrasts with the predicament of the person who has only formed a goal intention and thus needs to actively search for and identify good opportunities to act (Sheeran, Milne, Webb, & Gollwitzer, 2005b).

At the same time, specifying an effective goal-directed response in the then-component of the plan endows the control of this response with features of automaticity. The three features of automaticity that have been analyzed in various different studies are immediacy, efficiency, and lack of awareness (i.e., conscious intent is not required). For all three features, effect sizes were large. Apparently, furnishing goal intentions with implementation intentions switches the mode of goal-directed behavior from hesitant to immediate, from effortful to efficient, and from a conscious intent to act to direct response elicitation by the situation. Whereas the person who has only formed a goal intention still has to deliberate *in situ* about what goal-directed response to undertake and/or energize the self to perform it, forming an implementation intention means deciding these issues in advance, thereby delegating the control of goal-directed behavior to specified situational cues. Once these cues are encountered, action initiation is triggered automatically.

One might wonder whether a change in motivational factors (strength of respective goal intentions and/or self-efficacy) due to if–then plan formation may explain implementation intention effects on goal attainment – in addition to, or even instead of, the postulated component processes. However, at least two lines of research contradict this idea. First, studies that measured strength of goal intentions (commitment) or self-efficacy both before and after respective implementation intention inductions found no evidence that if–then plan formation increased scores on these variables in either within-participants analyses (differences within the if–then plan group over time) or between-participants analyses (differences between the if–then plan and control group at either time-point) (e.g., Brandstätter et al., 2001, Study 1; Milne et al., 2002; Oettingen et al., 2000, Study 2; Orbell et al., 1997; Sheeran & Orbell, 1999; Sheeran et al., 2005c, Study 1). Second, implementation intention formation enhanced rates of goal attainment even when participants had extremely high scores on goal intention and self-efficacy prior to plan formation. For instance, Sheeran and Orbell (2000) found that if–then planning increased attendance for cervical cancer screening even though the preintervention means for the if–then plan group were 4.60 and 4.63, respectively, on 1–5 scales. It is implausible to attribute the observed 33% improvement in attendance behavior among implementation intention participants to postmanipulation increases in goal intentions or self-efficacy (for equivalent findings see also Sheeran & Orbell, 1999; Verplanken & Faes, 1999). These results, together with findings showing that implementation intention effects do not exhibit the temporal decline of motivational interventions (e.g., Sheeran & Silverman, 2003; Sheeran et al., 2005b) and actually show stronger effects for difficult-to-implement as compared to easy-to-implement goals (e.g., Gollwitzer & Brandstätter, 1997, Study 1), all indicate that increases in goal intention strength and self-efficacy as a consequence of if–then plan formation cannot explain implementation intention effects on goal achievement.

3. Implementation intentions in everyday life

Two findings help to clarify when implementation intention formation is likely to especially benefit goal attainment. First, if–then planning has a significantly larger effect size among people who are known to have problems with action control (e.g., frontal lobe patients, schizophrenics). Second, implementation intentions exhibit a noticeably large effect size in tasks that are known to overextend people's capability to regulate their behavior (i.e., in ego-depletion and ironic rebound paradigms; $d = 1.28$). These findings speak to the idea that the presence of problems in goal striving is an important determinant of the strength of implementation intention effects. If the set goal is extremely easy to initiate and pursue, then simply forming the respective goal intention could satisfactorily facilitate goal achievement; in such instances, it is possible that forming an implementation intention may confer little additional benefit. If, on the other hand, person characteristics or task features make it difficult to execute goal-directed behaviors, then it is especially advantageous to engage in if–then planning. That is, forming implementation intentions is most likely to benefit goal achievement when regulating the behavior is difficult or people have chronic difficulties in regulating their behavior.

In the light of this analysis, and the overall support obtained in this review for the beneficial impact of implementation intentions on goal achievement, can we conclude that if–then planning will facilitate such attainment under any circumstances? In other words, is forming implementation intentions a foolproof self-regulatory strategy of goal striving? In everyday life, people may fail to form effective implementation intentions due to unfortunate specifications of opportunities and goal-directed responses. For instance, a person may identify an opportunity that hardly ever arises (e.g., when one rarely has the choice between walking vs. taking the elevator), or an opportunity in which it turns out to be impossible to act toward one's goal (e.g., one's boss insists that you ride the elevator together to discuss work). Similarly, a person may specify a behavior that has limited instrumentality with respect to reaching the goal (e.g., taking the stairs instead of the elevator is unlikely, on its own, to achieve the superordinate goal of reducing weight) or a behavior that, in reality, proves impossible for the person to perform (e.g., walk up 60 flights of stairs to one's office).

In addition, if–then plans may not be very effective because opportunities and responses are not specified precisely. For example, a plan that specifies "eat healthily" in the then-component and "tomorrow" in the if-component has hardly spelled out an unambiguous opportunity to act or a specific goal-directed response to initiate – the person still has to identify a particular behavior to perform in a particular situation to facilitate goal achievement (e.g., order a salad at lunch time tomorrow in my usual restaurant). Having to thus deliberate about when, where, and what to do *in situ* means that the person is unlikely to garner much benefit from the enhanced activation of critical cues or automation of responding conferred by forming precise if–then plans; the person seems no better off than having merely formed the goal intention to "eat healthily tomorrow." In sum, implementation intention formation should prove useful in promoting goal achievement provided components of the plan are precise (i.e., deliberation about appropriate opportunities and responses is not required *in situ*), viable (i.e., the specified situation will be encountered, the specified response can be performed), and instrumental (i.e., the specified situation permits action, and the specified response facilitates goal achievement). How often the if–then plans fashioned in people's everyday lives satisfy these conditions is an empirical issue.

Finally, it is important that people who specify obstacles in the if-component of their implementation intentions select those barriers and distractions that most hinder goal completion. In other words, it matters that people specify those obstacles that do indeed undermine goal striving. Research has demonstrated that the mental exercise of juxtaposing the desired future with the present negative reality (i.e., mental contrasting) is a particularly effective strategy for discovering powerful barriers and hindrances that stand in the way of realizing desired outcomes (Oettingen, 2000; Oettingen et al., 2001). Accordingly, inviting people to engage in mental contrasting prior to if–then planning should ensure that people gear their implementation intentions to precisely those obstacles that present the greatest obstruction to goal attainment.

4. Do implementation intentions engender rigid goal striving?

Assuming that implementation intentions create strong links between anticipated situations and goal-directed behaviors, does this mean that implementation intention formation undermines performance when flexible goal striving is called for? The idea that implementation intentions could engender costs in terms of rigidity has at least three aspects. First, action control by implementation intentions could be rigid in the sense that goal striving no longer takes into account the state (activation, strength) of participants' goal intentions. Research does not support this concern, however. Several studies have shown that goal intentions moderate the impact of implementation intentions on goal attainment such that strong effects of if–then plans only emerge when participants hold strong respective goal intentions (e.g., Koestner et al.,

2002b; Orbell et al., 1997; Sheeran et al., 2005c, Study 1). Similarly, studies that either activated (Bayer et al., 2004; Sheeran et al., 2005c, Study 2) or deactivated (Seehausen, Bayer, & Gollwitzer, 1994, cited in Gollwitzer, 1996) relevant goal intentions indicate that implementation intentions only affected performance when the respective goal intention was activated. For example, Sheeran et al. (2005c) showed that an if–then plan to enhance speed of responding on a puzzle task only affected response times when the goal intention to respond quickly had been primed in the situation. Thus, action control by implementation intentions does not involve a mechanistic elicitation of action in the presence of environmental cues but rather respects the presence versus absence of activated strong goal intentions. Apparently, the automaticity instigated by if–then plans is goal-dependent (Bargh, 1992, 1994) – concerns that if–then plans could engender rigid adherence to a course of action that does not serve a person's goals seem unfounded.

The second aspect of rigidity concerns the possibility that implementation intentions could facilitate one aspect of goal striving but do so at the expense of other aspects of goal striving. That is, forming an if–then plan to promote one dimension of performance could consume self-regulatory resources and thereby engender inflexible performance on other dimensions; as a consequence, overall goal attainment might be compromised. Again, evidence seems to contradict this idea. For example, although Sheeran et al. (2005c) found that implementation intentions enhanced response times on a puzzle task, accuracy of responses was not compromised. Similarly, Gollwitzer and Bayer (2000) showed that implementation intentions not only increased the number of solutions generated in a creativity task but also enhanced the conceptual variety of those solutions. These findings indicate that action control by implementation intentions does not induce rigidity in terms of inevitable trade-offs between dimensions of performance (speed vs. accuracy, quantity vs. quality). Rather, the automation of one aspect of goal striving seems to free up cognitive capacity such that other aspects of the focal striving are not compromised, and even can be enhanced (Brandstätter et al., 2001).

The third aspect of potential rigidity concerns whether implementation intention participants refrain from using alternative good opportunities to act toward the goal by insisting on acting only when the critical situation specified in the if-part of the implementation intention is encountered. Several features of if–then plans suggest that such rigid adherence to specified opportunities is unlikely. Because implementation intentions respect the activation and strength of participants' superordinate goal intentions, participants who have formed if–then plans should still be sensitive to the issue of identifying good opportunities to act. Moreover, because action control by implementation intentions is efficient and conserves self-regulatory capability, if–then planners should be in a good position to effectively process information about alternative opportunities, and to seize those opportunities judged suitable for execution of behavior. In sum, implementation intentions do not seem to engender rigid self-regulation in terms of mechanistic situational control, performance trade-offs, or neglecting suitable alternative opportunities to move toward the goal.

Finally, there may be a further fourth issue related to rigidity, this one having to do with how people deal with having acted on a faulty if–then plan. We do not know yet what happens when people recognize that they have formed an if–then plan that failed to lead to goal attainment (or even produced negative outcomes). Do people stubbornly adhere to the faulty if–then plan, or readily modify the if- and then-components of that plan, or do they even completely refrain from forming if–then plans? Also one wonders how the explicitness of the failure feedback and the strength of the respective goal intention affect whether people will adhere to or modify the plan, or stay away from planning altogether.

5. *Future research on if–then plans*

Although 94 independent tests of implementation intention effects on goal achievement were examined in this chapter, further research is warranted to exploit the benefits of implementation intentions in facilitating goal attainment and to enhance understanding of this mode of action control. Findings from 52 and 21 studies, respectively, showed that implementation intentions facilitated initiation of goal striving and effectively shielded ongoing goal pursuits from unwanted influences. However, there were fewer studies that addressed self-regulatory problems in disengaging from futile goal striving and conserving capability for future goal striving. Even considering the 21 tests to do with the problem of getting derailed, additional studies would help to corroborate the efficacy of if–then plans in dealing with the various aspects of the respective self-regulatory tasks (i.e., suppressing unwanted responses, blocking detrimental self-states, and blocking adverse contextual influences).

The same reasoning applies to research in different goal domains and using different samples. Most studies to date used laboratory tasks, and there have been relatively few applications to consumer, environmental, antiracist, and prosocial behaviors. Similarly, the 23 tests in relation to health goals predominantly concerned the initiation of health-protective behaviors (e.g., exercise, cancer screening). However, health-risk behaviors, such as smoking, excess alcohol consumption, and poor diet, are major contributors to mortality and morbidity in Western societies (Belloc, 1973; Breslow & Enstrom, 1980). How well implementation intentions can help people to assiduously avoid these actions constitutes an important avenue for future investigation. Previous studies also mainly used undergraduate samples, and although sample type did not generally moderate implementation intention effects, further tests among more representative groups would enhance the generality of the present analysis. The finding that people with chronic problems in action control (e.g., schizophrenics) were especially likely to benefit from implementation intention formation is encouraging and provides grounds for further rigorous tests of if–then planning interventions among other clinical samples (e.g., ADHD children, depressed individuals). More generally, although the present meta-analysis shows that implementation intentions are effective in enabling people to translate their "good" intentions into action, the review also reveals considerable scope for further tests in relation to long-standing self-regulatory problems (e.g., control of pain or stress), under-researched samples (e.g., people with physical illness), and new domains of application (e.g., educational, organizational, and clinical settings). In whatever context people's goal intentions are found to fall short of their goal achievement, applied psychologists might do well to consider deploying if–then plans to promote effective self-regulation of goal striving.

There is also room for further theoretical integration of the concept of implementation intentions with theories of motivation (e.g., Bandura, 1997) and willpower (e.g., Metcalfe & Mischel, 1999). For instance, with respect to motivation, future studies may want to explore whether implementation intentions can be used to elevate self-efficacy beliefs (e.g., "And if I run into problems with any of my homework, then I will tell myself 'I can do it!'"). With respect to willpower, implementation intentions can be used to turn off the hot system and activate the cool system when self-control is needed. For example, a person who wants to cope better with unpleasant social encounters could use implementation intentions to reduce feelings of frustration and anger (e.g., "And if I run into an obnoxious person, then I will try to understand this person as if I was a therapist!"). What distinguishes this approach from past research on implementation intentions is the fact that the then-component of the if–then plan does not specify one particular goal-directed response, but rather focuses on changing motivation-relevant beliefs and/or self-regulatory systems that can ultimately facilitate the performance of multiple and various goal-directed responses.

The present review obtained strong support for the component processes postulated to underlie implementation intention effects. Implementation intentions showed large effects on processes to do with heightened activation of the critical situation (accessibility, detection, discrimination, attention, memory) and automation of the goal-directed response (immediacy, efficiency, redundancy of intent). However, it would be valuable to conduct mediation analyses to explore whether these processes are indeed responsible for the positive effects of implementation intention formation on rates of goal achievement. One study that conducted this type of analysis measured the accessibility of situational cues specified in participants' if–then plans in a lexical decision task and subsequently measured rates of goal attainment (Aarts et al., 1999). Findings indicated that cue accessibility mediated the impact of implementation intention formation on goal completion. Recently, Webb and Sheeran (2005c) extended this paradigm to investigate the mediational role of both cue accessibility and the strength of cue-response links forged by if–then planning. In one experiment, participants had the goal intention to collect a coupon from a specified location as part of a series of laboratory tasks. A subset of participants also formed an implementation intention that specified the location for collecting the coupon in the if-component and the action of coupon collection in the then-component. Subsequently, an ostensibly unrelated lexical decision task had to be performed that assessed the accessibility of the critical cues (location words) and the accessibility of the target behavior when subliminally primed by the critical cues (i.e., the word "collect" preceded by location words). Findings indicated that implementation intention formation increased the rate of coupon collection (goal achievement) as well as the accessibility of both location cues and location-primed target behavior (i.e., the strength of the link between the if- and then-components of the plan). Most important, implementation intention effects on goal attainment were mediated by cue accessibility as well as the strength of respective cue-response links. These findings are consistent with the postulated theoretical mechanisms. Further tests are needed to explore the mediational role of the other hypothesized processes (e.g., immediacy, efficiency, and redundancy of conscious intent), however.

Moderators of implementation intention effects also warrant investigation. There are two aspects to moderation here. First, individual differences could either enhance or reduce the impact of implementation intentions on goal achievement. Individuals with personal attributes that make regulating their behavior more difficult, for instance, might especially benefit from implementation intention formation. Thus, people who score highly on measures of procrastination, distractability, or self-defensiveness may show higher rates of goal attainment when they form if–then plans compared to people who obtain low scores on these measures. On the other hand, individuals who spontaneously form implementation intentions may garner less advantage from inductions designed to prompt plan formation. Individual differences in conscientiousness, planfulness, or need for cognition could predict spontaneous if–then planning. It is also possible that individual difference variables could be identified that render if–then planning counterproductive. For instance, people who are poor at reality monitoring could form plans that are antithetical to effective goal striving. Similarly, people who set too much store by adherence to plans (e.g., perfectionist individuals) may be prone to self-evaluative ruminations that undermine the effective operation of their plans. Thus, standard individual difference variables could have an important influence on whether and how well implementation intentions are formed and how much of an effect they have on goal achievement.

If one conceives of personality in terms of "intra-individually stable, if…then…, situation–behavior relations" (Mischel & Shoda, 1995, p. 248), the question of how personality and if–then planning work together in the self-regulation of goal striving may get even more interesting. Let us assume that a person has the goal to reduce aggression in relating to others, and he also knows about his respective situation–behavior profile (i.e., he knows what kind of social situations elicit aggressive responses in him and which social situations allow him to stay calm and collected). Given this goal and knowledge, the person can now tailor his implementation intentions to those critical situations specifying any of the following goal-directed responses: "…then I will not get aggressive!" or "…then I will stay calm and collected!" or "…then I will ignore this situation!" Thus, it seems possible that people could maximize the self-regulatory benefits of forming implementation intentions by taking into account their unique chronic if–then (situation–behavior) profiles and specify implementation intentions exactly where they are needed. Exploring interactions between chronic and strategic situation–behavior links constitutes a promising direction for future studies.

The second aspect of moderation concerns degree of plan formation and refers both to the activation level of the if- and then-components of the plan and to the strength of the mental link between the if-component and the then-component of the plan. These features of implementation intentions are responsible for the enhanced identification of specified contextual cues and automated action control in the presence of these cues, thus determining how well if–then plans facilitate goal attainment. The implication of variations in degree of plan formation is that procedures that enhance the activation level of critical cues or the strength of cue–response associations should thereby increase the impact of implementation intentions on goal striving and goal completion. To date, only a small number of studies have tested this aspect of moderation. For instance, Gollwitzer et al. (2004a) manipulated the strength of participants' commitment to their implementation intentions presuming to thereby strengthen cue–response links. Findings from a cued recall paradigm showed that the high commitment group had superior memory for selected opportunities compared to the low commitment group. Similarly, Milne and Sheeran (2002c) manipulated cognitive rehearsal by having some participants concentrate on the cue–response link during plan formation; participants wrote down their plan to visit a particular website twice, and were instructed to concentrate on the link between the situation and action when they were writing the plan the second time. Another implementation intention group also wrote down their plan twice, but were instructed to take the second write-up of the plan with them and put it in a prominent place at home as a reminder. Findings indicated that participants who rehearsed the cue–response link were more likely to act on their plans compared to both participants who wrote their implementation intention on a reminder note and a control group who did not form implementation intentions (rates of visiting the Web site were 87%, 40%, and 20%, respectively).

Future studies should examine the effectiveness of strategies to aid encoding of if–then plans (e.g., different types of cognitive rehearsal, surprise recall tasks or plan reminders) and strategies to increase commitment to these plans (e.g., inducing anticipated regret about not following one's plan or making one's commitment public) in order to ensure that opportunities are highly accessible and opportunity–action links are strong. Some individuals are likely to be more in need of such strategies than others because people differ in their ability to generate strong if–then links when asked to form implementation intentions (Gollwitzer, Grant, & Oettingen, 2004b). But even if people's original if–then links are weak, it seems possible to strengthen these links by having people act repeatedly on their implementation intentions. Research by Orbell and Verplanken (2005) observed that whenever participants performed repeated actions (e.g., flossing one's teeth) on the basis of an implementation intention, they reported experiencing features of habitual action control (e.g., I do it without thinking, I start doing it before I realize I'm doing it, I do it automatically, I do it without having to think consciously, It would require effort not to do it,...) more so than participants who performed the repeated action on the basis of a mere goal intention. Further research along these lines would be valuable in order to ensure that implementation intentions are as effective as possible in facilitating the realization of goal intentions for particular people.

V. Conclusions

Goal intentions are not always successfully translated into behavior because merely making a commitment to attain a goal does not necessarily prepare people for dealing effectively with self-regulatory problems in goal striving. This chapter tested the idea that goal striving could benefit from a second act of willing – the formation of if–then plans – that focuses on the enactment of goal intentions. A meta-analysis of 94 studies showed that forming an implementation intention makes an important difference to whether or not people achieve their goals. This finding was robust across variations in study design, outcome measurement, and domains of goal attainment. Moreover, if–then planning facilitated goal striving no matter what self-regulatory problem was at hand. Medium-to-large effects were obtained in relation to initiating goal striving, shielding goals from unwanted influences, disengaging from failing goals, and preserving self-regulatory capability for future goal striving. There was also strong support for the if–then component processes. People who form implementation intentions are in a good position to recognize opportunities to act and respond to these opportunities swiftly and effortlessly. Thus, this chapter shows that the concept of implementation intentions is valuable both in understanding the processes of goal attainment and in providing a self-regulatory strategy to help people reach their goals. Notwithstanding the self-regulatory benefits of implementation intentions demonstrated here, there is considerable scope for further research to exploit the potential of if–then planning and to understand how implementation intentions can best be deployed to facilitate intention realization. Such research would seem to be a worthwhile goal pursuit for both basic and applied psychologists.

Acknowledgments

We thank Icek Ajzen, Christopher J. Armitage, Paul Dholakia, Rob Holland, Richard Koestner, Sonia Lippke, Andrew Prestwich, Falko Sniehotta, Liz Steadman, and Jochen Philipp Ziegelman for access to unpublished findings, and Tom Webb, Ute Bayer, Anja Achtziger, Inge Schweiger Gallo, Alex Jaudas, Georg Odenthal, Caterina Gawrilow, and Tanya Faude for comments on an earlier draft of the manuscript.

Preparation of this chapter was supported in part by National Institute of Health grant (R01–67100) and the Center for Research on Intentions and Intentionality at the University of Konstanz, Germany.

Appendix I

Examples of possible implementation intentions geared at resolving the four problems of goal striving

1 Failing to get started
  a Remembering to act
    To achieve the goal intention of sending a birthday card on time: *And if I walk by the institute's mail box, then I will drop in my card!*
  b Seizing opportunities
    To achieve the goal intention of complaining about poor service: *And if I see the manager walk into the restaurant, then I will go over to him and complain about the poor service!*
  c Overcoming initial reluctance
    To achieve the goal intention of completing course work on time: *And if it is Saturday morning at 10 a.m., then I will sit down at my computer and make an outline for my essay!*
2 Getting derailed
  a Suppressing unwanted attention responses
    To achieve the goal intention of behaving calmly in the face of scary spider pictures: *And if I see a spider, then I will ignore it!*
  b Suppressing unwanted behavioral responses
    To achieve the goal intention of behaving calmly in the wake of being insulted: *And if I feel my anger rise, then I will tell myself to stay calm and not aggress back!*
  c Blocking detrimental self-states
    To block the negative influence of ego-depletion on solving difficult anagrams: *And if I have solved one anagram, then I will immediately move onto the next one!*
  d Blocking adverse contextual influences
    To block the negative influence of loss framing on negotiation outcomes when having to share an attractive commodity (e.g., a fictitious island in the Lake of Constance): *And if I receive a proposal on how to share the island, then I will offer a cooperative counterproposal!*
3 Not calling a halt
  To prevent escalation of commitment to a certain strategy of performing a general knowledge test: *And if I receive disappointing feedback, then I will switch to a different strategy!*
4 Overextending oneself
  To prevent the emergence of ego-depletion in the wake of controlling one's emotions, such as not laughing at amusing cartoons: *And if an amusing scene is presented, then I will tell myself "these are just stupid, silly jokes!"*

References

Papers included in the meta-analysis are preceded by an asterisk.

Aarts, H., & Dijksterhuis, A. (2000a). Habits as knowledge structures: Automaticity in goal-directed behavior. *Journal of Personality and Social Psychology, 78*, 53–63.

Aarts, H, & Dijksterhuis, A. (2000b). On the automatic activation of goal-directed behavior: The case of travel habit. *Journal of Environmental Psychology, 20*, 75–82.

*Aarts, H., Dijksterhuis, A., & Midden, C. (1999). To plan or not to plan? Goal achievement or interrupting the performance of mundane behaviors. *European Journal of Social Psychology, 29*, 971–979.

Abraham, C., Sheeran, P., Norman, P., Conner, M., Otten, W., & de Vries, N. (1999). When good intentions are not enough: Modelling post-intention cognitive correlates of condom use. *Journal of Applied Social Psychology, 29,* 2591–2612.

Ajzen, I. (1991). The theory of planned behavior. *Organizational Behavior and Human Decision Processes, 50,* 179–211.

*Ajzen, I., Czasch, C., & Flood, M. G. (2002). *From intentions to behavior: Implementation intention, commitment, and conscientiousness.* Manuscript under review.

Arkes, H. R., & Blumer, C. (1985). The psychology of sunk cost. *Organizational Behavior and Human Performance, 35,* 129–140.

*Armitage, C. J. (2004). Implementation intentions and eating a low-fat diet: A randomized controlled trial. *Health Psychology, 23,* 319–323.

Armitage, C. J., & Conner, M. (2001). Efficacy of the theory of planned behaviour: A meta-analytic review. *British Journal of Social Psychology, 40,* 471–499.

Atkinson, J. W. (1957). Motivational determinants of risk taking behavior. *Psychological Review, 64,* 359–372.

Austin, J. T., & Vancouver, J. B. (1996). Goal constructs in psychology: Structure, process, and content. *Psychological Bulletin, 120,* 338–375.

*Bagozzi, R. P., Dholakia, U. M., & Basuroy, S. (2003). How effortful decisions get enacted: The motivating role of decision processes, desires, and anticipated emotions. *Journal of Behavioral Decision Making, 16,* 273–295.

*Bamberg, S. (2000). The promotion of a new behavior by forming an implementation intention: Results of a field experiment in the domain of travel mode choice. *Journal of Applied Social Psychology, 23,* 573–587.

*Bamberg, S. (2002). Implementation intention versus monetary incentive comparing the effects of interventions to promote the purchase of organically produced food. *Journal of Economic Psychology, 23,* 573–587.

Bandura, A. (1991). Self-regulation of motivation through anticipatory and self-reactive mechanisms. In R. A. Dienstbier (Ed.), *Nebraska symposium on motivation: Perspectives on motivation* (Vol. 38, pp. 69–164). Lincoln, NE: University of Nebraska Press.

Bandura, A. (1997). *Self-efficacy: The exercise of control.* New York: W. H. Freeman.

Bargh, J. A. (1990). Auto-motives: Preconscious determinants of social interaction. In E. T. Higgins and R. M. Sorrentino (Eds.), *Handbook of motivation and cognition: Foundations of social behavior* (Vol. 2, pp. 93–130). New York: Guilford Press.

Bargh, J. A. (1992). The ecology of automaticity: Towards establishing the conditions needed to produce automatic processing effects. *American Journal of Psychology, 105,* 181–199.

Bargh, J. A. (1994). The four horsemen of automaticity: Awareness, efficiency, intention, and control in social interaction. In R. S. Wyer, Jr. and T. K. Srull (Eds.), *Handbook of social cognition* (2nd ed., pp. 1–40). Hillsdale, NJ: Erlbaum.

Bargh, J. A., & Gollwitzer, P. M. (1994). Environmental control over goal-directed action. *Nebraska Symposium on Motivation, 41,* 71–124.

Bargh, J. A., Gollwitzer, P. M., Lee-Chai, A., Barndollar, K., & Trötschel, R. (2001). The automated will: Nonconscious activation and pursuit of behavioral goals. *Journal of Personality and Social Psychology, 81,* 1014–1027.

Baumeister, R. F., Bratlavsky, E., Muraven, M., & Tice, D. M. (1998). Ego-depletion: Is the active self a limited resource? *Journal of Personality and Social Psychology, 74,* 1252–1265.

*Bayer, U. C., Jaudas, A., & Gollwitzer, P. M. (2002, July). *Do implementation intentions facilitate switching between tasks?. Poster presented at the International Symposium on Executive Functions.* Konstanz, Germany.

*Bayer, U. C., Moskowitz, G. B., & Gollwitzer, P. M. (2004). *Implementation intentions and action initiation without conscious intent.* Manuscript under review.

Belloc, N. B. (1973). Relationship of physical health status and health status. *Preventive Medicine, 2,* 67–81.

Bem, D. J. (1972). Self-perception theory. *Advances in Experimental Social Psychology, 6,* 1–62.

Bless, H. (1997). *Stimmung und Denken: Ein Modell zum Einfluß von Stimmung auf Denkprozesse (Mood and reasoning: A model on the impact of mood on cognitive processes).* Bern: Hans Huber.

Bless, H., & Fiedler, K. (1995). Affective states and the influence of activated general knowledge. *Personality and Social Psychology Bulletin, 21,* 766–778.

Bobocel, D. R., & Meyer, J. P. (1994). Escalating commitment to a failing course of action: Separating the roles of choice and justification. *Journal of Applied Psychology, 79,* 360–363.

Bragger, J. D., Hantula, D. A., Bragger, D., Kirnan, J., & Kutcher, E. (2003). When success breeds failure: History, hysteresis, and delayed exit decisions. *Journal of Applied Psychology, 88,* 6–14.

*Brandstätter, V., Heimbeck, D., Malzacher, J. T., & Frese, M. (2003). Goals need implementation intentions: The model of action phases tested in the applied setting of continuing education. *European Journal of Work and Organizational Psychology, 12,* 37–59.

*Brandstätter, V., Lengfelder, A., & Gollwitzer, P. M. (2001). Implementation intentions and efficient action initiation. *Journal of Personality and Social Psychology, 81,* 946–960.

Brehm, J. W., & Self, E. (1989). The intensity of motivation. *Annual Review of Psychology, 40,* 109–131.

Breslow, L., & Enstrom, J. E. (1980). Persistence of health habits and their relationship to mortality. *Preventive Medicine, 9,* 469–483.

Brockner, J., Rubin, J. Z., & Lang, E. (1981). Face-saving and entrapment. *Journal of Experimental Social Psychology, 17,* 68–79.

*Brüwer, J., Bayer, U. C., & Gollwitzer, P. M. (2002). *Intentional control of the Simon effect. Poster presented at the International Symposium on Executive Functions.* Konstanz, Germany.

*Bulgarella, C., Oettingen, G., & Gollwitzer, P. M. (2003, February). *Reflexive competition and its self-regulation. Poster presented at the meeting of the Society for Personality and Social Psychology.* Los Angeles, CA.

Canary, D. J., & Seibold, D. R. (1984). *Attitudes and behavior: A comprehensive bibliography.* New York: Praeger.

Carver, C. S., & Scheier, M. F. (1982). Control theory: A useful conceptual framework for personality-social, clinical, and health psychology. *Psychological Bulletin, 92,* 111–135.

Carver, C. S., & Scheier, M. F. (1998). *On the self-regulation of behavior.* Cambridge, UK: University Press.

*Chasteen, A. L., Park, D. C., & Schwarz, N. (2001). Implementation intentions and facilitation of prospective memory. *Psychological Science, 12,* 457–461.

Cohen, J. (1992). A power primer. *Psychological Bulletin, 112,* 155–159.

COMMIT Research Group (1995). Community intervention trial for smoking cessation (COMMIT): I. Cohort results from a four-year community intervention. *American Journal of Public Health, 85,* 183–192.

De Dreu, C. K. W., Carnevale, P. J. D., Emans, B. J. M., & van de Vliert, E. (1995). Outcome frames in bilateral negotiation: Resistance to concession making and frame adoption. In W. Stroebe and M. Hewstone (Eds.), *European review of social psychology* (Vol. 6, pp. 97–125). Chichester, UK: Wiley.

Deci, E. L., & Ryan, R. M. (1991). A motivational approach to self: Integration in personality. *Nebraska Symposium on Motivation, 38,* 237–288.

*Dewitte, S., Verguts, T., & Lens, W. (2003). Implementation intentions do not enhance all types of goals: The moderating role of goal difficulty. *Current Psychology, 22,* 73–89.

*Dholakia, U. M., & Bagozzi, R. P. (2002). Mustering motivation to enact decisions: How decision process characteristics influence goal realization. *Journal of Behavioral Decision Making, 15,* 167–188.

*Dholakia, U. M., & Bagozzi, R. P. (2003). As time goes by: How goal and implementation intentions influence enactment of short-fuse behaviors. *Journal of Applied Social Psychology, 33,* 889–922.

*Dieffendorff, J. M., & Lord, R. G. (2003). The volitional and strategic effects of planning on task performance and goal commitment. *Human Performance, 16,* 365–387.

Dweck, C. S. (2000). *Self-theories: Their role in motivation, personality, and development.* Philadelphia, PA: Psychology Press.

Einstein, G. O., & McDaniel, M. A. (1996). Retrieval processes in prospective memory: Theoretical approaches and some new empirical findings. In M. Bradimonte, G. O. Einstein, and M. A. McDaniel (Eds.), *Prospective memory: Theory and applications* (pp. 115–141). Mahwah, NJ: Erlbaum.

*Einstein, G. O., McDaniel, M. A., Williford, C. L., Pagan, J. L., & Dismukes, R. K. (2003). Forgetting of intentions in demanding situations is rapid. *Journal of Experimental Psychology: Applied, 9,* 147–162.

Fishbein, M. (1980). Theory of reasoned action: Some applications and implications. In H. Howe and M. Page (Eds.), *Nebraska symposium on motivation, 1979* (pp. 65–116). Lincoln, NB: University of Nebraska Press.

Fishbein, M., & Ajzen, I. (1975). *Belief, attitude, intention, and behavior: An introduction to theory and research.* Reading, MA: Addison-Wesley.

Floyd, D. L., Prentice-Dunn, S., & Rogers, R. W. (2000). A meta-analysis of research on protection motivation theory. *Journal of Applied Social Psychology, 30,* 407–429.

Garner, D. M., & Wooley, S. C. (1991). Confronting the failure of behavioral and dietary treatments of obesity. *Clinical Psychology Review, 6,* 58–137.

Gibbons, F. X., Gerrard, M., Blanton, H., & Russell, D. W. (1998). Reasoned action and social reaction: Willingness and intention as independent predictors of health risk. *Journal of Personality and Social Psychology, 74,* 1164–1180.

*Gillholm, R., Ettema, D., Selart, M., & Garling, T. (1999). The role of planning for intention–behavior consistency. *Scandinavian Journal of Psychology, 40,* 241–250.

Godin, G., & Kok, G. (1996). The theory of planned behavior: A review of its applications in health-related behaviors. *American Journal of Health Promotion, 11,* 87–98.

Gollwitzer, P. M. (1990). Action phases and mindsets. In E. T. Higgins and J. R. M. Sorrentino (Eds.), *The handbook of motivation and cognition* (Vol. 2, pp. 53–92). New York: Guilford.

Gollwitzer, P. M. (1993). Goal achievement: The role of intentions. In W. Stroebe and M. Hewstone (Eds.), *European Review of Social Psychology* (Vol. 4, pp. 141–185). New York: Wiley.

Gollwitzer, P. M. (1996). The volitional benefits of planning. In P. M. Gollwitzer and J. A. Bargh (Eds.), *The psychology of action: Linking cognition and motivation to behavior* (pp. 287–312). New York: Guilford.

Gollwitzer, P. M. (1999). Implementation intentions: Strong effects of simple plans. *American Psychologist, 54,* 493–503.

*Gollwitzer, P. M., & Bayer, U. C. (2000, October). *Becoming a better person without changing the self. Paper presented at the Self and Identity Pre-conference of the Annual Meeting of the Society of Experimental Social Psychology.* Atlanta, Georgia.

Gollwitzer, P. M., Bayer, U. C., & McCulloch, K. C. (2005). The control of the unwanted. In R. R. Hassin, J. S. Uleman, and J. A. Bargh (Eds.), *The new unconscious* (pp. 485–515). New York: Oxford University Press.

*Gollwitzer, P. M., Bayer, U. C., Steller, B., & Bargh, J. A. (2004a). *Delegating control to the environment: Perception, attention, and memory for pre-selected behavioral cues.* Manuscript under review.

*Gollwitzer, P. M., & Brandstätter, V. (1997). Implementation intentions and effective goal pursuit. *Journal of Personality and Social Psychology, 73,* 186–199.

Gollwitzer, P. M., Grant, H., & Oettingen, G. (2004b, February). *An individual difference measure of the tendency to form implementation intentions. Poster presented at the 5th Annual Meeting of SPSP.* Austin, Texas.

Gollwitzer, P. M., & Moskowitz, G. B. (1996). Goal effects on action and cognition. In E. T. Higgins and A. W. Kruglanski (Eds.), *Social psychology: Handbook of basic principles* (pp. 361–399). New York: Guilford.

Gollwitzer, P. M., & Schaal, B. (1998). Metacognition in action: The importance of implementation intentions. *Personality and Social Psychology Review, 2,* 124–136.

*Gollwitzer, P. M., Sheeran, P., & Seifert, E. (2004c). *Intentions as symbols: How self-completion affects the translation of intentions into action.* Manuscript under review.

*Gollwitzer, P. M., Sheeran, P., Trötschel, R., & Webb, T. L. (2004d). *The control of behavior priming effects by implementation intentions.* Manuscript under review.

*Gollwitzer, P. M., Trötschel, R., Bayer, U. C., & Sumner, M. (2004e). *Potential costs of self-regulation by implementation intentions: Rebound and ego-depletion effects?* Manuscript under review.

Gollwitzer, P. M., & Wicklund, R. A. (1985). Self-symbolizing and the neglect of others' perspectives. *Journal of Personality and Social Psychology, 56,* 531–715.

Hagger, M. S., Chatzisarantis, N. L. D., & Biddle, S. J. H. (2002). A meta-analytic review of the theories of reasoned action and planned behavior in physical activity: Predictive validity and the contribution of additional variables. *Journal of Sport and Exercise Psychology, 24,* 3–32.

Hausenblas, H. A., Carron, A. V., & Mack, D. E. (1997). Application of the theories of reasoned action and planned behavior to exercise behavior: A meta-analysis. *Journal of Sport and Exercise Psychology, 19,* 36–51.

Heckhausen, H. (1991). *Motivation and action.* Heidelberg: Springer-Verlag.

Heckhausen, H., & Gollwitzer, P. M. (1987). Thought contents and cognitive functioning in motivational versus volitional states of mind. *Motivation and Emotion, 11,* 101–120.

*Henderson, M. D., Gollwitzer, P. M., & Oettingen, G. (2004). *Using implementation intentions to disengage from a failing course of action: The effects of planning on escalation of commitment.* Manuscript under review.

Hedges, L. V., & Olkin, I. (1985). *Statistical methods for meta-analysis.* New York: Academic Press.

Higgins, E. T. (2000). Making a good decision: Value from fit. *American Psychologist, 55,* 1217–1230.

*Holland, R., Aarts, H., & Langendam, D. (in press). Breaking and creating habits on the workfloor: A field experiment on the power of implementation intentions. *Journal of Experimental Social Psychology.*

Hunter, J. E. (1990). *Methods of meta-analysis: Correcting error and bias in research findings.* Newbury Park, CA: Sage.

Karau, S. J., & Williams, K. D. (1993). Social loafing: A meta-analytic review and theoretical integration. *Journal of Personality and Social Psychology, 65,* 681–706.

Kavanagh, D. J., Andrade, J., & May, J. (2005). Imaginary relish and exquisite torture: The elaborated intrusion model of desire. *Psychological Review, 112,* 446–467.

Kim, M. S., & Hunter, J. E. (1993). Attitude-behavior relations: A meta-analysis of attitudinal relevance and topic. *Journal of Communication, 43,* 101–142.

*Koestner, R., Downie, M., Horburg, E., & Hata, S. (2002a). *Self-construals and the pursuit of personal goals: The role of implementation intentions and self-concordance.* Manuscript in preparation. Quebec, Canada: McGill University.

*Koestner, R., Lekes, N., Powers, T. A., & Chicoine, E. (2002b). Attaining personal goals: Self-concordance plus implementation intentions equals success. *Journal of Personality and Social Psychology, 83,* 231–244.

*Koole, S., & Van't Spijker, M. (2000). Overcoming the planning fallacy through willpower: Effects of implementation intentions on actual and predicted task-completion times. *European Journal of Social Psychology, 30,* 873–888.

Kruglanksi, A. W., Shah, J. Y., Fishbach, A., Friedman, R., Chun, W. Y., & Sleeth-Keppler, D. (2002). A theory of goal systems. In M. P. Zanna (Ed.), *Advances in experimental social psychology* (Vol. 34, pp. 331–378). San Diego, CA: Academic Press.

Latané, B., Williams, K., & Harkins, S. (1979). Many hands make light work: The causes and consequences of social loafing. *Journal of Personality and Social Psychology, 37,* 822–832.

*Lengfelder, A., & Gollwitzer, P. M. (2001). Reflective and reflexive action control in patients with frontal brain lesions. *Neuropsychology, 15,* 80–100.

*Lippke, S., & Ziegelmann, J. P. (2002). *Self-regulation and exercise: A study on stages of change and successful ageing.* Unpublished manuscript. Germany: Free University of Berlin.

Lewin, K. (1926). Vorsatz, wille, und bedürfnis. *Psychologische Forschung, 7,* 330–385.

Locke, E. A., & Latham, G. P. (1990). *A theory of goal setting and task performance.* Englewood Cliffs, NJ: Prentice Hall.

Loewenstein, G. F., Weber, E. U., Hsee, C. K., & Welch, N. (2001). Risk as feelings. *Psychological Bulletin, 127,* 267–286.

Macrae, C. N., Bodenhausen, G. V., Milne, A. B., & Jetten, J. (1994). Out of mind but back in sight: Stereotypes on the rebound. *Journal of Personality and Social Psychology, 67,* 808–817.

McBroom, W. H., & Reid, F. W. (1992). Towards a reconceptualization of attitude-behavior consistency. *Social Psychology Quarterly, 55,* 205–216.

Metcalfe, J., & Mischel, W. (1999). A hot/cool-system analysis of delay of gratification: Dynamics of willpower. *Psychological Bulletin, 106,* 3–19.

Milne, S., Sheeran, P., & Orbell, S. (2000). Prediction and intervention in health-related behavior: A meta-analytic review of protection motivation theory. *Journal of Applied Social Psychology, 30,* 106–143.

*Milne, S., Orbell, S., & Sheeran, P. (2002). Combining motivational and volitional interventions to promote exercise participation: Protection motivation theory and implementation intentions. *British Journal of Health Psychology, 7,* 163–184.

*Milne, S., & Sheeran, P. (2002a, June). *Combining motivational and volitional interventions to prevent testicular cancer. Testing the interaction between protection motivation theory and implementation intentions.* Paper presented at the 13th general meeting of the European Association of Experimental Social Psychology. San Sebastian, Spain.

*Milne, S., & Sheeran, P. (2002b). *Unpublished raw data.* UK: University of Bath.

*Milne, S., & Sheeran, P. (2002c, October). *Making good implementation intentions: Comparing associative learning and prospective memory in remembering intentions.* Paper presented at the 16th conference of the European Health Psychology Society. Lisbon, Portugal.

Mischel, W., & Patterson, C. J. (1978). Effective plans for self-control in children. In W. A. Collins (Ed.), *Minnesota symposium on child psychology* (Vol. 11, pp. 199–230). Hillsdale, NJ: Lawrence Erlbaum Associates Inc.

Mischel, W., & Shoda, Y. (1995). A cognitive-affective system theory of personality: Reconceptualiszing situations, dispositions, dynamics, and invariance in personality structure. *Psychological Review, 102,* 246–268.

Muraven, M., & Baumeister, R. F. (2000). Self-regulation and depletion of limited resources. Does self-control resemble a muscle? *Psychological Bulletin, 126,* 247–259.

*Murgraff, V., White, D., & Phillips, K. (1996). Moderating binge drinking: It is possible to change behaviour if you plan it in advance. *Alcohol and Alcoholism, 6,* 577–582.

Neale, M. A., & Bazerman, M. H. (1985). The effects of framing and negotiator overconfidence on bargaining behaviors and outcomes. *Academy of Management Journal, 28,* 34–49.

Oettingen, G. (2000). Expectancy effects on behavior depend on self-regulatory thought. *Social Cognition, 18,* 101–129.

Oettingen, G., & Gollwitzer, P. M. (2001). Goal setting and goal striving. In A. Tesser and N. Schwarz (Eds.), *Intraindividual processes. Volume 1 of the Blackwell Handbook in Social Psychology.* M. Hewstone and M. Brewer (Eds.) (pp. 329–347). Oxford: Blackwell.

*Oettingen, G., Hönig, G., & Gollwitzer, P. M. (2000). Effective self-regulation of goal attainment. *International Journal of Educational Research, 33,* 705–732.

Oettingen, G., Pak, H., & Schnetter, K. (2001). Self-regulation of goal-setting: Turning free fantasies about the future into binding goals. *Journal of Personality and Social Psychology, 80,* 736–753.

*Orbell, S., Hodgkins, S., & Sheeran, P. (1997). Implementation intentions and the theory of planned behavior. *Personality and Social Psychology Bulletin, 23,* 945–954.

Orbell, S., & Sheeran, P. (1998). "Inclined abstainers": A problem for predicting health-related behavior. *British Journal of Social Psychology, 37,* 151–165.

*Orbell, S., & Sheeran, P. (1999). *Volitional strategies and the theory of planned behavior.* Unpublished manuscript. UK: University of Sheffield.

*Orbell, S., & Sheeran, P. (2000). Motivational and volitional processes in action initiation: A field study of the role of implementation intentions. *Journal of Applied Social Psychology, 30,* 780–797.

Orbell, S., & Verplanken, B. (2005). *Habituation of goal-directed behavior by implementation intentions.* Manuscript under review.

Ouellette, J. A., & Wood, W. (1998). Habit and intention in everyday life: The multiple processes by which past behavior predicts future behavior. *Psychological Bulletin, 124,* 54–74.

Patterson, C., & Mischel, W. (1976). Effects of temptation-inhibiting and task-facilitating plans on self-control. *Journal of Personality and Social Psychology, 33,* 209–217.

*Prestwich, A., Lawton, R., & Conner, M. (2003a). *Disguising the strength of implementation intentions: The effect of spontaneously arising plans.* Unpublished manuscript. UK: University of Leeds.

*Prestwich, A., Lawton, R., & Conner, M. (2003b). The use of implementation intentions and the decision balance sheet in promoting exercise behavior. *Psychology and Health, 18,* 707–722.

*Rise, J., Thompson, M., & Verplanken, B. (2003). Measuring implementation intentions in the context of the theory of planned behavior. *Scandinavian Journal of Psychology, 44,* 87–95.

Rogers, R. W. (1983). Cognitive and physiological processes in fear appeals and attitude change: a revised theory of protection motivation. In B. L. Cacioppo and L. L. Petty (Eds.), *Social psychophysiology: A sourcebook* (pp. 153–176). London: Guildford.

Rosenthal, R. (1984). *Meta-analytic procedures for social research.* Beverley Hills, CA: Sage.

*Schaal, B. (1993). *Impulskontrolle – Wie Vorsätze beherrschtes Handeln erleichtern.* [Impulse control – How implementation intentions facilitate the control of behavior]. Unpublished Master's Thesis. Munich, Germany: Ludwig-Maximilians-Universität.

Schwarz, N. (1990). Feelings as information: Informational and motivational functions of affective states. In E. T. Higgins and R. M. Sorrentino (Eds.), *Handbook of motivation and cognition: Foundations of social behavior* (Vol. 2, pp. 527–561). New York: Guilford.

Schwarz, N., Bless, H., & Bohner, G. (1991). Mood and persuasion: Affective states influence the processing of persuasive communications. In M. P. Zanna (Ed.), *Advances in Experimental Social Psychology* (Vol. 24, pp. 161–199). San Diego: Academic Press.

Shah, J. Y., Kruglanksi, A. W., & Friedman, R. (2003). Goal systems theory: Integrating the cognitive and motivational aspects of self-regulation. A goal systems approach to self-regulation. In S. J.

Spencer, S. Fein, M. P. Zanna, and J. M. Olson (Eds.), *Motivated social perception: The Ontario Symposium* (Vol. 9, pp. 247–275). New Jersey: Erlbaum.

Sheeran, P. (2002). Intention-behavior relations: A conceptual and empirical review. In W. Stroebe and M. Hewstone (Eds.), *European Review of Social Psychology* (Vol. 12, pp. 1–30). New York: Wiley.

Sheeran, P., Aarts, H., Custers, R., Rivis, A. J., Webb, T. L., & Cooke, R. (2005a). The goal-dependent automaticity of drinking habits. *British Journal of Social Psychology, 44,* 47–64.

Sheeran, P., Abraham, C., & Orbell, S. (1999). Psychosocial correlates of heterosexual condom use: A meta-analysis. *Psychological Bulletin, 125,* 90–132.

*Sheeran, P., & Milne, S. (2003). *Unpublished raw data.* UK: University of Sheffield.

*Sheeran, P., Milne, S., Webb, T. L., & Gollwitzer, P. M. (2005b). Implementation intentions. In M. Conner and P. Norman (Eds.), *Predicting health behavior: Research and practice with social cognition models* (2nd ed.). Milton Keynes, UK: Open University Press.

Sheeran, P., & Orbell, S. (1998). Do intentions predict condom use? A meta-analysis and examination of six moderator variables. *British Journal of Social Psychology, 37,* 231–250.

*Sheeran, P., & Orbell, S. (1999). Implementation intentions and repeated behavior: Augmenting the predictive validity of the theory of planned behavior. *European Journal of Social Psychology, 29,* 349–369.

*Sheeran, P., & Orbell, S. (2000). Using implementation intentions to increase attendance for cervical cancer screening. *Health Psychology, 19,* 283–289.

*Sheeran, P., & Silverman, M. (2003). Evaluation of three interventions to promote workplace health and safety: Evidence for the utility of implementation intentions. *Social Science and Medicine, 56,* 2153–2163.

*Sheeran, P., & Webb, T. L. (2003). *Implementation intentions versus ego-training as strategies for preventing ego-depletion.* Unpublished manuscript. UK: University of Sheffield.

*Sheeran, P., Webb, T. L., & Gollwitzer, P. M. (2005c). The interplay between goal intentions and implementation intentions. *Personality and Social Psychology Bulletin, 31,* 87–98.

Sheeran, P., White, D., & Phillips, K. (1991). Premarital contraceptive use: A review of the psychological literature. *Journal of Reproductive and Infant Psychology, 9,* 253–269.

Sheppard, B. H., Hartwick, J., & Warshaw, P. R. (1988). The theory of reasoned action: A meta-analysis of past research with recommendations for modifications and future research. *Journal of Consumer Research, 15,* 325–342.

*Sniehotta, F. F., Scholtz, U., & Schwarzer, R. (2002a). *The effects of planning on initiation and maintenance of physical activity in cardiac rehabilitation patients.* Unpublished research report. Germany: Free University Berlin.

*Sniehotta, F. F., Scholtz, U., & Schwarzer, R. (2002b). *Implementation intentions and coping intentions.* Unpublished research report. Germany: Free University Berlin.

*Steadman, L., & Quine, L. (2000, August). *Are implementation intentions useful for bridging the intention-behavior gap in adhering to long-term medication regimens? An attempt to replicate Sheeran and Orbell's (1999) intervention to enhance adherence to daily vitamin C intake. Paper presented at the British Psychological Society Division of Health Psychology annual conference, University of Kent.* Canterbury, UK.

*Steadman, L., & Quine, L. (2004). Encouraging young males to perform testicular self-examination: A simple, but effective, implementation intentions interventions. *British Journal of Health Psychology, 9,* 479–487.

*Stephens, A., & Conner, M. (1999, September). *A smoking prevention intervention in adolescents. Paper presented at the British Psychological Society Division of Health Psychology annual conference.* University of Leeds.

Sutton, S. (1998). Predicting and explaining intentions and behaviour: How well are we doing? *Journal of Applied Social Psychology, 28,* 1317–1338.

Sutton, S., & Sheeran, P. (2003). *Meta-analysis of the theory of planned behaviour and past behaviour.* UK: University of Cambridge. Manuscript in preparation.

Tan, H. T., & Yates, J. F. (2002). Financial budgets and escalation effects. *Organizational Behavior and Human Decision Processes, 87,* 300–322.

Trafimow, D., & Sheeran, P. (2004). A theory about the translation of cognition into affect and behavior. In G. Haddock and G. R. Maio (Eds.), *Contemporary perspectives on the psychology of attitudes* (pp. 57–76). Hove, UK: Psychology Press.

Triandis, H. C. (1980). Values, attitudes, and interpersonal behavior. In H. Howe and M. Page (Eds.), *Nebraska symposium on motivation* (Vol. 27, pp. 195–259). Lincoln, NB: University of Nebraska Press.

*Trötschel, R., & Gollwitzer, P. M. (2004). *Implementation intentions and the control of framing effects in negotiations.* Manuscript under review.

van den Putte, B. (1993). *On the theory of reasoned action.* Unpublished doctoral dissertation. The Netherlands: University of Amsterdam.

Verplanken, B., & Aarts, H. (1999). Habit, attitude, and planned behaviour: Is habit an empty construct or an interesting case of automaticity? In W. Stroebe and M. Hewstone (Eds.). *European review of social psychology* (Vol. 10, pp. 101–134). Chicester, England: Wiley.

Verplanken, B., Aarts, H., van Knippenberg, A., & Moonen, A. (1998). Habit versus planned behaviour: A field experiment. *British Journal of Social Psychology, 37,* 111–128.

*Verplanken, B., & Faes, S. (1999). Good intentions, bad habits, and effects of forming implementation intentions on healthy eating. *European Journal of Social Psychology, 29,* 591–604.

Vroom, V. H. (1964). *Work and motivation.* New York: Wiley.

*Webb, T. L., & Sheeran, P. (2003). Can implementation intentions help to overcome ego-depletion? *Journal of Experimental Social Psychology, 39,* 279–286.

*Webb, T. L., & Sheeran, P. (2004). Identifying good opportunities to act: Implementation intentions and cue discrimination. *European Journal of Social Psychology, 34,* 407–419.

*Webb, T. L., & Sheeran, P. (2005). Integrating concepts from goal theories to understand the achievement of personal goals. *European Journal of Social Psychology, 35,* 69–96.

*Webb, T. L., & Sheeran, P. (in press a). *Does changing behavioral intentions engender behavior change? A meta-analysis of the experimental evidence.* Psychological Bulletin.

*Webb, T. L., & Sheeran, P. (in press b). *How do implementation intentions promote goal attainment? Tests of component processes.* Journal of Experimental Social Psychology.

Wegner, D. M. (1994). Ironic processes in mental control. *Psychological Review, 101,* 34–52.

Wicklund, R. A., & Gollwitzer, P. M. (1982). *Symbolic self-completion.* Hillsdale, NJ: Erlbaum.

Wight, D. (1992). Impediments to safer heterosexual sex: A review of research with young people. *AIDS Care, 4,* 11–21.

*Williams, S. (2003). *Stand by your plan: A new approach to the planning fallacy.* Unpublished doctoral thesis. UK: University of Sussex.

Wood, W., Quinn, J. M., & Kashy, D. (2002). Habits in everyday life: The thought and feel of action. *Journal of Personality and Social Psychology, 83,* 1281–1297.

Wrosch, C., Scheier, M. F., Carver, C. S., & Schulz, R. (2003). The importance of goal disengagement in adaptive self-regulation: When giving up is beneficial. *Self and Identity, 2,* 1–20.

PART 3

Health care

Part contents

Commentary

Much research on health behaviour, as described in the previous parts, focuses on people who are well and healthy and have not yet come into contact with the health care system. Health psychology research is also concerned with the beliefs, behaviours and processes that are evoked as a person moves along the continuum from health to illness. The literature covering this area highlights factors such as symptom perception, help-seeking behaviour, illness cognitions, health professional–patient communication, adherence and screening. Further it is informed by theoretical perspectives such as risk communication, the self-regulatory model and the mechanisms of the placebo effect. For the purpose of this section I have selected the following five papers that illustrate some of the key constructs and theories and utilise a range of different methodologies. These are separated into those that relate to communication and those that focus on illness cognitions.

Communication

Central to the process of health care is the interaction between the patient and health professional and a core part of this is communication. Over the past few decades there has been a vast amount of research on health professional–patient communication which has varied in terms of whether it has **described** what happens in a consultation, whether it has attempted to **prescribe** what should go on or whether it has **evaluated** the impact of different ways of communicating. Descriptive research has used a range of methods including questionnaires, interviews and recordings. The more prescriptive works have tended to be based on reviews of the literature or have involved polemical pieces. The evaluative research has mainly involved trials and experimental designs. Together this literature has been published in journals relating to a range of disciplines including primary care, medical sociology, education and health psychology. This section contains three papers focusing on communication:

Roter, D.L., Stewart, M., Putnam, S.M. et al. (1997) Communication patterns of primary care physicians, *Journal of the American Medical Association*, 277 (4): 350–6.

Mead, N. and Bower, P. (2000) Patient-centredness: a conceptual framework and review of the empirical literature, *Social Science and Medicine*, 51: 1087–110. Reprinted with kind permission of Elsevier.

Marteau, T., Senior, V., Humphries, S.E. et al. (2004) Psychological impact of genetic testing for familial hypercholesterolemia within a previously aware population: a randomized controlled trial. *American Journal of Medical Genetics*, 128A: 285–93. Reprinted with kind permission of Wiley-Liss, Inc., a subsidiary of John Wiley & Sons, Inc.

Roter et al. (1997) represents a thorough and detailed attempt at describing and measuring what 'actually' happens in a primary care consultation using the Roter index which is a checklist of the kinds of micro-behaviours that a clinician may or may not perform while communicating with a patient. This index has subsequently been widely used in communication research and is now seen as a gold standard method for quantifying communication patterns. This is an interesting paper as it illustrates how the index was developed and tested. It also illustrates how a timely and well-thought-through construct can be picked up by subsequent research.

Also central to much research on the consultation is the notion of patient-centredness which is juxtaposed to that of doctor-centredness. In contrast to the Roter index, which was from the descriptive camp of research, patient-centredness has been taken up and used from a much more prescriptive perspective and is currently considered the gold standard for how clinicians should behave. In line with this when training to be a primary care doctor, videoed consultations are often assessed to explore the extent to which the trainee has been patient-centred with their patient. Parallels can be seen with education whereby teachers are encouraged to be learner-centred rather than teacher-centred. The concept of patient-centredness, however, is not as clearly defined or consistent as often assumed. Mead and Bower (2000) provide a thorough review of the literature that has defined, measured or tried to promote patient-centredness, and not only show the variability in how this term is used but also propose a useful synthesis of the different approaches. This narrative review is a useful overview of this literature and provides an excellent basis for exploring patient-centredness research further. In addition, it illustrates how reviews can be used to develop a construct and to identify key areas to provide a more coherent conceptual map.

The final paper in this section, by Marteau et al. (2004), evaluates the impact of different forms of communication. Patients who had already been given either a definite or possible diagnosis of familial hypercholesterolemia (FH) were randomly allocated to one of two conditions: routine clinical diagnosis or a routine clinical diagnosis plus genetic testing. The results were then analysed to explore whether being able to confirm a clinical diagnosis of FH with a genetic test influenced the ways in which the patients conceptualised their problem in terms of beliefs about control and adherence to medication and behaviour change recommendations. The results showed that being given a genetic confirmation of FH had no effect on patients' beliefs about how controllable their FH was but did make patients say that they were less confident that changing their diet would have an effect on their condition. This is an interesting paper for several reasons. Primarily it illustrates how different forms of information can influence patients in different ways. However, it also provides a good example of trial methodology and the process of randomisation: the interventions used, the outcome measures and the analyses are clearly presented. In addition, it shows how health psychology theories and measures can be used in real clinical situations and how research can directly inform routine clinical practice.

Roter, D.L., Stewart, M., Putnam, S.M. et al. (1997) Communication patterns of primary care physicians, *Journal of the American Medical Association*, 277 (4): 350–6.

Communication patterns of primary care physicians

Debra L. Roter, DrPH; Moira Stewart, PhD; Samuel M. Putnam, MD; Mack Lipkin, Jr, MD: William Stiles, PhD; Thomas S. Inui, MD

Abstract

Objectives: To use audiotape analysis to describe communication patterns in primary care, to relate these to ideal relationship types as described in the literature, and to explore the patterns' relationships with physician and patient characteristics and satisfaction.

Design: Description of routine communication in primary care based on audiotape analysis and patient and physician exit questionnaires.

Setting: A total of 11 ambulatory clinics and private practices.

Participants: The participants were 127 physicians and 537 patients coping with ongoing problems related to disease.

Main outcomes measures: Roter Interactional Analysis System (RIAS) and patient and physician exit satisfaction questionnaires.

Results: Cluster analysis revealed 5 distinct communication patterns: (1) "narrowly biomedical," characterized by closed-ended medical questions and biomedical talk occurring in 32% of visits; (2) "expanded biomedical," like the restricted pattern but with moderate levels of psychosocial discussion occurring in 33% of the visits; (3) "biopsychosocial," reflecting a balance of psychosocial and biomedical topics (20% of the visits); (4) "psychosocial," characterized by psychosocial exchange (8% of visits); and (5) "consumerist," characterized primarily by patient questions and physician information giving (8% of visits). Biomedically focused visits were used more often with more sick, older, and lower income patients by younger, male physicians. Physician satisfaction was lowest in the narrowly biomedical pattern and highest in the consumerist pattern, while patient satisfaction was highest in the psychosocial pattern.

Conclusions: Primary care communication patterns range from narrowly biomedical to consumerist patterns and parallel the ideal forms of patient-physician relationships described in the literature.

From the Department of Health Policy and Management, the Johns Hopkins University School of Hygiene and Public Health, Baltimore, Md (Dr Roter); the Department of Family Practice, University of Western Ontario, London, Ontario (Dr Stewart); the Department of Medicine, Boston University Medical Center, Boston, Mass (Dr Putnam); the Department of Medicine, New York University Medical Center, New York (Dr Lipkin): Miami University, Oxford, Ohio (Dr Stiles); and Harvard University, Boston (Dr Inui).

Reprints: Debra Roter, DrPH, Johns Hopkins University School of Hygiene and Public Health, 624 N Broadway, Baltimore, MD 21205 (e-mail: DROTER@phnet.sph.jhu.edu).

Inquiry into the most effective or desirable forms of the physician-patient relationship over the past 50 years has yielded controversy, debate, and little consensus. Much of the debate has centered around conflicting and shifting societal values regarding patient autonomy and medical paternalism.[1] The debate is important because the relationship shapes the expectations of physicians and patients, as well as ethical and legal standards for physician duties, informed consent, and medical malpractice.[2]

While there has been little consensus regarding the superiority of any particular model of the physician-patient relationship, Emanuel and Emanuel[2] have proposed 3 elements that represent core differences in ideal types. These core differences include the goals of the physician-patient interaction, the role of patients' values and conceptions of patient autonomy, and physicians' obligations in regard to their patients. Within this framework, the authors present 4 ideal relationship types. The paternalistic relationship delivers the most appropriate biomedical intervention as determined by the physician. The physician articulates and implements a course of action as the patient's guardian; patients' values are assumed consistent with those of the physician, and patient autonomy consists of assent to physician recommendations. In the informative or consumerist model, the interactions convey technical information so that patients may select the medical intervention they deem most appropriate. The physician's role is that of technical expert, patient values are unexamined, and patient autonomy is safeguarded. In the interpretive model, the interaction clarifies patients' values and needs so the physician may help the patients select an appropriate medical intervention. The physician provides technical expertise but also assists patients in interpreting and understanding their own values more fully. Finally, the deliberative model aims to help patients determine and choose the best health-related values possible within their clinical situations. The physician goes beyond the provision of technical expertise or values clarification to moral persuasion, suggesting why certain health-related values are more worthy and should be aspired to.

As ideal types, these 4 models were not empirically determined and have not been tested against the complicating details of the everyday real practice of medicine. This is not surprising. While thousands of medical encounters have been recorded by audio or video equipment and analyzed in some manner over the past 25 years, few of these studies have attempted more than an analysis of communication by individual categories relating to such things as amount of biomedical talk or social conversation. With the exception of a few investigators[3-6] who have derived broad topologies of physician style through quantitative analysis, the literature has been unidimensional, lacking in depth and richness. Inui and colleagues[7] maintain that the communication literature is akin to a description of *Hamlet* as a play including ghosts, witches, soldiers, lords, and ladies – one of whom is already dead, one of whom dies by drowning, one dies by poisoned drink, two die by sword, and one dies by sword and drink![7]

The current work addresses the question of whether patterns of style in the physician-patient relationship are recognizable in routine practice through the use of empirical, analytic techniques, and how such patterns correspond to the idealized approaches found in the literature. Specifically, the following aims are addressed: (1) to explore empirically the core communication elements that define varying models of the physician-patient relationship; (2) to describe the broader communication context within which these models may operate; (3) to describe patient and physician characteristics associated with these models; and (4) to explore the association between communication patterns and patient and physician satisfaction with care.

Methods

The Collaborative Study of Communication Dynamics was begun as a research effort by the Task Force on the Medical Interview of the Society of General Internal Medicine. The data were collected at 11 sites in the United States and Canada, including outpatient department clinics and private and group practice settings. Task force members recruited participating physicians through collegial networks. The data were collected in 1985 and 1986.

Participants

Physicians. Background information was available for 98 of the 127 physicians who volunteered for participation in the study and gave full informed consent. Included in this group were 35 second- and third-year residents, 60 physicians board certified in internal medicine, and 3 physicians certified in family practice. Physician participants were predominantly male (79%), and white (95%), averaging 35 years of age (range, 25–64 years). The majority of physicians (75%) were audiotaped in urban hospital-based clinic settings, while the remaining 25% were in private or small group practices. The physicians represent a convenience sample chosen by the coordinators at each site.

Patients. Adult patients with at least 2 prior visits to their physician and ongoing medical problems were included in the study to ensure that they would be seeing their primary care physician, and there would be something substantive to discuss. A majority of the patients in the study were female (58%), almost equally divided by race (55% white and 45% African American), with 65% earning less than $10 000 per year. The average age was 60 years, with a range from 21 years to 94 years. More than half the patients had at least 7 previous visits to their physician.

Patients were approached in the waiting room prior to their medical visit and recruited for the study and constituted a convenience sample. Participants signed informed consent for all aspects of the study, including audiotape recording of their visit. The medical visits were recorded on audiotape, and both physicians and patients completed questionnaires immediately after the visit. Individual patients were included in the study only once, and physicians were recorded with an average of 4 patients (range, 1–17 patients). Audiotapes of sufficient quality for analysis were obtained for 537 medical visits.

Sources of data

Audiotapes. The 537 study audiotapes were analyzed using the Roter Interaction Analysis System (RIAS), which codes each phrase or complete thought expressed during the visit by either patient or physician into 1 of 34 mutually exclusive and exhaustive categories. Coding is done directly from audiotapes, and, as in several other studies,[8–10] the coding system demonstrated adequate intercoder reliability. Reliability coefficients for physician categories averaged 0.76 (range, 0.58–0.90) and patient categories averaged 0.81 (range, 0.71–0.99), based on double coding of a random sample of 30 audiotapes.

For simplicity, only summary groupings of the RIAS coding categories are presented in this analysis. The summary groupings are composites of the individually coded categories that relate broadly to the content, affect, and process dimensions of the visit. Table 1 presents the content composites, the individual code categories included within the composites, and category examples of dialogue.

In addition to the composites, a measure of verbal dominance during the medical visit was derived by calculating a ratio of the count of physician statements divided by a total count of

Table 1 Categories of the Roter Interaction Analysis System

Functional grouping	Communication behavior	Example
Content categories	Question asking (medical condition, therapeutic regimen, psychosocial topics)	
	Open-ended questions	What can you tell me about the pain? How have you responded to medication? What's happening with your son?
	Close-ended questions	Does it hurt when you bend? Did the shot help? Are you sleeping any better?
	Biomedical information (medical condition, therapeutic regimen)	The medication may make you drowsy. You'll need to take the antibiotics every day for 10 days.
	Psychosocial exchange (problems of daily living, issues regarding social relations, feelings, and emotions)	It is important to get out and do something daily. The senior center is a place great for company and they'll give you lunch too.
Affective categories	Positive talk (agreements, approval, laughter, and jokes)	You look fantastic. You're doing great!
	Negative talk (disagreements, disapproval, criticisms, or corrections)	I think you're wrong. You weren't being careful. No, not like that; I want you to use it like this.
	Social talk (nonmedical subjects)	How about them O's, some game last night.
Process categories	Facilitation (asking for patient opinion, patient understanding, or paraphrase)	What do you think it is? Do you follow? Let me make sure I've got it right – you said the pain is less than before, but still bad.
	Orientation (directions or instructions)	Get up on the table; take a deep breath.

patient statements. Finally, a communication control score was calculated relating patient control (patients' questions and physicians' information giving and counseling, both biomedical and psychosocial) to physician control (physicians' questions and orientations and patients' biomedical information). This score is similar to a measure suggested by Greenfield et al[11] and reflects the description by Stewart[12] and Stewart et al[13] of the continuum between patient-centered and physician-centered interviewing.

Patient Questionnaire. After the medical visit, patients responded to a questionnaire that included sociodemographic and health status questions, as well as a 43-item patient satisfaction questionnaire. Earlier factor analysis found that the satisfaction items reflect 5 distinct and reliable dimensions of patient satisfaction: task-directed skill, attentiveness, interpersonal skill, emotional support, and physician-patient partnership.[14]

Physician Questionnaire. Study physicians completed a questionnaire immediately following each visit that included the patient's diagnosis, a rating of the patient's physical and emotional health (8-point scale), a rating of how successful the physician felt in accomplishing the main goal of the visit (4-point scale), and a 20-item visit satisfaction questionnaire. Earlier factor analysis found 4 distinct and reliable dimensions of physicians' visit satisfaction included in this measure: quality of relationship, patient's cooperative nature, adequacy of data collection, and appropriate use of time.[15]

Cluster Approach. The 3 categories of interaction, questions, biomedical information, and psychosocial talk (for patients and physicians), were chosen for entry in the cluster analysis.

These categories are most often considered in the patient-centered vs physician-centered interviewing continuum[13] and reflect the 3 functions of the medical interview: data gathering, patient education, and relationship building.[16,17]

The communication measures were analyzed using the SPSSx program for hierarchic cluster analysis (SPSS Inc, Chicago, Ill). The basic analytic model was analysis of variance (ANOVA), contrasting the pattern groups on a variety of measures consistent with the study's exploratory questions. In addition to an overall F statistic based on a comparison of the 5 patterns, planned contrasts were performed to compare each of the pattern groups against all the others combined. For analysis of dependent variables, physician and patient satisfaction and physician goal-success, analysis of covariance (ANCOVA) was performed, controlling for the significant correlates identified in preliminary regression analysis. The covariates of patient satisfaction included patient's sex, age, race, and number of prior visits. The covariates of physician satisfaction included patient income, number of prior visits, and patient's emotional health. The covariates of physician goal-success include patient's income, number of prior visits, and patient's physical health.

Results

Five distinct patterns emerged from the analysis – accounting for 95% of the visits and 99% of the physicians. The distinguishing characteristics of each pattern, based on mean levels of key communication variables, were used to derive 5 descriptive pattern names: narrowly biomedical, expanded biomedical, biopsychosocial, psychosocial, and consumerist.

As shown in Table 2, the 2 most common patterns, the narrowly biomedical and expanded biomedical, each account for one third of the visits and were used at least once by more than 60% of physicians. While less common than the biomedical patterns, the biopsychosocial pattern was evident in 20% of visits and was used by 42% of study physicians. The psychosocial and consumerist communication patterns were much less common than the others (7% and 8% of visits, respectively) and were used by fewer than one quarter of the study physicians.

The average length of the medical visit (including the physical exam that was tape-recorded and coded) was 21 minutes (range, 2.8–73.8 minutes). The narrowly biomedical visits averaged 20.5 minutes (range, 2.8–50.6 minutes); expanded biomedical visits averaged 21.8 minutes (range, 6.4–73.8 minutes); biopsychosocial visits averaged 19.3 minutes (range, 5.6–51.6 minutes); psychosocial visits averaged 22.9 minutes (range, 9.3–38.3); and consumerist visits averaged 21.9 minutes (range, 4.1–42.9). There were no overall significant differences among patterns (overall $F_{(4,499)} = 1.7$; $P=0.14$).

Table 2 Distribution of communication pattern use by visits and number of physicians across primary care visits

Pattern type	Visits, No. (%) ($n=537$)	Physicians, No. (%)* ($n=127$)
Narrowly biomedical	162 (32)	86 (68)
Expanded biomedical	168 (33)	77 (81)
Biopsychosocial	103 (20)	53 (42)
Psychosocial	35 (7)	24 (19)
Consumerist	40 (8)	29 (23)
Unclassified	29 (5)	1 (1)

*Number of physicians with at least 1 visit falling within the pattern.

Analysis of variance confirmed significant differences in the mean levels of all physician communication categories used in the cluster analysis across the 5 patterns (overall $F_{(4,503)}$ values ranged from 5.8 to 113.1; $P<0.001$). Patient categories used in the cluster analysis also showed significant differences across patterns (overall $F_{(4,503)}$ values ranged from 4.5 to 474.0; $P<0.001$). The percentage distribution of physician and patient talk categories used in the cluster analysis and described in the pattern characteristics below are shown in Table 3.

Although not used as cluster variables, clear differences in categories of physicians' and patients' social talk, positive talk, facilitation, and orientations were evident (overall $F_{(4,503)}$ values ranged from 3.7 to 14.0; $P<0.006$) (Table 3).

Pattern characteristics

Narrowly Biomedical. The narrowly biomedical pattern is notable for the extremely low percentage of both physician (2%) and patient (5%) talk devoted to psychosocial topics and high percentage of biomedical information given by physicians (27%) and patients (70%). Physician talk is also characterized by a high percentage (19%) of question asking.

Expanded Biomedical. The expanded biomedical pattern is similar to the narrow pattern in its high frequency of question asking by physicians (17%), but has more moderate levels of biomedical and psychosocial exchange for both physicians and patients.

Table 3 Percentage of talk in key communication categories across 5 communication patterns*

	Communication patterns					
	Narrowly biomedical	Expanded biomedical	Biopsychosocial	Psychosocial	Consumerist	Overall F
Physician categories						
Questions	19†	17†	11	9	10	48.3
Information	27†	22‡	23	20	43†	59.3
Psychosocial	2§	7‖	11†	19†	4¶	113.1
Social	4	5	7‡	5	3	5.3
Positive	21	23	23	28‡	17##	6.3
Facilitation††	7	7	6**	5	5††	5.7
Orientation††	12	13	11	8#	10	7.0
Patient categories						
Questions	4	5	4	3‡‡	6	4.5
Information	70†	58¶	39†	25†	53‖	459.2
Psychosocial	5†	18†	29†	55†	11†	474.0
Social	4	6	7§§	5	4	3.7
Positive	15	16	18	11‖‖‖	24†	14.0

* All differences based on Sheffe tests, $P<0.05$.
† Differs from every other group; all differences based on Sheffe tests, $P<0.05$.
‡ Differs from narrowly biomedical and consumerist patterns.
§ Differs from expanded biomedical, biopsychosocial, and psychosocial patterns.
‖ Differs from narrowly biomedical, biopsychosocial, and psychosocial patterns.
¶ Differs from biopsychosocial and psychosocial patterma.
# Differs from expanded biomedical, biopsychosocial, and psychosocial patterns.
Differs from expanded biomedical pattern.
†† Differs from narrowly biomedical and expanded biomedical patterns.
‡‡ Differs from expanded biomedical and consumerist patterns.
§§ Differs from narrowly biomedical pattern.
‖‖‖ Differs from expanded biomedical, biopsychosocial, and consumerist patterns.

Biopsychosocial. In the biopsychosocial pattern, there is relative balance between biomedical and psychosocial exchange in both physicians' and patients' communication. While physicians' communication is still predominantly biomedical with twice as much biomedical (23%) as psychosocial talk (11%), this is substantially less than the 14-fold difference in the narrowly biomedical pattern or the 3-fold difference in the expanded biomedical pattern. Fewer questions were also asked by physicians compared with the 2 biomedical patterns.

For patients, biomedical and psychosocial talk is in close balance in this pattern, reflecting a nearly equal emphasis. Finally, this pattern shows somewhat more of social talk than the other patterns for both patients and physicians.

Psychosocial. The psychosocial pattern is the most distinctive of the 5 patterns as its communication is clearly dominated by psychosocial exchange. Physician talk is almost evenly divided between the psychosocial and biomedical categories (20% vs 19%, respectively), while patients devote more than twice their talk to psychosocial compared with biomedical topics (55% vs 25%, respectively). This pattern shows the lowest level of question asking for both physicians and patients.

The psychosocial pattern has the highest level of physician positive talk and the lowest level of orientation statements. Here, the physician appears very positive and accepting of patient input, but less concerned with moving the visit along physically. The low level of patient positive talk reflect the lowered level of information giving by the physician.

Consumerist. The consumerist pattern suggests the use of the physician as a consultant who answers questions rather than one who asks them. The pattern is characterized by the combination of a comparatively low frequency of physician question asking (10%), a high frequency of patient question asking (6%), and the highest frequency of information being given by the physician (43%). This pattern is also characterized by low levels of psychosocial and social exchange.

In an almost mirror image of the psychosocial pattern, positive talk is very high for patients (in response to information being given by the physician), but low for physicians, indicating perhaps less needed effort in prompting patient input. It appears that the consumerist is the most "down to business" of the patterns, with little need for patient dialogue prompts or social exchange, but high patient question asking and receptivity to physician information.

Communication control and verbal dominance

A patient communication control score, relative to physician control, was calculated for all visits. The scores presented in Table 4 show the range of patient communication control

Table 4 Characteristics of prominent communication patterns and communication control scores*

Pattern	Mean control score (SD)[†]	95% CI	Score range
Narrowly biomedical	0.4420[‡] (0.1970)	0.4114 – 0.4726	0.0462 – 1.0896
Expanded biomedical	0.4889[‡] (0.2028)	0.4580 – 0.5198	0.1587 – 1.3148
Biopsychosocial	0.7286[§] (0.3067)	0.6687 – 0.7885	0.1471 – 1.6228
Psychosocial	0.9297[‖] (0.5078)	0.7553 – 1.1040	0.3125 – 2.1389
Consumerist	1.0090[‖] (0.2713)	0.9222 – 1.0957	0.3980 – 1.6610

* All differences based on Sheffe tests, $P < 0.05$.

† Mean control scores differ from all others. CI indicates confidence interval. Overall $F_{(4,500)} = 66.9917$: $P < 0.001$.

‡ Differs from biopsychosocial, and psychosocial and consumerist patterns.

§ Differs from every other group.

‖ Differs from narrowly biomedical expanded biomedical, and biopsychosocial patterns.

in relation to the patterns and are significant (overall $F_{(4, 507)} = 66.9$; $P < 0.001$). The lowest patient communication control in the narrowly biomedical pattern reflected a 0.44-to-1.0 ratio, indicating little patient control of the communication process. The highest relative patient control was in the consumerist pattern, reflecting an equally balanced 1-to-1 ratio. The psychosocial pattern was also nearly balanced in terms of communication control with a 0.93-to-1.0 ratio.

Tables 4 and 5 jointly reveal that, with the exception of the consumerist pattern, patient communication control and physician verbal dominance are inversely related. Table 5 presents the ratio of physician talk to patient talk calculated as a total count of physician statements divided by a total count of patient statements. The highest level of physician verbal dominance was evident in the consumerist pattern, while an almost equal distribution of patient and physician talk was notable in the psychosocial pattern group.

Demographic variables related to patterns

Patient age (overall $F_{(4, 494)} = 4.06$; $P = 0.003$) and patient annual income (overall $F_{(1, 363)} = 2.5$; $P = 0.04$) were related to pattern. Patients in the expanded biomedical pattern were older than others (mean age, 68.5 years; average age, 60 years; $P < 0.003$), while those in the biopsychosocial and consumerist patterns were younger (mean age, 56.7 years; $P < 0.008$; mean age, 55.9 years; $P < 0.07$, respectively). Patients in the narrowly biomedical pattern were more likely to be African American ($P < 0.03$) and poorer ($P < 0.02$) than patients in other patterns. Patient sex and number of prior visits were unrelated to patterns.

Pattern type, diagnoses, and ratings of health status

All health status analyses included patient age, race, sex, and number of prior visits as covariates. Physicians listed up to 3 main problems for each patient. Most patients suffered from at least 1 chronic disease. There was no difference in distribution of chronic disease diagnoses across patterns. There was a difference across patterns with respect to the number of patients for whom a psychosocial diagnosis was included. Psychosocial diagnoses in this study included any mention in the physician's list of the following: anxiety, depression, mood changes, nerves, stress, distinguishing somatic from nonsomatic complaints, check social situation, check living arrangements, provide support, provide reassurance, socialize with the patient, compliment patient on improvements, and discuss work concerns. As in Table 6, a high proportion of such diagnoses were made for patients falling within the psychosocial pattern, and the lowest frequency of such diagnoses was in the narrowly biomedical pattern.

Table 5 Prominent communication patterns and the ratio of physician to patient talk*

Pattern type	Physician to patient talk ratio (SD)	95% CI[†]	Ratio range
Narrowly biomedical	1.3682 (0.3951)	1.3069 – 1.4295	0.3506 – 2.6857
Expanded biomedical	1,3969 (0.5575)	1.3120 – 1.4819	0.6199 – 3.9032
Biopsychosocial	1.2916 (0.4161)	1.2103 – 1.3729	0.3939 – 2.5789
Psychosocial[†]	1.0841[‡] (0.4949)	0.9140 – 1.2541	0.4484 – 2.5079
Consumerist[‡]	1.6777[§] (0.8747)	1.3979 – 1.9574	0.7805 – 4.6234

* All differences based on Sheffe tests, $P < 0.05$.

† CI indicates confidence interval. Overall $F_{(4, 599)} = 7.003$; $P < 0.001$.

‡ Differs from expanded biomedical and consumerist patterns.

§ Differs from every other group.

Table 6 Communication patterns and psychological diagnosis*

Communication pattern	Psychosocial diagnosis patients, No. (%)[†]
Narrowly biomedical	10 (6)
Expanded biomedical	20 (12)
Biopsychosocial	17 (17)
Psychosocial	12 (34)[‡]
Consumerist	3 (8)

* All differences based on Sheffe tests; $P<0.05$.

† Overall $F_{(4.505)}=6.68$; $P<0.001$.

‡ Differs from narrowly biomedical, expanded biomedical, and consumerial patterns.

Patterns were also related to physicians' ratings of physical health status (overall $F_{(4,486)}=$ 3.29; $P=0.01$) and presence of social problems (overall $F_{(4,436)}=3.91$; $P=0.004$). Psychosocial-pattern patients were rated by their physicians as in better physical health, but with worse social problems than others. Patients in both the narrowly biomedical and expanded biomedical patterns were rated by physicians as in poorer physical health than other patients, but rated with fewer social problems.

Patterns were also related to patients' ratings of their own physical (overall $F_{(4,436)}=4.21$; $P=0.002$) and emotional health status (overall $F_{(4,436)}=2.36$; $P=0.05$). Somewhat different distinctions occurred than those made by physicians. Self-ratings by patients in the narrowly biomedical pattern reflected worse physical and emotional health than all other patients; self-ratings by psychosocial-pattern patients were close behind. In contrast, self-ratings by patients in the biopsychosocial and consumerist patterns were notably high for both physical and emotional health.

Communication patterns and patient and physician satisfaction

The ANCOVA analysis with patients' age, race, sex, and number of prior visits as covariates found that overall patient satisfaction with the medical visit was significantly higher for patients in the psychosocial pattern than others ($F_{(1,447)}=4.98$; $P<0.05$). Inspection of mean satisfaction scores showed the lowest ratings for the 2 biomedical patterns, followed by ratings for the biopsychosocial and consumerist pattern, and the highest levels of satisfaction for the psychosocial pattern. Specifically, satisfaction with the psychosocial pattern was significantly higher than any other pattern on the dimension of patient-physician partnership ($F_{(1,447)}=8.23$; $P=0.05$).

Communication patterns were also related to physicians' satisfaction with the medical visit. ANCOVA analysis, using patient income, number of prior visits, and physicians' rating of patients' emotional health as covariates, found that physicians rated narrowly biomedical pattern visits lower than other pattern visits on 2 of the 4 dimensions of physician satisfaction: satisfaction with appropriate use of time ($F_{(1,433)}=5.50$; $P=0.03$) and adequacy of data collection ($F_{(1,253)}=4.62$; $P=0.05$). In contrast, physician satisfaction with the consumerist pattern was significantly higher than all other patterns in relation to time ($F_{(1,439)}=5.09$; $P=0.03$) and data collection ($F_{(1,438)}=4.91$; $P<0.05$).

Using patient income, physical health, and number of prior visits as covariates, physicians' goals tended to be less successfully accomplished in the narrowly biomedical pattern than in all others ($F_{(1,448)}=3.3$; $P=0.10$).

Physician use of patterns

Physicians did not use the patterns in a random fashion; there was a significant tendency to use a particular pattern by most physicians. Analysis of 39 physicians seeing 5 or more patients revealed a nonrandom distribution of pattern use by individual physicians (χ^2, 214; *df*, 152; $P<$ 0.001). Virtually all physicians used more than 1 pattern, but half of the physicians used 1 pattern for the majority of their visits. This was most evident for the 2 biomedical patterns (each used by 8 physicians); 3 physicians favored the biopsychosocial pattern, and I favored the consumerist pattern. None of the physicians used the psychosocial pattern with the majority of their patients.

Physician age and sex were related to pattern use. Physicians using the 2 biomedical patterns were younger than those physicians using the other 3 patterns (mean age, 34 years vs 37 years, respectively; $F_{(1,214)}=6.9$; $P=0.009$), A higher proportion of male than female physicians used the biomedical patterns, while female physicians were more likely to use the other 3 patterns (χ^2, 3.5; *df*, 4; $P=0.05$).

Comment

The 5 communication patterns identified in this study are derived from actual medical practice and reflect the everyday business of medicine in the words of physicians and patients, The nature of the exchange and the balance it reflects between the voices of patients and physicians provides a basis for considering the physician-patient relationship. In this light, the 5 communication patterns described here are broadly suggestive of the ideal types of Emanuel and Emanuel.[2]

The narrowly biomedical pattern with its restricted focus and physician-dominated talk reflects the essential elements of the paternalistic model. The patient's voice is absent as reflected in the minimal psychosocial exchange and low patient communication control of the visit. High levels of physician question asking and physician verbal dominance overall further distinguish these visits as being physician directed and guided.

The expanded biomedical pattern, while still tightly controlled by the physician, allows for more patient input in the psychosocial arena than its restricted counterpart. Although still a physician-controlled model of exchange and dominated by a high level of physician question asking, the allowance of greater psychosocial dialogue may mark an intermediate pattern, a transition to more egalitarian models that more fully integrate the patient's perspective.

The biopsychosocial pattern includes visit balance with its mixed psychosocial and biomedical focus, lowered physician control, and lowered physician verbal dominance. This pattern appears as a collaborative model of exchange along the lines of the interpretive model of Emanuel and Emanuel.[2] Patients' health values and preferences are likely to be mutually negotiated and explored within these exchanges, with implication for patient autonomy, self-understanding, and self-discovery.

The psychosocial pattern also reflects aspects of the interpretive model, although more intensely than in the biopsychosocial patterns, and some aspects of the deliberative model of Emanuel and Emanuel.[2] With its preponderance of talk in the psychosocial domain, the 1-to-1 ratio of talk, and high patient control of communication, this pattern provides an opportunity for in-depth dialogue about the social and emotional implications of the patient's condition. The physician's role may be friend or therapist, engaging the patient in dialogue about life issues that go well beyond the biomedical circumstances.

Finally, the consumerist pattern suggests the informative model.[2] The physician acts as a competent technical expert and provides relevant factual information. The physician acts to implement the patient's selected intervention.

It is not surprising that some patterns were more commonly used than others. The biomedical pattern is almost always identified in the literature as the preeminent medical model, while the biopsychosocial model is a less practiced alternative. This appears to be the case here: 66% of the visits, with at least 60% of the study physicians, were characterized as physician dominated and narrowly focused on biomedical concerns. Brent and Beckett[5] similarly found that some two thirds of the medical students they studied used communication patterns that were heavily physician controlled and dominated relative to more egalitarian alternative styles available to them.

The expanded biomedical pattern may mark a transition in practice to more egalitarian models as advocated by Engle,[18] Lipkin,[19] and others. In this regard, the prevalence of the biopsychosocial pattern in 20% of the visits could reflect this advocacy over the past 25 years. Szasz and Hollender[20] stated in the 1950s that the mutual collaboration model was "essentially foreign to medicine." While this may have been true 40 years ago, it does not appear to be so now. Our study suggests that while collaborative models do not predominate, they are certainly evident in primary care practice. Since we lack databases of interviews that would allow a retrospective comparison of pattern frequencies, we will have to make current and future assessments to determine the trend in physician communication patterns.

The slight differences in length of visit across the patterns was a revelation. Many physicians think that "patient-centered" visits, particularly visits in which psychosocial issues are addressed, are more time-consuming than biomedical exchanges and more likely to overwhelm a tight schedule. This is clearly not the case here. Even the pattern in which dialogue was predominantly psychosocial did not result in significantly longer visits than the others. While we have found that length of visit is not associated with particular patterns, we don't know what will happen to patterns of interaction between patients and physicians with tighter schedules and shorter scheduled appointments. Patterns of care in many managed care organizations reduce face-to-face time to 10 to 12 minutes – clearly short of the average visits described here. From our data, we are unable to postulate whether physicians would shift from one interactional pattern to another with less time available to them. Some data suggest that when time is shortened in general practice, psychosocial talk drops out first.

Both patient and physician find dissatisfaction in common communication elements. The narrowly biomedical pattern was associated with the lowest levels of physician satisfaction and also was rated by patients as least satisfying. Indeed, physicians rated these patients as poor historians who provide low-quality data and make poor use of physician time. Physicians also saw these exchanges as least likely to achieve their visit goals. Perhaps related to poor goal attainment and satisfaction ratings was a disjuncture in physicians' ratings and patients' self-ratings of emotional health. The poor physical health status of these patients appears to dominate the visit, with little focus on patients' emotional health problems. Despite patients' self-ratings reflecting concern in the emotional domain, the very limited amount of psychosocial exchange in these visits makes it unlikely that these concerns are expressed or addressed. Consequently, an important aspect of the patient's history and condition may be overlooked.

This finding is consistent with the literature, which shows that physicians generally have low rates of or recognition of emotional distress among patients presenting with somatic complaints.[21,22] The high prevalence of visits of the narrowly biomedical pattern and the implications of missing emotional health concerns for morbidity, mortality, cost, and satisfaction makes these visits especially deserving of further study and possible remediation. Physician training through continuing medical education programs in communication skills have been associated with more accurate recognition of emotional distress.[23]

The psychosocial pattern was associated with the highest satisfaction ratings for patients overall and, particularly, in relation to a sense of partnership and support. The frequency of these visits is quite low (<10%) and appears to reflect an important, but small, proportion of routine visits.

Reflecting quite a different dimension of physician satisfaction and kind of visit, physicians were especially satisfied with the consumerist pattern, reporting that these visits made good use of their time. While not receiving the highest patient satisfaction ratings, patients were moderately pleased with these visits. Inasmuch as patients engaging in this pattern were younger than others, there may be a cohort effect, suggesting that the younger generation of patients will be "consumerist" in their relationships to physicians. As this pattern only reflects a small proportion of visits (<10%), its importance may be in anticipation of greater use as younger cohorts age into chronic conditions and become more frequent users of health services. Findings from the Medical Outcomes Study similarly report younger, nonminority patients as having medical visits characterized as participatory in decision-making style and that these visits are particularly satisfying.[24]

Limitations of the study should be noted. This was a convenience sample, not a random sample, of patients, and although we are not aware of any consistent bias in patient selection, this was possible. The coinvestigators who took responsibility for physician recruitment were members of the Task Force on the Medical Interview of the Society for General Internal Medicine. Members of the task force generally endorse an expansion of biomedical medicine into the biopsychosocial sphere. Recruitment efforts by coinvestigators were aimed at a broad collegial network at their home institution, and we do not know whether task force members have different local collegial networks than non-task force physicians.

Despite these qualifications, the patterns uncovered in this analysis are based on a large sample of patients and physicians. The sample reflects broad diversity of geographic location, representing all regions of the country, and a variety of practice settings, including hospital clinics and private practice.

We believe that the communication patterns described here reflect the routine business of medicine and provide a useful benchmark by which the evolution of physician-patient relationships and medical communication may be measured. The patterns identified in this study provide a starting point from which we can establish and follow trends in changing relations between doctors and patients over time. The implications of these changes are tremendous, and they must be given full and serious consideration in conceptualizing how the patient-physician relationship may be articulated in the future and how the dramatic current changes in health care delivery may affect care.

This research was supported by a grant from the National Fund for Medical Education.

Members of the Collaborative Study Group of the Task Force on Doctor and Patient of the Society for General Internal Medicine include Debra Roter, DrPH, Principal Investigator, Johns Hopkins University, Baltimore, Md; Klea Bertakis, MD, University of California, Davis; Rita Charon, MD, Columbia University, New York, NY; Steven Cole, MD, Long Island Jewish Hospital, New York, NY; Oliver Fein, MD, Columbia University; James Florek, MD, University of Massachusetts, Springfield; Michele Green, DrPH, Brooklyn College, Brooklyn, NY; Thomas Inui, MD, Harvard University, Boston, Mass; Mack Lipkin, Jr, MD. New York University, New York; Franklin Medio, PhD, Chicago College of Osteopathic Medicine, Chicago, Ill; Samuel Putnam, MD, Boston University Medical Center; Timothy Quill, MD, University of Rochester, Rochester, NY; Katherine Rost, PhD, University of Arkansas, Little Rock; David Simon, MD, Community General Hospital, Syracuse, NY; Michael Simon, EdD, Communities for People, Inc, Lincoln, Mass; Barbara Starfield, MD, Johns Hopkins University; Moira Stewart, PhD, University of Western Ontario, London, Ontario; William Stiles, PhD, Miami University, Oxford, Ohio; Bryce Templeton, MD, Hahnemann University, Philadelphia, Pa.

References

1 *President's Commission for the Study of Ethical Problems in Medicine and Biomedical and Behavioral Research.* Washington, DC: Government Printing Office; 1982;1.

2 Emanuel EJ, Emanuel LL. Four models of the physician-patient relationship. *JAMA.* 1992;267:2221–2296.

3 Byrne PS, Long BEL. *Doctors Talking to Patients.* London, England: Her Majesty's Stationery Office; 1976.

4 Buija R. Shija M, Verhaak PFM. Byrne and Long; a classification for rating the interview style of doctors. *Soc Sci Med.* 1984;7:683–690.

5 Brent EE, Beckett DE. Common response patterns of medical students in interviews of hospitalized patients. *Med Care.* 1986;24:981–989.

6 Campbell JD, Mauksch, HO, Neikirk HJ, Hosokawa MC. Collaborative practice and provider styles of delivering health care. *Soc Sci Med.* 1990;12:1359–1365.

7 Inui TS, Carter WR. Problems and prospects for health services research on provider patient communication. *Med Care.* 1985;23:521–538.

8 Roter D, Hall J, Katz N. Relations between physicians' behaviors and patients' satisfaction, recall, and impressions: an analogue study. *Med Care.* 1987:25;399–412.

9 Wissow LS, Roter DL, Wilson MEH. Pediatrician interview style and mothers' disclosure of psychosocial issues. *Pediatrics.* 1994;93:289–295.

10 Hall JA, Irish JT, Roter DL, Ehrlich CM, Miller LH. Gender in medical encounters: an analysis of physician and patient communication in a primary care setting. *Health Psychol.* 1994;13:384–392.

11 Greenfield S, Kaplan S, Ware JE, Jr. Expanding patient involvement in care: effects on patient outcomes. *Ann Intern Med.* 1985;102:520–528.

12 Stewart M. What is a successful doctor-patient, interview? a study of interactions and outcomes. *Soc Sci Med.* 1984;19:167–175.

13 Stewart M, Brown BJ, Weston WW. McWhinney I, McWilliam CL, Freeman TR. *Patient-Centered Medicine: Transforming the Clinical Method.* Thousand Oaks, Calif: Sage Publications; 1995.

14 Bertakis KD, Roter DL, Putnam SM, The relationship of physician medical interview style to patient satisfaction. *J Fam Pract.* 1991; 32:175 181.

15 Suchman AE, Roter DL, Green M, Lipkin M Jr. Physician satisfaction with primary care office visits. *Med Care.* 1993; 31:1088–1092.1.22.

16 Lazare A, Putnam S, Lipkin M. Functions of the medical interview. In: Lipkin M, Putnam S, Lazars A, eds. *The Medical Interview: Clinical Care, Education, and Research.* New York, NY: Springer-Verlag NY Inc: 1995:422–435.

17 Cohen-Cole S. *The Medical Interview: The Three Function Approach.* St Louis, Mo: Mosby–Year Book Inc: 1991.

18 Engel GL. How much longer must medicine's science be bound by a seventeenth century world view? In: White K, ed. *The Task of Medicine: Dialogue at Wickenburg.* Menlo Park, Calif: The Henry J Kaiser Foundation; 1988.

19 Lipkin M. The medical interview and related skills. In: Branch WT. Jr, ed. *Office Practice of Medicine.* 3rd ed. Philadelphia, Pa: WB Saunders Co: 1994;1287–1306.

20 Szasz PS, Hollender MH. A contribution to the philosophy of medicine: the basic model of the doctor-patient relationship. *Arch Intern Med.* 1956;97:586–592.

21 Ormel J., Giel R. Medical effects of nonrecognition of affective disorders in primary care. In: Sartorious N, Goldberg G, de Girolamo J, et al, eds. *Psychological Disorders in General Medical Settings.* Lewiston, NY: Hogrefe & Huber Publishers; 1990:146–158.

22 Bridges K, Goldberg D. Somatic presentation of DSM-III psychiatric disorders in primary care. *J Psychosom Res.* 1985;29:568–569.

23 Roter DL, Hall JA, Kern DE, Barker LR, Cole KA, Roca RP. Improving physicians' interviewing skills and reducing patients' emotional distress: a randomized clinical trial. *Arch Intern Med.* 1995;155:1877–1884.

24 Kaplan SH, Gandak B, Greenfield S, Rogers W, Ware JE Jr. Patient and visit characteristics related to physicians' participatory decision-making style: results from the Medical Outcomes Study. *Med Care.* 1995;83:1176–1187.

Mead, N. and Bower, P. (2000) Patient-centredness: a conceptual framework and review of the empirical literature, *Social Science and Medicine*, 51: 1087–110.

Patient-centredness

A conceptual framework and review of the empirical literature

Nicola Mead*, Peter Bower

National Primary Care Research and Development Centre, University of Manchester, 5th Floor Williamson Building, Oxford Road, Manchester M13 9PL, UK

Abstract

A 'patient-centred' approach is increasingly regarded as crucial for the delivery of high quality care by doctors. However, there is considerable ambiguity concerning the exact meaning of the term and the optimum method of measuring the process and outcomes of patient-centred care. This paper reviews the conceptual and empirical literature in order to develop a model of the various aspects of the doctor–patient relationship encompassed by the concept of 'patient-centredness' and to assess the advantages and disadvantages of alternative methods of measurement. Five conceptual dimensions are identified: biopsychosocial perspective; 'patient-as-person'; sharing power and responsibility; therapeutic alliance; and 'doctor-as-person'. Two main approaches to measurement are evaluated: self-report instruments and external observation methods. A number of recommendations concerning the measurement of patient-centredness are made. © 2000 Elsevier Science Ltd. All rights reserved.

Keywords: Patient-centred care; Process assessment; Literature review; Physician–patient relations; Quality of health care; Communication

Introduction

In the past 30 years, an extensive body of literature has emerged advocating a 'patient-centred' approach to medical care. Yet despite popularity of the concept there is little consensus as to its meaning. Edith Balint (1969) describes patient-centred medicine as "understanding the patient as a unique human being" while for Byrne and Long (1976) it represents a style of consulting where the doctor uses the patient's knowledge and experience to guide the interaction. McWhinney (1989) describes the patient-centred approach as one where "the physician tries to enter the patient's world, to see the illness through the patient's eyes". Giving information to patients and involving them in decision-making have also been highlighted (e.g. Lipkin, Quill & Napodano, 1984; Grol, de Maeseneer, Whitfield & Mokkink, 1990; Winefield, Murrell, Clifford & Farmer, 1996). For Laine and Davidoff (1996), patient-centred care is "closely congruent with, and responsive to patients' wants, needs and preferences". The most comprehensive description is provided by Stewart, Brown, Weston, McWhinney, McWilliam and Freeman

* Corresponding author. Tel.: + 44-161-275-7613; fax: + 44-161-275-7600.
E-mail address: Nicola.Mead@man.ac.uk (N. Mead).

(1995a) whose model of the patient-centred clinical method identifies six interconnecting components: (1) exploring both the disease and the illness experience; (2) understanding the whole person; (3) finding common ground regarding management; (4) incorporating prevention and health promotion; (5) enhancing the doctor–patient relationship; (6) 'being realistic' about personal limitations and issues such as the availability of time and resources.

Lack of a universally agreed definition of patient-centredness has hampered conceptual and empirical developments. This paper elucidates the key dimensions underlying published descriptions of patient-centredness, and critically reviews the empirical literature in order to explore relationships between the concept and its measurement. In 'taking stock' of the existing literature, the paper attempts to provide a clearer framework for future theoretical and empirical developments.

Key dimensions of patient-centredness

Development of the concept of patient-centredness is intimately linked to perceived limitations in the conventional way of doing medicine, often labelled the 'biomedical model'. Although inaccurate to view the 'biomedical model' as a single, monolithic approach (Friedson, 1970), it is generally associated with a number of broad concepts that determine the way in which medicine is practised (e.g. Siegler & Osmond, 1974; Engel, 1977; Cassell, 1982; McWhinney, 1989). These concepts exert particular influence on the content and style of the relationship between doctor and patient, where relationship is defined as "an abstraction embodying the activities of two interacting systems (persons)" (Szasz & Hollender, 1956).

In the 'biomedical model', patients' reports of illness are taken to indicate the existence of disease processes. This dictates a clinical method focused on identifying and treating standard disease entities. To this end, the patient's illness is reduced to a set of signs and symptoms which are investigated and interpreted within a positivist biomedical framework. Accurate diagnosis of the pathology permits selection of appropriate therapy which restores the diseased processes to (or near to) 'normal', thus curing (or improving) the patient's illness (Neighbour, 1987).

This paper proposes that 'patient-centred' medicine differs from the 'biomedical model' in terms of five key dimensions (described below), each representing a particular aspect of the relationship between doctor and patient.

Biopsychosocial perspective

Many illnesses presented in community settings cannot adequately be assigned to conventional disease taxonomies (Morrell, 1972; Bain, Bassett & Haines, 1973). In some cases, the exclusion of pathology and subsequent reassurance that there is nothing medically wrong may compound rather than relieve a patient's suffering. Conversely, people who do not feel ill may nonetheless have some classifiable disorder deemed worthy of medical treatment (e.g. hypertension). Furthermore, feeling ill and seeking help in response to illness appear to bear little relation to the type of condition or its clinical 'severity' (Rogers, Hassell & Nicolaas, 1999). Such findings challenge a key assumption of the 'biomedical model': that illness and disease are coterminous. This limitation has, in part, encouraged adoption of a wider explanatory framework by doctors, particularly in general practice. A combined biological, psychological and social perspective is regarded necessary to account for the full range of problems presented in primary care. For example, the UK Royal College of General Practitioners advocate composing 'triaxial diagnoses' of patients' problems (Royal College of General Practitioners, 1972). The concept is further developed in Engel's 'biopsychosocial model' (Engel, 1977, 1980) where disorders are conceptualised as existing at a number of interacting, hierarchical levels (from biological through to psychological and social levels).

Broadening the explanatory perspective on illness to include social and psychological factors has expanded the remit of medicine into the realm of ostensibly 'healthy' bodies. Again, this has been particularly evident in general practice. For Stott and Davis (1979) the 'exceptional potential' of the primary care consultation is not confined to managing acute and chronic (physical and psychosocial) disorders, but also includes possibilities for health promotion and the modification of help-seeking behaviour.

The biopsychosocial perspective is a key theme of many published accounts of 'patient-centredness'. Stewart et al. (1995a) assert that the patient-centred method requires a "willingness to become involved in the full range of difficulties patients bring to their doctors, and not just their biomedical problems". Furthermore, these authors regard health promotion as an essential component. Lipkin et al. (1984) emphasise the importance of being open to the patient's 'hidden agenda', reflecting the psychoanalytical influence of earlier work by Michael Balint (1964). According to Grol et al. (1990), the patient-centred doctor "feels responsible for non-medical aspects of problems". In short, the concept of patient-centredness can be seen as associated with a broadening of the scope of medicine from organic disease to a far wider range of 'dysfunctional' states (Silverman, 1987).

The 'patient-as-person'

A biopsychosocial perspective alone is not sufficient for a full understanding of the patient's experience of illness, which depends on his or her particular 'biography' (Armstrong, 1979). A compound leg fracture will not be experienced in the same way by two different patients; it may cause far less distress to the office worker than the professional athlete, for whom the injury potentially signifies the end of a career. Similarly, the medical treatment (even cure) of disease does not necessarily alleviate suffering for all patients. Cassell (1982) describes how one young woman's cancer treatment threatened her sense of self and perception of the future. The implication is that in order to understand illness and alleviate suffering, medicine must first understand the personal meaning of illness for the patient.

Clearly, personal meaning can have many dimensions. The social and behavioural sciences have contributed significantly to our understanding of how individuals interpret illness, and what significance it may hold for them. One cannot, for example, discount the impact of the particular rights and responsibilities which society attributes to those who occupy the 'sick role' (Parsons, 1951). Economic insecurity may make an individual reluctant to interpret symptoms as illness for fear of being labelled unfit to work. Similarly, culturally-determined norms and beliefs influence 'explanatory models'; that is, the conceptual and verbal tools used by lay people to describe, explain and predict illness (Helman, 1985; Croyle & Barger, 1993). While these models may sometimes be at odds with conventional medical explanations, they can predict how individuals act in response to illness. From the psychodynamic perspective, Balint stressed sensitivity to the patient's psychological world as crucial for insight into whatever unconscious motivations the patient may have for presenting, and for understanding "the patient's attitude towards his illness [which] is of paramount importance for any therapy" (Balint, 1964, p. 242).

Thus, patient-centred medicine conceives of the patient as an experiencing individual rather than the object of some disease entity. Attending to 'the patient's story of illness' (Smith &

Hoppe, 1991) involves exploring both the presenting symptoms and the broader life setting in which they occur (Lipkin et al., 1984; Stewart et al., 1995a). Levenstein, McCracken, McWhinney, Stewart and Brown (1986) stress the importance of eliciting each patient's expectations, feelings and fears about the illness. The goal, according to Balint, is to "understand the complaints offered by the patient, and the symptoms and signs found by the doctor, not only in terms of illnesses, but also as expressions of the patient's unique individuality, his conflicts and problems" (quoted in Henbest & Stewart, 1989).

To summarise, the first dimension of patient-centredness is concerned with understanding patients' illnesses in general within a broader biopsychosocial framework. This second dimension, however, is concerned with understanding the individual's experience of illness. Patients cannot wholly be characterised by a diagnostic label, whether that label is physical, psychological or social in nature (Balint, 1964). To develop full understanding of the patient's presentation and provide effective management the doctor should strive to understand the patient as an idiosyncratic personality within his or her unique context (Bower, 1998).

Sharing power and responsibility

Patient-centred medicine promotes the ideal of an egalitarian doctor–patient relationship, differing fundamentally from the conventional 'paternalistic' relationship envisaged by Parsons (1951). Parsons regards patient deference to medical authority is an important part of the social function of medicine, serving the interests of both parties. The asymmetrical relationship between doctor and patient (whereby authority and control lie with the former) is seen as an inevitable consequence of the 'competence gap' between medical expert and lay patient. However, Parsons' model of social relations has been much criticised for its assumptions of mutuality and reciprocity between the two parties. For example, Friedson (1960, 1970) argues that conflict between medical authority and patient autonomy is fundamental to the doctor–patient relationship.

Issues of power and control in the doctor–patient relationship were central to the sociopolitical critiques of medicine (particularly feminist critiques of medical patriarchy) that reached their zenith in the 1970s (e.g. Illich, 1976; Doyal, 1979; Ehrenreich & English, 1979). These critiques were translated into calls for greater medical recognition of the legitimacy of lay knowledge and experience, and greater respect for patient autonomy. Increasingly, physician behaviour came under scrutiny as a potential 'problem' in the consultation (May & Mead, 1999). Patient non-compliance and dissatisfaction with care were attributable to some failure on the part of doctors; for example, failure to regard patients as experts in their own illnesses (Tuckett, Boulton, Olson & Williams, 1985), to provide adequate information and explanation (Korsch, Gozzi & Francis, 1968) or to reach consensus through negotiation (Stimson & Webb, 1975). For Mishler (1984), the problem is one of an imbalance in the discourse of the consultation. By interrupting the patient's 'voice of the lifeworld' with response-constraining questions, the doctor's 'voice of medicine' effectively strips away the personal meaning of the illness.

What these and other authors advocate is a shift in doctor–patient relations from the 'co-operation–guidance' model (analogous to a parent–child relationship) to 'mutual participation' (analogous to a relationship between adults – Szasz & Hollender, 1956), where power and responsibility are shared with the patient. Related notions like 'user involvement', 'negotiation', 'concordance' and 'patient empowerment' have been particularly evident within the sphere of health policy in the 1980s and 90s (e.g. Department of Health, 1991; NHS Executive, 1996). Once passive recipients of medical care, patients are increasingly regarded as active 'consumers' (and potential critics) with the right to certain standards of service, including the right to full information, to be treated with respect and to be actively involved in decision-making about treatment. Aside from political and moral arguments, clinical justifications for sharing power and involving patients in care have been advanced. Kaplan, Greenfield and Ware (1989) report positive associations with health outcomes, while Grol et al. (1990) suggest that information enables patients to take greater responsibility for their health.

This particular dimension was first introduced to the concept of patient-centredness by Byrne and Long (1976), although the theme of sharing medical power and involving patients is an almost universal element of published descriptions since then (e.g. Lipkin et al., 1984; deMonchy, Richardson, Brown & Harden, 1988; Stewart et al., 1995a; Winefield et al., 1996; Laine & Davidoff, 1996; Kinmonth, Woodcock, Griffin, Spiegal, Campbell & Diabetes Care from Diagnosis Team, 1998). From analyses of audiotaped consultations, Byrne and Long describe a continuum of general practitioner (GP) consulting styles ranging from 'doctor-' to 'patient-centred'. In doctor-centred consultations the doctor's medical skills and knowledge predominate, reflected in behaviours such as direct and closed questioning of the patient and giving directions. These behaviours serve the doctor's control needs. Conversely, patient-centred consultations reflect recognition of patients' needs and preferences, characterised by behaviours such as encouraging the patient to voice ideas, listening, reflecting and offering collaboration (Byrne & Long, 1976). While it is unclear to what degree the doctor–patient relationship can, in practice, become genuinely symmetrical, patient-centred medicine is concerned to encourage significantly greater patient involvement in care than is generally associated with the 'biomedical model'.

The therapeutic alliance

In the 'biomedical model' the perceived value of the relationship between doctor and patient is somewhat ambiguous since diagnosis and treatment are essentially decision-making and procedural issues. Where the quality of the relationship is regarded as having value, this is largely in terms of mediating positive outcomes from management decisions. For example, a friendly and sympathetic manner may increase the likelihood of patient adherence to treatment. Conversely, negative emotional responses by either party (e.g. anger, resentment) may serve to complicate medical judgement (causing diagnostic error) or cause patients to default from treatment. Thus the impact of affect on outcome is indirect, mediated through medical management. Even in the absence of 'active' treatment, positive emotional responses may effect improvement in the patient's condition (the so-called 'placebo effect'; Crow, Gage, Hampson, Hart, Kimber & Thomas, 1999).

Patient-centred medicine affords far greater priority to the personal relationship between doctor and patient, based on psychotherapeutic developments around the concept of the 'therapeutic alliance'. Rogers (1967) proposed that the core therapist attitudes of empathy, congruence and unconditional positive regard are both necessary and sufficient for effecting therapeutic change in clients. More recent developments (Roth & Fonagy, 1996) emphasise the importance of aspects of the professional–patient relationship, including (a) the patient's perception of the relevance and potency of interventions offered, (b) agreement over the goals of treatment, and (c) cognitive and affective components, such as the personal bond between doctor and patient and perception of the doctor as caring, sensitive and sympathetic (Bordin, 1979; Squier, 1990).

Although the practise of conventional biomedicine can involve significant aspects of the therapeutic alliance, this is not regarded necessary. Moreover, effects of medical treatment are theoretically distinguishable from relationship effects: the former are 'real' while the latter a mysterious but potentially beneficial side-effect. In patient-centred care however, developing a therapeutic alliance is a fundamental requirement rather than a useful addition. A common understanding of the goals and requirements of treatment [what Balint (1964) termed the "mutual investment company"] is crucial to any therapy, whether physical or psychological. Furthermore, the alliance has potential therapeutic benefit in and of itself (hence Balint's famous aphorism "the drug, doctor").

Although the therapeutic alliance is a function of the relationship between doctor and patient, the patient-centredness literature focuses mainly on the doctor's role, particularly the skills required in order to achieve and develop the desired emotional 'context' in consultations (Lipkin et al., 1984; Smith & Hoppe, 1991; Stewart et al., 1995a).

The 'doctor-as-person'

The final dimension concerns the influence of the personal qualities of the doctor. In the 'biomedical model', the application of diagnostic and therapeutic techniques is a fundamentally objective issue: although lack of skill or unreliable instrumentation may cause error, there is no theoretical reason why well-trained doctors should not be essentially interchangeable since doctor subjectivity does not impact on diagnosis and treatment (Friedson, 1970). Where subjectivity (including the influence of the doctor's uncertainty) is apparent, it is regarded remediable through education and better instrumentation.

Balint, Courtenay, Elder, Hull & Julian (1993) describe the biomedical model as 'one person medicine' in that a satisfactory clinical description does not require consideration of the doctor. By contrast, patient-centred medicine is 'two-person medicine' whereby the doctor is an integral aspect of any such description: "the doctor and patient are influencing each other all the time and cannot be considered separately" (Balint et al., 1993, p. 13). Doctor subjectivity is therefore regarded inherent in the doctor–patient relationship, though it is not necessarily benign. The influence of the doctor may serve to constrain patient behaviour or provoke negative responses such as aggression. Nevertheless, sensitivity and insight into the reactions of both parties can be used for therapeutic purposes. Balint et al. (1993) describe how emotions engendered in the doctor by particular patient presentations may be used as an aid to further management (what is termed 'counter-transference' in the psychodynamic literature).

Winefield et al. (1996) describe this dimension of patient-centredness as "attention by the doctor to cues of the affective relationship as it develops between the parties, including self-awareness of emotional responses". However, they acknowledge that few efforts have been made to measure this aspect of patient-centredness. Reasons why the 'doctor-as-person' dimension may not be readily amenable to current measurement technologies are discussed later.

Summary

While many of the ideas that have shaped these five dimensions have origins in the social and behavioural sciences, most development of the patient-centredness concept has occurred within general practice. This is as much linked to professional concerns to differentiate general practice from specialist medicine (and subsequently, to establish a framework for GP vocational training) as with perceived limitations of the 'biomedical model' (May & Mead, 1999). However, interest in patient-centred medicine is rapidly emerging in other medical disciplines, notably oncology and paediatrics (e.g. Street, 1992; Ford, Fallowfield & Lewis, 1996; Fallowfield, Lipkin & Hall, 1998; Wissow et al., 1998). This may be a response to evidence suggesting that interpersonal aspects of care are key determinants of patient satisfaction. Patients report valuing highly such attributes as doctors' 'humaneness' (e.g. warmth, respect and empathy), being given sufficient information and time, being treated as individuals and involved in decision-making and aspects of the relationship with the doctor such as mutual trust (Hall & Dornan, 1988; Baker, 1990; Williams & Calnan, 1991; Wensing, Jung, Mainz, Olesen & Grol, 1998). Increasingly, patient-centredness is regarded as a proxy for the quality of such interpersonal aspects of care.

Measuring patient-centredness

Concerns about variation in standards of medical care, coupled with increasing managerialism throughout the public sector have served to encourage quantification of all aspects of quality of care (Roland, 1999). However, gaps can occur between the concepts put forward by theorists and measures of those concepts in empirical work (Meehl, 1978). This is particularly likely in the case of 'patient-centredness' where development of valid and reliable measures is constrained by lack of theoretical clarity and the inevitable difficulties of measuring complex relationship processes. The focus of the paper will now turn to a review of the empirical literature to examine how, and to what degree, the five proposed dimensions of patient-centredness have been measured, and assess the current and potential utility of such measures for quality assurance and medical education.

Methods
The search strategy

Relevant empirical literature was identified from searches of computerised databases (Medline and Psychlit) using both UK and US spellings of the term 'patient-centred(ness)'. Searches were restricted to English language (non-nursing) journals published within a 30-year period (1969–1998 inclusive). Studies were included in the review if they (1) utilised a quantitative measure of patient-centredness (however defined) and (2) provided sufficient detail concerning the measurement method to permit categorisation. Studies that measured hypothesised outcomes of patient-centred care but which did not attempt to measure the construct per se were not included in the review. A list of excluded studies is available from the authors.

Results

Studies employed two main methodological approaches: (a) self-report measures of doctors' patient-centredness and (b) measures involving external observation of the consultation process.

Self-report measures of doctors' patient-centredness

It has been suggested that a patient-centred approach to care is contingent on the doctor possessing certain attitudes and values (Grol et al., 1990), a particular type of personality (Crookshank, 1926; Balint, 1964) or cognitive style (McWhinney, 1985). Self-report inventories are traditionally used to measure such psychological attributes. Table 1 presents details of the content, reliability and validity of three such scales.

Table 1 Scales measuring doctors' patient-centred attitudes/values

Scale	Items	Content	Dimensions[a]	Reliability	Validity
Patient-centred attitudes (Grol et al., 1990)	7	Taking patients seriously; patient involvement in decisions; giving information to patients; responsibility for non-medical aspects of care	1, 3	$\alpha = 0.65$ ($n = 112$ GPs)	Correlations with interview behaviour such as prescribing, medical and psychosocial performance, openness to patient ideas and information-giving (r's from 0.29 to 0.46, $n = 57$ Dutch GPs). Sensitive to differences between doctors from different countries: UK ($n = 371$ GPs – 79% of all Avon GPs), Belgium ($n = 90$ volunteer GPs), Netherlands ($n = 75$ GPs – 71% of a regional sample)
Doctor–patient rating (deMonchy et al., 1988)	48	Medical versus humanistic role; scientific interests; status of doctor; equality in doctor–patient relationship; information-giving and sharing decisions; health care delivery	1,3,4	$\alpha = 0.62$ ($n = 92$ second year medical students), $\alpha = 0.65$ ($n = 54$ final year students), $\alpha = 0.64$ ($n = 39$ GP trainees), $\alpha = 0.81$ ($n = 29$ registrars)	GPs scored highest on patient-centredness, registrars scored lowest; final year medical students scored higher than second year students; female doctors scored higher than males. No demonstrated associations with clinical behaviour. No clear sampling information
Attitudes towards medical care (Cockburn et al., 1987)	21	Psychological orientation responsibility for decisions; appropriateness of consultations; preventive medicine; mutuality; communication; government role	1, 3, 4	$\alpha = 0.48–0.67$; $n = 387$ GPs (74% of a randomly-selected sample; Cockburn et al., 1987)	Three subscales defined as 'patient-centred' by Howie et al. (i.e. psychological orientation, responsibility for decisions and appropriateness of consultations) were associated with consultation length, 'process of care' and doctor stress (r's from 0.19 to 0.29, $n = 80$ – 19% of Lothian GPs; Howie et al., 1992)

[a] Dimensions (column 4) refers to those aspects of patient-centredness addressed by each instrument (in the opinion of the reviewers). See main text for full description of the five dimensions of patient-centredness.

Column 4 of the table shows which of the five proposed dimensions of patient-centredness each scale addresses (in the opinion of the reviewers). While all three scales contain items that map onto dimension 1 ('biopsychosocial perspective') and dimension 3 ('sharing power and responsibility'), the deMonchy et al. (1988) and Cockburn, Killer, Campbell and Sanson-Fisher (1987) scales also cover aspects of dimension 4 ('the therapeutic alliance').

With respect to the utility of self-report inventories, there are a number of important reliability issues to consider. Measures should exhibit satisfactory internal consistency (usually measured by Cronbach's alpha). However, to the extent that patient-centred attitudes are conceptualised as multi-dimensional, it is important that high alpha coefficients are not sought through excessive narrowing of item content (Cattell, 1978). A very short scale may have high internal reliability if its constituent items are similar in content, but relatively poor validity due to the restricted range of qualities measured. Although reported reliability is similar for the three scales in Table 1, the alpha quoted for the Grol et al. (1990) scale relates to a single overall construct, whereas those quoted for Cockburn et al. (1987) relate to the reliability of constituent subscales (which may be used as distinct variables). The deMonchy et al. (1988) scale has a similar alpha to the Grol scale despite a much higher number of items. This reflects the broad range of issues that are aggregated when scoring the scale (and which might benefit from some differentiation).

A further reliability issue centres on the implicit assumption that the psychological factors determining doctors' patient-centredness are relatively stable, at least in the absence of interventions. This requires information on the reliability of self-report scales over time. However, few would suggest that such attitudes are completely fixed. Sensitivity to change is therefore another relevant issue if scales are to have utility in evaluating educational interventions designed to enhance doctors' patient-centredness. None of the scales reviewed in Table 1 has published information on reliability over time or sensitivity to change.

Demonstrating the construct validity of self-report measures is crucial since there is no 'gold standard' criterion for patient-centredness. The relationship between self-report scores and a wide variety of external variables may have bearing on construct validity. For example, the deMonchy scale demonstrated associations with physician gender which may be interpretable with reference to theories of gender socialisation. The Grol scale differentiated between doctors from different countries which may reflect the influence of cultural differences in medical education or the social context of health care.

However, it is the link between doctors' self-reported attitudes and their actual clinical behaviour that is often of greatest interest. Without such a link, the utility of self-report measures may be unclear. Only the Grol and Cockburn scales report behavioural associations. The former was correlated with independent assessments of GPs' interview behaviour. Although the Cockburn scale was also associated with several process indicators of patient-centredness (Howie, Hopton, Heaney & Porter, 1992), some of these data relied on GPs' own subjective ratings (for example, of whether psychosocial problems were dealt with in the consultation) which may be less reliable than independent assessments.

A key problem with self-report scales concerns social desirability bias. As the characteristics of good interpersonal care are increasingly defined and disseminated by professional and patient groups and in government policy (e.g. patient involvement, negotiation, etc.), social desirability may mask real differences between doctors by encouraging particular responses from all doctors (Linn, DiMatteo, Cope & Robbins, 1987; Bucks, Williams, Whitfield & Routh, 1990). However, a key advantage of self-report scales is their feasibility. Instruments are relatively easy to administer. Thus large, representative samples of GPs can be surveyed, which may be more important than sensitivity in some contexts.

External observation methods

Most of the empirical literature conceptualises patient-centredness as a clinical method, reflected in the predominance of measures which involve observation of consultation behaviours. Two main approaches (or their combination) have been employed. Rating scales are concerned with how much or how well a specific behaviour was performed. Verbal behaviour coding systems involve categorising units of doctor and patient speech. Combined methods use elements of both approaches.

Rating scales

Table 2 presents details of the content, reliability and validity of six different scales. All the scales involve simple global ratings of behaviours defined as 'patient-centred', though they vary somewhat in focus and content. For example, the Verhaak (1988) scale is the only one not to focus explicitly on doctor behaviour. Rather it measures patient participation in the consultation (although this is likely to depend, to some degree, on facilitating behaviours of the doctor). The scales all tend to focus on evaluating 'instrumental' (i.e. task-oriented) behaviours rather than the emotional tone of the consultation.

Scale content was examined to judge which of the five proposed dimensions of patient-centredness each covers (see column 3). There was ambiguity regarding classification of some instruments due to lack of clarity about the exact processes being rated and their function (as perceived by the scale developers). For example, 'relating information to patient views' (Winefield et al., 1996) might be viewed as attempting to take account of the 'patient-as-person' (dimension 2) or as a means of enhancing the 'therapeutic alliance' (dimension 4). Pragmatically, it may relate to both dimensions. Thus, the dimensions assigned to each measure are judgements of the reviewers only and should be regarded as preliminary. It is also important to note that coverage of multiple dimensions by a single measure does not imply that all are measured adequately or with proven validity.

Reliable rating by observers is crucial. Although internal reliability is sometimes reported (e.g. Winefield et al., 1996), this reflects how constituent subscales or dimensions of an instrument inter-correlate, rather than the consistency of raters. In terms of inter-rater reliability, Table 2 shows the six measures generally report low to moderate levels, although a range of methods has been used. Measures of association such as Pearson's r (e.g. Verhaak, 1988) are less acceptable than measures of agreement such as kappa or intra-class correlations (e.g. Winefield et al., 1996; Mead & Bower, 2000) since the latter take into account the degree to which observers concur on the absolute 'level' of ratings, as well as their association. This is especially important where cut-offs of the 'adequacy' or 'quality' of behaviours are used: a high statistical correlation between two observers could mask the fact that one consistently rates a greater proportion of consultations as meeting a particular criterion.

The low inter-rater reliabilities reported for the Verhaak scale (1988) and the Euro-communication scale (Mead & Bower, 2000) may reflect the difficulty of rating relatively broadly defined behaviours. Generally, the reliability of a measure is inversely related to the amount of subjective judgement required on the part of observers. While it may be possible for observers to agree criteria for recognising a particular target behaviour (e.g. 'exploring patient ambivalence'), it may be more difficult to agree thresholds for scoring differing amounts or 'appropriateness' of that behaviour. To counter such problems, both the Farmer scale (used by Winefield et al., 1996) and the scale developed by Ockene et al. (1988) give relatively detailed criteria for scoring each behaviour. None of the scales has been assessed in terms of intra-rater reliability (i.e. the consistency of ratings by the same observer over time).

In terms of validity, the rating scales in Table 2 report various associations with consultation inputs and process such as type and length of consultation (Winefield et al., 1996; Mead & Bower, 2000), psychosocial content of communication (Verhaak, 1988), eye contact, acquaintance with the patient and GP age (Mead & Bower, 2000). One scale did not differentiate between doctors from different medical specialities (Ockene et al., 1988). Two scales were found to be sensitive to changes associated with training (Ockene et al., 1988; Langewitz et al., 1998) and one distinguished between consultations with real and simulated patients (Pieters et al., 1994). However, two of the scales have demonstrated low concurrent validity with other observation-based measures of patient-centredness (Winefield et al., 1996; Mead & Bower, 2000).

Of most interest is the degree to which patient-centredness is associated with consultation outcomes like participant satisfaction, patient compliance or health status. The Winefield et al. (1996) and Langewitz et al. (1998) scales both report positive associations with patient satisfaction.

Verbal behaviour coding

Many schemes for coding verbal behaviour have been developed. The best known include Bales' (1950) Interaction Process Analysis (IPA), Stiles' (1978) Verbal Response Modes (VRM) and Roter's (1977) Interaction Analysis System (RIAS). A useful comparison of these three techniques is provided by Inui, Carter, Kukull and Haigh (1982).

All coding schemes share the same broad function of sorting speech acts into mutually exclusive categories. While some categories deal implicitly with the content of talk (e.g. RIAS: shows disagreement/criticism) the main focus is on the instrumental intent and effect of speech rather than what is actually said. Generally used to code from literal transcripts, some schemes (e.g. RIAS) use audio- or videotapes, thus improving feasibility. Measurement is in terms of frequencies and proportions of speech units assigned to the different categories; that is, categories are not weighted in such a way that one type of verbal behaviour is valued as more or less important than another.

Various modifications of verbal coding schemes have been used to study patient-centredness in consultations (Table 3). In these studies, the verbal content of the consultation is first coded, then various combinations of categories defined by the authors as 'patient-centred' are used in analyses. The method employed by Cecil and Killeen (1997) differs in that all pre-coded verbal statements were subsequently categorised in terms of patient and physician 'controlling' behaviour.

Again, the content of instruments was examined in order to judge which of the five proposed dimensions of patient-centredness were measured by each (see column 3). The difficulties with such judgements, highlighted in the previous section, are compounded in relation to verbal coding methods because micro-processes such as 'open questions' (Winefield et al., 1996) are relatively unspecific and may relate to a number of dimensions, depending on the interpretative framework used. For example, doctors' 'talk about non-medical matters' (Butow, Dunn, Tattersall & Jones, 1995) may relate to the 'biopsychosocial perspective' (dimension 1) or function as a means of enhancing the 'therapeutic alliance' (dimension 4).

Although there is some consensus as to what types of behaviours reflect patient-centredness, there is also significant disagreement on the inclusion of particular behaviours and the role of the patient. Common to most systems are doctor behaviours that encourage patient talk (including question-asking), general empathic statements, non-medical discussion and affective

Table 2 Rating scales measuring patient-centred behaviour in consultations

Rating scale	Description	Dimensions	Reliability	Validity
Farmer scale (unpublished) – cited in Winefield et al. (1996)	Five behavioural dimensions: soliciting patient views; responding to patient views; relating information to patient views; involving patient; checking understanding. 5-point scale (-best performance rated across each dimension)	2, 3, (4)	Inter-rater: kappa = 0.84; internal: $\alpha = 0.61$ ($n = 67$; Winefield et al., 1996)	Low correlations with another measure of patient-centredness based on verbal behaviour coding (r's of 0.17 and 0.21). Associations with consultation length and patient satisfaction. Distinguished different consultation types: psychosocial or complex consultations were most patient-centred ($n = 210$ consultations with 21 volunteer GPs – 41% of invited random sample)
Verhaak (1988)	Two behavioural dimensions: patient participation in diagnostic decision-making; patient participation in therapy decision-making. Five-point scale (ratings made across each dimension for each complaint)	3	Inter-rater: $r = 0.45$ (sample size not reported)	Patient-centredness in both 'phases' of consultation correlated with psychosocial content of discussion. High correlations with other aspects of communication including: use of clarification, affective behaviour, use of 'purposive probing' ($n = 1866 – 1884$ somatic complaints; $406 – 496$ psychosocial complaints presented to a sample of 30 self-selecting GPs)
Langewitz, Phillipp, Kiss and Wossmer (1998)	Doctor's patient-centred communication style operationalised as: eliciting patient's explanatory model; eliciting patient's assumptions about diagnosis/treatment; following patient's ideas; checking patient's understanding. One rating (6-point scale) for entire consultation	2, 3	Mean inter-rater agreement (i.e. where difference between two raters does not exceed 1 scale point) = 88.5% (3 raters; number of consultations not reported)	Significant increase in ratings following training in patient-centred communication skills ($n = 19$ volunteer residents in internal medicine assessed across two pre- and two post-intervention consultations with simulated patients); significant improvement in patient-centred communication compared with control group ($n = 19$ vs $n = 23$). Patient-centred style correlated with patient satisfaction
Ockene et al. (1988)	Rating scale for evaluating a patient-centred 'Stop smoking' counselling intervention. Three skills rated on a 4-point scale (for each of six specific counselling 'content areas'): (1) eliciting information in exploratory sequences; (2) providing information pertinent to patient's concerns/requests/status; (3) eliciting patient's feelings and responding appropriately with empathy and assurance	2, 3, 4	Inter-rater: statistically significant correlations between three raters (Kendall's coefficient (W) – skill 1, $p < 0.01$; skill 2, $p < 0.02$; skill 3, $p < 0.05$). Number of consultations not reported	Significant pre- to post-training improvement in two skill areas: eliciting information and eliciting and responding to patient's feelings ($n = 23$ family medicine and 54 general medicine residents each assessed on one pre- and one post-training audiotaped consultation with a simulated patient). No differences between physician specialty

Table 2 Continued

Rating scale	Description	Dimensions	Reliability	Validity
'Euro-communication' scale – cited in Mead and Bower (2000)	Five behavioural dimensions: involving patient in problem definition, involving patient in decision-making, picking up patient 'cues', exploring patient ambivalence, overall 'responsiveness'. Doctor's performance on each dimension rated on 5-point scale. Summated score (as % of	1, 2, 3, (4)	Inter-rater: intraclass correlation coefficient=0.34 (intraclass=0.51 when average of two scores is used) – based on four observers rating 20 consultations	Poor concurrent validity with two other measures of patient-centredness (i.e. adaptation of Roter Interaction Analysis System r=0.37; Henbest & Stewart, 1989 r=0.35). Significant positive associations with: GP acquaintance with patient, GP age, consultation length, proportion of eye-contact and the degree to which psychological factors were judged important by the GP (r's between 0.27 and 0.51; n=55 videotaped consultations from 24 volunteer GPs)
Utrecht Consultation Assessment Method (UCAM) – cited by Pieters, Touw-Otten and Melker (1994)	Four dimensions of patient-centred behaviour: clarifying patient's reasons for attendance, making reasons explicit, finding common ground during problem formulation; finding common ground during management planning. Each item rated from 1 (='very inadequate') to 3 (='very adequate')	2, 3	Reliability not reported sufficiently clearly	Performance ratings for simulated patient encounters were higher than for matched 'real' encounters from GPs' everyday practice (n=20 trainee Dutch GPs each assessed over one simulated patient consultation and three real patient consultations)

Table 3 Schemes for coding patient-centred verbal behaviour in consultations

Study	Description of method used	Dimensions	Reliability	Validity
Stewart (1983, 1984)	*Doctor behaviour:* shows solidarity; shows tension release; agrees; asks for opinion; asks for suggestion; shows tension. *Patient behaviour:* gives opinion; disagrees; shows tension; shows antagonism; gives suggestion; gives orientation (adapted from Bales' IPA)	3, 4	Inter-rater: agreement for 90.3 of 100 utterances (two raters; number of transcripts not reported)	Doctor behaviour (especially 'agreeing') associated with patient-reported compliance. Doctor behaviour had more impact on patient satisfaction and compliance than patient behaviour. Doctors more likely to express tension release, ask about feelings/opinions with female patients. Female patients expressed more feelings/requests for help. Male patients expressed more facts. ($n = 140$ consultations, 24 volunteer family physicians)
Roter et al. (1987)	*Doctor behaviour:* gives information/ orientation/opinion related to procedures, medical condition, therapy or prevention; counsels/persuades about prevention, lifestyle or therapy (adapted from Roter's RIAS)	1, 3	Inter-rater: $r = 0.81$ (14 transcripts by second coder — median over 17 individual items)	Positive relationships with role-playing patients' satisfaction, impressions of affect and recall (r's from 0.27 to 0.62 for frequency-based measures; 0.11–0.58 for proportions; $n = 86$ consultations with 43 volunteer male primary care physicians)
Winefield et al. (1996)	*Doctor behaviour:* 'receptiveness' = reflections; open-questions; acknowledgements. *Patient behaviour:* 'involvement' = questions; positive/negative attitudes to treatment; private (unobservable) symptoms; accounts of action/experience; opinions (adapted from Stiles' VRM)	(1), 2, 3, 4	Inter-rater: Cohen's kappa = 0.84 for 'doctor receptiveness' 0.90 for 'patient involvement' (number of raters and transcripts not reported). Internal consistency: $\alpha = 0.70$ ('doctor receptiveness') and $\alpha = 0.58$ ('patient involvement')	Low correlations with Farmer scale (r's 0.17 and 0.21 — see Table 3). Moderate correlations between 'doctor receptiveness' and 'patient involvement' ($r = 0.44$). Doctor receptiveness related to patient age (older) and doctor knowledge of patient. Patient involvement related to age of patient (older), type of consultation (psychosocial or complex), longer consultations, and greater doctor dissatisfaction ($n = 210$ consultations with 21 volunteer GPs)
Ford et al. (1996)	Patient-centredness = *sum of:* doctor's psychosocial/lifestyle discussion + doctor's partnership-building statements + patient's questions + patient's psychosocial/lifestyle discussion *divided by sum of:* doctor's closed questions + doctor's biomedical information-giving + patient's biomedical information-giving (adapted from Roter's RIAS)	1, 2, 3, 4	Inter-rater: mean r for clinician utterance categories = 0.77 (range: 0.60–0.92); mean r for patient categories = 0.80 (range: 0.46–0.92) (two coders, $r = 20$ consultations)	Low ratios of patient-centred:doctor-centred behaviour reported for 'bad news' oncology outpatient consultations (mean ratio for first consultation = 0.33, rising to 0.41 at consultation 4 weeks later but remaining biomedically focused). No reported associations with consultation outcomes ($n = 113$ first and 95 second consultations, five volunteer clinicians)

Table 3 Continued

Study	Description of method used	Dimensions	Reliability	Validity
Street (1992)	*Doctor behaviour*: statements of reassurance, support, empathy, inter-personal sensitivity; soliciting/encouraging questions, opinions, expression of feelings (adapted from Stiles' VRM)	2, 3, 4	Inter-rater: Cohen's kappa of 0.69 (two raters over five transcripts)	Doctor behaviour positively associated with parents' satisfaction and perceptions of 'partnership-building' and 'inter-personal sensitivity' (*r*'s from 0.22 to 0.36, *n*=115 paediatric consultations with seven self-selected doctors)
Cecil and Killeen (1997)	Relational Communication Control Coding System – grammatical form and pragmatic function of each speaker's statements coded in terms of controlling/accepting/neutral behaviour. Paired statements (i.e. speaker-respondent) also coded in terms of control 'symmetry'	3	Inter-rater: Cohen's kappa of 0.85 (based on two raters coding 1024 doctor and patient statements)	Greater physician control associated with less patient self-reported compliance and satisfaction (*n*=50 patients and 15 volunteer family practice residents)
Wissow et al. (1998)	*Healthcare provider behaviour*: partnership; interpersonal sensitivity; information-giving. Scores above 50th percentile on these three combined categories of talk defined as 'patient-centred' (-adapted from Roter's RIAS)	3, 4	Inter-rater: mean *r* for all provider talk=0.74 and for provider's medical task-related talk=0.84; mean *r* for parent socio-emotional talk=0.81 and for parent's medical task-related talk=0.78 (*n*=15 audiotaped visits; number of raters not recorded)	Healthcare providers exhibited 'patient-centred' style with parent(s) in 33% of sampled visits and with the child patient in 36%. 'Patient-centred' style with parent(s) associated with: (i) more parent talk; (ii) higher parent ratings of provider informativeness and partnership. 'Patient-centred' style with child associated with: (i) more child talk with the provider; (ii) higher parent satisfaction with how good a job was done. (Total *n*=104 emergency room visits for childhood asthma with volunteer healthcare providers sampled across seven US cities).
Mead and Bower (2000)	Patient-centredness=*sum of*: doctor's psychosocial/lifestyle discussion+doctor's verbal attentiveness+doctor's clarifying+patient's biomedical questions+patient's psychosocial/lifestyle discussion *divided by sum of*: doctor's biomedical questions and information-giving+doctor's directive/orienting statements+patient's biomedical information-giving (adapted from Roter's RIAS)	1, 2, 3, 4	Inter-rater: intraclass correlation coefficient=0.71 (based on three raters coding 20 consultations)	Poor concurrent validity with two other measures of patient-centredness: *r*=0.37 (Euro-communication rating scale; Mead & Bower, 2000) and *r*=0.21 (Henbest & Stewart, 1989). Significant positive associations with: GP acquaintance with patient, patient emotional distress; consultation length, proportion of eye-contact and the degree to which psychological factors were judged important by the GP (*r*'s between 0.31 and 0.53; *n*=55 videotaped consultations from 24 volunteer GPs)

Table 3 Continued

Study	Description of method used	Dimensions	Reliability	Validity
Badger et al. (1994)	Interaction Analysis System for Interview Evaluation (ISIE-81). *Doctor behaviour:* narrow and broad psychosocial questions; all statements with affective focus. *Patient behaviour:* patient talk as proportion of total interview talk	1, 3, 4	Reported inter-rater: mean r's 0.72 – 0.82 (-number of raters and interviews not noted); intra-rater: mean $r = 0.84$ (all figures from original ISIE-81 development work)	No relationship with attitudes to psychosocial issues (measured using Physician Belief Scale). Affective interview behaviours, greater proportion of physician talk and broad psychosocial questioning were best predictors of depression diagnosis ($r = 47$ community physicians interviewing four patients standardised with symptoms of major depression)
Butow et al. (1995)	CN-LOGIT computer-based interaction analysis system for cancer consultations. *Patient-centred behaviour:* ratio of total patient to total doctor input (time); ratio of patient questions to doctor responses; all doctor talk about non-medical matters. Also rated global patient-centred style using visual analogue scale (0 – 100)	1, 3, (4)	Inter-rater: 66% agreement in number of identified speech units; 78 – 85% agreement on codes for matching speech units (two raters and 14 consultations). Intra-rater: 79% no. of speech units; 90 – 94% for matched units (14 consultations coded one year apart). Reliability of global scale not reported	Better psychological adjustment among patients whose questions were answered. No relationships between other verbal behaviour measures and patient satisfaction, recall or psychological adjustment. Global rating of consultation style associated with greater patient anxiety and female patient gender. No associations with patient age or preference for involvement in decision-making ($r = 142$ first in- or out-patient consultations with one medical oncologist)

statements. However, there is notable disagreement about doctors' information-giving. Street (1992) distinguishes patient-centredness from doctors' information-giving behaviour while Roter, Hall and Katz (1987) consider information-giving as a patient-centred skill. For Ford et al. (1996) and Mead and Bower (2000) the exchange of psychosocial information (by either party) is treated as patient-centred whereas biomedical information-exchange is not. Also, while some measures take account only of the doctor's verbal behaviour (e.g. Roter et al., 1987; Street, 1992; Wissow et al., 1998), others also take patient behaviour into consideration when calculating patient-centredness.

Inter-rater reliabilities reported for measures in Table 3 are generally acceptable, although (as with the rating scales discussed previously) assessments vary from percentage agreement to kappa calculations. It should be noted that many reported figures relate to the reliability of the initial verbal coding procedure rather than the method for subsequently scoring patient-centredness (which cannot be assumed to have equivalent reliability). However, generally speaking, verbal coding schemes are more reliable than rating scales since they reduce consultation behaviour to frequencies of specifically defined units, the categorisation of which usually requires less subjective judgement on the part of the observer.

Although the best known verbal coding schemes have been used many times in different studies of medical consultations, the precise methods by which each was modified specifically to study 'patient-centredness' (detailed in Table 3) have not been reproduced in other research. On a practical note, these methods can be rather time-consuming, especially since the whole consultation has to be coded first before 'patient-centredness' can be measured.

In terms of the validity of measures, greater levels of patient-centredness have been reported for consultations with patients who are female (Stewart, 1983, 1984; Butow et al., 1995), older (Winefield et al., 1996), more anxious or emotionally distressed (Butow et al., 1995; Mead & Bower, 2000) and better known to the doctor (Winefield et al., 1996; Mead & Bower, 2000). Associations are also reported with eye contact (Mead & Bower, 2000), type of consultation (Winefield et al., 1996) and consultation length (Winefield et al., 1996; Mead & Bower, 2000). In terms of outcomes, associations have been found with patient compliance (Stewart, 1983, 1984; Cecil & Killeen, 1997), satisfaction (Stewart, 1983, 1984; Roter et al., 1987; Street, 1992; Cecil & Killeen, 1997; Wissow et al., 1998) and recall (Roter et al., 1987). Patient-centredness has also been associated with a greater likelihood of diagnosing depression (Badger et al., 1994) and with doctor dissatisfaction (Winefield et al., 1996).

Combined assessment methods

Four combined assessment methods have been developed (Table 4), possibly as a response to criticisms that, used in isolation, no singular approach adequately captures the complexity of doctor–patient consultations (e.g. Wasserman & Inui, 1983; Waitzkin, 1990; Roter & Frankel, 1992). Because these methods have been specifically designed to measure patient-centredness, identifying the dimensions addressed by each is generally easier than for measures based on verbal coding schemes.

In Byrne and Long's (1976) method, individual doctor behaviours are categorised as either 'doctor-centred', 'patient-centred' or 'neutral'. An examination of the conceptual basis and content of the measure confirms that it examines dimension 3 ('sharing power and responsibility'). The frequency of different categories of behaviour are noted using separate checklists for the 'diagnostic' and 'prescriptive' phases of the consultation. Category weightings are used to score the consultation style for patient-centredness. However, Buijs, Sluijs and Verhaak (1984) are critical of this scoring procedure, rejecting the possibility that doctors' styles may be

Table 4 Combination methods for measuring patient-centred behaviour in consultations

Method	Dimensions	Reliability	Validity
Byrne and Long (1976)	3	Inter-rater (36 consultations rated by two independent observers): 'diagnostic' phase (frequently occurring categories only): r's = 0.43–0.87 (for 9 out of 11 categories, $r > 0.70$); 'prescriptive' phase (frequently occurring categories only): r's = 0.40–0.81 (for 5 out of 11 categories $r > 0.70$) – reported by Buijs et al. (1984) Inter-rater: 90% agreement for three observers based on 20 consultations – reported by Long (1985)	Scoring procedure for categorising consulting styles on a 'doctor-' to 'patient-centred' continuum failed to discriminate between different doctors and consultation types ($n = 36$ consultations by six GPs; Buijs et al., 1984) Detected improvements in GP interview style (significant for 'empathic behaviour') following Rogerian training aimed at encouraging patient expression of psychosocial problems ($n = 106$ pre- and 81 post-training consultations with six volunteer GPs; Bensing & Sluijs, 1985) Association between GP patient-centredness and (i) length of consultation, (ii) 'flexibility' of GP consulting style (defined by the author, $n = 53$ volunteer GPs supplying recordings of two complete surgeries six months apart; Long, 1985) No associations found between patient-centredness of consultations and (i) patients' own ratings of 'ease of communication' or 'doctor's degree of understanding', or (ii) length of consultation ($n = 88$ consultations with nine self-selected GPs; Cape, 1996)
Brown et al. (1986)	2, 3	Inter-rater: $r = 0.69–0.84$ for 3 coders ($n = 6$ tapes; Brown et al., 1986)	Physician patient-centredness moderately increased over 2-month period of training and practice in family medicine; significant increase in 'physician facilitating behaviours'; non-significant increase in overall patient-centredness ($n = 26$ pre- and 23 post-training interviews with 13 physicians; Stewart, Brown, Levenstein, McCracken & McWhinney, 1986)
Henbest and Stewart (1989)	2, 3	Inter-rater reliability: patient offers – 85% agreement; physician response scores: $r = 0.91$ (Henbest & Stewart, 1989); $r = 0.90$ (Law & Britten, 1995); intraclass correlation coefficient = 0.58 rising to 0.73 using average of two raters' Intra-rater reliability: $r = 0.88$ (after 2 weeks); $r = 0.63$ (after 6 weeks); correlation between scoring in first two min and score for entire interview: $r = 0.81$ (Henbest & Stewart, 1989); $r = 0.57$ (Law & Britten, 1995)	Moderate to high concurrent validity with Brown et al. (1986) measure (r's = 0.51 and 0.89) and empathy scale ($r = 0.89$); differentiated between doctors with respect to overall patient-centredness scores and in responses to different categories of patient offers ($n = 73$ taped consultations with six doctors; Henbest & Stewart, 1989) Patient-centredness correlated with doctors' ascertainment of patients' reasons for attending (r's from 0.3 to 0.42, $n = 73$); significant association between degree of patient-centredness in response to main symptom and resolution of patients' concerns; no associations with (i) doctor–patient agreement about the problem or (ii) patient satisfaction (Henbest & Stewart, 1990) Female GPs (especially trainers) scored higher on patient-centredness; female GPs ignored fewer patient offers and made more open-ended responses than males; highest median patient-centredness score for female GP/female patient dyad; lowest score for male GP/female patient dyad (Law & Britten, 1995) Poor concurrent validity with two other measures of patient-centredness (i.e. Euro-communication rating scale $r = 0.35$; RIAS-based measure $r = 0.21$); significant positive association with proportion of GP eye-contact ($r = 0.28$); no other associations with measured consultation input or process variables ($n = 55$ videotaped consultations from 24 volunteer GPs; Mead & Bower, 2000)
Brown, Stewart and Tessier (1995)	2, 3, (4)	Inter-rater: $r = 0.83$ ($n = 19$ consultations); intra-rater: $r = 0.73$ ($r = 20$ consultations; Stewart, Brown, Donner, McWhinney, Oates & Weston, 1995b)	Good concurrent validity with global scores of experienced communication researchers ($r = 0.85$, $n = 46$ consultations); some association with patients' subjective perceptions of 'finding common ground' but not with perceptions that the doctor 'explored the illness experience'; no association with any health outcomes ($n = 315$ consultations sampled from 39 doctors, i.e. 47% of a randomly selected sample; Stewart et al., 1995b)

classified on a patient-centred continuum. Only two published studies have used this instrument, neither using the original scoring system: instead, ratios of doctor- to patient-centred behaviour were determined (Long, 1985; Cape, 1996).

The next three methods represent successive developments of one instrument. Brown, Stewart, McCracken, McWhinney and Levenstein (1986) focused on eliciting and understanding the patient's experience of illness, thus tapping into dimension 2 ('patient-as-person'). The method involves categorising patients' verbal 'offers' into four mutually exclusive types: expectations, feelings, fears and prompts. The doctor's response to each offer is then scored as either an acknowledgement or a cut-off (i.e. block to further expression). A fifth dimension, physician facilitating behaviours, records any doctor comment encouraging further patient expression. To the degree that focusing on doctors' responses to patient 'offers' may be interpreted as measuring the amount of 'space' given to patients in the consultation, the instrument could also be said to tap into aspects of dimension 3 ('sharing power and responsibility'). Aside from the initial validation work, this measure has not been used in other published research.

Henbest and Stewart (1989) modified the Brown et al. (1986) measure to enable coding direct from video- or audiotape. They also added two more categories of patient 'offers' (symptoms and thoughts) and distinguished closed- from open-ended doctor responses. However, neither this nor the original Brown et al. (1986) instrument assesses the success (or otherwise) by which participants' respective 'agendas' are negotiated and integrated in the consultation.

The most recent version (Brown et al., 1995) now also includes patient 'offers' relating to impact on functioning/roles. A modified scoring method allows for the possibility that patients may not offer any symptoms or prompts during a consultation. This makes the measure applicable to a wider range of consultation types (e.g. doctor-initiated encounters). As well as measuring the degree to which the doctor elicits the patient's illness experience, the method now also contains two new sections. The first scores the doctor's attempts to 'understand the whole person' (still corresponding to the dimension we term 'patient-as-person'). The method requires verbatim transcription of patients' statements relating to family, personality, social support and life-cycle issues. The second additional section assesses the degree to which doctor and patient 'find common ground'. The method for scoring this involves consideration of the interaction between doctor and patient (e.g. mutual discussion of treatment goals). As such, the measure now also maps onto dimension 3 ('sharing power and responsibility') and possibly also dimension 4 ('therapeutic alliance').

All the reviewed combined methods have published reliability data, although samples are small and a number of reliability assessments have involved the developers of the scales rather than independent researchers. The Henbest and Stewart (1989) and Brown et al. (1995) measures have demonstrated acceptable intra-rater reliability. The Byrne and Long (1976) and Brown et al. (1986) methods have acceptable inter-rater reliability, although reliability of some categories in the Byrne and Long system is low. The high levels of inter-rater reliability reported for the Henbest and Stewart (1989) measure (both by its developers and by Law & Britten, 1995) could not be replicated by Mead and Bower (2000), although the latter report levels of actual agreement between observers rather than association. Brown et al. (1995) also report high inter-rater reliability.

In terms of validity, both the Byrne and Long (1976) and Brown et al. (1986) measures were sensitive to changes associated with training (Bensing & Sluijs, 1985; Stewart et al., 1986). Associations have also been reported with female gender and training status of doctors (Henbest & Stewart, 1989). Associations with consultation length are inconsistent (Byrne & Long, 1976; Cape, 1996). Concurrent validity with other measures of consultation processes include associations with flexibility of consulting style (Long, 1985), eye contact (Mead & Bower, 2000), measured empathy (Henbest & Stewart, 1989), ascertainment of patients' reasons for attendance (Henbest & Stewart, 1990) and 'global' communication skills (Stewart et al., 1995b). As would be expected, the Brown et al. (1986) and Henbest and Stewart (1989) measures are highly correlated, but the latter did not correlate highly with either a rating scale of patient-centredness nor a verbal coding measure based on RIAS (Mead & Bower, 2000). Finally, in terms of outcomes, Byrne and Long's (1976) system was not related to patients' ratings of the consultation; Henbest and Stewart (1989) was not related to doctor-patient agreement or patient satisfaction (Henbest & Stewart, 1990), and there was no association between the most recent Brown et al. (1995) measure and patient health outcomes (Stewart et al., 1995b).

Discussion

Focus of the review

The aim of this review was to explore relationships between the concept of patient-centredness and its measurement. Searches of empirical literature were therefore limited to explicitly defined measures of 'patient-centredness'. This effectively excluded work addressing related themes but using other labels (e.g. 'patient communication control' – Kaplan et al., 1989; 'relationship-centred care' – Tresolini, 1996). Only further theoretical and empirical work will determine whether such concepts require substantive modification to the proposed five-dimension framework or can be subsumed within it. In the opinion of the reviewers, limiting the search term to 'patient-centredness' did not result in omission of any important measures of the concept. Moreover, the strategy reduced a potentially huge body of empirical literature to proportions more suitable for journal publication.

Only quantitative systems were reviewed since the focus was on measuring patient-centredness using methods that might be part of professional evaluation or quality monitoring initiatives. However, this should not be interpreted as downplaying the role of qualitative work in furthering understanding of patient-centredness. Qualitative research may generate valuable explanatory insight into mechanisms underlying observed relationships, including hypotheses concerning null findings or discrepant results (e.g. where independent measures of patient-centredness are not associated with patients' ratings of their consultations). Additionally, qualitative methods may be the only way of fully examining some dimensions of patient-centredness (e.g. dimensions 2 and 5): this issue is discussed in greater detail below.

The review focused on patient-centredness in medicine (particularly general practice, where the bulk of the literature originates). However, the concept is described in the literature of other health care disciplines, notably nursing. Although there may be significant overlap between the two, this cannot be assumed. For example, doctors and nurses differ in their conceptualisation of related terms such as 'holism' (Williams, Robins & Sibbald, 1997). The specific context in which different health professionals work may influence the relevance of particular dimensions of patient-centredness. The applicability of the current model to other disciplines therefore requires further exploration.

The five dimensions of patient-centredness

To date, the term 'patient-centredness' has been used to refer to so many different concepts that its scientific utility may have been compromised. The proposed five-dimension framework provides conceptual clarity concerning the exact issues addressed by particular interventions or research tools. This should facilitate communication between different research groups, and between researchers and clinicians.

The framework has a number of strengths. Dimensions 3 and 4 ('sharing power and responsibility' and 'therapeutic alliance') have parallels in psychological theories of interpersonal relationships and in psychotherapy (Leary, 1957; Birtchnell, 1993; Roth & Fonagy, 1996), suggesting that aspects of patient-centredness reflect ways of relating not limited to the medical context. A wider literature may therefore be of relevance to further developments in this area.

In psychological theories of personality a distinction is often made between 'nomothetic' systems of understanding (i.e. those that apply to groups of people) and 'idiographic' systems (i.e. those concerned with understanding an individual). Dimension 1 of the proposed framework may be considered nomothetic in that it concerns the degree to which doctors use a biopsychosocial perspective to understand patients in general. Dimension 2 differs in that it is idiographic, relating to the doctor's understanding of the individual patient. Similarly, dimension 4 (nomothetic) concerns the caring, affiliative quality of the doctor–patient relationship in terms that can be applied to all patients, whereas dimension 5 (idiographic) is concerned with aspects of the relationship particular to the individual doctor–patient dyad.

Inter-relationships between the dimensions

Aside from the nomothetic/idiographic complementarity of dimensions 1 and 2, and dimensions 4 and 5, inter-relationships within individual doctors also requires consideration. If, as some authors suggest, patient- and doctor-centred approaches represent two qualitatively different types of practitioner (e.g. McWhinney, 1985), then all five dimensions might be expected to be highly correlated within individual doctors. Equally, inter-correlations might be expected to the degree that particular verbal behaviours may relate to more than one dimension (discussed below). Although in part this is an empirical issue, there is no theoretical reason why practitioners should not demonstrate behaviours indicative of one dimension but not another. Using a biopsychosocial perspective to account for problems presented by all patients (dimension 1) may be less complex a task than fully understanding each patient's subjective experience of illness (dimension 2). Thus with relatively simple training, doctors' skills may improve in some areas without significant progress in others. Although medical education may aim to create fully patient-centred practitioners, it is implicit in the current model that the five dimensions each represent distinct aspects of clinical work having their own determinants, correlates and outcomes.

On being 'patient-centred'

As befits such a complex construct, a large number of variables potentially influence a doctor's propensity to be patient-centred, both within the context of individual consultations and over the course of the professional career. Fig. 1 indicates some hypothesised influences.

At the centre of the model is the doctor–patient relationship expressed in the form of a behavioural interaction between the two parties. As proposed, these behaviours may be interpreted as more or less 'patient-centred' across five dimensions. Potential influences on these dimensions are hypothesised at a number of different levels. At the most remote level, 'shapers' (such as cultural norms or clinical experience) may impact on more specific determinants (like gender or attitudes). In Western culture, for example, norms relating to gender mean that it is more socially 'acceptable' for females to discuss feelings and emotions than males. Similarly, a doctor's attitude towards developing and maintaining a therapeutic alliance with drug misusers may become coloured by past negative experiences.

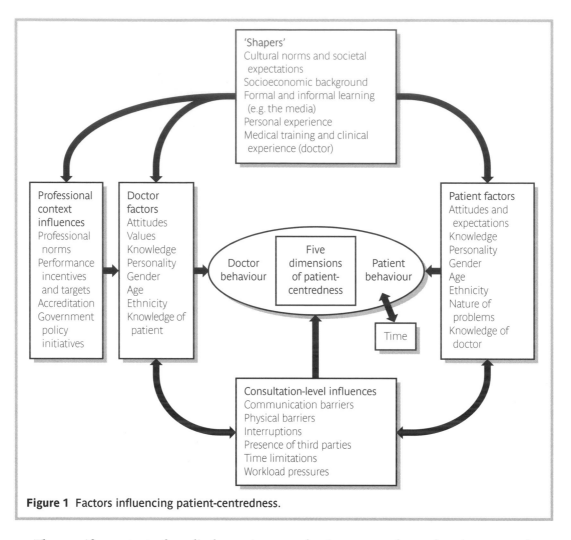

Figure 1 Factors influencing patient-centredness.

The specific context of medical practice may also impact on doctors' patient-centredness (Howie, 1996). For example, the introduction of videotaped consultation assessments into the membership examination for the UK Royal College of General Practitioners may encourage more systematic attention to interpersonal aspects of care by GPs. Recent policy initiatives to promote greater teamworking and role substitution among primary care professionals (e.g. Sibbald, 1996) may reduce possibilities for sustained personal contact with individual patients, in turn impacting on doctors' ability to attend to the more 'idiographic' aspects of patient-centred care. Increasing emphasis on 'evidence-based' clinical care may present problems for ensuring that patients have full information when deciding about treatment. As Toop (1998) points out, "concepts such as relative and absolute risk, number needed to treat, cost-effectiveness and resource allocation may not always be explainable to patients".

Finally, consultation-level influences have the most immediate impact on the propensity of doctors to be patient-centred. The mechanism for this may be direct or mediated via demographic and psychological characteristics of the patient or doctor. For example, ethnic differences may create barriers to effective communication. Time or workload pressures may limit possibilities for full negotiation and resolution of conflict between doctor and patient 'agendas'. Alternatively, such pressures may increase the value placed by a doctor on such aspects of clinical work, encouraging adoption of specific mechanisms (e.g. offering longer appointment slots) to facilitate patient-centred care.

The time dimension detailed in Fig. 1 explicitly recognises that the propensity of a doctor to be patient-centred will vary over time, and that some dimensions (especially 2 and 5) require significant time to develop between the doctor and individual patient.

As currently presented, the model is not fully specified in a number of respects. First, it only indicates hypothesised sources of influence on the broad construct of patient-centredness, without considering more in-depth relationships between specific elements of the model and each dimension. For example, dimension 3 ('sharing power and responsibility') may be relatively amenable to external influences such as policies that set standards for patient involvement in care. However, dimension 5 ('doctor-as-person') is far less amenable to such external influences since it requires a reflective approach on the part of the doctor which cannot be enforced from outside. Balint (1964) suggested that some aspects of patient-centredness require a "limited though considerable change in personality" (p. 121), whereas others suggest that patient-centred skills can be learned without such profound psychological change (Gask & McGrath, 1989). These conflicting points of view may relate to the relationship between training and the different dimensions: teaching techniques for improving the 'therapeutic alliance' may be simpler than teaching doctors to be insightful and reflective with individual patients.

Secondly, as in most models in the social sciences, many of the causal 'arrows' may function in both directions. Although full specification of relationships requires further theoretical and empirical work, a number of relationships have begun to be examined. For example, Howie et al. (1992) explored relationships between the context of care (i.e. consultation length and booking intervals), doctor attitudes and proxies of patient-centred behaviour.

Finally, the model concerns doctors' propensity to be patient-centred and does not consider outcomes. Nevertheless, proving the utility of patient-centred care requires consideration of its impact on a variety of outcomes. Howie (1996) suggests that patient outcomes such as health status, satisfaction and enablement and doctor outcomes such as stress and morale are both important.

Relationships between dimensions and measures

It is evident that the proposed conceptual framework does not map neatly onto some of the measures reviewed. This reflects the fact that non-specific verbal behaviours have no inherent relation to higher-order concepts such as 'sharing power and responsibility'. Such behaviours may be interpreted as relating to more than one dimension. Information-giving, for example, could imply 'sharing power and responsibility', in that information may provide patients with the resources to challenge or make decisions about their care. Alternatively it may relate to the 'therapeutic alliance', by enhancing the sense of partnership and increasing patient perception of the relevance or potency of an intervention. Greater specificity requires information about the context and motivations behind particular verbal processes, but it is unlikely that quantitative systems applied by external observers can ever adequately capture such complexity. This underscores the importance of validation with reference to appropriate variables that are 'external' to the consultation (e.g. measures of patient recall or adherence to treatment) as well as the triangulation of observer ratings of patient-centredness with doctor and patient reports.

None of the measures reviewed covers dimension 5 ('doctor-as-person'), reflecting the difficulty of operationalising such a complex and context-specific variable. On the other hand, dimension 1 ('biopsychosocial perspective') may be relatively straightforward to measure, despite the fact that some authors argue that extending the 'clinical gaze' to patients' social and psychological worlds is tantamount to increasing the social power and authority of doctors (e.g. Mishler, 1984). It is a common fact that complex theoretical concepts cannot be adequately translated into practical measures, but it is important to be clear about what is lost in translation and how this affects the interpretation of findings. The Henbest and Stewart (1989) measure, for example, focuses on eliciting the patient's illness experience, corresponding to dimension 2 ('patient-as-person'). However, dimension 2 concerns the doctor's understanding of the individual patient, an aspect which is lost to the degree that the Henbest and Stewart measure scores doctors' response modes to patients' 'offers' in general. More individualised (idiographic) methods are considered later.

As highlighted in the results section, even where observation-based measures appear to tap into the same dimension, they may differ in their focus on doctor or patient behaviour, and often include quite different combinations of variables. Such discrepancies in content and focus may go some way towards explaining inconsistent patterns of results in the literature. Identifying the particular conceptual dimensions addressed by each measure may assist in elucidating consistent relationships.

Another cause of inconsistency concerns differences in samples of clinicians and consultations studied. An association between patient-centredness and longer consultations (e.g. Long, 1985; Howie et al., 1992; Winefield et al., 1996) was not confirmed by Cape (1996), despite the fact that the latter used the same measure as Long (1985). However, it should be noted that Long's study of 53 GPs included all types of patient consultation, whereas Cape focused specifically on consultations for psychological problems submitted by a sample of nine GPs who all had particular interests in psychological care. It is therefore important that apparent inconsistencies are interpreted with sampling issues in mind.

A limitation of the all observer-based methods reviewed in this paper (at least as far as research in general practice is concerned) is the focus on single consultations. Balint (1964) and others in the field of general practice emphasise the importance of the long-term relationship between doctor and patient which develops over successive consultations. As mentioned above, some proposed dimensions of patient-centredness (e.g. 2 and 5) relate specifically to processes that cannot be expected to develop fully in a single encounter. Thus, observation measures applied to individual consultations are unlikely to be sensitive to aspects of the relationship not explicitly verbalised or which develop over time (e.g. mutual trust). Although practical problems have restricted exploration of this issue, it deserves serious attention if research in this area is not to ignore a key feature of general practice medicine in favour of logistical simplicity.

Utility of measures of patient-centredness

The utility of any measure depends on its validity, reliability, sensitivity and feasibility, and a trade-off between these criteria is often necessary (Mead & Bower, 2000). It is important to be clear about the context in which a measure is being used. For example, if patient-centredness scores were to influence decisions about individual doctors (e.g. for professional accreditation), then observer-based ratings need to be highly reliable so that individuals are not unfairly disadvantaged. Reliability can be lower in research contexts where individuals are not directly affected by scores. Nevertheless, while generally more reliable, methods based on verbal behaviour coding (including combined methods – see Tables 3 and 4) are less likely to be used for measuring individual doctors' performance than rating scales which evaluate more 'global' consultation skills (Table 2). Not only are rating scales less time-consuming and more feasible for quality assurance and professional accreditation, they lend themselves more readily to benchmarking and the prescription of quality standards.

While all the measures reviewed in this paper are relatively insensitive to the complexities of medical interactions, the importance attached to the issue of sensitivity depends, in part, on the intended function of a measure. Even a relatively insensitive instrument may have utility for professional monitoring if the focus is on very poorly performing doctors at the extreme of the distribution (providing that the measure is reliable). However, insensitive measures have much less utility when attempting to differentiate doctors closer to the mean.

Idiographic measurement methods

The idiographic/nomothetic distinction was discussed above. Conventional measurement in psychology and health services research prioritises the nomothetic perspective, but this cannot provide a full empirical account of patient-centredness as it is described in the conceptual literature. However, idiographic measurement methods do exist. Helman (1985) used a methodology which directly addressed the ability of the doctor to "see the illness through the patient's eyes" (McWhinney, 1985, p. 34). He explored the overlap between 'explanatory models' held by primary care physicians and patients suffering with gastrointestinal and respiratory problems. Qualitative interviews were used to elicit the clinician's model, the patient's model and the clinician's view of the patient's model. Helman then coded the degree of agreement between the two. Cohen, Tripp-Reimer, Smith, Sorofman and Lively (1994) undertook a similar study with diabetic patients. Such methods are time-consuming and require accurate coding of qualitative information about illness, but they do provide a direct estimate of the degree to which the doctor understands the patient's construction of the illness and are therefore face-valid measures of dimension 2.

The repertory grid (Fransella & Bannister, 1977; Bower & Tylee, 1997) is a quantitative method for examining idiographic characteristics such as doctors' psychological constructions of individual patients. Brooke and Sheldon (1985) report a grid study which seems to measure a 'doctor-' and 'patient-centred' distinction (although few details were provided), and a particular form of the grid (the dyad grid – Ryle & Lunghi, 1970) explicitly measures relationships. Schuffel, Egle, Schairer and Schneider (1977) used this form of grid to measure changes in medical students' perceptions of their relationships with patients, and such measures could provide a way of tackling the complexities of dimension 5.

Observer and patient report: the problem of the 'drug metaphor'

Observer measures of patient-centredness have yielded some inconsistent results in relation to patient satisfaction. While positive associations were found by Winefield et al. (1996), Street (1992) and Roter et al. (1987), Henbest and Stewart (1990) found none using their measure. To the degree that patients may be considered the final arbiters in evaluations of doctors' personal qualities, such disagreements throw doubt on the validity of these systems. However, patients' assessments cannot be used uncritically as a 'gold-standard'. Patient-centredness is, after all, generally perceived as a clinical method, and performance assessment is as much the responsibility of the medical profession as the healthcare 'consumer'. It may be that patient satisfaction is not an appropriate outcome for all dimensions of patient-centredness. Roter (1977) found that patients who were coached to ask more questions in their consultations reported lower satisfaction than a comparison group. Kaplan et al. (1989) also question the suitability of satisfaction as an outcome of patient involvement in care, suggesting that other measures (e.g. of health status and patient understanding) may be more appropriate. Furthermore, the measurement of patients' perceptions of care (including satisfaction) is not without its conceptual and methodological problems (e.g. Locker & Dunt, 1978; Fitzpatrick & Hopkins, 1983; Williams, 1994).

Discrepancies between measures of patient-centredness and patients' own perceptions may, however, reflect a deeper methodological issue. There is an implicit assumption in the literature that patient-centred behaviour and outcomes such as satisfaction and adherence to therapy will be associated in a simple linear fashion. This reflects the so-called 'drug metaphor' (Stiles & Shapiro, 1989), originally described in psychotherapy research (Stiles, Shapiro, Harper & Morrison, 1995), which conceives of consultation processes as analysable on the basis of their strength, integrity and effectiveness. Associations between process variables and outcomes are expected to elucidate the 'active' therapeutic ingredients in doctor–patient interactions. However, the drug metaphor is insensitive to the appropriateness of interventions, the particular requirements of individual patients and to the responsiveness of the two parties to one another in the consultation.

It is known, for example, that patient preferences for clinical style vary widely. Studies show that only a proportion of patients consider the GP a suitable person to talk to about personal problems, and that such attitudes are related to patient age, gender and social class (Cartwright, 1967; Fitton & Acheson, 1979; Cartwright & Anderson, 1981; Spence, 1992). Moreover, the same patient's preferences may vary depending on their reasons for consulting the doctor. Savage and Armstrong (1990) found that patients with simple physical complaints were significantly more satisfied with a 'directing' as opposed to 'sharing' consulting style from their GP, but this difference disappeared where patients' main complaints were of a chronic physical or psychosocial nature. Winefield et al. (1996), Winefield, Murrell, Clifford and Farmer (1997) found similar associations between patient-centredness and consultation 'type'. Although it has been suggested that clinician flexibility and responsiveness to patients' preferences for different consulting styles may be key to a patient-centred approach (Long, 1985), it is exceedingly difficult to develop measures that are sensitive to such contextual complexity while also remaining reliable and practical.

Inconsistent reports of relationships between consultation behaviour and outcomes may therefore represent insensitivity of the paradigm to the complexity of consultation processes. Analysis of the actual sequence of speech may represent one method of avoiding these problems (Wasserman & Inui, 1983). Other methods suggested by psychotherapy researchers include an 'events paradigm' (Elliott, 1984), involving both qualitative and quantitative description of micro-processes in the consultation (such as verbal exchange sequences explicitly identified as effecting patient change). However, such analyses are probably too complex and time-consuming for use in routine professional monitoring or accreditation.

In the absence of such methodological paradigm shifts, it may be more useful to consider in detail why disagreements occur in the present systems (for example, between patient evaluations and objective measures), rather than casting doubt on the validity of instruments. Winefield et al. (1996) call for further examination of factors external to the consultation which influence the behaviour and shape the goals and perceptions of each participant. Use of post-consultation interviews with doctors and patients, and techniques like inter-personal process recall (Elliott, 1984), may elucidate those aspects of the consultation that contribute to poor associations, such as patient preference for a more 'doctor-centred' style or perceived excessive intrusion into emotional issues too early in the doctor–patient relationship. Patients' perceptions are a useful external reality check on observer-based measures of consultation processes, but what is needed most is triangulation of the three perspectives (i.e. doctor, patient and independent observer) rather than affording particular priority to one.

Conclusion

This paper identifies a multiplicity of conceptual definitions and empirical measures of patient-centredness. It is proposed that these various approaches can be understood in terms of five distinct dimensions relating to the doctor–patient relationship. The measures reviewed can be seen to relate to these dimensions to varying degrees, though not all dimensions have proved accessible to current measurement technology. Overall, a significant number of measures have proved reliable, and a number of associations with external variables (such as participant characteristics and certain consultation processes) have been reported. Nevertheless, the pattern of findings is somewhat inconsistent, particularly in relation to patient outcomes like health status or satisfaction. Although further research will ameliorate some of these problems, it is likely that the more complex and contextual dimensions of patient-centredness require development of new measures and analytic methods if further advances are to be made.

Acknowledgements

The authors would like to thank Martin Roland, Anne Rogers and two anonymous referees for helpful comments on earlier drafts of this paper. This work was conducted as part of the programme of the National Primary Care Research and Development Centre, supported by the Department of Health. The views expressed are those of the authors and are not intended to represent the views of NPCRDC or its funders.

References

Armstrong, D. (1979). The emancipation of biographical medicine. *Social Science and Medicine, 13A*, 1–8.

Badger, L., deGruy, F., Hartman, J., Plant, M. A., Leeper, J., Ficken, R., Maxwell, A., Rand, E., Anderson, R., & Templeton, B. (1994). Psychosocial interest, medical interviews and the recognition of depression. *Archives of Family Medicine, 3*, 899–907.

Bain, D. J., Bassett, W., & Haines, A. (1973). Difficulties encountered in classifying illness in general practice. *Journal of the Royal College of General Practitioners, 23*, 474–479.

Baker, R. (1990). Development of a questionnaire to assess patients' satisfaction with consultations in general practice. *British Journal of General Practice, 40*, 487–490.

Bales, R. (1950). *Interaction process analysis: a method for the study of small groups.* Reading, MA: Addison-Wesley.

Balint, E. (1969). The possibilities of patient-centred medicine. *Journal of the Royal College of General Practitioners, 17*, 269–276.

Balint, E., Courtenay, M., Elder, A., Hull, S., & Julian, P. (1993). *The doctor, the patient and the group: Balint revisited.* London: Routledge.

Balint, M. (1964). *The doctor, his patient and the illness.* London: Pitman Medical.

Bensing, J., & Sluijs, E. (1985). Evaluation of an interview training course for general practitioners. *Social Science and Medicine, 20*, 737–744.

Birtchnell, J. (1993). *How humans relate: a new interpersonal theory.* Hove: Psychology Press.

Bordin, E. (1979). The generalizability of the psychoanalytic concept of the working alliance. *Psychotherapy, 16,* 252–260.

Bower, P. (1998). Understanding patients: implicit personality theory and the general practitioner. *British Journal of Medical Psychology, 71,* 153–163.

Bower, P., & Tylee, A. (1997). Measuring general practitioner psychology: the personal construct perspective. *Family Practice, 14,* 142–147.

Brooke, J., & Sheldon, M. (1985). Clinical decision = patient with problem + doctor with problem. In M. Sheldon, J. B. Brooke, & A. Rector, *Decision making in general practice.* London: Stockton.

Brown, J., Stewart, M., McCracken, E., McWhinney, I., & Levenstein, J. (1986). The patient-centred clinical method 2: definition and application. *Family Practice, 3,* 75–79.

Brown, J., Stewart, M., & Tessier, S. (1995). *Assessing communication between patients and doctors: a manual for scoring patient-centred communication.* Canada: Centre for Studies in Family Medicine, University of Western Ontario.

Bucks, R., Williams, A., Whitfield, M., & Routh, D. (1990). Towards a typology of general practitioners attitudes to general practice. *Social Science and Medicine, 30(5),* 537–547.

Buijs, R., Sluijs, E., & Verhaak, P. (1984). Byrne and Long: a classification for rating the interview style of doctors. *Social Science and Medicine, 19,* 683–690.

Butow, P., Dunn, S., Tattersall, M., & Jones, R. (1995). Computer-based interaction analysis of the cancer consultation. *British Journal of Cancer, 71,* 1115–1121.

Byrne, P., & Long, B. (1976). *Doctors Talking to Patients.* London: HMSO.

Cape, J. (1996). Psychological treatment of emotional problems by general practitioners. *British Journal of Medical Psychology, 69,* 85–99.

Cartwright, A. (1967). *Patients and their doctors.* London: Routledge.

Cartwright, A., & Anderson, R. (1981). *General practice revisited.* London: Tavistock.

Cassell, E. (1982). The nature of suffering and the goals of medicine. *The New England Journal of Medicine, 306,* 639–645.

Cattell, R. (1978). *The scientific use of factor analysis.* New York: Plenum.

Cecil, D., & Killeen, I. (1997). Control, compliance and satisfaction in the family practice encounter. *Family Medicine, 29,* 653–657.

Cockburn, J., Killer, D., Campbell, E., & Sanson-Fisher, R. W. (1987). Measuring general practitioners' attitudes towards medical care. *Family Practice, 4(3),* 192–199.

Cohen, M. Z., Tripp-Reimer, T., Smith, C., Sorofman, B., & Lively, S. (1994). Explanatory models of diabetes: patient–practitioner variation. *Social Science and Medicine, 38,* 59–66.

Crookshank, F. (1926). The theory of diagnosis. *Lancet, 2,* 939–942.

Crow, R., Gage, H., Hampson, S., Hart, J., Kimber, A., & Thomas, H. (1999). The role of expectancies in the placebo effect and their use in the delivery of health care: a systematic review. *Health Technology Assessment, 3(3).*

Croyle, R., & Barger, S. (1993). Illness Cognition. In S. Maes, H. Leventhal, & M. Johnston, *International review of health psychology.* New York: Wiley.

deMonchy, C., Richardson, R., Brown, R., & Harden, R. (1988). Measuring attitudes of doctors: the doctor–patient (DP) rating. *Medical Education, 22,* 231–239.

Department of Health (1991). *The patients' charter.* London: HMSO.

Doyal, L. (1979). *The political economy of health.* London: Pluto Press.

Ehrenreich, B., & English, D. (1979). *For her own good.* London: Pluto Press.

Elliott, R. (1984). A discovery-oriented approach to significant change events in psychological therapies: interpersonal process recall and comprehensive process analysis. In L. Rice, & L. Greenberg, *Patterns of change: intensive analysis of psychological therapies process.* New York: The Guildford Press.

Engel, G. (1977). The need for a new medical model: a challenge for biomedicine. *Science, 196,* 129–135.

Engel, G. (1980). The clinical application of the biopsychosocial model. *American Journal of Psychiatry, 137(5),* 535–543.

Fallowfield, L., Lipkin, M., & Hall, A. (1998). Teaching senior oncologists communication skills: results from phase I of a comprehensive longitudinal program in the United Kingdom. *Journal of Clinical Oncology, 16,* 1961–1968.

Fitton, F., & Acheson, H. (1979). *The doctor–patient relationship: a study in general practice.* London: HMSO.

Fitzpatrick, R., & Hopkins, A. (1983). Problems in the conceptual framework of patient satisfaction research: an empirical investigation. *Sociology of Health and Illness, 5,* 297–311.

Ford, S., Fallowfield, L., & Lewis, S. (1996). Doctor–patient interactions in oncology. *Social Science and Medicine, 42,* 1511–1519.

Fransella, F., & Bannister, D. (1977). *A manual for repertory grid technique.* London: Academic Press.

Friedson, E. (1960). Client control and medical practice. *American Journal of Sociology, 65,* 374–382.

Friedson, E. (1970). *Profession of medicine: a study of the sociology of applied knowledge.* New York: Harper & Row.

Gask, L., & McGrath, G. (1989). Psychotherapy and General Practice. *British Journal of Psychiatry, 154,* 445–453.

Grol, R., de Maeseneer, J., Whitfield, M., & Mokkink, H. (1990). Disease-centred versus patient-centred attitudes: comparison of general practitioners in Belgium, Britain and the Netherlands. *Family Practice, 7(2),* 100–104.

Hall, J., & Dornan, M. (1988). What patients like about their medical care and how often they are asked: a meta analysis of the satisfaction literature. *Social Science and Medicine, 27,* 935–939.

Helman, C. (1985). Communication in primary care: the role of patient and practitioner explanatory models. *Social Science and Medicine, 20(9),* 923–931.

Henbest, R., & Stewart, M. (1989). Patient-centredness in the consultation 1: a method for measurement. *Family Practice, 6,* 249–254.

Henbest, R., & Stewart, M. (1990). Patient-centredness in the consultation 2: does it really make a difference? *Family Practice, 7,* 28–33.

Howie, J. (1996). Addressing the credibility gap in general practice research: better theory; more feeling; less strategy. *British Journal of General Practice, 46,* 479–481.

Howie, J., Hopton, L., Heaney, D., & Porter, A. (1992). Attitudes to medical care, organisation of work, and stress among general practitioners. *British Journal of General Practice, 42,* 181–185.

Illich, I. (1976). *Limits to medicine.* London: Penguin.

Inui, T., Carter, W., Kukull, W., & Haigh, V. (1982). Outcome-based doctor–patient interaction analysis I: comparison of techniques. *Medical Care, 20,* 535–549.

Kaplan, S., Greenfield, S., & Ware, J. (1989). Assessing the effects of physician–patient interactions on the outcomes of chronic disease. *Medical Care, 27,* S110–S127.

Kinmonth, A., Woodcock, A., Griffin, S., Spiegal, N., Campbell, M., & Diabetes Care from Diagnosis Team (1998). Randomised controlled trial of patient centred care of diabetes in general practice: impact on current wellbeing and future disease risk. *British Medical Journal, 317,* 1202–1208.

Korsch, B., Gozzi, E., & Francis, V. (1968). Gaps in doctor–patient communication I: doctor–patient interaction and patient satisfaction. *Pediatrics, 42,* 855–871.

Laine, C., & Davidoff, F. (1996). Patient-centered medicine: a professional evolution. *Journal of the American Medical Association, 275,* 152–156.

Langewitz, W., Phillipp, E., Kiss, A., & Wossmer, B. (1998). Improving communication skills: a randomized controlled behaviorally-oriented intervention study for residents in internal medicine. *Psychosomatic Medicine, 60,* 268–276.

Law, S., & Britten, N. (1995). Factors that influence the patient-centredness of a consultation. *British Journal of General Practice, 45,* 520–524.

Leary, T. (1957). *Interpersonal diagnosis of personality.* New York: Ronald Press.

Levenstein, J., McCracken, E., McWhinney, I., Stewart, M., & Brown, J. (1986). The patient-centred clinical method 1: a model for the doctor–patient interaction in family medicine. *Family Practice, 3,* 24–30.

Linn, L., DiMatteo, R., Cope, D., & Robbins, A. (1987). Measuring physicians' humanistic attitudes, values and behaviours. *Medical Care, 25,* 504–515.

Lipkin, M., Quill, T., & Napodano, R. (1984). The medical interview: a core curriculum for residencies in internal medicine. *Annals of Internal Medicine, 100,* 277–284.

Locker, D., & Dunt, D. (1978). Theoretical and methodological issues in sociological studies of consumer satisfaction with medical care. *Social Science and Medicine, 12,* 283–292.

Long, B. (1985). A study of the verbal behaviour of family doctors. *International Journal of the Sociology of Language, 51,* 5–25.

May, C., & Mead, N. (1999). Patient-centredness: a history. In C. Dowrick, & L. Frith, *General practice and ethics: uncertainty and responsibility.* London: Routledge.

McWhinney, I. (1985). Patient-centred and doctor-centred models of clinical decision making. In M. Sheldon, J. Brook, & A. Rector, *Decision making in general practice.* London: Stockton.

McWhinney, I. (1989). The need for a transformed clinical method. In M. Stewart, & D. Roter, *Communicating with medical patients.* London: Sage.

Mead, N., Bower, P. (2000). Measuring patient-centredness: a comparison of three observation-based instruments, *Patient Education and Counseling, 39,* 71–80.

Meehl, P. (1978). Theoretical risks and tabular asterisks: Sir Karl, Sir Ronald and the slow progress of soft psychology. *Journal of Consulting and Clinical Psychology, 46,* 806–834.

Mishler, E. (1984). *The discourse of medicine: dialectics of medical interviews.* New Jersey: Ablex.

Morrell, D. (1972). Symptom interpretation in general practice. *Journal of the Royal College of General Practitioners, 22,* 297–309.

Neighbour, R. (1987). *The inner consultation.* Lancaster: MTP Press.

NHS Executive (1996). *Patient partnership: building a collaborative strategy.* Leeds: NHS Executive.

Ockene, J., Quirk, M., Goldberg, R., Kristeller, J., Donnelly, G., Kalan, K., Gould, B., Greene, H., Harrison-Atlas, R., Pease, J., Pickens, S., & Williams, J. (1988). A residents' training program for the development of smoking intervention skills. *Archives of Internal Medicine, 148,* 1039–1045.

Parsons, T. (1951). *The social system.* Glencoe, IL: Free Press.

Pieters, H., Touw-Otten, F., & Melker, R. (1994). Simulated patients in assessing consultation skills of trainees in general practice vocational training: a validity study. *Medical Education, 28,* 226–233.

Rogers, A., Hassell, K., & Nicolaas, G. (1999). *Demanding patients?: analysing the use of primary care.* Milton Keynes: Open University Press.

Rogers, C. (1967). *On becoming a person: a therapist's view of psychotherapy.* London: Constable.

Roland, M. (1999). Quality and efficiency: enemies or partners? *British Journal of General Practice, 49,* 140–143.

Roter, D. (1977). Patient participation in patient–provider interactions: the effects of patient question asking on the quality of interaction, satisfaction, and compliance. *Health Education Monographs, 5,* 281–315.

Roter, D., & Frankel, R. (1992). Quantitative and qualitative approaches to the evaluation of medical dialogue. *Social Science and Medicine, 34,* 1097–1103.

Roter, D., Hall, J., & Katz, N. (1987). Relations between physicians' behaviours and analogue patients' satisfaction, recall and impressions. *Medical Care, 25,* 437–451.

Roth, A., & Fonagy, P. (1996). *What works for whom? A critical review of psychotherapy research.* London: Guildford.

Royal College of General Practitioners (1972). *The future general practitioner: learning and teaching.* London: British Medical Association.

Ryle, A., & Lunghi, M. (1970). The dyad grid: a modification of repertory grid technique. *British Journal of Psychiatry, 117,* 323–327.

Savage, R., & Armstrong, D. (1990). Effect of a general practitioners' consulting style on patients' satisfaction: a controlled study. *British Medical Journal, 301,* 968–970.

Schuffel, W., Egle, U., Schairer, U., & Schneider, A. (1977). Does history- taking affect learning of attitudes. *Psychotherapy and Psychosomatics, 31,* 81–92.

Sibbald, B. (1996). Skill mix and professional roles in primary care. In *What is the future for a primary care-led NHS?.* Oxford: Radcliffe Medical Press.

Siegler, M., & Osmond, H. (1974). *Models of madness, models of medicine.* New York: MacMillan.

Silverman, D. (1987). *Communication and medical practice: social relations in the clinic.* London: Sage.

Smith, R., & Hoppe, R. (1991). The patient's story: integrating the patient- and physician-centered approaches to interviewing. *Annals of Internal Medicine, 115,* 470–477.

Spence, S. (1992). Problems that patients feel are appropriate to discuss with their Gps. *Journal of the Royal Society of Medicine, 85,* 669–673.

Squier, R. (1990). A model of empathic understanding and adherence to treatment regimens in practitioner-patient relationships. *Social Science and Medicine, 30,* 325–339.

Stewart, M. (1983). Patient characteristics which are related to the doctor–patient interaction. *Family Practice, 1,* 30–36.

Stewart, M. (1984). What is a successful doctor–patient interview? A study of interactions and outcomes. *Social Science and Medicine, 19,* 167–175.

Stewart, M., Brown, J., Levenstein, J., McCracken, E., & McWhinney, I. (1986). The patient-centred clinical method 3: changes in residents' performance over two months of training. *Family Practice, 3,* 164–167.

Stewart, M., Brown, J., Weston, W., McWhinney, I., McWilliam, C., & Freeman, T. (1995a). *Patient-centred medicine: transforming the clinical method.* London: Sage.

Stewart, M., Brown, J., Donner, A., McWhinney, I., Oates, J., & Weston, W. (1995b). *The impact of patient-centred care on patient outcomes in family practice (Final report).* Canada: Center for Studies in Family Medicine, University of Western Ontario.

Stiles, W. (1978). Verbal response modes and dimensions of interpersonal roles: a method of discourse analysis. *Journal of Personality and Social Psychology, 36,* 693–703.

Stiles, W., & Shapiro, D. (1989). Abuse of the drug metaphor in psychotherapy process-outcome research. *Clinical Psychology Review, 9,* 521–543.

Stiles, W., Shapiro, D., Harper, H., & Morrison, L. (1995). Therapist contributions to psychotherapeutic assimilation: an alternative to the drug metaphor. *British Journal of Medical Psychology, 68,* 1–13.

Stimson, G., & Webb, B. (1975). *Going to see the doctor: the consultation process in general practice.* London: Routledge and Kegan Paul.

Stott, N., & Davis, R. (1979). The exceptional potential in every primary care consultation. *Journal of the Royal College of General Practitioners, 29,* 201–205.

Street, R. (1992). Analyzing communication in medical consultations: do behavioral measures correspond to patients' perceptions? *Medical Care, 30,* 976–988.

Szasz, T., & Hollender, M. (1956). A contribution to the philosophy of medicine: the basic models of the doctor–patient relationship. *Archives of Internal Medicine, 97,* 585–592.

Toop, L. (1998). Patient-centred primary care. *British Medical Journal, 316,* 1882–1883.

Tresolini, C. (1996). Health care relationships: instruments for effective patient-focused care in the academic health center. *Journal of Dental Education, 60,* 945–950.

Tuckett, D., Boulton, M., Olson, C., & Williams, A. (1985). *Meetings between experts: an approach to sharing ideas in medical consultations.* London: Tavistock.

Verhaak, P. (1988). Detection of psychologic complaints by general practitioners. *Medical Care, 26*(10), 1009–1020.

Waitzkin, H. (1990). On studying the discourse of medical encounters: a critique of quantitative and qualitative methods and a proposal for reasonable compromise. *Medical Care, 28,* 473–488.

Wasserman, R., & Inui, T. (1983). Systematic analysis of clinician–patient interactions: a critique of recent approaches with suggestions for future research. *Medical Care, 21,* 279–293.

Wensing, M., Jung, H., Mainz, J., Olesen, F., & Grol, R. (1998). A systematic review of the literature on patient priorities for general practice care. Part 1: Description of the research domain. *Social Science and Medicine, 47,* 1573–1588.

Williams, A., Robins, T., Sibbald, B. (1997). Cultural differences between medicine and nursing: implications for primary care (summary report). NPCRDC, University of Manchester.

Williams, B. (1994). Patient satisfaction: a valid concept? *Social Science and Medicine, 38,* 509–516.

Williams, S., & Calnan, M. (1991). Key determinants of consumer satisfaction with general practice. *Family Practice, 8,* 237–242.

Winefield, H., Murrell, T., Clifford, J., & Farmer, E. (1996). The search for reliable and valid measures of patient-centredness. *Psychology and Health, 11,* 811–824.

Winefield, H., Murrell, T., Clifford, J., & Farmer, E. (1997). The usefulness of distinguishing different types of general practice consultation, or are the needed skills always the same? *Family Practice, 12,* 402–407.

Wissow, L., Roter, D., Bauman, L., Crain, E., Kercsmar, C., Weiss, K., Mitchell, H., & Mohr, B. (1998). Patient–provider communication during the emergency department care of children with asthma. *Medical Care, 36,* 1439–1450.

Marteau, T., Senior, V., Humphries, S.E. et al. (2004) Psychological impact of genetic testing for familial hypercholesterolemia within a previously aware population: a randomized controlled trial, *American Journal of Medical Genetics*, 128A: 285–93.

Psychological impact of genetic testing for familial hypercholesterolemia within a previously aware population

A randomized controlled trial

Theresa Marteau,[1]* Victoria Senior,[1] Steve E. Humphries,[8] Martin Bobrow,[10] Treena Cranston,[9] Martin A. Crook,[4,5] Lorna Day,[12] Maryam Fernandez,[1] Rob Horne,[11] Andrew Iversen,[6] Zoe Jackson,[1] Jacqui Lynas,[7] Helen Middleton-Price,[9] Richard Savine,[4] Jim Sikorski,[3] Melanie Watson,[1] John Weinman,[2] Anthony S. Wierzbicki,[4] and Richard Wray[7]

[1]*Psychology & Genetics Research Group, King's College London, London, United Kingdom*
[2]*Psychology Unit, King's College London, London, United Kingdom*
[3]*Department of General Practice and Primary Care, King's College London, London, United Kingdom*
[4]*Department of Chemical Pathology, Guy's & St. Thomas' Hospitals, London, United Kingdom*
[5]*Department of Chemical Pathology, Lewisham Hospital, London, United Kingdom*
[6]*Department of Chemical Pathology, Royal Sussex County Hospital, Brighton, United Kingdom*
[7]*Cardiology Department, The Conquest Hospital, East Sussex, United Kingdom*
[8]*Centre for Cardiovascular Genetics, British Heart Foundation Laboratories, Royal Free and University College London Medical School, London, United Kingdom*
[9]*Clinical Molecular Genetics, Great Ormond Street Hospital for Children, London, United Kingdom*
[10]*Cambridge Institute for Medical Research, University of Cambridge, Wellcome/MRC Building, Addenbrooke's Hospital, Cambridge, United Kingdom*
[11]*Centre for Health Care Research, University of Brighton, Brighton, United Kingdom*
[12]*Human Genetics, Level G, The Princess Anne Hospital, Southampton, United Kingdom*

The authors belong to the Genetic Risk Assessment for FH Trial (GRAFT) Study Group.

Grant sponsor: The Wellcome Trust; Grant number: 037006; Grant sponsor: British Heart Foundation; Grant numbers: RG2000015, RG95007, RG93008; Grant sponsor: Pfizer (Parke-Davis) Ltd.; Grant sponsor: Merck Sharp & Dohme.

*Correspondence to: Prof. Theresa Marteau, Ph.D., Psychology and Genetics Research Group, King's College London, 5th Floor Thomas Guy House, Guy's Campus, London SE1 9RT UK. E-mail: theresa.marteau@kcl.ac.uk

Abstract

This trial tests the hypothesis that confirming a clinical diagnosis of familial hypercholesterolemia (FH) by finding a genetic mutation reduces patients' perceptions of control over the disease and adherence to risk-reducing behaviors. Three hundred forty-one families, comprising 341 hypercholesterolemia probands and 128 adult relatives, were randomized to one of two groups: (a) routine clinical diagnosis; (b) routine clinical diagnosis plus genetic testing (mutation searching in probands and direct gene testing in relatives). The main outcome measures were perceptions of control over hypercholesterolemia, adherence to cholesterol-lowering medication, diet, physical activity, and smoking. There was no support for the main hypothesis: finding a mutation had no impact on perceived control or adherence to risk-reducing behavior (all P-values > 0.10). While all groups believed that lowering cholesterol was an effective way of reducing the risk of a heart attack, participants in whom a mutation was found believed less strongly in the efficacy of diet in reducing their cholesterol level ($P = 0.02$ at 6 months) and showed a trend in believing more strongly in the efficacy of cholesterol-lowering medication ($P = 0.06$ at 6 months). In conclusion, finding a mutation to confirm a clinical diagnosis of FH in a previously aware population does not reduce perceptions of control or adherence to risk-reducing behaviors. The pattern of findings leads to the new hypothesis that genetic testing does not affect the extent to which people feel they have control over a condition, but does affect their perceptions of how control is most effectively achieved. Further work is needed to determine whether similar results will be obtained in populations with little previous awareness of their risks.

Keywords: genetic testing; psychological consequences; familial hypercholesterolemia; health behavior; perceived control; illness perceptions

Introduction

Genetic mutations that increase the risk of developing potentially preventable conditions, including coronary heart disease (CHD) and cancer, have now been identified. While it is hoped that such genetic understanding will eventually result in better treatments tailored to individuals' genotypes, mutation testing is currently used mainly for prediction and diagnosis. There are concerns, however, about the psychological impact of using DNA as distinct from other biological markers to predict or diagnose disease, with fears that it will engender a sense of fatalism [McClure, 2002]. The potential value of detecting these mutations depends, in part, upon how individuals behave when they discover their increased, genetically influenced risk. Changes in motivation and behavior are largely determined by the perceptions that a recommended behavior is both effective in achieving risk reduction and personally controllable [Milne et al., 2000]. There is a common perception that genetic risks are uncontrollable [Blaxter and Paterson, 1982; Nelkin and Lindee, 1995; Hunt et al., 2000]. For example, students asked to rate a number of potential causes of disease, identified genetic causes as those over which people have least control, in contrast with behavioral causes such as smoking or low levels of physical activity where control is perceived as high [Shiloh et al., 2002]. Given this perception, using genetic tests to predict disease could potentially decrease motivation to engage in risk-reducing behaviors, by strengthening beliefs that a disease is neither preventable nor controllable. This would obviously be undesirable and would negatively affect the potential benefit of genetic testing. We therefore designed a randomized trial to evaluate the extent to which the use of genetic tests to predict common conditions may result in fatalism.

Currently there are no population-based predictive tests for treatable conditions. However, in anticipation of such tests, we designed a study to test this fatalism hypothesis by assessing the impact of confirming or making a clinical diagnosis of familial hycholestrolaemia (FH) using DNA. FH increases the risk of premature CHD, but this risk is modifiable by medication and lifestyle changes [Simon Broome Steering Committee, 1991]. FH is a dominantly inherited disorder, affecting about 1 in 500 of the general population. FH is diagnosed clinically by raised levels of low-density lipoprotein cholesterol (LDL-C), tendon xanthomata (TX), premature CHD, and a family history of hypercholesterolemia and premature CHD [Koivisto et al., 1992; Ward et al., 1996]. Recent advances make it possible to test for common mutations in two genes: the LDL-receptor gene (*LDLR*), which cause FH, and the apolipoprotein B gene (*APOB*), which causes a clinically indistinguishable disorder, familial defective apolipoprotein B100 (FDB) [Myant, 1993]. Patients with FH and FDB have significantly greater mortality than patients with polygenic hyperlipidaemia [Simon Broome Steering Committee, 1991, 1999], but lipid-lowering treatment is effective in reducing their risk [Simon Broome Steering Committee, 1999]. Thus early identification of at-risk individuals increases opportunities for dietary and physical activity interventions, smoking cessation advice, and drug treatment, which improve long-term prognosis [Durrington, 2001].

Although using genetic tests to confirm a clinically based diagnosis has several potential clinical advantages, the effect of this on an individual's motivation to reduce risks is unknown. We report here the first randomized controlled trial investigating the psychological impact of using genetic testing to make or confirm a clinical diagnosis. Following previous studies in general populations [Marteau, 1995; Lerman et al., 1997; Senior et al., 1999], we tested the hypothesis that finding a mutation that confirms a clinical diagnosis reduces perceptions of control over the disease and adherence to risk-reducing behaviors. The impact of using genetic testing in this diagnosis upon other salient illness perceptions was also assessed, alongside perceptions of the accuracy of the diagnosis, recall of genetic test results, and emotional state. When the study was planned, we expected to recruit sufficient undiagnosed first- and second-degree relatives of probands with FH to be able to assess the impact of genetic testing in an undiagnosed population as well as assessing the impact of genetic testing in confirming a clinical diagnosis of FH. There were, however, too few relatives that received a diagnosis of FH in the trial for this to be assessed. Thus, of the 128 relatives recruited into the trial, 107 had had previous cholesterol testing. Of the 41 completing the trial who had a diagnosis of FH confirmed or made, only 4 had no history of cholesterol testing.

Methods

Participants

Between October 1998 and February 2001, we recruited adults already clinically diagnosed with definite or possible heterozygous FH [Simon Broome Steering Committee, 1991], attending one of 5 lipid clinics in the South East of England, and their first- and second-degree adult relatives. Exclusion criteria were previous genetic diagnosis of FH and, in relatives only, previous CHD. A power calculation indicated that with 192 participants, the study would have 80% power to detect a medium effect on perceived control at the 5% significance level. This took into account the cluster randomization design and an anticipated 15% attrition rate.

Randomization and interventions

Families were randomized to one of two groups: (a) routine clinical diagnosis; or (b) routine clinical diagnosis plus genetic testing (mutation searching in probands and direct gene testing in relatives). In order to assess the impact of genetic testing, it was necessary to ensure that the comparison group underwent the same intervention minus the genetic testing. This resulted in patients with an existing clinical diagnosis undergoing a further routine clinical diagnosis, but often comprising more detailed testing and feedback than occurred at the time of their original diagnoses. The ratio of randomization to the two study groups was 3:1, based on the expectation that mutations would be identified in 30% of cases. The randomization list was prepared by a member of the independent data monitoring committee using incomplete blocks with randomization within blocks of 20 and random assignments allocated from consecutively numbered, opaque-sealed envelopes.

Routine clinical diagnosis. This comprised routine, clinical assessment for FH: analysis of fasting lipid profile and personal and family history of premature CHD and hyperlipidemia [Simon Broome Steering Committee, 1991]. This and other information (e.g., blood pressure and smoking status) was used to assess individuals' risks of having a coronary event in the next 10 years. Participants were informed of their diagnosis of FH, and given their cholesterol test results, an estimate of their risks of a coronary event in the next 10 years and a package of tailored life style advice to reduce the identified risks.

Routine clinical diagnosis plus genetic testing. Participants in this group received the same intervention as those in the "routine clinical diagnosis group" but in addition they underwent molecular analysis of DNA. Participants were informed of their diagnosis of FH, the results of the molecular analysis, and given their cholesterol test results, an estimate of their risks of a coronary event in the next 10 years and a package of tailored life style advice to reduce the identified risks.

All genetic analyses were carried out by one staff member (T.C.) at the Institute of Child Health DNA Diagnostic Laboratory (London, UK), using fully accredited laboratory guidelines, and methods piloted and fully described elsewhere [Heath et al., 2001]. Briefly, DNA samples were screened for point mutations in the LDLR gene by single strand confirmation polymorphism (SSCP) analysis [Heath et al., 2001], covering the promoter, all 18 exons, and the intron-exon boundaries. If an abnormal pattern was found, known polymorphisms were eliminated and the exon was sequenced using an ABI 377 DNA sequencer, to determine the nucleotide change. One mutation (R3500Q) in the *APOB* gene was tested for as described [Mamotte and van Bockxmeer, 1993]. DNA reports were scrutinized by a senior laboratory staff member (H.M.P.) and were sent to the Genetic Risk Assessment for FH Trial (GRAFT) co-ordinating center within 3 months of receipt of the blood sample [Heath et al., 2001].

Procedure

Multi-centre Research Ethics Committee approval was obtained. Eligible probands were sent information by letter and recruited by one of three research nurses, either at a routine lipid clinic appointment or at study-specific clinic appointment. Once informed consent had been obtained, the randomization envelope was opened by the recruiting research nurse. The specified tests were then undergone for the assessment of FH. On a second clinic visit 4 months later, they received the results of their diagnostic assessments and a package of tailored, lifestyle advice from a small clinical team using a standard protocol (available on request). A six-month follow-up assessment was conducted either at a routine clinic appointment or by telephone.

Consent to contact eligible relatives was obtained from the probands (Figure 1). The General Practitioners of relatives participating in the trial were informed of the diagnostic assessment.

Main outcome measures

Psychological responses were assessed at recruitment, one week and 6 months after testing (Figure 2).

Participants completed postal questionnaires. The research nurse assessed the risk-reducing behaviors of diet, activity level, and smoking.

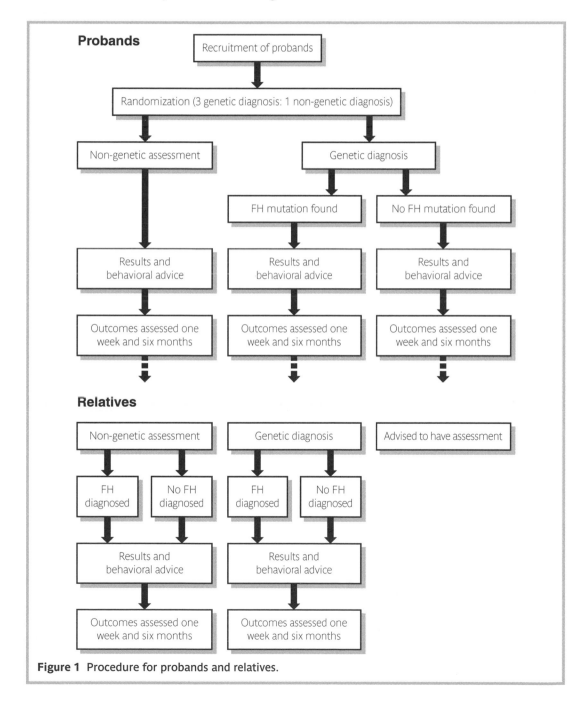

Figure 1 Procedure for probands and relatives.

	Recruitment	One week after diagnosis	Six months after diagnosis
Primary outcomes			
Perceived control over FH	✓	✓	✓
Perceived control over cholesterol	✓	✓	✓
Perceived control over heart disease	✓	✓	✓
Fatalism about FH	✓	✓	✓
Secondary outcomes			
Smoking	✓		✓
Diet	✓		✓
Exercise	✓		✓
Medication adherence	✓		✓
Emotional state	✓	✓	✓
Illness perceptions		✓	✓
Peceived relative risk of heart attack	✓	✓	✓
Perceived accuracy of diagnosis		✓	✓
Recall of genetic test results		✓	✓

Figure 2 Time points for assessment of outcomes.

Primary outcomes. Perceptions of control were assessed using four internally consistent scales (alphas > 0.70) assessing perceived control over (a) FH, (b) cholesterol, (c) heart disease, and (d) fatalism about FH. The five-item perceived control over FH scale and the six-item fatalism about FH scale were taken from the Revised Illness Perceptions Questionnaire [Moss Morris et al., 2002]. The two-item perceived control over cholesterol and two-item perceived control over heart disease scales were developed in a pilot study specifically for this study.

Secondary outcomes. Risk-reducing behavior. Standardized measures were used to assess self-reports of smoking [Lerman et al., 1997], diet [Roe et al., 1994], activity level [Godin and Shephard, 1985], and cholesterol-lowering medication adherence [Horne and Weinman, 1999].

Illness and treatment perceptions. Perceptions of the importance of genes in controlling cholesterol, and the perceived effectiveness of risk-reduction strategies (lowering cholesterol, dietary intervention, taking medication) were assessed and measured on seven-point response items. The perceived relative risk of a heart attack (relative to someone of the same age, sex, and with a family history of heart disease) was also assessed.

Perceptions of the diagnosis. The perceived accuracy of the diagnosis was assessed on a single seven-point scale ranging from *not at all accurate* to *completely accurate*. Recall of genetic test results was assessed using a checklist.

Emotional state. This was assessed using standardized measures of state anxiety [Marteau and Bekker, 1992] and depression [Zigmond and Snaith, 1983]. The scale range for state anxiety is from 20 to 80, with scores above 49 indicating clinically significant levels of anxiety. The scale range for depression is from 0 to 21, with scores above 10 indicating probable clinical depression.

Analysis

The trial was explanatory in design [Schwartz and Lellouch, 1967], and data analyses were conducted on participants who completed the three postal questionnaires and two behavioral assessments. The generalizability of findings was assessed by comparing (1) attendance versus non-attendance for the diagnostic assessment; and (2) completion versus non-completion of the trial.

Random effects models, with family as the random effect, were used to estimate associations between outcome measures and the results of the genetic testing, namely, mutation found, no mutation found, and non-genetic diagnosis (routine clinical diagnosis). Models were fitted using the "xtreg" command in STATA with the maximum likelihood option [Stata Corporation, 2001]. Analyses were adjusted for baseline scores at recruitment.

Results

Participant flow

Figure 3 shows the flow of participants through the trial.

Overall uptake rate for probands was 68%, comprising 225 (84% uptake) probands recruited at a routine lipid clinic appointment and 116 (50% uptake) probands recruited at a study-specific appointment. The final sample comprised 196 probands who underwent a genetic diagnostic assessment of FH, and 79 probands who underwent a non-genetic diagnostic assessment. Overall uptake rate for eligible relatives was 47% (128/274). Of the relatives who completed the trial, there were 37 in the genetic testing arm of whom 17 (46%) received a diagnosis of FH, and 57 relatives in the non-genetic diagnosis assessment arm of whom 24 (42%) received a diagnosis of FH. The relatives in whom a diagnosis of FH was not made (53/94) were excluded from the analyses reported in this study. Data from the 41 relatives with a diagnosis of FH were combined with those from probands, having checked that the pattern of responses on the main outcomes was similar.

Characteristics of the sample

Sample characteristics are shown in Table I. The randomization was successful: there were no significant differences in demographic, plasma lipids, clinical characteristics, or risk behaviors between the probands randomized to genetic or non-genetic diagnostic assessments.

Participants who did not attend for their results were more likely to be in the non-genetic arm of the trial ($P<0.05$), were younger ($P<0.05$) and more anxious at recruitment ($P<0.01$). There were no other differences. The largest proportion of participants lost to follow-up occurred between 1 week and 6 months. These participants, compared with those who completed the trial, were more likely to be in the genetic diagnosis arm of the trial ($P<0.01$) and, at recruitment, were more fatalistic ($P<0.05$) and perceived less control over heart disease ($P<0.05$).

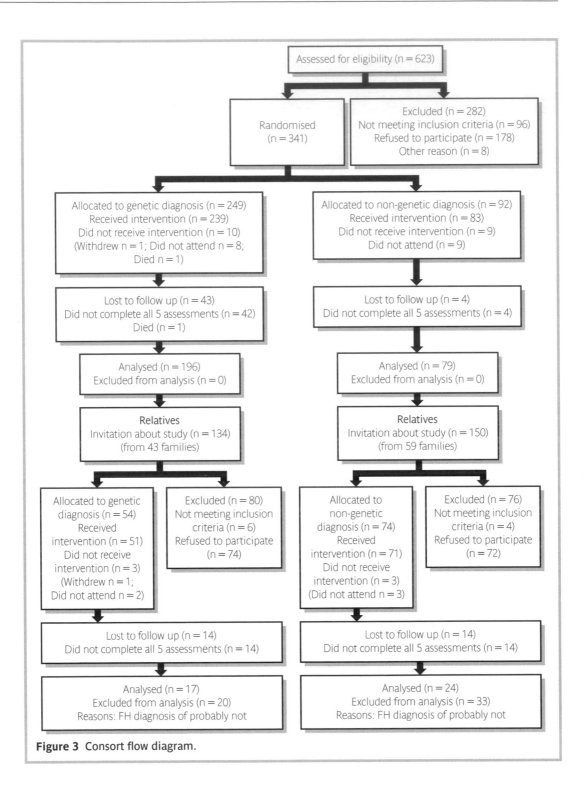

Figure 3 Consort flow diagram.

Table I Demographic characteristics and risk behavior at recruitment of probands and relatives

	Probands		Relatives	
	Genetic diagnosis (n=196)	Non-genetic diagnosis (n=79)	Genetic diagnosis (n=17)	Non-genetic diagnosis (n=24)
Demographic characteristics				
Gender				
Women	54% (105)	61% (48)	59% (10)	71% (17)
Men	46% (95)	39% (31)	41% (7)	29% (7)
Age (year)	56.2 (12.2)	55.9 (11.2)	44.1 (15.6)	48.9 (15.6)
Qualifications				
None	39% (73)	36% (28)	29% (5)	33% (8)
< Degree level	39% (74)	45% (35)	29% (5)	38% (9)
Degree level	22% (22)	18% (14)	41% (7)	29% (7)
Ethnicity				
White	95% (187)	96% (75)	88% (15)	100% (24)
Other	5% (9)	4% (3)	12% (2)	–
Total cholesterol (mmol/l)	6.46 (1.50)	6.23 (1.37)	6.96 (1.31)	6.69 (1.27)
LDL cholesterol (mmol/l)	4.24 (1.56)	3.90 (1.29)	4.75 (1.06)	4.73 (0.99)
Length awareness (month)	118.8 (102.9)	112.8 (85.2)	148.2 (99.2)	150.8 (121.6)
No. with xanthomata	50% (98)	38% (30)	18% (3)	25% (6)
No. with a history of heart events	29% (56)	29% (25)	0% (0)	0% (0)
Risk behavior				
Total fat intake				
Low	87% (171)	72% (57)	88% (15)	92% (22)
Medium	11% (22)	22% (17)	12% (2)	4% (1)
High	2% (3)	6% (5)	–	4% (1)
Unsaturated fat				
Low	1% (1)	3% (2)	–	4% (1)
Medium	17% (33)	24% (19)	12% (2)	8% (2)
High	82% (162)	73% (58)	88% (15)	88% (21)
Frequency of vigorous exercise				
Never/rarely	55% (108)	51% (40)	24% (4)	50% (12)
Sometimes	19% (37)	28% (22)	24% (4)	25% (6)
Often	15% (29)	5% (4)	35% (6)	21% (5)
No. of current smokers	12% (24)	14% (11)	12% (2)	13% (3)
No. prescribed cholesterol-lowering medication	88% (173)	91% (72)	77% (13)	50% (12)

Note: Table presents either percentage (frequency) or mean (standard deviation).

Perceptions of control. As can be seen from Table II, there was no support for the hypothesis that using genetic testing to confirm a diagnosis of FH resulted in lower perceptions of control over FH, cholesterol levels, or heart disease or that it increased perceptions of fatalism about FH.

Those who underwent genetic testing and for whom the mutation search was unsuccessful, perceived FH as less controllable ($P=0.01$) and perceived less control over heart disease ($P=0.03$) 1 week after receiving these results, compared with participants in whom a mutation was found. There were no significant differences between the groups 6 months later.

Risk-reducing behavior. There were no differences in smoking, diet, exercise, and medication adherence among the three groups, 6 months after the diagnostic assessment (see Table I for baseline data).

Table II Effect of genetic test results on perceptions of control: means (standard deviations) at each time point for all participants

	Mutation found (n=74)	No mutation found (n=139)	Non-genetic diagnosis (n=103)	Mutation found versus no mutation found Coefficient (95% CI; P-value)	Mutation found versus non-genetic diagnosis Coefficient (95% CI; P-value)
Perceived fatalism					
Baseline	1.75 (0.54)	1.80 (0.54)	1.72 (0.50)	–	–
One-week follow-up	1.74 (0.56)	1.82 (0.51)	1.78 (0.55)	0.02 (–0.02 to 0.05; 0.31)	0.01 (–0.02 to 0.05; 0.51)
Six-month follow-up	1.78 (0.65)	1.85 (0.52)	1.73 (0.44)	0.02 (–0.02 to 0.05; 0.29)	0.01 (–0.03 to 0.04; 0.75)
Perceived control over FH					
Baseline	4.01 (0.52)	4.07 (0.50)	4.06 (0.43)	–	–
One-week follow-up	4.08 (0.46)	3.95 (0.54)	4.11 (0.42)	0.05 (0.01 to 0.08; 0.01)	–0.01 (–0.05 to 0.034; 0.77)
Six-month follow-up	4.00 (0.63)	3.95 (0.47)	4.05 (0.43)	0.04 (–0.01 to 0.08; 0.10)	–0.00 (–0.05 to 0.05; 0.98)
Perceived control over cholesterol					
Baseline	3.89 (1.10)	4.16 (0.96)	4.17 (0.98)	–	–
One-week follow-up	4.03 (1.25)	4.25 (1.02)	4.21 (1.14)	–0.01 (–0.09 to 0.06; 0.75)	–0.02 (–0.10 to 0.07; 0.72)
Six-month follow-up	4.01 (1.01)	4.09 (1.02)	4.11 (1.11)	0.01 (–0.06 to 0.09; 0.70)	–0.00 (–0.08 to 0.08; 0.94)
Perceived control over heart disease					
Baseline	3.96 (1.13)	3.92 (0.91)	4.01 (0.92)	–	–
One-week follow-up	4.24 (0.84)	3.93 (1.02)	4.22 (0.82)	0.07 (0.01 to 0.14; 0.03)	–0.00 (–0.07 to 0.07; 0.96)
Six-month follow-up	4.01 (0.93)	3.89 (1.00)	3.97 (0.90)	0.02 (–0.05 to 0.10; 0.51)	0.01 (–0.07 to 0.09; 0.81)

Note: Higher scores indicate greater fatalism and greater perceived control over FH, cholesterol, and heart disease.

Illness perceptions. Illness perceptions, perceived relative risk of CHD, and perceptions of the accuracy of the diagnosis of FH are shown in Table III. Both 1 week and 6 months after the diagnostic assessment, participants in whom a mutation for FH was found believed more strongly that their cholesterol levels were controlled by their genetic make-up than either participants in whom no mutation was found, or participants having the non-genetic diagnosis (all $P < 0.01$). While all groups believed that lowering cholesterol was an effective way of reducing the risk of a heart attack, participants in whom a mutation was found believed less strongly in the efficacy of diet in reducing their cholesterol level ($P = 0.02$ at 6 months) and showed a difference of borderline significance in believing more strongly in the efficacy of cholesterol-lowering medication ($P = 0.06$ at 6 months). Perceived relative risk of a heart attack did not differ between groups.

Perceptions of the diagnosis. Participants in whom a mutation for FH was found perceived their diagnoses as more accurate and were more likely to recall correctly their test result (Table III). In this group, correct recall was 99% at 1 week and 100% at 6 months, compared with 87% ($P = 0.01$) and 77% ($P = 0.01$), respectively in those with unsuccessful mutation searches.

Emotional state. Mean levels of anxiety and depression were within the normal ranges for all groups (Table III). Participants in whom a mutation for FH was found were less anxious than the non-genetic diagnosis group 1 week after the diagnostic assessment ($P = 0.03$) but not at 6 months.

Discussion

The primary study hypothesis, that finding a mutation that confirms a clinical diagnosis of familial hypercholesterolemia (FH) reduces perceptions of control over the disease and adherence to risk-reducing behaviors, was not supported.

Perceived control and genetic susceptibility

Since the current trial commenced three other, less powerful studies, have reporting similar findings. One was a small observational study of 30 obese women undergoing testing for the b3-adrenergic reception gene, a gene variant thought to influence weight gain and energy expenditure. Women's confidence in the ability to lose weight was unaffected by knowledge of their genetic status [Harvey-Berino et al., 2001]. The other two studies comprised non-clinically based experimental studies [Hicken and Tucker, 2002; Wright et al., 2003]. An explanation for these findings and those of the current trial is that they reflect the powerful motivation in humans to perceive control over their fates [Malinowski, 1955; DeCharms, 1968]. When new information challenges the extent to which people can control their environment, people are adept at retaining control by altering their perceptions to fit their environment [Rothbaum et al., 1982]. Thus, while fatalism in relation to genetic conditions is common in general populations [Shiloh et al., 2002], those informed of a genetic predisposition do not perceive it as such. When the risk is not modifiable, as is the case for Huntington's disease, learning of the presence of the gene for this dominantly inherited condition does not result in depression or fatalism in the few who undergo such testing [Broadstock et al., 2000a], but rather appears to confer a sense of what has been termed secondary control in allowing the future to be predicted. Similar findings have been reported for predictive genetic testing for Alzheimer's disease [Brown et al., 2002]. When the risk is modifiable, as is the case for FH, learning of a genetic basis to this does not reduce perceptions of control but rather alters perceptions of how the control is most

Table III Impact of genetic diagnosis on illness perceptions, perceived accuracy of diagnosis, and perceived risk

	Mutation found (n=74)	No mutation found (n=139)	Non-genetic diagnosis (n=103)	Mutation found versus no mutation found Coefficient (95% CI; P-value)	Mutation found versus non-genetic diagnosis Coefficient (95% CI; P-value)
Lowering my cholesterol would reduce my risk of a heart attack					
One-week follow-up	5.45 (0.80)	5.45 (0.99)	5.54 (0.74)	−0.01 (−0.26 to 0.24; 0.94)	0.08 (−0.18 to 0.34; 0.54)
Six-month follow-up	5.56 (0.75)	5.56 (0.72)	5.59 (0.70)	0.00 (−0.20 to 0.20; 1.00)	0.03 (−0.19 to 0.25; 0.78)
Eating a lower fat diet would reduce my cholesterol level					
One-week follow-up	4.75 (1.32)	5.10 (1.31)	4.92 (1.33)	0.34 (−0.03 to 0.72; 0.07)	0.17 (−0.22 to 0.57; 0.40)
Six-month follow-up	4.79 (1.34)	5.19 (1.09)	5.08 (1.29)	0.40 (0.05 to 0.75; 0.02)	0.29 (−0.08 to 0.66; 0.12)
Taking medication would reduce my cholesterol level					
One-week follow-up	5.49 (0.71)	5.34 (0.93)	5.36 (0.94)	−0.14 (−0.40 to 0.11; 0.27)	−0.13 (−0.40 to 0.14; 0.34)
Six-month follow-up	5.54 (0.71)	5.31 (0.86)	5.35 (0.93)	−0.24 (−0.48 to 0.01; 0.06)	−0.19 (−0.44 to 0.07; 0.15)
My genetic make-up controls my cholesterol level					
One-week follow-up	4.86 (1.49)	4.32 (1.49)	4.37 (1.47)	−0.53 (−0.96 to −0.10; 0.01)	−0.48 (−0.94 to −0.02; 0.04)
Six-month follow-up	4.99 (1.16)	4.37 (1.47)	4.46 (1.39)	−0.61 (−1.01 to −0.22; 0.00)	−0.52 (−0.94 to −0.10; 0.01)
Perceived accuracy of diagnosis					
One-week follow-up	5.70 (0.54)	4.06 (1.57)	5.07 (0.93)	−1.64 (−1.98 to −1.31; 0.00)	−0.63 (−0.99 to −0.27; 0.00)
Six-month follow-up	5.54 (0.73)	4.41 (1.28)	4.79 (1.21)	−1.13 (−1.45 to −0.80; 0.00)	−0.75 (−1.10 to −0.40; 0.00)
Perceived relative risk of heart attack					
One-week follow-up					
Higher	18% (14)	27% (37)	23% (24)	χ^2=2.20, df=2, P=0.33	χ^2=0.83, df=2, P=0.66
Same	50% (38)	42% (58)	53% (55)	–	–
Lower	32% (24)	31% (43)	23% (24)	–	–
Six-month follow-up					
Higher	19% (14)	26% (36)	24% (24)	χ^2=1.86, df=2, P=0.39	χ^2=0.63, df=2, P=0.73
Same	51% (38)	51% (70)	49% (50)	–	–
Lower	30% (22)	23% (32)	27% (27)	–	–
Anxiety					
One-week follow-up	36.11 (14.12)	35.87 (13.81)	37.67 (12.76)	0.00 (−0.03 to 0.04; 0.88)	0.04 (0.00 to 0.07; 0.03)
Six-month follow-up	35.51 (10.71)	35.90 (13.25)	37.53 (13.07)	−0.01 (−0.04 to 0.03; 0.70)	0.03 (−0.01 to 0.07; 0.12)
Depression					
One-week follow-up	2.44 (2.40)	3.53 (3.58)	3.37 (3.09)	0.06 (−0.00 to 0.07; 0.07)	0.05 (−0.02 to 0.11; 0.16)
Six-month follow-up	2.88 (2.74)	3.57 (3.26)	3.44 (3.23)	0.02 (−0.03 to 0.08; 0.40)	−0.01 (−0.07 to 0.05; 0.84)

Note: Higher scores indicate greater perceived effectiveness of intervention strategies, greater belief that genes control cholesterol, greater perceived accuracy of the diagnosis, and greater anxiety and depression.

effectively achieved. Thus a diagnosis of FH reinforced by genetic testing was perceived as more accurate and seemed to weaken belief in the effectiveness of behavior change, namely altering diet, in reducing cholesterol, with a trend towards reinforcing belief in a biologically based way of reducing cholesterol, namely taking medication. In support of this, analyses of baseline data from this trial show that those who attributed more importance to genes in causing CHD, reported greater adherence to their cholesterol-lowering medication [V. Senior, T.M. Marteau, J. Weinman, unpublished data]. Thus we predict that confirming or making a diagnosis using DNA does not alter perceptions of control but rather alters how control is perceived as most effectively achieved. Evidence to support this hypothesis comes from a study of the impact on perceived control of testing for genetic vulnerability to nicotine addiction [Wright et al., 2003]. In this experimental analog study, smokers who were asked to imagine that they had tested positive for a mutation that confers an inherited predisposition to nicotine addiction did not perceive themselves as having less control over stopping smoking. They were, however, more likely to select the use of a pharmacological agent as effective in assisting quitting and less likely to select the use of willpower. Of concern is the possibility that genetic testing will reinforce biologically based ways of reducing risk when behavioral or environmental change is equally if not more effective.

Mutation searching

Mutation searches were successful in 29% of those with a clinical diagnosis of FH, which is comparable with other studies for FH reported in the UK and is common in the early stages of DNA testing for conditions with large numbers of mutations [Heath et al., 2001]. The pattern of results suggests that a successful search is associated with increased certainty about the diagnosis and with lower short-term levels of anxiety, although no group had clinical levels of anxiety. In contrast, an unsuccessful mutation search resulted in perceiving the diagnosis as less accurate and more difficult to recall. It should be noted, however, that we did not correct for the number of analyses performed. Other studies also suggest that failed mutation searches have psychological costs [Wiggins et al., 1992; Broadstock et al., 2000b]. While there may be clinical and psychological advantages of confirming a diagnosis using DNA, there may be some small, adverse psychological effects of unsuccessful searches. This raises the important question of what proportion of mutation searches need to be successful before they are offered as part of a clinical service.

Generalizability of the results

The study sample comprised families with a known predisposition to CHD. They were thus already aware of their genetic vulnerability to CHD. In addition, they had had experience of treatment that was effective in reducing high levels of cholesterol. Thus, their experience was of a genetic condition that can be controlled, as illustrated in a qualitative study in this sample of patients [Senior et al., 2002].

Furthermore, their self-reported dietary fat intake and smoking status showed them to have healthier lifestyles than a general population sample [Imperial Cancer Research Fund OXCHECK Study Group, 1991]. While the current study had sufficient power to detect a medium effect of genetic testing upon the main outcomes, it had insufficient power to detect this in relatives alone, particularly those very few who were unaware of their risks prior to this study. It remains to be determined whether the same pattern of results would occur in general population testing, or in testing at-risk groups where there is low awareness of CHD and its prevention.

Generalizability of the findings will be influenced by the fact that not all those invited to participate in the trial chose to do so. For those who did participate non-attendance for diagnosis were more likely among more anxious participants. Loss to follow-up was greater in those allocated to the genetic diagnosis trial arm. Their higher levels of fatalism and lower perceived control at recruitment suggest that these differences were exacerbated by participation in the trial, an effect that may have resulted in their dropout. It, therefore, remains an open question as to whether there is a small group of patients who will respond negatively to genetic testing.

Acknowledgments

The study was funded by The Wellcome Trust as part of a programme grant (No: 037006: Principal Investigator: Theresa Marteau). Steve Humphries is funded by the British Heart Foundation (RG2000015 RG95007 and RG93008). Richard Savine was supported by Pfizer (Parke-Davis) Ltd. Patients' and relatives' travelling expenses were paid through an unrestricted educational grant from Merck Sharp & Dohme. The authors are grateful to Martin Gulliford for statistical advice, to Fred Kavalier for comments on an earlier draft of this paper, to Margaret Thorogood and Andrew Neil for their work on the data monitoring committee, and to Kay Fearon for secretarial support at all stages of the trial.

References

Blaxter M, Paterson E. 1982. Mothers and daughters: A three generational study of health attitudes and behaviour. London: Heinemann Education Books.

Broadstock M, Michie S, Marteau T. 2000a. The psychological consequences of predictive genetic testing: A systematic review. Eur J Hum Genet 8:731–738.

Broadstock M, Michie S, Gray J, Mackay J, Marteau TM. 2000b. The psychological consequences of offering mutation searching in the family for those at risk of hereditary breast and ovarian cancer – A pilot study. Psycho-Oncology 9:537–548.

Brown T, Roberts S, LaRusse S, Barber M, Relkin N, Whitehouse P, Post S, Sadovnick AD, Quaid K, Ravdin L, Green R. 2002. Impact of genetic risk assessment for Alzheimer's disease. J Genet Counsel 11:446–447.

DeCharms R. 1968. Personal causation. New York: Academic Press.

Durrington PN.2001. Rigorous detection and vigorous treatment of familial hypercholesterolaemia. Lancet 357(9256):574–575.

Godin G, Shephard RJ. 1985. A simple method to assess exercise behavior in the community. Can J Appl Sport Sci 10:141–146.

Harvey-Berino JE, Casey Gold E, Smith West D, Shuldiner AR, Walston J, Starling RD, Nolan A, Silver K, Poehlman ET.2001. Does genetic testing for obesity influence confidence in the ability to lose weight: A pilot investigation. J Am Diet Assoc 101:1351–1353.

Heath KE, Humphries SE, Middleton-Price H, Boxer M. 2001. A molecular genetic service for diagnosing individuals with familial hypercholesterolaemia (FH). Eur J Hum Genet 9:244–252.

Hicken B, Tucker D. 2002. Impact of genetic risk feedback: Perceived risk and motivation for health protective behaviours. Psychol Health Med 7:725–736.

Horne R, Weinman J. 1999. Patients' beliefs about prescribed medicines and their role in adherence to treatment in chronic physical illness. J Psychosom Res 47:555–567.

Hunt K, Emslie C, Watt G. 2000. Barriers rooted in biography: How interpretations of family patterns of heart disease and early life experiences may undermine behavioural change in mid-life. In: Graham H, editor. Understanding Health Inequalities. Buckingham: Open University Press.

Imperial Cancer Research Fund OXCHECK Study Group. 1991. Prevalence of risk factors for heart disease in OXCHECK trial: Implications for screening in primary care. Br Med J 302:1057–1060.

Koivisto PVI, Koivisto U-M, Miettinen TA, Kontula K. 1992. Diagnosis of heterozygous familial hypercholesterolaemia. DNA analysis complements clinical examination and analysis of serum lipid levels. Arterioscler Thromb 12:584–592.

Lerman C, Gold K, Boyd NR, Orleans CT, Wilfond B, Louben G, Caporaso N. 1997. Incorporating biomarkers of exposure and genetic susceptibility into smoking cessation treatment: Effects of smoking-related cognitions, emotions, and behavior. Health Psychol 16:87–99.

Malinowski B. 1955. Magic, science, and religion. New York: Anchor Books.

Mamotte CDS, van Bockxmeer FM. 1993. A robust strategy for screening and confirmation of familial defective apolipoprotein B100. Clin Chem 39:118–121.

Marteau TM. 1995. Towards an understanding of the psychological consequences of screening. In: Croyle RT, editor. Psychosocial effects of screening for disease prevention and detection. New York: Oxford University Press. p 185–199.

Marteau TM, Bekker H. 1992. The development of a six-item short-form of the state scale of the Spielberger State-Trait Anxiety Inventory (STAI). Br J Clin Psychol 31:301–306.

McClure JB. 2002. Are biomarkers useful treatment aids for promoting health behavior change? An empirical review. Am J Prev Med 22:200–207.

Milne S, Sheeran P, Orbell S. 2000. Prediction and intervention in health related behavior: A meta-analytic review of protection motivation theory. J Appl Soc Psychol 30:106–143.

Moss Morris R, Weinman J, Petrie KJ, Horne R, Cameron LD, Buick D. 2002. The Revised Illness Perception Questionnaire (IPQ-R). Psychol Health 17:1–16.

Myant NB. 1993. Familial defective apolipoprotein B-100: A review, including some comparisons with familial hypercholesterolaemia. Atherosclerosis 104:1–18.

Nelkin D, Lindee MS. 1995. The DNA mystique. New York: WH Freeman & Company.

Roe L, Strong C, Whiteside C, Neil A, Mant D. 1994. Dietary intervention in primary care: Validity of the DINE method for dietary assessment. Fam Pract 11:375–381.

Rothbaum F, Weisz JR, Snyder SS. 1982. Changing the world and changing the self: A two-process model of perceived control. J Pers Soc Psychol 42:5–37.

Schwartz D, Lellouch J. 1967. Explanatory and pragmatic attitudes in therapeutic trials. J Chronic Dis 20:127–134.

Senior V, Marteau TM, Peters TJ. 1999. Will genetic testing for predisposition for disease result in fatalism? A qualitative study of parents responses to neonatal screening for familial hypercholesterolaemia. Soc Sci Med 48:1857–1860.

Senior V, Smith JA, Michie S, Marteau TM. 2002. Making sense of risk: An interpretative phenomenological analysis of vulnerability to heart disease. J Health Psychol 7:157–168.

Shiloh S, Rashuk-Rosenthal D, Benyamini Y. 2002. Illness causal attributions: An exploratory study of their structure and associations with other illness cognitions and perceptions of control. J Behav Med 25:373–394.

Simon Broome Steering Committee. 1991. Risk of fatal coronary heart disease in familial hypercholesterolaemia. Scientific Steering Committee on behalf of the Simon Broome Register Group. Br Med J 303:893–896.

Simon Broome Steering Committee. 1999. Steering committee on behalf of the Simon Broome Register Group. Mortality in treated heterozygous familial hypercholesterolaemia: Implications for clinical management. Atherosclerosis 142:105–112.

Stata Corporation. 2001. Stata release 7. Vol. 4. Su-Z. College Station, Texas: Stata Press. p 434–455.

Ward AJ, O'Kane M, Nicholls DP, Young IS, Nevin N, Graham CA. 1996. A novel single base deletion in the LDLR gene (211 del G). Effect on serum lipid profiles and the influence of other genetic polymorphisms in the ACE, APOE and APOB genes. Atherosclerosis 120:83–91.

Wiggins S, Whyte P, Huggins M, Adam S, Theilmann J, Bloch M, Sheps SB, Schechter MT, Hayden MR. 1992. The psychological consequences of predictive testing for Huntington's disease. N Engl J Med 327:1401–1405.

Wright AJ, Weinman J, Marteau TM. 2003. The impact of learning of a genetic vulnerability to nicotine addiction: An analogue study. Tob Control 12:227–230.

Zigmond AS, Snaith RP. 1983. The Hospital Anxiety and Depression Scale. Acta Psychiatr Scand 67:361–370.

Illness cognitions

As an individual moves along the continuum from health to illness, the ways in which they think about their health can impact upon a range of factors including communication, adherence to medication, willingness to attend a clinic, motivation to change their health-related behaviour or their levels of adjustment, coping and well-being. Much of this has been studied within health psychology with a focus on illness cognitions, particularly drawing upon the self-regulatory model. The following two papers have been selected to illustrate the role of beliefs and behaviour in the context of adherence:

Horne, R. and Weinman, J. (2002) Self-regulation and self-management in asthma: exploring the role of illness perceptions and treatment beliefs in explaining non-adherence to preventer medication, *Psychology and Health*, 17 (1): 17–32. Reprinted with kind permission of the Taylor & Francis Group.

Simpson, S.H., Eurich, D.T., Majumdar, S.R. et al. (2006) A meta-analysis of the association between adherence to drug therapy and mortality, *British Medical Journal*, 1 July, 333 (7557): 15–20. Reprinted with kind permission of the BMJ Publishing Group.

Within a self-regulatory framework, illness cognitions are described as predicting illness behaviours. In line with many studies in this field, Horne and Weinman (2002) test the self-regulatory model and present a study designed to explore the role of beliefs about asthma in predicting adherence to medication. In addition, this paper presents an interesting extension of the model and explores the extent to which treatment beliefs interact with illness cognitions and also relate to adherence. From this perspective, adherence, but also behaviours such as changes in diet, smoking or exercise, are more likely to occur if beliefs about treatment (i.e. does the treatment work, does it have side effects) are in line with beliefs about the illness (i.e. is it serious, how long will it last). Since the publication of this paper, research has built upon this idea and has emphasised the importance of a 'goodness of fit' between these different sets of cognitions. This paper provides a useful analysis of the self-regulatory model, and the measures of illness cognitions, treatment beliefs and adherence are described in a detailed and clear way. In addition, the paper presents an accessible description of structural equation modelling and how it can be used to build theory. Finally, the paper shows how research can be based on a theory but that, rather than simply testing that theory, the theory can be challenged and developed in useful ways.

The final paper in this section on health care is by Simpson et al. (2006) and is a meta-analysis of the effect of adherence on mortality. Much medical research emphasises how drugs can improve a patient's health status. Health psychology contributes to this literature by highlighting that even if the drug works, the patient has to take it for it to be effective. From this perspective adherence is treated as the dependent variable and health psychologists describe why patients do or do not take their medication and how they could be encouraged to do so. In contrast, Simpson et al. (2006) place adherence as the independent variable and suggest that the process of adherence itself, regardless of whether the drug actually works or not, may be linked to health status and mortality; in parallel to a placebo effect, taking a drug (of any sort) can be a helpful thing to do. This raises many new questions for health psychologists such as 'how can adherence in itself be beneficial?', 'what mechanisms are involved?', 'does taking a drug reflect a person's beliefs or does it change their beliefs?', 'could taking a drug influence an individual's physiology, even if that drug is a placebo?'. This paper is therefore interesting in many ways. Methodologically, it provides insights into the process of meta-analysis and shows how different studies can be synthesised. Theoretically, it offers up a new phenomenon which comes with a wealth of new research questions, all of which are at the centre of the discipline of health psychology. If adherence itself is related to mortality then an understanding of the many ways in which the mind and body are related, whether it be through cognitions, behaviour or physiology, must be core to understanding this association. Finally, this section has focused on health care. Adherence (and the placebo effect) are central to the health-care process and have a role to play at each stage as a person moves along the continuum from health to illness.

This section therefore focuses on health care in terms of communication and illness cognitions and the papers selected draw upon a range of perspectives, methodologies and theories to illustrate the place of health psychology in understanding the processes evoked as an individual interacts with a health-care system.

Horne, R. and Weinman, J. (2002) Self-regulation and self-management in asthma: exploring the role of illness perceptions and treatment beliefs in explaining non-adherence to preventer medication, *Psychology and Health*, 17 (1): 17–32.

Self-regulation and self-management in asthma

Exploring the role of illness perceptions and treatment beliefs in explaining non-adherence to preventer medication

Robert Horne[a,*] and John Weinman[b]

[a]Centre for Health Care Research, University of Brighton, I Great Wilkins, Falmer, Brighton, BNI 9PH, United Kingdom; [b]Psychology Unit, 5th Floor, Thomas Guy House, GKT Guys Campus, London, SEI 8RT, United Kingdom

Abstract

The present study was designed to evaluate the degree to which variations in reported adherence to preventer medication for asthma could be explained by two sets of beliefs: perceptions of asthma and perceptions of asthma medication (beliefs about its *necessity* and *concerns* over its use). It also begins the empirical testing of an extended self regulatory model, which includes treatment beliefs as well as illness perceptions. Using a cross-sectional design, 100 community-based patients completed validated questionnaires assessing their perceptions of asthma, beliefs about preventer inhalers and reported adherence to them. The findings showed that non-adherent behaviours were associated with doubts about the *necessity* of medication and *concerns* about its potential adverse effects and with more negative perceived *consequences* of illness. A hierarchical linear regression analysis revealed that socio-demographic and clinical factors explained only a small amount of variance in adherence whereas illness perceptions and treatment beliefs were both more substantial independent predictors. The best fit Amos analysis showed that illness perceptions influenced adherence both directly and indirectly via treatment beliefs, which, in turn, were the strongest predictors. The findings lend preliminary support for an extended self-regulatory model of treatment adherence, which incorporates beliefs about treatment as well as illness perceptions.

Keywords: Illness perceptions; Treatment beliefs; Asthma; Adherence; Preventer medication; Self-management

Introduction

It is estimated that over 150 million people worldwide have asthma (National Institute of Health, 1995). Approximately 3.5 million people in the UK alone suffer from asthma symptoms and the costs of asthma are high for patients, their carers and the health care system (National

* Corresponding author. Tel.: 00 44 1273 643985. Fax: 00 44 1273 643986.
E-mail: r.horne@brighton.ac.uk

Asthma Campaign, 1999). In asthma, good self-management is crucial, not only for dealing with symptoms, but also for preventing asthma attacks and related complications (Hand, 1998; Kaptein, 1997). Treatment usually combines two therapeutic modalities: 'reliever' medication for symptom relief during an asthma attack, and 'preventer' medication, which is designed to reduce the likelihood of an attack (Holgate, 1998). Both treatments are usually administered as dry powder or aerosol inhalers but need to be used in different ways. Reliever medication is usually prescribed on a 'use when necessary' basis and patients are often encouraged to adjust their dosage in response to symptoms. In contrast, preventer medication is prescribed to be taken regularly (typically twice a day) and usually contains a corticosteroid (British Thoracic Society, 1997).

Over the last decade, the emphasis in asthma care has shifted from symptom relief to the prevention of exacerbations and for many patients inhaled corticosteroids form the mainstay of their asthma treatment (Hand, 1998). However, adherence rates to preventer medication are often low (Rand and Wise, 1994) and this can result in increased morbidity (Horn, Clark and Cochrane, 1990) and mortality (British Thoracic Society, 1982). Thus, facilitating adherence to asthma prevention therapy is an important target in asthma care (Hand, 1998), which has been characterised by the development of self-management programmes (SMPs). A recent systematic review concluded that 'training in asthma self-management which involves self-monitoring by either peak expiratory flow or symptoms, coupled with regular medical review and written action plans, appears to improve health outcomes for adults with asthma' (Gibson *et al.*, 2000). However, other commentators have raised concerns about the content of SMPs (Clark and Nothwehr, 1997; Fay and Jones, 2000; Hand, 1998; Jones *et al.*, 2000). Most SMPs emphasise the didactic transfer of information and skills with little attempt to take account of patients' preferences or their views about asthma and self-management programmes. Recent work on patient information provision has recognised the limitations of a 'one size fits all' approach and the need to develop tailored approaches that take account of patients' beliefs, expectations and preferences (Kreuter *et al.*, 1999).

The benefits of existing self-management programmes in asthma might be enhanced by a better understanding of the types of beliefs that are associated with low adherence to preventer medication. The self-regulatory model (SRM) was formulated to explain illness-related behaviour, including adherence to treatment recommendations within the context of chronic illness (Leventhal *et al.*, 1992). In this context, adherence to treatment is viewed as one of a number of procedures that the patient can adopt to 'cope' with their illness. In the SRM, the patient is conceptualised as an 'active problem solver' whose coping behaviour (e.g., taking or not taking medication) represents a 'common sense' response to their cognitive and emotional interpretation of experiences (e.g., symptoms) or information (e.g., receiving a medical diagnosis). Continuation of the behaviour is dependent upon an appraisal of whether it has worked. The SRM also emphasises the importance of concrete symptom experiences in formulating representations and guiding appraisal of the efficacy of coping. Perceptions of the illness drive coping and subsequent appraisal and the question of how people conceptualise their illness is central to the SRM. Leventhal and colleagues suggest that illness representations are structured around five components. These are beliefs about the nature (*identity*), likely time-course (*timeline*), personal impact (*consequences*), causal factors (*cause*) and amenability to control or cure (*control/cure*).

Despite a cogently argued rationale for the study of illness perceptions as determinants of treatment adherence (Leventhal and Cameron, 1987; Leventhal *et al.*, 1992), relatively few studies have utilised this approach. However, there is some empirical support for the utility of self-regulatory theory in explaining adherence decisions. Illness perceptions were related to medication adherence in hypertension (Meyer *et al.*, 1985) and regimen adherence in diabetes (Gonder-Frederick and Cox, 1991). In separate prospective studies, adherence to recommendations to attend rehabilitation classes following a first myocardial infarction was predicted by illness perceptions (*identity, consequences* and *control/cure*) elicited during hospital convalescence (Cooper *et al.*, 1999; Petrie *et al.*, 1996).

It has been suggested that the ability of the SRM to explain treatment adherence may be enhanced by extending its scope to focus on specific treatment beliefs (Horne, 1997). It is likely that self-regulating patients will not just have their own ideas about the illness, but also about the treatment being offered. In deciding whether to adhere to a treatment schedule, the patient has to think not only about whether the illness warrants treatment but also about whether the treatment is appropriate for their illness. In particular, it is proposed that adherence decisions are influenced by an interaction of personal beliefs about the *necessity* of the treatment for maintaining or improving health and *concerns* about the potential adverse effects of adhering to it. Thus, the *necessity* and *concerns* constructs offer a means of operationalising some of the perceived benefits and costs associated with the adherence to treatment recommendations (Horne *et al.*, 1999). In a recent study involving patients from several illness groups (asthma, diabetes, cardiac disease and cancer), reported non-adherence was related to doubts about the *necessity* of prescribed medication and to *concerns* about potential adverse effects (Horne and Weinman, 1999).

Although studies have evaluated the separate roles of illness perceptions and treatment beliefs in adherence, as yet no published studies have explored the interaction between these two sets of beliefs. We have previously argued that beliefs about treatment *necessity* are directly related to perceptions of the illness. For example, patients who perceive their asthma to be an acute condition with minimal personal consequences may be less likely to perceive the need for regular use of the preventer inhaler, even if they believe that such treatments are effective (Horne and Weinman, 1998). While *necessity* beliefs are linked to illness perceptions, *concerns* are more likely to reflect perceptions and experiences of classes of treatment (Horne *et al.*, 1999). Previous studies have demonstrated the utility of patients' perceptions of respiratory problems in explaining variations in coping behaviour and outcome (Scharloo *et al.*, 2000) and have shown that low rates of adherence to asthma medication is related to concerns about the potential adverse effects of asthma medication (Hand and Bradley, 1996; Horne and Weinman, 1999). However, no published studies have evaluated the relative contribution of illness perceptions and treatment beliefs (necessity beliefs and concerns about preventer inhalers) in explaining non-adherence to preventer medication for asthma.

The present study was designed to evaluate the degree to which variations in reported adherence to preventer medication for asthma could be explained by two sets of beliefs: perceptions of asthma and perceptions of asthma medication (beliefs about its *necessity* and *concerns* over its use). It also begins the empirical testing of an extended self-regulatory model, which includes treatment beliefs as well as illness perceptions.

Hypothesis 1 Adherence to preventer medication will be related to treatment beliefs. It will be positively correlated with patients' perceptions of the necessity for preventer medication and negatively correlated with concerns about potential adverse effects.

Hypothesis 2 Patients' perceptions of the seriousness of their asthma (timeline and consequences) will influence their beliefs about the necessity of prescribed medication but not their concerns about potential adverse effects.

Hypothesis 2 arises from our expectation that patients' perceptions of their illness and beliefs about treatment will be related in a logically consistent way. Patients' beliefs about the necessity of their preventer medication are likely to be influenced by their perceptions of asthma. For example, patients may be more reluctant to accept the necessity of regular use of asthma preventers if they perceive their asthma to have few adverse consequences or to be a problem that is neither chronic nor consistently troublesome. However, medication concerns (e.g., worries about the potential side effects of corticosteroids or dependence) are more likely to arise from beliefs about the nature of medicines in general or from past experience of particular medicines than from views about illness (Horne, 1997). We will test the extent to which the data match the predicted relations between illness perceptions, treatment beliefs and reported adherence specified within the extended SRM, using structural equation modelling.

Hypothesis 3 Treatment beliefs will add to the proportion of variance in adherence that is explained by demographic variables, clinical factors and illness perceptions.

Method
Design and procedure

This was a cross-sectional study in which patients attending community based asthma clinics completed validated questionnaires assessing perceptions of asthma and beliefs about the necessity of preventer medication and their concerns about potential adverse effects of taking it. Adherence to preventer medication was assessed by patients' self report. Consecutive attenders at asthma clinics in two general practice surgeries in Mid Sussex were approached with the aim of recruiting a sample of 100. One hundred participants were recruited from 119 approaches, an acceptance rate of 84%. Most of the asthma clinics were run by practice nurses but a few were run by the general practitioners. A trained researcher invited patients to participate in a study of 'patients' views about asthma and its treatment'. Patients were eligible to take part if they had been given a confirmed diagnosis of asthma (obtained from the medical notes) and had been receiving preventer medication (corticosteroid inhaler) for a period of at least one month prior to attendance at the clinic. Patients were excluded from the study if they had noticeable difficulty in reading and understanding the study questionnaire. Those who agreed to take part were asked to complete the study questionnaire while waiting to see the practice nurse or doctor.

Measures
Illness Perceptions Questionnaire (IPQ) (Weinman et al., 1996)

The IPQ comprises five scales assessing the five dimensions underlying patients' models of illness (Leventhal and Nerenz, 1985). The IPQ has proven validity and reliability across a range of illness groups including asthma (Weinman *et al.,* 1996). The scales of the IPQ are described below.

Identity This was assessed by the number of symptoms that the patients endorse as being part of their asthma from a list of 14 symptoms. This list includes general symptoms such as aching joints and sleep difficulties as well as those which are commonly associated with asthma such as tight chest, wheezing and breathlessness.

Causal beliefs Patients' ideas about what caused their asthma were assessed by the degree to which they endorsed each of 10 causal items (pollution, heredity, chance, stress, own behaviour, other people, poor medical care, diet, my state of mind, and germ or virus). Responses were scores on a 5-point Likert-type scale (where 1 = strongly disagree, 2 = disagree, 3 = uncertain, 4 = agree, and 5 = strongly agree). Responses were re-coded on the basis of whether the patient endorsed each item as a cause of their asthma (where agree/strongly agree = 1 and uncertain/disagree/strongly disagree = 0). In this way, it was possible to identify which causal beliefs were endorsed by each patient as well as the number of causal attributions they perceived.

Timeline Personal ideas about the likely duration of the asthma were assessed by a 3-item 5-point Likert-type scale, ranging from strongly disagree to strongly agree. Total scores ranged from 3 to 15 with higher scores signifying a belief that the illness was chronic in nature. An example of an item on this scale is '*My asthma will last a long time*'.

Consequences Beliefs about the personal consequences and outcomes of asthma were assessed using a 9-item 5-point Likert-type scale, ranging from strongly disagree to strongly agree. Total scores ranged from 9 to 45 with higher scores indicating the perception of more serious consequences. Examples of items are '*My asthma is a serious condition*' and '*My asthma will have major consequences on my life*'.

Cure/Control Beliefs about the extent to which the asthma can be controlled or cured were assessed using a 6-item 5-point Likert-type scale, ranging from strongly disagree to strongly agree. Total scores ranged from 6 to 30 with higher scores indicating stronger beliefs that the illness can be controlled or cured. Examples of items are '*There is a lot I can do to control my symptoms*' and '*What I do can determine whether my illness gets better or worse*'.

To facilitate comparison between the *timeline, consequences* and *cure/control* scales, mean item scores were computed by dividing the total scale score by the number of items in the scale, giving a range of 1 to 5 for each.

Beliefs about Medicines Questionnaire (BMQ) (Horne et al., 1999)

Patients' beliefs about their inhaled preventer medication were assessed using the BMQ which has been validated for use in asthma samples. The BMQ comprises two scales: one assessing patients' beliefs about the necessity of preventer medication for controlling their asthma and the other assessing their concerns about the potential adverse consequences of using it. Each scale has five core items assessing beliefs that have been shown to be common across a range of chronic illness groups. Examples of items from the *necessity* scale are '*My health, at present, depends on this medicine*' and '*This medicine protects me from becoming worse*'. Examples of items from the *concerns* scale are '*I sometimes worry about the long term effects of this medicine*' and '*I sometimes worry about becoming too dependent on this medicine*'. Six asthma-specific items were added as recommended in the literature (Horne *et al.*, 1999) including '*This inhaler is harmless*' (reverse scored), '*I am concerned that this inhaler will be less effective if I use it regularly*' and '*People who use these inhalers should stop their treatment every now and again*'. One extra asthma-specific necessity item was also added ('*This inhaler is the most important part of my asthma treatment*'). Internal reliability data for these enlarged scales are shown in the Results section.

Respondents indicate their degree of agreement with each individual statement about medicines on a 5-point Likert-type scale (ranging from 1 = strongly disagree to 5 = strongly agree). Scores obtained for the individual items within each scale are summed to give a scale score. Thus, total scores ranged from 6 to 30 for the *necessity* scale and from 11 to 55 for the *concerns* scale. In order to facilitate comparison between scales, a mean item score was computed by dividing each scale score by the number of items, giving a range of 1 to 5. Scores can be interpreted in two ways: as a continuous scale where higher scores indicate stronger beliefs in the concepts represented by the scale, or by dichotomising at the scale mid-point. The latter method is a convenient way of categorising respondents according to the strength of their views about medication. However, the continuous scale was used in the statistical analyses as this provides richer information that is lost when the scale is dichotomised (Oppenheim, 1992).

Medication adherence

Adherence to medication was assessed using a 9-item Medication Adherence Report Scale (MARS) that elicits patients' reports of non-adherence; an approach that has been validated in previous studies (Kravitz *et al.*, 1993; Rand and Wise, 1994). The MARS items are shown in Table IV. In order to diminish the social pressure on patients to report high adherence, questions were phrased in a non-threatening manner and patients were assured that their responses would be anonymous and confidential, as recommended in the literature (Rand and Wise, 1994). The following statement prefaced the MARS items: '*Many people find a way of using their medicines which suits them. This may differ from the instructions on the label or from what their doctor had said. Here are some ways in which people have said they use their medicines. For each statement, please tick the box which best applies to you*'. Patients were asked to rate the frequency with which they engaged in each of the nine aspects of non-adherent behaviour, rated on 5-point scale (where 5=never, 4=rarely, 3=sometimes, 2=often and 1=very often). Scores for each item were summed to give a total score ranging from 9 to 45, where higher scores indicate higher levels of reported adherence. By focussing on specific aspects of non-adherence, the items challenge respondents to recall and report acts that obstruct the use of preventer medication, in contrast to focussing on adherence, which emphasises compliance with practitioner instruction. This technique has been used to elicit reports of non-adherence in previous work (Leventhal *et al.*, 1984). Adherence was measured as a continuous scale, as recommended in the literature, rather than as a dichotomous division into adherent/non-adherent categories (Oppenheim, 1992). This method of quantifying self-report has been validated by comparing reported adherence with tablet-count (Haynes *et al.*, 1980) and clinical outcome measures (Morisky *et al.*, 1986).

Statistical methods

Statistical analysis was carried out using the SPSS for Windows statistical software package. Examination of the distributions of the illness perception and treatment belief sub-scale scores showed that the data was suitable for parametric analysis. Group comparisons of reported adherence between patients endorsing or not endorsing each of the 10 possible causes of asthma were examined using independent sample *t*-tests. Relationships between illness perceptions, beliefs about medication and adherence were examined using Pearson correlation coefficients. The relative contribution of different predictors of reported adherence was evaluated using hierarchical linear regression analysis. Reported adherence to medication scores were entered as the dependent variable with groups of independent variables entered in the following order: demographic variables (gender, age, and educational status), clinical factors (number of visits to the family doctor and asthma-related hospital admissions in the previous year, duration of asthma), illness perceptions (*identity, timeline, consequences* and *control/cure*) and beliefs about medication (*necessity* and *concerns*).

The Amos structural equation modelling application (Arbuckle, 1997) was used to perform a path analysis to examine the structure of the relationships between illness perceptions, medication beliefs and self-reported adherence.

Results

Participants

Table I shows the demographic information and illness features of the participants. The sample represented a broad range of age and educational experience. The patients varied widely in the duration of their asthma from just under a year to 68 years with a mean of 22.4 years (SD = 18.8). The majority of the sample (67%) had made at least one asthma-related visit to their family doctor over the previous six months, and the mean number of family doctor visits was 1.53 (SD = 2.12). Only 10 patients had been admitted to hospital during that period (nine had been admitted on one occasion and one patient had been admitted twice). In this respect, the sample was typical of community managed asthma.

Perceptions of illness and beliefs about preventer medication

The descriptive statistics and Cronbach alpha values for all scales are shown in Table II. The internal reliability of each of the scales was acceptable with the exception of the IPQ *cure/control* scale ($\alpha = 0.50$).

The BMQ *necessity* and *concerns* scores were all normally distributed with a wide variation in the perceived benefits and costs of preventer medication. The percentage of patients scoring above the scale mid-point for each of the illness perception and medication belief scales is also shown in Table II. This provides an indication of the proportion of patients holding particularly strong views about the construct being measured by each particular scale. Most patients saw their asthma as a chronic condition (with 85% scoring greater mid-point on the IPQ *timeline* scale), a similar proportion felt that they could do much to control the illness, but only a quarter of the sample perceived their asthma as having particularly severe consequences. While most patients agreed that their preventer medication was necessary, 15% of the sample did not

Table I Demographic information and illness features (N = 100)

Gender (% female)	61
Age	
Mean	49.3
SD	18.1
Range	16.0 – 84.0
Duration of asthma (years)	
Mean	22.4
SD	18.8
Range	0.9 – 68
Educational status (%)	
Secondary	55
Tertiary	34
Higher	11
Number of reported visits to family doctor in last 6 months	
Mean	1.6
SD	2.1
Median	1.0
Range	0 – 15
Reported admissions to hospital in last year	
Mean	0.11
SD	0.34
Median	0.0
Range	0 – 2

Table II Scale descriptives

Scale	Number of items in scale	Cronbach's alpha	Mean	SD	Percentage scoring above scale mid-point
Illness Identity	14	0.75	5.75	2.78	NA
Illness Timeline	3	0.80	3.72	0.84	85
Illness Consequences	7	0.73	2.55	0.64	26
Illness Cure/Control	5	0.50	3.41	0.48	87
Treatment Necessity	6	0.82	3.56	0.65	85
Treatment Concerns	11	0.71	2.60	0.53	23
MARS	9	0.85	4.20	0.71	NA

Note: MARS = Medication Adherence Report Scale.

hold this view. Twenty three percent of patients has strong concerns about preventer medication. However, examination of the distribution of scores on individual items on the *concerns* scale showed that worries about the potential long-term effects and perceived risk of dependence were particularly prevalent. Forty-eight percent of the sample agreed with the statement '*I sometimes worry about the long-term effects of preventer medication*', and 37% agreed with the statement '*I sometimes worry about becoming too dependent on this inhaler*'.

Causal beliefs

The percentage of participants who endorsed each of the 10 possible causes for their asthma is shown in Table III. The most commonly endorsed causes were pollution of the environment, heredity, chance/fate and stress. Investigation of the relations between individual causal beliefs and other variables was limited to these four causal beliefs on the grounds that they were the only ones endorsed by more than 10% of the participants. Independent sample *t*-tests showed that none of these four causal beliefs were significantly related to illness perception scales, medication beliefs, reported adherence or general health status.

Participants endorsed relatively few causal beliefs (Mean = 1.78, SD = 1.28). Correlations between the number of causal beliefs endorsed by patients and other illness perceptions, treatment beliefs and reported adherence are shown in Table V. Although the number of causal beliefs endorsed was significantly correlated with illness *identity* ($r = 0.23$, $p < 0.05$), *consequences* ($r = 0.28$, $p < 0.01$) and *cure/control* ($r = 0.23$, $p < 0.05$), no significant correlations were found

Table III Causal attributions for asthma

Causal agent	Percentage of sample endorsing causal agent
Pollution of the environment	46
Heredity (asthma runs in the family)	42
Chance or fate	30
Stress	18
Own behaviour	10
Germ or virus	10
Other people	7
Poor medical care in the past	6
Diet	5
My state of mind	5

between the number of causal beliefs and patients' views about preventer medication or reported adherence to it. In view of these findings and the lack of significant relations between causal beliefs and other variables, these were omitted from the hierarchical regression analysis of predictors of reported adherence.

Illness perceptions and health care utilisation

IPQ identity scores were positively correlated with the number of asthma-related visits to the general practitioner (GP) over the previous six months ($r=0.39$, $p<0.01$). No other study variables were associated with the frequency of GP visits. As only eight patients reported an asthma-related admission to hospital during the previous year, the analysis of factors related to health care utilisation was limited to the frequency of asthma related visits to the GP.

Reported adherence to medication

Scores on the MARS were positively skewed (Mean$=4.20$, SD$=0.71$). The percentage of participants who reported that they engaged in each aspect of non-adherent behavior represented by the nine items of the scale is shown in Table IV.

Most patients (73.2%) reported that they sometimes, often or always engaged in one or more of the nine aspects of non-adherence assessed by the MARS. Patients endorsed a mean of 2.28 (SD$=2.41$) aspects of non-adherence (i.e., reporting that they engaged in the behaviour sometimes, often or always).

Testing the study hypotheses

Hypothesis 1   Adherence to preventer medication will be related to treatment beliefs. It will be positively correlated with patients' perceptions of the necessity for preventer medication and negatively correlated with concerns about potential adverse effects.

Reported adherence to preventer medication was found to correlate significantly with necessity beliefs ($r=0.32$, $p<0.01$) and *concerns* about potential adverse effects ($r=-0.43$, $p<0.001$), thus confirming hypothesis 1. Patients who has a strong belief in the necessity of taking their medication reported less non-adherence, whereas those who had greater concerns about their preventer medicine reported lower adherence.

Table IV Responses to individual items on the Medication Adherence Report Scale (MARS)

Type of non-adherent behaviour relating to corticosteroid (preventer) inhaler	Percentage of sample who admitted that they engaged in each form of non-adherent behaviour (sometimes, often or always)
I alter the dose	49
I forget to use it	29
I stop taking it for a while	28
I only use it when I feel breathless	27
I decide to miss out a dose	23
I take less than instructed	23
I avoid using it if I can	22
I use it only as a reserve, if my other inhaler doesn't work	15
I use it regularly every day*	14

Note: *Reverse scored.

Hypothesis 2 Patients' perceptions of the seriousness of their asthma (timeline and consequences) will influence their beliefs about the necessity of prescribed medication but not their concerns about potential adverse effects.

Intercorrelations between illness perceptions, medication beliefs and reported adherence are shown in Table V. Hypothesis 2 was confirmed by significant positive correlations between medication *necessity* beliefs and asthma *timeline* ($r=0.30$, $p<0.01$) and asthma *consequences* ($r=0.30$, $p<0.01$). Also, as predicted, the *concerns* about the potential adverse effects of medication were not significantly correlated with perceptions of asthma *timeline* ($r=-0.19$, ns) and asthma *consequences* ($r=0.16$, ns).

Hypothesis 3 Treatment beliefs will add to the proportion of variance in adherence that is explained by demographic variables, clinical factors and illness perceptions.

A hierarchical multiple linear regression was performed to evaluate whether medication beliefs added significantly to the amount of variance in reported adherence explained by demographic factors (gender, age and educational status), clinical factors (number of visits to the family doctor and asthma-related hospital admissions in the previous year, duration of asthma), illness perceptions (*identity, timeline, consequences* and *cure/control*) and beliefs about medication (*necessity* and *concerns*). As can be seen from Table VI, illness perceptions and treatment beliefs accounted for a significant amount of variance in reported adherence scores (13% and 17% respectively) above that already explained by demographic variables and clinical factors (6% in total).

Interactions between illness perceptions, medication beliefs and reported adherence were investigated by structural equation modelling using the Amos software package (see Table VII for observed and implied correlations). The model shown in Fig. 1 was confirmed as a good-fit for the data (RMSEA$=0.14$, $p=0.05$). This figure offers an insight into the interaction between patients' perceptions of their illness, their views about medication and their reported adherence to it. Beliefs about medication and scores on the IPQ *consequences* scale directly predicted 30% of the variance in reported adherence. However, scores on the IPQ *timeline* scale were found to have no direct effect on self-reported adherence. Indeed, the influence of illness perceptions was largely mediated by necessity beliefs about medication, accounting for 15% of variance in this measure.

These data provide a strong indication that patients' beliefs about their medicines are strongly associated with adherence to preventer medication in asthma. Although illness perceptions were less directly linked with adherence, they appear to play an important contributory

Table V Pearson correlation coefficients between perceptions of illness, beliefs about treatment and reported adherence (MARS)

	MARS	Illness identity	Illness timeline	Illness consequences	Illness cure/control	Illness causal beliefs	Medication necessity
Illness identity	−0.08	–	–	–	–	–	–
Illness timeline	0.17	−0.10	–	–	–	–	–
Illness consequences	−0.24*	0.27*	0.19	–	–	–	–
Illness cure/control	−0.11	0.34**	−0.24*	0.07	–	–	–
Illness causal beliefs	0.06	0.23*	−0.11	0.28**	0.23*	–	–
Treatment necessity	0.32*	0.19	0.30*	0.30*	−0.02	0.08	–
Treatment concerns	−0.43***	0.17	−0.19	0.16	0.12	0.10	−0.19

Note: MARS=Medication Adherence Report Scale.
*$p<0.05$: **$p<0.01$: ***$p<0.001$.

Table VI Hierarchical linear regression model of predictors of reported adherence to inhaled preventer medication

Predictor block	Significant predictors	β	p	Adjusted R^2	Increase in adjusted R^2
Demographic variables	Gender	−0.19	0.06	0.06	0.06
	Age	0.18	0.14	–	–
	Educational status	−0.12	0.29	–	–
Clinical factors	Number of family doctor visits in last 6 months	0.20	0.07	0.06	0.00
	Number of asthma-related hospital admissions in previous year	−0.24	0.03	–	–
	Duration of asthma	−0.08	0.45	–	–
Illness perceptions	Identity	0.01	0.92	0.19	0.13
	Timeline	0.09	0.43	–	–
	Consequences	−0.31	0.007	–	–
	Cure/control	0.11	0.31	–	–
Treatment beliefs	Necessity	0.28	0.01	0.36	0.17
	Concerns	−0.35	0.001	–	–

Table VII Observed and implied correlations for the Amos model

	Illness consequences	Illness timeless	Treatment concerns	Treatment necessity	MARS
Illness consequences	–	0.19*	0.16*	0.30*	−0.24*
Illness timeline	0.19**	–	−0.19*	0.30*	0.17*
Treatment concerns	0.00**	0.00**	–	−0.19*	−0.43*
Treatment necessity	0.30**	0.30**	0.00**	–	0.32*
MARS	−0.21**	0.05**	−0.31**	0.28**	–

Note: MARS = Medication Adherence Report Scale.

*Observed correlations.

**Implied correlations (best fit by generalised least squares method).

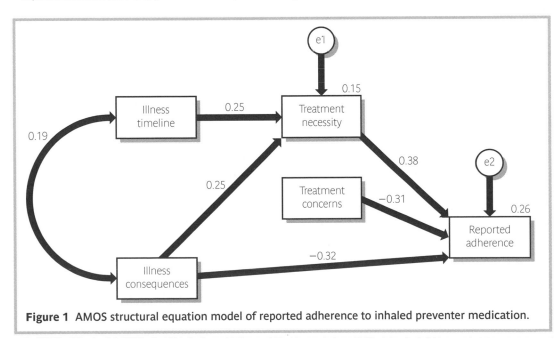

Figure 1 AMOS structural equation model of reported adherence to inhaled preventer medication.

role by influencing patients' beliefs about the *necessity* of their medicines. In particular, patients who perceive their asthma to be a relatively short-lived condition with relatively few adverse personal consequences are less likely to endorse the necessity of their preventer treatment and are less adherent to it.

Discussion

The main aim of the study was to examine the relative explanatory roles of illness and treatment beliefs in reported adherence to preventer medication in a community sample of patients with asthma. In common with previous studies, only relatively weak correlations were found between reported adherence and socio-demographic factors or clinical variables such as duration of asthma and frequency of GP and hospital visits (Horne and Weinman, 1999). However, significant associations were found between reported adherence and specific illness and treatment beliefs. The strongest correlations were obtained between reported adherence and treatment beliefs. Reported non-adherence was associated with doubts about the *necessity* for preventer medication to maintain health and with *concerns* about the potential adverse effects of this medication. Hierarchical linear regression analysis showed that illness perceptions and treatment beliefs added significantly to the amount of variance in reported adherence to preventer medication explained by demographic and clinical variables.

The observation that treatment beliefs were substantially and independently related to adherence is consistent with findings in a range of chronic illness samples (Horne and Weinman, 1999). Moreover, assessing treatment beliefs alongside illness perceptions has allowed us to evaluate the relative contribution of these two sets of beliefs to adherence. The relations between illness perceptions, treatment beliefs and reported adherence were consistent with an extended self-regulatory theory that includes treatment beliefs as well as illness perceptions. They provide preliminary support for the suggestion that the power of Leventhal's self-regulatory model (Leventhal *et al.*, 1992) to explain variations in adherence to treatment may be enhanced by taking account of patients' beliefs about the treatment as well as their perceptions of the illness (Horne, 1997; Horne and Weinman, 1998).

The lack of correlation between *necessity* beliefs and *concerns* indicates that they are separate constructs and not opposite poles of a more general attitude towards prescribed medication. Their independence has been confirmed in this study by the additional finding that they are related to illness perceptions in a clearly differential way.

Of the five components of illness representation identified by Leventhal *et al.*, (1980), only perceived *consequences* was directly related to reported adherence. However, against our prior expectations that higher perceived illness *consequences* would act as a stimulus to take prescribed medication, a negative correlation was found. Although we found that patients who perceived more negative consequences of asthma had stronger beliefs in the necessity of their preventer medication, high consequence scores were associated with lower reported adherence. One explanation of this is that, in this cross-sectional study, illness *consequence* scores may be the result rather than the determinant of medication adherence behaviour. Thus, adherence to preventer medication may have resulted in better asthma control, less health-related disability and hence fewer perceived consequences. Clearly a well-designed, prospective study is the only way to confirm this interpretation.

It is interesting to note that patients' models of illness and perceptions of treatment were related in a logically consistent way, as can be seen in the Amos analysis. For example, patients were more likely to perceive their preventer medication to be necessary if they viewed their asthma as a chronic condition with negative consequences. Thus, patients who are less inclined to take preventer medication may be doing so because their model of asthma is as an acute and possibly cyclical condition with fewer personal consequences which does not require regular preventive treatment. Surprisingly, *cure/control* beliefs were not associated with perceptions of the necessity of preventer medication nor with reported adherence to it. Moreover, the Amos model confirmed theoretical predictions that treatment beliefs add to the explanatory power of the SRM and that they should not be subsumed under cure/control beliefs (Horne, 1997). In this study, *cure/control* beliefs were not significantly associated with either medication beliefs or adherence. Unfortunately, the internal reliability of the *cure/control* scale was unsatisfactory in this data set, making it difficult to interpret these findings. In this respect, it should be noted that in a recent revision of the IPQ, the *cure/control* scale has been replaced by two separate scales, measuring personal control and treatment control beliefs (Moss-Morris *et al.*, in press).

The present study has a number of obvious limitations. The cross-sectional design makes it impossible to determine the direction of causality and this is particularly problematic in relation to the observed negative correlation between reported adherence and perceived consequences of asthma. An additional problem concerns the adherence measure that was based on self-report. Although patients' self-report is the most common method of assessment used in psychological research, it is subject to self-presentational and recall biases (Rudd, 1993). Patients may over-estimate the extent of their adherence in an attempt to 'please the doctor' or if they believe that admitting to non-adherence may result in adverse judgements or penalties. Nevertheless, reports of non-adherence are thought to be more accurate than reports of adherence (Haynes *et al.*, 1980), and other, more direct measures of adherence such as electronic monitoring or serum drug concentration assays have also been shown to be problematic (Bosley *et al.*, 1994; Matsui *et al.*, 1994).

Self-report measures of this type have been shown to have construct validity (Haynes *et al.*, 1980) and predictive validity as indicated by relations between self-reported adherence and biological markers of treatment efficacy (Haubrich *et al.*, 1999; Morisky *et al.*, 1986). It is clear from the analysis of responses to items on the Medication Adherence Report Scale that the prevalence of non-adherence behaviour reported by participants is similar to levels of non-adherence to asthma medication found in other studies using more 'objective' methods of assessment (Bosley *et al.*, 1994, 1995). Many patients in our study freely admitted that they did not adhere to preventer medication and our findings offer some insight into the possible psychological antecedents of this behaviour.

Despite its limitations, the study findings are relevant to clinical practice. Guidelines issued by the National Heart Lung and Blood Institute (NHLBI) in the USA (Fish *et al.*, 1997) and by commentators from the UK (Royal Pharmaceutical Society of Great Britain, 1997) and Europe (Lahdensuo, 1999), have identified the need for clinicians to gain a better understanding of their patients' views about their illness and treatment as a basis for clinician-patient partnership in asthma care. Our findings suggest that the illness and treatment perception approach used in this study offers a useful means of eliciting and understanding the patient's perception of asthma and its treatment. Moreover, if our findings can be replicated in prospective studies, they offer directions for developing interventions to facilitate adherence to preventer medication in asthma. They suggest that patients will be more likely to adhere to preventative medication in asthma if their beliefs in its necessity outweigh their concerns about potential adverse effects. Interventions could therefore address necessity beliefs and concerns. Our findings suggest that one strategy to shift patients' beliefs about the necessity of their treatment is via their illness perceptions. In particular, relations between *necessity* beliefs and *timeline* illness perceptions suggest that patients should be encouraged to perceive their asthma as a continuous underlying condition that needs to be treated even when symptoms are absent.

Acknowledgements

We are grateful to Professor Howard Leventhal for helpful discussions and advice. We would like to thank Deborah Morley and Lisa Doran for help with data collection. We are grateful to Matthew Hankins for providing statistical advice and for performing the structural equation modelling. Thanks also to Madeleine St Clair for identifying community asthma clinics and to Maeve Huttly and Richard Jenkins for help in preparing the manuscript. We are also very grateful to the clinicians who provided access to patients and, last but not least, to the patients who gave up their time to take part.

References

Arbuckle, J.L. (1997). *Amos users guide: version 3.6*. Chicago: Small Waters Corporation.

Bosley. C.M., Fosbury. J.A. and Cochrane, G.M. (1995). The psychological factors associated with poor compliance with treatment in asthma. *European Respiratory Journal*, **8**, 899–904.

Bosley, C.M., Parry, D.T. and Cochrane, G.M. (1994). Patient compliance with inhaled medication: does combining beta-agonists with corticosteroids improve compliance? *European Respiratory Journal*, **7**, 504–509.

British Thoracic Society (1982). Death from asthma in two regions of England. *British Medical Journal*, **285**, 1251–1255.

British Thoracic Society (1997). British guidelines on asthma management. *Thorax*, **52** [suppl. 1], 51–521.

Clark, N.M. and Nothwehr. F. (1997). Self-management of asthma by adult patients. *Patient Education and Counseling*, **32**, S5–S20.

Cooper, A., Lloyd, G., Weinman, J. and Jackson, G. (1999). Why patients do not attend cardiac rehabilitation: role of intentions and illness beliefs. *Heart*, **82**, 234–236.

Fay, J.K. and Jones, A. (2000). More information is needed on what patients think about self-management. *British Medical Journal*, **320**, 249.

Fish, J.E., Kaiser, H.B., Tinkelman, D. and Moyer, P. (1997). Asthma care: new treatment strategies, new expectations. *Patient Care*, **31**(16), 82.

Gibson, P.G., Coughlan, J., Wilson, A.J., Abramson, M., Bauman, A., Hensley, M.J. and Walters, E.H. (2000). Self-management education and regular practitioner review for adults with asthma. *Cochrane Review Cochrane Library*, **4.**

Gonder-Frederick, L.A. and Cox, D.J. (1991). Symptom perception, symptom beliefs and blood glucose discrimination in the self-treatment of insulin dependent diabetes. In: Skelton, J.A. and Croyle, R.T. (Eds.), *Mental representation in health and illness*, pp. 220–246. Springer-Verlag, New York.

Hand, C. (1998). Adherence and asthma. In: Myers, L. and Midence, K. (Eds.), *Adherence to treatment in medical conditions*, pp. 383–421. Harwood Academic, London.

Hand, C.H. and Bradley, C. (1996). Health beliefs of adults with asthma: toward an understanding of the difference between symptomatic and preventative use of inhaler treatment. *Journal of Asthma*, **33**, 331–338.

Haubrich, R.H., Little, S.J., Currier, J.S., Forthal, D.N., Kemper, C.A., Beall, G.N., Johnson, D., Dube, M.P., Hwang, J.Y. and McCutchan, J.A. (1999). The value of patient-reported adherence to antiretroviral therapy in predicting virologic and immunologic response. *AIDS*, **13**, 1099–1107.

Haynes, R.B., Taylor, D.W., Sackett, D.L., Gibson, E.S., Bernholtz, C.D. and Mukherjee, J. (1980). Can simple clinical measures detect patient non-compliance? *Hypertension*, **2**, 757–764.

Holgate, S. (1998). Asthma and allergy. *Quarterly Journal of Medicine*, **91**, 171–184.

Horn, C.R., Clark, T.J.H. and Cochrane, G.M. (1990). Compliance with inhaled therapy and morbidity from asthma. *Respiratory Medicine*, **84**, 67–70.

Horne. R. (1997). Representations of medication and treatment: advances in theory and measurement. In Petrie, K.J. and Weinman, J. (Eds.), *Perceptions of health and illness: current research and applications*, pp. 155–187. Harwood Academic, Amsterdam.

Horne, R. and Weinman, J. (1998). Predicting treatment adherence: an overview of theorietical models. In: Myers. L. and Midence, K. (Eds.), *Adherence to treatment in medical conditions*, pp. 25–50. Harwood Academic, London.

Horne, R. and Weinman. J. (1999). Patients' beliefs about prescribed medicines and their role in adherence to treatment in chronic physical illness. *Journal of Psychosomatic Research*, **47**, 555–567.

Horne, R., Weinman, J. and Hankins. M. (1999). The Beliefs about Medicines Questionnaire (BMQ): the development and evaluation of a new method for assessing the cognitive representation of medication. *Psychology and Health*, **14**, 1–24.

Jones, A., Pill, R. and Adams, S. (2000). Qualitative study of views of health professionals and patients on guided self-management plans for asthma. *British Medical Journal*, **321**, 1507–1510.

Kaptein, A.A. (1997). Asthma. In: Baum, A., Newman, S., Weinman, J., West, R. and McManus I., (Eds.), *Cambridge handbook of psychology, health and medicine*, pp. 371–372. Cambridge University Press, Cambridge.

Kravitz, R.L., Hays, R.D., Sherbourne, C.D., DiMatteo, M.R., Rogers, W.H., Ordway, L. and Greenfield, S. (1993). Recall of recommendations and adherence to advice among patients with chronic medical conditions. *Archives of Internal Medicine*, **153**, 1869–1878.

Kreuter, M., Strecher, V.J. and Glassman, B. (1999). One size does not fit all: the case for tailoring print materials. *Annals of Behavioral Medicine*, **21**, 276–283.

Lahdensuo. A. (1999). Guided self-management of asthma – how to do it. *British Medical Journal*, **319**, 759–760.

Leventhal, H. and Cameron, L. (1987). Behavioral theories and the problem of compliance. *Patient Education and Counseling*, **10**, 117–138.

Leventhal, H., Diefenbach, M. and Leventhal, E. (1992). Illness cognition: using common sense to understand treatment adherence and affect cognition interactions. *Cognitive Therapy and Research*, **16**, 143–163.

Leventhal, H., Mayer, D. and Nerenz, D. (1980). The common sense representation of illness danger. In: Rachman, S. (Ed.), *Contributions to medical psychology*, pp. 7–30. Pergamon Press, Oxford.

Leventhal, H. and Nerenz, D. (1985). The assessment of illness cognition. In: Karoly, P. (Ed.), *Measurement strategies in health psychology*, pp. 517–554. Wiley and Sons, New York.

Leventhal, H., Zimmerman, R. and Gutmann, M. (1984). Compliance: a self-regulation perspective. In: Gentry, D. (Ed.), *Handbook of behavioral medicine*, pp. 369–434. Pergamon Press, New York.

Mutsui, D., Hermann, C., Klein, J., Berkovitch, M., Olivieri, N. and Koren, G. (1994). Critical comparison of novel and existing methods of compliance assessment during a clinical trial of an oral iron chelator. *Journal of Clinical Pharmacology*, **34**, 944–949.

Meyer, D., Leventhal, H. and Gutmann, M. (1985). Common-sense models of illness: the example of hypertension. *Health Psychology*, **4**, 115–135.

Moss-Morris, R., Weinman, J., Petrie, K.J., Horne, R., Cameron, L. and Buck, D. (in press). The revised illness perception questionnaire (IPQ-R). *Psychology and Health.*

Morisky, D.E., Green, L.W. and Levine, D.M. (1986). Concurrent predictive validity of a self-reported measure of medication adherence. *Medical Care,* **24,** 67–74.

National Asthma Campaign (1999). *National Asthma Audit 1999/2000.* Cookham, Direct Publishing Solutions Ltd, Berkshire.

National Institutes for Health (1995). *Global initiative for asthma: global strategy for asthma management and prevention.* National Institutes of Health, Washington DC.

Oppenheim, A.N. (1992). *Questionnaire design, interviewing and attitude measurement.* Pinter, London.

Petrie, K., Weinman, J., Sharpe, N. and Buckley, J. (1996). Role of patients' views of their illness in predicting return to work and functioning after myocardial infarction: longitudinal study. *British Medical Journal,* **312,** 1191–1194.

Rand, C.S. and Wise, R.A. (1994). Measuring adherence to asthma medications. *American Journal of Respiratory and Critical Care Medicine,* **149,** 69–76.

Royal Pharmaceutical Society of Great Britain (1997). *From Compliance to Concordance: achieving shared goals in medicine taking.* Pharmaceutical Press, London.

Rudd, P. (1993). The measurement of compliance: medication taking. In: Krasnegor, N.A., Epstein, L.H., Johnson, S.B. and Yaffe, S.J. (Eds.), *Developmental aspects of health compliance behavior,* pp. 185–213. Lawrence Erlbaum Associates, Hillsdale, NJ.

Scharloo, M., Kaptein, A.A., Weinman, J., Willems, L.N.A. and Rooijmans, H.G.M. (2000) Physical and psychological correlates of functioning in patients with chronic obstructive pulmonary disease. *Journal of Asthma,* **37,** 17–29.

Weinman, J., Petrie, K.J., Moss-Morris, R. and Horne, R. (1996). The Illness Perception Questionnaire: a new method for assessing the cognitive representations of illness. *Psychology and Health,* **11,** 431–445.

Simpson S.H., Eurich D.T., Majumdar S.R. et al. (2006) A meta-analysis of the association between adherence to drug therapy and mortality, *British Medical Journal*, 1 July, 333 (7557): 15–20.

A meta-analysis of the association between adherence to drug therapy and mortality

Scot H Simpson, Dean T Eurich, Sumit R Majumdar, Rajdeep S Padwal, Ross T Tsuyuki, Janice Varney, Jeffrey A Johnson

Scot H Simpson, assistant professor
Faculty of Pharmacy and Pharmaceutical Sciences, University of Alberta, Edmonton, AB, Canada T6G 2N8
Janice Varney, librarian
Institute of Health Economics, Edmonton, AB
Dean T Eurich, research associate
Institute of Health Economics, Edmonton, AB
Rajdeep S Padwal, assistant professor
Division of Internal Medicine, Department of Medicine, Faculty of Medicine and Dentistry, University of Alberta
Sumit R Majumdar, associate professor
Division of Internal Medicine, Department of Medicine, Faculty of Medicine and Dentistry, University of Alberta
Ross T Tsuyuki, professor
Division of Cardiology, Department of Medicine, Faculty of Medicine and Dentistry, University of Alberta
Jeffrey A Johnson, professor
Department of Public Health Sciences, Faculty of Medicine and Dentistry, University of Alberta

Abstract

Objective: To evaluate the relation between adherence to drug therapy, including placebo, and mortality.

Design: Meta-analysis of observational studies.

Data sources: Electronic databases, contact with investigators, and textbooks and reviews on adherence.

Correspondence to: S H Simpson ssimpson@pharmacy.ualberta.ca

Review methods: Predefined criteria were used to select studies reporting mortality among participants with good and poor adherence to drug therapy. Data were extracted for disease, drug therapy groups, methods for measurement of adherence rate, definition for good adherence, and mortality.

Results: Data were available from 21 studies (46 847 participants), including eight studies with placebo arms (19 633 participants). Compared with poor adherence, good adherence was associated with lower mortality (odds ratio 0.56, 95% confidence interval 0.50 to 0.63). Good adherence to placebo was associated with lower mortality (0.56, 0.43 to 0.74), as was good adherence to beneficial drug therapy (0.55, 0.49 to 0.62). Good adherence to harmful drug therapy was associated with increased mortality (2.90, 1.04 to 8.11).

Conclusion: Good adherence to drug therapy is associated with positive health outcomes. Moreover, the observed association between good adherence to placebo and mortality supports the existence of the "healthy adherer" effect, whereby adherence to drug therapy may be a surrogate marker for overall healthy behaviour.

Introduction

About one in four people do not adhere well to prescribed drug therapy.[1] Following principles of evidence based medicine, clinicians use the most relevant and available evidence to guide decisions on drug therapy. Once the prescription is written, however, the fate of drug therapy is with the patient. Poor adherence is considered a critical barrier to treatment success and remains one of the leading challenges to healthcare professionals.[2]

Much of the literature on adherence focuses on methods for measuring adherence and identification of risk factors for poor adherence,[3–6] with the premise that good adherence must be associated with good health outcomes.[7] Although the most detailed systematic review on adherence in the literature included a wide array of disease states, drug therapy was only one element within a range of therapeutic interventions.[7] Combining adherence to drug therapy with adherence to other behavioural and therapeutic interventions limits the ability to examine specifically the relation between adherence to drug therapy and health outcomes.

Ideally the effect of adherence should be measured on an objective health outcome, such as mortality. Individual studies have reported that good adherence to prescribed drug therapy – even to placebo – was associated with a lower risk of mortality.[W1–W3] This is contrary to the proposition that a placebo has little effect on health outcomes[8] and has led to speculation that adherence to drug therapy may act as an identifiable marker for overall healthy behaviour, the so called healthy adherer effect.[W1–W4 8–10] We tested this hypothesis by summarising published observations of the relation between adherence to drug therapy and mortality, with a particular interest in placebo arms of controlled studies.

Methods

We used standard systematic review methods.[11] Eligible for inclusion in our study were randomised controlled trials, retrospective analyses of data from randomised controlled trials, and observational studies evaluating the association between adherence to drug therapy and mortality. We applied no language restrictions.

A professional librarian (JV) carried out the literature search. She searched several electronic databases from inception date to 20 June 2005: Allied and Complementary Medicine (AMED), Cumulative Index to Nursing and Allied Health Literature (CINAHL), Embase, Educational Research Information Center (ERIC), HealthSTAR, Medline, PsycINFO, and the Web of Science. Articles were identified using synonyms for adherence and mortality as database specific subject headings and keywords. We also checked references from textbooks[12–14] and review articles[1 7 9 10 15–17] on adherence for additional articles.

After excluding editorials, conference proceedings, letters, news articles, government reports, and practice guidelines, two investigators (SHS, DTE) independently screened titles and abstracts to identify potentially relevant citations. A citation was retained for further evaluation if either investigator selected it. Citations were excluded that did not report original data, have human participants, evaluate drug adherence, or report patient adherence.

Each potentially relevant article was reviewed to determine if it met the following inclusion criteria: described original research, explained the method used to measure adherence (for example, self report, electronic drug event monitoring system, pharmacy refill data, clinician estimation, tablet count), provided a clear definition for good adherence, stratified patients into good and poor adherence groups, and reported mortality according to adherence groups. Discrepancies were resolved by majority vote after review by a third investigator (JAJ).

Inter-reviewer agreement was measured during the initial screen to identify potentially relevant citations and on review of the full articles for study inclusion.[18] We characterised level of agreement using a qualitative scale developed by Landis and Koch.[19]

Data collection and outcome measures

Two investigators (DTE, RSP) used standardised forms to extract data from the included articles for disease state, drug therapy groups, methods used to measure adherence, definition for good adherence, and mortality. Accuracy of data collection was verified by comparing forms. We used the study authors' definition to stratify participants into good and poor adherence groups. When the number of deaths according to adherence group was not specifically stated in the article, we calculated this value from available information. If there was insufficient information in the article to calculate mortality according to adherence group, we contacted the corresponding author. The study was excluded if we were unable to obtain from the authors the number of deaths in each adherence group.

Statistical analysis

We analysed data using Rev Man 4.2.7. Each treatment arm in a randomised controlled trial was considered a discrete analysis of the relation between adherence and mortality. We used a random effects model to calculate pooled odds ratios and 95% confidence intervals.[20] Given the inclusion criteria, we anticipated including studies of a variety of diseases; therefore we examined heterogeneity using the Q and I^2 statistics.[20 21] We used a variation of Tobias' method to evaluate changes to the pooled odds ratio and tests for heterogeneity.[22] Rather than removing one study at a time, we used predetermined subgroups to identify potential sources of heterogeneity. For example, to test the theory of a healthy adherer effect,[W1–W4 8–10] we constructed a separate model to summarise the association between adherence to placebo and mortality. A priori subgroups included the effect of active treatment compared with placebo, study design, disease state, method used to measure adherence, and definition for good adherence.

Web references W1–W22 and author details are on bmj.com

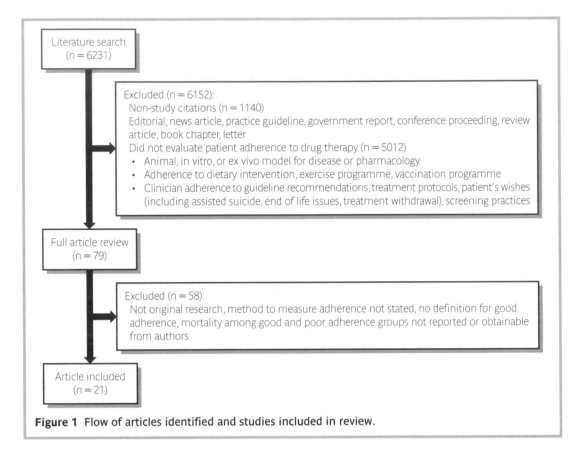

Figure 1 Flow of articles identified and studies included in review.

Results

Overall, 6231 unique citations were identified and 1140 ones related to non-studies were removed. In total, 5012 citations were excluded after review of the title and abstract (fig 1). Agreement to identify potentially relevant articles was 0.68, which is considered "substantial."[19] From the 79 potentially relevant articles, 21 studies with 46 847 participants met the inclusion criteria.[W1–W21] Agreement at this stage was 0.97, considered "almost perfect."[19]

Supplemental information on mortality was obtained from multiple sources for some studies. In the University Group Diabetes Program, mortality for participants with good adherence was available in a paper on statistical methods.[W18 W22] Supplemental mortality data according to adherence group were obtained from five corresponding authors.[W5 W7 W9 W10 W15]

Eight studies were randomised, placebo controlled trials (37 701 participants) reporting mortality according to adherence group for each treatment arm in a retrospective analysis.[W1–W4 W8 W16–W18 W22] Thirteen cohort studies (9146 participants) reported mortality according to adherence groups.[W5–W7 W9–W15 W19–W21] Table 1 lists the characteristics of the included studies. Eight studies evaluated drug therapy in participants with a recent myocardial infarction,[W1–W8] seven studies were in patients infected with HIV,[W9–W15] and two studies were in primary prevention of heart disease.[W16 W17] The remaining studies evaluated adherence to drug therapy for patients with type 2 diabetes,[W18 W22] hyperlipidaemia,[W19] heart failure,[W20] and immune suppression after heart transplant.[W21] Fifteen studies reported an adherence rate threshold to define good adherence.[W1–W5 W7 W8 W11 W13–W19 W22] All cause mortality was the primary

Table 1 Characteristics of included studies in meta-analysis of adherence to drug therapy and mortality

Study	Study type	Treatment groups (No of participants)	Adherence measures	Threshold for good adherence	Observation period
Post-myocardial infarction management:					
Coronary Drug Project Research Group 1980[w1]	Randomised controlled trial	Placebo (2695), clofibrate (1065)	Pill count, clinician's impression	≥80%	≥5 years
Wei et al 2002[w5]	Cohort	Statins (427)	Pharmacy refill	≥80%	Average 2.4 years
Cottar et al 2004[w6]	Cohort	Acetylsalicylic acid (64)	Thromboxane blood level	Less than healthy volunteer	1 year
β blocker heart attack trial (men) 1990[w2]	Randomised controlled trial	Placebo (1094), propranolol (1081)	Pill count	>75%	1 year
β blocker heart attack trial (women) 1993[w3]	Randomised controlled trial	Placebo (240), propranolol (265)	Pill count	≥75%	Median 26 months
Wei et al 2004[w7]	Cohort	β blockers (386)	Pharmacy refill	≥80%	Median 3.7 years
Canadian amiodarone myocardial infarction arrhythmia trial 1999[w8]	Randomised controlled trial	Placebo (538), amiodarone (573)	Pill count	≥66%	2 years
Cardiac arrhythmia suppression trial 1996[w4]	Randomised controlled trial	Placebo (579), encainide or flecainide (574)	Pill count	>80%	Average 10 months
HIV infection:					
San Andres Rebollo et al 2004[w9]	Cohort	Antiretroviral therapy (950)	Self report	Continued use	8 years
Cohn et al 2002[w10]	Cohort	Antiretroviral therapy) (626	Self report	No missed doses in previous 48 hours	56 weeks
Garcia de Olalla et al 2002[w11]	Cohort	Antiretroviral therapy (1219)	Self report and pharmacy refill	≥90%	3 years
Grimwade et al 2005[w12]	Cohort	Cotrimoxazole prophylaxis (1288)	Self report and frequency of clinic visits	Continued use, collection of new tablet supply, and ongoing attendance at clinic	6 months
Hogg et al 2002[w13]	Cohort	Antiretroviral therapy (1282)	Pharmacy refill	≥75%	1 year
Paterson et al 2000[w14]	Cohort	Protease inhibitors (81)	Medication event monitoring system	≥95%	Median 6 months
Wood et al 2003[w15]	Cohort	Antiretroviral therapy (1422)	Pharmacy refill	≥75%	4 years

continued

Table 1 Continued

Study	Study type	Treatment groups (No of participants)	Adherence measures	Threshold for good adherence	Observation period
Primary prevention of cardiovascular disease:					
Physicians' health study 1994[W16]	Randomised controlled trial	Placebo (10 989), acetylsalicylic acid (11 004)	Self report	≥95%	Average 60.2 months
West of Scotland prevention study 1997[W17]	Randomised controlled trial	Placebo (3293), pravastatin (3302)	Pill count	≥75%	Mean 4.9 years
Other disease states:					
University Group Diabetes Project 1970[W22] 1971[W18] (type 2 diabetes)	Randomised controlled trial	Placebo (205), tolbutamide (204)	Clinician's impression	≥75%	≥75% followed for ≥5 years
Howell et al 2004[W19] (hypercholesterolaemia)	Cohort	Statins (869)	Pharmacy refill	≥80%	11 years
Miura et al 2001[W20] (heart failure)	Cohort	Digoxin (431)	Blood levels of drug	Therapeutic range	72 months
Dobbels et al 2004[W21] (heart transplant)	Cohort	Immunosuppressive regimen (101)	Medication event monitoring system (for cyclosporin use)	No variation in dose compliance and no drug holidays	5 years

outcome in nine studies[W2][W3][W9–W13][W15][W19] and a secondary outcome in 12.[W1][W4][W5–W8][W14][W16–W18][W20–W22] The adherence substudy for the cardiac arrhythmia suppression trial reported arrhythmic mortality according to adherence group.[W4] Although 67% of the deaths in this trial were attributable to an arrhythmia, data for all cause mortality were not available.[W4][23]

The primary analysis of mortality risk according to adherence group was based on 2779 (5.9%) deaths in 46 847 participants. Overall, 1462 (4.7%) deaths occurred in 31 439 participants with good adherence to drug therapy and 1317 (8.5%) deaths in 15 408 participants considered to have poor adherence. The pooled odds ratio for mortality for good adherence compared with poor adherence was 0.56 (95% confidence interval 0.50 to 0.63). Some degree of heterogeneity was found: Q statistic P = 0.08 and $I^2 = 28.6\%$.

The placebo arms from eight studies contained 19 633 participants and reported 996 (5.1%) deaths.[W1–W4][W8][W16–W18][W22] Overall, good adherence to placebo was associated with a lower risk of mortality: pooled odds ratio 0.56, 0.43 to 0.74 (fig 2). Some heterogeneity of effect was found in this analysis: Q statistic P = 0.05 and $I^2 = 51.2\%$. A subgroup analysis restricted to studies of drug therapy after myocardial infarction reduced variance substantially: Q statistic P = 0.79 and $I^2 = 0\%$.[W1–W4][W8] The pooled odds ratio of these five studies was 0.45 (0.38 to 0.54).

Two studies were identified in which active drug therapy increased the risk of mortality compared with placebo.[W22][23] Therefore separate models were constructed to summarise the effect of adherence to active drug therapy found to be harmful compared with beneficial (fig 3). The two studies evaluating adherence to harmful drug therapy reported 53 (6.8%) deaths in 778 participants.[W4][W18][W22] The pooled odds ratio for mortality was 2.90 (1.04 to 8.11) for participants with good compared with poor adherence to the active treatment (fig 3).

The association between adherence to proved beneficial drug therapy and mortality was reported in 19 studies involving 26 436 participants and 1730 (6.5%) deaths.[W1–W3][W5][W17][W19–W21] The pooled odds ratio from these studies was 0.55 (0.49 to 0.62) for mortality in participants with good adherence compared with poor adherence (fig 3). These observations were homogeneous (Q statistic P = 0.71 and $I^2 = 0\%$) and further stratification by study characteristics did not result in substantive changes to these relations (table 2). However, moderate variance of the observed effects was found among the seven HIV studies ($I^2 = 50.2\%$) and among the four studies that used subjective methods to measure adherence ($I^2 = 61.0\%$).[21] Minor variance ($I^2 = 8.6\%$) was found among the 13 cohort studies (table 2).[21]

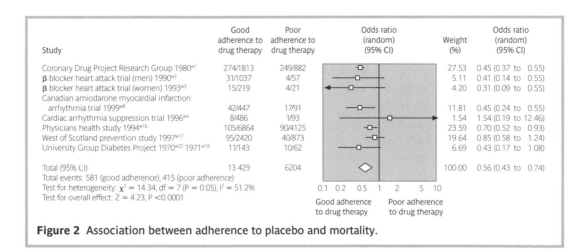

Figure 2 Association between adherence to placebo and mortality.

Study	Good adherence to drug therapy	Poor adherence to drug therapy	Odds ratio (random) (95% CI)	Weight (%)	Odds ratio (random) (95% CI)
Harmful drug therapy					
Cardiac arrhythmia suppression trial 1996[w4]	23/505	0/69		13.34	6.77 (0.4 to 112.72)
University Group Diabetes Project 1970[w22] 1971[w18]	26/151	4/53		86.66	2.55 (0.85 to 7.68)
Total (95% CI)	656	122		100.00	2.90 (1.04 to 8.11)
Total events: 49 (good adherence), 4 (poor adherence)					
Test for heterogeneity: $\chi^2 = 0.43$, df = 1 (P = 0.51), $I^2 = 0\%$					
Test for overall effect: Z = 4.03, P <0.04					
Beneficial drug therapy					
Coronary Drug Project Research Group 1980[w1]	106/708	88/357		12.11	0.54 (0.39 to 0.74)
Wei et al 2002[w5]	14/272	14/155		2.06	0.55 (0.25 to 1.18)
Cotter et al 2004[w6]	1/52	1/12		0.15	0.22 (0.01 to 3.72)
β blocker heart attack trial (men) 1990[w2]	14/1009	3/72		0.75	0.32 (0.09 to 1.15)
β blocker heart attack trial (women) 1993[w3]	11/242	2/23		0.49	0.50 (0.10 to 2.41)
Wei et al 2004[w7]	24/226	26/160		3.43	0.61 (0.34 to 1.11)
Canadian amiodarone myocardial infarction arrhythmia trial 1999[w8]	33/445	19/128		3.35	0.46 (0.25 to 0.84)
San Andres Rebollo et al 2004[w9]	69/197	300/753		11.39	0.81 (0.59 to 1.13)
Cohn et al 2002[w10]	8/585	2/41		0.49	0.27 (0.06 to 1.32)
Garcia de Olalla et al 2002[w11]	156/831	105/388		15.13	0.62 (0.47 to 0.83)
Grimwade et al 2005[w12]	12/743	27/545		2.56	0.31 (0.16 to 0.63)
Hogg et al 2002[w13]	62/955	44/327		7.29	0.45 (0.30 to 0.67)
Paterson et al 2000[w14]	0/23	1/58		0.12	0.82 (0.03 to 20.75)
Wood et al 2003[w15]	117/1067	76/355		12.04	0.45 (0.33 to 0.62)
Physicians health study 1994[w16]	89/6608	102/4396		14.80	0.57 (0.43 to 0.77)
West of Scotland prevention study 1997[w17]	66/2435	40/867		7.59	0.58 (0.39 to 0.86)
Howell et al 2004[w19]	24/654	12/215		2.65	0.55 (0.28 to 1.08)
Miura et al 2001[w20]	17/218	32/213		3.15	0.48 (0.26 to 0.89)
Dobbels et al 2004[w21]	9/84	2/17		0.46	0.90 (0.18 to 4.59)
Total (95% CI)	17 354	9082		100.00	0.55 (0.49 to 0.62)
Total events: 832 (good adherence), 898 (poor adherence)					
Test for heterogeneity: $\chi^2 = 14.34$, df = 7 (p = 0.05), $I^2 = 51.2\%$					
Test for overall effect: Z = 4.23, P <0.0001					

0.1 0.2 0.5 1 2 5 10

Good adherence to drug therapy   Poor adherence to drug therapy

Figure 3 Association between adherence to harmful or beneficial drug therapy and mortality.

Discussion

This meta-analysis of 21 studies, involving 46 847 participants, showed a consistent association between adherence to drug therapy and mortality. For participants with good adherence to placebo or beneficial drug therapy, the risk of mortality was about half that of participants with poor adherence. Conversely, the risk of mortality was more than doubled for participants with good adherence to proved harmful drug therapy compared with participants with poor adherence.

The association between adherence to harmful therapy and mortality is important in the light of recent issues of patient safety and post-marketing drug surveillance. Our observation suggests that stratification by adherence group may facilitate earlier identification of harmful therapies if the rate of adverse events is higher in participants with good adherence. According to the consolidated standards of reporting trials statement, investigators should, at a minimum, report the number of participants receiving the intended treatment.[24] Although randomised clinical trials will often measure adherence – either through pill count from returned vials or information on frequency of refills – this information is usually reported only as an overall adherence rate.[25] Many authors have identified that an array of adherence rates can confound the association between treatment and response and substantially affect generalisability.[25–27] Therefore we would encourage clinical trialists to consider reporting treatment effects stratified by adherence group.

Table 2 Subgroup analysis of active treatment arms considered beneficial

Analysis group	No of studies	Pooled odds ratio (95% CI)	Tests for heterogeneity	
			P value (Q statistic)	I²(%)
Active treatment arm considered beneficial	19	0.55 (0.49 to 0.62)	0.71	0
Post-myocardial infarction studies only[W1–W3 W5–W8]	7	0.52 (0.41 to 0.66)	0.96	0
HIV studies only[W9–W15]	7	0.53 (0.41 to 0.69)	0.06	50.2
Primary prevention studies only[W16 W17]	2	0.58 (0.46 to 0.73)	0.99	0
Method used to measure adherence: Objective method (pill count, pharmacy refill, blood level, medication event monitor system)[W1–W3 W5–W8 W11 W13–W15 W17 W19–W21]	15	0.53 (0.46 to 0.60)	0.99	0
Subjective method (patient self report, clinician impression)[W9 W10 W12 W16]	4	0.55 (0.37 to 0.83)	0.05	61.0
Threshold used to define good adherence group: ≥75%[W1–W3 W5 W7 W11 W13–W17 W19]	12	0.54 (0.48 to 0.61)	0.97	0
≥80%[W1 W5 W7 W11 W14 W16 W19]	7	0.58 (0.50 to 0.68)	1.00	0
≥90%[W11 W14 W16]	3	0.60 (0.49 to 0.73)	0.91	0
Study design: Randomised controlled studies only[W1–W3 W8 W16 W17]	6	0.55 (0.46 to 0.65)	0.95	0
Cohort studies only[W5–W7 W9–W15 W19–W21]	13	0.55 (0.47 to 0.64)	0.36	8.6

In 1997 McDermott and colleagues reviewed the literature on cardiovascular disease that reported admission to hospital and mortality according to adherence groups.[9] They found that seven of 12 studies had a significant association between adherence and outcomes and noted that adherence to placebo was associated with improved outcomes in three studies. More recently DiMatteo and colleagues determined that the risk of a poor health outcome was 26% lower in participants with good adherence.[7] Although that meta-analysis included studies from a wide range of medical conditions, drug therapy was included with a variety of other healthcare interventions. In addition, the placebo arms from controlled trials were excluded from their analysis. Our study confirms, updates, and extends these observations by including studies from across several disease states and summarises the observations between adherence to drug therapy (both active drug and placebo) and mortality.

Our study shares limitations inherent with meta-analyses in general and with studies of adherence specifically. Firstly, important studies relevant to the research question may have been missed during the literature search, although this was unlikely. Secondly, as with previous reviews,[7 9] our data sources were observational studies, thus restricting our ability to explore fully the influence of unmeasured confounding variables. For example, participants with good adherence to study drugs (even placebo) may also have good adherence to other healthy behaviours such as diet, exercise, regular follow-up with healthcare professionals, immunisations, screening, and use of other drugs.[W1–W4 8–10] All of these could independently affect the risk of mortality. Conversely, participants with poor adherence may have consciously chosen to use a lower dosage[28 29] or have other conditions, such as depression, that affect adherence.[10 30] In the absence of individual patient data to control for these factors, we tested the healthy adherer effect hypothesis and assumed that the presence of good adherence is a marker for overall healthy behaviour.[W1–W4 8–10] Thirdly, in the absence of an ideal method to measure adherence,[31] we observed a wide variety of measurement methods and definitions for good adherence. Grouping studies according to measurement method and definition for good adherence did not, however, result in substantive changes to our overall observation. Finally, with the exception of two studies,[W6 W20] all studies used indirect methods to measure adherence. These methods are limited by the assumption that drug acquisition is a reasonable surrogate for consumption. This assumption would, however, overestimate exposure and bias our observation towards the null.

With these limitations in mind, our findings support the tenet that good adherence to drug therapy is associated with positive health outcomes. Moreover, the observed association between good adherence to placebo and lower mortality also supports the existence of the healthy adherer effect, whereby adherence to drug therapy may be a surrogate marker for overall healthy behaviour. Our findings set the stage for future studies to address the causal relation between adherence and health outcomes, but, more importantly, quantify for patients and providers how important it is to take drugs of proved efficacy as prescribed.

Acknowledgements

We thank the individual trialists for providing information from their study databases and Maria Santana, who translated three Spanish papers.

Contributors: SHS had the idea for the article. All authors took part in the planning and design of the study. SHS, DTE, RSP, and JV did the data collection. MS (listed in the acknowledgements) assisted in data collection from articles printed in Spanish. SHS carried out the statistical analyses. SHS, DTE, SRM, RSP, RTT, and JAJ had access to the data and participated in the interpretation of the data. SHS wrote the first draft of the paper. SHS provided leadership for the study and is guarantor.

What is already known on this topic

About one in four people do not adhere well to prescribed drug therapy

Poor adherence is considered a critical barrier to treatment success and remains an important challenge to healthcare professionals

What this study adds

Good adherence to drug therapy is associated with positive health outcomes

The observed association between adherence to placebo and mortality supports the premise of a healthy adherer effect, where adherence to drug therapy may be a surrogate marker for overall healthy behaviour

References

1 DiMatteo MR. Variations in patients' adherence to medical recommendations: a quantitative review of 50 years of research. *Med Care* 2004;42:200–9.

2 Miller NH, Hill M, Kottke T, Ockene IS. The multilevel compliance challenge recommendations for a call to action. A statement for healthcare professionals. *Circulation* 1997;95:1085–90.

3 Morris IS. Schulz RM. Patient compliance – an overview. *J Clin Pharm Ther* 1992;17:285–95.

4 Donovan JL. Patient decision making. The missing ingredient in compliance research. *Int J Technol Assess Health Care* 1995;11:443–55.

5 Ellis S, Shumaker S, Sieber W, Rand C. Adherence to pharmacological interventions. Current trends and future directions. The Pharmacological Intervention Working Group. *Control Clin Trials* 2000;21:S218–25.

6 Osterberg L. Blaschke T. Adherence to medication. *N Engl J Med* 2005;353:487–97.

7 DiMatteo MR, Giordani PJ. Lepper HS, Croghan TW. Patient adherence and medical treatment outcomes: a meta-analysis. *Med Care* 2002;40:794–811.

8 Czajkowski SM. Chesney MA. Smith AW. Adherence and the placebo effect. In: Shumaker SA, Schron EB. Ockene JK, eds. *The handbook of health behavior change.* New York: Springer, 1990;519–34.

9 McDermott MM, Schmitt B, Wallner E. Impact of medication nonadherence on coronary heart disease outcomes. A critical review. *Arch Inlern Med* 1997:157:1921–9.

10 Hays RD, Kravitz RL, Mazel RM, Sherbourne CD, DiMatteo MR, Rogers WH, et al. The impact of patient adherence on health outcomes for patients with chronic disease in the medical outcomes study: *J Behav Med* 1994;17:347–60.

11 In: Higgins JPT, Green S, eds. *Cochrane handbook for systematic reviews of interventions 4.2.5* [updated May 2005]. www.cochrane.dk/cochrane/handbook/hbook.htm (accessed 3 Apr 2006).

12 Shumaker SA. Schron EB, Ockene JK. *The handbook of health behavior change.* New York: Springer, 1990.

13 Cramer JA, Spilker B. *Patient compliance in medical practice and clinical trials.* New York: Raven, 1991.

14 Myers LB, Midence K. *Adherence to treatment in medical conditions.* Australia: Harwood Academic, 1998.

15 Cramer JA. A systematic review of adherence with medications for diabetes. *Diabetes Care* 2004;27:1218–24.

16 Fogarty L. Roter D, Larson S, Burke J, Gillespie J, Levy R. Patient adherence to HIV medication regimens: a review of published and abstract reports. *Patient Educ Couns* 2002;46:95–108.

17 Simoni JM, Frick PA, Pantalone DW, Turner BJ. Antiretroviral adherence interventions: a review of current literature and ongoing studies. *Top HIV Med* 2003;11:185–98.

18 Cohen JA. A coefficient of agreement for nominal scales. *Educ Psychol Meas* 1960;20:37–46.

19 Landis JR, Koch GG. The measurement of observer agreement for categorical data. *Biometrics* 1977;33:159–74.

20 DerSimonian R, Laird N. Meta-analysis in clinical trials. *Control Clin Trials* 1986;7:177–88.

21 Higgins JP, Thompson SG, Deeks JJ. Altman DG. Measuring inconsistency in meta-analyses. *BMJ* 2003;327:557–60.

22 Tobias A. Assessing the influences of a single study in meta-analysis. *Stata Tech Rull* 1999;47:15–7.

23 Echt DS, Liebson PR, Mitchell LB, Peters RW, Obias-Manno D. Barker AH, et al. Mortality and morbidity in patients receiving encainide, flecainide, or placebo. The cardiac arrhythmia suppression trial. *N Engl J Med* 1991;324:781–8.

24 Moher D, Schulz KF, Altman D. The CONSORT statement: revised recommendations for improving the quality of reports of parallel-group randomized trials. *JAMA* 2001;285:1987–91.

25 Boudes P. Drug compliance in therapeutic trials: a review. *Control Clin Trials* 1998;19:257–68.

26 Haynes RB, Dantes R. Patient compliance and the conduct and interpretation of therapeutic trials. *Control Clin Trials* 1987;8:12–9.

27 Efron B, Feldman D. Compliance as an explanatory variable in clinical trials *J Am Stat Assoc* 1991;86:9–26.

28 Weintraub M. Intelligent noncompliance with special emphasis on the elderly. *Contemp Pharm Pract* 1981;4:8–11.

29 Conrad P. The meaning of medications: another look at compliance. *Soc. Sci Med* 1985;20:29–37.

30 Ciechanowski PS, Katon WJ, Russo JE. Depression and diabetes: impact of depressive symptoms on adherence, function, and costs. *Arch Intern Med* 2000;160:3278–85

31 Rudd P. In search of the gold standard for compliance measurement. *Arch Intern Med* 1979;139:627–8.

PART 4

Stress and health

Part contents

Commentary

So far, this book has explored the role of psychology in health with a focus on beliefs and behaviours. Much of health psychology, however, also explores physiological pathways as a means to understand why people become ill in the first place and why the progression and impact of an illness varies between people. Stress research takes such a psychobiological approach and assesses the relationship between stress and illness and explores possible mechanisms for this association. This part focuses on stress, health and illness. It draws upon research on different illnesses including coronary heart disease, cervical cancer and wound healing, and covers a range of mechanisms including cardiovascular reactivity, behaviour, immune function and emotional expression.

Everson, S.A., Lynch, J.W., Chesney, M.A. et al. (1997) Interaction of workplace demands and cardiovascular reactivity in progression of carotid atherosclerosis: population based study, *British Medical Journal*, 314: 553–8. Reprinted with kind permission of the BMJ Publishing Group.

Pereira, D.B., Antoni, M.H., Danielson, A. et al. (2003) Life stress and cervical squamous intraepithelial lesions in women with human papillomavirus and human immunodeficiency virus, *Psychosomatic Medicine*, 65 (1): 1–8. Reprinted with kind permission of Lippincott Williams & Wilkins.

Ebrecht, M., Hextall, J., Kirtley, L.G. et al. (2004) Perceived stress and cortisol levels predict speed of wound healing in healthy male adults, *Psychoneuroendocrinology*, 29: 798–809. Reprinted with kind permission of Elsevier.

Pennebaker, J.W. (1997) Writing about emotional experiences as a therapeutic process, *Psychological Science*, 8 (3): 162–6. Reprinted with kind permission of Blackwell Publishing Ltd.

Petrie, K.J., Booth, R.J. and Pennebaker, J.W. (1998) The immunological effects of thought suppression, *Journal of Personality and Social Psychology*, 75 (5): 1264–72. Reprinted with kind permission of the American Psychological Association.

Research illustrates that stress can cause illness. From this perspective studies have particularly examined the impact of work stress and have drawn upon the job–control–demand approach, mostly in the context of coronary heart disease. Everson et al. (1997) carried out a large-scale prospective study over four years to explore the extent to which work stress was related to the progression of carotid atherosclerosis in 591 middle-aged men. They also assessed the role of cardiovascular reactivity in explaining the stress–illness link which is a measure of an exaggerated blood pressure increase to stress. The results showed that the progression of carotid atherosclerosis was greatest in those who reported greatest job stress and showed highest levels of cardiovascular reactivity. Stress did cause illness, particularly in those who showed the greatest cardiac reactivity. This paper is interesting as it answers some of the research questions fundamental to understanding the stress–illness link. It also provides clear descriptions of the physiological measures used to assess blood pressure, reactivity and atherosclerosis which are fairly accessible even to a non-physiologist. It also fulfils many of the 'best case' criteria for stress research in that it involves a large sample, the outcome variables are objective, the design is prospective and it explores a range of mediating variables. Finally, the paper illustrates a clear interaction between psychological and biological variables.

Pereira et al. (2003) also explored the impact of stress on illness but in this paper they focus on the progression and/or persistence of squamous intraepithelial lesions (SIL) which are the markers for the human papillomavirus and are linked with cervical cancer. Further, people who are HIV positive are more susceptible to SIL. In this study Pereira et al. (2003) followed up 32 women who were infected with the HIV virus and examined whether life stress predicted a progression in SIL after one year. The results showed that higher life stress increased the odds of developing SIL sevenfold, even when other biological and behavioural variables were controlled for. This paper illustrates a strong link between stress and illness progression. It also provides details of a number of immunological measures and describes a range of important biological and behavioural variables that should be included in research from a physiological perspective. The paper is also interesting as it illustrates an interaction between different illnesses. Most research takes a single illness as its focus. This study illustrates how HIV can make a person more susceptible to cervical cancer and how the progression of cervical cancer can be promoted by stress.

The third paper in this section, by Ebrecht et al. (2004), also explores the relationship between stress and illness but in this case focuses on wound healing which is a useful outcome variable as it can be measured objectively, reflects a 'real' process of recovery and integrates a range of perspectives including the stress paradigm and psychoneuroimmunology (PNI). Ebrecht et al. (2004) also examine the role of cortisol, health behaviours and personality factors as possible mediating variables. The study used a prospective design and participants were given a 4mm punch biopsy to generate a wound. The process of wound healing was then assessed over a two-week period using ultrasound scanning. The results showed that higher stress levels were related to slower wound healing and that this seemed to be influenced by elevated cortisol levels rather than changes in health-related behaviours. The studies by Everson et al. (1997) and Pereira et al. (2003) explore the link between stress and illness in a naturalistic setting. Although this means that the results are generalisable to other people suffering from the same condition, it introduces the possibility of individual variability. Ebrecht et al. (2004) used an experimentally induced wound which reduces this variability, at least in the participant's illness state. This paper is therefore a useful example of how 'healthy' participants can be used to explore the stress–illness link and how experimental procedures can be used in psycho physiological research. The paper also provides clear descriptions of the measures used and the results take a step-by-step approach and illustrate how to analyse repeated measures data. Finally the paper presents a good overview of the literature on wound healing and describes the pros and cons of the different ways of measuring changes in wound status.

The papers described so far in this section focus on whether stress causes illness and what variables may influence this relationship. There is also, however, a body of literature that has explored how stress can be reduced as a means to avoid illness onset or prevent disease progression. Some of this has drawn upon stress management interventions which use strategies such as relaxation, cognitive behavioural therapy and mindfulness. Some research over recent years has explored the impact of a very simple intervention which seems to have had some fairly profound effects on a range of health outcomes. This intervention is the 'writing paradigm' and Pennebaker, who developed this approach, offered a detailed description in his paper in 1997. Pennebaker (1997) describes how the basic writing paradigm involves asking participants to write about 'their very deepest thoughts and feelings about an extremely important emotional issue' for 3–5 consecutive days for a 15–30 min period. The effects of this are then compared to a control group who are asked to write about a superficial topic such as how they spend their time. Pennebaker (1997) describes how the writing paradigm is akin to a process of disclosure that can happen in therapy and may work by encouraging the individual to stop inhibiting negative or problematic thoughts, by changing cognitions or by creating a coherent narrative which may reduce rumination or flashbacks. Pennebaker (1997) also describes how simply writing about an emotional experience seems to have an effect on a vast range of outcome variables ranging from a reduction in distress to being able to get a new job more quickly or an improvement in college grades. In a similar vein, the paper by Petrie, Booth and Pennebaker (1998) also explores the writing paradigm but uses an experimental design to assess the impact of emotional expression through writing on immune function which locates the writing paradigm within a framework of psychoneuroimmunology (PNI). The study also examines whether the benefits of writing were undermined by a thought suppression task in which participants were asked to 'put any thoughts about what you have been writing completely out of your mind'. The results showed that emotional writing improves immune function. The results also showed that thought suppression decreases immune function. Pennebaker (1997) is an interesting review of the writing paradigm research which set the scene for numerous subsequent studies exploring the impact of writing and emotional expression on a multitude of outcome variables. Petrie et al. (1998) made a useful experimental contribution to both the writing and PNI literature and illustrates how experimental designs can be used to establish causality. Furthermore, Petrie et al. (1998) highlight the impact of thought suppression, which has implications for understanding a range of issues central to health psychology such as stopping smoking, eating less, exercising more, etc., which all involve imposing denial (and therefore thought suppression) by trying not to do activities that most people really prefer to be doing.

This part therefore focuses on associations between psychological and biological factors with a particular emphasis on the stress–illness link, and presents research exploring different mechanisms. The papers selected cover a range of illnesses and assess a number of different possible mechanisms including cardiovascular reactivity, immune function, behaviour and emotional expression.

Everson, S.A., Lynch, J.W., Chesney, M.A. et al. (1997) Interaction of workplace demands and cardiovascular reactivity in progression of carotid atherosclerosis: population based study, *British Medical Journal*, 314: 553–8.

Interaction of workplace demands and cardiovascular reactivity in progression of carotid atherosclerosis

Population based study

Susan A Everson, John W Lynch, Margaret A Chesney, George A Kaplan, Debbie E Goldberg, Starley B Shade, Richard D Cohen, Riitta Salonen, Jukka T Salonen

Human Population Laboratory, Public Health Institute, Berkeley, CA 94704, USA
Susan A Everson, associate research scientist
John W Lynch, associate research scientist
George A Kaplan, chief
Debbie E Goldberg, senior research associate
Starley B Shade, graduate assistant
Richard D Cohen, senior research scientist
Prevention Sciences Group, University of California, San Francisco, CA 94105, USA
Margaret A Chesney, professor of medicine
Research Institute of Public Health, University of Kuopio, 70211 Kuopio, Finland
Riitta Salonen, research scientist
Jukka T Salonen, professor of epidemiology

Abstract

Objective: To examine the combined influence of workplace demands and changes in blood pressure induced by stress on the progression of carotid atherosclerosis.

Design: Population based follow up study of unestablished as well as traditional risk factors for carotid atherosclerosis, ischaemic heart disease, and other outcomes.

Setting: Eastern Finland.

Subjects: 591 men aged 42–60 who were fully employed at baseline and had complete data on the measures of carotid atherosclerosis, job demands, blood pressure reactivity, and covariates.

Main outcome measures: Change in ultrasonographically assessed intima-media thickness of the right and left common carotid arteries from baseline to 4 year follow up.

Correspondence to: Dr Everson.

Results: Significant interactions between workplace demands and stress induced reactivity were observed for all measures of progression (P<0.04). Men with large changes in systolic blood pressure (20 mm Hg or greater) in anticipation of a maximal exercise test and with high job demands had 10–40% greater progression of mean (0.138 v 0.123 mm) and maximum (0.320 v 0.261 mm) intima-media thickness and plaque height (0.347 v 0.264) than men who were less reactive and had fewer job demands. Similar results were obtained after excluding men with prevalent ischaemic heart disease at baseline. Findings were strongest among men with at least 20% stenosis or non-stenotic plaque at baseline. In this subgroup reactive men with high job demands had more than 46% greater atherosclerotic progression than the others. Adjustment for atherosclerotic risk factors did not alter the results.

Conclusions: Men who showed stress induced blood pressure reactivity and who reported high job demands experienced the greatest atherosclerotic progression, showing the association between dispositional risk characteristics and contextual determinants of disease and suggesting that behaviourally evoked cardiovascular reactivity may have a role in atherogenesis.

Introduction

People's susceptibility to disease varies widely and may be a reflection of differences in biological predispositions, personality, behaviour, and environmental exposures. In addition, psychological stress is commonly believed to play an important part in illness and premature death, particularly with respect to cardiovascular diseases.

One model that may explain why some people under great stress develop cardiovascular diseases or other illnesses and others do not is the diathesis-stress model of disease susceptibility. This model assumes that a biological predisposition to disease will be expressed only if a predisposed individual is exposed to unusual or prolonged stress.[1] One mechanism by which stress may be associated with cardiovascular diseases is hyperreactivity of the sympathetic nervous system, which manifests as exaggerated increases in blood pressure or heart rate in response to psychological or behavioural stressors.[23] In the diathesis-stress framework behaviourally evoked reactivity is considered to be a biological predisposition of an individual that is expressed and consequently leads to cardiovascular diseases only under high stress conditions.[1]

Situations in which stress induced reactivity may be elicited differ between people. The work environment is probably an important source of stress for most adults.[4] Furthermore, previous studies indicate that stressful jobs have a role in the illness and death caused by cardiovascular disease.[4-6] We used the diathesisstress model to examine the interactive effects of blood pressure reactivity to stress and high workplace demands on the progression of carotid atherosclerosis. This report is from the Kuopio ischaemic heart disease risk factor study, an ongoing, population based study of previously unestablished risk factors for carotid atherosclerosis, ischaemic heart disease, mortality, and other outcomes among middle aged men from the Kuopio region in Eastern Finland, an area of high coronary morbidity and mortality.[78]

Subjects and methods

A total of 2682 men aged 42, 48, 54, and 60 (82.9% of those eligible) were recruited for the baseline examination, which occurred between March 1984 and December 1989. Follow up examinations were conducted between March 1991 and December 1993 in men who had undergone ultrasound examination of the right and left carotid arteries at baseline. Of the 1229 men who were eligible for the follow up examination, 1038 (88.2%) participated, 107 refused, 52 could not participate because they had died, had severe illness, or had moved, and 32 could not be contacted. Average time to follow up was 4.2 years (range 3.9–5.1 years).

We excluded subjects if they were not fully employed at the time of the baseline examination (348 men), did not participate in the bicycle ergometer test because of scheduling difficulties (72), or had missing data on the covariates at baseline (27). Therefore, the results reported here are based on 591 men who were fully employed and had complete data on the job demands scale, the measure of anticipatory blood pressure reactivity, all covariates at baseline, and measurements of intima-media thickness at baseline and follow up. A comparison of the 447 subjects who were excluded with the 591 subjects with complete data found no significant differences in resting systolic blood pressure, body mass index, or mean intima-media thickness at baseline, although the subjects who were excluded were older (55.1 v 48.6 years, $P < 0.0001$).

Baseline and follow up examinations

Examinations were carried out over two days, one week apart, at both baseline and follow up and consisted of a wide variety of biochemical, physiological, anthropometric, and psychosocial tests, including a questionnaire on workplace demands and characteristics (see job demands scale). In addition, a maximal exercise tolerance test on an upright bicycle ergometer was administered at baseline. Medical history and drug treatment were checked during a medical examination at both baseline and follow up.

Blood pressure measurement

Blood pressure readings were obtained on two occasions by a trained observer using a random zero muddler sphygmomanometer (Hawksley). The protocol on the first examination day was as follows. Subjects rested supine for 15 minutes and blood pressure was measured at 5, 10, and 15 minutes; they then stood at rest and blood pressure was taken once after 1 minute; they finally sat at rest for 10 minutes, and blood pressure was measured at 5 and 10 minutes. Blood pressure while subjects were seated was also measured on the second examination day, one week later, after the subject had been seated on the bicycle ergometer for 5 minutes but before the exercise test protocol was begun. Measurements on both examination days were taken in the mornings.

Cardiovascular reactivity

The measure of reactivity used in this study was change in systolic blood pressure in anticipation of the exercise test (blood pressure after five minutes of seated rest on the bicycle ergometer before the start of the exercise test), which was calculated as the difference between the blood pressure reading while seated before exercise and the average of the two resting blood pressure readings while seated on the first examination day. The anticipation of exercise is characterised by emotional, behavioural, and physiological arousal attendant to the impending challenge. Blood pressure increases during this anticipatory period thus reflect cardiovascular adjustments in response to psychological and behavioural stress. In this study men with a systolic response of 20 mm Hg or greater were considered to be high reactors (45.7%). This measure of reactivity is a significant, independent predictor of incident hypertension in this population.[9]

Job demands scale

As part of the baseline examination participants completed a detailed questionnaire that included items about their work environment. The measure of job demands used in this study was an 11 item scale developed by Lynch *et al*[10] that conformed to important theoretical dimensions of the work environment.[4 5 11] Using a four point Likert response, respondents indicated how much stress they experienced from excessive supervision of time schedules, troublesome supervisors, troublesome coworkers, job responsibilities, poorly defined tasks and responsibilities, risk of accidents, risk of unemployment, and irregular work schedules. They were also asked to indicate how often they had work deadlines and how much stress this caused them and to rate both the mental and physical strenuousness of their work. Individual items were dichotomised such that only men reporting more than average strain or stress for any given item were considered positive for that item. The 11 dichotomised items were then summed to create the job demands scale score, which had a mean of 3.0 and range of 0–11 in the full sample, with Cronbach's α of 0.78. We considered men with a score of 4 or greater on the job demands scale to have high job demands. This cut off point was selected because it represented the upper quartile (26%) of the distribution of job demands scores in this population. Scores on the job demands scale were imputed based on non-missing items for men who had two or fewer items with missing responses (5%); those with more than two missing items were excluded from analyses. This scale predicts mortality and acute myocardial infarction in this population.[10]

Measurement of carotid atherosclerosis

The extent of carotid atherosclerosis was assessed by high resolution B mode ultrasonography of the right and left common carotid arteries in a 1.0–1.5 cm section at the distal end, proximal to the carotid bulb. Images were focused on the posterior wall of the right and left common carotid arteries and recorded on videotape for later analysis. Near wall images were not obtained because of their greater variability in measurement.[12] Ultrasound examinations at baseline and follow up were conducted by one of four sonographers who had been trained for a minimum of six months, and they were performed with the subject lying supine after a 15 minute rest. Details of the scanning protocol, technical aspects of measurement, and their reliability have been described elsewhere.[13]

At baseline arterial images were obtained using the ATL UM4 duplex ultrasound system with a 10 MHz sector transducer (Advanced Technology Laboratories, Bothell, WA). At follow up images were obtained with a Biosound Phase 2 scanner equipped with a 10 MHz annular array probe.[13] Wedge phantom studies of this system, calibrated against a 414B tissue phantom (Radiation Measurement, Middleton, WI), have shown measurement precision of 0.03 mm.[14 15]

Intima-media thicknesses were measured at baseline and follow up by computerised analysis of the videotaped ultrasound images using Prosound software (University of Southern California, Los Angeles, CA). This software uses an edge detection algorithm specifically designed for use with ultrasound imaging and permits automatic detection, tracking, and recording of the interfaces between intima and lumen and media and adventitia.[16] Intima-media thickness, calculated as the mean distance between these interfaces, was estimated at around 100 points in both the right and left common carotid arteries.

We used three measures of intima-media thickness: (*a*) mean intima-media thickness, calculated as the mean of all estimates from the right and left common carotid arteries and considered an overall measure of the atherosclerotic process in the carotid arteries; (*b*) maximum intima-media thickness, the average of the points of maximum thickness from the right and left common carotid arteries and indicative of the depth of intrusion of atherosclerotic thickening into the lumen in this part of the arteries; and (c) plaque height, the average of plaque height in the right and left common carotid arteries, calculated as the difference between maximum and minimum thickness, and an assessment of how steeply atherosclerotic lesions protruded into the lumen. Progression of atherosclerosis was estimated as follow up minus baseline values for each of these measures.

Baseline covariates

Biological risk factors – Resting systolic blood pressure was calculated as the average of the last two supine and the two seated blood pressure measurements obtained on the first examination day. Apolipoprotein B concentration was determined by an immunoturbidimetric method (KONE, Espoo, Finland). High density lipoprotein cholesterol-2, the protective subfraction of high density lipoprotein cholesterol, was separated from fresh plasma using ultracentrifugation and precipitation and its concentration measured enzymatically (CHOI)-PAP cholesterol method, Boehringer Mannheim, Mannheim, Germany). Blood glucose concentration was measured in whole blood samples after at least 12 hours of overnight fasting by the glucose dehydrogenase method after precipitation of the proteins with trichloroacetic acid (Granutest 100, Merck, Darmstadt, Germany). Body mass index was calculated as weight divided by height squared (kg/m^2).

Behavioural and educational factors – Alcohol consumption was assessed by a questionnaire on drinking behaviour over the previous 12 months and from dietary records over four days. Cigarette smoking was assessed by self report of never, former, and current smoking (measured in pack years). Education was assessed by self report of completed years of schooling.

Drug treatment – The use of drugs to treat hypertension and hyperlipidaemia was assessed at baseline by interview.

History of diabetes – A participant was considered to have a history of diabetes if he reported having taken drugs for or used diet to control diabetes or if he had a fasting blood glucose concentration of 6.7 mmol/l or greater at baseline.

Evaluation of prevalent ischaemic heart disease – Participants were considered to have prevalent ischaemic heart disease at baseline if they had a history of angina or myocardial infarction; if they currently took drugs for angina; or if they had positive findings of angina according to the Rose questionnaire.[17]

Data analyses

We examined the influence of workplace demands and cardiovascular reactivity on the progression of atherosclerosis over four years by estimating the mean change in each measure of intima-media thickness (mean, maximum, plaque height) according to low *v* high job demands and low *v* high reactors. These dichotomous variables and their product interaction term were entered as predictors into our linear regression models. Two sets of regression models were calculated. The initial model included adjustments for age, baseline intima-media thickness, zooming depth of the ultrasound scan, sonographer, and participation in the placebo or treatment arm of an unrelated clinical trial of pravastatin.[18] The second model included all variables in the initial model plus variables representing systolic blood pressure, apolipoprotein B concentration, high density lipoprotein cholesterol-2 concentration, body mass index, cigarette smoking, alcohol consumption, use of antihypertensive or antihyperlipidaemic drugs, and history of diabetes.

Analyses were performed using the general linear models procedure in SAS, version 6.09,[19] installed on a Sun Sparcstation 20. This procedure allowed least square mean values of intima-media thickness to be estimated and contrasted for each job demands/reactor group while simultaneously controlling for age and other covariates.

Results

Table 1 shows scores on the job demands scale, change in systolic blood pressure in anticipation of exercise, age, intima-media thicknesses at baseline, and other covariates by job demands and reactivity.

Demands, reactivity, and atherosclerotic progression

Table 2 shows age adjusted scores for changes in mean and maximum intima-media thickness and plaque height for the four groups from both the initial and fully adjusted models. Significant interactions between self reported job demands and reactivity were noted for progression of mean intima-media thickness ($\beta = 0.052$, 95% confidence interval 0.011 to 0.093, SE 0.021,

Table 1 Baseline covariates according to job demands and reactivity. Values are means (SD) unless stated otherwise

	Low job demands		High job demands	
	Low reactors (n=233)	High reactors (n=192)	Low reactors (n=88)	High reactors (n=78)
Job demands scale	1.7 (0.8)	1.8 (0.8)	5.0 (1.3)	5.0 (1.1)
Systolic pressure response (mm Hg)	8.5 (7.2)	31.6 (9.5)	9.3 (7.3)	33.0 (10.5)
Age (years)	47.6 (5.4)	50.7 (5.9)	47.8 (5.4)	51.6 (5.6)
Education (years)	10.9 (3.9)	9.5 (3.4)	9.4 (3.6)	9.3 (4.0)
Intima-media thickness (mm):				
Mean	0.70 (0.13)	0.76 (0.15)	0.73 (0.20)	0.77 (0.21)
Maximum	0.87 (0.17)	0.94 (0.20)	0.91 (0.27)	0.97 (0.29)
Plaque height (mm)	0.35 (0.13)	0.37 (0.14)	0.37 (0.17)	0.41 (0.22)
Resting systolic pressure (mm Hg)	131.2 (16.2)	131.9 (13.5)	132.2 (15.6)	130.8 (12.8)
Apolipoprotein B (mmol/l)	2.58 (0.60)	2.63 (0.53)	2.57 (0.54)	2.62 (0.51)
High density lipoprotein cholesterol 2 (mmol/l)	0.89 (0.30)	0.88 (0.27)	0.87 (0.28)	0.87 (0.26)
Blood glucose (mmol/l)	4.70 (1.08)	4.72 (1.21)	4.57 (0.54)	4.51 (0.46)
Body mass index (kg/m^2)	26.9 (3.6)	26.7 (3.2)	26.2 (2.9)	26.6 (3.1)
No (%) of subjects:				
Drinking alcohol (drinks/day):				
None	21 (9)	22 (12)	8 (9)	8 (10)
>2	61 (26)	37 (19)	18 (21)	15 (19)
Smoking:				
Never	76 (33)	52 (27)	29 (33)	23 (30)
Formerly	80 (34)	70 (37)	31 (35)	32 (41)
Currently	77 (33)	70 (36)	28 (32)	23 (30)
Receiving drug treatment:				
Antihyperlipidaemic agent	0	2 (1)	1 (10)	1 (1)
Antihypertensive agent	24 (10)	25 (13)	10 (11)	13 (17)
With diabetes	10 (4)	5 (3)	1 (1)	2 (3)

P < 0.014), maximum intima-media thickness ($\beta = 0.076$, 0.012 to 0.141, SE 0.033, P < 0.021), and plaque height ($\beta = 0.067$, 0.003 to 0.131, SE 0.033, P < 0.04). Men who reported high job demands and who were high reactors had the largest increases in mean and maximum intima-media thickness and plaque height over the four years of follow up (Table 2). Results were essentially unchanged after including adjustments for education, resting systolic blood pressure, apolipoprotein B concentration, high density lipoprotein cholesterol-2 concentration, body mass index, former and current smoking, alcohol consumption, use of drugs for hypertension or hyperlipidaemia, and history of diabetes. Indeed, the group with high demands and high reactivity showed 10–40% greater atherosclerotic progression than the other groups, even after adjustment for the various risk factors.

Demands, reactivity, and atherosclerotic progression in men without prevalent ischaemic heart disease

Table 3 shows mean (SE) changes in mean and maximum intima-media thickness and plaque height for the four groups, excluding 73 men with prevalent ischaemic heart disease at baseline.

Table 2 Progression of carotid atherosclerosis over four years according to job demands and reactivity in 591 Finnish men. Values are mean (SE) increases in millimetres

	Low job demands		High job demands		P value for interaction
	Low reactors (n=233)	High reactors (n=192)	Low reactors (n=88)	High reactors (n=78)	
Model 1* *Intima-media thickness:*					
Mean	0.123 (0.008)	0.109 (0.009)	0.099 (0.013)	0.138 (0.013)	<0.014
Maximum	0.261 (0.013)	0.267 (0.013)	0.238 (0.020)	0.320 (0.021)	<0.021
Plaque height	0.264 (0.013)	0.289 (0.013)	0.255 (0.020)	0.347 (0.021)	<0.04
Model 2† *Intima-media thickness:*					
Mean	0.122 (0.008)	0.106 (0.009)	0.093 (0.013)	0.134 (0.013)	<0.008
Maximum	0.261 (0.013)	0.262 (0.013)	0.228 (0.020)	0.312 (0.021)	<0.013
Plaque height	0.264 (0.013)	0.282 (0.013)	0.246 (0.020)	0.340 (0.020)	<0.022

*Adjusted for age, baseline intima-media thickness, ultrasound zooming depth, sonographer, and participation in placebo or treatment arms of Kuopio artherosclerosis prevention study.[18]

†Includes adjustments from model 1 plus covariates representing education, resting systolic blood pressure, apolipoprotein B concentration, high density lipoprotein cholesterol-2 concentration, fasting blood glucose concentration, former and current smoking, body mass index, alcohol consumption, use of antihyperlipidaemic or antihypertensive drugs, and history of diabetes.

Table 3 Progression of carotid atherosclerosis over four years according to job demands and reactivity in 518 men without prevalent ischaemic heart disease. Values are mean (SE) increases in millimetres*

	Low job demands		High job demands		P value for interaction
	Low reactors (n=216)	High reactors (n=168)	Low reactors (n=77)	High reactors (n=57)	
Intima-media thickness:					
Mean	0.122 (0.008)	0.110 (0.008)	0.112 (0.012)	0.126 (0.014)	<0.15
Maximum	0.256 (0.012)	0.255 (0.012)	0.252 (0.019)	0.290 (0.021)	<0.20
Plaque height	0.262 (0.013)	0.276 (0.013)	0.257 (0.020)	0.324 (0.022)	<0.12

*Adjusted for age, baseline intima-media thickness, ultrasound zooming depth, sonographer, and participation in placebo or treatment arms of Kuopio artherosclerosis prevention study.[18]

The pattern of findings was similar, albeit slightly weaker, to that in the full sample, with interactions between job demands and reactivity noted for each measure of atherosclerotic progression ($\beta = 0.03$, −0.011 to 0.070, SE 0.021, P < 0.15 for mean intima-media thickness; $\beta = 0.04$, −0.021 to 0.100, SE 0.031, P < 0.20 for maximum intima-media thickness; and $\beta = 0.052$, −0.013 to 0.117 SE 0.033, P < 0.12 for plaque height). Men with high job demands and high reactivity had a 13–15% greater increase in maximum intima-media thickness and a 17–26% greater increase in plaque height relative to the other groups. Adjustment for atherosclerotic risk factors in this subgroup did not alter the size of these differences (data not shown).

Demands, reactivity, and atherosclerotic progression by degree of stenosis at baseline

Table 4 shows the mean values of the three measures of atherosclerotic progression for the four groups according to the presence of carotid stenosis or non-stenotic atherosclerotic plaque at baseline.

Among the 121 men with at least 20% carotid stenosis or evidence of non-stenotic atherosclerotic plaque at baseline there were significant interactions between job demands and reactivity for progression of mean and maximum media-intima thickness ($\beta = 0.189$, 0.065 to 0.313, SE 0.063, P < 0.003 and $\beta = 0.284$, 0.073 to 0.495, SE 0.108, P < 0.0095 respectively); the interaction for plaque height was almost significant ($\beta = 0.121$, −0.080 to 0.323, SE 0.103, P < 0.24). Men with high job demands and reactivity showed the greatest increases in mean and maximum intima media thickness and plaque height from baseline to follow up, being more than 46% larger than those in the other groups. Models that included adjustments for atherosclerotic risk factors produced essentially the same patterns of results for both strata (data not shown). No interactions between job demands and reactivity were seen in the men without advanced thickening at baseline. However, high reactors showed greater progression of plaque height than low reactors (0.303 v 0.255 mm, P < 0.037). No differences were noted for mean or maximum intima-media thickness in this subgroup.

Table 4 Progression of carotid atherosclerosis over four years according to job demands and reactivity and degree of stenosis at baseline. Values are mean (SE) increases in millimetres*

	Low job demands		High job demands		P value for interaction
	Low reactors	High reactors	Low reactors	High reactors	
Carotid stenosis ≥20% or presence of non-stenotic atherosclerotic plaque					
No of subjects	34	54	13	20	
Intima-media thickness:					
Mean	0.118 (0.026)	0.097 (0.021)	0.004 (0.044)	0.173 (0.034)	<0.003
Maximum	0.250 (0.044)	0.252 (0.037)	0.134 (0.074)	0.420 (0.059)	<0.0095
Plaque height	0.255 (0.040)	0.272 (0.035)	0.280 (0.070)	0.418 (0.056)	<0.24
Carotid stenosis < 20%					
No of subjects	199	138	75	58	
Intima-media thickness:					
Mean	0.123 (0.009)	0.113 (0.010)	0.112 (0.013)	0.120 (0.014)	<0.40
Maximum	0.262 (0.013)	0.276 (0.015)	0.254 (0.020)	0.279 (0.021)	<0.71
Plaque height	0.257 (0.014)	0.296 (0.014)	0.253 (0.019)	0.310 (0.021)	<0.56

*Adjusted for age, baseline intima-media thickness, ultrasound zooming depth, sonographer, and participation in placebo or treatment arms of Kuopio artherosclerosis prevention study.[18]

Discussion

We found a significant interaction between cardiovascular reactivity and reported job demands such that men who showed a heightened increase in systolic blood pressure before an exercise stress test and who reported a highly demanding work environment experienced greater progression of carotid atherosclerosis than men who were less reactive or had fewer job demands, or both. This interaction was observed for the measures of mean and maximum intima-media thickness and plaque height and was largely unaffected by adjustment for known atherosclerotic risk factors. A similar, albeit slightly weaker, pattern of findings was seen in the subset of healthy men without prevalent ischaemic heart disease at baseline. However, the strongest associations were seen among men with early evidence of atherosclerosis, suggesting that the combined effects of stress induced reactivity and high job demands may be more pronounced once atherosclerotic plaque or measurable stenosis has occurred.

Support for diathesis-stress model of disease

Our data clearly show that dispositional characteristics of the individual, in combination with the work environment, are importantly related to disease progression. These findings support the diathesisstress model of disease susceptibility, which emphasises the synergistic relation between dispositional risk characteristics and contextual determinants of diseases. Moreover, our results provide some of the clearest human evidence to date that stress induced cardiovascular reactivity may play a part in atherogenesis. Additional support for this hypothesis comes from research in cynomolgus macaques which has shown that heightened sympathetic nervous system arousal and endothelial injury induced by psychosocial stressors (threat of capture, social disruption, and reorganisation) potentiate diet induced coronary and carotid atherosclerosis.[20–22] Interestingly, these psychosocially mediated effects are abolished after administration of β adrenergic antagonists.[3 22]

Interpretation of results

Our consistent results across the measures of mean and maximum intima-media thickness and plaque height suggest that the interactive effects of heightened blood pressure responses and high job demands influence the overall atherosclerotic process and contribute to the development or progression of focal lesions of the common carotid arteries. Increased arterial wall roughness with steeply projecting lesions may lead to greater shear stress and flow turbulence on the vessel walls, thereby increasing the likelihood of plaque rupture and thrombus formation.[22] Furthermore, although the differential pathological and clinical significance of the three measures of carotid atherosclerosis used in this study remains to be determined, cross sectional data from the entire Kuopio ischaemic heart disease risk factor study sample showed that each 0.10 mm difference in maximum thickness was associated with an 11% increase in risk of acute myocardial infarction ($P < 0.001$).[13]

The relations between behaviourally evoked reactivity and high job demands and atherosclerotic progression identified in our study were essentially unchanged after adjustments for known atherosclerotic risk factors, including resting blood pressure, lipoprotein concentrations, alcohol and cigarette consumption, body mass index, and education. This relative lack of confounding is somewhat surprising because of the strength of the known associations between these risk factors and atherosclerosis.[24 25] However, the cumulative effect of these variables on atherosclerosis may be accounted for by their associations with baseline intima-media thickness, which is a highly significant covariate in all models.

Conclusions

Our findings are limited to employed, middle aged white men. Additional research is needed to determine if these relations are also evident in non-white or female populations or among other age groups. Given that men and women are often employed in different occupational sectors and may perceive and experience workplace demands and job stress differently from one another, it is particularly important to examine the influence of sex differences on these associations. Furthermore, work is only one aspect of life. Therefore, it is important to consider a variety of social and interpersonal contexts that may be potential sources of stress in individuals' daily lives. The diathesis-stress model offers a valuable framework within which future research may be conducted and for examining the relations between various dispositional traits and work or other environments in relation to cardiovascular diseases and other illnesses.

Key messages

- Psychological stress plays an important part in the illness and premature death associated with cardiovascular disease, but individual susceptibility to disease varies according to biological predispositions, personality, behaviour, and environmental exposures

- This study found that a demanding work environment in combination with a predisposition to exaggerated blood pressure reactivity to stress was significantly related to progression of carotid atherosclerosis over four years among employed middle aged men and was independent of known atherosclerotic risk factors

- These findings support the role of stress induced reactivity in human atherogenesis

- Future research needs to confirm these findings in other populations and to examine the influence of other risk factors and environments on the progression of disease

References

1 Manuck SB, Kasprowicz AL, Muldoon MF. Behaviorally-evoked cardiovascular reactivity and hypertension: conceptual issues and potential associations. *Annals of Behavioral Medicine* 1990;12:17–29.

2 Lovallo WR, Wilson MF. The role of cardiovascular reactivity in hypertension risk In: Turner JR, Sherwood A, Light KC, eds. *Individual differences in cardiovascular response to stress.* New York: Plenum Press, 1992:165–86.

3 Manuck SB. Cardiovascular reactivity in cardiovascular disease: "Once more unto the breach." *International Journal of Behavioral Medicine* 1994;1:4–31.

4 Schnall PL, Landsbergis PA, Baker D. Job strain and cardiovascular disease. *Ann Rev Public Health* 1994;15:381–411.

5 Karasek R, Baker D, Marxer F, Ahlbom A, Theorell T. Job decision latitude, job demands, and cardiovascular disease: a prospective study of Swedish men. *Am J Public Health* 1981;71:694–705.

6 Karasek RA, Theorell T, Schwartz JE, Schnall PL, Pieper CF, Machela JL. Job characteristics in relation to the prevalence of myocardial infarction in the US health examination survey (HES) and the health and nutrition examination study (HANES). *Am J Public Health* 1988;78:910–8.

7 Salonen JT. Is there a continuing need for longitudinal epidemiologic research? The Kuopio ischemic heart disease risk factor study. *Ann Clin Res* 1988;20:46–50.

8 Keys A. *Seven countries: a multivariate analysis of death and coronary heart disease.* Cambridge, MA: Harvard University Press, 1980.

9 Everson SA, Kaplan GA, Goldberg DE, Salonen JT. Anticipatory blood pressure response to exercise predicts future high blood pressure in middle-aged men. *Hypertension* 1996;27:1059–64.

10 Lynch JL, Krause N, Kaplan GA, Tuomilehto J, Salonen JT. Workplace demands and resources, economic reward and the risk of mortality and acute myocardial infarction. Prospective evidence from the Kuopio ischemic heart disease risk factor study. *Am J Public Health* (in press).

11 Siegrist J, Peter R, Junge A, Cremer P, Seidel D. Low status control, high effort at work and ischaemic heart disease: Prospective evidence from blue-collar men. *Soc Sci Med* 1990;31:1127–54.

12 Wikstrand J, Wendelhag L. Methodological considerations of ultrasound investigation of intima-media thickness and lumen diameter. *J Intern Med* 1994;236:555–9.

13 Salonen JT, Salonen R. Ultrasound B-mode imaging in observational studies of atherosclerotic progression. *Circulation* 1993;87(suppl II): 50–65.

14 Salonen R, Salonen JT. Intima-media changes in a population study: KIHD. In: Boccalon H. ed. *Vascular medicine.* Amsterdam: Elsevier Science Publishers, 1993:301–4.

15 Salonen JT, Korpela H, Salonen R, Nyyssönen K. Precision and reproducibility of ultrasonographic measurement of progression of common carotid artery atherosclerosis. *Lancet* 1993;341:1158–9.

16 Blankenhorn DH, Selzer RH, Crawford DW, Barth JD, Liu CR, Liu CH, *et al.* Beneficial effects of colestipol-niacin therapy on the common carotid artery. Two- and four-year reduction of intima-media thickness measured by ultrasound. *Circulation* 1993;88:2–8.

17 Rose GA, Blackburn H, Gillum RF, Prineas RJ. *Cardiovascular survey methods.* Geneva: World Health Organisation, 1982.

18 Salonen R, Nyyssönen K, Porkkala E, Rummukainen J, Belder R, Park J, *et al.* Kuopio atherosclerosis prevention study (KAPS). *Circulation* 1995;92:1758–64.

19 SAS Institute. *SAS user's guide: statistics.* Version 6.09. Cary, NC:SAS, 1990.

20 Manuck SB, Kaplan JR, Clarkson TB. Behaviorally induced heart rate reactivity and atherosclerosis in cynomolgus monkeys. *Psychosom Med* 1983;45:95–108.

21 Manuck SB, Kaplan JR, Clarkson TB. Behaviorally elicited heart rate reactivity and atherosclerosis in female cynomolgus monkeys (Macaca fascicularis). *Psychosom Med* 1989;51:306–18.

22 Kaplan JR, Pettersson K, Manuck SB, Olsson G. Role of sympathoadrenal medullary activation in the initiation and progression of atherosclerosis. *Circulation* 1991;84(suppl VI):23–52.

23 Lynch JL, Kaplan GA, Salonen R, Salonen JT. Socioeconomic status and progression of carotid atherosclerosis. Prospective evidence from the Kuopio ischaemic heart disease risk factor study. *Arteriosclerosis, Thrombosis and Vascular Biology* (in press).

24 Salonen JT, Seppänen K, Rauramaa R, Salonen R. Risk factors for carotid atherosclerosis: The Kuopio ischaemic heart disease risk factor study. *Ann Med* 1989;21:227–9.

25 Evans GW, Chambless LE, Szklo M, Folsom AR, Hutchinson RG, Heiss G, *et al.* Risk factors for carotid atherosclerosis progression: The ARIC study. *Circulation* 1996;93:629.

Pereira, D.B., Antoni, M.H., Danielson, A. et al. (2003) Life stress and cervical squamous intraepithelial lesions in women with human papillomavirus and human immunodeficiency virus. *Psychosomatic Medicine*, 65 (1): 1–8.

Life stress and cervical squamous intraepithelial lesions in women with human papillomavirus and human immunodeficiency virus

Deidre Byrnes Pereira, PhD, Michael H. Antoni, PhD,
Aimee Danielson, PhD, Trudi Simon, ARNP,
JoNell Efantis-Potter, ARNP,
Charles S. Carver, PhD, Ron E. F. Durán, PhD, Gail Ironson, MD, PhD,
Nancy Klimas, MD, and Mary Jo O'Sullivan, MD

Abstract

Objective: Human immunodeficiency virus (HIV)-infected women are at risk for cervical intraepithelial neoplasia (CIN) and cancer due to impaired immunosurveillance over human papillomavirus (HPV) infection. Life stress has been implicated in immune decrements in HIV-infected individuals and therefore may contribute to CIN progression over time. The purpose of this study was to determine whether life stress was associated with progression and/or persistence of squamous intraepithelial lesions (SIL), the cytologic diagnosis conferred by Papanicolaou smear, after 1-year follow-up among women co-infected with HIV and HPV.

Method: Thirty-two HIV-infected African-American and Caribbean-American women underwent a psychosocial interview, blood draw, colposcopy, and HPV cervical swab at study entry. Using medical chart review, we then abstracted SIL diagnoses at study entry and after 1-year follow-up.

Results: Hierarchical logistic regression analysis revealed that higher life stress increased the odds of developing progressive/persistent SIL over 1 year by approximately seven-fold after covarying relevant biological and behavioral control variables.

Conclusions: These findings suggest that life stress may constitute an independent risk factor for SIL progression and/or persistence in HIV-infected women. Stress management interventions may decrease risk for SIL progression/persistence in women living with HIV.

From the Department of Psychology (D.B.P., M.H.A., A.D., C.S.C., R.E.F.D., G.I., N.K.), University of Miami, Coral Gables, Florida; and Department of Obstetrics and Gynecology (D.B.P., T.S., J.E-P., M.J.O.), Department of Psychiatry (M.H.A., G.I.), and Departments of Microbiology and Immunology (N.K.), University of Miami School of Medicine, Miami, Florida.

Address reprint requests to: Deidre Byrnes Pereira, PhD, Department of Clinical and Health Psychology, University of Florida, P.O. Box 100165, 101 S. Newell Dr., Room 3137, Gainesville, FL 326100165. Email: dpereira@hp.ufl.edu

▶ **Keywords:** HIV, squamous intraepithelial lesions (SIL), human papillomavirus (HPV), stress, psychoneuroimmunology (PNI), women.
AIDS=acquired immune deficiency syndrome; CI=confidence interval; CIN=cervical intraepithelial neoplasia; HAART=highly active antiretroviral therapy; HGSIL=high-grade SIL; HIV=human immunodeficiency virus; HPV=human papillomavirus; LES=Life Experiences Survey; LGSIL=low-grade SIL; NKCC=natural killer cell cytotoxicity; SIL=squamous intraepithelial lesions.

HIV-infected women have high prevalence, incidence, and persistence rates of both human papillomavirus (HPV) infection and cervical intraepithelial lesions (CIN) (1–6). HIV-infected women also experience high rates of CIN recurrence (7) and treatment complications (8). Although recent studies have not observed high-grade CIN and invasive cervical carcinoma with great frequency in HIV-infected women (2, 6), Maiman et al. (9) found that cervical cancer was the most common acquired immune deficiency syndrome (AIDS)-related malignancy among HIV-infected women in New York City from 1987 to 1995. They also reported that cervical cancer was more likely to recur despite adequate therapy and was associated with a greater risk of death.

Low socioeconomic status African-American women living with HIV may be at especially high risk for CIN progression, recurrence, and treatment complications. African-American women are disproportionately affected by HIV (10) and HPV infections (4) and have the second highest cervical cancer mortality rates in the United States (11). Therefore, primary and secondary prevention of CIN are crucial to maximizing the health and quality of life of minority women co-infected with HIV and HPV.

HPV infection, impaired immune functioning, and behaviors such as smoking have been identified as risk factors for CIN in HIV-infected women. However, virtually no research has examined the possible role of psychosocial factors, such as life stress. Life stress and other psychosocial factors such as depression have been implicated in the reactivation of latent viruses (12–14), immune decrements in both HIV+ men and women (15, 16), faster progression to AIDS in HIV+ men and women (17–19), and more advanced CIN in HIV– women (20). The purpose of the present study was to determine whether life stress was associated with the progression and/or persistence of squamous intraepithelial lesions (SIL), the cytologic diagnosis conferred by Papanicolaou smear, in African-American and Caribbean-American women living with HIV and HPV[1].

Materials and methods
Participants

Participants were 32 HIV-1 seropositive African-American, Haitian, Jamaican, and Bahamian women between the ages of 15 and 50 enrolled in a National Cancer Institute funded study of psychosocial, viral, and immune risk factors for CIN. Participants were recruited from an immunology clinic in the Department of Obstetrics and Gynecology at the University of Miami. This study was conducted in accordance with the rules and regulations of the Human Subjects Committee of the Institutional Review Board at the University of Miami School of Medicine.

---

1 For the purposes of this paper, CIN and SIL will be used interchangeably.

Inclusion criteria included one abnormal Papanicolaou smear in the 2 years before study enrollment, a CD4 + CD3 + cell count ≥ 150 cells/mm³, and fluency in English. Exclusion criteria included past or current clinical AIDS (ie, Category C) diagnosis (21), a history of high-grade SIL (HGSIL) or cervical cancer, hysterectomy, treatment for SIL in the year before enrollment, and intravenous drug use in the 6 months before enrollment.

We used a prospective study design. At study entry, participants completed informed consent and underwent a psychosocial assessment interview, peripheral venous blood draw, and colposcopy and HPV cervical swab. A 10-item abbreviated version of the Life Experiences Survey (LES) (22) was used to measure stressful life events. The LES has been used successfully in prior cross-sectional research examining the association between psychosocial factors and cervical dysplasia (23). In the present study, we used a modified 10-item version of the LES. This shortened version of the LES was developed by researchers at the University of Miami in the early 1990s to assess the unique stressors of HIV + women of color in obstetric-gynecology settings, particularly HIV + postpartum women. To this end, focus groups were convened to determine the most frequent and salient life events listed on the full 57-item LES for this specific population. Focus group responses revealed that stressors associated with the peripartum period, such as changes in eating and sleeping habits, pregnancy, addition of a new family member, and an outstanding personal achievement (eg, "being a good mom") were cited as most frequent and salient. Other stressors included changing a work situation, residence, and church activities. These were often cited as indirectly caused by or complicated by pregnancy or childbirth. Deaths of family members and close friends were also cited as frequent and salient. The LES-10 comprised these items. Although not all of our participants in the current study were postpartum, we elected to use the LES-10 due to the similarities between our sample and focus group respondents in socioeconomic status, health concerns, and recruitment setting (special immunology obstetrics-gynecology clinic). A secondary benefit of using this instrument was decreased participant burden, an important concern when working with hard-to-access populations.

For each event that occurred in the past year, participants rated its impact from "extremely negative" (−3) to "extremely positive" (+3). An average subjective impact score for negative life events experienced in the 6 months before enrollment was computed. This stress score equaled the sum of the impact scores for all negatively rated events divided by the total number of negative life events experienced. If a participant did not experience a negative event listed on the LES-10, she was assigned a life stress score of "0," or "no impact." Higher life stress scores indicated higher impact of negative life events (ie, 0 = no impact; 1 = slightly negative; 2 = moderately negative; 3 = extremely negative).

The distribution of lymphocyte phenotypes was determined by flow cytometry at study entry as described in detail by Ironson et al. (24). Given the relationship between greater immunosuppression and risk for SIL promotion in HIV-infected women (6), we measured the decline in CD4 + CD3 + % as a possible control variable. CD4 + CD3 + % after 1-year follow-up was abstracted using chart review.

At study entry, a colposcopic examination was conducted by two colposcopy-trained nurse practitioners according to standard colposcopy protocol (25). Before the application of acetic acid solution, an HPV cervical swab was collected for detection and subtyping of HPV. HPV detection and subtyping utilized dot blot (DB) hybridization analysis as described previously by Byrnes et al. (26). Briefly, this procedure allowed for the detection of HPV types 6/11/42/43/44 ("6/11"), the types conferring low risk for SIL progression, and types 16/18/31/33/35/45/51/52/56 ("16/18"), the types conferring intermediate and high risk for SIL progression (3). For the purposes of this study, we operationalized risk for SIL progression as presence of HPV types 16/18. Presence of these types was coded as "1," while absence of these types (including presence of HPV 6/11) was coded as "0."

We used medical chart review to follow SIL diagnoses prospectively for 8 to 16 months based on cytology[2]. This time frame was selected because our prospective data collection was linked to patient care, and patients averaged approximately one Papanicolaou smear every 8 months[3].

SIL outcome was operationalized in terms of whether the participant experienced the progression and/or persistence of SIL at 1-year follow-up. If a participant experienced the progression or persistence of SIL at 1 year, she was assigned a "1" for the outcome variable, while a "0" was assigned for participants who remained free of SIL or regressed to no SIL over this period.

To control for the possible effects of immunosuppression on SIL progression over the follow-up period (6), we also followed CD4+CD3+% prospectively for 6 to 18 months. We utilized this time frame because our prospective data collection was linked to patient care, and participants averaged approximately one T-cell subset analysis every 6 months.

We began by conducting independent-samples t tests and χ^2 analyses between progression and/or persistence at 1-year follow-up and demographic (ie, age, income, education); viral (ie, presence of HPV 16/18); behavioral (eg, cigarette smoking and medication use); immune (ie, CD4+CD3+% decline); and gynecological (eg, number of genital herpes simplex virus outbreaks) control variables relevant to SIL. We then used hierarchical logistic regression analysis to predict progression and/or persistence after 1 year from life stress. If a control variable was related to progression and/or persistence after 1 year ($p \leq 0.10$), it was entered as a covariate in the regression equation before entry of life stress. Covariates were entered in blocks with similar variables. The predictor of interest, subjective impact of negative life events in the 6 months before study entry ("life stress"), was added in the last block.

Results

Demographic characteristics

The 32 participants included African-American (78%), Haitian (13%), Bahamian (3%), and Jamaican (6%) women with a mean age of 28.2 years (SD=6.3). The vast majority described themselves as single/never married (78%) and reported having one current sex partner (71%). The mean level of education was a high-school degree (mean years of education=11.6, SD= 1.7), and 72% of the participants reported a yearly income of less than $10,000. Eighty-seven percent (N=27) of the women reported having at least one child, and 59% reported parturition in the past year. The mean time since last delivery was 3.5 years (SD=6.0). One participant became pregnant during the 1-year follow-up period. She did not carry the pregnancy to term.

Health status

Clinical and immunologic status. At study entry, the mean time since HIV diagnosis was 3.0 years (SD=2.1), and all participants were in the asymptomatic or symptomatic (pre-AIDS) phase of HIV infection. Thirty-five percent of the participants reported experiencing at least

---

2 We utilized a histopathologic diagnosis for one participant who did not have a cytologic SIL diagnosis during follow-up. Exclusion of her data did not alter the findings in this paper.

3 One participant had 5 months between SIL diagnoses at study entry and follow-up. Exclusion of her data did not alter the findings in this paper.

one current HIV-related symptom at baseline. The mean CD4 + CD3 + cells/mm³ at baseline was 526.9 (SD = 254.3). One participant had a CD4 + CD3 + cell count below 200 cells/mm³, 13 (43%) had counts between 200 and 500 cells/mm³, and 16 (57%) had counts greater than 500 cells/mm³. The mean baseline CD4 + CD3 + percentage was 27.2% (SD = 9.3) with a statistically significant decline to 23.7% (SD = 10.3) after 1 year [$t(31) = 3.5$, $p = 0.002$].

HPV status and squamous intraepithelial lesions. Fifty percent of the women were infected with HPV 16/18 at baseline. Seventy-five percent had no SIL at baseline, whereas 25% had (low-grade SIL) LGSIL. At 1-year follow-up, 78% had no SIL, 19% had LGSIL, and 3% had HGSIL. Sixty-three percent remained free of SIL at baseline and 1 year, while 15% regressed from LGSIL at baseline to no SIL at 1 year. This group was designated the "no SIL at follow-up" group. In contrast, 22% either developed new SIL or showed evidence of persistent LGSIL or HGSIL at 1-year follow-up. This group was designated the "progressed or persistent SIL at follow-up" group.

Health-related behaviors

At study entry, 16 participants (50%) were not on antiretrovirals or protease inhibitors, while 7 (22%) were on one antiretroviral ("monotherapy"), and 9 (28%) were on double or triple combination therapy. Only two women on combination therapy reported taking a protease inhibitor. Twenty-eight percent of women had at least one diagnostic procedure (ie, cervical biopsy and/or endocervical curettage)[4] for SIL during the follow-up period. No participants had treatment (ie, LEEP procedure or cone biopsy) for CIN during the follow-up period.

Eleven women (34%) reported cigarette smoking at baseline. Of the women who smoked, the average number of cigarettes smoked in the month before baseline interview was 325.5 (SD = 237.3) or approximately four packs per week. Only eight women (25%) reported alcohol use and three (9%) reported marijuana use in the month before study entry. No participants reported use of crack cocaine in the month before study entry, although eight (26%) reported a prior history of crack cocaine use.

Life stress

Forty-four percent (N = 14) reported no negative impact of life events in the past 6 months, 19% (N = 6) reported a slightly negative impact, 18% (N = 6) reported a moderately negative impact, and 19% (N = 6) reported an extremely negative impact. The most common negatively rated life event was the death of a close friend or family member. Thirty-one percent (N = 10) reported being aversively impacted by a death in the past 6 months. The frequency of each negatively rated life stressor is listed in Table 1.

Relations between progression/persistence of SIL and control variables

Table 2 presents the means and standard deviations (SDs) of continuous control variables by SIL status at 1-year follow-up (ie, progressive and/or persistent SIL vs. regressive and/or absent SIL). Independent-samples *t* tests revealed that women with progressive and/or persistent SIL at 1 year experienced greater declines in CD4 + CD3 + % [$t(30) = 2.36$, $p = 0.03$] and reported

---

4 Unlike treatment procedures, such as LEEP procedure or cone biopsy, neither of these diagnostic procedures would be expected to affect the risk of SIL progression/persistence during follow-up.

Table 1 Frequency of negatively-rated life stressors experienced in the past 6 months by HIV+ women in an obstetric-gynecology setting

Life stressor	Frequency
Death of a family member	6
Death of a close friend	4
Major change in eating habits	3
Major change in sleeping habits	3
Change in a work situation	3
Pregnancy*	3
Major change in church activities	2
Change in residence	2
Addition of a new family member	0
Outstanding personal achievement	0

* Of the three women who reported pregnancy as a negative life stressor in the past 6 months, only one carried the pregnancy to term.

higher negative life stress scores before study entry [$t(30) = 2.27$, $p = 0.03$]. Decline in CD4 + CD3 + % was retained as a control variable in further analyses. In contrast to other research (27), the number of cigarettes smoked in the month before study entry was not significantly associated with SIL status.

Likelihood ratio tests between SIL status at 1-year follow-up and highly active antiretroviral therapy (HAART) status, income bracket, and presence of HPV 16/18 revealed that only the presence of HPV 16/18 was significantly associated with progression and/or persistence of SIL at 1 year [$\chi^2 (2) = 4.97$, $p = 0.03$]. This was retained as a control variable. HAART usage was marginally associated with regression and/or absence of SIL at 1-year follow-up [$\chi^2 (2) = 5.37$, $p = 0.07$]. HAART usage was retained as a control variable in further analyses as a conservative measure due to its documented relationship with SIL (28). Income was unrelated to SIL status at 1-year follow-up.

Predicting progression/persistence of SIL with life stress

Our regression equation contained three blocks of variables. The first block included biological control variables (ie, HPV 16/18, declines in CD4 + CD3 + %); and the second block included behavioral control variables (ie, antiretroviral usage). Life stress was entered in the third block. After controlling for biological and behavioral control variables, hierarchical logistical regression revealed that life stress accounted for 27% of the variance in progression and/or persistence of SIL at 1 year. Higher life stress increased the odds of developing progressive and/or persistent SIL over 1 year by approximately nine-fold (95% CI = 1.07–69.08)[5]. The overall model was significant [$\chi^2 (4) = 18.36$, $p = 0.001$] (Table 3).

The possibility existed that several life stressors, namely major changes in eating habits and sleeping habits, could be manifestations or consequences of HIV disease progression. In addition, although no study to date has shown that pregnancy is associated with significantly

5 We were initially concerned that multicollinearity between our predictors may have produced inflation of the standard error of the regression coefficients, leading to wide confidence intervals. However, we tested for this and found that the tolerance associated with life stress was 0.93, indicating that only a small percentage of the variance in life stress was accounted for by other independent variables in the equation. The wide confidence intervals are likely due to our small sample size.

Table 2 Means and standard deviations of potential control variables by SIL status at 1 year

Potential control variable	Progressive/persistent SIL group		Regressive/absent SIL group		t	df	p Value (2-tailed)
	Mean	SD	Mean	SD			
Age (yrs)	28.00	6.68	28.24	6.34	−0.09	30	0.94
Education (yrs)	11.86	1.95	11.58	1.67	0.37	29	0.72
No. of HIV-related symptoms at study entry	0.14	0.38	0.88	1.45	−1.31	29	0.21
Length of time since HIV diagnosis (yrs)	3.14	2.67	2.91	1.94	0.26	29	0.80
No. of sex partners at study entry	0.57	0.53	0.83	0.48	−1.24	29	0.23
No. of episodes of unprotected sex in month prior to study entry	0.00	0.00	2.42	10.18	−0.62	29	0.54
Age at first coitus (yrs)	16.43	2.82	15.90	1.76	0.61	30	0.55
No. of cigarettes smoked in month prior to study entry	50.00	65.57	129.20	229.82	−0.89	30	0.38
No. of Pap smears in 24 months prior to study entry	2.57	1.90	2.84	1.03	−0.50	30	0.62
CD4+CD3+% decline over 1-year follow-up (log transformed)	−7.93	3.60	−2.36	5.79	−2.40	30	0.03*
No. of HSV-2 outbreaks over 1-year follow-up	0.20	0.45	0.08	0.27	0.80	28	0.44
No. of drinks of alcohol consumed in month prior to study entry	1.43	2.30	3.60	11.26	−0.50	30	0.62
No. of times of marijuana usage in month prior to study entry	0.00	0.00	3.70	13.17	−0.73	30	0.47
Negative life stress impact score [0 (none) −3 (extremely negative)]	1.96	1.02	0.88	1.13	2.27	30	0.03*

* $p \leq .05$.

Table 3 Predicting progression and/or persistence of SIL after 1 year from life stress in the past 6 months

(Step number) predictor	Wald statistic	Odds ratio	95% CI	p Value
(1) Biological variables				
Presence of HPV 16/18 at study entry	2.07	0.18	0.02–1.88	0.15
Decline in CD4+CD3+% during 1-year follow-up	2.86	0.81	0.64–1.03	0.10
(2) Behavioral variable				
Antiretroviral medication use at study entry[a]	0.73	0.50	0.10–2.46	0.40
(3) Psychological variable life stress[b]	4.08	8.58	1.07–69.08	0.05

$N=32$. Significance of model, $\chi^2 (4)=18.36$, $p=0.001$.

[a] 0=no use of antiretrovirals; 1=use of 1 antiretroviral; 2=use of 2 or more antiretrovirals.

[b] Average impact rating of all negatively rated events in the past year as measured by a modified 10-item version of the Life Experiences Survey (Sarason et al., 1979) (0=no impact or no negatively rated life events; 1=slightly negative; 2=moderately negative; 3=extremely negative).

elevated risk for mortality or AIDS incidence in HIV+ women, pregnancy carried to term is associated with immunologic changes (29) that could possibly alter risk for SIL progression/ persistence. As a conservative measure, we eliminated negativity ratings associated with major changes in eating and sleeping habits. Of the three women who reported pregnancy as a negative life event in the 6 months before study entry, only one carried the pregnancy to term. To eliminate the possibility that pregnancy-induced alterations in immune functioning may have influenced risk for SIL at follow-up, we removed this participant from our logistic regression analysis. With our revised life stress score and removal of this participant, hierarchical logistical regression revealed that life stress accounted for 26% of the variance in progression and/or persistence of SIL after 1 year. Higher life stress increased the odds of developing progressive and/or persistent SIL over 1 year by approximately seven-fold (95% CI = 1.00−45.14). The overall model was significant [$\chi^2 (4) = 18.14$, $p=0.001$].

Discussion

For many years, life stress has been posited and examined as a possible cofactor in the initiation and promotion of neoplastic processes, particularly those that are virally mediated and therefore immunogenic (12). Life stressors have been associated with the reactivation of latent viruses, such as herpesviruses (12–14), immune decrements in HIV+ men and women (15–16), faster progression to AIDS in HIV+ men and women (17–19), and more advanced cervical intraepithelial neoplasia in HIV-seronegative women (20). There is substantial evidence that CIN is initiated by HPV, a latent DNA virus that is commonly sexually transmitted. Psychosocial factors, such as life stress, may be associated with impaired immunosurveillance over HPV infection and increased risk for CIN progression. Among women co-infected with HIV and HPV, preliminary evidence exists that psychosocial factors are associated with lower natural killer cell cytotoxicity (NKCC) and percentages of cytotoxic/suppressor T cells (23), two immune markers linked to viral and neoplastic control (30).

Therefore, in the present study, we evaluated the effects of life stress on the progression and/or persistence of squamous intraepithelial lesions in African-American and Caribbean-American women living with human immunodeficiency virus and human papillomavirus. In doing so, we observed high rates of oncogenic HPV infection and SIL prevalence at study entry, which is consistent with other research (3). Fifty percent of women were infected with oncogenic HPV types, and 25% of women had SIL at baseline. These numbers are higher than those found by Minkoff et al. (3) (HPV prevalence: 38.5%; abnormal Papanicolaou smear prevalence: 22.5%), perhaps because we specifically recruited women with at least one recent abnormal Papanicolaou smear from an immunology obstetric and gynecology clinic. Contrary to other published research (31), however, only 22% had SIL that progressed and/or persisted over the year. This may be due to several factors. First, our sample was relatively healthy because we excluded women with AIDS-related opportunistic infections and CD4+CD3+ cell counts below 150 cells/mm^3. The overall health of our sample may have created an unfavorable environment for SIL progression and persistence. Second, our reliance on Papanicolaou smears may have underestimated the percentages of women with SIL (32–33). Third, given the components of the study (eg, psychosocial interview) and time commitment required, selection bias may have resulted in a sample that was more adherent with medical recommendations (eg, colposcopies, medication) or more knowledgeable or concerned about their health. Fourth, because these women were attending an immunology clinic because they had been identified as especially high risk for SIL, they represented patients receiving medical care more aggressive than normal throughout the follow-up period. Despite these potential sources of bias, we were able to identify a subgroup who still revealed evidence of disease progression and/or persistence at follow-up.

As predicted, women experiencing life stress in the 6 months before study entry had a seven-fold risk of developing progressive/persistent SIL 1 year later. This finding held after we controlled for the presence of oncogenic HPV types, declines in CD4+CD3+% over follow-up, and antiretroviral medication usage. This is the first study to our knowledge to demonstrate a longitudinal relationship between stress and SIL in women living with HIV.

The most common negative life stressor in the sample was the death of a close friend or family member. Multiple AIDS-related bereavements are common experiences for HIV+ women (34). Bereavement is associated with a rapid decline of CD4+CD3+ cell count (35) and decrements in NKCC and lymphocyte proliferate responses in HIV+ gay men (36). Psychosocial interventions for HIV+ bereaved men, conversely, exhibit beneficial effects on immune status, neuroendocrine functioning, and distress in HIV+ men (37–39). Few, if any, studies have examined the impact of bereavement on health outcome in HIV+ women. The present data may be among the first to suggest that bereavement is a risk factor for cervical dysplasia, an AIDS-related and gender-specific condition.

Life stress may be associated with SIL progression and persistence in this sample through neuroendocrine and immune pathways or through health behavior pathways. Life stress may cause decrements in natural immunity (eg, NKCC) and/or cell-mediated immunity (eg, CD4+ CD3+ cells, CD8+CD3+ cells) through elevations in glucocorticoid hormones, such as cortisol (34–35, 40–41). Decreases in these components may affect immunosurveillance over HPV infection and may allow SIL to persist or progress (36, 42).

Life stress may also affect SIL persistence through behavioral pathways. High levels of life stress may interfere with self-care behaviors, which are vital to health maintenance for women living with HIV. For instance, women with high levels of life stress and distress may have difficulty following through with medical recommendations for Papanicolaou smear screenings, colposcopy, and antiretroviral medication usage (37–40, 43–46), thus leading to SIL progression and/or persistence.

Although the present findings do not reveal the pathways through which stress is associated with SIL, they do suggest that HIV+/HPV+ women who are experiencing life stress may benefit from psychosocial assessment and counseling as an adjunct to standard medical care. Obstetric and gynecology practitioners may consider referring highly stressed patients to group-based cognitive-behavioral stress management interventions (41, 47). Within a supportive group atmosphere, such interventions emphasize increasing awareness of the effects of stress and changing appraisals of stressful situations in order to impact mood, behavior, and interpersonal relationships. Furthermore, these interventions seek to improve coping skills, social support, anger management, and assertiveness skills. Prior work has demonstrated potentially beneficial psychological, hormonal, and immunologic changes in HIV + individuals participating in this form of intervention (42–44, 48–50). The present research broaches the possibility that honing these skills may buffer SIL progression and/or persistence in women living with HIV and HPV.

The present study has several limitations. The low sample size may have produced unstable findings and lack of generalizability. Replication with a larger sample is needed. In addition, the LES-10 does not represent all of the potentially important life events experienced by HIV + women, such as poverty, racism, domestic violence, and unsafe neighborhoods. It also contained several items that could be manifestations of HIV disease progression (eg, changes in eating habits) or could potentially alter risk of SIL progression/persistence (eg, pregnancy). Future research in this area should utilize life stress measures that provide greater variation in type, chronicity, and severity of life events and less potential for confounding with disease status. Given the fact that much of our data were collected before HIV viral load was routinely measured in HIV + individuals, we were unable to control for the possible effects of HIV viral load on SIL progression/persistence. Future research should examine the possibility that life stress affects SIL through decreases in HAART adherence and increases in HIV viral load. Furthermore, the prospective design of our research necessitated the use of chart review to obtain SIL diagnoses. The quantity and quality of follow-up data in charts are confounded with illness factors and access to medical care, which may have biased our data in unknown ways. We also did not have histopathologic confirmation of SIL at study entry or follow-up. Reliance solely on Papanicolaou smears for follow-up may have underestimated the percentages of women with SIL at follow-up (32–33). Finally, this research would be better served by gauging lifetime history of cigarette smoking (eg, through pack-years of smoking), rather than cigarette smoking in the month before study entry. Pack-years of smoking may be related to progression/persistence of SIL unlike recent cigarette smoking. Despite these limitations, it seems plausible that psychosocial assessment and stress management may emerge as important components of primary care and gynecologic treatment for women living with HIV and HPV.

Acknowledgements

This work was supported by Grants T32-MH18917, P01-MH49548, P30CA14395, and P50CA84944-01 from the National Institutes of Health. The authors thank the nursing and social work staff of the Department of Obstetrics and Gynecology at the University of Miami for their help in conducting this research.

References

1 Hankins C, Coutlee F, Lapointe N, Simard P, Tran T, Samson J, Hum L. Prevalence of risk factors associated with human papillomavirus infection in women living with HIV. Canadian Women's HIV Study Group. CMAJ 1999;160:185–91.

2 Massad LS, Riester KA, Anastos KM, Fruchter RG, Palefsky JM, Burk RD, Burns D, Greenblatt RM, Muderspach LI, Miotti P. Prevalence and predictors of squamous cell abnormalities in Papanicolaou smears from women infected with HIV-1. Women's Interagency HIV Study Group. J Acquir Immune Defic Syndr 1999;21:33–41.

3 Minkoff HL, Eisenberger-Matityahu D, Feldman J, Burk R, Clarke L. Prevalence and incidence of gynecologic disorders among women infected with human immunodeficiency virus. Am J Obstet Gynecol 1999;180:824–36.

4 Palefsky JM, Minkoff H, Kalish LA, Levine A, Sacks HS, Garcia P, Young M, Melnick S, Miotti P, Burk R. Cervicovaginal human papillomavirus infection in human immunodeficiency virus-1 (HIV)-positive and high-risk HIV-negative women. J Natl Cancer Inst 1999;91:226–36.

5 Rezza G, Giuliani M, Branca M, Benedetto A, Migliore G, Garbuglia AR, D'Ubaldo C, Pezzotti P, Cappiello G, Pomponi Formiconi D, Suligoi B, Schiesari A, Ippolito G, Giacomini G. Determinants of squamous intraepithelial lesions (SIL) on Pap smear: the role of HPV infection and of HIV-1 induced immunosuppression. DIANAIDS Collaborative Study Group. Eur J Epidemiol 1997;13:937–43.

6 Stratton P, Gupta P, Riester K, Fox H, Zorrilla C, Tuomala R, Eriksen N, Vajaranant M, Minkoff H, Fowler MG. Cervical dysplasia on cervicovaginal Papanicolaou smear among HIV-1-infected pregnant and nonpregnant women. Women and Infants Transmission Study. J Acquir Immune Defic Syndr Hum Retrovirol 1999;20:300–7.

7 Maiman M, Fruchter RG, Serur E, Levine PA, Arrastia CD, Sedlis A. Recurrent cervical intraepithelial neoplasia in human immunodeficiency virus-seropositive women. Obstet Gynecol 1993;82:170–4.

8 Cuthill S, Maiman M, Fruchter RG, Lopatinsky, Cheng CC. Complications after treatment of cervical intraepithelial neoplasia in women infected with the human immunodeficiency virus. J Reprod Med 1995;40:823–8.

9 Maiman M, Fruchter RG, Clark M, Arrastia CD, Matthews R, Gates EJ. Cervical cancer as an AIDS-defining illness. Obstet Gynecol 1997;89:76–80.

10 Centers for Disease Control and Prevention. HIV/AIDS Surveillance Report. 1999;11:1–44.

11 Ries LAG, Eisner MP, Kosary CL, Hankey BF, Miller BA, Clegg L, Edwards BK. SEER Cancer Statistics Review, 1973–1997. Bethesda (MD): National Cancer Institute; 2000.

12 Antoni MH, Goodkin K. Cervical neoplasia, human papillomavirus and psychoneuroimmunology. In: Friedman H, Klein TW, Friedman AL, editors. Psychoneuroimmunology, stress, and infection. Boca Raton: CRC Press; 1996. p. 243–62.

13 Glaser R, Kiecolt-Glaser JK. Stress-associated immune modulation: relevance to viral infections and chronic fatigue syndrome. Am J Med 1998;105:35S–42S.

14 Glaser R, Friedman SB, Smyth J, Ader R, Bijur P, Brunell P, Cohen N, Krilov LR, Lifrak ST, Stone A, Toffler P. The differential impact of training stress and final examination stress on herpes virus latency at the United States military academy at West Point. Brain Behav Immun 1999;13:240–51.

15 Leserman J, Petitto JM, Perkins DO, Folds JD, Golden RN, Evans DL. Severe stress, depressive symptoms, and changes in lymphocyte subsets in human immunodeficiency virus-infected men. A 2-year follow-up study. Arch Gen Psychiatry 1997;54: 279–85.

16 Kimerling R, Calhoun KS, Forehand R, Armistead L, Morse E, Morse P, Clark R, Clark I. Traumatic stress in HIV-infected women. AIDS Educ Prev 1999;11:321–30.

17 Leserman J, Jackson ED, Petitto JM, Golden RN, Silva SG, Perkins DO, Cai J, Folds JD, Evans DL. Progression to AIDS. The effects of stress, depressive symptoms, and social support. Psychosom Med 1999;61:397–406.

18 Kemeny ME, Dean L. Effects of AIDS-related bereavement on HIV progression among New York City gay men. AIDS Educ Prev 1995;7:36–47.

19 Ickovics JR, Hamburger ME, Vlahov D, Schoenbaum EE, Schuman P, Boland RJ, Moore J. Mortality, CD4 cell count decline, and depressive symptoms among HIV-seropositive women: longitudinal analysis from the HIV Epidemiology Research Study. JAMA 285:1466–74.

20 Goodkin K, Antoni MH, Blaney PH. Stress and hopelessness in the promotion of cervical intraepithelial neoplasia to invasive squamous cell carcinoma of the cervix. J Psychosom Res 1986;30:67–76.

21 Centers for Disease Control and Prevention. 1993 Revised classification system for HIV infection and expanded surveillance case definition for AIDS among adolescents and adults. MMWR Recomm Rep 1992;41:1–19.

22 Sarason IG, Johnson JH, Siegel JM. Assessing, the impact of life change: development of the Life Experiences Survey. J Consult Clin Psychol 1978;46:932–46.

23 Antoni MH, Goodkin K. Host moderator variables in the promotion of cervical neoplasia. II. Dimensions of life stress. J Psychosom Res 1989;33:457–67.

24 Ironson G, Wynings C, Schneiderman N, Baum A, Rodriguez M, Greenwood D, Benight C, Antoni M, LaPerriere A, Huang HS, Klimas N, Fletcher MA. Posttraumatic stress symptoms, intrusive thoughts, loss, and immune function after Hurricane Andrew. Psychosom Med 1997;59:128–41.

25 Wright VC, Lickrish GM. Basic and advanced colposcopy: a practical handbook for diagnosis and treatment. Houston: Biomedical Communications, Inc.; 1989.

26 Byrnes D, Antoni MH, Goodkin K, Ironson G, Asthana D, Efantis-Potter J, Simon T, Munajj J, Fletcher M. Stressful events, pessimism, and natural killer cell cytotoxicity in HIV+ Black women at risk for cervical cancer. Psychosom Med 1998;60:714–22.

27 Cerqueira EM, Santoro CL, Donozo NF, Freitas BA, Pereira CA, Bevilacqua RG, Machado-Santelli GM. Genetic damage in exfoliated cells of the uterine cervix. Association and interaction between cigarette smoking and progression to malignant transformation? Acta Cytol 1998;42:639–49.

28 Heard I, Schmitz V, Costagliola D, Orth G, Kazatchkine MD. Early regression of cervical lesions in HIV-seropositive women receiving highly active antiretroviral therapy. AIDS 1998;12:1459–64.

29 Ahdieh L. Pregnancy and human immunodeficiency virus. Clin Obstet Gynecol 2001;44:154–66.

30 Abbas A, Lichtman A, Pober J. Cellular and molecular immunology. Philadelphia: Saunders; 1991.

31 Heard I, Bergeron C, Jeannel D, Henrion R, Kazatchkine MD. Papanicolaou smears in human immunodeficiency virus-seropositive women during follow-up. Obstet Gynecol 1995;86:749–53.

32 Gullotta G, Margariti PA, Rabitti C, Balsamo G, Valle D, Capelli A, Mancuso S. Cytology, histology, and colposcopy in the diagnosis of neoplastic non-invasive epithelial lesions of the cervix. Eur J Gynaecol Oncol 1997;18:36–8.

33 Mayeaux EJ Jr, Harper MB, Abreo F, Pope JB, Phillips GS. A comparison of the reliability of repeat cervical smears and colposcopy in patients with abnormal cervical cytology. J Fam Pract 1995;40:57–62.

34 Ickovics JR, Druley JA, Morrill AC, Grigorenko E, Rodin J. "A grief observed": the experience of HIV-related illness and death among women in a clinic-based sample in New Haven, Connecticut. J Consult Clin Psychol 1998;66:958–66.

35 Kemeny ME, Dean L. Effects of AIDS-related bereavement on HIV progression among New York City gay men. AIDS Educ Prev 1995;7:36–47.

36 Goodkin K, Feaster DJ, Tuttle R, Blaney NT, Kumar M, Baum MK, Shapshak P, Fletcher MA. Bereavement in associated with time-dependent decrements in cellular immune function in asymptomatic human immunodeficiency virus type 1-seropositive homosexual men. Clin Diagn Lab Immunol 1996;3:109–18.

37 Goodkin K, Feaster DJ, Asthana D, Blaney NT, Kumar M, Baldewicz T, Ruttle RS, Maher KJ, Baum MK, Shapshak P, Fletcher MA. A bereavement support group intervention is longitudinally associated with salutary effects on the CD4 cell count and number of physician visits. Clin Diagn Lab Immunol 1998;5:382–91.

38 Goodkin K, Blaney NT, Feaster DJ, Baldewicz T, Burkhalter JE, Leeds B. A randomized controlled clinical trial of a bereavement support group intervention in human immunodeficiency virus type 1-seropositive and -seronegative homosexual men. Arch Gen Psychiatry 1999;56:52–9.

39 Goodkin K, Baldewicz TT, Asthana D, Khamis I, Blaney NT, Kumar M, Burkhalter JE, Leeds B, Shapshak P. A bereavement support group intervention affects plasma burden of human immunodeficiency virus type 1. Report of a randomized controlled trial. J Hum Virol 2001;4:44–54.

40 Antoni MH, Goodkin K. Host moderator variables in the promotion of cervical neoplasia. I. Personality facets. J Psychosom Res 1988;32:327–38.

41 Meier CA. Mechanisms of immunosuppression by glucocorticoids. Eur J Endocrinol 1996;134:50.

42 Olaitan A, Johnson MA, Reid WM, Poulter LW. Changes to the cytokine microenvironment in the genital tract mucosa of HIV+ women. Clin Exp Immunol 1998;112:100–4.

43 Demas P, Schoenbaum EE, Wills TA, Doll L, Klein RS. Stress, coping, and attitudes toward HIV treatment in injecting drug users: a qualitative study. AIDS Educ Prev 1995;7:429–42.

44 Lerman C, Miller SM, Scarborough R, Hanjani P, Nolte S, Smith D. Adverse psychologic consequences of positive cytologic cervical screening. Am J Obstet Gynecol 1991;165:658–62.

45 Mehta S, Moore RD, Graham NMH. Potential factors affecting adherence with HIV therapy. AIDS 1997;11:1665–70.

46 Schneiderman N, Antoni MH, Ironson G. Cognitive behavioral stress management and secondary prevention in HIV/AIDS. Psych AIDS Exch 1997;22:1–8.

47 West-Edwards CAC, Byrnes-Pereira D, Greenwood DU. Tailoring a psychosocial intervention for HIV+ African-American women. Invited address at the 105th Convention of the American Psychological Association; August 1997; Chicago (IL).

48 Lutgendorf SK, Antoni MH, Ironson G, Klimas N, Kumar M, Starr K, McCabe P, Cleven K, Fletcher MA, Schneiderman N. Cognitive-behavioral stress management decreases dysphoric mood and herpes simplex virus type 2 antibody titers in symptomatic HIV-seropositive gay men. J Consult Clin Psychol 1997;65:31–43.

49 Antoni MH, Cruess S, Cruess DG, Kumar M, Lutgendorf S, Ironson G, Dettmer E, Williams J, Klimas N, Fletcher MA, Schneiderman N. Cognitive-behavioral stress management reduces distress and 24-hour urinary free cortisol output among symptomatic HIV-infected gay men. Ann Behav Med 2000;22:1–11.

50 Antoni MH, Cruess DG, Cruess S, Lutgendorf S, Kumar M, Ironson G, Klimas N, Fletcher MA, Schneiderman N. Cognitive-behavioral stress management intervention effects on anxiety, 24-hr urinary norepinephrine output, and T-cytotoxic/suppressor cells over time among symptomatic HIV-infected gay men. J Consult Clin Psychol 2000;68:31–45.

Ebrecht, M., Hextall, J., Kirtley, L.G. et al. (2004) Perceived stress and cortisol levels predict speed of wound healing in healthy male adults, *Psychoneuroendocrinology*, 29: 798–809.

Perceived stress and cortisol levels predict speed of wound healing in healthy male adults

Marcel Ebrecht[a,*], **Justine Hextall**[b], **Lauren-Grace Kirtley**[a], **Alice Taylor**[a], **Mary Dyson**[c], **John Weinman**[a]

[a]*Unit of Psychology, Kings College, London, UK*
[b]*Unit of Dermatology, Kings College, London, UK*
[c]*Department of Physical Therapy, University of Kansas, USA*

Abstract

Summary: The main purpose of the present study was to investigate the association between perceived stress and impaired cutaneous wound healing in humans using a novel wound assessment technique, and taking into account putative mediating factors such as cortisol levels, health behaviours, and personality factors.

The study made use of a prospective, within-subjects design in which 24 male non-smokers participated. Every subject received a standard 4mm-punch biopsy, and the healing progress was monitored via high-resolution ultrasound scanning. Participants completed questionnaires on perceived stress, health behaviours, and personality factors, and sampled saliva for cortisol assessment after awakening at 2 weeks prior, directly after, and 2 weeks after the biopsy.

The overall results showed a significant negative correlation between speed of wound healing, and both Perceived Stress scale (PSS) scores ($r=-0.59$; $p<0.01$), and General Health Questionnaire (GHQ) scores ($r=-0.59$; $p<0.01$) at the time of the biopsy. The area under the morning cortisol response curve was negatively correlated with speed of wound healing ($r=-0.55$; $p<0.05$), indicating a clear elevation in the morning cortisol slope of those whose wounds were slowest to heal. A median split of the complete sample yielded that the 'slow healing' group showed higher stress levels (PSS $t=3.93$, $p<0.01$, GHQ $t=2.50$, $p<0.05$), lower trait optimism ($t=3.25$, $p<0.05$), and higher cortisol levels to awakening ($F=5.60$, $p<0.05$) compared with the 'fast healing' group. None of the health behaviours investigated (i.e. alcohol consumption, exercise, healthy eating, and sleep) were correlated with healing speed at any time point.

Our data hint at a considerable influence of stress on wound healing, and suggests that elevated cortisol levels, rather than altered health behaviours, play a role in this effect.

Keywords: Stress; Wound healing; Glucocorticoids; Cortisol; Steroids; Ultrasound

* Corresponding author: Dr. Marcel Ebrecht, Department of Psychological Medicine, Unit of Psychology, 5th Floor Thomas Guy House, Guy's Campus, Guy's, King's, and St. Thomas' School of Medicine, Kings College, London SE1 9RT, UK, Tel.: (+44) 020 7955 4922, Fax: (+44) 020 7955 2727.
E-mail address: marcel.ebrecht@gmx.net (M. Ebrecht).

1. Introduction

Cutaneous wound healing in mammals can be subdivided into three successive overlapping phases: acute inflammation, proliferation and granulation tissue formation, and tissue remodelling. During the early inflammatory phase, platelet aggregation and blood coagulation leads to the formation of a clot. The extravasational part of the blood clot provides a provisonal matrix for the migration of cells such as polymorphnuclear leucocytes, lymphocytes, monocytes, fibroblasts, endothelial cells and pericytes (Dyson, 1997). Platelets secrete PDGF, TGF-alpha, and TGF-beta, which promote tissue generation, while pro-inflammatory agents enhance recruitment of leukocytes such as granulocytes and macrophages to the wound (Wolpe and Cerami, 1989).

During granulation tissue formation, new blood vessels grow into the wound bed. Granulation tissue is a well-vascularised, soft connective tissue in which the key cells are macrophages, fibroblasts and endotheliocytes. Cytokines derived from macrophages and fibroblasts, such as IL-1α, IL-1β, IL-8 and TNF-α orchestrate the formation of a fibroblast matrix, which replaces the provisional matrix provided by the blood clot (Hubner et al., 1996; Schaffer and Barbul, 1998; Agaiby and Dyson, 1999). In parallel, wound contraction, re-epithelisation, and angiogenesis occur. The remodelling phase of wound repair is characterised by collagen fibrillogenesis and development of extra-cellular matrix. The cellularity and vascularity of the reparative tissue decreases until finally the granulation tissue is replaced by scar tissue (Dyson, 1997).

Recent studies have confirmed a negative effect of stress on the rate of wound healing in animals (Padgett et al., 1998) and humans. One human study examined levels of chronic stress and wound healing in a group of Alzheimer's caregivers and compared them with matched controls (Kiecolt-Glaser et al., 1995). Carers who exhibited high scores on the Perceived Stress Scale (PSS) showed slower wound healing rates and this difference was particularly marked at 14 days after a standardised punch biopsy. Likewise, in a sample of elderly people, individuals scoring high on the Hospital Anxiety and Depression Scale (HADS) exhibited significantly impaired healing of chronic wounds (Cole-King and Harding, 2001). Another study reported an intra-individual comparison of medical students during a phase of high psychosocial stress (i.e. during the exam period) versus a phase of relatively low stress (i.e. holiday period) (Marucha et al., 1998). In this study, standardised wounds to the dental palate during a holiday period healed significantly faster than equivalent wounds incurred during an exam period.

While these findings provide evidence for a clear relationship between heightened perceived stress and delayed wound healing in humans, some putative mediating factors have not been taken into account in previous studies. For example, health-risk behaviours such as smoking, alcohol consumption, poor sleep and lack of physical exercise have been associated with psychological distress (Hellerstedt and Jeffery, 1997; Baum and Posluszny, 1999; Vitaliano et al., 2002). The wound healing progress is highly dependent on the host's nutritional status; especially glucose, polyunsaturated fatty acids, protein, and the vitamins A, C, E, and Zinc are essential dietary components during the healing progress (Russell, 2001; Scholl and Langkamp-Henken, 2001). Therefore, a lack of intake of these substances due to unhealthy eating habits (i.e. high saturated fat/low protein and vitamins), or vitamin depletion due to increased smoking and alcohol consumption could compromise wound healing (van den Berg et al., 2002). Additionally, disturbed sleep patterns due to stress could result in reduced growth hormone release and further downregulation of tissue repair processes (Lee and Stotts, 1990; Rose et al., 2001). Therefore, it is possible that the reported correlations between psychological distress and impaired wound healing could be secondary to stress-induced changes in health behaviours, which suppress the individual's immune functions, thus delaying the repair process of the wound.

Most of the previous studies involved the use of macrophotography and hydrogen peroxide foaming to assess wound healing. However, hydrogen peroxide interacts with non-epithelial tissues causing tissue damage, and macrophotography only records the surface appearance of the wound. It has recently been demonstrated, that high resolution ultrasound (HRUS) scanning of a standard punch biopsy wound is a more valid measure of healing activity in deeper tissue layers than surface photography (Dyson et al., in press). Measures obtained by photography of the wound diameter were influenced by variable contractions of the wound scab, and especially by increases in wound diameter after the scab detaches. In contrast, non-invasive HRUS scans obtained at the base (i.e. at the level of the dermal/hypodermal junction) of a standard punch biopsy wound yielded measures documenting a more stable wound healing progress unaffected by changes in surface contractions (Dyson et al., in press).

Another putative mediating factor between psychological stress and wound healing are glucocorticoid levels. Glucocorticoid-induced suppression of the wound healing process has been documented in humans and animals (Goforth and Gudas, 1980; Gupta et al., 1999). This down-regulating effect might be due to inhibition of cytokines such as IL-1, IL-6, IL-8 and TNF-α (Sapolsky et al., 2000) or growth factors, such as keratinocyte growth factor (KGF) 1 (Brauchle et al., 1995; Chedid et al., 1996), all of which play a pivotal role during the inflammatory-, re-epithelisation-, and fibroblast matrix-formation phase of wound regeneration (Dyson, 1997; Schaffer and Barbul, 1998). This hypothesis is supported by animal data demonstrating that glucocorticoid-induced immunosuppression leads to impaired dermal wound healing (Gupta et al., 1999). Studies in humans have shown that IL-1 β levels were downregulated in individuals who exhibited slow wound healing (Kiecolt-Glaser et al., 1995; Marucha et al., 1998). Further, blister chamber fluid levels of the cytokines IL-1α and IL-8 were lower in participants with high perceived stress levels, and participants with the lowest levels of both cytokines at the induced blister wound site showed elevated cortisol levels in saliva (Glaser et al., 1999).

The cortisol response to awakening has been established as a reliable and stable marker of HPA axis activity in humans (Pruessner et al., 1997). Since this response has been found to be associated with levels of reported psychological distress (Schulz et al., 1998; Steptoe et al., 2000; Wüst et al., 2000), we investigated cortisol levels directly after awakening in relation to wound healing speed and levels of perceived stress.

In sum, the present study aimed to confirm and extend previous reports on positive associations between stress on wound healing. The effects of recent life stress during the preceding month on wound healing in a young adult sample were investigated using high resolution ultrasound (HRUS) scans to assess wound healing, controlling for health behaviours and cortisol levels. The goal of the study was to examine the relationship between perceived stress, emotional distress and wound healing over 21 days, using a longitudinal within-groups design.

2. Materials and methods

2.1. Participants

Participants consisted of staff and students recruited via circular e-mails and posters at Kings College London. The mean age of the 24 participants was 29.42 (minimum 19, maximum 59, standard deviation 11.53 years). To minimise inter-individual variation in cortisol levels due to gender (Kirschbaum et al., 1992), only males were recruited. Participants were screened for the following exclusion criteria via short interviews: Smoking, intake of glucocorticoid medication during the last month, chronic inflammatory disorders, allergies, clinical depression, acute illness such as infections, allergic reactions to local anaesthetics, bleeding disorders, and risk of keloid scarring.

2.2. Experimental procedure

On the first day of the experiment, participants reported to the Unit of Psychology for an introductory meeting. The experimental procedure was explained and written informed consent was obtained from each participant. The following questionnaires were completed on the first visit: the Perceived Stress Scale (PSS, Cohen et al., 1983), the General Health Questionnaire (GHQ, Goldberg, 1992), a health behaviour questionnaire to assess reported health behaviours such as alcohol consumption, diet, sleep, and exercise as described previously in (Ogden and Mtandabari, 1997), the Life Orientation Test (LOT, Scheier and Carver, 1985), the Short-form Social Support Scale (SSS, Sarason et al., 1987), the Rosenberg Self Esteem Scale (RSE, Rosenberg, 1989), and the UCLA Loneliness Scale (UCLA-LC, Russell, 1996). Participants received a batch of saliva sampling devices (Salivettes®) to assess their cortisol levels after awakening and throughout the day on the following day (see below for a detailed description of the sampling procedure).

On the second visit two weeks later, participants were seen at the Dermatology Unit to have their biopsies performed. Each participant completed the PSS, the GHQ and the Health Behaviour Questionnaire a second time. After this, participants received a local anaesthetic of Lignocaine, and a standard 4mm punch biopsy was performed at the inner aspect of the upper non-dominant arm by a trained dermatologist. The wound site was sealed with a standard plaster, and participants received their second batch of Salivettes® to sample saliva for the analysis of cortisol levels on the following day.

Seven, 14, and 21 days after the biopsy, participants attended follow up visits at the Unit of Psychology. During these visits, short (10 min) ultrasound scans of the wound sites were performed to monitor wound-healing progress (see below for detailed description). At the 14-day follow up visit, participants filled in the PSS, GHQ and Health Behaviour questionnaire a third time, and received a third batch of Salivettes® to collect saliva samples on the following day. After the 21-day follow-up visit, participants received monetary compensation for travel expenses and inconveniences. This study protocol was approved by the Guy's Hospital Research Ethics Committee.

2.3. Ultrasound scanning of the wound site

At days 7, 14, and 21 after the punch biopsy, the participant's wounds were scanned using high resolution ultrasound (HRUS). We used a prototype of the EPISCAN™ HRUS-Scanner (Longport Intl. Ltd., Silchester, UK), operating at a frequency of 20 MHz. The scanner consists of a handheld ultrasound probe, a custom designed proprietary amplifier/analogue to digital converter (ADC) board, standard PC components (motherboard, display, disk drives, communication ports) and the operating software (Windows Skin Scanner V. 2.05, © 2000 Longport Intl. Ltd.).

Eight mm deep, and 15 mm wide 2D digitised scans were taken through the centre of the wound bed and the adjacent intact skin. Using the scanner's calibrated measurement capability, the wound width was measured at its base, defined as being level with the dermal/hypodermal junction. Scanning of the wound base by HRUS has been shown to be a more accurate marker of wound healing progress, when compared to surface photography (Dyson et al., in press). HRUS has previously been used for assessment of surgical wounds in renal transplant patients (Calvin et al., 1997).

2.4. Cortisol sampling and assay

Free cortisol levels after awakening have been reported to reliably reflect the individual's adrenocortical activity. Normative data for the early morning cortisol response to awakening is available (Wüst et al., 2000).

Participants were instructed to sample saliva for cortisol assessment on three days (the day after the first visit, the day after the biopsy and the day after the 14-day follow-up visit). In order to safeguard against any influence of anticipatory stress on cortisol levels on the morning of the biopsy day, we scheduled the cortisol sampling to take place on the morning after the biopsy day. The participants obtained saliva samples using Salivette® sampling devices (Sarstedt, Rommelsdorf, Germany). The first sample on each day was collected immediately after awakening. Four additional samples were collected 10, 20, 30 and 60 minutes later. Saliva samples were stored at −20°C until assay.

After thawing, saliva samples were centrifuged at 3000 rpm for 5 minutes, which resulted in a clear supernatant of low viscosity. A 50μl sample of saliva was used for duplicate analysis. Cortisol levels were determined employing a time-resolved immunoassay with fluorometric end point detection (DELFIA, Wallac, Turku, Finnland) with an intra assay coefficient of variance below 10% as described in detail elsewhere (Dressendorfer et al., 1992). This assay has a lower detection limit of 0.78 nmol/l, an intra assay variation of 4.0% to 6.7% and an inter assay variation of 7.1 to 9.0%. To reduce error variance caused by intra assay inaccuracies all samples of one participant were analysed in the same run.

2.5. Questionnaires
2.5.1. Perceived stress

The Perceived Stress Scale (PSS, Cohen et al., 1983) is a 14-item scale, which has been shown to possess test-retest reliability, adequate internal consistency and concurrent and predictive validity (Cohen et al., 1983). Participants were asked to indicate how often they felt or thought a certain way in the past month. Scores range from 0 to 40, with higher scores indicating more perceived stress. Perceived stress scores were calculated for each participant, at baseline, the day of biopsy and 14 days after the biopsy, creating the variables 'PSS1', 'PSS2' and 'PSS3'. The internal consistency was Cronbach's $\alpha=0.72$ for PSS1, $\alpha=0.66$ for PSS2, and $\alpha=0.49$ for PSS3. Obtaining repeated PSS scores in 14 days intervals leads to high intercorrelations since the retrospective measurement periods (1 month) overlap (see also results section). However, we did not favour changing the instructions of the PSS to cover the past 2 weeks (instead of 4 weeks) since we did not want to alter this frequently used and well known scale. Thus we maintained high comparability of our results at the expense of enhanced intercorrelation between repeated measures on this scale.

2.5.2. Emotional distress

The General Health Questionnaire (GHQ-12, Goldberg, 1992), a shortened version of the well-validated full version, was used to detect the degree of emotional distress in participants. Each of the 12 items asks whether the respondent has experienced a particular symptom or item of behaviour over the past few weeks and whether this is usual. Scores range from 0 to 36 with higher scores indicating a greater probability of clinical disorder. GHQ scores were calculated for each participant, at baseline, the day of biopsy and 14 days after the biopsy, creating the variables 'GHQ1' (Cronbach's $\alpha=0.90$), 'GHQ2' ($\alpha=0.78$) and 'GHQ3' ($\alpha=0.91$).

2.5.3. Health behaviours

Fourteen days before the biopsy, on the day of the biopsy and 14 days after the biopsy participants were asked to complete questions about four health related behaviours: alcohol consumption; sleep; exercise and eating behaviour. Based on a similar format to that used by Ogden and Mtandabari, (1997) participants were required to indicate how many alcoholic drinks they consumed per week (variables 'Drink1', 'Drink2' and 'Drink3'); on average, how many hours they had slept per night (variables 'Sleep1', 'Sleep2' and 'Sleep3'); and how many hours they had spent exercising per week (variables 'Exercise1', 'Exercise2' and 'Exercise3'). Participants were also asked to indicate how often they had practised the following eating behaviours on a scale from 'never' to 'all the time': Eat three meals; Eat fruit; Eat vegetables; Eat snack foods between meals; Eat high fat foods; Have a healthy diet. These items formed an eating behaviour score (variables 'Eat3'; Cronbach's $\alpha=0.70$, 'Eat2'; $\alpha=0.69$ and 'Eat3'; $\alpha=0.65$) that ranged from 6 to 30, with high scores indicating healthier eating behaviour.

2.5.4. Dispositional optimism

Dispositional optimism (the habitual style of anticipating favourable outcomes) was assessed by the 8-item Life Orientation Test (LOT) designed by Scheier and Carver (1985). The questionnaire requires participants to report how much they agree with each statement. For instance, 'In uncertain times, I usually expect the best'. The LOT has been shown to have satisfactory internal consistency and test-retest reliability (Scheier and Carver, 1985). Scores range from 0 to 32 with higher scores indicating higher dispositional optimism. Cronbach's α for the sample reported here was 0.41.

2.5.5. Social support

To measure social support, the short form Social Support Questionnaire (SSQ6, Sarason et al., 1987) was administered. This six-item questionnaire consists of two sub-scales: a quasi-structural measure (number of social supports, variable SSSa, Cronbach's $\alpha=0.86$) by asking participants which people in their environment provide help or support, and a global functional measure (satisfaction with support, variable SSSb, Cronbach's $\alpha=0.93$) by asking how satisfied they are with the support that they receive. The score for number of social supports sub-scale ranges from 0 to 54 with higher score indicating more support. The satisfaction with support score ranges from 6 to 36 with higher scores indicating higher satisfaction with support.

2.5.6. Self-esteem

The Rosenberg Self-Esteem Scale (RSE, Rosenberg, 1989) is one of the most widely used measures of self-esteem/self-worth. The scale requires participants to indicate the extent to which they agree with statements dealing with their general feelings about themselves such as 'At times I think I am no good at all'. Scores range from 10 to 40 with low scores indicating high self-esteem. Cronbach's α for the sample reported here was 0.40.

2.5.7. Loneliness

To assess loneliness, the UCLA Loneliness Scale (Version 3), developed by (Russell, 1996), was implemented. Analyses have indicated that this 20-item measure is highly reliable and has convergent and construct validity (Russell, 1996). The UCLA Loneliness Scale asks participants to indicate how often they feel the feeling described in each item e.g. '*How often do you feel that you are no longer close to anyone?*' Scores range from 20 to 100. High scores indicate greater degree of loneliness. Cronbach's α for the sample reported here was 0.45

2.6. Statistical analysis

Cumulative measures for the cortisol responses and the healing progress were established as follows: The area under the reaction curve (AUC) for the saliva samples 0, 10, 20, 30, and 60 minutes after awakening on the three days was computed employing the trapezoid formula (AUC_1 for the response on the baseline day, AUC_2 for the day after the biopsy and AUC_3 for the 14-days follow-up after the biopsy). The rate of healing was calculated as the difference in wound diameter at the base of the wound between the 7-day follow up and the 21-day follow up visit (=HEAL).

A median split of the total sample was performed employing the variable HEAL to create a group of fast healing and a group of slow healing individuals. ANOVAs for repeated measures were computed to detect differences in cortisol responses after awakening between groups defined by the median split, with Greenhouse-Geisser corrections applied for repeated measures factors. Correlations between biological, psychometric and other markers were computed using Pearson correlations. Due to the relatively small sample size, and to control for the effect of outliers, nonparametric Spearman correlations were computed in addition. To account for the influence of a third variable on a correlation between two variables, partial correlations were calculated. To compare group differences in the questionnaire data, t-tests for independent samples were calculated. Since the data presented here was analysed to test specific hypotheses rather than in an exploratory way, Bonferroni correction of α-levels were not applied when more than one comparison of means, or more than one correlation was computed at a time. Data are presented as mean ± standard error of the mean (SEM) unless stated otherwise. The statistical package SPSS v.10 was used for the calculation of all statistical procedures.

3. Results

All participants showed a significant progression of wound healing over the time between day 7 and day 21 after the biopsy. Average diameters of the wound base changed from 4.38 mm (std. dev. 0.58 mm) on day 7 to 3.52 mm (std. dev. 0.60 mm) on day 14 and to 2.80 mm (std. dev. 0.74 mm) on day 21. A repeated measures ANOVA confirmed a highly significant within subjects reduction in wound base diameter over time ($F = 49.9$, $p < 0.001$).

Table 1 summarises the correlations between speed of wound healing and the psychological variables measured in this experiment. We observed high negative correlations between the participants' scores on the PSS and on the GHQ 14 days before the biopsy, at the day of the biopsy, and 14 days after the biopsy and the total amount of wound healing measured between days 7 and 21 after the biopsy. The strongest correlation was found between the amount of healing and the scores on the PSS and the GHQ on the day of the biopsy. Scores on both subscales of the SSS were not correlated with any of the wound healing measures. Similarly, participant's scores on the UCLA-LC, and the RSE were not found to be significantly associated with wound

Table 1 Pearson and Spearman correlations between psychological measures (distress: PSS, GHQ) (assessed 14 days prior (1), at the biopsy day (2), and 14 days after the biopsy (3)), social support (SSS), loneliness (UCLA-LC), self esteem (RSE) and life optimism (LOT) (assessed 14 days prior to the biopsy) and the healing progress between the days 7 and 21 after the biopsy (HEAL)

		HEAL Pearson	HEAL Spearman
PSS_1	Correlation	−0.547*	−0.541*
	p	0.013	0.014
PSS_2	Correlation	−0.587**	−0.593**
	p	0.006	0.006
PSS_3	Correlation	−0.517*	−0.492*
	p	0.023	0.032
GHQ_1	Correlation	−0.392	−0.352
	p	0.088	0.128
GHQ_2	Correlation	−0.591**	−0.572**
	p	0.006	0.008
GHQ_3	Correlation	−0.490*	−0.468*
	p	0.033	0.043
SSS_A	Correlation	0.354	0.304
	p	0.126	0.193
SSS_B	Correlation	0.400	0.381
	p	0.090	0.108
UCLA-LC	Correlation	−0.047	−0.069
	p	0.845	0.773
RSE	Correlation	0.261	0.343
	p	0.265	0.149
LOT	Correlation	0.435	0.411
	p	0.056	0.072

*Correlation is significant at the 0.05 level (2-tailed).
**Correlation is significant at the 0.01 level (2-tailed).

healing in this sample. There was a nonsignificant trend towards a positive correlation between high scores on the LOT and faster wound healing between days 7 and 21 after the biopsy.

Table 2 shows the correlations between the aggregated cortisol responses on the three test days and the healing progress between the days 7 and 21 after the biopsy. There was no association between the cortisol responses 14 days before the biopsy and any measure of healing progress. Also no association was observed between the cortisol response 14 days after the biopsy and any of the healing measures. However, strong negative correlations emerged between the cortisol response directly after awakening one day after the biopsy and the total healing progress.

Table 2 Pearson and Spearman correlations between aggregated cortisol responses 14 days prior, 1 day after, and 14 days after the biopsy ($AUC_{1,2,3}$) and the healing progress between the days 7 and 21 after the biopsy (HEAL)

		HEAL Pearson	HEAL Spearman
AUC_1	Correlation	0.235	0.097
	P	0.348	0.692
AUC_2	Correlation	−0.550*	−0.510*
	p	0.018	0.024
AUC_3	Correlation	−0.024	−0.180
	p	0.923	0.461

The cortisol responses to awakening ($AUC_{1,2,3}$) were not correlated with PSS scores obtained on any of the test days. However, the cortisol response after the biopsy day was significantly correlated with the GHQ score obtained at the day of the biopsy ($r = 0.49$, $p < 0.05$). Social support (SSS), loneliness (UCLA-LC) and optimism (LOT) showed no correlation with the AUC of the cortisol responses measured on any of the test days. Although there was a significant negative correlation between the participants' self esteem-scores (RSE) and cortisol responses after awakening at day 14 after the biopsy ($r = -44$, $p < 0.05$), cortisol responses on the other two test days were not associated with RSE scores. As expected, intra-individual Pearson correlations were mostly significant between the 2 measures of distress (PSS and GHQ) and repeated scores on the same questionnaire. Further, a consistent negative correlation was found between measures of distress and dispositional optimism scores (LOT) (see Table 3).

A median split of the total sample was performed employing the variable HEAL. Participants showing less than 1.5mm wound healing progress between days 7 and 21 after the biopsy were defined as the 'slow healing'-group, whereas those healing 1.5mm or more during this period were defined as the 'fast healing'-group. Table 4 shows the comparison of means of the cortisol responses to awakening and various psychological variables between the 'slow healing', and the 'fast healing' group.

T-test analysis revealed a significantly higher cortisol response to awakening on the day after the biopsy in the 'slow healing'-group when compared to the 'fast healing'-group (AUC_2). Further, the 'slow-healing' group yielded significantly higher scores on the PSS scale 14 days before the biopsy (PSS_1), on the day of the biopsy (PSS_2) and 14 days after the biopsy (PSS_3) when compared with the 'fast healing'-group. Likewise, scores on the GHQ were significantly elevated on the day of the biopsy (GHQ_2) and 14 days after the biopsy (GHQ_3) in the 'slow healing' group. There was a nonsignificant trend towards a more diverse social network (SSS_A-score), a more satisfactory perceived social support (SSS_B-score), and higher self-esteem (RSE-score) in the 'fast healing'-group when compared with the 'slow healing'-group. Further, participants in the 'fast healing'-group scored significantly higher than the 'slow healing'-group on the LOT (e.g. life optimism scale).

An ANOVA for repeated measures was calculated comparing the cortisol levels to awakening between the 'slow healing' and 'fast healing' groups. On the first cortisol measurement 14

Table 3 Pearson correlations between measures of distress and dispositional optimism (PSS 1 – 3, GHQ 1 – 3, and LOT)

		PSS1	PSS2	PSS3	GHQ1	GHQ2	GHQ3
PSS_2	Correlation	0.704**	–	–	–	–	–
	p	0.000	–	–	–	–	–
PSS3	Correlation	0.631**	0.920**	–	–	–	–
	p	0.001	0.000	–	–	–	–
GHQ_1	Correlation	0.742**	0.380	0.318	–	–	–
	p	0.000	0.067	0.140	–	–	–
GHQ_2	Correlation	0.660**	0.515*	0.547**	0.533**	–	–
	p	0.000	0.010	0.007	0.007	–	–
GHQ_3	Correlation	0.403	0.390	0.523*	0.309	0.613**	–
	p	0.056	0.066	0.013	0.151	0.002	–
LOT	Correlation	−0.773**	−0.862**	−0.770**	−0.426*	−0.437*	−0.310
	p	0.000	0.000	0.000	0.038	0.033	0.150

*Correlation is significant at the 0.05 level (2-tailed).
**Correlation is significant at the 0.01 level (2-tailed).

Table 4 Comparison of means for the groups 'slow healing' vs. 'fast healing' based on a median split employing the variable HEAL

Variables	'slow healing'-group		'fast healing'-group		t	df[1]	p
Mean	SEM	Mean	SEM	Mean			
AUC_1	107.40 AU[2]	12.61 AU	103.94 AU	4.35 AU	0.26	11.13	0.800
AUC_2	115.63 AU	11.21 AU	84.66 AU	6.76 AU	2.37*	14.96	0.032
AUC_3	91.66 AU	7.86 AU	91.05 AU	5.07 AU	0.06	17.82	0.950
PSS_1	27.42	2.10	19.00	2.00	2.90**	21.00	0.008
PSS_2	28.08	1.66	17.73	2.04	3.93**	19.76	0.001
PSS_3	26.91	1.95	18.09	1.98	3.18**	19.99	0.005
GHQ_1	13.42	1.53	9.82	1.39	1.74	20.94	0.099
GHQ_2	12.42	1.04	9.09	0.83	2.50*	20.34	0.021
GHQ_3	13.91	1.80	8.91	0.88	2.49*	14.50	0.025
SSS_A	20.33	3.26	29.82	3.63	−1.95	20.51	0.065
SSS_B	29.17	1.58	32.90	1.23	−1.86	19.59	0.078
UCLA-LC	45.08	3.10	41.00	2.66	1.00	19.95	0.330
RSE	29.42	1.57	33.30	1.21	−1.95	19.52	0.065
LOT	26.58	1.72	36.36	2.47	−3.25*	18.18	0.004

[1] Adjusted for equal variances not assumed

[2] AU: arbitrary units (area under the curve)

*Difference is significant at the 0.05 level (2-tailed).

**Difference is significant at the 0.01 level (2-tailed).

days before the biopsy, both groups showed a significant rise in cortisol levels in the morning ($F = 10.39$, $p < 0.01$), but the groups did not differ in the magnitude of the total response, and the interaction was not significant. On the second measurement (in the morning after the biopsy), both groups showed a significant elevation in cortisol levels ($F = 14.71$, $p < 0.01$), and the 'slow healing' group exhibited significantly higher overall cortisol levels than the 'fast healing' group (significant group effect: $F = 5.60$, $p < 0.05$, see Fig. 1). The interaction was not significant in this analysis. On the third cortisol measurement 14 days after the biopsy, both groups showed a significant rise in cortisol levels in the morning ($F = 40.09$, $p < 0.05$), but the groups did not differ in the magnitude of the total response, and the interaction was not significant.

Pearson and Spearman correlations were calculated for health behaviours measured by the 'Health Behaviour Questionnaire' at 14 days prior to the biopsy, on the day of the biopsy, and 14 days after the biopsy. The scores on the four scales ('exercise', 'sleep', 'alcohol consumption' and 'healthy eating') were not significantly correlated with the variable HEAL.

The means for the variable age and all health behaviours were compared between the 'fast' and 'slow' healing groups. Table 5 shows a series of 13 t-tests, out of which only the variable EAT 2 was significant, suggesting that participants in the 'fast healing' group reported significantly more healthy eating behaviour on the day of the biopsy, but none of the other group comparisons for health behaviours reached statistical significance.

Discussion

In the sample reported here, wound healing assessed by repeated ultrasound scans was negatively correlated with perceived stress measured by the PSS and the GHQ, and positively with dispositional optimism. Further, the cortisol response in the morning of the day after the

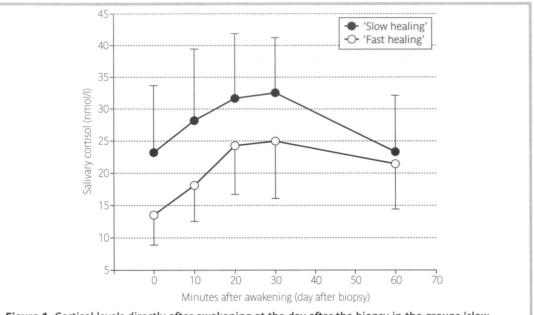

Figure 1 Cortisol levels directly after awakening at the day after the biopsy in the groups 'slow healing' and 'fast healing', created by a median split of the sample using the variable HEAL. Repeated measures ANOVA yielded an overall significant main effect for group and time, but not a significant interaction (see text for details).

Table 5 Comparison of means for the groups 'slow healing' vs. 'fast healing' based on a median split employing the variable HEAL

Variables	'slow healing'-group			'fast healing'-group		t^2	df^2	p^2
	Mean[1]	SEM	Mean[2]	SEM	Mean			
Age	31.08	3.17	29.82	4.01		0.25	19.47	0.807
Exer 1	4.08	0.85	3.90	1.36		0.11	17.03	0.915
Exer 2	3.64	0.89	3.36	0.91		0.26	19.99	0.832
Exer 3	4.42	1.06	4.18	1.25		0.14	20.12	0.888
Sleep 1	7.33	0.31	7.00	0.27		0.81	20.83	0.426
Sleep 2	6.67	0.45	6.45	0.31		0.38	19.25	0.703
Sleep 3	6.75	0.30	6.82	0.23		−0.18	19.84	0.859
Eat 1	19.16	0.99	21.27	1.02		−1.48	20.88	0.153
Eat 2	18.33	0.78	21.45	0.91		−2.60*	20.22	0.017
Eat 3	18.67	0.74	20.91	1.45		−1.38	14.99	0.189
Drink 1	2.08	0.29	2.00	0.33		0.19	20.30	0.851
Drink 2	2.00	0.25	2.09	0.37		−0.20	17.72	0.840
Drink 3	2.00	0.28	1.82	0.35		0.41	19.38	0.689

[1] Arbitrary units except for age (years).
[2] Adjusted for equal variances not assumed.
*Difference is significant at the 0.05 level (2-tailed).

biopsy was negatively correlated with speed of wound healing. However, only inconsistent associations were observed between levels of cortisol after awakening and levels of perceived stress. Similarly, various health behaviours such as diet, alcohol consumption, sleep, and healthy eating were not consistently correlated with healing speed, suggesting that a moderating influence of these behaviours on the healing progress was absent in our sample.

Thus, the present findings replicate the well-documented association between psychosocial stress and impaired wound healing in animals (Padgett et al., 1998), as well as in human studies using cross sectional- (Kiecolt-Glaser et al., 1995), and within groups-designs (Marucha et al., 1998). Moreover, our data extends those comparisons between extreme groups or conditions to a sample which can be regarded as normal in terms of perceived stress levels.

As described in the introduction, the successive phases of wound healing are each dependent on the respective preceding phase. Therefore, one could speculate that a slowing of the initial inflammatory phase delays onset of the following phases thus slowing the overall healing process. It has been demonstrated, that topical glucocorticoids slow down the healing process of dermal wounds (Goforth and Gudas, 1980).

Further, there is abundant evidence, that production of inflammatory cytokines such as IL-1, IL-6, IL-8 and TNF-α can be suppressed by glucocorticoids *in vivo* and *in vitro* (Sapolsky et al., 2000). These findings have been replicated in various wound healing paradigms. In an immunocompromised host model, rats were treated with 40mg intramuscular hydrocortisone (HC). In contrast to control animals, the HC treated rats exhibited signs of immunosuppression and significantly impaired healing of a 8mm punch biopsy wound (Gupta et al., 1999). Also, wound healing is greatly delayed in IL-6 deficient (IL-6 KO) mice. Treatment with recombinant murine IL-6 restored the wound healing capacity not only in IL-6 KO mice, but also in wild type animals previously immunocompromised by dexamethasone (DEX) treatment (Gallucci et al., 2000).

In a human blister chamber paradigm, it has been shown that blister fluid levels of the cytokines IL-1α and IL-8 were lower in participants with high perceived stress levels. Participants with the lowest levels of both cytokines at the wound site showed elevated cortisol levels in saliva (Glaser et al., 1999). Reduced responses of IL-1β to LPS stimulation in whole blood were associated with poorer wound healing in two other human studies (Kiecolt-Glaser et al., 1995; Marucha et al., 1998). It should be pointed out, however, that other ways in which glucocorticoids could affect dermal wound healing might exist. For example, the inhibition of keratinocyte growth factor (KGF) by glucocorticoids has been demonstrated both *in vitro* and *in vivo* (Brauchle et al., 1995; Chedid et al., 1996).

It appears likely that stress-induced elevation of glucocorticoid levels are responsible for the slowing of the cutaneous healing process. However, in our sample there was only an inconsistent correlation between the cortisol response in the morning and scores on questionnaires measuring perceived stress, with significant positive correlations between GHQ scores and morning cortisol responses, and nonsignificant correlations between PSS scores and morning cortisol responses. Likewise, findings from other groups provide a mixed picture of the influence of stress on diurnal HPA axis activity. For example, school teachers with high job strain according to the demand/control model of work stress, exhibited higher levels of cortisol early during a working day (0800 h – 0830 h), compared with their less stressed colleagues (Steptoe et al., 2000). In this study, cortisol, was only sampled once in the early morning with no reference to the time of awakening. In contrast, other studies have found lower levels of cortisol in the morning in women with high home and work demands (Adam and Gunnar, 2001), and in workers in the retail industry who reported high job strain (Steptoe et al., 1998). However individuals with high chronic burnout seem to exhibit elevated salivary cortisol levels in the morning (0800 h) and afternoon (1600 h) (Melamed et al., 1999).

Employing a sampling procedure similar to the one reported in our study, Schulz et al. (1998) compared cortisol levels directly after awakening in students reporting high and low chronic work overload. In this study, one hundred students were divided into two groups based on a median split of their scores on the 'chronic work overload' scale of the 'Trier Inventory of Chronic Stress' (TICS; Schulz and Schlotz, 1999). The students reporting more chronic work overload showed significantly higher cortisol levels directly after awakening, when arithmetic means of the morning cortisol response over three separate days were compared between groups (Schulz et al., 1998).

These findings have been supported by results obtained in a sample of 104 twin pairs (Wüst et al., 2000). Scores on three different scales of the (TICS), namely 'worries', 'social stress', and 'lack of social recognition' were all significantly associated with an elevated morning salivary cortisol response after awakening. The studies by Schulz et al. (1998), and Wüst et al. (2000) used a stress questionnaire assessing chronic stress and specifically work overload over a time span of 1 year, and it is possible that abnormalities of HPA axis after awakening are only associated with long term stressors. Therefore, in the study presented here, it may not have been possible to differentiate morning cortisol responses using scores on the Perceived Stress Scale (PSS), which only assessed levels of perceived stress during the previous month. This hypothesis is supported by a finding of Pruessner et al. (1999), who reported no differences in morning cortisol levels between school teachers with high and low PSS scores using the same cortisol sampling technique as described here. It is possible that a questionnaire focusing on more work-related, chronic stress would have differentiated between participants with high and low morning cortisol responses.

In contrast to a number of previous studies in the literature on stress and wound healing in humans, our study attempted to control for the possible mediating effects of health behaviours. Since stress can lead to a less healthy lifestyle, with increased alcohol consumption, poorer sleep, and a less healthy diet, this can indirectly compromise bodily functions such as wound healing. However, even though two distinct measurements of reported health behaviours were correlated with the healing progress in our sample, partial correlations showed that they did not account for the association between perceived stress and wound healing. It is of course possible, that longer term changes in health behaviours associated with chronic stress may have stronger effects on wound healing. Further, more accurate outcome measures of health behaviours might have yielded group differences on variables such as blood levels of nutrients or detailed analysis of sleep quality between the "high-" and "low stress" group. Another limitation of our study is the relatively small sample size. Even though the sample size provides the power to detect an effect comparable to the ones reported in previous studies which have compared high- and low-stressed individuals on wound healing speed, this might have been insufficient to uncover more subtle group differences or correlations in the other variables investigated (e.g. cortisol, health behaviours). Finally, our data provides a hint to a mediation of the effect of stress on wound healing by cortisol, even though correlations between measures of psychosocial stress and cortisol proved inconsistent in our sample.

In our study we were able to demonstrate the usefulness of ultrasound B-scans for the monitoring of wound healing over time. Digitised ultrasound scans have proven superior to surface photography as demonstrated recently (Dyson et al., in press). The use of a ultrasound imaging in combination with measurement software can be regarded as a promising new method to obtain quantifiable data in an *in vivo* human wound healing paradigm.

In conclusion, our study supports the hypothesis of a relation between perceived stress and wound healing in humans. This effect has previously been demonstrated by comparing extremely stressed individuals with controls, and our data extend these findings in a sample of healthy individuals who exhibit a normal distribution of perceived stress. From our data, it appears that this association is less likely to be caused by compromising health behaviours, but by increased cortisol levels, which could influence healing processes by well documented physiological mechanisms.

Due to the longitudinal design of this study, a cautious interpretation can be drawn in terms of a causal link between perceived stress and wound healing, since the perceived stress levels measured before the event of wounding were predictive for the healing process over the three weeks after the biopsy. Considerable implications for the health sector arise from our findings, particularly for interventions aiming at reducing psychosocial stress before surgical procedures. An influence of psychosocial stress on post-surgical recovery has been described (George and Scott, 1982; Kiecolt-Glaser et al., 1998), and beneficial effects of interventions reducing state anxiety and cortisol levels have been reported in clinical trials (Field et al., 1998; Holden-Lund, 1988; Whitney and Heitkemper, 1999).

Acknowledgements

We would like to thank Paul Wilson from Longport Intl. for technical support and scientific advice regarding the use of the portable ultrasound scanner.

References

Adam, E.K., Gunnar, M.R., 2001. Relationship functioning and home and work demands predict individual differences in diurnal cortisol patterns in women. Psychoneuroendocrinology 26, 189–208.

Agaiby, A.D., Dyson, M., 1999. Immuno-inflammatory cell dynamics during cutaneous wound healing. J. Anat. 195, 531–542, ((Pt 4)).

Baum, A., Posluszny, D.M., 1999. Health psychology: mapping biobehavioral contributions to health and illness. Annu. Rev. Psychol. 50, 137–163.

Brauchle, M., Fassler, R., Werner, S., 1995. Suppression of keratinocyte growth factor expression by glucocorticoids in vitro and during wound healing. J. Invest Dermatol. 105, 579–584.

Calvin, M., Modari, B., Young, S.R., Koffman, G., Dyson, M., 1997. Pilot study using high-frequency diagnostic ultrasound to assess surgical wounds in renal transplant patients. Skin. Res. Technol. 3, 60–65.

Chedid, M., Hoyle, J.R., Csaky, K.G., Rubin, J.S., 1996. Glucocorticoids inhibit keratinocyte growth factor production in primary dermal fibroblasts. Endocrinology 137, 2232–2237.

Cohen, S., Kamarck, T., Mermelstein, R., 1983. A global measure of perceived stress. J. Health. Soc. Behav. 24, 385–396.

Cole-King, A., Harding, K.G., 2001. Psychological factors and delayed healing in chronic wounds. Psychosom. Med. 63, 216–220.

Dressendorfer, R.A., Kirschbaum, C., Rohde, W., Stahl, F., Strasburger, C.J., 1992. Synthesis of a cortisol-biotin conjugate and evaluation as a tracer in an immunoassay for salivary cortisol measurement. J. Steroid Biochem. Mol. Biol. 43, 683–692.

Dyson, M., 1997. Advances in wound healing physiology: the comparative perspective. Vet. Dermatol. 8, 227–233.

Dyson, M., Moodley, S., Verjee, L., Verling, W., Weinman, J., Wilson, P. Wound healing assessment using 20MHz ultrasound and photography. Skin. Res. Technol., in press.

Field, T., Peck, M., Krugman, S., Tuchel, T., Schanberg, S., Kuhn, C., Burman, I., 1998. Burn injuries benefit from massage therapy. J. Burn Care Rehabil. 19, 241–244.

Gallucci, R.M., Simeonova, P.P., Matheson, J.M., Kommineni, C., Guriel, J.L., Sugawara, T., Luster, M.I., 2000. Impaired cutaneous wound healing in interleukin-6-deficient and immunosuppressed mice. FASEB J 14, 2525–2531.

George, J.M., Scott, D.S., 1982. The effects of psychological factors on recovery from surgery. J. Am. Dent. Assoc. 105, 251–258.

Glaser, R., Kiecolt-Glaser, J.K., Marucha, P.T., MacCallum, R.C., Laskowski, B.F., Malarkey, W.B., 1999. Stress-related changes in proinflammatory cytokine production in wounds. Arch. Gen. Psychiatry 56, 450–456.

Goforth, P., Gudas, C.J., 1980. Effects of steroids on wound healing: a review of the literature. J. Foot Surg. 19, 22–28.

Goldberg, D., 1992. General Health Questionnaire (GHQ-12). NFER Nelson, Windsor.

Gupta, A., Jain, G.K., Raghubir, R., 1999. A time course study for the development of an immuno-compromised wound model, using hydrocortisone. J. Pharmacol. Toxicol. Methods 41, 183–187.

Hellerstedt, W.L., Jeffery, R.W., 1997. The association of job strain and health behaviours in men and women. Int. J. Epidemiol. 26, 575–583.

Holden-Lund, C., 1988. Effects of relaxation with guided imagery on surgical stress and wound healing. Res. Nurs. Health 11, 235–244.

Hubner, G., Brauchle, M., Smola, H., Madlener, M., Fassler, R., Werner, S., 1996. Differential regulation of pro-inflammatory cytokines during wound healing in normal and glucocorticoid-treated mice. Cytokine 8, 548–556.

Kiecolt-Glaser, J.K., Marucha, P.T., Malarkey, W.B., Mercado, A.M., Glaser, R., 1995. Slowing of wound healing by psychological stress. Lancet 346, 1194–1196.

Kiecolt-Glaser, J.K., Page, G.G., Marucha, P.T., MacCallum, R.C., Glaser, R., 1998. Psychological influences on surgical recovery. Perspectives from psychoneuroimmunology. Am. Psychol. 53, 1209–1218.

Kirschbaum, C., Wüst, S., Hellhammer, D., 1992. Consistent sex differences in cortisol responses to psychological stress. Psychosom. Med. 54, 648–657.

Lee, K.A., Stotts, N.A., 1990. Support of the growth hormone-somatomedin system to facilitate healing. Heart Lung 19, 157–162.

Marucha, P.T., Kiecolt-Glaser, J.K., Favagehi, M., 1998. Mucosal wound healing is impaired by examination stress. Psychosom. Med. 60, 362–365.

Melamed, S., Ugarten, U., Shirom, A., Kahana, L., Lerman, Y., Froom, P., 1999. Chronic burnout, somatic arousal and elevated salivary cortisol levels. J. Psychosom. Res. 46, 591–598.

Ogden, J., Mtandabari, T., 1997. Examination stress and changes in mood and health related behaviours. Psychol. Hlth. 12, 288–299.

Padgett, D.A., Marucha, P.T., Sheridan, J.F., 1998. Restraint stress slows cutaneous wound healing in mice. Brain Behav. Immun. 12, 64–73.

Pruessner, J.C., Hellhammer, D.H., Kirschbaum, C., 1999. Burnout, perceived stress, and cortisol responses to awakening. Psychosom. Med. 61, 197–204.

Pruessner, J.C., Wolf, O.T., Hellhammer, D.H., Buske-Kirschbaum, A., von Auer, K., Jobst, S., Kaspers, F., Kirschbaum, C., 1997. Free cortisol levels after awakening: a reliable biological marker for the assessment of adrenocortical activity. Life Sci. 61, 2539–2549.

Rose, M., Sanford, A., Thomas, C., Opp, M.R., 2001. Factors altering the sleep of burned children. Sleep 24, 45–51.

Rosenberg, M., 1989. Society and the adolescent self-image. Wesleyan Univ Press, Miidletown, CT.

Russell, D.W., 1996. UCLA Loneliness Scale (Version 3): reliability, validity, and factor structure. J. Pers. Assess. 66, 20–40.

Russell, L., 2001. The importance of patients' nutritional status in wound healing. Br. J. Nurs. 10 (542), 544–549.

Sapolsky, R.M., Romero, L.M., Munck, A.U., 2000. How do glucocorticoids influence stress responses? Integrating permissive, suppressive, stimulatory, and preparative actions. Endocr. Rev. 21, 55–89.

Sarason, B.R., Shearin, E.N., Pierce, G.R., Sarason, G.I., 1987. Interrelationship of social support measures: Theoretical and practical implications. J Personal Soc Psychol 52, 813–832.

Schaffer, M., Barbul, A., 1998. Lymphocyte function in wound healing and following injury. Br. J. Surg. 85, 444–460.

Scheier, M.F., Carver, C.S., 1985. Optimism, coping, and health: assessment and implications of generalized outcome expectancies. Health Psychol 4, 219–247.

Scholl, D., Langkamp-Henken, B., 2001. Nutrient recommendations for wound healing. J. Intraven. Nurs. 24, 124–132.

Schulz, P., Kirschbaum, C., Prussner, J., Hellhammer, D.H., 1998. Increased free cortisol secretion after awakening in chronically stressed individuals due to work overload. Stress Med. 14, 91–97.

Schulz, P., Schlotz, W., 1999. Trierer Inventar zur Erfassung von chronischem Streß (TICS): Skalenkonstruktion, test-statistische Überprüfung und Validierung der Skala "Arbeitsüberlastung". Diagnostica 45, 8–19.

Steptoe, A., Cropley, M., Griffith, J., Kirschbaum, C., 2000. Job strain and anger expression predict early morning elevations in salivary cortisol. Psychosom. Med. 62, 286–292.

Steptoe, A., Wardle, J., Lipsey, Z., Mills, R., Oliver, G., Jarvis, M., Kirschbaum, C., 1998. A longitudinal study of work load and variations in psychological well-being, cortisol, smoking, and alcohol consumption. Ann. Behav. Med. 20, 84–91.

van den Berg, H., van der Gaag, M., Hendriks, H., 2002. Influence of lifestyle on vitamin bioavailability. Int. J. Vitam. Nutr. Res. 72, 53–59.

Vitaliano, P.P., Scanlan, J.M., Zhang, J., Savage, M.V., Hirsch, I.B., Siegler, I.C., 2002. A path model of chronic stress, the metabolic syndrome, and coronary heart disease. Psychosom. Mcd. 64, 418–435.

Whitney, J.D., Heitkemper, M.M., 1999. Modifying perfusion, nutrition, and stress to promote wound healing in patients with acute wounds. Heart Lung 28, 123–133.

Wolpe, S.D., Cerami, A., 1989. Macrophage inflammatory proteins 1 and 2: members of a novel superfamily of cytokines. FASEB J. 3, 2565–2573.

Wüst, S., Federenko, I., Hellhammer, D.H., Kirschbaum, C., 2000. Genetic factors, perceived chronic stress, and the free cortisol response to awakening. Psychoneuroendocrinology 25, 707–720.

Pennebaker, J.W. (1997) Writing about emotional experiences as a therapeutic process, *Psychological Science*, 8 (3): 162–6.

Writing about emotional experiences as a therapeutic process

James W. Pennebaker
Southern Methodist University

Abstract

For the past decade, an increasing number of studies have demonstrated that when individuals write about emotional experiences, significant physical and mental health improvements follow. The basic paradigm and findings are summarized along with some boundary conditions. Although a reduction in inhibition may contribute to the disclosure phenomenon, changes in basic cognitive and linguistic processes during writing predict better health. Implications for theory and treatment are discussed.

Virtually all forms of psychotherapy – from psychoanalysis to behavioral and cognitive therapies – have been shown to reduce distress and to promote physical and mental well-being (Mumford, Schlesinger & Glass, 1983: Smith, Glass, & Miller, 1980). A process common to most therapies is labeling the problem and discussing its causes and consequences. Further, participating in therapy presupposes that the individual acknowledges the existence of a problem and openly discusses it with another person. As discussed in this article, the mere act of disclosure is a powerful therapeutic agent that may account for a substantial percentage of the variance in the healing process.

Parameters of writing and talking associated with health improvements

Over the past decade, several laboratories have been exploring the value of writing or talking about emotional experiences. Confronting deeply personal issues has been found to promote physical health, subjective well-being, and selected adaptive behaviors. In this section, the general findings of the disclosure paradigm are discussed. Whereas individuals have been asked to disclose personal experiences through talking in a few studies, most studies involve writing.

The basic writing paradigm

The standard laboratory writing technique has involved randomly assigning each participant to one of two or more groups. All writing groups are asked to write about assigned topics for 3 to 5

Address correspondence to James W. Pennebaker, Department of Psychology. Southern Methodist University, Dallas, TX 75275; e-mail: pennebak@mail.smu.edu.

consecutive days, 15 to 30 min each day. Writing is generally done in the laboratory with no feedback given. Participants assigned to the control conditions are typically asked to write about superficial topics, such as how they use their time. The standard instructions for those assigned to the experimental group are a variation on the following:

> For the next 3 days. I would like for you to write about your very deepest thoughts and feeling about an extremely important emotional issue that has affected you and your life. In your writing. I'd like you to really let go and explore your very deepest emotions and thoughts. You might tie your topic to your relationships with others, including parents, lovers, friends, or relatives: to your past, your present, or your future; or to who you have been, who you would like to be, or who you are now. You may write about the same general issues or experiences on all days of writing or on different topics each day. All of your writing will be completely confidential. Don't worry about spelling, sentence structure, or grammar. The only rule is that once you begin writing, continue to do so until your time is up.

The writing paradigm is exceptionally powerful. Participants – from children to the elderly, from honor students to maximum-security prisoners – disclose a remarkable range and depth of traumatic experiences. Lost loves, deaths, incidents of sexual and physical abuse, and tragic failures are common themes in all of the studies. If nothing else, the paradigm demonstrates that when individuals are given the opportunity to disclose deeply personal aspects of their lives, they readily do so. Even though a large number of participants report crying or being deeply upset by the experience, the overwhelming majority report that the writing experience was valuable and meaningful in their lives.

Effects of disclosure on outcome measures

Researchers have relied on a variety of physical and mental health measures to evaluate the effect of writing. As depicted in Table 1, writing or talking about emotional experiences, relative to writing about superficial control topics, has been found to be associated with significant drops in physician visits from before to after writing among relatively healthy samples. Writing or talking about emotional topics has also been found to have beneficial influences on immune function, including t-helper cell growth (using a blastogenesis procedure with the mitogen phytohemagglutinin), antibody response to Epstein-Barr virus, and antibody response to hepatitis B vaccinations. Disclosure also has produced short-term changes in autonomic activity (e.g., lowered heart rate and electrodermal activity) and muscular activity (i.e., reduced phasic corrugator activity).

Self-reports also suggest that writing about upsetting experiences, although painful in the days of writing, produces long-term improvements in mood and indicators of well-being compared with writing about control topics. Although a number of studies have failed to find consistent effects on mood or self-reported distress. Smyth's (1996) recent meta-analysis on written-disclosure studies indicates that, in general, writing about emotional topics is associated with significant reductions in distress.

Behavioral changes have also been found. Students who write about emotional topics show improvements in grades in the months following the study. Senior professionals who have been laid off from their jobs get new jobs more quickly after writing. Consistent with the direct health measures, university staff members who write about emotional topics are subsequently

Table 1 Effects of disclosure on various outcome parameters

Outcome	Studies
Physician visits (comparison of number before and after writing)	
Reductions lasting 2 months after writing	Cameron and Nicholls (1996); Greenberg and Stone (1992); Greenberg, Wortman, and Stone (1996); Krantz and Pennebaker (1996); Pennebaker and Francis (1996); Pennebaker, Kiecolt-Glaser, and Glaser (1988); Richards, Pennebaker, and Beal (1995)
Reductions lasting 6 months after writing	Francis and Pennebaker (1992); Pennebaker and Beall (1986); Pennebaker, Colder, and Sharp (1990)
Reductions lasting 1.4 years after writing	Pennebaker, Barger, and Tiebout (1989)
Physiological markers	
Long-term immune and other serum measures	
Blastogenesis (t-helper cell response to phytohemagglutinin)	Pennebaker et al. (1988)
Epstein-Barr virus antibody titers	Esterling, Antoni, Fletcher, Margulies, and Schneiderman (1994); Lutgendorf, Antoni, Kumar, and Schneiderman (1994)
Hepatitis B antibody levels	Petrie, Booth, Pennebaker, Davison, and Thomas (1995)
Natural killer cell activity	Christensen et al. (1996)
CD-4 (t-lymphocyte) levels	Booth, Petrie, and Pennebaker (in press)
Liver enzyme levels (SGOT)	Francis and Pennebaker (1992)
Immediate changes in autonomic and muscular activity	
Skin conductance, heart rate	Dominguez et al. (1995); Hughes, Uhlmann, and Pennebaker (1994); Pennebaker, Hughes, and O'Heeron (1987); Petrie et al. (1995)
Corrugator activity	Pennebaker et al. (1987)
Behavioral markers	
Grade point average	Cameron and Nicholls (1996); Krantz and Pennebaker (1996); Pennebaker et al. (1990); Pennebaker and Francis (1996)
Reemployment following job loss	Spera, Buhrfeind, and Pennebaker (1994)
Absenteeism from work	Francis and Pennebaker (1992)
Self-reports	
Physical symptoms	Greenberg and Stone (1992); Pennebaker and Beall (1986); Richards et al. (1995). Failure to find effects: Pennebaker et al. (1988, 1990); Petrie et al. (1995)
Distress, negative affect, or depression	Greenberg and Stone (1992); Greenberg et al. (1996); Murray and Segal (1994); Rimé (1995); Spera et al. (1994). Failure to find effects: Pennebaker and Beall (1986); Pennebaker et al. (1988); Pennebaker and Francis (1996); Petrie et al. (1995)

Note. Only studies published or submitted for publication are included. Several studies found effects that were qualified by a second variable (e.g., stressfulness of topic). See also Smyth (1996) for a detailed account.

absent from their work at lower rates than control participants. Interestingly, relatively few reliable changes emerge using self-reports of health-related behaviors. That is, after writing, experimental participants do not exercise more or smoke less. The one exception is that the study with laid-off professionals found that writing reduced self-reported alcohol intake.

Procedural differences that affect the disclosure effects

Writing about emotional experiences clearly influences measures of physical and mental health. In recent years, several investigators have attempted to define the boundary conditions of the disclosure effects. Some of the most important findings are as follows:

- *Writing versus talking about traumas.* Most studies comparing writing versus talking either into a tape recorder (Esterling, Antoni, Fletcher, Margulies, & Schneiderman, 1994) or to a therapist (Donnelly & Murray, 1991; Murray, Lamnin, & Carver, 1989) find comparable biological, mood, and cognitive effects. Talking and writing about emotional experiences are both superior to writing about superficial topics.

- *Topic of disclosure.* Whereas two studies have found that health effects occur only among individuals who write about particularly traumatic experiences (Greenberg & Stone, 1992; Lutgendorf, Antoni, Kumar, & Schneiderman, 1994), most studies have found that disclosure is more broadly beneficial. Choice of topic, however, may selectively influence the outcome. For beginning college students, for example, writing about emotional issues related to coming to college influences grades more than writing about traumatic experiences (Pennebaker & Beall, 1986; Pennebaker, Colder, & Sharp, 1990).

- *Length or days of writing.* Different experiments have variously asked participants to write for 1 to 5 days, ranging from consecutive days to sessions separated by a week: writing sessions have ranged from 15 to 30 min in length. In Smyth's (1996) meta-analysis, he found a promising trend suggesting that the more days over which the experiment lapses, the stronger the effects. Although this was a weak trend, it suggests that writing once each week over a month may be more effective than writing four times within a single week. Self-reports of the value of writing do not distinguish shorter from longer writing sessions.

- *Actual or implied social feedback.* Unlike psychotherapy, the writing paradigm does not employ feedback to the participant. Rather, after individuals write about their own experiences, they are asked to place their essays into an anonymous-looking box with the promise that their writing will not be linked to their names. In one study comparing the effects of having students either write on paper that would be handed in to the experimenter or write on a "magic pad" (on which the writing disappears when the person lifts the plastic writing cover), no autonomic or self-report differences were found (Czajka, 1987).

- *Individual differences.* No consistent personality or individual difference measures have distinguished who does versus who does not benefit from writing. The most commonly examined variables that have not been found to relate to outcomes include sex, age, anxiety (or negative affectivity), and inhibition or constraint. The one study that preselected participants on hostility found that those high in hostility benefited more from writing than those low in hostility (Christensen et al., 1996).

- *Educational, linguistic, or cultural effects.* Within the United States the disclosure paradigm has benefited senior professionals with advanced degrees at rates comparable to those for maximum-security prisoners with sixth-grade educations (Richards, Pennebaker, & Beal, 1995; Spera, Buhrfeind, & Pennebaker, 1994). Among college students, no differences have been found as a function of the students' ethnicity or native language. The disclosure paradigm has produced consistently positive results among French-speaking Belgians (Rimé, 1995), Spanish-speaking residents of Mexico City (Dominguez et al., 1995), and English-speaking New Zealanders (Petrie, Booth, Pennebaker, Davison, & Thomas, 1995).

Summary

When individuals write or talk about personally upsetting experiences in the laboratory, consistent and significant health improvements are found. The effects are found in both subjective and objective markers of health and well-being. The disclosure phenomenon appears to generalize across settings, most individual differences, and many Western cultures, and is independent of social feedback.

Why does writing work?

Most of the research on disclosure has been devoted to demonstrating its effectiveness rather than on identifying the underlying mechanisms. Two very broad models that have been proposed to explain the value of disclosure invoke inhibitory processes and cognitive processes.

Inhibition and disclosure

The original theory that motivated the first studies on writing was based on the assumption that not talking about important psychological phenomena is a form of inhibition. Drawing on the animal and psychophysiological literatures, we posited that active inhibition is a form of physiological work. This inhibitory work, which is reflected in autonomic and central nervous system activity, could be viewed as a long-term low-level stressor (cf. Selye. 1976). Such stress, then, could cause or exacerbate psychosomatic processes, thereby increasing the risk of illness and other stress-related disturbances. Just as constraining thoughts, feelings, or behaviors linked to an emotional upheaval is stressful, letting go and talking about these experiences should, in theory, reduce the stress of inhibition (for a full discussion of this theory, see Pennebaker, 1989).

Findings to support the inhibition model of psychosomatics are accumulating. Individuals who conceal their gay status (Cole, Kemeny, Taylor, & Visscher, 1996), conceal traumatic experiences in their past (Pennebaker, 1993a), or are considered inhibited or shy by other people (e.g., Kagan, Reznick, & Snidman, 1988) exhibit more health problems than those who are less inhibited. Whereas inhibition appears to contribute to long-term health problems, the evidence that disclosure reduces inhibition and thereby improves health has not materialized. For example, Greenberg and Stone (1992) found that individuals benefited as much from writing about traumas about which they had told others as from writing about traumas that they had kept secret. Self-reports of inhibition before and after writing have not consistently related to health changes. At this point, then, the precise role of inhibition in promoting health within the writing paradigm is not proven.

Cognitive changes associated with writing

In the past decade, several studies have persuasively demonstrated that writing about a trauma does more than allow for the reduction of inhibitory processes. For example, in a recent study, students were randomly assigned either to express a traumatic experience using bodily movement, to express a traumatic experience first through movement and then in written form, or to exercise in a prescribed manner for 3 days, 10 min per day (Krantz & Pennebaker, 1996). Whereas participants in the two movement-expression groups reported that they felt happier and mentally healthier in the months after the study, only the movement-plus-writing group showed significant improvements in physical health and grade point average. The mere expression of a trauma is not sufficient. Health gains appear to require translating experiences into language.

In recent years, we have begun analyzing the language that individuals use in writing about emotional topics. Our first strategy was to have independent raters evaluate the essays' overall contents to see if it was possible to predict who would benefit most from writing. Interestingly, judges noted that essays of people who benefited from writing appeared to be "smarter," "more thoughtful," and "more emotional" (Pennebaker, 1993b). However, the relatively poor inter-judge reliability led us to develop a computerized text-analysis system.

In 1991, we created a computer program called LIWC (Linguistic Inquiry and Word Count) that analyzed essays in text format. LIWC was developed by having groups of judges evaluate the degree to which about 2,000 words or word stems were related to each of several dozen categories (for a full description, see Pennebaker & Francis, 1996). The categories included negative emotion words (*sad, angry*), positive emotion words (*happy, laugh*), causal words (*because, reason*), and insight words (*understand, realize*). For each essay that a person wrote, we were able to quickly compute the percentage of total words that represented these and other linguistic categories.

Analyzing the experimental subjects' data from six writing studies, we found three linguistic factors reliably predicted improved physical health. First, the more that individuals used positive emotion words, the better their subsequent health. Second, a moderate number of negative emotion words predicted health. Both very high and very low levels of negative emotion words correlated with poorer health. Third, and most important, an increase in both causal and insight words over the course of writing was strongly associated with improved health (Pennebaker, Mayne, & Francis, in press). Indeed, this increase in cognitive words covaried with judges' evaluations of the construction of the narratives. That is, people who benefited from writing began with poorly organized descriptions and progressed to coherent stories by the last day of writing.

The language analyses are particularly promising in that they suggest that certain features of essays predict long-term physical health. Further, these features are congruent with psychologists' current views on narratives. The next issue, which is currently being addressed, is the degree to which cohesive stories or narratives predict changes in real-world cognitive processes. Further, does a coherent story about a trauma produce improvements in health by reducing ruminations or flashbacks? Does a story ultimately result in the assimilation of an unexplained experience, thereby allowing the person to get on with life? These are the theoretical questions that psychologists must address.

Implications for treatment

Almost by definition, psychotherapy requires a certain degree of self-disclosure. Over the past 100 years, the nature of the disclosure has changed depending on the prevailing therapeutic winds. Whether the therapy is directive or evocative, insight-oriented or behavioral, the patient and therapist have worked together to derive a coherent story that explains the problem and, directly or indirectly, the cure. As the research summarized here suggests, the mere disclosing of the person's problem may have tremendous therapeutic value in and of itself.

The writing paradigm points to one of several possible active ingredients associated with psychotherapy. Most studies that have been conducted using this technique have not examined individuals with major emotional or physical health problems or substance abuse problems. One obvious question is the degree to which writing can serve as a supplement to – or even a substitute for – some medical and psychological treatments. Translating important psychological events into words is uniquely human. Therapists and religious leaders have known this intuitively for generations. Psychologists specializing in language, cognition, social processes, and psychotherapy can work together in better understanding the basic mechanisms of this phenomenon.

References

Booth, R.J., Petrie, K.J., & Pennebaker, J.W. (in press). Changes in circulating lymphecyte numbers following emotional disclosure: Evidence of buffering? *Stress Medicine.*

Cameron, L.D., & Nicholls, G. (1996). *Expression of stressful experiences through writing: A self-regulation approach.* Manuscript submitted for publication.

Christensen. A.J., Edwards, D.L., Wiebe, J.S., Benotsch, E.G., McKelvey, L., Andrews, M., & Lubaroff, D.M. (1996). Effect of verbal self-disclosure on natural killer cell activity: Moderation influence on cynical hostility, *Psychosomatic Medicine.* 58, 150–155.

Cole, S.W., Kemeny, M.W., Taylor, S.E., & Visscher, B.R. (1996). Elevated health risk among gay men who conceal their homosexual identity. *Health Psychology, 15,* 243–251.

Czajka, J.A. (1987). *Behavioral inhibition and short term physiological responses.* Unpublished master's thesis. Southern Methodist University, Dallas, TX.

Dominguez, B., Valderrama, P., Meza, M.A., Perez, S.L., Silva, A., Martinez, G., Mendez, V.M., & Olvera, Y. (1995). The roles of emotional reversal and disclosure in clinical practice. In J.W. Pennebaker (Ed.). *Emotion, disclosure, and health* (pp. 255–270). Washington, DC: American Psychological Association.

Donnelly, D.A., & Murray, E.J. (1991). Cognitive and emotional changes in written essays and therapy interviews. *Journal of Social and Clinical Psychology, 10,* 334–350.

Esterling, B.A., Antoni, M.H., Fletcher, M.A., Margulies, S., & Schneiderman, N. (1994). Emotional disclosure through writing or speaking modulates latent Epstein-Barr virus antibody titers. *Journal of Consulting and Clinical Psychology, 62,* 130–140.

Francis, M.E., & Pennebaker, J.W. (1992). Putting stress into words: Writing about personal upheavuls and health. *American Journal of Health Promotion, 6,* 280–287.

Greenberg, M.A., & Stone, A.A. (1992). Writing about disclosed versus undisclosed traumas: Immediate and long-term effects on mood and health. *Journal of Personality and Social Psychology, 63,* 75–84.

Greenberg, M.A., Wortman, C.B., & Stone, A.A. (1996). Emotional expression and physical health: Revising traumatic memories or fostering self-regulation. *Journal of Personality and Social Psychology, 71,* 588–602.

Hughes, C.F., Uhlmann, C., & Pennebaker, J.W. (1994). The body's response to psychological defense. *Journal of Personality, 62,* 565–585.

Kagan, J., Reznick, J.S., & Snidman., N. (1988). Biological bases of childhood shyness. *Science, 240,* 167–171.

Krantz, A., & Pennebaker, J.W. (1996). *Bodily versus written expression of traumatic experience.* Manuscript submitted for publication.

Lurgendorf, S.K., Antoni, M.H., Kumar, M., & Schneiderman, N. (1994). Changes in cognitive coping strategies predict EBV-antibody titre change following a stressor disclosure induction. *Journal of Psychosomatic Research, 38,* 63–78.

Mumford, E., Schlesinger, H.J., & Glass, G.V. (1983). Reducing medical costs through mental health treatment: Research problems and recommendations. In A. Broskowski, E. Marks, & S.H. Budman (Eds.), *Linking health and mental health* (pp. 257–273). Beverly Hills, CA: Sage.

Murray, E.J., Lumnin, A.D., & Carver, C.S. (1989). Emotional expression in written essays and psychotherapy. *Journal of Social and Clinical Psychology, 8,* 414–429.

Murray, E.J., & Segal, D.L. (1994). Emotional processing in vocal and written expression of feelings about traumatic experiences. *Journal of Traumatic Stress, 7,* 391–405.

Pennebaker, J.W. (1989). Confession, inhibition, and disease. In L. Berkowitz (Ed.). *Advances in experimental social psychology* (Vol. 22, pp. 211–244). New York: Academic Press.

Pennebaker, J.W. (1993a). Mechanisms of social constraint. In D.M. Wegner & J.W. Pennebaker (Eds.), *Handbook of mental control* (pp. 200–219). Englewood Cliffs, NJ: Prentice Hall.

Pennebaker, J.W. (1993b). Putting stress into words: Health, linguistic, and therapeutic implications. *Behaviour Research and Therapy, 31*, 539–548.

Pennebaker, J.W., Barger, S.D., & Tiehout, J. (1989). Disclosure of traumas and health among Holocaust survivors. *Psychosomatic Medicine, 51*, 577–589.

Pennebaker, J.W., & Beall. S.K. (1986). Confronting a traumatic event: Toward an understanding of inhibition and disease. *Journal of Abnormal Psychology, 95*, 274–281.

Pennebaker, J.W., Colder, M., & Sharp. L.K. (1990). Accelerating the coping process, *Journal of Personality and Social Psychology, 58*, 528–537.

Pennebaker, J.W., & Francis, M.E. (1996). Cognitive, emotional, and language processes in disclosure. *Cognition and Emotion, 10.* 601–626.

Pennebaker, J.W., Hughes, C.F., & O'Heeron, R.C. (1987). The psychophysiology of confession: Linking inhibitory and psychosomatic processes. *Journal of Personality and Social Psychology, 52*, 781–793.

Pennebaker, J.W., Kiecolt-Glaser. J., & Glaser, R. (1988). Disclosure of traumas and immune function: Health implications for psychotherapy. *Journal of Consulting and Clinical Psychology, 56*, 239–245.

Pennebaker, J.W., Mayne, T.J., & Francis, M.E. (in press). Linguistic predictors of adaptive bereavement. *Journal of Personality and Social Psychology.*

Petrie, K.J., Booth, R.J., Pennebaker, J.W., Davison, K.P., & Thomas, M.G. (1995). Disclosure of trauma and immune response to a hepatitis B vaccination program. *Journal of Consulting and Clinical Psychology, 63*, 787–792.

Richards, J.M., Pennebaker, J.W., & Beal, W.E. (1995. May). *The effects of criminal offense and disclosure of trauma an anxiety and illness in prison inmates.* Paper presented at the annual meeting of the Midwest Psychological Association. Chicago.

Rimé, B. (1995). Mental rumination, social sharing, and the recovery from emotional exposure, in J.W. Pennebaker (Ed.). *Emotion, disclosure, and health* (pp. 271–292). Washington, DC: American Psychological Association.

Selye, H. (1976). *The stress of life.* New York: McGraw-Hill.

Smith, M.L., Glass, G.V., & Miller, R.L. (1980). *The benefits of psychotherapy.* Baltimore: Johns Hopkins University Press.

Smyth, J.M. (1996). *Written emotional expression: Effect sizes, outcome types, and moderating variables.* Manuscript submitted for publication.

Spera, S.P., Buhrfeind, E.D., & Pennebaker. J.W. (1994). Expressive writing and coping with job loss. *Academy of Management Journal, 37*, 722–733.

Petrie, K.J., Booth, R.J. and Pennebaker, J.W. (1998) The immunological effects of thought suppression, *Journal of Personality and Social Psychology*, 75 (5): 1264–72.

The immunological effects of thought suppression

Keith J. Petrie and Roger J. Booth
University of Auckland

James W. Pennebaker
University of Texas

Abstract

Individuals often suppress emotional thoughts, particularly thoughts that arouse negative emotions, as a way of regulating mood and reducing distress. However, recent work has highlighted the complexities and unexpected cognitive and physiological effects of thought suppression. In a study designed to examine the short-term immunological effects of thought suppression, participants wrote about either emotional or nonemotional topics with or without thought suppression. Blood was drawn before and after each experimental session on 3 consecutive days. Results showed a significant increase in circulating total lymphocytes and CD4 (helper) T lymphocyte levels in the emotional writing groups. Thought suppression resulted in a significant decrease in CD3 T lymphocyte levels. The implications of the results for the role of the expression and suppression of emotion in health are discussed.

Suppression of emotional thoughts, particularly those thoughts that arouse negative emotions, is often invoked as a way of regulating mood and reducing distress. Emotional suppression has played an important role in psychosomatic models of disease, in which the active suppression of strong emotions has been proposed to increase susceptibility to illness (Schwartz, 1990). Reports from clinicians working with cancer patients and research studies suggest that a personal coping style that suppresses negative emotion may increase the risk of cancer (e.g., Gross, 1989; Kune, Kune, Watson, & Bahnson, 1991; Shaffer, Graves, Swank, & Pearson, 1987). The mechanisms by which suppression is associated with disease are far from clear, but a likely mechanism is via the immune system (Petrie, Booth, & Davison, 1995).

To date, there has been little experimental work examining the effect of suppression on immunity, but a number of recent studies have highlighted the complexities and unexpected physiological and cognitive effects of thought suppression. Research suggests that suppression

Keith J. Petrie, Department of Psychiatry and Behavioural Science, University of Auckland, Auckland, New Zealand; Roger J. Booth, Department of Molecular Medicine, University of Auckland, Auckland, New Zealand; James W. Pennebaker, Department of Psychology, University of Texas.

This research was supported by the Auckland Medical Research Foundation and by National Institutes of Health Grant MH52391.

Correspondence concerning this article should be addressed to Keith J. Petrie, Department of Psychiatry and Behavioural Science, Faculty of Medicine and Health Science, University of Auckland, Private Bag 92019, Auckland, New Zealand. Electronic mail may be sent to kj.petrie@auckland.ac.nz.

of emotional thoughts magnifies the emotionality and accompanying physiological reaction of the suppressed thoughts (Wegner & Zanakos, 1994). Wegner, Shortt, Blake, and Page (1990) found that the suppression of exciting thoughts, specifically thoughts about sex, resulted in short-term increases in levels of sympathetic system arousal as measured by skin conductance. It seems that the process of suppression, perhaps because of the accompanying cognitive monitoring process, heightens the impact of any emotion attached to the thought.

Previous studies have also found that efforts to suppress target thoughts often result in a "rebound effect" in which the suppressed thought increases in frequency after the suppression period (e.g., Clark, Ball, & Pape, 1991; Wegner, Schneider, Carter, & White, 1987; Zeitlin, Netten, & Hodder, 1995). Moreover, when the target thought has emotional significance (e.g., a thought about a still-desired ex-lover), the rebound effect has been linked with increased physiological activity (Wegner & Gold, 1995).

In a study examining the physiological effects of suppressing emotions during emotional arousal, Gross and Levenson (1993) found reliable physiological differences between participants asked to suppress their emotional response to a disgust-inducing film and controls. Although suppression did not affect subjective emotional reports, it produced a mixed physiological state distinguished by increased skin conductance and decreased heart rate. In a more recent study, Gross and Levenson (1997) examined the responses of participants inhibiting emotions while watching sad, neutral, and amusing films and the responses of control participants who watched the films without suppressing. They found no physiological changes between the groups while watching the neutral film. However, suppression of both positive and negative emotions produced increased sympathetic activation of the cardiovascular system and other effects specific to the emotion being suppressed. Participants suppressing emotions while watching an amusing film exhibited less somatic activity and slower heart rates but no difference in skin conductance or respiratory activation; those watching the sad film also exhibited less somatic activity, but they evidenced higher levels of skin conductance and respiratory activation. Both of these studies raise the possibility that suppression, as well as affecting sympathetic and parasympathetic activity, may influence other areas of physiological functioning such as the immune system. This possibility was investigated in the present study.

To date, there is little direct experimental evidence on this issue, although there is some indication that circumstances or personality styles that inhibit the disclosure of stressful or traumatic experiences are associated with changes in immune function and an increased risk of poor health. After major stressful events, the vast majority of individuals experience intrusive thoughts about the episode (Tait & Silver, 1989) and feel a need to talk to others about their experience (Ersland, Weisaeth, & Sund, 1989; Rimé, 1995). A number of studies have found that poorer immunological function after stressful experiences is associated with lower levels of social or spousal support and, thus, restricted opportunities to talk with others (Glaser et al., 1993; Kennedy, Kiecolt-Glaser, & Glaser, 1988; Kiecolt-Glaser, Dura, Speicher, Trask, & Glaser, 1991). Furthermore, studies of victims of major life events that are difficult to confide to others, such as rape and sexual abuse, suggest that such individuals may be at greater risk of poor health (Golding, Stein, Siegel, Burnam, & Sorenson, 1988; Kimerling & Calhoun, 1994; Pennebaker & Susman, 1988).

As well as suppressing emotional thoughts because of the nature of the traumatic experience, individuals may also do so because of their usual coping style or personality. Here there is also some evidence to suggest that a personality style that consistently represses negative emotion is associated with differences in immune function consistent with poorer health outcomes. Studies have found individuals classified as repressors to have lower cell-mediated immune responses (Shea, Burton, & Girgis, 1993), decreased numbers of blood monocytes, and elevated eosinophil counts, serum glucose levels, and self-reported reactions to medication (Jamner, Schwartz, & Leigh, 1988). In two studies examining antibody titers in individuals with latent Epstein-Barr virus (EBV) infection, Esterling, Antoni, Kumar, and Schneiderman (1990, 1993) found repression of negative affect and defensiveness to be associated with higher serum EBV antibody titers, indicating poorer immunological control of the virus. Repression of negative emotion has also been associated with poorer natural killer (NK) cell activity (Levy, Herberman, Maluish, Schlien, & Lippman, 1985).

Although there is evidence that suppression of emotions and emotional thoughts leads to physiological and immunological changes, there are now a number of studies showing that the expression of emotions leads to immune changes associated with positive health outcomes. Emotional expression has been associated with reliable decreases in autonomic system activity (Pennebaker, 1993), elevations in NK cell activity (Futterman, Kemeny, Shapiro, Polonsky, & Fahey, 1992), and changes in blood lymphocyte reactivity to mitogens (Knapp et al., 1992).

Experimental studies have also assessed immunological changes in individuals randomly assigned to write or talk about emotional issues. Investigations have shown that, in comparison with controls, those in emotional disclosure groups have lower titers to EBV (Esterling, Antoni, Fletcher, Margulies, & Schneiderman, 1994), increased proliferative response capacity of blood T lymphocytes to phytohemagglutinin (PHA; Pennebaker, Kiecolt-Glaser, & Glaser, 1988), and greater development of antibodies to hepatitis B after vaccination (Petrie, Booth, Pennebaker, Davison, & Thomas, 1995). The limited data available on this issue suggest that emotional expression may have important links with the functioning of the immune system.

Evidence in this area to data points to the possibility of two different processes affecting immune functioning. The first is that simply attempting to suppress one's thoughts could be construed as a stressful activity, and acute stressors have been found to affect circulating lymphocyte numbers (Marsland et al., 1997) and activities (Herbert et al., 1994). The second possibility is that suppression of emotional and nonemotional thoughts, perhaps through differential effects on autonomic activity, could alter immune variables in different ways.

Recently, attention has been given to how the nature of an individual's writing may be related to health outcomes. A text analysis of six previous writing studies that included health outcomes as dependent variables showed that the use of more self-reflective and causal thinking from the first to the last day of writing was associated with greater health improvements, as assessed by lower symptom reports and fewer doctor visits (Pennebaker, Mayne, & Francis, 1997). It has been proposed that these changes may reflect more efficient cognitive processing of a trauma or may come about as the person integrates and makes a more coherent construction of the emotional components of the event.

In the present study, we sought to identify whether any short-term immunological effects are associated with the suppression of emotional or control thoughts. In our previous work, we found changes in numbers of circulating lymphocytes but not other blood cells after emotional writing (Booth, Petrie, & Pennebaker, 1997). Circulating leukocyte populations change in response to acute stressors, characteristically with increases in total white blood cells, CD8 cells (cytotoxic-suppressor T lymphocytes), and CD56 cells (NK lymphocytes) but not CD4 (helper T lymphocytes) cells (Brosschot et al., 1994; Cacioppo et al., 1995; Herbert et al., 1994; Marsland et al., 1997). Interestingly, the changes we observed to be associated with emotional expression were typical of those associated with acute stressors, suggesting that aspects of emotional expression may have overridden acute stressor effects. Because of this, we were particularly interested in the influence of emotional expression and thought suppression on circulating lymphocyte populations. The experimental design of the study involved participants writing about emotional or control topics and, immediately after this writing period, suppressing or thinking about their topic. In this way, we were able to examine the effects of both emotional disclosure and thought suppression.

Method
Participants

Sixty-five 1st-year medical school students from the University of Auckland volunteered for the study. The sample comprised 47 women and 18 men with an average age of 19.66 years ($SD=$ 2.67). There were 37 Caucasians, 24 Asians, and 4 Maori in the sample. The study was completed during winter in the middle of the medical school year, and participants received NZ$30 for taking part.

Procedure

Participants were randomly assigned to one of four experimental groups: emotional writing with or without thought suppression and control writing with or without thought suppression. After arrival at the lab, participants completed brief questionnaires and had blood (10 ml) collected by a trained hospital phlebotomist immediately before the 20-min experimental session. Directly after the session, another blood sample was taken. Blood was collected into ethylenediaminetetraacetic acid (EDTA; anticoagulant) tubes for immunological analysis. All participants completed the study writing at a personal computer in a private computer laboratory carrel. All writing was anonymous, and participants identified themselves by a four-digit alphanumeric code. This code was used as an identifier on all writing, blood tests, and questionnaires.

A computer program was written that gave participants instructions for their particular experimental group. Participants in the two emotional writing conditions were given instructions based on those outlined in previous writing studies (e.g., Pennebaker et al., 1988):

> For each of the three days of the study we want you to write about an emotional issue that is personally meaningful for you. The topic may be a traumatic experience in your life, a difficult or tragic emotional event, or an issue related to close interpersonal relationships, sex, death and so on. Ideally, this topic should be something you haven't talked about very much or at all with other people. The topic should be one that still bothers you at some level and that you still think about from time to time. The most important aspect is that the topic is personally meaningful for you.

Participants in the control writing conditions were instructed to write on their use of time over the previous 24 hr. Their instructions included the following:

> The topic you will write about is what you did in the past 24 hours. In your writing we want you to write in a purely descriptive way about your day without the use of emotions. So you might describe what you did at lunchtime yesterday, then what you did in the afternoon and so forth. The most important aspect is that you write in a purely descriptive way without the use of emotions.

Participants in all groups wrote for 15 min at the same time of day for 3 consecutive days. At the end of the writing period, participants in the emotional and control thought-suppression groups were instructed as follows:

> For the next 5 minutes we want you to concentrate on putting any thoughts about what you have been writing completely out of your mind. What we want you to do is to concentrate on suppressing those thoughts and pushing them completely out of your mind. Try and do this without looking around the room but by closing your eyes and focusing totally on controlling these thoughts. Sometimes people find it difficult to block out thoughts. If at any time you think of any of the things you have been writing about, please press the space bar then carry on suppressing the thoughts and trying to put them out of your mind.

In the 5 min after the writing, participants in the no-suppression groups were asked to think about what they had just written:

> For the next 5 minutes we want you to sit and just allow your mind to think over the things that you've been writing about. You need do nothing else but sit and think about your writing. Try and do this without looking around the room but by closing your eyes and focusing on what you've written about.

Questionnaires. Before beginning the study, participants completed a demographic and health behavior questionnaire asking them how often they had restricted their activity as a result of their health in the previous 2 months, their current alcohol consumption, hours of sleep per night, and how often they had engaged in strenuous exercise each week.

Participants completed the Profile of Mood States (McNair, Lorr, & Droppleman, 1971) before the experimental session each day. Participants were asked to describe their mood "right now" using 65 descriptors on 5-point Likert scales ranging from *not at all* (0) to *very much* (4). Items were summed to form six mood scales: tension, depression, anger, vigor, fatigue, and confusion.

Eight weeks after completion of the study, participants were sent a follow-up questionnaire. This questionnaire, completed and returned by 61 of the 65 participants (94%), contained the same health behavior questions as the initial questionnaire. It also asked participants to rate the following item on a 7-point scale ranging from *not at all* (1) to *a great deal* (7): "Since completing the study how much have you thought about what you wrote and how much have you talked to other people about what you wrote?" Participants also rated the degree to which the study had positive effects and negative effects, as well as how happy and sad they had felt since the study finished and how valuable or meaningful the study had been for them.

Content analysis of writing. Text analysis was carried out with the second version of Linguistic Inquiry and Word Count (LIWC; Pennebaker & Francis, 1996), a text analysis program. As with the first version of LIWC, the program analyzes text on a word-by-word basis and categorizes words into multiple psychologically relevant high-level categories (Pennebaker & Francis, 1996; Pennebaker et al., 1997). Although the more than 2,100 words and word stems in the dictionaries are able to measure 72 different linguistic dimensions, we focus here on 4 that have been discussed in previous writing studies: positive emotions (e.g., happy, good, and love), negative emotions (e.g., guilt, sad, and hate), insight (e.g., realize, understand, and know), and causation (e.g., cause, because, and reason). In addition, we examined self-discrepancy word use (e.g., would, could, and ought), which has recently been implicated in health outcomes (Higgins, Vookles, & Tykocinski, 1992), as well as a general cognitive process category made up of words from each of the insight, cause, and self-discrepancy subcategories together with other general cognitive words that connote thinking (see Pennebaker & Francis, 1996, for details).

Blood samples and hematological and lymphocyte surface markers. Blood (10 ml) was drawn into heparinized tubes immediately before and immediately after each writing session. Standard hematological markers relating to white blood cells, red blood cells, and platelets, together with white blood cell differential counts, were determined with a Bayer Technicon H1 hematology analyzer (Bayer Corporation, Pittsburgh, PA). Proportions of mononuclear cells in the blood bearing the markers CD3 (T lymphocytes), CD4 (T helper lymphocytes), CD8 (T cytotoxic–suppressor lymphocytes), and CD16/56 (NK cells) were determined using flow cytometry in a Becton Dickinson FACScan cell analyzer with Becton Dickinson Simultest fluorescent antibody reagents (Becton Dickinson and Company, Franklin Lakes, NJ). Absolute numbers of CD3, CD4, CD8, and NK cells were calculated by means of these proportions and lymphocyte concentrations from the hematological screen.

Results

The results fall into four broad categories. The first focuses on the nature of the writing and suppression task itself. The second deals with the impact of the manipulations on the primary immune outcome measures. The third class of results includes long-term measures of health and adjustment. Finally, we focus on possible psychological processes implicated in the links among emotion, suppression, and immunity.

Nature of writing and suppression

Individuals were randomly assigned to write about either traumatic or control topics for 3 consecutive days. As in previous studies, the participants in the trauma conditions wrote about a wide range of objectively distressing events. Overall, 34% wrote about problems in close personal relationships, 16% wrote about family difficulties, 12% wrote about sexual issues, 11% wrote about the death of someone close, and 17% wrote about other miscellaneous topics. The Profile of Mood States was administered to participants daily before they began writing. A series of 2 (emotion vs. nonemotion writing) $\times$ 2 (suppression vs. no suppression) $\times$ 3 (day) between-subjects–within-subject repeated measures analyses of variance (ANOVAs) were computed on the subscales. The only scale to yield significant effects was self-ratings of tension. Specifically, those in the emotion writing conditions reported higher levels of tension than those in the control cells, $F(1, 57) = 3.75$, $p = 0.058$ (emotion group mean: 8.43; control mean: 6.17). In addition, there was a significant Suppression $\times$ Day interaction, $F(2, 114) = 4.75$, $p = 0.01$, such that those in the suppression cells maintained stable levels of tension across the 3 days (suppression means: 7.20, 6.61, and 6.97), whereas those in the no-suppression conditions showed drops in self-reported tension across the 3 writing days (no suppression means: 10.21, 5.86, and 7.09).

Each writing sample was separately analyzed using the LIWC text analysis program. On the basis of previous writing studies, only five text dimensions were examined in the present experiment: percentage of total words categorized as (a) negative emotion, (b) positive emotion, (c) overall cognitive processes, (d) insight, and (e) causal. Note that the cognitive processes dimension was a general cognitive category attempting to assess the degree to which participants were actively thinking. This dimension included words in both the insight and causal word categories as well as words that tapped self-discrepancies (e.g., would, should, and could), markers of tentative thinking (perhaps and guess), and certainty (unquestionably and always). Averaging across the 3 days of writing, individuals in the emotion conditions used significantly more negative, $F(1, 61) = 111.24$, $p < 0.01$, and positive, $F(1, 61) = 55.68$, $p < 0.01$, emotion words than those in the control conditions (see Table 1). No interactions with day or the suppression manipulation emerged for the negative or positive emotion words. Cognitive word analyses indicated that emotion participants, in comparison with control participants, used more cognitive process words in general, $F(1, 61) = 204.74$, $p < 0.01$, as well as more insight, $F(1, 61) = 123.99$, $p < 0.01$; causal, $F(1, 61) = 41.3$, $p < 0.01$; and self-discrepancy words, $F(1, 61) = 142.8$, $p < 0.01$. Three intriguing interactions also emerged. First, as can be seen in Table 1, a marginal Emotion × Suppression interaction was obtained for the use of insight words, $F(1, 61) = 3.37$, $p = 0.07$. In addition, significant Emotion × Suppression × Day interactions emerged for self-discrepancy words, $F(2, 122) = 3.87$, $p = 0.02$, and overall cognitive processes, $F(2, 122) = 2.76$, $p = 0.06$. Although not significant, similar interactions emerged in the same direction for causal words ($p = 0.10$) and insight words ($p = 0.18$). The patterns of these effects were all in the same direction, and they are depicted in Figure 1 using the overall cognitive processes dimension. As can be seen, no-suppression participants writing about emotional topics demonstrated an overall drop in cognitive processes over time, whereas those in the suppression cells were increasing in terms of their use of these words over time.

Recall that participants in the suppression conditions were asked to press the space bar on their keyboards during the suppression phase whenever they became aware of the target thoughts related to their writing. As can be seen in Figure 2, the pattern of thought suppression failure differed as a function of condition. Overall, participants in the emotion condition had

Table 1 Text analyses and self-reports by experimental group averaged across writing days

Measure	Emotion – no suppression (n = 14)		Emotion – suppression (n = 18)		Control – no suppression (n = 17)		Control – suppression (n = 16)		Significant effect(s)
	M	SD	M	SD	M	SD	M	SD	
LIWC category word count percentages[a]									
Negative emotion	2.9	1.3	2.6	1.1	0.6	0.5	0.5	0.3	E
Positive emotion	2.8	0.9	2.8	1.3	1.0	0.7	1.3	0.5	E
Cognitive processes	8.8	1.3	9.1	1.9	3.7	1.6	3.5	1.0	E, E × S × D[b]
Insight	2.8	0.8	3.3	0.8	1.2	0.6	1.1	0.4	E, E × S[b]
Cause	1.3	0.5	1.4	0.6	0.6	0.4	0.5	0.2	E
Self-discrepancy	3.1	0.6	2.9	1.0	0.9	0.5	1.0	0.5	E, E × S × D
Total word count	457.0	134.2	414.8	80.6	411.0	121.3	434.8	89.9	
Self-reports									
Meaningful experience	3.2	1.6	2.7	1.6	1.8	1.2	2.2	1.4	E
Thought about writing topic	3.7	2.2	3.7	1.7	1.5	0.8	1.5	0.9	E
Talked about writing topic	2.8	2.7	2.1	1.5	1.6	0.8	1.6	0.7	E
Positive effects of study	3.4	1.7	3.6	1.7	1.6	1.2	2.3	1.6	E
Negative effects of study	2.0	1.5	1.6	1.1	1.4	1.1	1.5	0.9	
Happy since study	4.9	1.7	4.3	1.1	4.2	1.1	5.0	1.0	E × S
Sad since study	3.4	1.7	3.4	1.2	3.3	1.3	2.6	1.2	

Note. The significant effects column refers to the statistically significant ($p < 0.05$) effects of the respective variables. E = emotion main effect; S = suppression main effect; D = day main effect. Self-reports were provided along a 7-point unipolar scale (7 = *a great deal*). LIWC = Linguistic Inquiry and Word Count.
[a] Reflects percentage of total words. [b] Significant at $p \leq 0.07$.

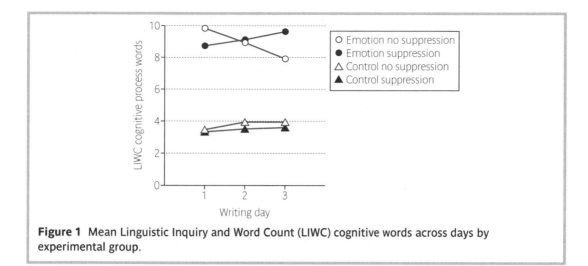

Figure 1 Mean Linguistic Inquiry and Word Count (LIWC) cognitive words across days by experimental group.

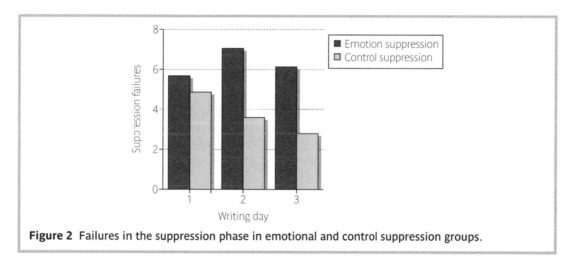

Figure 2 Failures in the suppression phase in emotional and control suppression groups.

more difficulty suppressing thoughts than those in the control cells, $F(1, 32) = 4.28$, $p = 0.047$. Interestingly, a trend emerged suggesting that control participants improved in their abilities to suppress over the course of the study in comparison with the emotion participants, $F(2, 64) = 2.66$, $p = 0.078$.

Immunological markers

Immunological measures were assayed from the blood samples drawn before and again after the writing and suppression–no suppression sessions each day. Preliminary analyses on each of the assays indicated no significant interactions between day and condition. Consequently, scores for each measure were averaged across days, yielding mean presession and postsession values. To simplify the data, we ran multiple regressions on each assay using the postmeasure as the criterion and the premeasure as the predictor. The residual adjusted scores, then, served as the dependent measures for the immunological markers. An initial overall 2 (emotion)×2 (suppression) multivariate analysis of variance was computed on the eight adjusted immune markers collected for the study. A significant marker effect emerged, $F(7, 427) = 4,616.32$, $p < 0.01$, as well as significant Emotion × Marker, $F(7, 427) = 1.98$, $p = 0.055$, and Suppression ×

Marker, $F(7, 427) = 4.14$, $p < 0.01$, interactions. To evaluate these patterns, we conducted separate ANOVAs on each marker.

Recall that the primary focus of the study centered around changes in circulating lymphocyte counts following the writing sessions, after control for prewriting levels. Whereas total lymphocytes refers to the general count of circulating white blood cells, the most commonly studied subpopulations of lymphocytes include CD3 (a general lymphocyte measure), CD4 (T helper cells), CD8 (T suppressor), and CD16 (NK cells). As shown in Table 2, a 2 (emotion) $\times$ 2 (suppression) ANOVA on the adjusted lymphocyte measures yielded a significant emotion effect, $F(1, 61) = 4.77$, $p = 0.03$, and a marginal suppression condition effect, $F(1, 61) = 3.21$, $p = 0.078$. Thus, writing about emotional topics and not having to suppress the writing topic were associated with higher total lymphocyte counts.

The counts of each class of lymphocyte were affected by the manipulations, albeit in somewhat different ways (see Table 2). Consistent with the T suppressor pattern, analyses of CD3 lymphocytes revealed a significant main effect for the suppression condition, $F(1, 61) = 5.11$, $p = 0.027$, but no emotion main effect ($p = 0.16$). CD4 levels after the manipulations were elevated in the two emotion conditions relative to the controls, $F(1, 61) = 3.77$, $p = 0.057$. No other CD4 effects approached significance. CD8 levels, on the other hand, tended to be lower in the suppression conditions, as evidenced by a marginal suppression main effect, $F(1, 61) = 3.65$, $p = 0.10$. The emotion main effect did not attain significance ($p = 0.17$). Finally, analyses of CD16 levels indicated that the patterns of means were in the same directions as for the total lymphocytes, although neither the emotion ($p = 0.16$) nor suppression ($p = 0.19$) main effect attained significance. In none of the preceding analyses did the Emotion $\times$ Suppression interaction approach significance. In addition, we explored sex differences by adding this variable separately. Although the cell sizes were uneven, no consistent sex effects or interactions emerged for immune, language, or self-report data.

Longer term study effects

Participants completed a postexperimental questionnaire 8 weeks after the writing phase of the study and before debriefing. Using a 7-point scale ranging from *not at all* (1) to *a great deal* (7), individuals responded to a series of questions about the long-term effects of the study. As can be seen in Table 1, participants in the emotion condition reported that the experiment was

Table 2 Means for immunological measures, as a function of groups, before and after experimental session

Immunological measure	Emotion – no suppression		Emotion – suppression		Control – no suppression		Control – suppression		Significant effect(s)
	M	SD	M	SD	M	SD	M	SD	
Total lymphocytes	2.4	0.3	2.3	0.2	2.2	0.2	2.2	0.2	E, S[a]
CD3 (T lymphocytes)	160.7	18.9	150.5	20.1	154.1	18.9	144.7	10.1	S
CD4 (helper T lymphocytes)	90.9	10.3	90.4	13.5	85.7	9.2	85.7	5.4	E
CD8 (cytotoxic T lymphocytes)	80.6	11.0	74.8	10.3	75.3	10.7	73.0	7.2	S[a]
CD16 (natural killer cells)	25.6	6.5	23.8	5.4	23.7	4.2	21.9	5.5	
Monocytes	0.7	0.2	0.7	0.2	0.7	0.2	0.6	0.1	
Red blood cells	4.9	0.1	4.9	0.1	5.0	0.2	4.9	1.0	
Hemoglobin	140.4	5.5	142.4	2.5	140.8	8.2	143.1	3.2	S[a]

Note. The significant effects column refers to the statistically significant ($p \leq 0.05$) effects of the respective variables. E = emotion main effect; S = suppression main effect.
[a] Significant at $p < 0.06$ to $p < 0.11$.

more valuable and meaningful than did control participants, $F(1, 57)=6.80$, $p=0.01$. Emotion-group participants also reported that they had thought about, $F(1, 57)=33.72$, $p<0.01$, and talked about, $F(1, 57)=4.91$, $p=0.03$, the experiment more than the control group. In addition, the emotion participants were more likely to endorse the item "Looking back on the study, to what degree do you feel it has had positive effects on you?" than controls, $F(1, 57)=14.63$, $p< 0.01$. Somewhat unexpectedly, an Emotion × Suppression interaction emerged on the responses to the item assessing the degree to which participants had felt happy since the study, $F(1, 57)= 5.67$, $p=0.01$, such that emotion–no-suppression and control–suppression participants reported greater happiness. No main effects or interactions attained significance in terms of questions assessing negative effects of the study or feelings of sadness or depression since the study.

Other relevant data

As noted earlier, previous studies have found a particular "linguistic fingerprint" to be associated with long-term improved health among people writing about emotional topics. Specifically, Pennebaker et al. (1997) reported that an increasing use of cognitive words over 3 days of writing (specifically, insight and causal words) and a relatively high rate of positive emotion words to negative emotion words were optimally linked to long-term health. Through the algorithm from the Pennebaker et al. study, changes in insight and causal words from the first to last day of writing were standardized within condition and then summed, yielding an overall cognitive change measure. Similarly, the mean rates of positive and emotion words across the 3 days of writing were standardized and then subtracted (positive minus negative emotion word use). These two word use scores, cognitive change and relative positive emotion word use, were then correlated with mean standardized lymphocyte counts as well as long-term self-reports separately by condition. As can be seen in Table 3, strikingly different patterns emerged.

Table 3 Correlations of cognitive change and positive emotion words with immune and self-report measures

Measure	Emotion – no suppression		Emotion – suppression		Control – no suppression		Control – suppression	
	COG	EMO	COG	EMO	COG	EMO	COG	EMO
Lymphocyte counts								
Total lymphocytes	0.60**	0.47[†]	−0.02	−0.55**	0.37	0.29	0.31	−0.26
CD3 (T lymphocytes)	0.64**	0.24	−0.10	−0.43[†]	0.21	0.09	0.54**	−0.03
CD4 (helper T lymphocytes)	0.39	0.44	−0.24	−0.41[†]	0.41[†]	0.08	0.32	0.04
CD8 (cytotoxic T lymphocytes)	0.57**	0.28	0.06	−0.41[†]	−0.01	0.24	0.24	−0.57**
CD16 (natural killer cells)	0.59**	0.23	−0.02	−0.12	0.26	0.42[†]	0.16	−0.23
Self-reports								
Meaningful experience	0.10	0.35	−0.02	0.04	0.70**	0.50**	0.03	0.10
Thought about writing topic	−0.09	0.13	0.20	−0.02	0.11	0.04	−0.25	−0.21
Talked about writing topic	−0.06	0.17	0.00	0.57**	0.08	−0.25	−0.13	0.05
Positive effects of study	−0.23	0.24	−0.30	−0.31	0.50**	0.52**	−0.07	0.02
Negative effects of study	0.34	−0.40	0.24	0.55**	0.21	0.20	0.08	0.35
Happy since study	−0.15	0.77**	0.28	−0.12	−0.01	0.11	−0.34	−0.22
Sad since study	0.14	−0.40	−0.01	0.39	−0.20	−0.20	0.32	0.38

Note. COG and EMO were standardized scores within condition. COG=increased use of insight and causal words on the last day of writing relative to the first day; EMO=relatively higher rate of positive emotion words to negative (positive minus negative emotion words across the 3 days of writing). [†] $p \leq 0.10$ (marginally significant). **$p \leq 0.05$ (two-tailed).

Consistent with effects reported by both Pennebaker et al. (1997) and Pennebaker and Francis (1996), an increasing rate in the use of cognitive words and higher rates of positive emotion words were generally positively correlated with the various measures of lymphocyte counts as well as selected long-term self-reports. In contrast, participants in the emotional suppression condition generally showed opposite patterns. That is, higher positive emotion words and increased cognitive words tended to be linked to poorer long-term measures. Although less clear cut, similar effects appeared to be at work in the two control conditions.

Discussion

The results of this study suggest that the act of thought suppression produced measurable effects on circulating immune variables independent of whether the thoughts suppressed were of an emotional or control nature. Suppression caused a significant decrease in circulating T lymphocytes (CD3) as well as marginal decreases in CD8 (T suppressor) cells and total lymphocyte numbers. Emotional writing, on the other hand, increased the levels of circulating CD4 (T helper) cells and the number of total lymphocytes. No significant differences were observed in CD16 NK cells or other blood markers.

We found that difficulty in suppressing thoughts differed by condition, with participants in the emotion condition having more difficulty suppressing thoughts related to personal emotional issues than participants suppressing thoughts about what they had done over the previous 24 hr. This finding is similar to that of Wegner and Gold (1995) but contrasts with the findings of Kelly and Kahn (1994). Consistent with this result, subjective reports after the experiment indicated that participants in the emotional writing groups thought about and talked to others about what they had written more than controls. These participants also saw the study as more meaningful and having more positive effects than did those in the control groups. These aspects are consistent with results from previous writing studies (e.g., Booth et al., 1997; Petrie et al., 1995).

The finding that suppression of thoughts leads to a reduction in certain circulating lymphocyte populations is intriguing and worthy of further investigation. It is consistent with earlier work showing that suppression is associated with a significant increase in sympathetic nervous system activation (Gross & Levenson, 1993, 1997; Wegner et al., 1990). The circulating pool of lymphocytes constitutes approximately 10% of the total number of lymphocytes in the body. Mobilization of lymphocytes into and out of the peripheral circulation can be quite rapid and is affected by a variety of physiological factors, such as blood pressure, vascular endothelial changes, hemoconcentration, neuroendocrine hormones, and autonomic nervous system activity. The effects of acute stressors on circulating lymphocyte populations have been well studied, and the accumulated evidence suggests that total white blood cells, CD8 T cells, and CD56 (NK) cells increase in response to acute stress (Brosschot et al., 1994; Cacioppo et al., 1995; Herbert et al., 1994; Marsland et al., 1997), whereas CD4 T cells and B cells remain unchanged (Marsland et al., 1997) or decrease (Mills, Dimsdale, Nelesen, & Dillon, 1996). These effects have been attributed in part to elevated catecholamine levels (Cacioppo et al., 1995), cardiovascular changes (Herbert et al., 1994), changes in plasma concentration (Marsland et al., 1997), and sympathetic activation (Cacioppo et al., 1995; Herbert et al., 1994). Although we did not include measurements of neuroendocrine, autonomic, or hemodynamic stress reactivity in this investigation, our circulating lymphocyte measurements indicate that the short-term effects of emotional expression and of thought suppression cannot be attributed solely to classical stress reactivity effects. Moreover, they raise the possibility that suppression over a longer term may cause changes in immune function that could compromise health. This issue is clearly worthy of exploration in future studies.

In this study, the immune effects of suppression were independent of whether the participants were suppressing emotional or control thoughts. However, the distinction between emotional and neutral topics may have less relevance than might be first thought. In day-to-day experience, the goal of thought suppression is usually to regulate emotional responses so that upsetting thoughts do not dominate and interfere with everyday function and activity. Normally, one seldom needs to suppress thoughts that do not arouse strong emotional reactions, because such thoughts do not typically return or demand further attention. Individuals can be required to suppress daily events in an experimental setting, but this artificially constructed situation would not occur normally. The fact that thought suppression has immune consequences is most relevant to emotional thoughts, because it is this activity that thought suppression is used most frequently to regulate.

Data from this study point to the fact that the processes of emotional disclosure and suppression do not appear to have directly opposing effects on immune measures over the short term but, rather, may affect aspects of the circulating lymphoid pool. In this study, emotional disclosure, as opposed to control writing, influenced total circulating lymphocyte numbers (mostly T and B lymphocytes), whereas suppression mostly affected T lymphocyte counts. As discussed earlier, these effects cannot be explained solely in terms of stress reactivity. Although it is difficult to relate short-term changes, in terms of minutes, to longer term effects over weeks or months, we have consistently found the CD4 and CD8 circulating T lymphocyte populations to be most often affected by emotional disclosure (Booth et al., 1997; Petrie et al., 1995). Clearly, measures of T lymphocyte functional activity warrant further investigation in terms of the capacity to produce both helper and cytotoxic immune activities in response to an antigenic stimulus.

Previous writing studies have found the increased use of causal and insight words to be associated with markers of improved health (Pennebaker & Francis, 1996; Pennebaker et al., 1997). It has been proposed that changes in these word categories reflect greater cognitive integration of the emotional issue as the person processing the event gains perspective on the experience through his or her writing. The correlations between cognitive word use and both the immune measures and the long-term self-reports bolster this argument. Specifically, those individuals in the emotion–no-suppression condition replicated previous studies, suggesting that constructing a story over time with an increasing rate of cognitive words within an overall positive emotional state may be associated with improved health outcomes. Interestingly, the suppression manipulation brought about very different cognitive and, perhaps, emotional dynamics. For participants in the emotional suppression condition, the suppression period resulted in an increased use of cognitive words over the course of the study. This may indicate that the suppression period interfered with the natural processing of the issue participants were writing about after the session. Moreover, the pattern of correlations in Table 3 suggests that the suppression period disrupted the relationship between cognitive writing and immune changes and thus may have interfered with changes brought about naturally when emotional topics are aired and processed.

Previous research has demonstrated that thought suppression, particularly of emotional topics, has a number of accompanying effects. These effects include physiological changes while the individual is suppressing the emotional thought (Gross & Levenson, 1997; Wegner et al., 1990) and thought rebound after the suppression period (Wegner et al., 1987). The current study extends these findings and suggests that thought suppression also may have distinctive effects on the immune system. Our results indicate the need for further work to examine the cumulative effects of suppression on immunity over longer time periods and the effect of suppression on functional immune activity.

References

Booth, R. J., Petrie, K. J., & Pennebaker, J. W. (1997). Changes in circulating lymphocyte numbers following emotional disclosure: Evidence of buffering? *Stress Medicine,* 13, 23–29.

Brosschot, J. F., Benschop, R. J., Godaert, G. L., Olff, M., De Smet, M., Heijnen, C. J., & Ballieux, R. E. (1994). Influence of life stress on immunological reactivity to mild psychological stress. *Psychosomatic Medicine,* 56, 216–224.

Cacioppo, J. T., Malarkey, W. B., Kiecolt-Glaser, J. K., Uchino, B. N., Sgoutas Emch, S. A., Sheridan, J. F., Berntson, G. G., & Glaser, R. (1995). Heterogeneity in neuroendocrine and immune responses to brief psychological stressors as a function of autonomic cardiac activation. *Psychosomatic Medicine,* 57, 154–164.

Clark, D. M., Ball, S., & Pape, D. (1991). An experimental investigation of thought suppression. *Behaviour Research and Therapy,* 29, 253–257.

Ersland, S., Weisaeth, L., & Sund, A. (1989). The stress upon rescuers involved in an oil rig disaster: "Alexander Kielland" – 1980. *Acta Psychiatrica Scandinavica,* 80, 38–49.

Esterling, B. A., Antoni, M. H., Fletcher, M. A., Margulies, S., & Schneiderman, N. (1994). Emotional disclosure through writing or speaking modulates latent Epstein-Barr virus antibody titers. *Journal of Consulting and Clinical Psychology,* 62, 130–140.

Esterling, B. A., Antoni, M. H., Kumar, M., & Schneiderman, N. (1990). Emotional depression, stress disclosure responses, and Epstein-Barr viral capsid antigen titers. *Psychosomatic Medicine,* 52, 397–410.

Esterling, B. A., Antoni, M. H., Kumar, M., & Schneiderman, N. (1993). Defensiveness, trait anxiety, and Epstein-Barr viral capsid antigen antibody titers in healthy college students. *Health Psychology,* 12, 132–139.

Futterman, A. D., Kemeny, M. E., Shapiro, D., Polonsky, W., & Fahey, J. L. (1992). Immunological variability associated with experimentally-induced positive and negative affective states. *Psychological Medicine,* 22, 231–238.

Glaser, R., Pearson, G. R., Bonneau, R. H., Esterling, B. A., Atkinson, C., & Kiecolt-Glaser, J. K. (1993). Stress and the memory T-cell response to the Epstein-Barr virus in healthy medical students. *Health Psychology,* 12, 435–442.

Golding, J. M., Stein, J. A., Siegel, J. M., Burnam, M. A., & Sorenson, S. B. (1988). Sexual assault history and the use of health and mental health services. *American Journal of Community Psychology,* 16, 625–644.

Gross, J. (1989). Emotional expression in cancer onset and progression. *Social Science and Medicine,* 28, 1239–1248.

Gross, J., & Levenson, R. W. (1993). Emotional suppression: Physiology, self-report, and expressive behavior. *Journal of Personality and Social Psychology,* 64, 970–986.

Gross, J., & Levenson, R. W. (1997). Hiding feelings: The acute effects of inhibiting negative and positive emotion. *Journal of Abnormal Psychology,* 106, 95–103.

Herbert, T. B., Cohen, S., Marsland, A. L., Bachen, E. A., Rabin, B. S., Muldoon, M. F., & Manuck, S.B. (1994). Cardiovascular reactivity and the course of immune response to an acute psychological stressor. *Psychosomatic Medicine,* 56, 337–344.

Higgins, E. T., Vookles, J., & Tykocinski, O. (1992). Self and health: How "patterns" of self-beliefs predict types of emotional and physical problems. *Social Cognition,* 10, 125–150.

Jamner, L. D., Schwartz, G. E., & Leigh, H. (1988). The relationship between repressive and defensive coping styles and monocyte, eosinophile, and serum glucose levels: Support for the opioid peptide hypothesis of repression. *Psychosomatic Medicine, 50,* 567–575.

Kelly, A. E., & Kahn, J. H. (1994). Effects of suppression of personal intrusive thoughts. *Journal of Personality and Social Psychology, 66,* 998–1006.

Kennedy, S., Kiecolt-Glaser, J. K., & Glaser, R. (1988). Immunological consequences of acute and chronic stressors: Mediating role of interpersonal relationships. *British Journal of Medical Psychology, 61,* 77–85.

Kiecolt-Glaser, J. K., Dura, J. R., Speicher, C. E., Trask, O. J., & Glaser, R. (1991). Spousal caregivers of dementia victims: Longitudinal changes in immunity and health. *Psychosomatic Medicine, 55,* 395–409.

Kimerling, R., & Calhoun, K. S. (1994). Somatic symptoms, social support and treatment seeking among sexual assault victims. *Journal of Consulting and Clinical Psychology, 63,* 333–340.

Knapp, P. H., Levy, E. M., Giorgi, R. G., Black, P. H., Fox, B. H., & Heeren, T. C. (1992). Short-term immunological effects of induced emotion. *Psychosomatic Medicine, 54,* 133–148.

Kune, G. A., Kune, S., Watson, L. F., & Bahnson, C. B. (1991). Personality as a risk factor in large bowel cancer: Data from the Melbourne Colorectal Cancer Study. *Psychological Medicine, 21,* 29–41.

Levy, S. M., Herberman, R. B., Maluish, A. M., Schlien, B., & Lippman, M. (1985). Prognostic risk assessment in primary breast cancer by behavioral and immunological parameters. *Health Psychology, 4,* 99–113.

Marsland, A. L., Herbert, T. B., Muldoon, M. F., Bachen, E. A., Patterson, S., Cohen, S., Rabin, B., & Manuck, S. B. (1997). Lymphocyte subset redistribution during acute laboratory stress in young adults – Mediating effects of hemoconcentration. *Health Psychology, 16,* 341–348.

McNair, D., Lorr, M., & Droppleman, L. (1971). *Profile of mood states.* San Diego, CA: EDITS.

Mills, P. J., Dimsdale, J. E., Nelesen, R. A., & Dillon, E. (1996). Psychologic characteristics associated with acute stressor-induced leukocyte subset redistribution. *Journal of Psychosomatic Research, 40,* 417–423.

Pennebaker, J. W. (1993). Social mechanisms of constraint. In D. M. Wegner & J. W. Pennebaker (Eds.), *Handbook of mental control* (pp. 200–219). Englewood Cliffs, NJ: Prentice Hall.

Pennebaker, J. W., & Francis, M. E. (1996). Cognitive, emotional, and language processes in disclosure. *Cognition and Emotion, 10,* 601–626.

Pennebaker, J. W., Kiecolt-Glaser, J. K., & Glaser, R. (1988). Disclosure of trauma and immune function: Health implications for psychotherapy. *Journal of Consulting and Clinical Psychology, 56,* 239–245.

Pennebaker, J. W., Mayne, T. J., & Francis, M. E. (1997). Linguistic predictors of adaptive bereavement. *Journal of Personality and Social Psychology, 72,* 863–871.

Pennebaker, J. W., & Susman, J. R. (1988). Disclosure of trauma and psychosomatic processes. *Social Science and Medicine, 26,* 327–332.

Petrie, K. J., Booth, R. J., & Davison, K. P. (1995). Repression, disclosure, and immune function: Recent findings and methodological issues. In J. W. Pennebaker (Ed.), *Emotion, disclosure, and health* (pp. 223–237). Washington, DC: American Psychological Association.

Petrie, K. J., Booth, R. J., Pennebaker, J. W., Davison, K. P., & Thomas, M. G. (1995). Disclosure of trauma and immune response to a hepatitis vaccination program. *Journal of Consulting and Clinical Psychology, 63,* 787–792.

Rimé, B. (1995). Mental rumination, social sharing and recovery from emotional exposure. In J. W. Pennebaker (Ed.), *Emotion, disclosure, and health* (pp. 271–291). Washington, DC: American Psychological Association.

Schwartz, G. E. (1990). Psychobiology of repression and health: A systems approach. In J. L. Singer (Ed.), *Repression and dissociation* (pp. 405–434). Chicago: University of Chicago Press.

Shaffer, J. W., Graves, P. L., Swank, R. T., & Pearson, T. A. (1987). Clustering of personality in youth and the subsequent development of cancer among physicians. *Journal of Behavioral Medicine, 10,* 441–447.

Shea, J. D., Burton, R., & Girgis, A. (1993). Negative affect, absorption, and immunity. *Physiological Behavior, 53,* 449–457.

Tait, R., & Silver, R. C. (1989). Coming to terms with major negative life events. In J. S. Uleman & J. A. Bargh (Eds.), *Unintended thoughts* (pp. 351–382). New York: Guilford Press.

Wegner, D. M., & Gold, D. B. (1995). Fanning old flames: Emotional and cognitive effects of suppressing thoughts of a past relationship. *Journal of Personality and Social Psychology, 68,* 782–792.

Wegner, D. M., Schneider, D. J., Carter, S. R., & White, T. L. (1987). Paradoxical effects of thought suppression. *Journal of Personality and Social Psychology, 53,* 5–13.

Wegner, D. M., Shortt, J. W., Blake, A. W., & Page, M. S. (1990). The suppression of exciting thoughts. *Journal of Personality and Social Psychology, 58,* 409–418.

Wegner, D. M., & Zanakos, S. (1994). Chronic thought suppression. *Journal of Personality, 62,* 615–640.

Zeitlin, S. B., Netten, K. A., & Hodder, S. L. (1995). Thought suppression: An experimental investigation of spider phobics. *Behaviour Research and Therapy, 33,* 407–413.

PART 5

Chronic illness

Part contents

Commentary

A biomedical view of the role of psychology in health and illness emphasises psychological factors as the consequence of being ill; having a heart attack or being diagnosed as having diabetes may make the person anxious or upset. Health psychology challenges this perspective and clearly places psychological factors as having a role to play in the cause, contribution and consequence of illness. For example, a person's beliefs and behaviours may contribute to the onset of their illness; how they make sense of their symptoms could then influence whether they seek help and adhere to any recommendations, and the ways in which they subsequently cope and behave could influence how the illness progresses. Furthermore, such psychological variables may have a direct effect upon their physiology in terms of their stress hormones, wound healing or immune system. In line with this, much health psychology research is concerned with understanding the role that psychology plays in chronic illness and has focused upon a vast array of illnesses including coronary heart disease, cancer, diabetes, obesity, asthma, HIV, chronic fatigue syndrome and COPD. Research also explores patients' experiences of pain which is relevant to all these different illnesses. For the purpose of this chapter I have selected papers on pain, CHD, cancer and HIV. This section also contains a paper on response shift which highlights how quality of life changes over time. There is obviously a vast literature on each of these illnesses and identifying one paper for each is inevitably idiosyncratic. I have therefore chosen seven papers which vary in terms of illness, method and design and whether they are concerned with the impact of an illness or its treatment. I have also chosen papers that I feel have something different and interesting to say:

Eccleston, C., Morley, S., Williams, A. et al. (2002) Systematic review of randomised controlled trials of psychological therapy for chronic pain in children and adolescents with a subset meta-analysis of pain relief, *Pain*, 99 (1–2): 157–65. Reprinted with kind permission of the International Association for the Study of Pain.

Smith, J.A. and Osborn, M. (2007) Pain as an assault on the self: an interpretative phenomenological analysis of the psychological impact of chronic benign low back pain, *Psychology and Health*, 22 (5): 517–34. Reprinted with kind permission of the Taylor & Francis Group.

Taylor, S.E. (1983) Adjustment to threatening events: a theory of cognitive adaptation, *American Psychologist*, 38 (11): 1161–73. Reprinted with kind permission of the American Psychological Association.

Petrie, K.J., Cameron, L.D., Ellis, C.J. et al. (2002) Changing illness perceptions after myocardial infarction: an early intervention randomized controlled trial, *Psychosomatic Medicine*, 64: 580–6. Reprinted with kind permission of Lippincott Williams & Wilkins.

Antoni, M.H., Carrico, A.W., Durán, R.E. et al. (2006) Randomized clinical trial of cognitive behavioral stress management on human immunodeficiency virus viral load in gay men treated with highly active antiretroviral therapy, *Psychosomatic Medicine*, 68: 143–51. Reprinted with kind permission of Lippincott Williams & Wilkins.

Ogden, J., Clementi, C. and Aylwin, S. (2006) The impact of obesity surgery and the paradox of control: a qualitative study, *Psychology and Health*, 21 (2): 273–93. Reprinted with kind permission of the Taylor & Francis Group.

Rapkin, B.D. and Schwartz, C.E. (2004) Toward a theoretical model of quality-of-life appraisal: implications of findings from studies of response shift. *Health and Quality of Life Outcomes*, 2: 14. Reproduced with kind permission of BioMed Central.

Chronic pain is an interesting phenomenon for psychologists as the individual's beliefs, expectations, past experiences and behaviour can have a profound effect on how pain is experienced. In line with this, pain clinics have been established which have a strong psychological component and many chronic pain patients are now offered psychological support and interventions such as relaxation, cognitive behavioural therapy and reinforcement alongside more traditional pain relief. Eccleston et al. (2002) carried out a systematic review of trials using psychological therapies for children and adolescents who were suffering from problems such as chronic headache, abdominal pain and sickle cell pain. They located 18 randomised control trials and concluded that psychological therapies are effective at reducing headaches but that there remained no evidence for their effectiveness for other pain problems. Eccleston et al. (2002) offers a clear example of a systematic review and illustrates the importance of synthesising across studies where possible rather than relying upon the results from individual research projects. The paper also highlights how systematic reviews are most reliable when they address simple questions and when the independent and dependent variables are similar enough across studies to enable them to be combined. The paper also illustrates how psychological theory and therapy can have a direct impact upon clinical practice and patient care.

Smith and Osborn (2007) also focus on pain but from a very different perspective. Rather than exploring the effectiveness of pain management, Smith and Osborn (2007) are concerned with patients' experiences of chronic pain and use a qualitative method with semi-structured interviews being conducted with six patients suffering from chronic benign low back pain. Smith established interpretative phenomenological analysis (IPA) as a method for analysing qualitative data and uses this approach in the current study. The analysis illustrates the ways in which chronic pain is experienced and Smith and Osborn (2007) locate this experience within the individual's sense of self and identity and explore both how their experience is affected and how it affects their relationships with others. This paper provides a detailed insight into pain from the patient's perspective. It also provides a clear example of how to carry out IPA and how to present the findings in an interesting and accessible way. Finally, it illustrates how qualitative methods can be used in health psychology not only to inform our understanding of the patient's perspective but also to illuminate core constructs, in this case identity, shame and acceptance, which are pertinent to numerous other health- and non-health-related areas.

Taylor (1983) also uses a qualitative approach to explore women's experiences of breast cancer. This paper is a summary of the findings from this study which Taylor then uses to build a theory of coping called 'a theory of cognitive adaptation'. The results show that, when faced with a threatening event, in this case breast cancer, people respond by showing a search for meaning ('Why me?'), a search for mastery ('How can I stop it from happening again?') and a process of self-enhancement ('I am better off than many people I know'). In addition, these processes enable them to form illusions about their illness which facilitates a sense of adaptation and an ability to move on. This paper (and the studies that it draws upon) is interesting in many ways. First, it provides a detailed description of what it feels like to have breast cancer, and the paper offers many illuminating examples and quotes. Further, the paper places the quotes at the centre of the analysis which makes the analysis feel 'data led'. In addition, the paper illustrates how qualitative data can be used to develop theory that can be tested subsequently using a more quantitative approach. Finally, the paper also illustrates how results from different qualitative studies can be pooled together as Taylor in subsequent work draws parallels between patients who have had breast cancer, those who have been raped and cardiac patients to further develop and build her theory of cognitive adaptation.

While Smith and Osborn (2007) and Taylor (1983) explore patients' experiences of pain and cancer, the next three papers in this section are concerned with interventions and their effectiveness at changing a patient's health status in the broadest sense. The first of these, by Petrie et al. (2002), describes an intervention designed to elicit and change patients' illness cognitions after they have had a heart attack and explores the impact of this on a range of outcomes including leaving hospital, return to work, angina pain and attendance at cardiac rehabilitation. The study was based on the premise that patients may have illness cognitions that are detrimental to their recovery which could be changed in an intervention. For example, if a patient believes that their heart attack was caused by stress they might be reluctant to change their diet or stop smoking, or if they believe that their heart muscle has been overstretched, they might be fearful of taking up an exercise regimen. The results showed that the intervention was effective at changing illness cognitions which in turn was related to patient health outcomes. This paper provides a clear description of how to carry out a randomised control trial. It is also an excellent example of how psychological theory (in this case the self-regulatory model) can be used in clinical practice to have a direct impact upon patient health outcomes. Finally, it also illustrates how health psychologists can work in the health-care setting and be involved in setting up and running interventions.

Antoni et al. (2006) also present the results from a randomised control trial but this paper uses cognitive behavioural stress management for men who are HIV positive. The paper describes a study whereby 130 men who were HIV positive and being treated with highly active antiretroviral therapy (HAART) were randomly allocated to receive either medication adherence training (MAP) only or MAP and stress management. The results showed that for those men with a detectable viral load at baseline, stress management resulted in a greater reduction in viral load than those who received MAP only. Research drawing on a PNI perspective suggests that stress may exacerbate the progression of HIV to AIDs. This paper illustrates how the psychological factors that may exacerbate illness progression can be modified through a psychological intervention. The paper also supports the effectiveness of a PNI approach and illustrates the use of psychological variables in a clinical context to produce definite changes in disease status. Finally, the paper provides clear descriptions of the randomisation process and offers insights into the practicalities of coordinating a trial in a clinical setting.

Much health psychology research in the area of chronic illness examines the impact of psychological interventions on either psychological factors (e.g. does CBT influence pain perception?) or physical factors (e.g. does stress management influence immune status?). In contrast, Ogden et al. (2006) explore the psychological consequences of a surgical intervention – in this case obesity surgery. Obesity is mainly treated with psychological therapies including behavioural management, CBT and counselling designed to change the cognitions and behaviour of the patient. This is seen as appropriate as the perceived causes of the problem are matched to the offered solution. In contrast, obesity surgery is sometimes seen as letting the obese person off the hook but is becoming more common as the number of obese people increases and behavioural interventions are deemed relatively ineffective. Ogden et al. (2006) carried out qualitative interviews with 15 men and women who had had surgery in the past four years and described four main themes: personal weight histories; the decision-making process; the impact of surgery on eating behaviour and their relationship with food; the impact of weight loss on health status, self-esteem and relationships with others. In addition, the authors highlight how the theme of control permeated all areas of the interviews. In particular, they conclude that while a sense of lack of control can contribute to the development of obesity, by imposing control and limiting choice, obesity surgery can paradoxically result in a sense of enhanced control both over food and other areas of the patient's life. This is obviously my own paper and I am therefore biased in finding it worth including in this reader. These are my justifications for this. First, it highlights the psychological consequences of a non-psychological intervention, which, though a fairly obvious area for study, remains a relatively unexplored aspect of the patient experience and has implications for many illnesses that are treated in medical or surgical ways. Second, it was a qualitative study which produced surprising and counter-intuitive findings. On embarking upon this project I would have assumed that by making their stomach very small, the obese person would be hungry, preoccupied with food and would feel more out of control over their eating behaviour. The finding that the patients felt less hungry, less preoccupied with food and more in control was unpredicted and emerged directly from the transcripts rather than from my own expectations or the existing literature. Finally, the paper illustrates how small-scale qualitative studies can be used to develop theories that can subsequently be tested using quantitative methods as we are currently collecting quantitative prospective data to test the effects described in the qualitative paper.

The last paper in this section, by Rapkin and Schwartz (2004), provides a review of the literature on the response shift and offers a new model concerned with quality-of-life appraisal. Quality of life and its measurement plays a major role in chronic illness research with studies examining how illness and interventions impact on a person's quality of life or how quality of life changes over the course of illness progression. There are many inconsistencies, however, within the quality-of-life research which have presented challenges to those involved in its measurement. For example, subjective and objective measures of quality of life are often very different; those with more physical impairment often report better quality of life than those with less impairment and there is also much variation in quality-of-life assessment even within the same person. Some of this variation has been attributed to measurement error, researcher bias or responder bias. Increasingly, however, it is seen as an illustration of the appraisal processes involved in making quality-of-life assessments. The literature on the response shift has specifically addressed this appraisal process and has focused on how an individual's rating of their own quality of life can change over time. For example, some may show an improvement in their quality of life as they recover from their illness. Some, however, may show an improvement in their quality of life even as their health status deteriorates. Rapkin and Schwartz (2004) focus on the response shift and provide a detailed analysis of what appraisal mechanisms are involved in making a quality-of-life judgement and how changes in the appraisal process can account for changes in quality of life. In particular, they argue that each time a person judges their quality of life they must establish a 'frame of reference' which determines how they comprehend the questions being asked (what do the words 'health', 'mood', 'family', 'work' mean to them?). Next they decide upon a 'sampling strategy' to determine which parts of their life they should assess (should I think of right now or how far back should I go?). Then they decide upon 'standards of comparison' to decide whether to judge their quality of life in terms of their own past history, their expectations or other people or patients they know or have known (am I better off or worse off than I have been or than other people?). Finally, it is argued that people then combine these three sets of appraisal components to formulate a response. Rapkin and Schwartz (2004) then offer formal equations for assessing these appraisal processes and present a tool for measuring them.

They argue that by explicitly assessing the different appraisal processes that are evoked when making a quality-of-life assessment, changes in quality of life over time as well as differences in quality of life between patients and between patients and health professionals can be tested directly. From this perspective, inconsistencies in the quality-of-life literatures are no longer seen as a product of measurement error. In addition, they need no longer be seen as the product of unknown variables causing differences in the ways in which questions are answered. If this more formal and explicit approach is used these inconsistencies can be analysed to provide further insights into how judgements are made and what these judgements say about an individual's quality of life. This paper therefore offers a new and interesting way of understanding both quality of life and the response shift. It also presents a framework for research in the form of a tool for measuring the appraisal processes involved in making assessments about quality of life. Furthermore, it also provides insights into how people answer any questions for any research as all the processes described in this paper in the context of quality of life are equally relevant to all other aspects of both health- and non-health-related research.

This section therefore focuses on chronic illness and presents papers on pain, CHD, cancer, AIDS, obesity, quality of life and the response shift. The papers selected do not reflect the vast amount of research on each of these areas but have been selected as they use a range of methods and have something interesting to contribute to the literature.

Eccleston, C., Morley, S., Williams, A. et al. (2002) Systematic review of randomised controlled trials of psychological therapy for chronic pain in children and adolescents, with a subset meta-analysis of pain relief, *Pain*, 99 (1 – 2): 157 – 65.

Systematic review of randomised controlled trials of psychological therapy for chronic pain in children and adolescents, with a subset meta-analysis of pain relief

Christopher Eccleston[a,*], Stephen Morley[b], Amanda Williams[c], Louise Yorke[a], Kiki Mastroyannopoulou[d]

[a]*Pain Management Unit, University of Bath, UK*
[b]*School of Medicine, University of Leeds, UK*
[c]*Guys, Kings & St. Thomas' Medical and Dental Schools, University of London, UK*
[d]*School of Health Policy and Practice, University of East Anglia, UK*

Abstract

A systematic review and subset meta-analysis of published randomised controlled trials of psychological therapies for children and adolescents with chronic pain is reported. A search of four computerised abstracting services recovered 123 papers from which 28 potential trials were identified. Eighteen met the criteria for inclusion in the review. The majority of these papers reported brief behavioural and cognitive behavioural interventions for children with headache and many were conducted in community (i.e. school) settings. Meta-analysis was applicable for 12 headache trials and one trial of recurrent abdominal pain using the Pain Index. The odds-ratio for a 50% reduction in pain was 9.62 and the number needed to treat was 2.32, indicating that the psychological treatments examined are effective in reducing the pain of headache. The quality of the 18 trials retrieved is narratively reviewed and suggestions for the development of trials in this field are made. © 2002 International Association for the Study of Pain. Published by Elsevier Science B.V. All rights reserved.

Keywords: Systematic review: Meta-analysis; Children; Chronic pain; Headache; Psychology

* Corresponding author. Tel.: + 44-1225-826439; fax: + 44-1225-826752.
E-mail address: c.eccleston@bath.ac.uk (C. Eccleston).

1. Introduction

Children and adolescents frequently experience and report pain (e.g. Goodman and McGrath, 1991; Fearon et al., 1996). A minority become patients who report significant pain and pain-associated distress and disability. This paper reports a systematic review of the randomised controlled trials (RCTs) of psychological therapies for children and adolescents with chronic pain and associated distress and disability.

Chronic pain, pain-related distress, and pain related disability are thought to be commonly under-reported by children and adolescents (Varni et al., 1996; Elliott et al., 1999). However, a number of well-designed studies have found that children and adolescents do report persistent or recurrent chronic pain. For example, in a recent investigation, Perquin et al. (2000, 2001) analysed a large representative sample of school children for all pain experiences and found that 25% of the sample reported chronic or recurrent pain of 3 months or longer. They also found evidence in support of earlier findings that the most common locations of pain are head, limb, and gut; that the report of chronic pain increases with age; and that chronic pain is more common amongst older girls. Of interest to the present study was the finding that 8% of this large school-attending sample reported their experience of pain to be both chronic and severe.

Older children with chronic pain also report chronic disability and emotional distress due to recurrent or persistent pain (Bursch et al., 1998); distress that is often also reported by family members (e.g. Walker and Greene, 1989). Psychological therapies have recently been promoted as potentially effective interventions for the management of severe pain and its disabling consequences (McGrath and Finley, 1999). However, although there is an established systematically reviewed evidence base for the effectiveness of psychological treatments for chronic pain in adults (Morley et al., 1999), there is no similar evidence base for chronic pain in children and adolescents.

There is both indirect and direct evidence for the idea that psychological therapies may have a role to play in paediatric chronic pain management. Indirect evidence comes from the field of paediatric psychotherapy. Kazdin and Weisz (1998), in a thoughtful and challenging narrative review of child and adolescent psychotherapy outcome research, report that there is good evidence for the effectiveness of cognitive behavioural therapy in treating childhood anxiety disorders, childhood depression, and oppositional behaviour. Perhaps of most relevance to the current review is their conclusion that the results are promising for the psychological treatments that are aimed at reducing the anxiety and symptom reporting associated with medical and dental procedures (see also Kibby et al., 1998).

Direct evidence for the claim that psychological therapies may have a role to play in paediatric chronic pain management is provided in a number of recent review articles. Holden et al. (1999) reviewed 31 studies of treatments for children with chronic headache and found good evidence for the efficacy of relaxation and self-hypnosis in reducing pain. The authors included non-randomised trials, and did not analyse pooled data. In their review of paediatric migraine Hermann et al. (1995) did employ data-pooling techniques and found biofeedback and muscle relaxation to be more efficacious than placebo treatments and prophylactic drug treatments in controlling headache. Recurrent abdominal pain is a difficult area of study due to the heterogeneity of presentation and the lack of consensus on a standard treatment approach (Walker, 1999). Nevertheless, some attempts have been made at intervention studies. Janicke and Finney (1999) reported on nine studies, of which four employed control groups. The authors included uncontrolled studies and studies of dietary fibre supplements. No data were available for pooling, although these authors judge the cognitive behavioural approach taken by Sanders et al. (1994) to be promising. Walco et al. (1999) undertook the difficult task of reviewing the literature on interventions for disease related pain, including patients with oncologic, rheumatologic and hematologic disorders. No data pooling was performed and no study met standards from which to extract evidence of treatment effectiveness. Usefully these authors conclude that there is promise in recent trial work from established research groups (e.g. Gil et al., 2001) and in recent theoretical developments of a psychobiological perspective (Zeltzer et al., 1997).

In this paper, we report a systematic review of the published RCTs for psychological therapy of children and adolescents with chronic pain. Systematic review is a specific approach within evidence based medicine that has three related goals: first, it aims to review comprehensively the world literature. Second, where possible, it aims to produce a statement of the efficacy of specific treatments or classes of treatment. If data are combinable meta-analytic techniques are often appropriate. Where data are not combinable narrative review is appropriate. Finally, the most important aim is to describe the quality of the evidence base for all the interventions in a field, paying attention to the omissions in equal measure to the inclusions (Chalmers and Altman, 1995). This last aim is particularly important because the product of such a systematic review is rarely a clear statement of treatment efficacy in all domains of outcome, but more usually a detailed description of the methodological strengths and weakness of trials that can inform trial development.

We chose to review all trials that examine a psychological intervention, and that have pain as an outcome variable, across all treatments, for all chronic pain conditions. Chronic pain in children and adolescents was accepted as a label for pain that persists or recurs for 3 months or longer in people of 21 years or under. The aim of this review is to provide a systematic overview of the current evidence base for psychological interventions in child and adolescent chronic pain, focussing on methodological details of existing trials. An explicit objective is to provide information and guidance that will help shape the next generation of trials in the field.

2. Methods

2.1. Search strategy

A search was conducted for published RCTs of psychological therapies for children and adolescents with chronic pain. A priori decisions were made to search only for papers reported in full, in peer reviewed journals, and to search electronically across databases. In order to maximise the number of papers we adopted a three-stage search strategy, similar to that employed by Morley et al. (1999). First, the Cochrane register of controlled trials, Medline on Ovid from 1966 to 1999, Psychlit on silver platter from 1987 to 1999, Embase from 1980 to 1999, and the Social Science Indices from 1981 to 1999 were all electronically searched. Full search strategies using the available data-management techniques for each abstracting service are available from the authors on request. This search yielded 3715 papers of which 123 were identified as possible trials and eight were identified as relevant review articles. Nineteen of the 123 papers examined were relevant. Second, reference lists of the recovered 19 articles and eight review papers were searched yielding a further ten papers. Finally, a list of possible papers was compiled and sent to the first named author of each paper and review asking them to cross-check these with their own records for missing trials. This produced one more paper. A total of 30 papers, representing 28 studies was reached. All papers were read initially by four of the authors and a consensus on the suitability of the paper for inclusion in the review was reached, based on whether the paper was an RCT of a psychological treatment for child and adolescent chronic pain. Trials were included if they had a clearly defined psychological treatment even when this treatment was concomitant with other non-psychological treatments given as standard care. Trials without a clearly defined psychological treatment, for instance, made only mention to a psychological component of a multi-component treatment package, were excluded. Ten studies were discarded: one proved to be a treatment of acute pain in a chronic pain population, five were single case studies, three compared two active treatments without a no-treatment control, and one had fewer than five patients in each group. This procedure left a total of 18 studies considered to be RCTs (see Table 1). Of these 18 RCTs only 13 provided data suitable for meta-analysis (see below for criteria).

2.2. Coding

Coding schemes were developed from the scheme used by Morley et al. (1999) and were piloted on 11 papers. The version used in this study comprised several sections to record the following aspects of study design: *Verification of study eligibility* e.g. randomisation, appropriate treatment and control groups, sample size > 5 per group, quantitative outcomes; *Design and method* e.g. statement of inclusion and exclusion criteria, sample sizes from recruitment through to endpoint, demographic characteristics of the sample and caregivers, therapist characteristics, manualisation, manipulation, and credibility checks; *Interventions* e.g. individual or group treatment, hours of therapy, treatment components – relaxation, biofeedback, behavioural and cognitive interventions, homework and maintenance strategies; *Outcomes* e.g. details of power calculations, attrition and loss in groups, duration of therapy and follow-up, intention-to-treat or endpoint analysis, measures used; *Individual outcomes* – details for each identified outcome e.g. reliability, origin of data (self-report, observer, assessor), and available summary statistics. (Copies of the coding scheme are available electronically from the corresponding author.) The resultant coding scheme was applied to all 18 papers from the first three authors. The mean inter-rater reliability across all of the separate measurements was $\kappa = 0.68$. Fleiss (1981) suggests that as per a rule of thumb a κ between 0.60 and 0.75 is 'good' (0.4–0.6 is 'fair' and greater than 0.75 is 'excellent'). Consensus was reached on non-agreements through discussion.

3. Results
3.1. Trial design

Table 1 gives summary data for the 18 studies. These studies involved 11 lead investigators in five countries. A total of 808 patients entered trials, 438 in treatment conditions, and 370 in comparison conditions. The trials were relatively simple: ten trials used three arms and eight trials used two arms. The most common comparison group was a waiting list control (eight trials). The mean number of subjects entered into each condition was 18 (SD = 11.8, range 6–65). Fifteen trials treated patients with headache, two recurrent abdominal pain, and one sickle cell pain.

The treatments examined were described as relaxation (11 trials), relaxation with biofeedback (four trials), cognitive behavioural therapy (nine trials), and cognitive behavioural family intervention (one trial). Twelve trials took place in a clinic setting and six in a community setting. Treatment contact time was relatively brief with a mean duration of 3 h (range 45 min–9 h, 20 min).

Table 1 Eighteen studies included in further analyses[a]

Study	Setting	Sample description[b]; mean age, age range, gender ratio (f:m)	Groups and sizes (n); number and labels	Duration of treatment	Outcome measures	Included in meta-analysis
Barry and van Bayer (1997)	Clinic	$M = 9.4$; range $= 7-12$; gender 19:10	Abbreviated cognitive therapy (12); WLC (17)	3 h	Diary: included; mood, school attendance, activity, medication, pain management strategies used	✓
Fentress et al. (1986)	Clinic	$M = 10.1$; range = not given; gender = 11:7	Relaxation (6); relaxation + biofeedback (6); WLC (6)	9 h	Diary	✓
Gil et al. (1997)	Clinic	$M = 11.9$; range = 10–12; gender = 23:26	Cognitive coping skills (25); standard care (24)	One 45 min session	Modified Coping Strategies Questionnaire: Pain sensitivity test	✗
Griffiths and Martin (1996)	Clinic	$M = 11.3$; range 10–12; gender = 21:21	CBT @ clinic (15); CBT @ home (15); WLC (12)	12 h	Diary; mood (anxiety and depression); coping	✓
Labbé and Williamson (1984)	Clinic	$M = 10.7$; range 7–16; gender = 14:14	Autogenic biofeedback (14); WLC (14)	6.67 h	Diary; medication	✓
Labbé (1995)	Clinic	$M = 12.0$; range 8–18; gender = 13:17	Temperature biofeedback + autogenic training (10); autogenic training (10); WLC (10)	7.5 h	Diary	✓
Larsson and Carlsson (1996)	School	M = not given; range 10–15; gender = 25:1	Relaxation (13); NTC (13)	3.3 h	Diary	✓
Larsson and Melin (1986)	School	M = not given; range = 16–18; gender = 30:2	Relaxation (11); information – contact[c,d] (13); NTC[e] (7)	6.75 h	Diary; medication; mood	✓
Larsson et al. (1990)	School	M = not given; range = 16–18; gender = 43:5	Self-help relaxation (31); WLC (17)	1.67 h	Diary; medication; somatic complaints; anxiety; depression; daily stress	✓
Larsson et al. (1987a)	School	M = not given; range 16–18; gender = 35:6	Self-help relaxation (16); therapist assisted relaxation (14); self-monitoring control (11)	6.75 h	Diary; medication; school attendance; mood (anxiety – depression)	✓

Table 1 Continued

Study	Setting	Sample description[b], mean age, age range, gender ratio (f:m)	Groups and sizes (n); number and labels	Duration of treatment	Outcome measures	Included in meta-analysis
Larsson et al. (1987b)	School	M=not given; range=16–18; gender=34:0	Self-help relaxation (12); problem discussion[c] (10); self-monitoring control (12)[c,d]	3 and 7 h	Diary; medication; school attendance; mood (anxiety–depression); psychosomatic symptoms; social relationship	✓
McGrath et al. (1988)	Clinic	M=13.1; range=9–17; gender=69:30	Relaxation (32); 'Own best efforts' (130); placebo: attention control (37)	6 h	Diary	✓
McGrath et al. (1992)	Clinic	M=not given; +range=11–18; +gender=63:24	CBT self-administered[e] (24); CBT therapist administered[e] (23); attention control (26)	8 h	Diary; depression	✓
Osterhaus et al. (1997)	Clinic	M=15.2; range 12–22; gender=29:10	CBT+temperature biofeedback (20); WLC (15)	9.33 h	Diary	✓
Passchier et al. (1990)	School	M=13.7; range=not given; gender=65:54	Relaxation – teacher presented (65); placebo – physical exercises (54)	2.5 h	Diary; medication; school problems; fear of failure	✗
Richter et al. (1986)	Clinic	+M=12.9;+range=9–18; +gender=34:17	Relaxation (15); cognitive coping (15); attention control placebo (12)	9 h	Diary	✗
Sanders et al. (1989)	Clinic	M=9.0; range=6–12; gender=not given	CBT (8); WLC (8)	Eight sessions	Diary; parent and observer behaviour ratings; Problem Behaviour Checklist; Connors CBCL	✓
Sanders et al. (1994)	Clinic	+M=9.3;+range=7–14; +gender=28:16	Cognitive behavioural family intervention (22); standard paediatric cure (22)	6 h	Pain diary; interference; parent observation of pain behaviour; child behaviour checklist	

[a] WLC, waiting list control; NTC, no-treatment control; CBT, cognitive behaviour therapy.

[b] Numbers based on trial completers unless indicated by+where data are available for entrants only.

[c] Used as separate control treatment contrasts in first analysis.

[d] Used as contrast in second analysis.

[e] Groups pooled in second analysis.

3.2. Trial quality

All the 18 trials reported that randomisation had taken place, but in no case was the exact method of randomisation given. Eight trials explicitly reported restrictions on randomisation e.g. to produce equal numbers per group, or restricting allocation within a school class group. In five other trials randomisation took place after stratification or a matching procedure. Finally, there was one study in which cluster randomisation of whole school classes occurred. None of the studies was double blind. This conventional methodological criterion is inapplicable to most psychological interventions. Eight of the trials stated either that the credibility of the treatment or the expectation of therapeutic improvement had been assessed. In no trial was there mention of the therapeutic allegiance of the trial therapist although this may influence the outcome of the trial.

3.3. Treatment delivery

Ten trials reported treatment delivered to individuals or parent–child couples, in one to one contacts with a therapist. In seven trials a group-based intervention was used: included in this were interventions applied to a whole school class or a subset of members of that class as well as groups which were formed de novo for the purposes of the trial. There was one trial in which individuals received a mixture of individual and group treatment. Eleven of the trials used a treatment manual, and where this was not explicitly stated the authors either referred to another authority on which the treatment was based (e.g. Bernstein and Borkovec, 1973), or gave details of the structure and content of treatment within the paper. Studies that tested the effectiveness of self-help strategies used a combination of manual and audio taped instructions. In contrast to this high level of manualisation, only three studies explicitly mentioned checks for therapist adherence to the manual. One study conducted a partial check on initial sessions.

The trials employed a variety of therapists ranging from undergraduate assistants to experienced psychological and medical personnel. The major group used as therapists were graduate trainees in clinical psychology (six trials). Other trials employed non-psychologists specifically trained for the trials (e.g. school nurses and teachers) to deliver structured interventions. The level of therapist training was not stated in six trials. Only three trials explicitly mentioned that therapists received supervision during the trials. This coupled with the general failure to note whether checks on adherence were made must be considered a weakness when judging the overall quality of the trials.

3.4. Measurement domains

A number of measures were employed in a range of domains of chronic pain. Only pain experience was measured in all trials. Recent practice in the conduct of many trials in medical settings is to provide an unequivocal statement of the primary outcome measure. This has not been the tradition in trials of psychological treatments and this was reflected in these studies. We could find only two trials (McGrath et al., 1992; Larsson and Carlsson, 1996) where the authors explicitly stated a 'primary' or 'major' outcome. However, given the prevalence of the use and analysis of pain diaries it seems reasonable to infer that pain was the primary outcome variable, but we note that there is considerable uncertainty as to the primary variable used by authors. Most report multiple parametric analyses of frequency, intensity, and duration (but did not provide sufficient information for meta-analysis) as well as the compound Pain Index.

In total, 47 distinct measurement instruments were employed; the modal number of instruments used in each study was one (range one to six). The second most common measurement domain represented was mood, reported in eight trials. Only six papers reported medication use, and only four papers reported school attendance as outcomes. Despite the number of measurement instruments employed sufficient data for statistical meta-analysis were available in only 13 trials for the single domain of pain experience. All trials used a version of a daily pain diary derived from Budzynski's early research on biofeedback for headache and subsequently widely adopted (Budzynski et al., 1973). The diary records the frequency, duration, and intensity characteristic of pain episodes. There was some variation in the diaries e.g. use of 0–4 or 0–5 scale points, frequency of rating (1, 3 or 4 times per day but most authors report using some transformation to capture a function of the total amount of pain experience which we denote as the Pain Index). The most common transformation was a simple summation of intensity ratings over a set period, usually a week. While the precise scaling of the diary data varies, outcomes were expressed as a ratio representing the percentage change from baseline in the Pain Index. In all studies where this metric was reported the authors use a 50% reduction in the Pain Index as a criterion of clinically significant improvement. This value is widely used in many studies of treatment for acute pain (McQuay and Moore, 1998) and enables the outcome to be expressed as the number of participants in each group achieving a clinically significant gain. These data were reported as a dichotomous outcome variable (improved vs. unimproved) for treatment and control groups in 13 studies and are therefore susceptible to meta-analysis using odds ratios (OR) as the outcome statistic. A number of papers reported continuous (mean, SD) outcome data but in most cases the additional data (SD and/or sample size) were not available in a form suitable for analysis, and attempts to retrieve suitable data from authors were not successful.

3.5. Meta-analysis

Our intended analytic strategy was to explore the effects of treatments on a range of outcomes, but we were unable to do this because of limited analysable data. For example, although mood was assessed in a number of trials, and in general the mood scores decreased from pre- to post-treatment assessments for both treatment or control groups, these data are not of a quality to perform statistical meta-analysis, due largely to incomplete reporting, or the use of unreliable measurement instruments. Pain experience data were, however, analysable. We conducted two analyses using a random effects model. The pooled OR was computed using the DerSimonian and Laird (1986) method. Tests for combinability, bias detection (OR against 1/trial weight), and funnel plots were examined for the pooled data. The tests for combinability indicated that the data could be legitimately pooled but both the bias detection and funnel plots suggested that the OR was systematically related to the size of the trials with smaller trials having larger ORs. The first analysis was the comparison between a treatment group and the designated control. For studies with more than one arm the data are confounded because there is a common control group used to compute the effect size. A second analysis pooled the treatment arms within each study and estimated a common treatment effect against a single control group. This procedure assumes that the outcome of the treatment groups is similar irrespective of differences in treatment content. Indeed, there was no evidence within the trials of differences between treatments. The small number of trials precluded an analysis based on variations in the content of control groups, i.e. active treatment controls vs. waiting list and vs. no treatment controls.

The first analysis gave a pooled OR = 9.2 (approximate 95% CI = 5.64–15.00; $X^2 = 78.97$, d.f. = 1, $P < 0.0001$). The second analysis produced a similar estimate: pooled OR = 9.62 (approximate 95% CI = 5.17–17.92; $X^2 = 50.95$, d.f. = 1, $P < 0.0001$). A partial Cochrane plot for the latter analysis is shown in Fig. 1. Both analyses indicate that psychological treatments are effective when compared with a pooled group of control conditions. As OR are not intuitively easy to interpret we also computed the number needed to treat (NNT) statistic from the pooled data set. The NNT = 2.32 (95% CI 1.96–2.88), which implies that therapists need to treat just over two people for one to benefit who would not have done so in the non-treatment control condition. Inspection of the ORs for studies conducted in the clinic and those conducted in the community showed no systematic difference according to setting. We also inspected the ORs associated with various methods of recording the pain diary. There appeared to be no systematic variation of OR with method and the subsamples were too small for statistical analysis.

4. Discussion

4.1. Resume

From the 30 papers reviewed, 18 trials met criteria for inclusion in the review and 13 provided data suitable for meta-analysis. The trials were relatively simple in design, with one or two treatment conditions in comparison to a waiting list, standard care or placebo control group. No trial was fully blinded, indeed, this criterion that is generally applied to evaluate pharmacological interventions would seem to be largely misplaced in the trials of psychosocial interventions. Nevertheless, it is important for the design of these trials to consider ways in which the equivalence of the trial arms can be assessed. This requires the careful design of control treatments (Schwartz et al., 1997) and the assessment of critical components. However, in the sample of trials reported in this study credibility of the therapy, therapist allegiance, therapist training, allocation of therapist to treatments, and supervision of therapists were rarely mentioned. The use of treatment manuals was relatively common but adherence to manuals was measured in only three studies. Although 47 separate measurement instruments were used covering the range of chronic pain experience, data from these instruments were rarely reported in full.

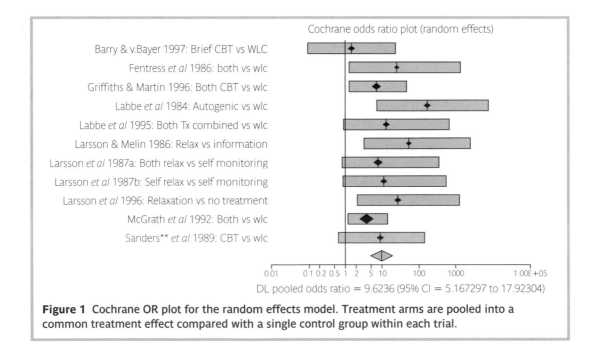

Figure 1 Cochrane OR plot for the random effects model. Treatment arms are pooled into a common treatment effect compared with a single control group within each trial.

Domains of measurement that one might have expected to be well reported such as function or school attendance were either not included or not reported. Pain was the most common domain assessed, followed by mood. Twelve papers provided self-report data of pain severity in children and adolescents with headache and one paper reported data in children with recurrent abdominal pain. There was an NNT of 2.32 for psychological therapies producing more than 50% relief in pain. This compares favourably with other published NNTs in chronic pain (McQuay and Moore, 1998). There was only one non-headache trial with meta-analysable data and there were insufficient non-pain outcome data from all trials to subject to meta-analysis. A striking feature of the set of trials examined was the inclusion of six community trials, five from a Scandinavian research group working in a school setting. There were no differences between studies conducted in the clinic and the community.

We made a number of decisions that should be taken into account when interpreting the findings (Fishbain et al., 2001; Thompson et al., 1995). Hand searching was not undertaken, but multiple electronic databases and author contact were used. In line with the primary questions, we chose to include a heterogeneous sample of treatments and patients. Data were independently abstracted and reliability of the data extraction measured. Reliable study quality criteria were employed. Both effect sizes and NNTs were calculated and the heterogeneity between studies was controlled for. Where insufficient data were reported these were simply omitted from the review.

4.2. Current status and future investigations

The provision of a reliable evidence base of paediatric pain treatments is a shared goal of the paediatric pain research community. If one takes account of the complexities involved in undertaking psychological research in paediatric chronic pain, we would argue that the current status of the evidence base for psychological treatments is good. Particularly impressive was the use of simple designs and the use of well-validated pain measures. This systematic review raises a number of implications for the design of trials of psychological therapy for children with chronic pain.

First, the lack of a tradition in psychological research for specifying primary outcomes causes problems for interpretation. In the present studies, no data were analysable from non-pain outcome domains suggesting that pain relief alone was the most important goal of treatment. In some trials pain relief may be the only target. However, children, adolescents, and their families normally present for treatment with more than only pain severity and frequency as primary complaints (McGrath and Hillier, 2001). For many, improvements in pain relief, function, and mood are legitimate outcomes of psychological therapies. The current evidence base does not allow for a judgement of the effectiveness of psychological therapy in improving mood, function, and school attendance, nor in reducing disability.

All studies included and reported standardised pain data. However, there is no similar standardised multidimensional instrument designed to measure the impact of chronic pain on the life of a child or adolescent or family members. Instead, in all of the reviewed studies single domain instruments were employed. The development of a multidimensional outcome tool may provide agreement on the importance of including domains of pain experience other than pain severity and frequency.

Second, a striking result of this study was the finding that therapy contact was typically individual, brief, and well manualised. The relatively frequent mention of manualisation may be due to the brief skill-based type of interventions. For example, the 13 treatments that were labelled relaxation were relatively well defined and referenced. In contrast, the more time consuming 11 treatments that were labelled as having a cognitive component were more poorly described. The active components of psychological treatments labelled cognitive behavioural therapy for children remain somewhat of a mystery. To better specify the content of therapy will strengthen the evidence base.

Third, a relatively small number of patients have been exposed to controlled treatments ($n=$ 438) with an average sample size of an active treatment arm of 15 patients. However, what will be of interest to the development of the field is a further level of analysis to determine exactly which treatment components are effective for which patients on which outcomes. We recognize that this is not a problem specific to chronic pain but is true for many child and adolescent treatment domains (Durlak et al., 1995; Kazdin and Weisz, 1998). It is unlikely that treatment components will match directly to specific outcomes. Trials that assess the addition of a psychological treatment to existing non-psychological treatments are required (e.g. Olness et al., 1987). This second level of analysis will require studies with larger sample sizes. Multicentre trials may be a necessity in this field.

Fourth, there is an urgent need for well-designed, conducted, and reported trials of behavioural and cognitive behavioural therapies for children and adolescents with chronic pain other than headache, in which the management of pain-associated disability and distress is a primary aim of treatment (Walco et al., 1999). The current evidence base is representative of patients mostly with headache that does not lead to chronic limitations on social and family functioning, and that does not lead to prolonged psychological distress. Trials are required for children and adolescents whose complaints are of chronic pain that is more severely limiting and distressing, in which pain relief is not the only, and not always the important outcome. Important to consider will be the design of trials that focus treatment not upon the child or adolescent alone, but on combinations of parents, carers, and children (Malleson et al., 2001).

Finally, the apparent effectiveness of simple psychological interventions for headache applied in school settings raises the possibility of whether such interventions could be applied as a method of secondary prevention to ameliorate the development of chronicity in the population. The simplicity of the intervention and the apparent ease with which non-pain specialists can implement it suggests the possibility that a preventive psychosocial intervention could be developed (Masek, 1999).

4.3. Conclusions

There is insufficient evidence to judge the effectiveness of psychological therapies in improving mood, function, or disability associated with chronic pain in children and adolescents. Well-designed and comprehensively reported RCTs of psychological therapy for non-headache chronic pain in children and adolescents are urgently needed. There is strong evidence that psychological treatments, principally relaxation and cognitive behavioural therapy, are highly effective in reducing the severity and frequency of chronic pain in children and adolescents. There is a strong case for these treatments to be offered to patients with headache as a matter of routine care (McGrath, 1999).

References

Barry J, von Bayer CL. Brief Cognitive-Behavioural group treatment for children's headache. Clin J Pain 1997;13:215–220.

Bernstein DA, Borkovec TD. Progressive relaxation training: a manual for the helping professions, Champaign, IL: Research Press, 1973.

Budzynski TH, Stoyva JM, Adler CS, Mullancy DJ. EMG biofeedback and tension headache: a controlled outcome study. Psychosom Med 1973;35:483–496.

Bursch B, Walco GA, Zeltzer L. Clinical assessment and management of chronic pain and Pain-Associated Disability Syndrome. Dev Behav Pediatr 1998;19:45–53.

Chalmers I, Altman DG, editors. Systematic Reviews London: BMJ, 1995.

DerSimonian R, Laird N. Meta-analysis in clinical trials. Control Clin Trials 1986;7:177–188.

Durlak JA, Wells AM, Cotton JK, Johnson S. Analysis of selected methodological issues in child psychotherapy research. J Clin Child Psychol 1995;24:141–148.

Elliott AM, Smith BH, Kay PI, Cairns Smith W, Chambers WA. The epidemiology of chronic pain in the community. Lancet 1999;354:1248–1252.

Fearon I, McGrath PJ, Achat H. Booboos: the study of everyday pain among young children. Pain 1996;68:55–62.

Fentress DW, Masek BJ, Mehegan JE, Benson H. Biofeedback and relaxation-response training in the treatment of pediatric migraine. Dev Med Child Neurol 1986;28:139–146.

Fishbain D, Cutler RB, Rosomoff HL, Rosomoff RS. What is the quality of the implemented meta-analytic procedures in chronic pain treatment meta-analyses? Clin J Pain 2001;16:73–85.

Fleiss JL. Statistical methods for rates and proportions, New York, NY: Wiley, 1981.

Gil KM, Wilson JJ, Edens JL, Workman E, Ready J, Sedway J, Redding-Lallinger R, Daeschner C. Cognitive coping skills training in children with sickle cell disease pain. Int J Behav Med 1997;4:364–377.

Gil KM, Carson AKK, Redding-Lallinger JW, Daeschner CW, Ware RE. Coping skills training in children with sickle cell disease: daily coping practice predicts treatment effects. J Pediatr Psychol 2001;26:163–173.

Goodman JE, McGrath PJ. The epidemiology of pain in children and adolescents: a review. Pain 1991;46:247–264.

Griffiths JD, Martin PR. Clinical versus home-based treatment formats for children with chronic headache. Br J Health Psychol 1996;1:151–166.

Hermann C, Kim M, Blanchard EB. Behavioral and prophylactic pharmacological intervention studies of pediatric migraine: an exploratory meta-analysis. Pain 1995;60:239–256.

Holden EW, Deichmann MM, Levy J. Empirically supported treatments in pediatric psychology: recurrent pediatric headache. J Pediatr Psychol 1999;24:91–109.

Janicke DM, Finney JQ. Empirically supported treatments in pediatric psychology: recurrent abdominal pain. J Pediatr Psychol 1999;24:115–127.

Kazdin AE, Weisz JR. Identifying and developing empirically supported child and adolescent treatments. J Consult Clin Psychol 1998;66:19–36.

Kibby MY, Tye VL, Mulhern RK. Effectiveness of psychological intervention for children and adolescents with chronic medical illness: a meta-analysis. Clin Psychol Rev 1998;18:103–117.

Labbé EE. Treatment of childhood migraines using autogenic training and skin temperature biofeedback: a component analysis. Headache 1995;35:10–13.

Labbé EE, Williamson DA. Treatment of childhood migraines using autogenic feedback training. J Consult Clin Psychol 1984;52:968–976.

Larsson B, Carlsson J. A school-based, nurse administered relaxation training for children with chronic tension-type headache. J Pediatr Psychol 1996;21:603–614.

Larsson B, Melin L. Chronic headaches in adolescents: treatment in a school setting with relaxation training as compared with information contact and self-registration. Pain 1986;25:325–336.

Larsson B, Daleflod B, Hakansson L, Melin L. Therapist assisted versus self-help relaxation treatment of chronic headaches in adolescents: a school-based intervention. J Child Psychol Psychiatry 1987a;28:127–136.

Larsson B, Melin L, Lamminen M, Ullstedt F. A school-based treatment of chronic headaches in adolescents. J Pediatr Psychol 1987b;12:553–566.

Larsson B, Melin L, Doberl A. Recurrent tension headache in adolescents treated with self-help relaxation training and a muscle relaxant drug. Headache 1990;30:665–671.

Malleson PN, Connell H, Bennett SM, Eccleston C. Chronic musculoskeletal and other idiopathic pain syndromes. Arch Dis Child 2001;84:189–192.

Masek BJ. Commentary: the pediatric migraine connection. J Pediatr Psychol 1999;24:110.

McGrath PJ. Commentary: recurrent headaches: making what works available to those who need it. J Pediatr Psychol 1999;24:111–112.

McGrath PJ, Finley GA, editors. Chronic and recurrent pain in children and adolescents Seattle, WA: IASP Press, 1999.

McGrath PA, Hillier LMH, editors. The child with headache: diagnosis and treatment Seattle, WA: IASP Press, 2001.

McGrath PJ, Humphreys P, Goodman JT, Keene D, Firestone P, Jacob P, Cunningham SJ. Relaxation prohphylaxis for childhood migraine: a randomized placebo-controlled trial. Dev Med Child Neurol 1988;30:626–631.

McGrath PJ, Humphreys P, Keene D, Goodman JT, Lascelles MA, Cunningham SJ, Firestone P. The efficacy and efficiency of a self-administered treatment for adolescent migraine. Pain 1992;49:321–324.

McQuay HJ, Moore RA. An evidence-based resource for pain relief, Oxford: Oxford University Press, 1998.

Morley S, Eccleston C, Williams AC de C. Systematic review and meta-analysis of randomized controlled trials of cognitive behaviour therapy for chronic pain in adults, excluding headache. Pain 1999;80:1–13.

Olness K, Macdonald JT, Uden DL. Comparison of self-hypnosis and propranolol in the treatment of juvenile classic migraine. Pediatrics 1987;79:593–597.

Osterhaus SO, Lange A, Wim HJP, Passchier J, van der Helm Hylkema H, de Jong KT, Orlebeke JF. A behavioral treatment of young migrainous and nonmigrainous headache patients: prediction of treatment success. Int J Behav Med 1997;18:698–715.

Passchier J, van den Bree MB, Emmen HH, Osterhaus SO, Orlebeke JF, Verhage F. Relaxation training in school classes does not reduce headache complaints. Headache 1990;30:660–664.

Perquin CW, Hazebroek-Kampscheur AAJM, Hunfeld JAM, Bohnene AM, van Suijlekom-Smit LWA, Passchier J, van der Wouden JC. Pain in children and adolescents: a common experience. Pain 2000;87:51–58.

Perquin CW, Hazebroek-Kampscheur AAJM, Hunfeld JAM, van Suijlekom-Smit LWA, Passchier J, van der Wouden JC. Chronic pain among children and adolescents: physician consultation and medication use. Clin J Pain 2001;16:229–235.

Richter IL, McGrath PJ, Humphreys PJ, Goodman JT, Firestone P, Keene D. Cognitive and relaxation treatment of pediatric migraine. Pain 1986;25:195–203.

Sanders MR, Rebgetz M, Morrison M, Bor W, Gordon A, Dadds M, Shepherd R. Cognitive-behavioral treatment of recurrent nonspecific abdominal pain in children: an analysis of generalization, maintenance and side-effects. J Consult Clin Psychol 1989;57:294–300.

Sanders MR, Shepherd RW, Cleghorn G, Woolford H. The treatment of recurrent abdominal pain in children: a controlled comparison of cognitive-behavioral family intervention and standard pediatric care. Consult Clin Psychol 1994;62:306–314.

Schwartz CE, Chesney MA, Irvine J, Keefe FJ. The control group dilemma in clinical research: applications for psychosocial and behavioral medicine trials. Psychosom Med 1997;59:362–371.

Thompson SG. Why sources of heterogeneity in meta-analysis should be investigated. In: Chalmers I, Altman DG, editors. Systematic reviews, London: BMJ, 1995. pp. 48–63.

Varni JW, Rapoff MA, Waldron SA, Gragg RA, Bernstein BH, Lidsley CB. Chronic pain and emotional distress in children and adolescents. Dev Behav Pediatr 1996;17:154–161.

Walco GA, Sterling CM, Conte PM, Engel RG. Empirically supported treatments in pediatric psychology: disease related pain. J Pediatr Psychol 1999;24:155–167.

Walker L. The evolution of research on recurrent abdominal pain: history, assumptions, and new directions. In: McGrath PJ, Finley GA, editors. Chronic and recurrent pain in children and adolescents, Seattle, WA: IASP Press, 1999. pp. 141–172.

Walker L, Greene J. Children with recurrent abdominal pain and their parents: more somatic complaints, anxiety, and depression than other patient families? J Pediatr Psychol 1989;14:231–293.

Zeltzer L, Bursch B, Walco G. Pain responsiveness and chronic pain: a psychobiological perspective. J Dev Behav Pediatr 1997;18:413–422.

Smith, J.A. and Osborn, M. (2007) Pain as an assault on the self: an interpretative phenomenological analysis of the psychological impact of chronic benign low back pain, *Psychology and Health*, 22 (5): 517–34.

Pain as an assault on the self

An interpretative phenomenological analysis of the psychological impact of chronic benign low back pain

Jonathan A. Smith[1] & Mike Osborn[2]

[1]School of Psychology, Birkbeck University of London, UK and [2]Pain Management Unit, University of Bath and Pain Clinic, Royal United Hospital, Bath, UK

Abstract

This paper presents an in-depth, idiographic study illustrating how chronic benign low back pain may have a serious debilitating impact on the sufferer's sense of self. Semi-structured interviews were conducted with six patients and the resultant transcripts subjected to interpretative phenomenological analysis. The analysis points to the powerful ways in which chronic pain has negative impact on patients' self and identity. This impact is made worse in the public arena. Some of the participants describe how the ensuing derogatory self image also seems to lead to their directing negative affect towards other people. The results section gives a detailed account of these processes at work. The results are then considered in relation to relevant constructs in the extant literature, including work on illness and identity, shame and acceptance.

Keywords: Pain, back, self, shame, interpretative phenomenological analysis

Introduction

Chronic benign pain is any pain that has persisted for longer than six months and is not related to an ongoing peripheral disease process (I.A.S.P., 1986). Unlike acute pain (of duration under three months) it has no 'biological utility' (Gatchel & Epker, 1999, p. 413), it is rarely diagnostic and tends not to respond to medical treatment to the extent that it is relieved completely. The sufferer experiences chronic pain as the seamless persistence of acute pain and as such it does not necessarily feel any different to them, it simply endures long after the point at which it 'should' have receded. In this way the experience of chronic pain often involves a long and drawn out process where it is defined over time by exclusion and by the cumulative failure of interventions. This process of acquiring and then living with a diagnosis of chronic pain plays a role in the 'unpleasantness' of chronic benign pain and informs the meanings that the pain has for the sufferer as they try to make sense of what is happening to them.

Correspondence: Dr Jonathan A. Smith, School of Psychology, Birkbeck University of London, Malet St, London, WC1E 7HX, UK. E-mail: ja.smith@bbk.ac.uk

Not everyone with chronic benign low back pain suffers clinical levels of pain sensation, distress and disability, but a significant number do. Their lives and the meaning it has for them can change beyond recognition, ranging from finding it difficult to sit in a chair, to having to leave work or decide not to have children. Immobility, worry, frustration, pessimism, powerlessness and cognitive interference are matched by a struggle to retain paid employment, supportive relationships, social status and any kind of valued self-view. When at its worst chronic pain sufferers are often described as having chronic pain syndrome (I.A.S.P., 1994).

Chronic pain is a major public health problem and has been described as having reached epidemic proportions in western society. Chronic benign lower back pain is a particular problem as it is most often a mid-life condition which disables people during their most economically active years. It is the single largest cause of disability and time lost at work in western society (Clabber Moffat, Richardson, Sheldon, & Maynard, 1995). Maniadakis and Gray (2000) in a study of the economic burden of back pain in the UK concluded that it was "one of the most costly conditions for which an economic analysis had been carried out in the UK" (p. 95). They estimated that direct care costs in 1998 were £1632 million but that this was dwarfed by the cost of informal care and loss of production which amounted to £10668 million.

The relationship between chronic pain sensation, distress and disability is a complex, dynamic and unpredictable one involving many psychosocial factors (Turk & Flor, 1999). It has probably generated the largest single body of health psychology and clinical health psychology research; yet it retains much of its mystery and the challenge remains how to best understand and manage something which causes so much morbidity and is so notable for its variability and idiosyncrasy.

Recently some writers have been arguing for the importance of considering the concepts of self and identity in relation to pain (Morley & Eccleston, 2004). Although psychological models and theories that reference the self are common, concise and consensual, definitions of the self are elusive and it has been neglected as a central focus of study. Definitions of the self have to be broad to capture its dynamic complexity and not represent it falsely as an inert monolith (Kihlstrom & Kihlstrom, 1999). It is most often referred to as a stable but dynamic collection of core beliefs, affects or cognitions that are utilized by the individual to define or represent themselves both privately and in their presentation to the outside world (Ashmore & Jussim, 1997). In this way the self is central to the sense-making process and serves as a useful concept for exploring the inter-relationship between individuals, their bodies, larger relational, social and cultural systems and between the private and the public domains of our own experience.

Pincus and Morley (2001) theorised that the experience of chronic pain related to the degree to which the three schemas of pain, self and illness over-lapped, ultimately leading to a form of enmeshment where the activation of elements from one would influence the other. A pathway, via the self, was hypothesized between the physical and psychological dimensions of chronic pain. Consonant with this notion of the centrality of the self, Morley and Eccleston (2004) argued that one of the key 'objects of fear' in chronic pain was a threat to identity and the potential of pain to both overwhelm the self permanently and threaten its social legitimacy has also been established (Aldrich, Eccleston, & Crombez, 2000; Eccleston, Williams, & Stainton-Rogers, 1997).

A small number of qualitative studies have explored the personal experience of chronic pain and an emergent theme has been the impact of the experience of living with chronic pain on the self (e.g., Gustafsson, Ekholm, & Ohman, 2004; Hellstrom, 2001; Hellstrom, Jansson, & Carlsson, 1999; Osborn & Smith, 1998; Paulson, Danielson, & Soderberg, 2002). These studies have highlighted the value of exploring the subjective experience of chronic pain and the importance of looking beyond disease-specific beliefs to see how concepts of the self and self-conscious affect might help to understand chronic pain. Retaining a stable and valued self and managing the emergence of a range of new and potentially problematic selves as a chronic and disabling condition persists over time is a common feature of these studies. For example, Hellstrom (2001) showed how, in chronic conditions, different selves developed over time which were problematic if they contrasted too much with the contemporary reality of the pain. The self appeared to lag behind the changes in the body and did not automatically accommodate for the presence of pain. Aspects of it were rejected, resisted or avoided and a range of selves developed in response to its development over time, some of which were unhelpful and an obstacle to constructive management and acceptance. Loss of function and social role, the uncertainty of aetiology and diagnosis and the stigma of the illness have all been suggested as factors in this process (Charmaz, 1983, 1991; Kotarba, 1983; Osborn & Smith, 1998).

A strong argument has been made for exploring the self-concept in more detail in chronic benign pain but more needs to be known about how the two inter-relate on an individual or psychological level. Much of the qualitative work to date has taken a sociological focus or looked at chronic disease in general rather than chronic pain specifically. Similarly the cognitive work on 'enmeshment' (Pincus & Morley, 2001) highlights the need to know more about how such a process operates for the person involved and what contextual and subjective phenomena are involved. Further idiographic study, focusing on benign chronic low back pain from a psychological perspective and exploring the personal accounts of sufferers in depth would help build upon the work to date. It would explore the manner in which the pain sufferer's sense of self unfolded and developed as their pain progressed and contribute to our understanding of the unpleasantness of pain and its management.

The aim of this study is to explore the relationship between the participants' chronic benign low back pain and their sense of self from an idiographic, phenomenological perspective, dedicated to fore-grounding the subjective experience of the participant. The study is qualitative and employs Interpretative Phenomenological Analysis (IPA) (Smith, 2004). IPA has been developed specifically within psychology and combines a dedication to understanding the 'lived' experience of the participant with a belief that to achieve such understanding requires interpretative work on the part of the researcher and it offers a systematic approach to doing this (Smith & Osborn, 2003). It is committed to idiographic inquiry (Lamiell, 1987; Smith, Harre, & Van Langenhove, 1995; Smith 2004) where each case is examined in great detail as an entity in its own right before a move to more general claims are made in a narrative account that includes detailed extracts from the individual participants' accounts.

IPA has been used extensively, although not exclusively, within health psychology and there is now a growing corpus of IPA research examining aspects of the psychology of health (see Brocki & Wearden, 2006 for a review). Among topics examined thus far are: the experience of chronic illness (Bramley & Eatough, 2005; Reynolds & Prior, 2003); psychosocial aspects of the new genetics (Michie, Smith, Senior, & Marteau, 2003; Smith, Michie, Allanson, & Elwy, 2000); sexual and reproductive health (Flowers, Duncan, & Knussen, 2003; Jarman, Walsh, & De Lacey, 2005; Lavie & Willig, 2005); the experience of health professionals (Carradice, Shankland, & Beail, 2002; Michie, Hendy, Smith, & Adshead, 2004).

IPA is particularly useful where the topic under study is dynamic, contextual and subjective, relatively under-studied and where issues relating to identity, the self and sense-making are important (Smith, 2004). By focusing in more depth on the specific experience of the self in chronic pain this study builds upon the small number of qualitative studies published to date. Through a detailed, idiographic and in-depth analysis of the participants' personal experiences the complex interrelationship between chronic pain and the self will be examined further.

Method

Participants

The participants represent a reasonably homogeneous, purposive sample (Smith & Osborn, 2003). They were European, Caucasian, from a working class background and in middle adulthood. All had recently been referred to the same pain clinic in the UK. They had all stopped paid employment due to their pain. Names have been changed to protect confidentiality. The ages of the participants, plus the length of time they had been in pain are listed in Box 1. The participants had no prior experience of pain management clinics or any psychological interventions for pain, had no significant psychological co-morbidity, and were neither taking any major opiates for their pain nor awaiting any further medical interventions or investigations. The participants' pain was not associated with any litigation, ongoing disease process or previous trauma. Each participant was considered by the staff at the pain clinic to have chronic benign low back pain associated with high levels of distress and disability.

Local ethical approval had been secured for the study and the appropriate consent and information forms were administered. Patients were approached by the second author while waiting in the clinic, informed about the study and asked if they would consider participating. The participants in this paper represent the first six to agree to participate. No patients declined. The sample size is normative for IPA (see e.g., Brocki & Wearden, 2006; Turpin et al., 1997). There is no necessary correct number of participants for a qualitative study. With IPA the emphasis is on the detailed analysis of each case and therefore sample sizes are usually small.

Procedure

Data was collected through semi-structured interviews. The participants were asked to talk as widely as possible about the different ways their pain had affected or influenced their feelings, attitudes or beliefs about themselves. The interviews were semi-structured in that the researcher was informed by the schedule (see Appendix 1) but participants were encouraged to talk in detail about their particular concerns and were probed on important individual topics which arose. Verbatim transcripts of the semi-structured interviews served as the raw data for the study.

The data was analysed using IPA. The analysis followed very closely the four-stage process described in detail in Smith and Osborn (2003). Analysis began with a close interpretative reading of the first case where initial responses to the text are annotated in one margin. These initial notes are translated into emergent themes at one higher level of abstraction and recorded in the other margin. The themes were interrogated in order to make connections between them. This resulted in a table of super-ordinate themes for the first case within which were nested the subordinate themes with identifying information – that is, where the instances supporting the theme can be found within the interview transcript.

Box 1 The participants

Anonymised name (to protect identity)	Age	Pain duration (years)
Helen	37	5
Lynette	52	9
Simon	45	11
Frank	51	7
Kevin	36	13
Tony	44	15

This process is repeated for each case. After analysis has been conducted on each case, patterns were established cross-case and documented in a master table of themes for the group. One researcher reviewed and audited the themes to ensure that they were grounded and well represented in the transcripts. The master table was then transformed into a narrative account; the analytic account is supported by verbatim extracts from each participant.

Results

The negative impact of pain on the self

We will start with the detailed examination of one passage from one participant – Helen. We are placing this here as it illustrates all the main features which also crop up in the other accounts though of course each instance also has its own idiosyncratic flavour. The effect of the passage is cumulatively therefore to vividly demonstrate the central thesis of this paper – that pain can have dramatic effect on the patient's sense of self and identity:

> It's not who I am it's just who I am if you know what I mean, it's not really me, I get like that and I know like, you're being mean now but I can't help it. It's the pain, it's me, but it is me, me doing it but not me do you understand what I'm saying?
> If I was to describe myself like you said, I'm a nice person, but then I'm not, am I?
>
> And there's other stuff, stuff I haven't told you, if you knew you'd be disgusted I just get so hateful. […]
>
> I know your gonna say it's all me, but I can't help it even though I don't like it. It's the mean me, my mean head all sour and horrible, I can't cope with that bit, I cope with the pain better. […]
>
> [Tearful] Look do you mind if we stop now, I didn't think it would be like this, I don't want to talk any more.

There is a great deal going on in this extract. Helen introduces two selves: 'a nice person' and the 'mean me, my mean head all sour and horrible' and seems to be engaged in a wrestle over the degree to which each applies to her. At this point the status of the different selves seems somewhat equivocal. It may be that Helen is convinced that she is still a nice person but is worried that publicly other people perceive her to be something else – and that negative image can therefore be attributed to something outside the self – the pain itself. Alternatively and more distressing, she may see herself as engaged in a battle for her identity itself, an attempt to retain the old 'nice' self against the onslaught of the new 'mean' self.

What is striking in the extract is just how far the self-denigration goes. She is already describing herself in considerably pejorative terms and yet insists it is in fact even worse but that shame prevents her revealing the full extent of the depravity.

The way the passage unfolds strongly suggests that this is not a cool detached account of herself Helen has come to live with but rather is something that she is still wrestling with in the present. This is reflected in how she works through the contradictions in real-time at the beginning of the extract and then in the way in which she draws the interviewer into the debate: 'Stuff I haven't told you … I know you're gonna say' and then most dramatically at the end where she asks for the interview to be stopped. Helen's battle comes alive in the contemporaneous interview with the researcher.

Helen neatly encapsulates the essence of her distress when she says: "I can't cope with that bit, I cope with the pain better." Remember this is a person who has a high level of disability from her pain. Yet she argues that the pain itself is not the main problem. Rather what is worse is the impact it is having on her sense of self and the struggle she is having to retain a good self.

As suggested earlier, this passage in some way speaks for all the participants – each of whom echoes Helen's struggle. See this passage from Kevin:

> The bits that aren't me, I can't be me. The hardest part is the pain obviously, but the fact that I'm like this monster, I get mean, I do things and I think things which are mean, things which I'd never tell anyone and I'll not tell you so don't ask, [...] that's the hardest part now you ask.

We see a similar mental struggle in relation to identity. There is the same unspeakable shame and loathing; the same invocation of the interviewer. And finally a similar plea that the effect on self is more distressing than the pain itself.

Continuum and trajectory?

While all participants demonstrate the debilitating impact of pain on self and identity, there are differences in how this impact is portrayed. Indeed there is the suggestion of the possibility of a developmental process, patients beginning with a fight to retain the positive original self, then beginning to doubt the possibility and finally resigning themselves to a new less desirable self taking over. Let us look at an extract from Simon:

> It's like living with this guy who follows you around all the time. [...] You're cursed with him and he gets in the way, he embarrasses me, he's unsociable and sometimes downright rude. If I can't be the image that I think I am then I'm in trouble. [...] Worse than it is now, I'm sure, when you think about it, it just feels horrible. I know when I'm mean it is me, I know there is no 'guy', I'm not mad, but it's not me, that's not me, I'm not like that

Simon seems to move in and out of self-identification with the pain. He has attempted to cope with the negative effects of pain by attributing them to a different agent 'this guy' who is separate yet follows Simon around. Of course Simon has considerable self-awareness and so the strategy is fairly precarious.

Lynette seems engaged in a similar battle of identification:

> I am a nice person, but the pain takes over and stops it sucks it all out and leaves me miserable and tired and those who know me know its not me but I suppose it is and if you didn't know me you'd think I was a miserable cow, so maybe I was a nice person and now I'm a cow. [...] I've become a cow.

So we witness the same binary forces at work 'a nice person' versus 'a miserable cow'. Follow how Lynette's thinking seems to change during the passage. She begins with the assertion that she is a good person battling with the negative impact of the pain and concerned about others' perception of her. However by the end of the passage, Lynette acknowledges that the corrosive process may have gone on for so long and to such an extent that it may have actually changed her into the 'miserable cow' she fears other people see.

Finally, we hear Frank who seems almost to have given up the battle and resigned to the fact that his sense of self has now been changed as a result of the debilitating process of pain:

> I hate the way I am now, I've never been like this before, no, I hate it, drives me up the wall. [...] Yeah, being miserable all the time, I used to have a laugh, [...] I'm a miserable git.

So we see some suggestion that different participants, while engaged in the same battle to preserve a positive sense of self against the ravages of pain, differ in where they are in this battle. Speculatively we can propose a continuum from on the one hand employing coping strategies to protect the self from erosion by the pain (Simon) to, on the other side, a resignation to pain having changed ones identity completely (Frank). There is evidence suggesting something like this continuum even in this study. However whether it actually represents a developmental process, a trajectory, where one might expect patients to move from a position something like Simon's to one more like Frank's over time cannot be ascertained from the present study and would require a larger longitudinal study.

The public arena makes it worse

The threats to the participants' self-regard were at their most acute when in a social or relational context. Their uncomfortable feelings emerged into their consciousness most strongly when they were in the presence of others and they worried about how they were seen in the minds of others.

Tony felt he could manage his situation more easily if he avoided any interaction with others, most specifically his children. Social isolation appealed to him because, when alone, his punitive feelings emerged into his consciousness less and the pressure to behave in certain ways was reduced:

> I'd love that [being alone on a desert island] [...] but to be away from people and not have to be something else you're not, that would be bliss. [...] I'd still be a miserable old git but it wouldn't matter, its only when other people come around that it matters.

Managing with himself in different social contexts was, to Tony, an additional task that required a conscious element of acting. Tony's overt social behaviour did not reflect how he felt privately, but concealed it. It was the expression of an alternative self which was exhausting to the point that he dreaded the prospect of having to engage with other people:

> When you go out you end up like you can't wait to get home. [...] People ask you or invite you and you think oh god do I have to and [...] you think, well I should make the effort. So you put a front on and you go out but all the time you're looking at your watch and thinking about when you can go home and go upstairs and lay on the bed and get some relief.

Simon also managed his lifestyle in such a way as to remain as isolated as possible. He made no reference to the behaviour of the people he met, but described the discomfort he felt about himself when with others and the way this compelled him to behave, to withdraw:

I just can't do it. It makes me sick to be around them and look them in the eye. If I stay in the house, in the garden I'm ok, you should see my house, it's like Fort Knox, if someone came to the house they wouldn't think any one was in.

Simon has found a way to protect himself but the analogy is telling – he ends up living in a cold impersonal prison, a house rather than a home. Other participants had also retreated into their homes and become anxious at the prospect of talking to anyone as this triggered their most punitive and uncomfortable feelings:

I don't go out, I don't answer the phone, I live at the back of the house and I dread it when the postman comes. [...] I don't know what to say, or anything, I just feel embarrassed. You just think what do they think of me?

(Kevin)

Participants also worried about the impact of the pain on their social familial responsibilities. Tony felt he had become a poor role model to his children:

I'm some waster, they should have someone who's impressive, to look up to but how can they look up to me with what I do all bad tempered and crippled, dossing about lying down every 10 minutes. All they see is a bit of a man [...] terrible. I try and keep out of their way or when they're around I make sure I try to do lots so at least they have something to look up to, but I can't bear to have them see me like this, it's pitiful.

So Tony is concerned he cannot fulfil his role as a father and imagined his children saw him as inferior, as 'a bit of a man'. Since this feeling was at its most unbearable when his children were around, he avoided them when he could.

Each of the participants felt in some way that having pain left them inferior to others and vulnerable to scorn or punishment. Frank did not feel as if other people saw him as guilty of having pain but he found his disability and the way it denied him the opportunity to fulfil his social roles threatening and described himself as a burden, having no social value or virtue:

I'm just useless, I can't help out my mother, can't kick a ball in the garden with the kids. I'm just a burden [...] what's the point if you can't contribute, you may as well not be there, everyone is missing out because of me [...] it's me not them, although I'm sure they get tired, its me feeling pointless because I can't do my bit, [...] Now I need people, but they don't need me, in fact their life would be easier if I wasn't there, they'd have less to do, so I'm a burden.

Directing it at others

A number of participants show a possible consequence of this process whereby their concern is that the negativity becomes so strong and so centrally implicated in the self that it also becomes directed outward towards other people, begins to contaminate those around them:

This pain, it hurts but its evil gives me a nasty head and makes me hateful, irrational. I hate it when they all leave in the morning and I'm left on my own and I hate it when they all come back in the evening. [. . .] If something sad happens to someone, I'm not sad, sometimes I'm pleased, [. . .] I'm just glad someone else is miserable and you have these stupid rows about nothing and you know they're stupid but you have them anyway because you get to spray a bit of hate about.

(Kevin)

Notice how the first sentence beautifully captures the developmental process suggested earlier. The pain starts as somatic but develops malevolent agency. Its impact is then also to change Kevin's psychological 'state' but then this in turn becomes stronger and more menacing so that in the end the pain has impact on 'trait' and makes Kevin 'hateful'.

However here the impact goes further. Kevin's discomfort at being alone is transferred into similar negative affect when with his family. And powerfully the inward directed self-loathing we have seen in a number of participants is now in turn also directed outward, projected onto others he meets as Kevin suggests he takes pleasure at the suffering of others. The end of the extract suggests this is done deliberately, almost as though it is cathartic, as Kevin deliberately fuels rows in order 'to spray a bit of hate about'.

Tony felt that his bitterness and frustration had left him unable to care for other people.

You stop caring, if someone else gets a pain you're not sad for them, you're glad that someone else knows how you feel, [. . .] that's awful, [. . .] people come to the door collecting money and you think, why is it never for chronic pain, [. . .] it might be cancer in children or something but you just think I don't care anymore, I'm not just miserable to know I am miserable, miserable old git.

At times, Tony only thought ill towards others; he welcomed their misfortune and pain, rejected their need for help and wished pain upon them. Tony actively felt 'glad' at the suffering of others rather than indifference or sympathy and was appalled to have such feelings. Notice how he uses a particular rhetorical device to emphasize the corrosive extent of his self-loathing. He suggests he would not even care about children with cancer (a pinnacle object of compassion) and so underlines his view of himself as undesirable and unworthy.

And again notice how in the final sentence the talk makes manifest the thinking and the process. The attribute descriptor 'miserable' metamorphoses from a situational state, 'just miserable to know', through a generic state, 'miserable', to a generic trait as Tony resigns himself to being a 'miserable old git'.

The sting in the tail

The participants' fear of social judgement is extremely strong. This is most powerfully captured in an extraordinary statement from Kevin:

I need to be careful about people and a bit worried about what's going to happen to me. Are we all going to get rounded up and taken to a camp somewhere?

Kevin concealed his pain from others for fear of suffering severe social consequences. His expression 'rounded up and taken to a camp' seems to suggest an allusion to the persecution of those sent to the concentration camps during the Holocaust, and this seems totally disproportionate to the reality of his situation.

How can Kevin end up feeling like this? The sequence appears to be:

1 Pain leads to the person having negative thoughts

2 These become internalized, part of the self, and so turned to self loathing

3 This also gets discharged relationally as the negativity is directed at significant others

4 And so through an implied model of a form of fate or justice, 'what goes around comes around'. A participant may believe that he/she will, in the end, have to be punished for behaving so negatively towards other people. Given the fact that Kevin has reached the point where he can say of himself 'I'm like this monster', it is perhaps less surprising that he portrays such a strong suggestion of the possible consequences of social judgement and that he in turn will be treated monstrously by others.

Discussion

The participants in this study illustrate the debilitating impact of chronic pain on their sense of self. Their self-concept had deteriorated and continued to endure further assaults in the form of undesirable experiences, beyond the sensation of pain that could not be accommodated into a contemporary valued self. The new, rejected, experiences were ascribed to a new, unwelcome self, a 'self with pain' that contained the elements that were incompatible with their preferred self, or 'the real me'. The degree to which the new 'self with pain' dominated the preferred 'real me' varied. The new 'self with pain' was socially undesirable, shameful and intruded into the participant's consciousness most acutely when they were in a social or relational context. The participants felt confused and powerless at times to influence the emergent self and, during those times, found it more difficult to manage than the pain sensation itself.

The participants' experience in this study related closely to those described by Hellstrom (2001) who described a nostalgia for a past self and a contemporary struggle with both an 'entrapped self' (that which felt unable to progress or communicate with people) and a 'projected self' (that was vulnerable to the judgements of others). In this study the participants articulated ways in which having chronic pain could overwhelm the self and engage the sufferer in a struggle to preserve their morality and security from condemnation. Their problems with the self were not related just to disability and a loss of functioning or social role but were exposed as a daily process of managing experiences that were felt to be threatening, intrusive and beyond control.

The difficulties related to the loss of a positive social identity over time in chronic illness is documented in the sociological literature (Bury, 1982; Kelly, 1992), although Cuthbert (1999) rejected any implication that such a process was inevitable and gave examples of those with chronic illness who maintained high levels of self-regard and productivity despite their condition. Charmaz (1991) described how over time the self could become out of step with contemporary experience in chronic conditions, become unrepresentative of the person's situation and instead reflect a preferred (usually past) self. This study showed that such resistance to change went beyond the self lagging behind change and a struggle to grieve to involve a daily defence of a self under assault. The participants were unable to assimilate or accommodate some of their emergent pain experiences into their preferred self. To have done so would have involved adopting a critical and punitive set of self-definitions. This has significant implications for pain management as the unacceptability of these definitions would represent a palpable obstacle to the acceptance of the chronic nature of the pain which has been shown to be important for a positive clinical outcome (McCracken & Eccleston, 2003). The individual detail present in the participants' accounts articulated powerfully both the shared contemporary immediacy of the threats involved in their pain and their unique and personal quality. They highlighted a significant but overlooked aspect of the distress and suffering related to chronic pain and the ways in which the two inter-relate.

The participants' experience of their self was at its most conscious and disabling when in the social domain and seen from a relational perspective that involved the perceived judgements of others. Their most 'unpleasant' experiences were all inherently socially undesirable and this highlighted the 'socialness' of their chronic pain. Both illness and the self have a recognised social dimension (Ashmore & Contrada, 1999; Ashmore & Jussim, 1997) and maintaining a felt sense of social virtue, which is important in the experience of chronic illness (Williams, 1993), reveals the extent to which it must be defined as a moral as well as a biomedical condition (Kugelmann, 1997). The participants struggled to fulfil any valued roles in their everyday life and felt their private experiences were abnormal and left them vulnerable to hostile judgement. They lived in disabling fear of being judged critically by others, abhorred or pitied. An omnipotent anticipation of such judgements often dictated their behaviour and prompted them to either withdraw from social contact, or over-compensate in the presence of others and do too much, according to the situation. The way they lived in the minds of others pre-occupied their thoughts. They appeared to share the paralysing problems of living with the kind of 'projected' and 'entrapped' selves that were described by Hellstrom (2001) and this highlighted the importance of the social and cultural context involved in chronic pain and the degree of shame with which it is associated.

The concept of shame is a useful one in this regard as it places the private experience of the individual within a social context. It has been described as the 'affect of inferiority' and is associated with major disturbances of the self (Kaufman, 1989). Shame has been defined as the anxiety derived from beliefs that create a negative self image in the eyes of potential evaluators (Lewis, 1987). Gilbert (1992) added to this by broadening the concept to relate it to a predisposition towards rank and status judgements and the consequences of such judgements. Gilbert, Pehl and Allan (1994) defined the threat inherent in shame:

> In shame one sees oneself in the inferior position. Shame is characterised by the self being unable, the helpless object of another's ridicule, scorn or punishment.
>
> (p. 25)

Shamed individuals feel inferior, powerless, bad in comparison to others, vulnerable to punishment and unattractive. Shame promotes concealment and resentment and has been related to distress and social anxiety (Gilbert, 2000). It incorporates the individual's evaluation of their relationships with others, their appraisal and anticipation of the beliefs of others about them and their evaluation of themselves in relation to others. It places the individual's self-judgements and definitions firmly within a social context and shows how that can be inherently threatening and distressing for the individual. The shame felt by the participants' in this study was, at times, more uncomfortable and unbearable than their pain sensation or immobility. And indeed 'shame' seems to under-represent the valence of the affective response illustrated in these accounts. 'Loathing' or 'disgust' would seem closer to the mark.

Shame is private and personal but also set within a social context and it provides a bridge between the two (Leeming & Boyle, 2004). Social and cultural constructs such as culpability, blame and being disbelieved are prominent themes in the experience of chronic benign low back pain where, in the absence of a clear medical diagnosis of pathology, the sufferer is held responsible for their own condition (Eccleston et al., 1997; Kugelman, 1997; Osborn & Smith,

1998), something Kotarba (1983) referred to as 'victim blaming'. This has important clinical implications as evidenced by Gustafsson et al. (2004) who described how moving from a state of shame to one of self-respect was one of the positive processes experienced by participants in a pain rehabilitation programme.

The prominence of the self in the participants' experiences relates quite closely to the notion of self-pain enmeshment theorised by Pincus and Morley (2001) and tested later by Morley, Davies and Barton (2005). It also provides strong support for Morley and Eccleston's (2004) argument that one of the objects of fear in chronic pain is the threat to identity. This places the self (potentially) at the centre of the experience of chronic pain and an important part of the inter-connection between its physical and psychological aspects. In particular the very social-ness of chronic pain and the self emerges in this study and the relationship between chronic pain and shame would be worth pursuing in further research.

Their chronic pain was described by the participants as a social and moral condition which had the potential to place them in significant jeopardy. Their anxieties about their socially undesirable and destructive behaviour, their social withdrawal and self-criticism suggested that a significant part of their experience involved feeling ashamed of themselves, embarrassed about their situation, vulnerable to criticism and fearful of punishment.

The participants' accounts showed that their chronic pain experience involved more than the loss of function, status or role. The presence of ongoing fear, shame and sensitivity to punishment or rejection emphasised the degree to which their pain was also laden with an ongoing sense of threat. This could perhaps play an active role in the disruptiveness, intensity and unpleasantness of their chronic pain. It is possible perhaps that through this fear of social punishment, a height-ened vigilance could develop towards pain (of the kind described by Van Damme, Crombez, Eccleston, & Roelofs, 2004) that reinforced and entrenched its place within the consciousness of the sufferer and defied their attempts to disengage from it. From a psychological perspective, the participants' chronic pain was imbued with a malignant and threatening meaning.

Limitations and suggestions for further research and interventions

We want to be quite cautious in the claims we make from this study. The sample is small and it should not be assumed that similar findings would come from all patients in a similar situation. At the same time the fact that all participants spoke similarly and with such intensity indicates the strength of the impact on these individuals and is suggestive about wider applicability. And it is possible for the reader to think in terms of theoretical generalizability – to consider the results in the light of their own professional experience when assessing the potential prevalence of the phenomenon.

It would be useful to conduct a subsequent study with carefully selected cells of participants in order to help test the breadth of possible applicability. A study purposively selecting in terms of e.g., age, class, ethnicity from the same geographical region as the current study would provide a logical next stage and offer useful direct comparison with the results in this study.

Given the apparent corrosive impact of pain on self, it would also be useful to conduct a longitudinal study following a set of patients from referral at the pain clinic, through the inter-vention phase and for two or three years into the future. What impact would intervention have on self perception? How constant is the derogatory self image? How does it develop over time?

The study also suggests implications for interventions. The degree of the impact upon the self which participants point to suggests that psychological interventions to tackle the experience of pain may be usefully supplemented by addressing the self experiencing the pain as well as the pain itself. To date pain management programmes have not addressed the self explicitly but the accounts of the participants suggest that their experience of their pain was situated within a disintegrating and threatened self and that this was also very much a social and relational phenomenon (something that is best understood in a "public arena").

The evidence in this study supports the development of more 'contextual' or mindful approaches to pain management (McCracken, 2005) which address not just the content of the pain sufferer's thoughts but endeavour to help them to re-contextualise and make sense of their experience in a more helpful way, a way which is perhaps less self-persecutory, threatening and shameful and more accepting of the lived experience of chronic pain. Such an intervention could, within session, introduce the notion of a 'normal psychology of pain' and help patients to develop a more compassionate self-view. It would also help them to see that their pain experience was not a function of a characterological flaw and something to be criticised or ashamed of but was an integral part of the experience of pain which cannot be controlled, ignored or 'cured' but could be accepted, managed and worked with. Including close family members in this process may also prove fruitful in some cases and this also connects with the suggestion, supported by the accounts, of a move towards adopting a more relational perspective to the experience of pain, helping patients to place their private and personal experience of pain within a public and relational context. In addition, adopting a phenomenological approach in the early stages of any intervention that enabled patients to recognise their own experience could well promote engagement and rapport and reduce attrition.

Conclusions

The notion of the self emerged in this study as an important aspect of the participants' experience of chronic pain sensation, distress and disability. Their chronic pain assaulted and undermined their sense of self and the struggle to maintain a valued or coherent self was, at times, more unpleasant than enduring the physical sensation of pain. The assault on the self involved the participants' difficulties assimilating their experiences into a socially valued or coherent sense of self. Participants worried about how their degraded self was also responsible for polluting those around them and were concerned, in turn, that they might come to be judged and punished by others for carrying this new malignant self.

Acknowledgements

We would like to thank the journal editor and two anonymous reviewers for helpful comments on a previous version of this article. We would also like to thank all participants for their contribution to the study.

Appendix 1: The interview schedule

1 Could you, to begin with, describe your pain to me in your own words please?
    – What does it feel like?
    – How long have you had it?
    – Does it change in any way?

2 How did your pain start?
  – How long have you had it?
  – How did it come on?
  – Has it changed over time?

3 Does anything affect your pain?
  – Does anything make it better?
  – Does anything make it worse?

4 Do you know why your pain persists?
  – What causes your pain?
  – Why hasn't your pain been cured?

5 Has your pain changed things for you at all?
  – Is anything different now?
  – Do you do anything or feel differently since you had the pain?

6 How would you describe yourself as a person?
  – What would sum you up?
  – How do you think/feel about yourself?

7 Has having pain changed the way you think or feel about yourself?
  – Are you any different now as a person after having pain?
  – Do you see yourself differently?
  – In what ways are you a different person now?

8 Why do you think that change has happened (if it has)?
  – What has caused the change?
  – What has brought that change about?

Appendix 2: Transcript extract notation

[…] indicates editorial elision where non-relevant material has been omitted. [text] indicates explanatory text added by authors.

References

Aldrich, S., Eccleston, C., & Crombez, G. (2000). Worrying about chronic pain: Vigilance to threat and misdirected problem solving. *Behaviour Research and Therapy, 38,* 457–470.

Ashmore, R. D., & Contrada, R. J. (1999). Self, social identity, and the analysis of social and behavioural aspects of physical health and disease. In R. J. Contrada & R. D. Ashmore (Eds), *Self, social identity and physical health: Interdisciplinary explorations* (Vol. 2, Rutgers series on self and identity, pp. 240–256). New York: Oxford University Press.

Ashmore, R. D., & Jussim, L. (Eds), (1997). *Self and identity: Fundamental issues* (Vol. 1). New York: Oxford University Press.

Bramley, N., & Eatough, V. (2005). The experience of living with Parkinson's Disease: An interpretative phenomenological analysis case study. *Psychology & Health, 20,* 223–236.

Brocki, J., & Wearden, A. (2006). A critical evaluation of interpretative phenomenological analysis (IPA) in health psychology. *Psychology & Health, 21,* 87–108.

Bury, M. (1982). Chronic illness as biographical disruption. *Sociology of Health and Illness, 4,* 167–182.

Carradice, A., Shankland, M., & Beail, N. (2002). A qualitative study of the theoretical models used by UK mental health nurses to guide their assessments with family caregivers of people with dementia. *International Journal of Nursing Studies, 39,* 17–26.

Charmaz, K. (1983). Loss of self: A fundamental form of suffering in the chronically ill. *Sociology of Health and Illness, 5,* 168–195.

Charmaz, K. (1991). *Good days, bad days: The self in chronic illness and time.* New York: Rutgers University Press.

Clabber Moffat, J., Richardson, G., Sheldon, T., & Maynard, A. (1995). *The cost of back pain.* York: Centre for Health Economics.

Cuthbert, K. (1999). Experience of self in the context of chronic illness and disability. *Health Psychology Update, 36,* 11–15.

Eccleston, C., Williams, A., & Stainton-Rogers, W. (1997). Patients' and professionals' understandings of the causes of chronic pain: Blame, responsibility and identity protection. *Social Science & Medicine, 45,* 699–709.

Flowers, P., Duncan, B., & Knussen, C. (2003). Reappraising HIV testing: An exploration of the psychosocial costs and benefits associated with learning one's HIV status in a purposive sample of Scottish gay men. *British Journal of Health Psychology, 8,* 179–194.

Gatchel, R. J., & Epker, J. (1999). Psychosocial predictors of chronic pain and response to treatment. In R. J. Gatchell & D. C. Turk (Eds), *Psychosocial factors in pain: Critical perspectives* (pp. 412–434). New York: Guilford Press.

Gilbert, P. (1992). *Depression: The evolution of powerlessness.* Hove, Erlbaum/New York: Guilford Press.

Gilbert, P. (2000). The relationship of shame, social anxiety and depression: The role of the evaluation of social rank. *Clinical Psychology & Psychotherapy, 7,* 174–189.

Gilbert, P., Pehl, J., & Allan, S. (1994). The phenomenology of shame and guilt: An empirical investigation. *British Journal of Medical Psychology, 67,* 23–36.

Gustafsson, M., Ekholm, J., & Ohman, A. (2004). From shame to respect: Musculoskeletal pain patients' experience of a rehabilitation programme, a qualitative study. *Journal of Rehabilitation Medicine, 36,* 97–103.

Hellstrom, C. (2001). Temporal dimensions of the self-concept: Entrapped and possible selves in chronic pain. *Psychology & Health, 16,* 111–124.

Hellstrom, C., Jansson, B., & Carlsson, S. G. (1999). Subjective future as a mediating factor in the relation between pain, pain-related distress and depression. *European Journal of Pain, 3,* 221–233.

International Association for the study of Pain (I.A.S.P.) (1986). Classifications of chronic pain. Descriptions of chronic pain syndromes and definitions of pain terms. *Pain,* 27(Suppl. 3), S1–S226.

International Association for the study of Pain (I.A.S.P.) (1994). Task force on Taxonomy. In *Classification of chronic pain: Descriptions of chronic pain syndromes and definitions of pain terms* (2nd Edn). Seattle, USA: IASP Press.

Jarman, M., Walsh, S., & De Lacey, G. (2005). Keeping safe, keeping connected: A qualitative study of HIV positive women's experiences of partner relationships. *Psychology & Health, 20,* 533–551.

Kaufman, G. (1989). *The psychology of shame: Theory and treatment of shame based syndromes.* London: Routledge.

Kelly, M. (1992). Self, identity and radical surgery. *Sociology of Health & Illness, 14,* 390–415.

Kihlstrom, J. F. & Kihlstrom, L. C. (1999). Self, sickness, somatization, and systems of care. In R. J. Contrada & R. D. Ashmore (Eds), *Self, social identity and physical health: Interdisciplinary explorations* (Rutgers series on self and identity Vol. 2) (pp. 23–42). New York: Oxford University Press.

Kotarba, J. A. (1983). *Chronic pain: Its social dimensions.* London: Sage.

Kugelmann, R. (1997). The psychology and management of pain. *Theory and Psychology, 7,* 43–65.

Lamiell, J. (1987). *The psychology of personality.* New York: Columbia University Press.

Lavie, M., & Willig, C. (2005). "I don't feel like melting butter": An interpretative phenomenological analysis of the experience of inorgasmia. *Psychology & Health, 20,* 115–128.

Leeming, D., & Boyle, M. (2004). Shame as a social phenomenon: A critical analysis of the concept of dispositional shame. *Psychology and Psychotherapy, Theory, Research and Practice, 77*(3), 375–396.

Lewis, H. B. (1987). Introduction: Shame – the 'sleeper' in psychopathology. In H. B. Lewis (Ed.), *The role of shame in symptom formation.* Hillsdale: Erlbaum.

Maniadakis, N., & Gray, A. (2000). The economic burden of back pain in the UK. *Pain, 84,* 95–103.

McCracken, L. (2005). *Contextual cognitive-behavioral therapy for chronic pain.* Seattle: I.A.S.P.

McCracken, L., & Eccleston, C. (2003). Coping or acceptance: What to do about chronic pain? *Pain, 105,* 197–204.

Michie, S., Hendy, J., Smith, J. A., & Adshead, F. (2004). Evidence into practice: A theory based study of achieving national health targets in primary care. *Journal of Evaluation in Clinical Practice, 10,* 447–456.

Michie, S., Smith, J. A., Senior, S., & Marteau, T. (2003). Understanding why negative genetic test results sometimes fail to reassure. *American Journal of Medical Genetics, 119A,* 340–347.

Morley, S., Davies, C, & Barton, S. (2005). Possible selves in chronic pain: Self-pain enmeshment, adjustment and acceptance. *Pain, 115,* 84–94.

Morley, S., & Eccleston, C. (2004). The object of fear in pain. In J. G. Asmundsen, J. W. S. Vlaeyen & G. Crombez (Eds), *Understanding and treating fear of pain* (pp. 163–188). NY: Oxford University Press.

Osborn, M., & Smith, J. A. (1998). The personal experience of chronic benign lower back pain: An interpretative phenomenological analysis. *British Journal of Health Psychology, 3,* 65–83.

Paulson, M., Danielson, E., & Soderberg, S. (2002). Struggling for a tolerable existence: The meaning of men's lived experiences of living with pain of fybromyalgia type. *Qualitative Health Research, 12,* 238–249.

Pincus, T., & Morley, S. (2001). Cognitive-processing bias in chronic pain: A review and integration. *Psychological Bulletin, 127,* 599–617.

Reynolds, F., & Prior, S. (2003). Sticking jewels in your life: Exploring women's strategies for negotiating an acceptable quality of life with multiple sclerosis. *Qualitative Health Research, 13,* 1225–1251.

Smith, J. A. (2003). Validity and qualitative psychology. In J. A. Smith (Ed.), *Qualitative psychology: A practical guide to research methods* (pp. 232–235). London: Sage.

Smith, J. A. (2004). Reflecting on the development of interpretative phenomenological analysis and its contribution to qualitative research in psychology. *Qualitative Research in Psychology, 1,* 39–54.

Smith, J. A., Harre, R., & Van Langenhove, L. (1995). Idiography. In J. A. Smith, R. Harre & L. Van Langenhove (Eds), *Rethinking psychology.* London: Sage.

Smith, J. A., Michie, S., Allanson, A., & Elwy, R. (2000). Certainty and uncertainty in genetic counselling: A qualitative case study. *Psychology & Health, 15,* 1–12.

Smith, J. A., & Osborn, M. (2003). Interpretative phenomenological analysis. In J. A. Smith (Ed.), *Qualitative psychology: A practical guide to research methods* (pp. 51–80). London: Sage.

Turk, D. C., & Flor, H. (1999). Chronic pain: A biobehavioural perspective. In R. J. Gatchell & D. C. Turk (Eds), *Psychosocial factors in pain: Critical perspectives* (pp. 18–34). New York: Guilford Press.

Turpin, G., Barley, V., Beail, N., Scaife, J., Slade, P., Smith, J. A., et al. (1997). Standards for research projects & theses involving qualitative methods: Suggested guidelines for trainees & courses. *Clinical Psychology Forum, 108,* 3–7.

Van Damme, S., Crombez, G., Eccleston, C., & Roelofs, J. (2004). The role of hypervigilance in the experience of pain. In G. J. G. Asmundsen, J. W. S. Vlaeyen & G. Crombez (Eds), *Understanding and treating fear of pain* (pp. 71–90). Oxford: OUP.

Williams, G. H. (1993). Chronic illness and the pursuit of virtue in everyday life. In A. Radley (Ed.), *Worlds of illness: Biographical and cultural perspectives on health and disease.* London: Routledge.

Taylor, S.E. (1983) Adjustment to threatening events: a theory of cognitive adaptation,
American Psychologist, 38 (11): 1161 – 73.

Adjustment to threatening events

A theory of cognitive adaptation

Shelley E. Taylor
University of California, Los Angeles

Abstract

A theory of cognitive adaptation to threatening events is proposed. It is argued that the adjustment process centers around three themes: A search for meaning in the experience, an attempt to regain mastery over the event in particular and over one's life more generally, and an effort to restore self-esteem through self-enhancing evaluations. These themes are discussed with reference to cancer patients' coping efforts. It is maintained that successful adjustment depends, in a large part, on the ability to sustain and modify illusions that buffer not only against present threats but also against possible future setbacks.

One of the most impressive qualities of the human psyche is its ability to withstand severe personal tragedy successfully. Despite serious setbacks such as personal illness or the death of a family member, the majority of people facing such blows achieve a quality of life or level of happiness equivalent to or even exceeding their prior level of satisfaction.[1] Not everyone readjusts, of course (Silver & Wortman, 1980), but most do, and furthermore they do so substantially on their own. That is, typically people do not seek professional help in dealing with personal problems. They use their social networks and individual resources, and their apparent cure rate, if self-reports of satisfaction are to be trusted, is impressive even by professional standards (Gurin, Veroff, & Feld, 1960; Wills, 1982).

These self-curing abilities are a formidable resource, and our recent work with cancer patients, cardiac patients, rape victims, and other individuals facing life-threatening events has explored them. The consequence of these investigations is a theory of cognitive adaptation. I will argue that when an individual has experienced a personally threatening event, the readjustment

---

1 See Turk (1979); Visotsky, Hamburg, Goss, and Lebovits (1961); Tavormina, Kastner, Slater, and Watt (1976); Andreasen and Norris (1972); Weisman (1979); Follick and Turk (Note 1); Katz (1963); Myers, Friedman, and Weiner (1970); see also Silver and Wortman (1980); Leon, Butcher, Kleinman, Goldberg, and Almagor (1981).

This article is based on the 10th Katz-Newcomb lecture delivered at the University of Michigan, April 28, 1982. Its preparation was supported in part by NIMH Research Grant MH 34167 and Research Scientist Development Award MH 00311. I am grateful to a large number of individuals for their comments on this article, especially Philip Brickman, Barry Collins, Norma Haan, Richard Lazarus, Rosemary Lichtman, Joanne Wood, and Robert Zajonc.

Requests for reprints should be sent to Shelley E. Taylor, Department of Psychology, University of California, Los Angeles, California 90024.

process focuses around three themes: a search for meaning in the experience, an attempt to regain mastery over the event in particular and over one's life more generally, and an effort to enhance one's self-esteem – to feel good about oneself again despite the personal setback.

Specifically, meaning is an effort to understand the event: why it happened and what impact it has had. The search for meaning attempts to answer the question, What is the significance of the event? Meaning is exemplified by, but not exclusively determined by, the results of an attributional search that answers the question, What caused the event to happen? Meaning is also reflected in the answer to the question, What does my life mean now? The theme of mastery centers around gaining control over the event and one's life. It is exemplified by, but not exclusively served by, beliefs about personal control. Efforts at mastery center on the questions, How can I keep this or a similar event from happening again? and What can I do to manage it now? The third theme is self-enhancement. Victimizing events often reduce self-esteem (e.g., Briar, 1966; Pearlin & Schooler, 1978; Ryan, 1971) even when the individual had no responsibility for bringing the event about. Many intrapsychic efforts at recovery accordingly involve finding ways to feel good about oneself again. The theme of self-enhancement is not addressed by one particular cognition (it is served by many), but in our own work, social comparisons have been a chief vehicle by which self-enhancement occurred.

Before turning to an analysis of these three themes, an important quality that they share merits mention. I will maintain that the individual's efforts to successfully resolve these three themes rest fundamentally upon the ability to form and maintain a set of illusions. By illusions, I do not mean that the beliefs are necessarily opposite to known facts. Rather, their maintenance requires looking at the known facts in a particular light, because a different slant would yield a less positive picture, or the beliefs have yet to yield any factual basis of support. The viewpoint that successful recovery from tragedy rests on illusion may seem overly cynical, but I hope to convince the reader that it is not.

The following analysis draws heavily on the responses of 78 women with breast cancer and many of their family members whom Rosemary Lichtman, Joanne Wood, and I have intensively interviewed during the past two years (Taylor, Lichtman, & Wood, Note 2). Some of these women have good prognoses, others do not. Some have achieved a high quality of life following their illness (although it may have taken them several years to do so), others have not. But virtually all of them have shown some attempt to resolve the three issues of meaning, mastery, and self-enhancement.

In the remainder of the article I will first describe the processes that contribute to cognitive adaptation, namely those that center around these three themes. Next, I will address the issue of illusion and maintain that, far from impeding adjustment, illusion may be critical to mental health. Then, I will focus on the very important question: What happens if the illusions upon which one's satisfaction is based are disconfirmed? I will suggest that disconfirmation of one's beliefs, such as a belief in personal control, may not be as psychologically problematic as currently popular models of the disconfirmation process would lead us to believe. Using principles of cognitive adaptation, I will offer an alternative model of the disconfirmation process.

The search for meaning

The search for meaning involves the need to understand why a crisis occurred and what its impact has been. One of the ways in which meaning is addressed is through causal attributions. Attribution theory (Heider, 1958; Kelley, 1967) maintains that following a threatening or dramatic event, people will make attributions so as to understand, predict, and control their environment (Wong & Weiner, 1981). By understanding the cause of an event, one may also begin to understand the significance of the event and what it symbolizes about one's life. In the case of cancer, of course, no one knows the true cause or causes. There are a number of known causes, such as heredity, diet, or specific carcinogens, but a search for the cause of cancer on the part of a patient would seem to be a fruitless endeavor.

Nonetheless, cancer patients do try to understand why they developed cancer. Ninety-five percent of our respondents offered some explanation for why their cancer occurred. In an effort to have some comparison group against which to judge this rate, we also asked the spouses of these patients whether they had any theory about the cause of their partner's cancer. One would also expect spouses' rates of making attributions to be inflated, relative to an uninvolved person, since they, like the patients, have been strongly affected by the cancer experience. Nonetheless, their rate of making causal attributions was significantly less (63%), suggesting that the need for an explanation was more insistent among the patients themselves.

Does any particular form of the attributional explanational meet the search for meaning better than others? This question can be partially addressed by looking at the specific content of the cancer patients' explanations and then relating those explanations to overall psychological adjustment.[2] The largest number (41%) attributed their cancer either to general stress or to a particular type of stress. When a particular stressor was mentioned, it was often either an ongoing problematic marriage or a recent divorce. Thirty-two percent of the sample attributed their cancer to some particular carcinogen, including ingested substances such as birth control pills, DES, or primarin (which is an estrogen replenisher prescribed for menopausal women) or to environmental carcinogens such as having lived near a chemical dump, a nuclear testing site, or a copper mine. Twenty-six percent of the women attributed their cancer to hereditary factors. Another 17% attributed it to diet (usually to a diet high in protein and fat and low in vegetables), and 10% blamed some blow to the breast such as an automobile accident, a fall, or in one case, being hit in the breast by a frisbee. (The numbers exceed 100% because a number of people had multiple theories.) It is noteworthy that with the exception of heredity, all of these causes are either past, rather than ongoing events, or they are events over which one currently has some control, such as stress or diet. This fact anticipates a point to be made shortly – that meaning and mastery may often be intertwined.

When one relates these specific attributions to overall psychological adjustment to the cancer, no single attribution stands out as more functional than any other. All are uncorrelated with adjustment. It would be premature to conclude from this information that these attributional explanations are functionally interchangeable. However, the high frequency of making attributions, coupled with the fact that no specific attribution produces better adjustment, suggests that causal meaning itself is the goal of the attributional search rather than the specific form through which it is realized.

The search for meaning involves not only understanding why the event occurred, but what its implications for one's life are now. Slightly over half of our respondents reported that the cancer experience had caused them to reappraise their lives. Here is one example from a 61-year-old woman:

---

2 Psychological adjustment is operationalized in this study as a factor score. The high-loading items are: The physician's rating of the patient on a standardized measure of adjustment termed the Global Adjustment to Illness Scale (GAIS; Derogatis, 1975); the interviewer's independent rating on that same scale; the patient's self-rated adjustment on a 5-point scale; patient self-reports of various psychological symptoms, such as anxiety and depression; the patient's score on the Profile of Mood States (McNair & Lorr, 1964); and the Campbell, Converse, and Rodgers (1976) Index of Well-Being.

You can take a picture of what someone has done, but when you frame it, it becomes significant. I feel as if I were for the first time really conscious. My life is framed in a certain amount of time. I always knew it. But I can see it, and it's made better by the knowledge.

For many, the meaning derived from the cancer experience brought a new attitude toward life:

I have much more enjoyment of each day, each moment. I am not so worried about what is or isn't or what I wish I had. All those things you get entangled with don't seem to be part of my life right now.

For others, the meaning gained from the experience was self-knowledge or self-change:

The ability to understand myself more fully is one of the greatest changes I have experienced. I have faced what I went through. It's a bit like holding up a mirror to one's face when one can't turn around. I think that is a very essential thing.

I was very happy to find out I am a very strong person. I have no time for game-playing any more. I want to get on with life. And I have become more introspective and also let others fend for their own responsibilities. And now almost five years later, I have become a very different person.

Typically, individuals have reordered their priorities, giving low priority to such mundane concerns as housework, petty quarrels, and involvement in other people's problems and high priority to relationships with spouse, children, and friends, personal projects, or just plain enjoyment of life (Lichtman, Note 3):

You take a long look at your life and realize that many things that you thought were important before are totally insignificant. That's probably been the major change in my life. What you do is put things into perspective. You find out that things like relationships are really the most important things you have – the people you know and your family – everything else is just way down the line. It's very strange that it takes something so serious to make you realize that.

Not everyone can construe positive meaning from the experience:

I thought I was a well-cared-for, middle-class woman who chose her doctors carefully and who was doing everything right. I was rather pleased with myself. I had thought I could handle pretty much what came my way. And I was completely shattered. My confidence in myself was completely undermined.

However, when positive meaning can be construed from the cancer experience, it produces significantly better psychological adjustment. The cancer threat, then, is perceived by many to have been the catalytic agent for restructuring their lives along more meaningful lines with an overall beneficial effect.

To summarize, the attempt to find meaning in the cancer experience takes at least two forms: a causal analysis that provides an answer to the question of why it happened and a rethinking of one's attitudes and priorities to restructure one's life along more satisfying lines, changes that are prompted by and attributed to the cancer.

Gaining a sense of mastery

A sudden threatening event like cancer can easily undermine one's sense of control over one's body and one's life generally (e.g., Leventhal, 1975). Accordingly, a second theme of the adjustment process is gaining a feeling of control over the threatening event so as to manage it or keep it from occurring again. This theme of mastery is exemplified by beliefs about personal control.

Many cancer patients seem to solve the issue of mastery by believing that they personally can keep the cancer from coming back. Two thirds of the patients we interviewed believed they had at least some control over the course of or recurrence of their cancer, and 37% believed they had a lot of control. Some of the remaining one third believed that although they personally had no control over the cancer, it could be controlled by the doctor or by continued treatments. Hence, belief in direct control of the cancer is quite strong. Again, using the significant others as a comparison population, belief in both the patient's ability to control the cancer and the physician's ability to control the cancer are less strong, suggesting that mastery needs are greater among patients. Significantly, both the belief that one can control one's own cancer and the belief that the physician or treatments can control it are strongly associated with overall positive adjustment, and both together are even better.

Many of the patients' efforts at control were mental. One of the most common manifestations was a belief that a positive attitude would keep the cancer from coming back:

> I believe that if you're a positive person, your attitude has a lot to do with it. I definitely feel I will never get it again.

> My mental attitude, I think, is the biggest control over it I have. I want to feel there is something I can do, that there is some way I can control it.

> I think that if you feel you are in control of it, you can control it up to a point. I absolutely refuse to have any more cancer.

A substantial number attempted to control their cancer by using specific techniques of psychological control. These techniques included meditation, imaging, self-hypnosis, positive thinking, or a combination of factors. Many had read the Simonton and Simonton (1975) work suggesting that people can control their own cancers using these kinds of methods, and they saw no harm in trying them on their own; a number had great faith in them.

Causal attributions can also contribute to a sense of mastery if the perceived initial cause is believed to be no longer in effect. Apropos of this point, for many patients the perception of a discontinuity between the time before their cancer and their present life is very important. They need to be able to say that "things are different now." For some, this perceived temporal discontinuity was tied to a relationship. One woman, for example, characterized her first husband as a "boorish rapist" and believed that this destructive relationship had produced the cancer; her new involvement with her "wonderful" second husband, she felt, would keep her cancer-free.

Another woman, who attributed her cancer to a poor immune system, believed that the cancer had structurally altered her body – she called it "realigning the cells." As a consequence, she felt she would no longer be vulnerable to cancer. This expression of a discontinuity between pre-cancer and postcancer time – the sense that things are different now – is echoed many times and seems to be important to producing a sense of mastery by maintaining, in part, that the initial cause is no longer in effect.

Although many patients have regained a sense of mastery by thinking about their cancer differently, others adopt direct behavioral efforts to keep the cancer from coming back. In a number of cases, patients made changes in their lives that both enabled them to reduce the likelihood of recurrence (they believed) and gave them something to control now. For some, these were dietary changes; a full 49% of our sample had changed their diet since the cancer bout, usually in the direction of adding fresh fruit and vegetables and cutting down on red meats and fats. For others, eliminating the medications they had taken like birth control pills or estrogen replenishers fulfilled the same function. The relationship of these changes to the need for mastery was verbalized by some patients:

> [Where the cancer came from] was an important question to me at first. The doctor's answer was that it was a multifaceted illness. I looked over the known causes of cancer, like viruses, radiation, genetic mutation, environmental carcinogens, and the one I focused on very strongly was diet. I know now why I focused on it. It was the only one that was simple enough for me to understand and change. You eat something that's bad for you, you get sick.

A sense of mastery can be fulfilled by other than direct efforts to control the cancer. Assuming control over aspects of one's cancer care can meet the same need. One such effort at control is acquiring information about cancer, so one can participate in or be knowledgeable about one's care. As one woman put it:

> I felt that I had lost control of my body somehow, and the way for me to get back some control was to find out as much as I could. It really became almost an obsession.

One spouse described his wife:

> She got books, she got pamphlets, she studied, she talked to cancer patients, she found out everything that was happening to her, and she fought it. She went to war with it. She calls it taking in her covered wagons and surrounding it.

Attempting to control the side effects of one's treatments represents another effort at mastery. For example, 92% of the patients who received chemotherapy did something to control its side effects. For slightly under half, this involved simply medications or sleep, but the remaining half used a combination of mental efforts at control. These included imaging, self-hypnosis, distraction, and meditation. Similar efforts were made to control the less debilitating but still unpleasant side effects of radiation therapy. For example, one woman who was undergoing radiation therapy would imagine that there was a protective shield keeping her body from being burned by the radiation. Another woman imaged her chemotherapy as powerful cannons which blasted away pieces of the dragon, cancer. One 61-year-old woman simply focused her attention on healing with the instruction to her body, "Body, cut this shit out."

A sense of mastery, then, can be achieved by believing that one can control the cancer by taking active steps that are perceived as directly controlling the cancer or by assuming control over related aspects of one's cancer, such as treatment. This belief in mastery and its relationship to adjustment ties in with a large body of literature indicating that manipulated feelings of control enhance coping with short-term aversive events (Averill, 1973; see Thompson, 1981, for a recent review). The cancer patients' experiences suggest that self-generated feelings of control over a chronic condition can achieve the same beneficial effects.

The process of self-enhancement

The third theme identified in our patients' adjustment process was an effort to enhance the self and restore self-esteem. Researchers exploring a range of threatening events from the death of one's child (Chodoff, Friedman, & Hamburg, 1964) to going on welfare (Briar, 1966) have documented the toll such events can take on self-regard. Even when the events can be legitimately attributed to external forces beyond the individual's control, there is often a precipitous drop in self-esteem. After experiencing such a drop, however, many individuals then initiate cognitive efforts to pull themselves back out of their low self-regard.

In some cases, esteem-enhancing cognitions are quite direct. During our interviews, we asked our respondents to describe any changes that had occurred in their lives since the cancer incident. To digress momentarily, I think people are always curious about how others change their lives when they have had a life-threatening experience. Popular images would have patients changing jobs, changing spouses, moving, or squandering all their money on a series of self-indulgent adventures. In fact, these major changes are fairly rare, and when they do occur, they are associated with unsuccessful overall adjustment. Frequently, a couple will have one "binge" such as taking a cruise or buying a Cadillac, but otherwise there are typically few overt dramatic changes. After people reported the changes they had experienced in their lives since cancer, we asked them to indicate whether those changes were positive or negative. Only 17% reported *any* negative changes in their lives. Fifty-three percent reported only positive changes; the remainder reported no changes. We also asked our patients to rate their emotional adjustment before any signs of cancer, at various points during the cancer bout, and at the time of the interview. Not only did patients see themselves as generally well adjusted at the time of the interview and as better adjusted than they were during the cancer bout, they also saw themselves as better adjusted than before they had any signs of cancer! When you consider that these women usually had had disfiguring surgery, had often had painful follow-up care, and had been seriously frightened and lived under the shadow of possible recurrence, this is a remarkable ability to construe personal benefit from potential tragedy.

Some of the most intriguing illusions that contribute to self-enhancement are generated by social comparisons (Festinger, 1954; Latané, 1966; Suls & Miller, 1977). Drawing on some provocative suggestions by Wortman and Dunkel-Schetter (1979) concerning cancer patients' needs for social comparison, we hypothesized that if we could identify the women's objects of comparison we could predict who would perceive themselves as coping well or badly. The media highlight people who are models of good adjustment to crises. With respect to breast cancer, women such as Betty Ford, Shirley Temple Black, or Marvella Bayh come to mind. We reasoned that such models might demoralize normal women by making them feel they were not doing well by comparison (Taylor & Levin, 1976). In contrast, comparisons with average women who might be experiencing a number of more negative reactions to cancer should yield more favorable self-evaluations. An alternative prediction derived from Festinger's (1954) social comparison theory (Wheeler, 1966) is that people will compare themselves with someone doing slightly better than they are – in other words, make upward comparisons in order to learn how to cope more effectively.

What we found conformed neither to our analysis nor to the upward comparison prediction (Wood, Taylor, & Lichtman, Note 4). Instead, virtually all the women we interviewed thought they were doing as well as or somewhat better than other women coping with the same crisis. Only two said they were doing somewhat worse. If we had an unusually well-adjusted sample, of course, these perceptions could be veridical, but we know from other information that this was not true.[3] These results suggest that these women are making downward comparisons, comparing themselves with women who were as fortunate or less fortunate than they. These results tie in with a more general body of literature recently brought together by Wills (1981) indicating that when faced with threat, individuals will usually make self-enhancing comparisons in an apparent effort to bolster self-esteem. Downward comparisons, then, would seem to be a fairly robust method of self-protection against threat.

In some cases, these downward comparisons were drawn explicitly. For example, one woman took great glee from the fact that her Reach to Recovery volunteer (the woman sent in by the American Cancer Society to serve as a model of good adjustment) seemed to be more poorly adjusted than she was. Despite some direct comparisons, however, many of the social comparisons seem to be made against hypothetical women:

> Some of these women just seemed to be devastated. And with really less problems than I encountered, you know, smaller tumors.

> You read about a few who handle it well, but it still seems like the majority really feel sorry for themselves. And I really don't think they cope with it that well. I don't understand it, because it doesn't bother me at all.

> I think I did extremely well under the circumstances. I know that there are just some women who aren't strong enough, who fall apart and become psychologically disturbed and what have you. It's a big adjustment for them.

It seems, then, that the need to come out of the comparison process appearing better off drives the process itself; the process does not determine the outcome. If a comparison person who makes one appear well adjusted is not available from personal experience, such a person may be manufactured.

Choice of comparison target is not the only way that social comparison processes can operate to enhance self-esteem. One must also consider the dimensions selected for evaluation. Conceivably, one could select a dimension that would make one appear more advantaged than others or one could select a dimension for evaluation that would put one at a disadvantage. To illustrate what our patients did, let me offer a few of their statements. The following is a comparison made by a woman whose cancer was treated with a lumpectomy (removal of the lump itself) rather than a mastectomy (which involves the removal of the entire breast):

> I had a comparatively small amount of surgery. How awful it must be for women who have had a mastectomy. I just can't imagine, it would seem it would be so difficult.

3 Comparison of participants in the study with nonparticipants from the same practice on a large number of disease-related and adjustment-related variables revealed no significant differences between the two (Taylor, Lichtman, & Wood, Note 2).

These are the remarks of a woman who had a mastectomy:

> It was not tragic. It's worked out okay. Now if the thing had spread all over, I would have had a whole different story for you.

An older woman:

> The people I really feel sorry for are these young gals. To lose a breast when you're so young must be awful. I'm 73; what do I need a breast for?

A young woman:

> If I hadn't been married, I think this thing would have really gotten to me. I can't imagine dating or whatever knowing you have this thing and not knowing how to tell the man about it.

The point, of course, is that everyone is better off than someone as long as one picks the right dimension. In our study, several women with lumpectomies compared themselves favorably to women with mastectomies; no woman with a mastectomy ever evaluated herself against a woman with a lumpectomy. Older women considered themselves better off than younger women: no younger woman expressed the wish that she had been older. Married women pitied the single woman; no single woman pointed out that it would have been easier if she'd been married. The women who were the worst off consoled themselves with the fact that they were not dying or were not in pain. The amount of self-enhancement in these dimensional comparisons is striking. Not only choice of comparison target, then, but also choice of comparison dimension is important for restoring self-enhancement in the face of threat. The issue of dimension selection in social comparisons is one that has been almost entirely ignored in the social comparison literature. This would seem to be an important oversight, particularly for research that examines social comparisons made under threat (Taylor, Wood, & Lichtman, in press).

The fact that social comparison processes can be used to enhance oneself is important, because it meshes social psychological processes with clinically significant outcomes. However, these social comparisons appear to serve important functions other than just self-enhancement. Several researchers (e.g., Fazio, 1979; Singer, 1966) have made a distinction between social comparisons that are made to validate one's self-impression versus social comparisons that are drawn to construct self-impressions. The results just described can be construed as efforts to validate a favorable self-image. However, one can also see evidence of constructive social comparisons among the respondents. Specifically, some of the comparisons involved instances in which women selected as comparison objects other women who were worse off physically (such as women with nodal involvement, women with metastatic cancer, or women with double mastectomies) but who were coping very well. Such comparisons are self-enhancing, but they are also instructive and motivating. That is, the fact that women worse off are coping well seems to inspire the person drawing the comparison to try to do as well and to pattern her own behavior after the comparison person. These comparisons are particularly important because self-enhancement, and indeed cognitive illusion generally, is often written off as defensive and dysfunctional. Instead, these illusions may have multiple functions. In addition to self-enhancement, they can instill motivation and provide information, as these downward comparisons apparently did for some of our respondents (see Brickman & Bulman, 1977). I will discuss this point more fully in a later portion of the article.

What, then, can be learned from the analysis of cancer patients' comparative processes? These women made downward comparisons instead of upward ones, and appear to have selected their comparison persons to enhance their self-esteem rather than letting their self-esteem be determined by who was available for comparison. If other appropriate persons were not readily available for comparison, they manufactured a norm that other women were worse off than they were. The dimensions singled out for comparison were ones on which they appeared better, rather than worse, off. Physically disadvantaged but successful copers also were selected as models. One, then, has the best of both worlds: The comparisons enable one to feel better about oneself, but one does not lose the advantage of having a successful model on which to pattern one's efforts at adjustment.

Implications of cognitive adaptation for cognitive processing

Given these themes that constitute the tasks of cognitive adaptation to threatening events, it is now useful to examine the form of these cognitive adaptations more generally and discuss their implications for cognitive processing. The themes of meaning, mastery, and self-enhancement could be observed in nearly every patient as a consequence of the threat she was experiencing, and yet the form through which the theme was expressed differed from patient to patient. For example, although the specific attributions made by our cancer patients were varied, virtually every patient had a theory about her cancer. Likewise, although cognitions about what one could control varied from patient to patient, an effort at control was present for most. Although the specific form of social comparisons varied, their self-enhancing quality was highly robust. These findings imply that the specific form of the cognitions patients hold about their illness may matter less than the functions those cognitions serve.

Indeed, cognitions are both the easiest and the hardest thing to study empirically. They are easy because there are so many of them, and they are hard because it is so difficult to know which ones are important and when. The meaning of specific cognitions can vary substantially from situation to situation. To take an empirical example, consider the specific cognition of self-blame for a negative outcome. Self-blame may serve some needs under some circumstances and other needs under others. In Bulman and Wortman's (1977) research on quadriplegics and paraplegics, self-blame was associated with good coping outcomes, perhaps because it signified a restored sense of mastery. In our cancer work (Taylor, Lichtman, & Wood, Note 2), self-blame was uncorrelated with adjustment; for some, self-blame may have produced guilt and self-recrimination (cf. Abrams & Finesinger, 1953), whereas for others it was associated with mastery. In recent research Buf Meyer and I conducted on rape victims (Meyer & Taylor, Note 5), self-blame was associated with poor coping, because it may well have led people to question their sense of mastery. Note, then, the robustness of the mastery need, but the different ways that the specific cognition of self-blame related to it. Thus, a particular cognition may mean one thing under one set of circumstances and something completely different under others.

Moreover, specific cognitions (such as attributions, beliefs about control, or social comparisons) are in some cases functionally equivalent or at least functionally overlapping. The need for self-enhancement can conceivably be served by believing one has control or by making downward comparisons. Likewise, the need to find meaning in the experience can be served by finding an explanation for the event or by laying out a plan for controlling things in the future. Not only do specific cognitions functionally overlap, but individual cognitions may serve several needs simultaneously. For example, a causal explanation can simultaneously provide meaning for an experience and increase one's sense of mastery. Rothbaum, Weisz, and Snyder (1982) have argued that attempts to find meaning in an aversive experience actually represent an effort at interpretive control, a secondary form of control that involves flowing with the experience rather than trying to change it.

Perhaps the best example of meeting dual needs through a single cognition is the downward social comparisons our cancer patients made. By selecting someone worse off physically but who was coping very well, these women both came off looking advantaged and also provided themselves with a model of how to cope, thus contributing to their mastery needs. To summarize, specific cognitions may mean different things under different circumstances, they may be functionally overlapping rather than functionally distinct, and they may satisfy several functions simultaneously.

This portrait of cognitions is very different from that typically provided by psychological research on social cognitions. These usually laboratory-based efforts often portray specific cognitions as if they were highly robust rather than fluid and ephemeral (cf. Wortman & Dintzer, 1978). Cognitions are often discussed as if they had a fixed meaning across situations rather than multiple and changing meanings. The functions specific cognitions serve, such as those identified in the present study, are almost entirely ignored in laboratory investigations. The present results argue, at the very least, for expanding the study of cognitions to include field situations of high involvement; such situations may more properly capture the function–cognition interface that is necessary for interpreting the specific form through which a cognitive theme is expressed. There are other implications as well. As will be seen shortly, the preceding points regarding the form of specific cognitions assume increasing importance in the context of the disconfirmation of cognitions. Before that issue is discussed, however, an important attribute of cognitive adaptations to threatening events merits extended comment, and that is their illusion-based nature.

Illusion as essential to normal cognitive functioning

The cognitions upon which meaning, mastery, and self-enhancement depend are in a large part founded on illusions. Causes for cancer are manufactured despite the fact that the true causes of cancer remain substantially unknown. Belief in control over one's cancer persists despite little evidence that such faith is well placed. Self-enhancing social comparisons are drawn, and when no disadvantaged person exists against whom one can compare oneself, she is made up. I have argued that these illusions are beneficial in bringing about psychological adaptation. However, in the past, mental health researchers and clinicians have assumed that positive mental functioning depends upon being in touch with reality (e.g., Erikson, 1950; Haan, 1977; Jahoda, 1958; Maslow, 1954; Menninger, 1963; Vaillant, 1977; see Lazarus, 1983, for a discussion of this point). Indeed, one goal of therapy has been considered to be the stripping away of illusions so that a more accurate view of the world and one's problems can emerge. As Lazarus (1983) put it: "to be sophisticated [meant] accepting accurate reality testing as the hallmark of mental health....Everyone knew that self-deception was tantamount to mental disorder" (p. 1).

However, the idea that normal mental functioning depends upon illusion is gaining increasing support. In his new look at denial, Lazarus (1983) points out that denial is no longer denounced as the primitive, ultimately unsuccessful defense it once was; rather, clinicians and health psychologists are now recognizing its value in protecting people against crises, both in the initial stages of threat and intermittently when people must come to terms with information that is difficult to accept, such as the diagnosis of a terminal illness.

Greenwald's (1980) recent analysis of the totalitarian ego points out how the maintenance of the self-concept depends upon the revision of one's personal history. One remembers oneself as more successful and more often correct than one really is. Attribution research reveals that good outcomes are attributed to oneself much more than are bad outcomes (e.g., Bradley, 1978; Miller & Ross, 1975; Snyder, Stephan, & Rosenfield, 1978). Optimism pervades our thinking (Tiger, 1979). People believe that the present is better than the past and that the future will be even better (Brickman, Coates, & Janoff-Bulman, 1978; Free & Cantril, 1968; Weinstein, 1980). People expect to succeed and improve in the future. All these views of oneself and the world become even more extreme under ego-involving conditions (see Greenwald, 1980).

Perhaps the clearest evidence for the benefits of illusions comes from the study of depressive cognitions. Independent work by several investigators has shown that relative to depressives, normals show several characteristics. Normals inflate others' views of them (Lewinsohn, Mischel, Chaplin, & Barton, 1980). They are more prone to an illusion of control – that is, the perception that they can control objectively uncontrollable outcomes (Alloy & Abramson, in press; Alloy, Abramson, & Viscusi, 1981; Golin, Terrell, & Johnson, 1977; Golin, Terrell, Weitz, & Drost, 1979). Nondepressives underestimate the amount of negative feedback they have received (DeMonbreun & Craighead, 1977; Nelson & Craighead, 1977). Nondepressives overestimate the predictability of and control they have over positive outcomes and underestimate the predictability of undesired outcomes (Alloy & Abramson, 1979, 1980; Alloy et al., 1981). They reward themselves more than their objective performance warrants (Rozensky, Rehm, Pry, & Roth, 1977), and they tend to attribute their successes to internal stable causes and their failures to external, unstable, specific ones (Abramson & Alloy, 1981). Finally, on an issue quite similar to the cancer experience, Silver and Wortman (1980) found that often unrealistic beliefs among quadriplegics and paraplegics about the relationship between their own efforts and likelihood of improving led to better emotional functioning and better coping.

Illusion clearly pervades normal cognitive functioning, and the researchers who have investigated this area have suggested several reasons why. Such illusions may have evolutionary significance: As Greenwald (1980) notes, they contribute to maintaining the self as a highly organized information processing system, and they produce behavioral persistence. Behavioral persistence may also be the adaptive significance of the illusion of control and other exaggerated perceptions of contingency (Lewinsohn et al., 1980) in that high expectations of control should enhance efforts at control. Self-enhancement biases likewise are functional: Positive self-perceptions can make one behave more favorably toward both the self and others, such as by increasing helping behavior (Isen, Shalker, Clark, & Karp, 1978; Rosenhan, Underwood, & Boore, 1974). Self-reinforcement, which normals appear to do to excess, increases rate of responding at a task (see Rozensky et al., 1977). The so-called "warm glow" produced by these illusion-based perceptions, then, may have implications for a wide variety of adaptive self-regulatory mechanisms (Lewinsohn et al., 1980). In our own work, it is clear that the sense of meaning, mastery, and self-enhancement, and the specific cognitions through which they are achieved, enable people to make sense of the cancer, to take controlling efforts to attempt to forestall a recurrence, to assert control in aspects of their lives where control is possible, and to change perceptions of themselves and their lives in ways that are self-enhancing and psychologically beneficial. The effective individual in the face of threat, then, seems to be one who permits the development of illusions, nurtures those illusions, and is ultimately restored by those illusions.

The disconfirmation of the cognitive management of threat

There is one potential problem in arguing for the adaptive significance of illusion, which is that beliefs that rest on illusion are vulnerable to disconfirmation. The belief that one can control one's cancer can, for example, be abruptly disconfirmed by a recurrence. The belief that one's cancer came from a particular cause, such as an auto accident, can be quickly disconfirmed by a physician or a knowledgeable acquaintance. If people's adjustment to threat depends on the maintenance of illusions, what happens when these illusions are challenged or destroyed?

This has been an extremely important issue in social cognition, especially in work on psychological control (e.g., Wortman & Brehm, 1975). Whereas considerable research highlights the benefits of control (Thompson, 1981), there is growing suspicion that when efforts at control are exerted in an environment where no control exists, controlling efforts will lead to poorer rather than more successful adjustment (e.g., Seligman, 1975; Wortman & Brehm, 1975). A sense of mastery may be fine so long as nothing happens to undermine it. This suspicion about the potential adverse effects of control is sustained by two models of the disconfirmation process furnished by psychological theory. The first is reactance (Brehm, 1966; Brehm & Brehm, 1981), which maintains that threats to freedom or loss of it produce arousal, hostility, and direct or indirect efforts to restore those freedoms. The second, more widely researched, model is learned helplessness (Abramson, Seligman, & Teasdale, 1978; Seligman, 1975), which maintains that after repeated, unsuccessful efforts at control, the individual will give up responding. Motivational, cognitive, and emotional deficits may then arise that will interfere with learning in a new environment. Central to these models is the belief that when lack of control exists in reality, those who attempted to exercise it will be worse off behaviorally, emotionally, cognitively, and motivationally than those who do not.

Both reactance theory and learned helplessness theory, however, suffer from the problems of laboratory-based investigations of social cognition described earlier. Both greatly simplify the environments within which loss of control is introduced, creating several difficulties in interpreting both the meaning of loss of control and the cognitive and behavioral responses to loss of control. For example, potential controlling efforts are often limited to a restricted set of responses, such as a bar press or a verbalized choice. In the world in which loss of control is usually experienced, however, a range of response options is often available to an individual. Accordingly, the potential responses to loss of control are far greater than the range made available in typical studies of learned helplessness or reactance. It is therefore hard to know how to interpret persistence or giving up when those are the only possible responses available. A greater conceptual problem of both theories is that they focus attention on the controlling response itself and the fact that it has been blocked, rather than on the goal or function that the response was designed to serve. In life, however, controlling responses are not made in a vacuum; they are made in response to some goal that achieves some value or function. From the standpoint of cognitive adaptation theory, the specific response (and its blocking) has no fixed meaning independent of the goals or functions it serves. The specific form matters little or not at all. Knowing the value or function of the goal can enable one to look for its expression elsewhere, if expression through some specific form is blocked.

Accordingly, let me propose a third model of the disconfirmation process that more fully captures the fluidity of cognitive adaptations. This model owes its genesis, in part, to some observations on mundane plans. Barbara and Frederick Hayes-Roth, two cognitive psychologists, have studied mundane plans extensively (Hayes-Roth, 1981; Hayes-Roth & Hayes-Roth,

1979), and they report one highly robust and quite curious finding. It is that people grossly overestimate how much they can accomplish in a given period of time and continue to do so in the face of repeated negative feedback. Anyone who makes a daily "to-do" list must be aware of the following phenomenon. Each morning, one makes an extensive list of what one plans to do for the day. One then does perhaps 40% of the items, starts another 40%, and leaves 20% completely untouched. One then shifts the uncompleted items over to the next day or, if the day was particularly unproductive, crosses out the name of the day at the top of the list – for example, Monday – and changes it to the next day! What is interesting is that this process goes on day after day with no disruption to one's functioning, little if any emotional upset, and more to the point, no modification in behavior. Disconfirmation of our expectations of getting things done is a fact of life about which we are apparently unperturbed.

I believe this model of cheerful ineptitude, which associates have variously dubbed "learned haplessness" or "proactance," similarly characterizes the disconfirmation of illusions in the adjustment to threat. The model is appropriately derived from behavior in complex environments. It conceives of specific cognitions, like control or attributions, not as individual responses to be observed in isolation, but rather outlines general themes that are themselves made up of a number of potential specific cognitive responses. It conceptualizes disconfirmation not as the violation of a single expectation, but as a temporary frustration. According to the model, disconfirmation of a single effort at control or a single attribution would be little more frustrating than would finding a particular store closed when one was running one's errands.

An additional important feature of the planning literature that makes it an appropriate source for a model of the disconfirmation process is its emphasis on the plan–goal relationship. Specific plans (which here function as analogues to specific cognitions) have no meaning independent of the goals or values they serve. Accordingly, when a particular plan is thwarted, some alternative plan is substituted that accomplishes the same goal or achieves the same value. It is only when the goal or value itself is blocked, as by the blockage of *all* possible tactics or plans, that one may see goal frustration rather than response substitution as the consequence of loss of control. Even then, goal substitution or value substitution may occur (see Schank & Abelson, 1977; Wilensky, 1981).[4]

Applying the model to the cancer experience leads to specific predictions. If one's belief about the cause of one's cancer is disconfirmed, one finds another potential cause to satisfy one's search for meaning. If one felt that one could control one's cancer, and a recurrence occurred, then one would shift to control something else that *was* controllable, such as one's responses to chemotherapy. Before I create an incorrect impression, let me hasten to add that I do not mean that people face setbacks with aplomb. One does not, for example, react calmly to a recurrence of cancer. What I mean is that people who believed they understood the cause of their cancer, believed they could control it, or believed they were handling it well, and who then discover their beliefs are untrue, are not worse off for having thought so. In fact, they may be better off.

This possibility first suggested itself in our examination of causal attributions among the seriously ill. Having been wedded to laboratory models of the attribution process, we believed that the specific attribution an individual made for his or her cancer would predict adjustment. It was therefore somewhat unnerving that when we asked people what they thought caused their cancer, a large number of them listed several possibilities. More to the point, they encompassed the entire range of dimensions thought to be theoretically important in understanding

---

4 The author apologizes to these planning investigators for vastly oversimplifying their models.

the consequences of causal attributions. Furthermore, some of the theories people had originally advanced for their cancer had been disconfirmed by a physician or other knowledgeable individual with no apparent emotional costs. For example, one woman who had been in an auto accident just prior to the detection of her tumor wanted to file suit against the other driver for causing her cancer. Her doctor and lawyer, of course, quickly disabused her of this notion. She promptly came up with another explanation. She is one illustration of the general point: People often hold multiple or serial theories about their cancer that would seem to have vastly different psychological consequences, but which apparently do not. Moreover, having one or more theories disconfirmed does not seem to be particularly bothersome.

The issue of disconfirmation is most important in the area of psychological control, and at present, our own investigations do not provide a large data base on the effects of failure of control. One example, however, is particularly illustrative of the point I want to make. One of the women I interviewed told me that after detection of her breast tumor, she had believed she could prevent future recurrences by controlling her diet. She had, among other things, consumed huge quantities of Vitamin A through the singularly unappetizing medium of mashed asparagus. A year and a half later, she developed a second malignancy. This, of course, is precisely the situation all control researchers are interested in: a dramatic disconfirmation of efforts to control. I asked her how she felt when that happened. She shrugged and said she guessed she'd been wrong. She then decided to quit her dull job and use her remaining time to write short stories – something she had always wanted to do. Having lost control in one area of her life, she turned to another area, her work life, that *was* controllable.

This example is raised not as proof, but as an instance of what was observed several times. Disconfirmation of efforts at control did not produce the emotional upset or inactivity that one might predict from reactance or learned helplessness theory. Rather, there are many things that can potentially be controlled, and if one's need to control a situation is great, one will control what one can and give up attempting to control what one cannot (cf. Rothbaum et al., 1982).

Cognitive adaptation theory, then, is proposed as an alternative model of the disconfirmation process, not because it has been proven to be better – it has not yet – but because it offers a very different view of the human organism than do currently available models. It views people as adaptable, self-protective, and functional in the face of setbacks.

Conclusion

I have offered a theory of cognitive adaptation to threatening events. The theory maintains that when individuals experience personal tragedies or setbacks, they respond with cognitively adaptive efforts that may enable them to return to or exceed their previous level of psychological functioning. The themes around which such adaptations occur include a search for meaning, an effort to gain mastery, and an attempt to enhance the self. Meaning is addressed by such cognitive processes as finding a causal explanation for the experience and restructuring the meaning of one's life around the setback. Mastery involves efforts to gain control over the threatening event in particular and over one's life more generally by believing that one has control and by exerting behavioral control over threat-related events. Self-enhancement occurs by construing personal benefit from the experience, by comparing oneself with others who are less fortunate, and by focusing on aspects of one's own situation that make one appear to be well off.

I have maintained that these cognitive restructurings are in large part based on illusions, that is, beliefs that have no factual basis or that require looking at known facts in a particular way. Illusion has, in the past, been treated with mild contempt. In the psychological community, illusion is often equated with defensiveness, relegated to being primarily of clinical interest, and is seen as ignorant, static, and as ineffective for learning and action. Even in literature in which the need for illusion is a common theme, the self-deluded characters are often portrayed as naive or pathetic (see Lazarus, 1983). Consider as examples *Don Quixote* (Cervantes, 1605, 1615/1956), *The Iceman Cometh* (O'Neill, 1946), or *Who's Afraid of Virginia Woolf?* (Albee, 1964). In contrast, I maintain that illusions can have a dynamic force. They can simultaneously protect and prompt constructive thought and action. As the literature on depression and on the self makes clear, normal cognitive processing and behavior may depend on a substantial degree of illusion, whereas the ability to see things clearly can be associated with depression and inactivity. Thus, far from impeding adjustment, illusion may be essential for adequate coping.

Perhaps the most important implication of cognitive adaptation theory is its metatheoretical stance regarding the nature of cognitions themselves. Specific cognitions are viewed not as robust elements that maintain a cross-situational meaning, but as strategic changing elements that serve general value-laden themes. Specific cognitions may change their meanings from situation to situation, they may be functionally overlapping rather than functionally distinct, and they may serve several functions simultaneously. Viewed from this perspective, the disconfirmation of a specific cognition, such as a belief in personal control over a recurrence of cancer, may not be as psychologically problematic as previous models of the disconfirmation process (reactance, learned helplessness) have suggested. Rather, given the flexibility of the relationship between cognitions and themes, the individual may find an alternative response that serves the same function and thus continue to adapt as well as or better than the individual who makes no adaptive effort at all.

As a theoretical and empirical venture, cognitive adaptation theory is still in its infancy. It suggests a general strategy for studying adaptation to threatening events by focusing on multiple cognitively adaptive efforts simultaneously, rather than upon the adaptive value of particular cognitions in isolation. It also takes a stand against laboratory-based examinations of reactions to threat that fail to acknowledge the relation of particular cognitions to overriding goals or values. More specifically, the theory points to some directions for beginning research. Systematically documenting the themes of meaning, mastery, and self-enhancement in adjustment to threatening events other than cancer is an important empirical step. In this context, it is encouraging to note that evidence for each of the three themes – meaning (Chodoff et al., 1964; Frankl, 1963; Mechanic, 1977; Visotsky et al., 1961; Weisman & Worden, 1975), mastery (Bulman & Wortman, 1977; Janoff-Bulman, 1979; Rothbaum et al., 1982), and self-enhancement (Pearlin & Schooler, 1978; Wills, 1981) – has already been reported by investigators exploring misfortunes as varied as economic difficulty, marital problems, rape, and physical illness other than cancer. A second beginning line of research stems from the different predictions that cognitive adaptation theory generates for reactions to disconfirmation of cognitions, as compared with reactance or learned helplessness theory. The theory suggests, for example, that in field settings where people have multiple response options at their disposal, they will turn their frustrated efforts at control, understanding, or self-enhancement to tasks on which they are more likely to be successful. Our current empirical work focuses on this very question: What happens when people's efforts to exert control in a threatening environment are unsuccessful?

My biologist acquaintances frequently note that the more they know about the human body, the more, not less, miraculous it seems. The recuperative powers of the mind merit similar awe. The process of cognitive adaptation to threat, though often time-consuming and not always successful, nonetheless restores many people to their prior level of functioning and inspires others to find new meaning in their lives. For this reason, cognitive adaptation occupies a special place in the roster of human capabilities.

Reference notes

1 Follick, M. J., & Turk, D. C. *Problem specification by ostomy patients.* Paper presented at the meeting of the Association for Advancement of Behavior Therapy, Chicago, November 1978.

2 Taylor, S. E., Lichtman, R. R., & Wood, J. V. *Adjustment to breast cancer: Physical, socio-demographic, and psychological predictors.* Manuscript submitted for publication, 1982.

3 Lichtman, R. R. *Close relationships after breast cancer.* Unpublished doctoral dissertation, 1982.

4 Wood, J. V., Taylor, S. E., & Lichtman, R. R. *Social comparison processes in adjustment to cancer.* Manuscript submitted for publication, 1982.

5 Meyer, B., & Taylor, S. E. *Adjustment to rape.* Manuscript submitted for publication, 1982.

References

Abrams, R. D., & Finesinger, J. E. Guilt reactions in patients with cancer. *Cancer,* 1953, *6,* 474–482.

Abramson, L. Y., & Alloy, L. B. Depression, nondepression, and cognitive illusions: Reply to Schwartz. *Journal of Experimental Psychology: General,* 1981, *110,* 436–447.

Abramson, L. Y., Seligman, M. E. P., & Teasdale, J. Learned helplessness in humans: Critique and reformulation. *Journal of Abnormal Psychology,* 1978, *87,* 49–74.

Albee, E. *Who's afraid of Virginia Woolf?* New York: Atheneum, 1964.

Alloy, L. B., & Abramson, L. Y. Judgment of contingency in depressed and nondepressed students: Sadder but wiser? *Journal of Experimental Psychology: General,* 1979, *108,* 441–485.

Alloy, L. B., & Abramson, L. Y. The cognitive component of human helplessness and depression: A critical analysis. In J. Garber & M. E. P. Seligman (Eds.), *Human helplessness: Theory and application.* New York: Academic Press, 1980.

Alloy, L. B., & Abramson, L. Y. Learned helplessness, depression, and the illusion of control. *Journal of Personality and Social Psychology,* in press.

Alloy, L. B., Abramson, L. Y., & Viscusi, D. Induced mood and the illusion of control. *Journal of Personality and Social Psychology,* 1981, *41,* 1129–1140.

Andreasen, N. J. C., & Norris, A. S. Long-term adjustment and adaptation mechanisms in severely burned adults. *Journal of Nervous and Mental Disease,* 1972, *154,* 352–362.

Averill, J. R. Personal control over aversive stimuli and its relationship to stress. *Psychological Bulletin,* 1973, *80,* 286–303.

Bradley, G. W. Self-serving biases in the attribution process: A reexamination of the fact or fiction question. *Journal of Personality and Social Psychology,* 1978, *36,* 56–71.

Brehm, J. W. *Response to loss of freedom: A theory of psychological reactance.* New York: Academic Press, 1966.

Brehm, S. S., & Brehm, J. W. *Psychological reactance: A theory of freedom and control.* New York: Academic Press, 1981.

Briar, S. Welfare from below: Recipient's views of the public welfare system. *California Law Review,* 1966, *54,* 370–385.

Brickman, P., & Bulman, R. J. Pleasure and pain in social comparison. In J. M. Suls & R. L. Miller (Eds.). *Social comparison processes: Theoretical and empirical perspectives.* Washington, D.C.: Hemisphere, 1977.

Brickman, P., Coates, D., & Janoff-Bulman, R. Lottery winners and accident victims: Is happiness relative? *Journal of Personality and Social Psychology,* 1978, *36,* 917–927.

Bulman, R. J., & Wortman, C. B. Attributions of blame and coping in the "real world": Severe accident victims react to their lot. *Journal of Personality and Social Psychology,* 1977, *35,* 351–363.

Campbell, A., Converse, P. E., & Rodgers, W. L. *The quality of American life: Perceptions, evaluations, and satisfactions.* New York: Russell Sage Foundation, 1976.

Cervantes, S. M. de. *The adventures of Don Quixote* (J. M. Cohen, trans.). Baltimore. Md.: Penguin Books, 1956. (Original publications in Spanish: Part 1, 1605; Part II, 1615.)

Chodoff, P., Friedman, P. B., & Hamburg, D. A. Stress, defenses and coping behavior: Observations in parents of children with malignant disease. *American Journal of Psychiatry*, 1964, *120*, 743–749.

DeMonbreun, B. G., & Craighead, W. E. Distortion of perception and recall of positive and neutral feedback in depression. *Cognitive Therapy and Research*, 1977, *1*, 311–329.

Derogatis, L. R. *The global adjustment to illness scale (GAIS)*. Baltimore, Md.: Clinical Psychometric Research, 1975.

Erikson, E. H. *Childhood and society*. New York: Norton, 1950.

Fazio, R. H. Motives for social comparison: The construction–validation distinction. *Journal of Personality and Social Psychology*, 1979, *37*, 1683–1698.

Festinger, L. A theory of social comparison processes. *Human Relations*. 1954, *7*, 117–140.

Frankl, V. E. *Man's search for meaning*. New York: Washington Square Press, 1963.

Free, L. A., & Cantril, H. *The political beliefs of Americans: A study of public opinion*. New York: Clarion, 1968.

Golin, S., Terrell, F., & Johnson, B. Depression and the illusion of control. *Journal of Abnormal Psychology*. 1977, *86*, 440–442.

Golin, S., Terrell, F., Weitz, J., & Drost, P. L. The illusion of control among depressed patients. *Journal of Abnormal Psychology*, 1979, *88*, 454–457.

Greenwald, A. G. The totalitarian ego: Fabrication and revision of personal history. *American Psychologist*, 1980, *35*, 603–618.

Gurin, G., Veroff, J., & Feld, S. *Americans view their mental health*. New York: Basic Books, 1960.

Haan, N. *Coping and defending*. New York: Academic Press, 1977.

Hayes-Roth, B. A cognitive science approach to improving planning. In *Proceedings of the third annual conference of the Cognitive Science Society*. Berkeley, Calif.: Cognitive Science Society, August 19–21, 1981.

Hayes-Roth, B., & Hayes-Roth, F. A cognitive model of planning. *Cognitive Science*, 1979, *3*, 275–310.

Heider, F. *The psychology of interpersonal relations*. New York: Wiley, 1958.

Isen, A. M., Shalker, T. E., Clark, M., & Karp. L. Affect, accessibility of material in memory, and behavior: A cognitive loop? *Journal of Personality and Social Psychology*, 1978, *36*, 1–12.

Jahoda, M. *Current conceptions of positive mental health*. New York: Basic Books, 1958.

Janoff-Bulman, R. Characterological versus behavioral self-blame: Inquiries into depression and rape. *Journal of Personality and Social Psychology*, 1979, *37*, 1798–1809.

Katz, A. H. Social adaptation in chronic illness: A study of hemophilia. *American Journal of Public Health*, 1963, *53*, 1666–1675.

Kelley, H. H. Attribution theory in social psychology. In D. Levine (Ed.), *Nebraska Symposium on Motivation* (Vol. 15). Lincoln: University of Nebraska Press; 1967.

Latané, B. Studies in social comparison: Introduction and overview. *Journal of Experimental Social Psychology*, 1966, *Supplement 1*, 1–5.

Lazarus, R. S. The costs and benefits of denial. In S. Breznitz (Ed.), *Denial of stress*. New York: International Universities Press, 1983.

Leon, G. R., Butcher, J. N., Kleinman, M., Goldberg, A., & Almagor, M. Survivors of the Holocaust and their children: Current status and adjustment. *Journal of Personality and Social Psychology*, 1981, *41*, 503–516.

Leventhal, H. The consequences of depersonalization during illness and treatment. In J. Howard & A. Strauss (Eds.), *Humanizing health care*. New York: Wiley, 1975.

Lewinsohn, P. M., Mischel, W., Chaplin, W., & Barton, R. Social competence and depression: The role of illusory self-perceptions. *Journal of Abnormal Psychology*, 1980, *89*, 203–212.

Maslow, A. H. *Motivation and personality*. New York: Harper & Row, 1954.

McNair, D. M., & Lorr, M. An analysis of mood in neurotics. *Journal of Abnormal Psychology*, 1964, *69*, 620–627.

Mechanic, D. Illness behavior, social adaptation, and the management of illness. *Journal of Nervous and Mental Disease*. 1977, *165*, 79–87.

Menninger, K. *The vital balance*. New York: Viking, 1963.

Miller, D. T., & Ross, M. Self-serving biases in the attribution of causality: Fact or fiction? *Psychological Bulletin*, 1975, *82*, 213–225.

Myers, B. A., Friedman, S. B., & Weiner, I. B. Coping with a chronic disability: Psychosocial observations of girls with scoliosis. *American Journal of Diseases of Children*, 1970, *120*, 175–181.

Nelson, R. E., & Craighead, W. E. Selective recall of positive and negative feedback, self-control behaviors, and depression. *Journal of Abnormal Psychology*, 1977, *86*, 379–388.

O'Neill, E. *The iceman cometh*. New York: Random House, 1946.

Pearlin, L. I., & Schooler, C. The structure of coping. *Journal of Health and Social Behavior*, 1978, *19*, 2–21.

Rosenhan, D., Underwood, B., & Boore, B. Affect moderates self-gratification and altruism. *Journal of Personality and Social Psychology*, 1974, *30*, 546–552.

Rothbaum, F., Weisz, J. R., & Snyder, S. S. Changing the world and changing the self: A two-process model of perceived control. *Journal of Personality and Social Psychology*, 1982, *42*, 5–37.

Rozensky, R. H., Rehm, L. P., Pry, G., & Roth, D. Depression and self-reinforcement behavior in hospitalized patients. *Journal of Behavioral Therapy and Experimental Psychiatry*, 1977, *8*, 31–34.

Ryan, W. *Blaming the victim*. New York: Vintage Books, 1971.

Schank, R. C., & Abelson, R. P. *Scripts, plans, goals, and understanding: An inquiry into human knowledge structures*. Hillsdale, N.J.: Erlbaum, 1977.

Seligman, M. E. P. *Helplessness: On depression, development, and death*. San Francisco: Freeman, 1975.

Silver, R. L., & Wortman, C. B. Coping with undesirable life events. In J. Garber & M. E. P. Seligman (Eds.), *Human helplessness: Theory and applications*. New York: Academic Press, 1980.

Simonton, O. C., & Simonton, S. Belief systems and management of the emotional aspects of malignancy. *Journal of Transpersonal Psychology*, 1975, *7*, 29–48.

Singer, J. E. Social comparison: Progress and issues. *Journal of Experimental Social Psychology*, 1966, *Supplement 1*, 103–110.

Snyder, M. L., Stephan, W. G., & Rosenfield, C. Attributional egotism. In J. H. Harvey, W. J. Ickes, & R. F. Kidd (Eds.), *New directions in attribution research* (Vol. 2). Hillsdale. N.J.: Erlbaum, 1978.

Suls, J. M., & Miller, R. L. M. *Social comparison processes: Theoretical and empirical perspectives*. New York: Wiley, 1977.

Tavormina, J. B., Kastner, L. S., Slater, P. M., & Watt, S. L. Chronically ill children: A psychologically and emotionally deviant population? *Journal of Abnormal Child Psychology*, 1976, *4*, 99–110.

Taylor, S. E., & Levin, S. *The psychological impact of breast cancer: Theory and practice*. San Francisco: West Coast Cancer Foundation, 1976.

Taylor, S. E., Wood, J. V., & Lichtman, R. R. It could be worse: Selective evaluation as a response to victimization. *Journal of Social Issues*, in press.

Thompson, S. C. Will it hurt less if I can control it? A complex answer to a simple question. *Psychological Bulletin*, 1981, *90*, 89–101.

Tiger, L. *Optimism: The biology of hope*. New York: Simon & Schuster, 1979.

Turk, D. C. Factors influencing the adaptive process with chronic illness: Implications for intervention. In I. G. Sarason & C. D. Spielberger (Eds.), *Stress and anxiety* (Vol. 6). Washington, D.C.: Hemisphere, 1979.

Vaillant, G. *Adaptation to life.* Boston: Little, Brown, 1977.

Visotsky, H. M., Hamburg, D. A., Goss, M. E., & Lebovits, B. Z. Coping behavior under extreme stress. *Archives of General Psychiatry,* 1961, *5,* 423–448.

Weinstein, N. D. Unrealistic optimism about future life events. *Journal of Personality and Social Psychology,* 1980, *39,* 806–820.

Weisman, A. D. *Coping with cancer.* New York: McGraw-Hill, 1979.

Weisman, A. D., & Worden, J. W. Psychological analysis of cancer deaths. *Omega,* 1975, *6,* 61–75.

Wheeler, L. Motivation as a determinant of upward comparison. *Journal of Experimental Social Psychology,* 1966, *Supplement 1,* 27–31.

Wilensky, R. A model for planning in everyday situations. In *Proceedings of the third annual conference of the Cognitive Science Society.* Berkeley, Calif.: Cognitive Science Society, August 19–21, 1981.

Wills, T. A. Downward comparison principles in social psychology. *Psychological Bulletin.* 1981, *90,* 245–271.

Wills, T. A. Social comparison and help-seeking. In B. M. DePaulo, A. Nadler, & J. D. Fisher (Eds.), *New directions in helping: Vol. 2. Help-seeking.* New York: Academic Press, 1982.

Wong, P. T. P., & Weiner, B. When people ask "why" questions, and the heuristics of attributional search. *Journal of Personality and Social Psychology,* 1981, *40,* 650–663.

Wortman, C. B., & Brehm, J. W. Responses to uncontrollable outcomes: An integration of reactance theory and the learned helplessness model. In L. Berkowitz (Ed.), *Advances in experimental social psychology* (Vol. 8). New York: Academic Press. 1975.

Wortman, C. B., & Dintzer, L. Is an attributional analysis of the learned helplessness phenomenon viable? A critique of the Abramson–Seligman–Teasdale reformulation. *Journal of Abnormal Psychology,* 1978, *87,* 75–90.

Wortman, C. B., & Dunkel-Schetter, C. Interpersonal relationships and cancer. A theoretical analysis. *Journal of Social Issues,* 1979, *35,* 120–155.

Petrie, K.J., Cameron, L.D., Ellis, C.J. et al. (2002) Changing illness perceptions after myocardial infarction: an early intervention randomized controlled trial, *Psychosomatic Medicine*, 64: 580–6.

Changing illness perceptions after myocardial infarction

An early intervention randomized controlled trial

Keith J. Petrie, PhD, Linda D. Cameron, PhD, Chris J. Ellis, BM, Deanna Buick, PhD and John Weinman, PhD

Abstract

Objective: This study was designed to examine whether a brief hospital intervention designed to alter patients' perceptions about their myocardial infarction (MI) would result in a better recovery and reduced disability.

Design: In a prospective randomized study, 65 consecutive patients with their first MI aged were assigned to receive an intervention designed to alter their perceptions about their MI or usual care from rehabilitation nurses. Patients were assessed in hospital before and after the intervention and at 3 months after discharge from hospital.

Results: The intervention caused significant positive changes in patients' views of their MI. Patients in the intervention group also reported they were better prepared for leaving hospital ($p < 0.05$) and subsequently returned to work at a significantly faster rate than the control group ($p < 0.05$). At the 3-month follow-up, patients in the intervention group reported a significantly lower rate of angina symptoms than control subjects (14.3 vs. 39.3, $p < 0.03$). There was no significant differences in rehabilitation attendance between the two groups.

Conclusions: An in-hospital intervention designed to change patients' illness perceptions can result in improved functional outcome after MI.

Keywords: myocardial infarction, illness perceptions, return to work, disability, rehabilitation.
MI = myocardial infarction; CHD = coronary heart disease; IPQ = Illness Perception Questionnaire; LDL = low density lipoproteins.

From the Department of Health Psychology (K.J.P.), Department of Psychology (L.D.C.), Department of Medicine (C.J.E.), University of Auckland, New Zealand; Centre for Health Care Research (D.B.), University of Brighton, Brighton, and Unit of Psychology (J.W.), Guy's, King's, and St. Thomas' School of Medicine, London, United Kingdom.

Address reprint requests to: Keith J. Petrie, Faculty of Medical and Health Sciences, Department of Health Psychology, The University of Auckland, Private Bag 92019, Auckland, New Zealand. Email: kj.petrie@auckland.ac.nz

Received for publication December 5, 2000; revision received July 20, 2001.

Introduction

Recent advances in medical treatment for myocardial infarction have resulted in fewer patients dying in the acute stage of the illness. However, progress has been slower in improving functional recovery after MI. A large number of patients fail to return to work and normal functioning after myocardial infarction despite being physically well, and vocational disability remains one of the important negative consequences of MI (1, 2). Furthermore, many patients do not attend rehabilitation programs after their MI even when such services are readily available (3), and for those patients who do attend rehabilitation, a recent survey has found psychosocial issues are poorly addressed (4). Functional disability after MI is generally associated with higher levels of reported symptoms and lower levels of well-being. A recent follow-up study found only 44% of MI patients were free of chest pain symptoms after 4 years, and chest pain was associated with impaired quality of life and a failure to return to work (5).

Patients' beliefs and perceptions about their illness are key determinants of recovery after a MI (6). In recent years, many studies investigating patients' illness beliefs or perceptions have been based on Leventhal's self-regulatory model (7). This starts from the premise that individuals are active problem solvers who make sense of a threat to their health, such as symptoms or an illness, by developing their own cognitive representation of the threat, which, in turn, determines how they then respond. There is now a convergence of evidence showing that these representations consist of five distinct but interrelated components that serve to define the nature of the health threat for the individual. The identity component comprises the label that the individual uses to describe the condition (eg, heart attack) and the associated symptoms (eg, chest pain, breathlessness), which are linked in a reciprocal way and illustrate the bilevel nature of illness representations (the abstract label and the concrete symptoms). The other linked components of the illness representation are the individual's beliefs about the cause(s) of their condition and their expectations about its likely duration (timeline), its physical, social, and psychological effects (consequences), and the extent to which it is amenable to cure and/or control. Theses five components of illness representation form a schema that determines the patient's coping procedures (eg, adhering or not adhering to medical advice). Patients' illness representations vary considerably within any illness population; they not only determine the selection of illness-related behavior but also serve as a conceptual framework for making sense of information from health care professionals and for evaluating the appropriateness and efficacy of recommended treatment or advice.

In our earlier work with MI patients, we were able to show that patients' perceptions of illness, assessed a few days after their MI, had important effects on different aspects of recovery. Those patients who believed that their MI would have more serious long-lasting consequences were found to have greater levels of illness-related disability and were slower to return to work (8). Similarly, those patients who had weaker beliefs in the control or cure of their heart condition were subsequently found to be less likely to attend cardiac rehabilitation (8, 9). In this context it is important to note that patients' illness representations were not linked to objective indicators of MI severity nor did the latter significantly predict the outcomes that were predicted by illness representations.

The specificity of these belief-behavior links and the fact that they can be identified early on after the onset of the MI is important. Unlike other factors such as personality or sociodemographic variables, these links provide considerable potential for developing cognitively based interventions at an early stage after MI. Thus, if negative thinking about MI can be identified early in the recovery process and an intervention instituted to foster more adaptive models and expectations, then improved levels of functioning and return to work could be expected.

In this study, we tested whether a brief psychological hospital-based intervention designed to change inaccurate and negative illness perceptions of MI would result in an earlier return to work, less long-term disability, and improved cardiac rehabilitation attendance. The intervention was conducted during the normal hospital stay and used first-time MI patients who had not previously been exposed to cardiac care. It used the patient's model of their illness as a starting point to deliver information. The intervention was specifically structured to change highly negative perceptions and to alter the patient's views of the timeline and consequences of their MI.

In contrast with other interventions that typically deliver the same behavioral or cognitive intervention to each patient, the present study used an individualized approach in which the content of each patient's intervention was based on an assessment of their perception of their MI. The latter was achieved by using the Illness Perception Questionnaire, a recently developed measure that assesses the five components of illness representation (10).

Methods

Participants and procedure

Sixty-five first-time MI patients aged < 65 years admitted to Auckland Hospital over a 12-month period were enrolled in the study. Participants were consecutive admissions to the hospital; 12 patients declined to participate in the study before randomization. With informed consent and ethics committee approval, patients were randomly assigned into either an intervention or control group using a computer-generated allocation code.

After being enrolled in the study, subjects completed the initial questionnaire and were randomly assigned to receive either standard care, which involved cardiac rehabilitation nurse in-hospital visits and standard MI educational material, or three 30- to 40-minute intervention sessions conducted by a psychologist in addition to the routine education material. A further research questionnaire was completed by 62 of the 65 patients before leaving hospital. Patients were contacted at 12 weeks and asked to complete a follow-up mail assessment. This questionnaire was returned by 56 patients (86%), and nonrespondents did not differ significantly from respondents on any baseline variables.

Intervention

The intervention contained a broadly equivalent structure for all patients, but its exact content was also individualized according to patients' responses on the Illness Perception Questionnaire. The first session consisted of a brief explanation of the pathophysiology of MI, which included the use of drawings to provide a concrete image of the illness as well as an explanation of common MI symptoms and terminology. A distinction was drawn between cardiac and noncardiac symptoms because many patients ascribe all symptoms to their MI.

This session also explored the patient's beliefs about the cause of the MI. Attention was given to addressing the common misconception that stress was singularly responsible for the patient's MI and broadening the patient's causal model by including the importance of lifestyle factors in the etiology of CHD underlying the MI. This was done by asking the patient to think of other factors that may have contributed to the development of the MI apart from stress (such as poor diet, smoking, lack of exercise) to try to expand the patient's causal model and provide more avenues for future personal control and management of the disease.

The second session built on the causes identified by the patient and focused on developing a plan of minimizing future risk by altering risk factors relevant to the patient and increasing beliefs about control of the condition. This session used data from the patient's scores on the consequences and time line subscales of the Illness Perception Questionnaire (see below) and focused on these aspects of the patient's heart disease. Highly negative beliefs about the consequences of the MI, particularly the belief that the patient will need to significantly reduce activities over the long term, were challenged and a recovery action plan was developed personalized to the patient's own circumstances. For example, the plan included an explicit plan of exercise, dietary change, and return to work tailored to the patient. The linking of the timeline and consequences of the illness was achieved by explaining that, as patients recovered from the illness, they could expect to return to their work and normal activities. The use of a written action plan for self-management has been used in a number of illnesses. A recent systematic review of asthma patients, eg, has shown that patients who had a personalized written plan were more adherent to medication, less likely to be hospitalized, and had better lung function than those who did not have a personalized plan (11).

In the third session, this action plan was reviewed and symptoms of recovery were discussed. Symptoms that are a normal part of the healing and recovery process were distinguished from symptoms that may be warning signs of a further MI. For example, symptoms that may be experienced during exercise, such as slight breathlessness but still being able to speak, were distinguished from symptoms that are not expected, such as severe chest pain. Concerns the patient had about their medication were also explored. The need to take medications consistently and the hazards of relying on symptoms as guides for medications were also discussed in this final session along with concerns about going home.

Measures

In-hospital assessment: IPQ. On enrolling into the study and at hospital discharge, patients completed the IPQ (10) to assess the identity, time line, consequences, and cure/control dimensions that underlie the patient's representations of illness. The IPQ provides a quantitative assessment of the nature and strength of their beliefs about each of the components of their illness representation. The identity subscale is the number of symptoms from a 15-item symptom checklist that the patient associates with the illness (scores range from 0 to 15). The timeline subscale contains four items (eg, "My illness is likely to be permanent rather than temporary"), with scores ranging from 4 to 20 and higher scores representing a belief that the illness is going to last for a longer time. The consequences subscale contains nine items (eg, "My illness will have major consequences on my life"), and scores ranged from 9 to 45, with higher scores representing a stronger belief that the illness will have serious consequences. The cure/control subscale contains seven items (eg, "My treatment will be effective in curing my illness," "There is very little that can be done to improve my illness"). Scores ranged from 7 to 35, with higher scores indicating a higher level of belief in control or potential for cure of the illness. Patients also rated their distress about their symptoms on a two-item scale ("The symptoms of my heart condition are distressing to me," "The symptoms of my heart condition are puzzling to me"; $r = 0.82$). Scores on this scale ranged from 2 to 10, with higher scores indicating greater distress.

The IPQ has been used quite extensively in different illness populations, including a number of studies of MI patients, and fairly extensive psychometric data have been published for all the subscales. The internal reliability for each subscale is satisfactory, with Cronbach alpha coefficients ranging from 0.73 to 0.82 in MI samples (8, 9). Similarly, good test–retest data for each subscale have been obtained in patients with established chronic illness, and a range of concurrent, discriminant, and predictive validity data have been published for different chronic illness groups, including patients with MI (10).

Hospital ratings. At hospital discharge, patients were also asked to rate on a seven-point scale the following questions: "How satisfied were you with the information you received concerning your heart attack and heart condition?" "How satisfied were you with the amount of information that you received?" "How well do you understand the information given to you about your heart attack and heart condition?" "Do you feel prepared for leaving the hospital and returning to your normal activities and work?" "What extent do you still have questions about your heart attack and heart condition?" "How well do you feel you understand your heart attack and heart condition?" "How likely is it you will attend the rehabilitation program?"

Three-month assessment. Information about the time taken until return to work was collected in the 3-month questionnaires. At 3 months, 13 control patients and 19 intervention patients who were employed at the time of hospitalization had returned to work and 6 others (3 from each group) who were employed at the time of hospitalization had not returned to work. Delay in return to work was calculated as the number of days from hospital discharge until the first day back to work.

At the 3-month follow-up, patients completed the IPQ and symptom distress scale and were also asked how often they had angina pain in the past week and, on average, how severe the pain was, rated on a seven-point scale from "not at all severe" to "extremely severe." Data on attendance at the six-session outpatient cardiac rehabilitation program were obtained from program records.

Data analysis

The SPSS for Windows 9 statistical software package was used for all analyses. Treatment group differences in demographic and clinical characteristics were assessed with χ^2 tests and one-way analysis of variance. One-way ANOVA was used to assess treatment group differences in baseline illness perception scores and evaluation ratings obtained at the time of discharge. Treatment-group differences in changes in illness perceptions by the time of discharge and at 3 months were assessed using analysis of covariance; in each analysis, the covariate was the baseline measure of the illness perception component in question. The Cox regression model with the forward stepwise procedure was used to identify demographic and medical variables that predict delay in return to work during the 3 months after discharge for the 38 patients who were employed at the time of hospitalization. These variables were then included as covariates in a Cox regression model assessing treatment-group differences in delay in return to work for the 38 employed patients.

Results

The demographic and clinical characteristics of the intervention and control groups are shown in Table 1. There were no significant differences between the groups other than the proportion of subjects who were married or in de facto relationships, which was significantly greater in the intervention condition than in the control condition (χ^2 (1, $N=65$) $=9.23$, $p<0.002$). Marital/de facto relationship (yes/no) was therefore included as a covariate in preliminary analyses of experimental group differences in illness perceptions, program evaluations, angina symptoms, and return to work. However, it was not a significant covariate for any of these outcome measures and its inclusion did not alter the significance of the experimental group effects, so it was dropped in the final analyses.

The changes in illness perceptions after the intervention and at the 3-month follow-up are shown in Table 2. The intervention significantly altered patients' beliefs about their illness.

Table 1 Demographic and clinical characteristics of the sample at baseline

	Control	Intervention
Gender	24 M, 10 F	23 M, 8 F
Age	55.9 (10.0)	55.3 (8.8)
Ethnicity (%) Caucasian	64.7	71.0
Maori/Pacific Island	5.9	19.4
Other	29.4	9.6
Marital status (%) Single	8.8	0.0
Married/de facto	61.8	93.5
Divorced/separated	23.5	6.5
Widowed	5.9	0.0
Employment status (%) Full-time	47.1	71.0
Part-time	11.8	9.7
Retired	23.5	9.7
Unemployed	17.6	9.7
Family history of heart disease (%)	64.7	67.7
Current smoker (%)	32.4	25.8
Prior angina (%)	14.7	16.1
Hypertension[a] (%)	44.1	38.7
Diabetes mellitus (%)	17.6	12.9
Peak CPK (iu/liter)	1720.3 (1194.0)	2162.3 (2260.8)
ST segment elevation (%)	73.5	71.0
ST segment depression (%)	61.8	77.4
SK or TPA thrombotic therapy (%)	52.9	54.8
Site of MI (%) Anterolateral	52.9	32.3
Inferoposterior	44.1	48.4
Other	3.0	19.3
HDL-C (mmol/liter)	1.2 (0.4)	1.2 (0.4)
LDL-C (mmol/liter)	3.6 (0.9)	4.1 (1.7)
Triglycerides (mmol/liter)	2.2 (1.6)	2.2 (1.4)
Total cholesterol	5.5 (0.9)	6.3 (1.6)
Time in hospital (days)	9.3 (6.2)	7.7 (4.0)

[a] On treatment or blood pressure > 160/95.

Values are mean (SD) or %. SK = streptokinase; TPA = tissue plasminogen activator.

Significant group differences in scores on the consequences, timeline, control/cure, and symptom distress subscales at the time of discharge indicate that intervention (relative to control) participants had lower levels of belief that their heart condition would cause serious consequences and last a long time or indefinitely, higher levels of belief that their heart condition could be controlled, and lower levels of distress about symptoms. Timeline and control-cure beliefs remained significantly different between the two groups at the 3-month follow-up. These data show that the illness perception intervention was successful in changing patients' beliefs to a more positive and controllable view of a MI.

Table 2 Mean (SE) illness perception percentile scores at baseline, discharge, and 3 months

IPQ Subscales	Baseline			Discharge			3 Months		
	Control	Intervention	$F_{(1, 63)}$	Control	Intervention	$F_{(1, 59)}$	Control	Intervention	$F_{(1, 53)}$
Consequences	44.6 (0.03)	47.6 (0.03)	0.63	48.1 (0.02)	41.8 (0.02)	4.32*	41.3 (0.02)	38.1 (0.02)	0.05
Timeline	35.0 (0.03)	35.6 (0.03)	0.02	40.9 (0.02)	34.2 (0.02)	4.28*	46.3 (0.03)	33.0 (0.03)	12.62***
Control/cure	61.3 (0.02)	60.8 (0.02)	0.03	57.3 (0.02)	63.4 (0.02)	8.54**	56.8 (0.01)	62.4 (0.01)	8.10**
Identity symptoms	38.4 (0.04)	31.9 (0.04)	1.64	31.9 (0.03)	28.0 (0.03)	0.72	28.3 (0.04)	20.5 (0.04)	2.46
Distress	43.8 (0.03)	48.1 (0.03)	0.88	43.2 (0.03)	32.2 (0.03)	7.10**	31.8 (0.03)	26.8 (0.03)	1.10

Note: Discharge and 3-month means are adjusted for baseline values.
* $p < 0.05$; ** $p < 0.01$; *** $p < 0.001$.

Before hospital discharge, patients completed ratings of their understanding of their MI and preparedness to leave hospital. These ratings are presented in Table 3 and show that the intervention group, while not differing from the control group in their satisfaction with the amount of information received, rated themselves as having a higher level of understanding of their heart condition and feeling better prepared to leave hospital. Patients in the intervention group also rated themselves as more likely to attend rehabilitation. A higher percentage of intervention patients (74.2%) attended rehabilitation compared with the control patients (55.9%), but this difference did not reach statistical significance (χ^2 (1, $N=65$) $=2.38$, $p<0.13$).

Of the 56 subjects followed up at 3 months, 26.8% reported experiencing angina pain at least once within the previous week. Angina pain at 3 months was not associated with a diagnosis of angina before the MI (χ^2 (1, $N=56$) $=0.1$), NS), but it was positively associated with an anterolateral site of the MI (χ^2 (1, $N=56$) $=5.96$, $p<0.02$) and high LDL levels at baseline (point biserial correlation $r=0.33$, $p<0.05$). Intervention subjects (14.3%) were significantly less likely than control subjects (39.3%) to report angina pain at 3 months (χ^2 (1, $N=56$) $=4.46$, $p<0.05$). A binary logistic regression assessed whether this experimental group difference would remain significant after controlling for the effects of MI site and LDL levels. The three variables were entered simultaneously, and the results revealed a trend for MI site to predict angina pain reports ($B=1.20$, SE $B=0.74$, Wald ($df=1$) $=2.63$, $p<0.10$, exp $B=3.32$) and a significant effect of LDL levels on angina pain reports (B$=0.84$, SE B 0.39, Wald ($df=1$) $=4.68$, $p<0.04$, exp B$=2.31$). This analysis further revealed that, controlling for these two variables, the group effect on angina pain reports was significant ($B=1.96$, SE $B=0.88$, Wald ($df=1$) $=4.89$, $p<0.03$, exp $B=7.08$). Analysis of pain severity ratings reported by subjects experiencing angina pain revealed no significant difference between intervention subjects ($M=2.50$) and control subjects ($M=2.18$); t(13) $=-0.76$, NS.

Preliminary Cox regression analyses individually assessed the significance of each of the demographic and clinical variables (Table 1) in predicting delay in return to work for the patients employed full time before their MI (control $N=16$; intervention $N=22$). These analyses revealed that delay in return to work was significantly predicted by longer hospital stays and higher triglyceride levels. The final Cox model (χ^2 (3, $N=38$) $=11.82$, $p<0.01$), which included hospital stay, triglyceride levels, and experimental group, revealed that all three variables were significantly associated with delay in return to work. Consistent with the preliminary analyses, longer length of hospital stay was positively associated with longer delays in return to work ($B=-0.18$, SE $B=0.06$, Wald ($df=1$) $=9.21$, $p<0.01$, exp $B=0.84$). For every additional day spent in hospital, the relative risk of returning to work was 0.84. Similarly, there was a

Table 3 Mean evaluation ratings prior to hospital discharge

Evaluation	Control	Intervention	$F(1, 60)$
Satisfaction with quality of information	5.47 (0.26)	6.27 (0.16)	6.58*
Satisfaction with amount of information	4.37 (0.23)	4.47 (0.16)	0.10
Understanding of information	5.40 (0.29)	6.27 (0.14)	7.05**
Feel prepared	4.91 (0.29)	5.63 (0.17)	4.65*
Still have questions	3.75 (0.32)	3.03 (0.24)	3.48*
Understanding of heart attack/condition	5.00 (0.28)	5.83 (0.11)	7.49**
Likelihood of attending cardiac rehabilitation	5.72 (0.28)	6.67 (0.10)	9.16**

Note: Higher scores correspond to positive evaluations or affirmative responses.

*$p<0.10$; *$p<0.05$; ** $p<0.01$.

significant effect of triglyceride levels on delay in return to work ($B=-0.29$, SE $B=0.14$, Wald ($df=1)=4.15$, $p<0.04$, exp $B=0.74$). Every increase in triglyceride level by one unit was associated with a relative risk of return to work of 0.74. Controlling for these factors, the intervention group had a shorter delay in return to work rate ($B=-0.80$, SE $B=0.40$, Wald ($df=1)=4.03$, $p=0.05$, exp $B=0.45$). This effect indicates that the estimated rate (risk) of returning to work for the control group was 0.45 times the rate (risk) of returning to work for the intervention group. The addition of treatment group to the model yielded a significant increase in prediction over the model containing only the two covariates (χ^2 (3, N=38)$=4.18$, $p<0.05$). The Cox regression survival curves estimating delay in returning to work for the two groups are shown in Figure 1.

Discussion

This study shows that a brief in-hospital intervention was successful in changing patients' perceptions of their MI. Before leaving hospital, patients in the intervention group had significantly modified their perceptions about how long their illness would last and the personal consequences of the MI on their life compared with the control group. The intervention group was also more optimistic than the control group that their illness could be controlled or cured. The changes in time-line and control-cure were maintained at the 3-month follow-up assessment. The intervention also had a positive effect on patients' reported understanding of their MI and their preparedness to leave hospital.

At 3 months, there was a significant difference between the intervention and control groups in the speed at which patients returned to work. Patients in the intervention group started to return to work earlier, and this difference was maintained over the follow-up period. In addition, the reported rates of angina symptoms were also significantly different between the two groups, with the control group reporting symptoms at a higher frequency. The intervention, while significantly increasing patients' intentions to go to the rehabilitation program, also resulted in higher attendance at rehabilitation, but this difference did not reach significance in this relatively small sample.

The illness-perception intervention has a number of differences from conventional approaches to improving recovery after MI. Most formal rehabilitation programs after MI are

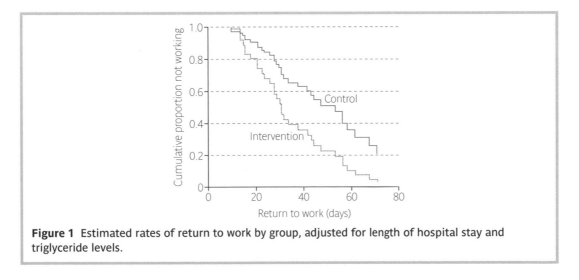

Figure 1 Estimated rates of return to work by group, adjusted for length of hospital stay and triglyceride levels.

not theoretically based but tend to comprise a number of fixed components, usually including education about cardiac disease as well as advice regarding exercise and lifestyle change. It is not always clear what patient attitudes are being targeted and what components are critical to achieving behavior change. In contrast, the illness perception program used the patient's view of his/her illness as a starting point for the intervention and built the material around these existing perceptions. Illness perceptions provide both an initial target for change and a way of evaluating the effectiveness of the intervention, as we know that these beliefs are related to later recovery of function and behavioral change (8, 12).

The reduction of angina symptoms in the intervention group is an interesting finding. Note that reported angina pain may represent chest pain due to cardiac or noncardiac origin. Fewer angina symptoms may be due to the lower level of worry about symptoms in the intervention group or may be associated indirectly through the higher levels of confidence and work functioning in this group. The frequency of chest pain does seem to be critical in the decision to return to work (5), so the time spent in the intervention discussing symptoms expected during recovery may have normalized the symptom experience for patients in the intervention group.

This intervention differs from normal cardiac rehabilitation programs in that it is conducted within the patient's normal hospital stay. We believe this has a number of therapeutic advantages. First, previous research suggests patients' perceptions of their MI are already developed before hospitalization, possibly from previous contact with MI patients or from media depictions of MI (8). The hospital intervention allows for misperceptions and negative beliefs to be modified early in the recovery process. Second, immediately after a major illness or health threat, such as a heart attack, individuals are often more amenable to interventions that encourage changes in behaviors. During this window of vulnerability, future risks are seen less optimistically and individuals are more receptive to change (13). Third, many patients with high levels of risk factors for future MI fail to attend outpatient rehabilitation program and so do not get exposed to a formal intervention process. Although an outpatient cardiac rehabilitation service is available to Auckland Hospital patients, a recent audit found 56% of patients did not attend any session and only 19% completed the six sessions (14).

Generalization from this study is limited by a small sample size and by the postal nature of the follow-up assessment. The focus of this study is on illness perceptions and return to work rather than quality of life and depression after MI, and the effect of the intervention on these outcomes needs to be evaluated in future research. Furthermore, the importance of individual differences such as anxiety level in the response to the intervention is also an area that needs further work.

This study suggests that an inpatient intervention program designed to change behavior by altering patients' illness perceptions of MI has considerable potential to reduce work-related disability. The intervention is acceptable to patients and results in patients feeling better prepared for leaving hospital. It also appears to be compatible with other aspects of inpatient MI treatment. Furthermore, this approach provides a theoretical framework within which inpatient rehabilitation efforts can be directed and evaluated. Further work is needed to evaluate the extent to which the illness perception approach may be usefully incorporated into current hospital treatment regimens for MI patients to complement existing rehabilitation programs.

This research was supported by The Heart Foundation of New Zealand.

References

1 Lipkin DP. Is cardiac rehabilitation necessary? Br Heart J 1991; 65:237–8.

2 Shanfield SB. Return to work after an acute myocardial infarction: a review. Heart Lung 1990;19:109–17.

3 Ades PA, Waldmann ML, McCann WJ, Weaver SO. Predictors of cardiac rehabilitation participation in older coronary patients. Arch Intern Med 1996;152:1033–5.

4 Lewin RJP, Ingleton R, Newens AJ, Thompson DR. Adherence to cardiac rehabilitation guidelines: a survey of rehabilitation programmes in the United Kingdom. BMJ 1998;316:1354–5.

5 Brown N, Melville M, Gray D, Young T, Munro J, Skene AM, Hampton JR. Quality of life four years after acute myocardial infarction: short form 36 scores compared with a normal population. Heart 1999;81:352–8.

6 Maeland JG, Havik OE. Psychological predictors for return to work after a myocardial infarction. J Psychosom Res 1987;31: 471–81.

7 Leventhal H, Meyer D, Nerenz D. The common sense representation of illness danger. In: Rachman S, editor. Contributions to medical psychology. New York: Pergamon Press; 1980. p. 17–30.

8 Petrie KJ, Weinman J, Sharpe N, Buckley J. Role of patients' view of their illness in predicting return to work and functioning after myocardial infarction: longitudinal study. BMJ 1996;312: 1191–4.

9 Cooper A, Lloyd G, Weinman J, Jackson G. Why do patients not attend cardiac rehabilitation: role of intentions and illness beliefs. Heart 1999;82:234–6.

10 Weinman J, Petrie KJ, Moss-Morris R, Horne R. The illness perception questionnaire: a new method for assessing the cognitive representation of illness. Psychol Health 1996; 11: 114–29.

11 Gibson PG, Coughlan J, Wilson AJ, Abramson M, Bauman A, Hensley MJ, Walters EH. Self-management education and regular practitioner review for adults with asthma. Cochrane Database Syst Rev 2000;2:CD001117.

12 Weinman J, Petrie KJ, Sharpe N, Walker S. Causal attributions in patients and spouses after a heart attack and subsequent lifestyle changes. Br J Health Psychol 2001;5:263–73.

13 Weinstein ND. Optimistic biases about personal risks. Science 1989;246:1232–3.

14 Parks D, Allison M, Doughty R, Cunningham L, Ellis CJ. An audit of phase II cardiac rehabilitation at Auckland Hospital. N Z Med J 2000;113:158–61.

Antoni, M.H., Carrico, A.W., Durán, R.E. et al. (2006) Randomized clinical trial of cognitive behavioral stress management on human immunodeficiency virus viral load in gay men treated with highly active antiretroviral therapy, *Psychosomatic Medicine*, 68: 143–51.

Randomized clinical trial of cognitive behavioral stress management on human immunodeficiency virus viral load in gay men treated with highly active antiretroviral therapy

Michael H. Antoni, PhD, Adam W. Carrico, MS, Ron E. Durán, PhD, Susan Spitzer, PhD, Frank Penedo, PhD, Gail Ironson, MD, PhD, Mary Ann Fletcher, PhD, Nancy Klimas, MD, and Neil Schneiderman, PhD

Abstract

Objective: Human Immunodeficiency Virus (HIV)-positive individuals treated with highly active antiretroviral therapy (HAART) may experience psychological burdens and negative mood states, which could impair their ability to derive maximum benefits from their medical treatment. We tested whether a cognitive behavioral stress management (CBSM) intervention in combination with antiretroviral medication adherence training (MAT) from a clinical pharmacist influences HIV viral load more than MAT alone.

Methods: HIV-positive men who have sex with men were randomized to either a 10-week CBSM+MAT intervention ($n=76$) or a MAT-Only condition ($n=54$). Data were collected at baseline immediately following the 10-week intervention period, at 9 months post-randomization, and at 15 months postrandomization.

Results: We found no differences in HIV viral load among the 130 men randomized. However, in the 101 HIV+men with detectable viral load at baseline, those randomized to CBSM+MAT ($n=61$) displayed reductions of 0.56 $\log_{10}$ units in HIV viral load over a 15-

From the Department of Psychology (M.H.A., A.W.C., R.E.D., S.S., F.P., G.I., N.S.), Department of Psychiatry (M.H.A., G.I., N.S.), and Department of Medicine (M.A.F., N.K., N.S.), University of Miami, Coral Gables, FL.

Address correspondence and reprint requests to Michael H. Antoni, PhD, Department of Psychology, 5665 Ponce De Leon Blvd, Coral Gables, FL 33146. E-mail: Mantoni@miami.edu

Received for publication March 28, 2005; revision received May 19, 2005.

This research was supported by National Institute of Mental Health grants P01 MH49548 and T32 MH18917.

month period after controlling for medication adherence. Men in the MAT-Only condition (*n* = 40) showed no change. Decreases in depressed mood during the intervention period explained the effect of CBSM + MAT on HIV viral load reduction over the 15 months.

Conclusions: A time-limited CBSM + MAT intervention that modulates depressed mood may enhance the effects of HAART on suppression of HIV viral load in HIV + men with detectable plasma levels.

Keywords: depression, HIV/AIDS, HIV viral load, intervention.
AIDS = acquired immunodeficiency syndrome; ACTG = Adherence to Combination Therapy Guide; BDI = Beck Depression Inventory; CBSM = cognitive behavioral stress management; CET = coping effectiveness training; EDTA = ethylenediaminetetraacetic acid; HAART = highly active antiretroviral therapy; HIV = human immunodeficiency virus; MAT = medication adherence training; MEMS = medication event monitoring system; POMS = Profile of Mood States.

Introduction

With substantial reductions in morbidity and mortality following the advent of highly active antiretroviral therapy (HAART), clinical care of human immunodeficiency virus (HIV)-positive individuals has improved dramatically such that the disease is now commonly conceptualized as a chronic illness (1,2). However, not all HIV-positive patients receiving HAART show adequate viral suppression, which may be due in large part to suboptimal levels of adherence, as well as the emergence of drug-resistant strains of the virus (3,4). Questions also remain regarding the appropriate time to initiate HAART in HIV-positive patients due to variability in the extent of immune reconstitution, increased incidence of opportunistic infections in the months following initiation, and reports of potentially profound drug-related toxicities (5). Consequently, difficulties in adhering to demanding HAART regimens have been associated with a variety of psychosocial factors such as low perceived social support (6), depressed mood and poor emotional functioning (7), and avoidant-oriented coping (8). Effective management of depressive symptoms may be especially relevant because HIV-positive persons are at increased risk for developing an affective or adjustment disorder across the disease spectrum (9). While reductions in mood disturbance have been observed following the introduction of HAART (10), the risk of developing major depressive disorder is 2 times higher in HIV-positive persons (11). Lending further support to the relevance of mood disturbance in HIV-positive persons are observations that depressive symptoms are associated with decrements in immune status, progression to acquired immunodeficiency syndrome (AIDS), and mortality (12).

Many of the psychosocial and behavioral difficulties experienced by HIV-positive persons may be addressed with stress management and behavioral interventions that improve functioning across a variety of domains (13). In particular, group-based interventions appear to be well suited for HIV-positive populations as they provide opportunities for enhanced skill acquisition and received social support (14). We have previously reported that group-based cognitive behavioral stress management (CBSM) teaches stress reduction skills, decreases depressed mood, provides social support, and is associated with increases in indicators of immune system reconstitution in a cohort of mildly symptomatic men who have sex with men (15,16). Specifically, men reported reductions in distress and increases in perceived social support during the 10-week intervention period, which appeared to explain the effect of CBSM on a measure of antiviral immunity (17,18). Other trials have observed that HIV-positive men in group-based coping effectiveness training (CET) reported lower perceived stress and burnout, as well as higher coping self-efficacy following the 10-week intervention period, when compared with an HIV informational control group (19). Over the maintenance phase, where men in both conditions received six booster sessions, CET effects on enhanced positive morale were sustained through the 12-month follow-up. It is noteworthy, however, that these trials were conducted before the availability of HAART, and hence the findings may not generalize to contemporary cohorts of HIV-positive men who have sex with men.

In the HAART era, a variety of behavioral interventions for HIV-positive persons has also been developed specifically to support medication adherence. Although psychological adjustment has not uniformly been conceptualized as a mechanism of enhanced adherence outcomes, research has supported the efficacy of pharmacist-led individualized medication adherence training (MAT) interventions and those that employ cognitive-behavioral principles based on self-efficacy theory (20). We theorized that a modified form of CBSM may offer benefits in improving mood, health behaviors, and immune status in the era of HAART. As a result, the present trial was designed to test the added value associated with providing stress management training by comparing the combination of CBSM and MAT (i.e., CBSM+MAT) to MAT alone in a cohort of HAART-treated HIV-positive men who have sex with men. We hypothesized that the CBSM+MAT intervention would decrease HIV viral load more than MAT-Only over the 15-month investigation period. Intervention-related increases in adherence were hypothesized to be one plausible mechanism of reductions in HIV viral load. Another was intervention-related decreases in depressed mood, a known predictor of HIV disease progression, which was a major focus of this study. In order to examine intervention-related reductions in depressed mood as a potential mediator of intervention effects on disease progression, we tested the effects of CBSM+MAT on HIV viral load against a MAT-Only condition and after controlling for adherence at four time points over a 15-month observation period. By examining CBSM+MAT effects after controlling for adherence training and adherence levels, we were able to determine whether there was any remaining variance in viral load reductions which could be associated with changes in depressed mood.

Methods

Procedure

Because the current trial was designed to investigate immunologic outcomes, participants were excluded if they (A) were prescribed medications with immunomodulatory effects (e.g., interferon-α, γ globulin), (B) had a history of chemotherapy or whole-body radiation treatment for cancer that was not AIDS-related, or (C) had a history of chronic illness associated with permanent changes in the immune system. Temporary exclusion criteria included antibiotic use for an acute infection within the past 2 weeks, changes in the HAART regimen or acute bodily infection during the past month, hospitalization for surgery within the past 3 months, and intravenous drug use within the previous 6 months. Additional exclusionary criteria, determined at the initial appointment, included (A) cognitive impairment; (B) inability to read at a sixth-grade level; (C) current psychosis, drug or alcohol dependence, and panic disorder; and (D) active suicidality.

During the initial visit, men between the ages of 18 and 65 who reported no changes in their HAART regimen during the past month completed an informed consent, provided morning peripheral venous blood samples, and received a physical examination from a physician.

Participants were assessed using the HIV Dementia Scale (21) and selected modules of the Structured Clinical Interview for DSM-IV (22) to determine eligibility. Eligible participants were randomized into either a 10-week CBSM + MAT intervention or a MAT-Only condition. To facilitate within group analyses, we randomized approximately 40% more of the eligible participants to CBSM + MAT. Randomization procedures were conducted by a master's-level project manager and overseen by the principal investigator. Participants' identification numbers were drawn from a box for assignment to the study conditions. Participants completed self-report measures of mood and adherence, as well as provided morning peripheral venous blood samples at baseline (i.e., month 0), during the week following the intervention period (i.e., 3 months), at 9 months postrandomization, and at 15 months postrandomization. Research personnel were blind to participants' experimental condition. At baseline, participants were provided with a medication event monitoring system (MEMS) cap and continued to meet with a licensed clinical pharmacist at 3 months and 9 months postrandomization to download these in conjunction with MAT sessions held during assessment visits. At each of the four assessment visits, men were provided with a $50 incentive for their participation, as well as $10 compensation for travel expenses ($60 total).

CBSM intervention

Participants attended 10 weekly 135-minute group sessions (90 minutes' stress management and 45 minutes' relaxation) and were instructed to practice relaxation exercises twice daily between sessions. Guided by a detailed training manual, postdoctoral fellows and advanced clinical health psychology graduate students led groups of four to nine participants. Group facilitators were supervised weekly by a licensed psychologist or board-certified psychiatrist using audiotapes to monitor intervention fidelity. Sessions included a didactic component, as well as group discussion, with opportunities provided to apply newly learned techniques. Homework was assigned to provide opportunities for participants to practice techniques and increase self-efficacy.

This modified form of CBSM focused extensively on eliciting participant experiences with adherence and medication side effects. Throughout the 10 sessions, facilitators encouraged participants to examine potentially distorted cognitions and how these may influence adherence to HAART (as well as other relevant self-care behaviors). During cognitive restructuring exercises, participants were asked to examine medication-relevant thoughts both in session and through homework exercises. Adherence was also a key target during the skills training sessions. For example, participants were encouraged to break down the larger stressor of adherence into smaller, more manageable components and then match these to a productive coping response (i.e., emotion-focused versus problem-focused). Finally, participants were also taught a variety of relaxation exercises, including progressive muscle relaxation, autogenic training, meditation, and deep breathing. Relaxation exercises were presented as an important form of emotion-focused coping that may be particularly effective in managing HAART side effects (e.g., peripheral neuropathy). Although 10 CBSM sessions were conducted, men attended a median of six CBSM group sessions. Men randomized to CBSM + MAT received a $5 incentive for their participation and $10 compensation for travel expenses ($15 total) at each of the group sessions.

MAT intervention

All participants received MAT from a licensed clinical pharmacist in a 1-hour session at baseline, as well as a half-hour maintenance sessions at 3 months and 9 months postrandomization, respectively. MAT was delivered in conjunction with regularly scheduled assessment visits. All 130 participants attended at baseline, 98 (CBSM + MAT = 64; MAT-Only = 34) attended at 3 months, and 77 (CBSM + MAT = 51; MAT-Only = 26) attended at 9 months. The MAT aims to increase information about HIV and HAART, including how the medications work, why they must be taken on time and at the proper dose, how to recognize possible side effects, and explore medication-related concerns with one's health care provider (23). Information is provided in a context that attempts to build on intrinsic motivation for change by addressing potential strategies that will support adherence to HAART. Two weeks after the posttreatment assessment, MAT-Only participants were offered a 1-day educational seminar that consisted of a condensed version of the 10-week CBSM. This was done to ensure that all men had access to information regarding stress management and relaxation training, which may be helpful in the management of HIV disease. At the 1-day seminar, men randomized to MAT-Only received a $5 incentive for their participation and a $10 compensation for travel expenses ($15 total). In total, 38 men attended the 1-day seminar.

Recruitment and retention

From 1998 to 2004, we approached 257 HIV-positive men who have sex with men via fliers at health care facilities, as well as through referrals from current participants, physicians, and HIV/AIDS service organizations (see Figure 1). After a preliminary telephone contact, 81 refused participation due to scheduling conflicts, travel requirements, and lack of interest. The 81 men who refused participation after an initial telephone contact did not significantly differ in age, education, employment status, and time since diagnosis from those who elected to participate (all $p > 0.10$). Of the 176 participants who expressed further interest, 46 were excluded for the following reasons: positive urine screen for illicit substances ($n = 12$), presence of a comorbid medical condition known to affect immune function or no current prescription for antiretroviral medications ($n = 9$), active suicidal ideation ($n = 6$), panic disorder ($n = 5$), AIDS-related dementia ($n = 4$), less than a sixth-grade reading level ($n = 3$), antisocial personality disorder ($n = 2$), active psychosis ($n = 2$), men who were not gay/bisexual or participating in another behavioral intervention trial with HIV-positive men ($n = 2$), and refused randomization ($n = 1$). Thus, we began the trial with 130 men who were randomized to CBSM + MAT ($n = 76$) and MAT-Only ($n = 54$).

Throughout the present trial, we employed a number of commonly utilized strategies to enhance retention of participants (24). At consent, study staff emphasized the long-term follow-up period for the trial and highlighted the importance of participation for helping others with HIV/AIDS. We also provided the aforementioned incentives for participation, reimbursement for travel expenses, and small tokens of our appreciation (e.g., holiday cards) to participants. At baseline, each participant provided a weekly schedule, and we made every effort to accommodate group sessions, as well as study assessment visits to match availability. A detailed log of contacts for each participant was kept in a secure location, and participant appointments were tracked with a computer-generated calendar. However, due to the fact that data collection required morning peripheral venous blood samples drawn by medical staff at our Behavioral Medicine Research Center, we were unable to schedule assessment appointments at offsite locations (e.g., a participant's home).

For the present investigation, a participant was classified as a completing follow-up if he returned at either 9 or 15 months postrandomization ($n = 78$; 60%). Of those who returned during the follow-up period, 77 provided data at 9 months and 71 at 15 months. These retention rates are comparable to those reported in a trial of CET with HIV-positive men who have

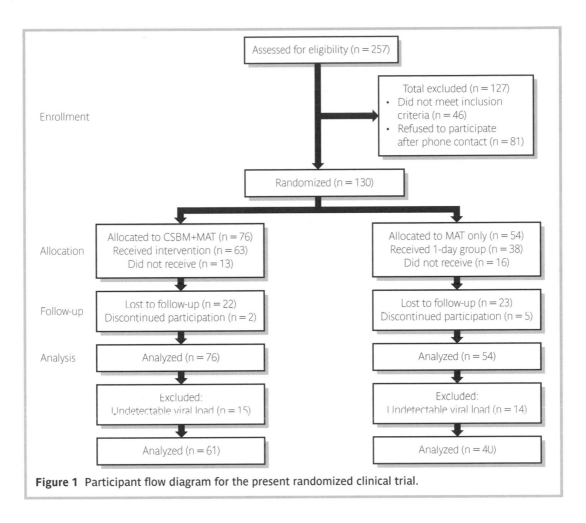

Figure 1 Participant flow diagram for the present randomized clinical trial.

sex with men (i.e., 67%) where maintenance data were collected through a 12-month follow-up (19). Interestingly in that study it appears that all participants received six booster sessions throughout the maintenance phase. This enhanced contact with the study team across the conditions may have resulted in slightly higher retention rates when compared with the present trial where men received only one half-hour MAT session at 9 months postrandomization. For those men who did not complete follow-up, staff spoke with 7 who indicated they were no longer interested in participating. In addition, staff were unable to contact 45 men via telephone or mail (CBSM + MAT = 22; MAT-Only = 23) to schedule follow-up assessments.

Control measures
Demographics
Age, ethnicity, education, income, relationship status, sexual orientation, and religion were assessed.

Health status
Lowest historical CD3+CD4+ cell counts, HIV symptoms, prescription of psychotropic medications, prescription of acyclovir, and time since HIV diagnosis were assessed during a physical examination with study physicians at baseline.

AIDS diagnosis

As per the current Centers for Disease Control and Prevention criteria, study physicians made a diagnosis of AIDS with historical or current evidence of a $CD3^+CD4^+$ count below 200 cells/mm^3 or an AIDS-related condition (25).

Medication adherence

The Adult AIDS Clinical Trial Group Adherence to Combination Therapy Guide (ACTG) was used to assess self-reported HAART adherence (26). Interviewers asked each participant to report the number of doses skipped for each day over the past 4 days. The percentage of pills missed was subtracted from 100 to calculate percent adherence.

MEMS caps contain a pressure-activated microprocessor which records the date, time, and duration of each opening. A licensed clinical pharmacist (collaborating with study physicians) selected the most potent antiretroviral in a participant's regimen to monitor using the MEMS. MEMS cap data were electronically downloaded (MEMS View version 2.61; Aprex Corporation). Percent adherence was calculated for three periods: (1) between baseline and 3 months; (2) 90 days following the 3-month assessment; and (3) from 90 days after the 3-month assessment through 9 months postrandomization. We also calculated percent adherence with the MEMS over the 4 days before each assessment (3 months and 9 months postrandomization) to examine data comparable to that obtained using the ACTG.

Depressed mood and anxiety

The Profile of Mood States (POMS), a 65-item scale, assesses six different mood states during the past week using a variety of adjectives that participants were asked to rate using a 5-point Likert-type scale: 0 = not at all to 4 = extremely. The POMS has internal consistencies close to or greater than 0.90, as well as high external validity (27). We selected the POMS to measure depressed mood and anxiety because these subscales are not confounded with HIV symptoms. Both the depressed mood and anxiety subscales displayed adequate internal consistency in this sample (Cronbach's α = 0.94 and 0.78, respectively).

The Beck Depression Inventory (BDI), a 21-item scale, assesses somatic, affective, behavioral, and cognitive dimensions of dysphoria during the past 2 weeks (28). The BDI is reliable and has shown good concurrent validity with the Hamilton Rating Scale for Depression (0.73 to 0.80 for nonpsychiatric patients). The internal consistency of the BDI for the present investigation was adequate (Cronbach's α = 0.90). In addition, we examined selected symptoms measured by the BDI as a means of cross-validating any observed effects of CBSM + MAT on depressed mood as measured by the POMS. Specifically, we selected BDI items assessing sadness, hopelessness, dissatisfaction, and guilt because these most closely reflected in the adjectives used in the POMS-depressed mood subscale. When summed, these items displayed adequate internal consistency (Cronbach's α = 0.72) and were examined as a modified BDI-Affective composite score (range = 0–12). This score was viewed as less likely than the total BDI score to be confounded by physical disease status because it was free of somatic symptoms.

HIV disease status
CD3$^+$ CD4$^+$ T-lymphocyte counts

Morning peripheral blood samples were collected from all subjects in ethylenediaminetetraacetic acid (EDTA) tubes (Vacutainer-EDTA, Becton-Dickinson, Rutherford, NJ).

CD3$^+$CD4$^+$ lymphocyte count was determined by whole blood four-color direct immunofluorescence using a Coulter XL and flow cytometer (29).

HIV viral load

HIV-1 viral load was determined on EDTA plasma using an in vitro reverse transcriptase polymerase chain reaction assay (AMPLICOR, Roche Laboratories, US #83088). This ultrasensitive assay has a lower limit of 50 copies/ml.

Statistical analyses

Analyzing repeated measures in randomized clinical trials can present challenges due to the increased likelihood of having missing data at distal follow-up points. A major concern with using split-plot, repeated-measures ANOVA to analyze effects of interventions is that because it requires listwise deletion of cases, this methodology yields potentially biased parameter estimates due to attrition over time. The mixed-model methodology provides a valid test of the intent-to-treat hypothesis because it does not require listwise deletion and as a result is able to use all available data at each assessment time (30). This methodology can also account for unequal time intervals, makes less stringent assumptions regarding within-subject correlation patterns and enables one to utilize parameter estimates of change per 1-month increase in time to predict dependent variable values. Predicted values are a function of unstandardized parameter estimates based on the likelihood of obtaining the observed data. In preliminary, mixed-model analyses for this study, fixed effects were time (either 0, 3, 9, and 15 months or just 0 and 3 months), group (CBSM + MAT versus MAT), and the interaction of group–time. Where we observed CBSM + MAT effects on depressed mood or adherence in preliminary mixed-model analyses, these were to be examined as potential mediators of treatment effects on HIV viral load using the MPlus statistical package for structural equation modeling (31). We specified a latent growth curve model with the trajectory of change in HIV viral load over time (i.e., slope) and HIV viral load at 15 months (i.e., intercept) as two latent variables, both of which are required for model identification. The 15-month values for HIV viral load were specified as the intercept for this model by employing accepted modifications to the time structure (i.e., −15, −12, −6, 0). Thus, we could examine the mechanisms of change in HIV viral load and outcomes at 15 months. This flexible, innovative statistical methodology has been reviewed in depth elsewhere (32).

Results
Preliminary analyses

We observed no baseline differences between the CBSM + MAT and MAT-Only conditions in demographics, health status variables, AIDS diagnosis, adherence, depressed mood, and HIV viral load (all p values > 0.10). Results of Pearson X^2 and independent samples t-tests indicated that completers did not differ significantly from noncompleters in age, ethnicity, religion, education, income, sexual orientation, time since diagnosis, lowest historical CD3$^+$CD4$^+$ T cell counts, and number of HIV-related symptoms at baseline (all p values > 0.10). The CBSM + MAT condition was implemented in 12 separate cohorts of participants. Cohort status (i.e., 1–12) was unrelated to changes in HIV viral load, measures of mood, and adherence across the 15-month investigation (all p values > 0.20).

Using structural equation modeling, we examined the association between the 2 measures of adherence (i.e., ACTG and MEMS) and HIV viral load separately. We specified a latent variable of MEMS using the three available indicators measured over the investigation period and examined its association with a latent variable of HIV viral load (which was composed of four indicators over the 15-month investigation period). We determined that this model was a good fit for the data (x^2 [13] = 15.289, p = 0.29; CFI = 0.99; RMSEA = 0.037). Results indicated that the latent variable of MEMS was not significantly related to the latent variable of HIV viral load (β = −0.052, t = −1.10, p values > 0.05). Next, we specified a latent variable for the ACTG (composed of four indicators over the 15-month period) and examined its association with the latent variable of HIV viral load. We determined that this model was an adequate fit for the data (X^2 [18] = 24.10, p = 0.15; CFI = 0.97; RMSEA = 0.051). In contrast to MEMS data, the latent variable of ACTG was significantly related to the latent variable of HIV viral load (β = −1.558, t = −3.18, p < 0.01). Thus, self-reported adherence (i.e., ACTG) appeared to be the most valid method of assessment in this sample of HIV-positive men who have sex with men.[1]

HIV viral load and CD3⁺ CD4⁺ T-cell counts

After controlling for adherence, we examined intervention effects for HIV viral load and $CD3^+$ $CD4^+$T-cell counts across the 15-month investigation period and found no differences between conditions (p > 0.10). Next, we conducted a secondary analysis by excluding 29 men with undetectable viral load at baseline. It is plausible that we were unable to detect potential intervention-related reductions in HIV viral load due to floor effects in those men who already presented with undetectable levels at baseline.

CBSM + MAT effects in men with a detectable HIV viral load

A majority of the 101 participants with a detectable HIV viral load at baseline were non-Hispanic white (52%), but a sizeable minority were African American (21%) and Hispanic (20%). A majority of the sample (84%) indicated they were predominantly or exclusively homosexual in orientation. Most participants were single (65%) and reported being raised with Christian religious traditions (59%). Mean age was 41.6 (SD = 8.3) years, and the sample was largely well educated, with 75% of participants having completed at least some college. The majority of participants (70%) reported that they were not working at study entry. The modal income was $5,000 to $20,000 per year. The average time since HIV diagnosis was 7.8 (SD = 5.1) years, and participants reported an average of 6 (range = 0 to 12) HIV symptoms. The majority of participants (54%) were diagnosed with AIDS at baseline. The mean baseline $CD3^+CD4^+$ T cell count was 422 (SD = 240) cells/mm³, and we observed a mean viral load of 17,047 (SD = 33,938) copies/ml at baseline. We observed no baseline differences between the CBSM + MAT and MAT-Only conditions in demographics, health status variables, AIDS diagnosis, adherence, depressed mood, or HIV viral load (all p values > 0.10).

Among this subsample of 101 men, completers did not differ significantly from noncompleters in ethnicity, religion, education, employment status, income, sexual orientation, time since diagnosis, psychotropic medications, AIDS category C status, number of HIV-related symptoms, lowest historical $CD3^+CD4^+$ T-cell counts, $CD3^+CD4^+$ T-cell counts, and HIV viral load (all p values > 0.10). Completers (M = 43.8, SD = 9.3 years) were significantly older than noncompleters (M = 38.4, SD = 8.3 years; p < 0.01). Consistent with previous findings (8),

---

1 A similar pattern of results was obtained when medications skipped using the MEMS during the past 4 days was utilized as a predictor of adherence. Self-reported adherence (ACTG) continued to be a superior predictor of HIV viral load. We also determined that the MEMS and ACTG were not significantly correlated at any point during the investigation period (all p values > 0.10).

younger age was associated with decreased adherence at baseline ($r=0.30$, $p<0.01$) but was unrelated to HIV viral load, $CD3^+CD4^+$ counts, or depressed mood (all p values >0.10).

HIV viral load and CD3⁺ CD4⁺ T-cell counts

For the 101 men with detectable plasma HIV levels at baseline, we observed a significant group × time interaction for HIV viral load across the investigation period after controlling for HIV medication adherence ($\beta=-0.056$, $t(131)=-2.10$, $p<0.05$). Men in CBSM displayed significant reductions in HIV viral load through the 15 months ($\beta=-0.037$, $t(131)=-2.40$, $p<0.05$), whereas controls displayed no change ($\beta=0.02$, $t(131)=0.87$, $p>0.30$).[2] Men in CBSM+MAT displayed a 0.037 $\log_{10}$ reduction in HIV viral load per month, yielding a 0.56 $\log_{10}$ reduction in HIV viral load (i.e., more than a three-fold decrease) over the investigation period (see Figure 2). In fact, a 0.50 $\log_{10}$ decrease in HIV viral load has been identified as the minimum criterion for determining the short-term effectiveness of a HAART regimen (33). Descriptive statistics for observed, untransformed HIV viral load are summarized in Table 1. It is noteworthy that in contrast to those assigned to MAT-only, men in CBSM+MAT achieved median viral loads that were below the detectable range of our assays at 15 months. Within the CBSM+MAT condition, attending more group sessions was associated with greater reductions in HIV viral load, $\beta=-0.004$, $t(100)=-2.48$, $p<0.05$. At the same time, however, we found no intervention-related changes in $CD3^+CD4^+$ T-cell counts over the 15 months ($p>0.50$).

Medication adherence

Among men with detectable viral load at study entry, the experimental conditions did not differ significantly in participant-reported medication adherence throughout the 15-month investiga-

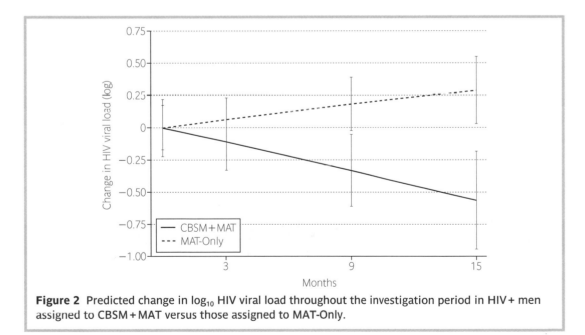

Figure 2 Predicted change in $\log_{10}$ HIV viral load throughout the investigation period in HIV+ men assigned to CBSM+MAT versus those assigned to MAT-Only.

2   This was similar to the pattern of results observed when analyses of CBSM+MAT effects on HIV viral load were restricted to study completers. We observed a marginally significant group × time interaction ($p=0.080$) and a marginally significant reduction in the CBSM+MAT group ($p=0.088$).

Table 1 Observed untransformed measures of central tendency for HIV viral load and CD3+ CD4+ cell counts

Group	Month	HIV viral load					CD3⁺CD4⁺
		Mean	SE	Median	Mean	SE	Median
CBSM + MAT (n=61)	0	13,224	3,088	365	392	28	405
	3	12,894	3,503	66	435	38	402
	9	5,438	3,017	54	437	51	388
	15	5,632	3,054	<50ᵃ	450	49	421
MAT-Only (n=40)	0	22,982	7,339	215	386	42	340
	3	12,818	5,879	313	398	55	348
	9	30,096	14,102	494	413	47	416
	15	31,956	16,218	2,108	439	69	449

ᵃ Median HIV viral load value is less than the detectable range for the assay.

tion period, even after controlling for age ($p > 0.50$). Each group reported nonsignificant increases in adherence over time (CBSM + MAT reported 91% at baseline, 93% at 15 months; MAT-Only reported 89% at baseline, 94% at 15 months). Approximately 70% of men reported levels of adherence that met or exceeded 95% of those medication doses prescribed. No differences between the experimental conditions were observed throughout the investigation period for the number of participants reporting greater than or equal to 95% adherence (all p values > 0.10). Observed values for measures of medication adherence across the 15-month investigation period are reported in Table 2.

Depressed mood

For the POMS-Depression subscale, we observed a significant group × time interaction over the 10-week intervention period ($\beta = -2.30$, $t(64) = -3.20$, $p < 0.01$), but no concurrent effects on anxiety ($\beta = -0.05$, $t(62) = -0.11$, $p > 0.90$). Men in CBSM reported significant reductions in depressed mood ($\beta = -1.21$, $t(64) = -2.83$, $p \leq 0.01$) from a predicted mean of 14.8 (SE = 1.4) at baseline to a predicted mean of 11.2 (SE = 1.6) immediately following the 10-week intervention. Controls reported marginally significant increases ($\beta = 1.10$, $t(64) = 1.90$, $p = 0.06$) from a predicted mean of 10.7 (SE = 1.8) at baseline to a predicted mean of 14.0 (SE = 2.1) immediately following the 10-week intervention period. Intervention-related reductions in depressed mood were not maintained through 15 months postrandomization ($\beta = -0.36$, $t(149) = -1.34$, $p \geq 0.10$). Observed values for POMS measures across the 15-month investigation period are reported in Table 2.

Table 2 Observed means for measures of mood and adherence over the 15-month investigation period

Group	Month	M (SD)					
		POMS-D	POMS-Anx	BDI	BDI-Mood	Hopelessness	ACTG
CBSM + MAT (n=61)	0	14.6 (12.3)	11.0 (5.8)	11.6 (8.0)	1.9 (1.9)	0.4 (0.6)	90.1 (20.2)
	3	11.6 (11.1)	10.4 (5.8)	8.8 (7.5)	1.4 (1.5)	0.2 (0.5)	92.0 (20.9)
	9	11.3 (12.4)	10.8 (8.0)	9.2 (7.2)	1.2 (1.6)	0.3 (0.6)	96.4 (9.8)
	15	13.1 (13.6)	11.9 (7.0)	10.8 (9.2)	1.8 (2.1)	0.4 (0.7)	92.3 (20.1)
MAT-Only (n=40)	0	10.7 (9.4)	10.0 (4.6)	12.4 (9.2)	1.6 (1.8)	0.3 (0.6)	90.0 (24.3)
	3	13.6 (11.5)	8.9 (4.9)	10.8 (8.6)	1.5 (1.7)	0.4 (0.8)	92.2 (19.8)
	9	10.4 (10.0)	8.6 (5.3)	12.6 (10.5)	2.4 (3.1)	0.5 (0.9)	92.8 (14.5)
	15	17.4 (16.6)	11.7 (7.2)	14.7 (11.1)	2.5 (2.8)	0.7 (1.1)	95.3 (9.6)

We observed no intervention-related changes in BDI scores ($\beta = -0.48$, $t(65) = -0.98$, $p > 0.30$) during the 10-week training period. We did note, however, that as a group, only men in CBSM + MAT reported mean BDI values at 10 weeks that were below the clinically significant level (i.e., BDI < 10). Next, we examined the modified BDI-affective composite score (composed of sadness, hopeless, dissatisfaction, and guilt) to cross-validate observed intervention effects on depressed mood. We observed a nearly significant group × time interaction ($\beta = -0.20$, $t(64) = -1.95$, $p = 0.056$) over the 10-week intervention period. Men in CBSM + MAT reported significant reductions in these depressive symptoms ($\beta = -0.16$, $t(64) = -2.65$, $p = 0.01$), while those in MAT-Only reported no changes ($\beta = 0.04$, $t(64) = 00.51$, $p > 0.10$). Interestingly, it appears that the symptom showing the greatest group × time change during the 10 weeks was hopelessness ($\beta = -0.11$, $t(65) = -2.27$, $p < 0.05$). Men in CBSM + MAT reported significant reductions in hopelessness ($\beta = -0.07$, $t(65) = -2.54$, $p = 0.013$), while those in MAT-Only reported no changes ($\beta = 0.04$, $t(65) = 0.96$, $p > .10$). Observed values for these mood measures across the 15-month investigation period are reported in Table 2.

Structural equation modeling was used to determine if changes in depressed mood during the intervention period could explain decreases in viral load over and above the influence of medication adherence. Because we did not observe intervention-related effects on medication adherence, we were unable to examine this as a potential comediator. However, bearing in mind the potent effects of even mild fluctuations in adherence on HIV viral replication, we included this as an important covariate in the model. The final model (see Figure 3) fit adequately (X^2 [38] = 47.41, $p = 0.14$; CFI = 0.94; RMSEA = 0.050), and men in CBSM + MAT reported significant reductions in POMS-Depression over the 10-weeks ($\beta = -7.44$, $t = -3.48$, $p < 0.01$), which were in turn associated with decreases in HIV viral load over the 15 month investigation ($\beta = -0.002$, $t = 2.50$, $p < 0.05$). For each 1-point reduction in POMS-Depression during the 10-week intervention period, we observed a drop of 0.03 $\log_{10}$ viral load units over the 15 months. Because men in CBSM + MAT experienced a 3.6-point decrease in depressed mood on average, reductions in depressed mood may account for an average decrease of 0.11 $\log_{10}$ viral load units. After setting the previously significant path from group membership to the slope of HIV viral load at zero, the decrement in model fit was nonsignificant (ΔX^2 [1] = 0.46, $p > 0.10$), consistent with the hypothesis that intervention-related reductions in depressed mood explained the effect of CBSM + MAT on HIV viral load over the 15-month period. Interestingly, the latent variable of adherence was unrelated to change in HIV viral load over the investigation ($p > 0.10$) but was significantly related to HIV viral load at 15 months postrandomization ($\beta = -1.13$, $t = -2.61$, $p < 0.05$). Thus, the maintenance of stable medication adherence was important, and this was evident across study conditions. The reduction in depressed mood during CBSM + MAT, however, contributed to further decrements in viral load above and beyond sustained adherence over time.

Discussion

In the era of HAART, HIV-positive persons are under a great deal of burden to manage a challenging medication regimen and are at a markedly elevated risk for depressive conditions when compared with their HIV-negative peers (11). The relevance of interventions designed to assist individuals with managing depressed mood is further supported by findings which indicate that depressive symptoms are associated with faster disease progression: $CD3^+CD4^+$ T-cell-count decline, higher viral load, progression to AIDS, and mortality (12). The current investigation provides the first evidence that a behavioral intervention enhances the effectiveness of HAART

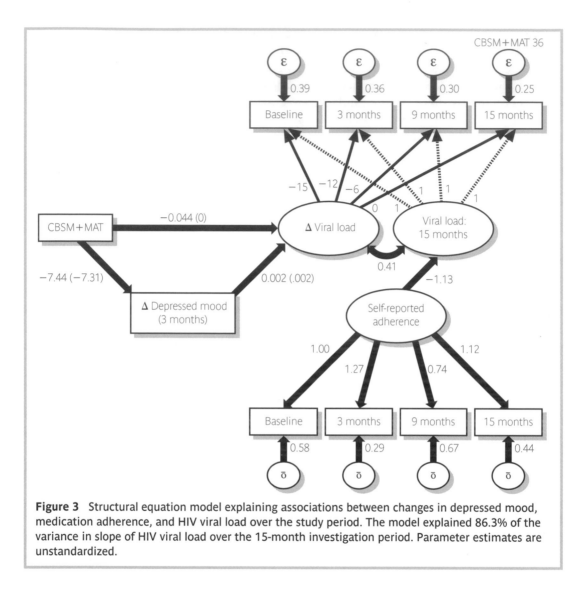

Figure 3 Structural equation model explaining associations between changes in depressed mood, medication adherence, and HIV viral load over the study period. The model explained 86.3% of the variance in slope of HIV viral load over the 15-month investigation period. Parameter estimates are unstandardized.

on HIV viral load suppression via reductions in depressed mood in HIV-positive men who have sex with men. Although we did not observe concurrent intervention-related increases in CD3⁺ CD4⁺ cell counts, the effects of HAART on specific elements of immune repertoire reconstitution are influenced by a variety of factors (5). Future investigations should examine the efficacy of CBSM+MAT with respect to relevant CD3⁺ CD4⁺ T-cell subsets, being that reductions in depressed mood during a similar intervention predated increases in transitional naïve T cells over time in HIV-positive men treated in the pre-HAART era (34).

Just how reductions in depressed mood influence HIV viral load remains unclear. The association between depressed mood and viral load seemed to be independent of changes in medication adherence, due in large part to the relatively high levels of antiretroviral medication adherence (approximately 90%) reported by all participants throughout investigation period. It is also noteworthy that we determined that self-reported adherence (i.e., ACTG) as compared with electronic monitored adherence was a superior predictor of HIV viral load in this cohort of men who have sex with men. These data highlight, as other investigators have noted, that each measure of adherence possesses relative strengths and limitations (26,35). Anecdotally, men in the present study reported difficulties using the MEMS caps because medication bottles provided by the study were perceived as bulky, made it clear to others that participants were taking medications, and did not easily fit into their medication routines. It should also be noted that the MEMS caps were only used on a single medication in a multimedication regimen, thus explaining in part the lack of association between the two adherence indicators in the present study. It may be that the validity of specific adherence measures varies as a function of the medication regimen, as well as the population being examined. Future investigations should seek to examine the differential validity of MEMS and ACTG in single-dose antiretroviral regimens (e.g., Trizivir) among diverse cohorts of HIV-positive persons.

The relationship between decreases in depressed mood and slower HIV disease progression may be explained, in part, by alterations in hypothalamic-pituitary-adrenal axis functioning. In fact, reductions in cortisol have been shown to accompany depression (36) and to covary with reductions in depressed mood during a similar intervention in HIV-positive men (37). A burgeoning literature has also demonstrated that cortisol may influence immune status and health outcomes in HIV-positive persons. Elevated serum cortisol has previously been associated with faster progression to AIDS, increased likelihood of developing an AIDS-related condition, and increased mortality over a 9-year period (38). Furthermore, lower 15-hour urinary-free cortisol levels have been related to long-term survival with AIDS (39). Other in vitro data indicate that cortisol decreases maturational selection of $CD3^+CD4^+$ T cells in lymphoid organs (40), synergizes with HIV capsid glycoprotein-120 to enhance rates of cell decline (41), facilitates HIV infection of $CD3^+CD4^+$ T cells (42), and is associated with high rates of apoptosis in $CD3^+$ $CD4^+$ T cells and accessory cells in the lymphoid tissue (43). Thus, neuroendocrine-induced impairments in cellular-immune control of HIV infection are another plausible pathway for explaining the effects of depressed mood reductions on HIV viral load.

A major limitation of the present study was the lack of complete follow-up data on many participants. We determined that there were no evident, systematic biases related to whether participants provided follow-up data, but the possibility remains that some unexamined variable differentially influenced follow-up. We were able to partially address this concern by utilizing a mixed-model methodology in which all available data were included in intent-to-treat analyses. However, the relatively low proportion of men returning for follow-up across trials highlights the need for innovative methods to enhance follow-up in behavioral interventions with HIV-positive persons (24). An additional limitation is that intervention-related effects were observed only in a subsample of men with detectable viral load at study entry. Although it is likely that HIV replication continues in men with an undetectable viral load (particularly in latent reservoirs such as the testes), the sensitivity of current immunologic measures may not allow for adequate detection of fluctuations in low-range viral load values for these participants. Consequently, it may be unrealistic to expect behavioral interventions to produce meaningful viral activity changes in the subgroup of HIV + men with an undetectable viral load. Practically, these individuals may not require as intensive of an intervention in order to maintain optimal viral load levels; they appeared to fare well with MAT only.

Because of the difference in contact time between the two study conditions, we cannot ascertain whether group differences in outcomes are attributable to the inclusion of stress management techniques or differential attention and/or social support; this should be explored in future work. Although we were unable to account for group differences in viral load changes as a function of medication adherence, there remains the possibility that these groups differed in other health behaviors such as substance use and unprotected sexual behaviors, which could affect viral load. This is supported, in part, by the results of previous investigations which have determined that increased cocaine use mediated the association between baseline depression and increases in HIV viral load over a 2-year period (44).

Overall, the finding that a 10-week CBSM + MAT intervention can reduce HIV viral load in men with detectable viral loads by more than 0.5 $\log_{10}$ units is clinically interesting. In order to replicate these preliminary findings, there is a need for a multisite trial to examine the efficacy CBSM + MAT in a large sample of HIV-positive men who have sex with men, who present with a detectable viral load. Future trials should also incorporate a no-treatment control group to determine if MAT alone is efficacious. Studying a cohort of HIV-positive persons with a history of nonadherence may be helpful in order to examine the efficacy of both CBSM + MAT and MAT-Only in the most vulnerable clinical population. Other relevant HIV-positive populations for similar efficacy trials include women, those with clinical depression, and those with a history of substance dependence. The initiation of HAART in more recently diagnosed populations may be a crucial window of opportunity to begin behavioral interventions, at a point before drug resistance develops and when behavior patterns may be amenable to change.

References

1 Mannheimer SB, Matts J, Telzak E, Chesney M, Child C, Wu AW, Friedland G. Quality of life in HIV-infected individuals receiving antiretroviral therapy is related to adherence. AIDS Care 2005;17:10–22.

2 Centers for Disease Control. Update: trends in AIDS incidence, deaths, and prevalence: United States, 1996. Morb Mortal Wkly Rep 1997;46:165–74.

3 Bangsberg DR, Perry S, Charlebois ED, Clark RA, Robertson M, Zolopa AR, Moss A. Non-adherence to highly active antiretroviral therapy predicts progression to AIDS. AIDS 2000;15:1181–3.

4 Tamalet C, Fantini J, Tourres C, Yashi N. Resistance of HIV-1 to multiple antiretroviral drugs in France: a 6-year survey (1997–2002) based on an analysis of over 7000 genotypes. AIDS 2003;17:2383–8.

5 Yeni PG, Hammer SM, Carpenter CCJ, Cooper DA, Fischl, MA, Gatell JM, et al. Antiretroviral treatment for adult HIV-infection in 2002. JAMA 2002;288:137–42.

6 Gordillo V, del Amo J, Soriano V, Gonzalez-Lahoz J. Sociodemographic and psychological variables influencing adherence to antiretroviral therapy. AIDS 1999;13:1763–9.

7 Catz SL, Kelly JA, Bogart LM, Benotsch EG, McAuliffe TL. Patterns, correlates, and barriers to medication adherence among persons prescribed new treatments for HIV disease. Health Psychol 2003;19:124–33.

8 Weaver KE, Llabre MM, Durán RE, Antoni MH, Ironson G, Penedo FJ, Schneiderman N. A stress and coping model of medication adherence and viral load in HIV + men and women on highly active antiretroviral therapy (HAART). Health Psychol 2005;24:385–92.

9 Bing EG, Burnam MA, Longshore D, Fleishman JA, Sherbourne CD, London AS, Turner BJ, Eggan F, Beckman R, Vitiello B, Morton SC, Orlando M, Bozzette SA, Ortiz-Barron L, Shapiro M. Psychiatric disorders and drug use among human immunodeficiency virus-infected adults in the United States. Arch Gen Psychiatry 2001;58:721–8.

10 Rabkin JG, Ferrando SJ, Lin SH, Sewell M, McElhiney M. Psychological effects of HAART: a 2-year study. Psychosom Med 2000;62:413–22.

11 Cielsa JA, Roberts JE. Meta-analysis of the relationship between HIV infection and the risk for depressive disorders. Am J Psychiatry 2001;158:725–30.

12 Leserman J. HIV disease progression: depression, stress, and possible mechanisms. Biol Psychiatry 2003;54:295–306.

13 Antoni MH. Stress management and psychoneuroimmunology in HIV infection. CNS Spectr 2003;8:40–51.

14 Bower JE, Kemeny ME, Fawzy FI. Group interventions for individuals with serious medical illness. In: Chesney MA, Antoni MH, eds. Innovative Approaches to Health Psychology: Prevention and Treatment Lessons from AIDS. Washington, DC: American Psychological Association; 2002.

15 Antoni MH, Cruess DG, Klimas N, Maher K, Cruess S, Kumar M, Lutgendorf S, Ironson G, Schneiderman N, Fletcher MA. Stress management and immune system reconstitution in symptomatic HIV-infected gay men over time: effects on transitional naïve T-cells (CD4$^+$CD45RA$^+$CD29$^+$). Am J Psychiatry 2002;159:143–5.

16 Lutgendorf S, Antoni M, Ironson G, Starr K, Costello N, Zuckerman M, Klimas N, Fletcher MA, Schneiderman N. Changes in cognitive coping skills and social support during cognitive behavioral stress management intervention and distress outcomes in symptomatic HIV-seropositive gay men. Psychosom Med 1998;60:204–14.

17 Cruess S, Antoni M, Cruess D, Fletcher MA, Ironson G, Kumar M, Lutgendorf S, Hayes A, Klimas N, Schneiderman N. Reduction in herpes simplex virus type 2 antibody titers after cognitive behavioral stress management and relationships with neuroendocrine function, relaxation skills, and social support in HIV-positive gay men. Psychosom Med 2000;62:828–37.

18 Lutgendorf SK, Antoni MH, Ironson G, Klimas N, Kumar M, Starr K, McCabe P, Cleven K, Fletcher MA, Schneiderman N. Cognitive behavioral stress management intervention decreases dysphoria and herpes simplex virus-type 2 titers in symptomatic HIV-seropositive gay men. J Consult Clin Psychol 1997;65:23–31.

19 Chesney MA, Chambers DB, Taylor JM, Johnson LM, Folkman S. Coping effectiveness training for men living with HIV: results from a randomized clinical trial testing a group-based intervention. Psychosom Med 2003;65:1038–46.

20 Simoni JM, Frick PA, Pantalone DW, Turner BJ. Antiretroviral adherence interventions: a review of current literature and ongoing studies. Top HIV Med 2003;11:185–97.

21 Power C, Selnes O, Grim J, McArthur J. HIV Dementia Scale: a rapid screening test. J AIDS Hum Retrovirus 1995;8:273–8.

22 First MB, Spitzer RL, Gibbon M, Williams JBW. Structured Clinical Interview for DSM-IV Axis I Disorders (SCID-I). Washington, DC: American Psychiatric Press; 1997.

23 McPherson-Baker S, Jones D, Duran RE, Klimas N, Schneiderman N. Development and implementation of a medication adherence training instrument for persons living with HIV: the MATI. Behav Modif 2004;29:286–317.

24 Coday M, Boutin-Foster C, Sher TG, Tennant J, Greaney ML, Saunders SD, Somes GW. Strategies for retaining study participants in behavioral intervention trials: retention experiences of the NIH Behavior Change Consortium. Ann Behav Med 2005; special supplement:55–65.

25 Centers for Disease Control and Prevention. 1993 Revised classification system for HIV infection and expanded surveillance case definition for AIDS among adolescents and adults. MMWR Morb Mortal Wkly Rep 1992;41:RR-171–19.

26 Chesney MA, Ickovics JR, Chambers DB, Gifford AL. Self-reported adherence to antiretroviral medications among participants in HIV clinical trials: the AACTG adherence instruments. AIDS Care 2000;12:255–66.

27 McNair DM, Lorr M, Droppleman LF. EITS Manual for the Profile of Mood States. San Diego: Educational and Industrial Testing Service; 1971.

28 Beck AI, Ward CH, Mendelson M, Mock J, Erbaugh E. An inventory for measuring depression. Arch Gen Psychiatry 1961;47:720–5.

29 Fletcher MA, Maher K, Patarca R, Klimas N. Comparative analysis of lymphocytes in lymph nodes and peripheral blood of patients with chronic fatigue syndrome. J Chronic Fatigue Syndr 2000;7:65–75.

30 Littell RC, Henry PR, Ammerman CB. Statistical analysis of repeated measures data using SAS procedures. J Anim Sci 1998;76:1216–31.

31 Muthen LK, Muthen BO. Mplus: Statistical Analysis with Latent Variables. Los Angeles, CA: Muthen & Muthen; 1998.

32 Llabre MM, Spitzer S, Siegel S, Saab PG, Schneiderman N. Applying latent growth curve modeling to the investigation of individual differences in cardiovascular recovery from stress. Psychosom Med 2004;66:29–41.

33 Dybul M, Fauci AS, Bartlett JG, Kaplan JE, Pau AK. Guidelines for using antiretroviral agents among HIV-infected adults and adolescents. Ann Intern Med 2002;137:381–433.

34 Antoni MH, Cruess D, Klimas N, Carrico AW, Maher K, Cruess S, Lechner SC, Kumar M, Lutgendorf S, Ironson G, Fletcher MA, Schneiderman N. Increases in a marker of immune system reconstitution are predated by decreases in 24-hour urinary cortisol output and depressed mood during a 10-week stress management intervention in symptomatic gay men. J Psychosom Res 2005;58:3–13.

35 Samet JH, Sullivan LM, Traphagen ET, Ickovics JR. Measuring adherence among HIV-infected persons: is MEMS consummate technology? AIDS Behav 2001;5:21–30.

36 Gorman JM, Kertzner R, Cooper T, Goetz RR, Lagomasino I, Novacenko H, Williams JBW, Stern Y, Mayeux R, Ehrhardt EA. Glucocorticoid level and neuropsychiatric symptoms in homosexual men with HIV infection. Am J Psychiatry 1991;148:41–5.

37 Antoni MH, Cruess S, Cruess DG, Kumar M, Lutgendorf S, Ironson G, Dettmer E, Williams J, Klimas N, Fletcher MA, Schneiderman N. Cognitive behavioral stress management reduces distress and 24-hour urinary free cortisol among symptomatic HIV-infected gay men. Ann Behav Med 2000;22:29–37.

38 Leserman J, Petitto JM, Gu H, Gaynes BM, Barroso J, Golden RN, Perkins DO, Folds JD, Evans DL. Progression to AIDS, a clinical AIDS condition, and mortality: psychological and physiological predictors. Psychol Med 2002;32:1059–73.

39 Ironson G, Solomon GF, Balbin EG, O'Cleirigh CO, George A, Kumar M, Kumar M, Larson D, Woods TE. The Ironson-Woods Spirituality/Religiousness Index is associated with long survival, health behaviors, less distress, and low cortisol in people with HIV/AIDS. Ann Behav Med. 2002;24:34–48.

40 Norbiato G, Bevilacqua M, Vago T, Taddei A, Clerici M. Glucocorticoids and immune function in human immunodeficiency virus infection: a study of hypercortisolemic and cortisol-resistant patients. J Clin Endocrinol Metabol 1997;82:3260–3.

41 Nair MPN, Mahajan S, Hou J, Sweet AM, Schwartz SA. The stress hormone, cortisol synergizes with HIV-1 gp-120 to induce apoptosis of normal human peripheral mononuclear cells. Cell Mol Biol 2000;46:1227–38.

42 Markham PD, Salahuddin SZ, Veren K. Hydrocortisone and some other hormones enhance the expression of HTLV-III. Int J Cancer 1986;37:67–72.

43 Gougeon ML. Programmed cell death in HIV infection: dysregulation of the BCL-2 and FAS pathways and contribution to AIDS pathogenesis. Psychoneuroendocrinology 1997;22:S33–9.

44 O'Cleirigh C, Ironson G, Fletcher MA, Balbin E, Schneiderman N. An examination of drug/alcohol use as a mechanism relating depression to HIV disease progression (CD4 and HIV-1 viral load) over 2 years in a diverse HIV + sample. Psychosom Med. 2005;67:A–18.

Ogden, J., Clementi, C. and Aylwin, S. (2006) The impact of obesity surgery and the paradox of control: a qualitative study, *Psychology and Health*, 21 (2): 273–93.

The impact of obesity surgery and the paradox of control

A qualitative study

Jane Ogden[1], Cecilia Clementi[1], & Simon Aylwin[2]

[1]*Kings College London, Kings College Hospital, Denmark Hill, London, UK*
[2]*Department of General Practice, 5 Lambeth Walk, London, UK*

Abstract

In light of the failure of psychological approaches to obesity some clinicians and patients are turning to surgery. The present qualitative study aimed to explore patients' experiences of having obesity surgery and in-depth interviews were carried out with 15 men and women, who had had surgery in the past four years. The data were analysed using Interpretative Phenomenological Analysis (IPA). The patients described their experiences in terms of four broad themes: personal weight histories; the decision-making process, which involved general motivations such as worries about health and specific triggers such as symptoms; the impact of surgery on eating behaviour and their relationship with food; the impact of weight loss on health status, self-esteem and relationships with others. The central theme of control permeated all areas of the interviews. The current clinical climate highlights the importance of self-control and patient choice as the path to patient empowerment. Obesity surgery illustrates that in contrast to this perspective, imposed control and limited choice can sometimes paradoxically result in a renewed sense of control.

Keywords: Obesity, surgery, control, patient experiences

Introduction

Most obese patients are managed through behavioural interventions, which include dietary advice and information, behavioural skills training, relapse prevention and self-monitoring. Some individual studies show that such an approach can produce good initial weight loss and some degree of weight maintenance (e.g., Perri et al., 2001). A broader analysis of the effectiveness of multidimensional treatment approaches suggests that average weight loss during the treatment programme is 0.5 kg per week and that ≈60–70% of the weight loss is maintained during the first year (Brownell and Wadden, 1992). At three- and five-year follow ups, however,

Correspondence: Jane Ogden, Professor in Health Psychology, Department of Psychology, University of Surrey, Guildford, GU2 7XH, UK. Tel.: 01483 300800. E-mail: J.Ogden@surrey, ac.uk the data tend to show weight regain back to baseline weight (Brownell & Wadden, 1992; Wadden, 1993; Wilson, 1995). In real terms between 90 and 95% of those who lose weight regain it within several years (Garner & Wooley, 1991; NHS Centre for Reviews and Dissemination, 1997). Furthermore, some research also suggests that not only may behavioural interventions fail to produce sustained weight loss they may also exacerbate problems with eating control and result in weight cycling and overeating (e.g., Garner & Wooley, 1991; Herman & Polivy, 1984; Lissner & Brownell, 1992; Ogden, 2003). In light of the general failure of behavioural interventions, some clinicians have turned to surgery, which is reserved for the morbidly obese and is offered when all other attempts at weight loss have repeatedly failed. Although there are 21 different surgical procedures for obesity (Kral, 1995), the two most popular are the gastric bypass and laparoscopic gastric banding (e.g., Kral, 1995; Mason, 1987). Both these procedures provide a physical limitation to the amount the patient can eat and therefore reduce the need for the patient to voluntarily restrict their own eating behaviour. In addition, the gastric bypass may reduce food absorption after ingestion and can lead to an unpleasant flushing sensation ('dumping') if the patient has a high calorie load. In terms of the effectiveness of surgery, Halmi, Stunkard and Mason (1980) reported high levels of weight loss and maintenance following surgery and Stunkard, Stinnett and Smoller (1986) indicated that after one year weight losses average at 50% of excess weight. Stunkard (1984) also stated that 'Severe obesity...is most effectively treated by surgical measures, particularly ones that reduce the size of the stomach and of its opening into the large gastrointestinal tract' (p. 171). More recently researchers in Sweden have carried out the large scale Swedish Obese Subjects (SOS) study which explored ≈1000 matched pairs of patients, who received either surgery or conventional treatment for their obesity (Torgerson & Sjostrom, 2001). The results showed an average weight loss of 28 kg in the surgical group after two years compared to only 0.5 kg in the conventional group. After eight years the weight loss in the surgical group remained high (average of 20 kg), whilst the control group had gained an average of 0.7 kg. The weight loss in the surgical group was associated with a reduction in diabetes and hypertension at two years and diabetes at eight years. This study indicated that surgery can be effective for both weight loss and maintenance and brings with it a reduction in the risk factors for cardiovascular disease. The surgical management of obesity has been endorsed by expert committees in the US (Institute of Medicine, 1995) and the UK (Garrow, 1997) and is recommended for those with a BMI over 40 kg m^{-2} (or >35 with complications of obesity), who have not lost weight with dietary or pharmacological interventions as long as they were made aware of the possible side effects.

Obesity surgery, however, does not only affect weight. Some research has also explored post operative changes in aspects of the individual's psychological state, such as quality of life, psychological morbidity and eating behaviour. In terms of health status and quality of life a series of studies have shown significant improvements, particularly in those patients who show sustained weight loss. For example, cross-sectional research has illustrated improved quality of life in surgical patients compared to control subjects (De Zwann et al., 2002; Ogden, Clementi, Aylwin & Patel, 2005), which has been supported by studies using either retrospective or longitudinal designs. In particular, in a large scale follow up of the SOS patients Karlsson, Sjostrom and Sullivan (1998) reported an improvement in health-related quality of life operationalised in terms of mood disorders, mental well-being, health perceptions and social interaction, and Boan, Kolotkin, Westman, McMahon and Grant (2004) reported improvements in weight related quality of life and physical activity. Similarly positive results have also been reported for psychological morbidity. For example, Holzwarth, Huber, Majkrazak and Tareen (2002) reported a decrease in antidepressant use following surgery, and Vallis, Butler, Perey, Veldhuyzen van Zenten and MacDonald (2001) and van Gemert, Severeijns, Greve, Groenman and Soeters (1998) reported a reduction in psychological functioning including depression and emotional distress. In terms of the impact of surgery on aspects of eating behaviour, however, the research shows a less consistent pattern of results. For example, some studies show benefits of aspects of eating behaviour, such as post surgical decreases in hunger (e.g., Lang, Hauser, Buddeberg & Klaghofer, 2002; Rand, MaCgregor & Hankins, 1987), binge eating (Boan et al., 2004; Lang et al., 2002), emotional and external eating and flexible control (Horchner, Tuine-breijer & Kelder, 2002; Lang et al., 2002). In contrast, however, other studies suggest that pre-surgical eating problems persist after surgery with patients showing either a return to loss of control over eating and binge eating (Kalarchian et al., 2002; Saunders, 2001) or the development of frequent eating, which has been labelled 'grazing' (Saunders, 2004). Bocchieri, Meana and Fisher (2002a) carried out a comprehensive review of much of the literature examining the impact of obesity surgery on psychosocial outcomes and concluded that in general 'the empirical evidence...seems to be pointing in a positive direction' (p. 164).

Research, therefore, shows that obesity surgery can result in weight loss and maintenance, and results in fairly consistent improvements in aspects of quality of life and psychological functioning. Surgery also seems to have a more variable impact upon aspects of eating behaviour. However, to date the majority of work in this area has been quantitative using pre-existing validated measures taken from other health problems. Such research provides useful insights into changes in pre-defined broad psychological domains and enables statistical predictors of success to be identified. However, it cannot provide detailed insights into the patient's own experience of obesity surgery as defined by the individual themselves. Furthermore, such research, by the nature of the statistical analysis used aims to minimise rather than explore individual differences. Two previous studies have used qualitative methods (Bocchieri, Meana & Fisher, 2002b; Glinski, Wetzler & Goodman, 2001) and have explored how patients describe the impact of surgery on their lives. For example, Bocchieri et al. (2002b) concluded that all patients not only highlighted many positive consequences of surgery and considered the process as one of being reborn but also described some life changes that generated tensions, which needed to be negotiated. To build upon this previous research, the present qualitative study aimed to explore how patients experience obesity surgery with a focus on both their quality of life and aspects of their eating behaviour. In addition, the study aimed to locate these experiences within the patients' decision to have surgery in the first place and their previous attempts at weight loss.

Method
Design
The study used a qualitative design with in-depth interviews.

Sample
Fifteen patients who had undergone surgery in the past four years were interviewed about their reasons for having surgery and their subsequent experiences. Fourteen patients had shown significant weight loss but two had regained weight recently due to problems with the banding. Their profile characteristics are shown in Table I. All patients have been given a pseudonym.

Table I Details of the interviewees

Name	Sex	Age	BMI at operation	Time since operation	Type of surgery	BMI now
Caroline	F	35	47	10 months	Gastric banding	36.14
Angela	F	37	50.4	10 months	Gastric banding	38.57
Emma	F	33	58	5 months	Vertical stapled bypass	42.38
Ellen	F	40	46.6	23 months	Gastric banding	41.11
Lucy	F	48	53.5	31 months	Gastric banding	51.0
Cathy	F	33	48.9	13 months	Vertical stapled gastroplasty	35.88
Jenny	F	25	45.8	8 months	Gastric bypass	31.12
Mia	F	48	39.5	13 months	Gastric bypass	29.75
Pat	F	43	42	12 months	Gastric bypass	32.04
Alison	F	46	48.2	32 months	Gastric banding	28.1
Ann	F	34	44.1	33 months	Gastric banding	43.12
Fiona	F	54	49	15 months	Gastric banding	38.56
Sonia	F	49	45.9	31 months	Gastric banding	26.62
Michael	M	41	47	10 months	Gastric bypass	28
Jane	F	50	46.2	4 months	Gastric bypass	33.55

Procedure

All patients ($n=22$) who had completed the questionnaire for a quantitative cross-sectional study of the impact of surgery on health status (Ogden et al., 2005) were invited to be interviewed and 17 agreed. Two were moving abroad so a mutually convenient time was arranged with the remaining 15. The interviews took place either at the patient's home or at the hospital clinic. All interviews were audiotaped and transcribed. The interviews lasted between 40 and 90 min. After 15 interviews it was felt that saturation had been reached as no new themes were emerging and similar stories were being told therefore no new interviews were arranged. Approval was obtained from the Hospital Research Ethics Committee.

The interview schedule

The interview schedule included open ended questions such as 'Why did you decide to have the operation?', 'How have you felt since the operation?', 'Has the operation changed how you feel about food?', 'Has the operation changed how you feel about yourself?'

Data analysis

The interviews were analysed using Interpretative Phenomenological Analysis (IPA, Smith, 1996). The transcripts were read and re-read by JO and CC to ensure familiarity with the data. For each interview a coding sheet was constructed. This sheet contained all possible themes and sub-themes for each interview. References to transcripts were recorded under each theme. From the individual summary sheets an overall list of themes was constructed. With continuous reference to the transcripts, connections across the list of themes were made. A table of themes with their various sub-themes was consequently constructed. All the verbatim transcripts were re-read to ensure that the themes were representative of the original material. Instances of each theme in the transcripts were recorded. Throughout the write-up process, themes and sub-themes were adjusted.

The IPA was chosen as it emphasises 'sense making' (Smith & Osborn, 2003) and enables an analysis of the individual's own experience and the ways in which they derive meaning from this experience whilst acknowledging the role of the researchers' own perspective. In the case of the present study it is acknowledged that whilst none of the researchers are either obese or have had surgery all had gained sufficient experience of obese patients through clinical and research work to believe that severe obesity was not a desirable condition. Furthermore, all were aware of the limitations of other non-surgical treatment interventions. In addition, as both the quantitative and qualitative studies progressed (Ogden et al., 2005) all researchers became increasingly impressed with the effectiveness of surgery and increasingly regarded surgery as a positive treatment alternative. It is therefore possible that such views influenced the nature of the analysis. However, although it was expected that surgery would impact upon health status and eating behaviour in the ways described in previous research, the impact upon the individual's broader psychological state and their sense of control (described below) was surprising.

Results and discussion

The patients described obesity surgery in terms of four broad areas; their personal weight histories, the processes involved in deciding to undergo obesity surgery, the impact of surgery and the impact of weight loss. These will now be considered.

1. Personal histories

People described their personal histories prior to having surgery in terms of weight gain, the weight loss methods they had used and weight cycling.

All patients described how long they had been overweight for and how their weight problem had developed. Some reported a clearly defined start to their weight problem. For some this was identified as pregnancy:

> 'I put on more of my weight when I had the children...I'm pregnant again so now I'm going to put on weight again'

(Cathy)

For others it related to illness and the inability to exercise:

> 'I'd been dancing all my life and I gave up dancing and my metabolic rate changed because of lack of exercise and I started putting on weight...then I broke my foot very badly and I got even less exercise and my weight piled on and then I had to go on insulin for diabetes...and the insulin just made me just bigger and bigger and hungrier and hungrier'

(Jane)

Others described how the process of weight gain had been a more gradual one:

> 'My weight did not come in one year. My weight came over thirty years'

(Cathy)

Many also described how they had been overweight since being a child:

> 'I was born overweight and I've always been overweight....I was a fat child and then a fat teenager and fat adult and my weight has never decreased it always just went up.... I was never a normal weight'
>
> (Jenny)

Patients also described the vast range of weight loss methods that they had tried:

> 'I went to Slimmer's World, Weight Watchers. I went to sessions at the Health Centre, I went to ... aerobic classes, I went to health centres, I started doing swimming.... I'd lost a little bit and then it went back on and more.... I went to one of those clubs ... and you're given tablets, these appetite suppressant tablets, I went for counselling'
>
> (Ann)

For all patients these attempts had resulted in some short term success but most described a long history of weight cycling:

> 'being on diets and yo yoing up and down, up and down and always getting heavier and heavier and heavier'
>
> (Ellen)

Patients therefore described their histories of weight gain, failed attempts at weight loss and weight cycling. The majority attributed their weight problem to factors such as illness, pregnancy or their genetics and illustrated a preference for a biological model of the etiology of obesity and one that shifts responsibility away from their own behaviour. This supports research indicating that, whereas as doctors prefer a more psychological model of obesity, patients endorse a more medical perspective (Ogden et al., 2001). The patients also provided detailed accounts of the vast array of interventions, which had been tried and had failed, which support the extensive literature on the failure of more traditional weight loss interventions (NHS Centre for Reviews and Dissemination, 1997). Throughout these personal histories emerges a central sense of a lack of control, with patients feeling out of control both of their weight gain and also of any subsequent weight loss.

2. Decision making

Patients also described which factors had resulted in them deciding to have surgery. Some of these factors reflect general motivation and the negative effects of being overweight whilst other reflect specific triggers to action.

General motivations. Patients described a range of experiences relating to being overweight that had acted as general motivations for them to seek surgical help. For many these involved the impact of their body weight on aspects of their psychological health. Some described how their weight affected their self-confidence:

> 'I was starting to lose confidence really because I felt so overweight and it got to a stage really where every time I met someone I thought all that they could see was this fat person'
>
> (Mia)

Many described how they felt 'miserable', 'depressed' and 'upset' by their weight:

> 'I was miserable for a lot of reasons but it was all to do with my weight, my weight affected every area of my life....I spent so many miserable years as a teenager....I missed the whole socialising thing because I was miserable with myself all the time...I was worried about people looking at me'
>
> (Jenny)

Some also described how they were unhappy with their body image and the way they looked:

> 'It was self esteem, how I looked. I couldn't buy clothes, I couldn't wear tights, I couldn't find my feet, I was wearing big shoes'
>
> (Ellen)

Some focused more on their physical health and the impact that their weight had on their general health and their ability to carry out their daily lives. Many expressed concerns about a range of weight related health problems:

> 'I was getting trouble, pains in my knees, in my back, in my groin and I could hardly walk at all'
>
> (Fiona)

Some described how their weight had limited what they could do:

> 'I couldn't walk very far, I couldn't bend down, I couldn't tie my shoe laces, I couldn't walk upstairs...if my shoelaces came undone I would have to wait until I could find something to put my leg...on to reach. You can't live like that'
>
> (Sonia)

Finally many patients described how they realised that they were not going to lose weight on their own and stated how they wanted to hand over control and responsibility for their weight loss to someone else. Some described their 'lack of will power', a feeling of 'having no hope', and 'feeling powerless':

> 'I knew really that the answer was with me but I just didn't feel that I could do anything'
>
> (Mia)

And many described the need for external factors to control their problem:

> 'I knew that nothing was going to change unless something stopped me'
>
> (Pat)

And:

> 'I just said to him (the GP) 'look I'm fed up with being like this. I want something done. I want somebody to do something. I need some medical help'
>
> (Angela)

However, one patient described how she had been reluctant to admit defeat over her weight for a long time and had believed that it was her responsibility to bring about a change:

> 'I felt that I internalised a lot of negativity…always thought that it was my fault that I was overweight and it was my responsibility to do something about it.…They [the GPs] consolidated the belief that it was my fault that I was the way that I was'
>
> (Emma)

Therefore patients described several general motivations including concerns about psychological and physical health. These motivations were conceptualised as ongoing and persistent and as influencing patients' decision to have surgery in a gradual 'drip drip' fashion. They operated by generating dissatisfaction with the patient's current self and created a gradual realisation that something needed to change. Such factors find reflection in the distal cognitions described by some decision making models as they are removed from decision itself but help to create a cognitive context in which the final decision becomes increasingly inevitable (e.g., Ajzen, 1988; Schwarzer, 1992). The patients also reveal a sense of being out of control of their problem and express a need to hand over control to someone or something else. This supports research indicating that whilst a more psychological self-help model of obesity may be associated with the success of such self-help strategies a more medical model prompts the search for medical solutions (Ogden, 2000; Ogden et al., 2001).

Triggers. In contrast to these background motivations, the patients also described a series of triggers that had directly prompted their contact with their GP or the surgeon. For many patients their decision had been triggered by the onset of symptoms.

> 'I was diagnosed with intracranial pressure so I was beginning to get more health problems.…When I went for the pre check…the doctor found a small heart murmur…and listening to the heart murmur I thought that's it. If I've got a heart murmur because of the weight already, that's why I did the operation'
>
> (Ellen)

And:

> 'It was to get rid of the diabetes. I wasn't interested in image…because I was getting to the stage where I would have ended up with gangrene in my toes, having toes taken off surgically…one toe in particular…was starting to go black'
>
> (Jane)

Such symptoms raised the salience of the threat of obesity and made patients more fearful of illness:

> 'My mum had diabetes, hypertension and angina and my father had diabetes hypertension, kidney failure so I'd thought I'd lessen my chances of getting those diseases'
>
> (Angela)

And some described how they had started to consider the real possibility of their own death:

'I felt if I didn't do something I would die or at least just be confined to a wheel chair or something'

(Pat)

One woman described a specific health crisis in the form of a desire to get pregnant:

'I wouldn't have been able to get pregnant naturally so that sort of spurred me on and then when I read about the operation.... I decided to go for it'

(Jenny)

Therefore patients described a range of factors that triggered their help-seeking behaviour. These triggers are more temporally linked to the decision than the background motivations and find reflection in the notion of proximal cognitions, which can have an immediate impact upon the desire to change or seek help (e.g., Schwarzer, 1992). Central to these triggers is the role of symptoms in raising the salience of the threat of obesity resulting in a subsequent realisation that immediate outside help is now required. For example, symptoms of heart problems or diabetes resulted in the severity of obesity becoming a personal reality and led to fears of illness and death. This finds reflection in the work of Leventhal and colleagues (Leventhal, Benyamini & Brownlee, 1997) who emphasise the role of symptoms in seeking help and argue that symptoms can often precipitate action, above and beyond the individual's health beliefs.

In summary, the decision making processes involved in seeking surgery included a role for background motivations and immediate triggers. This pathway towards surgery reflects a shift from seeing obesity as an unpleasant consequence of biology to a serious threat to health and life itself precipitated by the onset of symptoms. It also illustrates a concurrent change in patients' understanding of responsibility from a patient reliant upon self help to one with a desire to hand over control to the 'experts'. This in line with the patients' analysis of their personal histories, as it reflects a central role for control as they describe feeling out of control of their weight, out of control of any attempts at weight loss and express a desire to shift the control of their problem over to something outside to themselves.

3. The impact of surgery

The third area to emerge from the interviews was the patients' experiences of surgery that can be understood in terms of two distinct phases, the initial impact of the surgery involving feelings of shock and a range of negative side effects and a subsequent phase of adjustment involving changes in eating behaviour and a shift in their relationship with food.

Initial impact. Immediately after the operation, many patients described how they felt shocked at the change in themselves. Some described how ill they felt and how they wondered whether they had made the right choice:

'after the operation I did think, Oh my god, what have I done because I felt so unwell, I didn't quite realise the effect surgery would have on me.... It completely zapped me and I did think what have I done?'

(Mia)

And some felt that they were unprepared:

'I wasn't told that it was going to be the way it actually is....I feel a bit angry... because I don't think there was enough information given before the operation'

(Deidra)

Some also described how they couldn't eat anything:

'I really couldn't eat anything, I could eat maybe half a water cracker, nothing else.... It was really hard getting fluids down and I felt really unwell for about six weeks'

(Mia)

Some also described the immediate side effects such as 'pain', 'feeling sick' and 'feeling hungry'

'The pain is even worse than the sickness...you just get so cramped up, your stomach just really cramps up...it just will not go away, I have to lay down, I use a hot water bottle on my stomach'

(Caroline)

Most people described how these immediate side effects subside and how they adjust to their new capacity to eat. However, one patient described how she had to have the band removed:

'It had stopped me eating and drinking anything. I went for about three weeks....I went on a drip because I was getting very dehydrated and...it wouldn't work in the end, I had to have it out and since I have put on four or five stone in six months... which is worse than before'

(Ellen)

The initial stage was therefore characterised by shock and a range of negative side effects. One patient eventually had the band removed, and one was still in the initial stage at the time of the interviews. The majority of patients however described how after a few weeks some of the side effects subsided as they adjusted to their new stomach size and relearned how to eat smaller portions.

Adjustment. After the initial stage of shock, patients described a multitude of changes, which occurred as they adjusted to their new stomach size. The surgery makes the stomach much smaller and results in changes in eating behaviour, such as unpleasant consequences of eating and a reduction and change in the amount eaten. The patients described such factors and also analysed how the operation fundamentally changed their relationship with food in terms of the place of food in their lives, control and hunger.

Surgery reduces the size of the stomach and some patients described unpleasant consequences of eating. For example, one woman said:

'The only bad thing is the vomiting and I now I suffer from heartburn'

(Sonia)

One woman described how she had had to learn how to cope with being sick so frequently:

'You'd be sick all the time...where could I be sick? How could I be sick quietly? I developed how to be sick, you'd flush the chain and be sick at the same time'

(Ellen)

For many these consequences were a deterrent to overeating and offered a form of negative feedback. For example, Fiona said:

'If I eat too much I start to feel sick and full up and uncomfortable so it's not worth it now'

(Fiona)

A couple of patients, however, who had regained some weight, described how the negative consequences of eating had subsided resulting in overeating and subsequent regain.

'At the moment it doesn't seem as though there's a band there so that's why I've got to keep coming regularly to get it tightened because the volume that I can eat is a lot more than I used to'

(Ann)

The majority of patients also described how surgery had changed their eating behaviour using emphatic terms such as 'drastically', 'completely', 'utterly'. For most patients the surgery had resulted in them having to eat much less and many patients described how their food intake was 'ridiculously small' and involved 'tiny portions'. For example one woman said:

'I can eat half a sandwich, and if I eat a few crisps I start feeling uncomfortable so I have to stop'

(Pat)

However, several described how this was not the case for them and how they could still manage normal size portions:

'People told me…you can only eat little portions. That's not true.…I can eat a plate full…not mounded but…a reasonable plate full of spaghetti bolognese'

(Michael)

The inability to eat much was described by many as resulting in an increased need to make considered choices about what was eaten rather than simply eating whatever was available. For example, Cathy described how:

'I eat 'selective eating'…because I know my stomach can only take a little bit I have to choose very carefully what I'm gong to eat because if I take pizza by the time I bite the base I cannot eat anything else so I have to not bother eating pizza'

(Cathy)

Some also described how they found it difficult to find anything to eat that did not make them feel ill:

'Fried meat, like steak or pork chop, you know I can't eat that.…Occasionally I buy fresh fruit salad but I just I find it so difficult to chew.…I find it too difficult to digest'

(Fiona)

For about half the sample this careful selection, along with the negative feedback provided by the unpleasant side effects resulted in patients eating a more healthy diet. Some described eating diets lower in fat:

> 'I'm in the supermarket and I'm looking at the calories and I don't want that and I look at the fat content'
>
> (Michael)

Some described eating more healthily in general:

> 'I eat more salads, more vegetables, more pickles....I eat plates of boiled vegetables and I eat a lot of salads. I like that. I put horseradish with it sometimes. Sometimes chilli sauce....I don't have cake, I don't have chocolate...everything I eat now is either brown or natural'
>
> (Jane)

One woman also described how her own healthier eating habits had also influenced the rest of her family:

> 'We don't go to McDonalds anymore, we don't have pizzas. We used to go to Greggs and buy donuts and we don't do that....Me and my family are being healthy now'
>
> (Angela)

For others, however, the surgery had resulted in them eating less healthily:

> 'I actually love fruit and I used to eat a lot of fruit before but I can't eat fruit. I can't eat vegetables now...now I find that fattier foods I can actually eat better....I still think I like the same foods I just can't eat all the same foods'
>
> (Sonia)

This was also the case for one woman who had regained a lot of her lost weight:

> 'I couldn't eat bread, I couldn't eat rice, I couldn't eat meat. I couldn't eat any fruit or vegetables....I ate custard, yoghurts, rice pudding, sweet stuff....I could eat biscuits, cake, chocolate,...anything that was sweet well very sweet'
>
> (Ellen)

For many, these changes in eating behaviour were due to the avoidance of side effects:

> 'The food I like now is totally different to the food I liked before....I didn't have a sweet tooth before....I do tend to eat sweeter things because they are easier to digest...savoury things like meat, cheese rolls, bacon rolls, proper dinners like steak and kidney pie and vegetables, I find them difficult to eat....I loved salads before....I can't eat a salad now'
>
> (Fiona)

For some the changes reflected a radical shift in food preferences:

'My tastes are completely different.... The major changes are I detest any fried foods like McDonalds, fried chicken, bacon, I absolutely detest it... Everything I like is low calorie.... All the fatty food I just don't like them'

(Michael)

However, one woman described how because she had had to eat differently to avoid the side effects she had learned to like her new and healthier diet:

'I eat a lot more vegetables and salads now. I do like them now whereas I never used to eat any of them... you sort of acquire the taste whereas before I don't think I ever did try to acquire the taste'

(Angela)

Surgery therefore seemed to have a profound effect upon patients' eating behaviour. Many experienced unpleasant consequences to eating such as sickness and pain that provided a negative feedback system to discourage overeating. However, above and beyond a change in the volume of food consumed, patients also described some very specific shifts in food preferences and diet. However, these shifts were not consistent across all patients but seemed to be idiosyncratic with some preferring low fat foods and other preferring the opposite. Previous research has pointed to a detrimental impact of surgery on the patient's subsequent diet with a post surgical rise in a preference for sweets foods and dairy products. Such shifts in food preferences have mainly been explained in terms of physiological mechanisms and changes in the stomach's ability to digest and absorb food (Halmi, Mason, Falk & Stunkard, 1981; Shai, Henkin, Weitzman & Levi, 2002). The results from the present study indicate much greater variability in shifts in food preferences than previously recognised suggesting that a physiological explanation may not be the whole story. If patients are being forced into making careful choices about their food intake given their reduced capacity for food, such choices may relate more to their beliefs about foods and the meanings attributed to certain foods. The idiosyncratic nature of such beliefs and meanings would more readily translate into idiosyncratic food preferences than more systematised physiological changes. If one can only eat a small amount of food, then the careful selection of a food that has the most salient meaning whether it be pleasure, comfort, health or hunger would seem a sensible use of reduced stomach capacity.

In addition to changes in actual food intake, all patients also described how surgery had altered their relationship with food. Many described how before the surgery they had been quite preoccupied with food and many used words such as 'addiction' and 'obsession'. For example, Pat described how:

'I used to think about food all the time... before I got married.... I'd sit in bed and read recipe books thinking oh that sounds really nice'

(Pat)

All patients described how this was no longer the case. Some stated that food had no place in their lives and had become 'just eating' and 'just food':

'Food has no role in my life, it just has no meaning, I just don't think about it'

(Sonia)

Others described how they now had a pragmatic relationship with food relating to necessity and the practicalities of staying alive. For example, Angela described how:

> 'It's not the first thing I think of in the morning when I wake up its not the last thing I think of at night when I go to sleep....I eat to live whereas before I used to be Oh what can I have now what can I have now'
>
> (Angela)

For some this meant that they no longer enjoyed eating as it had become a very mundane activity:

> 'Before, I used to get pleasure out of eating. Now I don't get hardly any pleasure out of eating because you can't eat much'
>
> (Fiona)

For many, they still found food a pleasure and had learned to enjoy smaller amounts:

> 'I'm still a foodie, I'm still interested in food, I've always enjoyed food....I've become more selective about the type of food that I can eat'
>
> (Emma)

Central to this changed relationship with food was the concept of control. Many patients described a separation between their mind and their body and indicated a tension between the two in terms of controlling their food intake. Some described how 'the stomach is now controlling the mind': For example,

> 'My brain wants me to eat and my mouth wants me to eat, I'm still like that but my body doesn't
>
> (Fiona)

And:

> 'Now I feel that the control is taken out of my hands. I didn't have that control over my body because my stomach controlled everything. If I eat too much I'm sick so I don't have the control anymore...that's a good thing because I couldn't control on my own'
>
> (Jenny)

In contrast, others described how they felt they were truly more in control of their eating behaviour. These patients recognised that their stomach was imposing a limit on what they could eat but they felt that this imposed control had been internalised resulting in a shift in their psychological state:

> 'I can control the amount that I eat, the portions that I eat are small, they're satisfying....I don't obsess about food anymore....I think about what I'm putting in my mouth but not the point where it controls me. I feel that I am back in control of my body....It's about learning about how to eat from scratch and it's a new start for me'
>
> (Emma)

And some described how this renewed control made them feel 'liberated' and pleased with themselves:

> 'I've had to work with the operation. I mean I am proud of myself in that I could have just sat down and ate hundreds and hundreds of bars of chocolate…so I have worked at it as well'
>
> (Alison)

Given the reduction in food intake and the smaller portions being consumed due to a shift in food preferences and the avoidance of unpleasant side effects, it could be predicted that patients would feel excessive hunger. This was the case for two patients who described how they had not adjusted to their operation.

One woman had been taking a range of medicines described how she felt excessive hunger:

> 'The constant hunger…I'm literally sick with hunger.…I'm not interested in the food itself, I'm only interested in not being hungry'
>
> (Lucy)

However, in line with the reduced role that food now played in many patients' lives, the majority were surprised at how their hunger had subsided. For example, one woman said:

> 'The most incredible thing that has happened is lack of appetite…the hunger pangs have gone, I'm sated when I eat.…I know that my stomach is smaller so I know in my head, that if I have that food it will satisfy my hunger'
>
> (Emma)

Many also described they were having to learn to respond to their new found fullness:
For example, Pat described how she now could tell when she was full:

> 'I'll start thinking 'Oh I'm feeling full' and I actually listen to that whereas I didn't before, I mean I could just eat'
>
> (Pat)

And several described how they were learning new eating patterns and discovering what it felt like to be full:

> 'You feel hungry in your head because you know you haven't eaten a lot…it's just something to remember, that you might be hungry in your head but you're not hungry in your stomach'
>
> (Angela)

Given the unpleasant consequences experienced after eating and the reduction in food intake, it could be predicted that food would acquire an even greater importance in the patients' lives. However, paradoxically, the majority of patients described how surgery had resulted in a fundamental shift in their relationship with food in terms of the role of food, control and hunger with food and eating becoming increasingly related to a biological necessity rather than a psychological support. This supports previous research that has shown a post surgical reduction in hunger (e.g., Lang et al., 2002; Rand et al., 1987) but indicates that it is not only hunger that decreases but also a preoccupation with food and feelings of lack of control. Furthermore, the results suggest that although, for some, this increase in control was experienced as relating directly to their new stomach size, others believed that they had relearned to control their eating behaviour in addition to any physically imposed limitations.

4. Impact of weight loss

Finally, the fourth area described related to the impact of weight loss. These included changes in their confidence, body image, energy and general quality of life.

All patients who had lost weight described how their confidence had grown and how they now felt much more positive about themselves. For some this was an added bonus to a life, which had always been a happy one:

> 'I was a happy person before and I am now ecstatic'
>
> (Angela)

However, for many this represented a shift from feeling 'miserable', 'depressed', 'worthless' and sometimes 'feeling like killing myself':

> 'I didn't feel like a person, I felt like just one great big blob wobbling around, I hated myself absolutely hated myself...I just thought that I was worthless, worthless, not good to anyone. Often I felt like killing myself....Now I beginning to feel that I might have a future and I don't feel like killing myself anymore'
>
> (Fiona)

And many referred to the experience as a 'rebirth'.

> 'I feel more confident...I'm less embarrassed and not self conscious anymore and body language has changed...I can just lean back in my chair and talk....I feel like I've got a new life, new chances, new opportunities. I'm a new person....It is rebirth really'
>
> (Michael)

Some also described how they now felt that they were just back to being themselves and normal:

> 'I just feel normal now. I don't feel slim, I don't feel fat I just feel like average and that's all I wanted really'
>
> (Mia)

This shift in confidence was closely bound up with a parallel change in body image and in general a new found enjoyment in how both the men and women now looked.

> 'Before I was ashamed of the way I looked. Now I'm proud....I think I look....I feel and think I look good'
>
> (Michael)

Many also described a range of behaviours aimed at improving appearance that were often described as 'taking care' or 'making more effort'.

'I go to the hairdressers, I have manicures, I have pedicures, I look after my body totally differently'

(Sonia)

However, not all patients felt so positively and one woman felt pleased with her new body whilst at the same time believed that she had betrayed herself by having the operation:

'I do feel more attractive, more vibrant and more confident, more flexible. . . . I feel in a way I've self mutilated my body. I feel that it is totally against everything that I believed in, that I had to change my physical appearance by surgery because I wasn't happy. . . . I still feel like I've let myself down'

(Emma)

Therefore the majority of patients described improved confidence and body image. However, for many this was still an ongoing process and many described how they were still coming to terms with the changes. For many this adjustment process was highlighted by their confusion in clothes shops and their need to constantly rediscover how much weight they had lost:

'I can't focus on what I really look like because I still see myself in a size thirty dress. . . . I went out shopping with my daughter and I went to go into the same old shop, like the big shop, and she went to me, Mum you don't need to go in there'

(Alison)

The adjustment process was also highlighted by their continuing surprise when looking in the mirror:

'I still look in the mirror and see a fat person. . . . I still can't tally up the way I look and the person in my head'

(Emma)

The patients also described how their weight loss had improved their health status in terms of pain, mobility, illness and most commonly energy:

'I used to get home from work . . . and just fall in the chair in front of the telly, flick flick flick . . . now I can do the dinner. . . . I go to the gym. . . . I do the ironing'

(Angela)

Some also described how their weight loss had affected their work lives:

'I realised there was a life and I would be able to work because I was petrified of losing my career, my life, everything. . . . Now I'm well. . . . I've got self esteem, I've got confidence and the more weight I lose the better I feel'

(Jane)

And many also described how their relationships with others had improved and how they felt more 'respected', 'accepted' and 'valued'. In particular, many described how their relationships with family and friends had improved:

'I feel that I am able to be a proper mum to them and if they want to go to the park...
before it was I'm not going to the park I'm tired....I now feel part of the family
whereas it used to be you go with them'

(Angela)

Finally, the majority of patients described how they were pleased that they had decided to have
surgery. Some acknowledged that they had had initial reservations whilst adjusting to the side
effects but the majority felt that it was the best thing that they had ever done:

'I'd recommend it to anyone who was morbidly obese – it's a life saver'

(Jane)

And many wished that they could have had it done earlier:

'I would have got myself into debt to pay for it and now I say to anybody if you can
afford it, have it done. I wish I'd have had it done when I was twenty and that's the
truth'

(Alison)

Surgery therefore was described as improving confidence, body image and factors contributing
to quality of life. This supports much previous research that has indicated the positive effect
that successful weight loss can have and illustrates that surgery is seen by many of its patients as
a 'rebirth' (e.g., Boan et al., 2004; Bocchieri et al., 2002b; Karlsson et al., 1998). Further, the
present study illustrates that the transition towards a new more confident and positive identity
is a journey, which requires a period of adjustment often tempered by confusion and a tendency to resort to the old sense of self.

Conclusion

The present study aimed to explore the patient's experience of having obesity surgery and the
decision making processes involved in embarking upon this solution to a weight problem. The
results show that people decide upon obesity surgery as a result of repeated failed attempts at
alternative more traditional solutions and report extensive histories of weight cycling and failed
dieting. In addition, patients report the influence of a range of distal background motivations,
such as concerns about weight and health and the role of proximal triggers such as symptoms
that raise the salience of the threat associated with excess weight. Patients also provided detailed
accounts of their experiences of surgery that focused both on the consequences specific to
surgery and those resulting from weight loss. Surgery was seen as influencing eating behaviour
by enforcing a reduction in food intake through stomach size and the negative feedback offered
by unpleasant consequences, such as nausea and pain. This resulted in a range of new eating
preferences and whilst for some surgery had led to less healthy eating practices for others it had
resulted in a preference for healthier foods. In addition, patients described how surgery had had
a profound effect on their relationship with food making it much less of a focus, causing a
reduction in hunger and for many enabling them to regain control over what and how much
they ate. Finally, patients also described the positive consequences of weight loss including
renewed confidence, self-esteem, energy and overall improved quality of life. These findings
support much of the previous quantitative research that has reported changes in hunger, eating

behaviour and health status but suggest that the experiences of surgery are more varied and less consistent than previously described. Research, particularly that highlighting shifts in food preferences, has mainly drawn upon a physiological explanation emphasising changes in the stomach's ability to digest and absorb food (Halmi, Mason, Falk, & Stunkard, 1981; Shai, Henkin, Weitzman, & Levi, 2002). The variability highlighted by the present study suggests that a physiological explanation may not be the whole story. If one is forced into making careful choices about which and how much food to eat due to a smaller stomach capacity then it is likely that post surgical food preferences reflect those foods that have the most salient meaning for the individual. Accordingly, patient's eating behaviour and relationship with food post surgery may reflect the idiosyncratic meanings attached to foods whether it is pleasure, comfort, health or hunger at this particular time.

Central to all themes emerging from the interviews was the concept of control. Patients conceptualized weight gain as a result of uncontrollable factors and chose to have surgery through a belief that they were out of control of their weight and eating and through a desire to hand over control to an external force. Further, although the initial stage post surgery was characterized by a sense of shock, the majority of patients described how they adjusted to the physical limitations imposed by the operation and developed a new sense of control over both their weight and eating. This new sense of control appears to take two forms. For some, it took the form of an externally imposed control that was welcomed as a release from their previous sense of responsibility and ongoing battle with themselves. For many however, this reflected an internalization of control resulting in a new psychological state. In addition, this new state of mind appeared to generalize to other areas of life with many reporting not only feeling more in control over what they ate but also over their lives in the broadest sense. Over the past few years much has been written about patient self-control across a range of theoretical perspectives. For example, whilst researchers exploring the consultation have focused on patient partnerships, shared decision making and patient centredness (Coulter, 1999; Guadagnoli & Ward, 1998; Mead & Bower, 2000), within the psychological literature researchers have developed concepts, such as locus of control, behavioural control and self-efficacy as a means to capture this cognitive set (Bandura, 1977; Wallston & Wallston, 1982). Furthermore, within sociology, the terms power and empowerment have predominated (e.g., Lukes, 1974; Oakley, 1980). Although such terms differ in their disciplinary emphasis they all centre around the notion of control. In addition, they all emphasise the importance of patient choice in facilitating the development of control. Choice is seen as central if patients are to take part in shared decision making and if doctors are to offer a patient centred approach. Similarly, the absence of choice undermines self-efficacy and behavioural control and without choice a person is deemed powerless and unempowered. In contrast, the results from the present study suggest that the relationship between choice and control may not be this straightforward; by taking away choice obesity surgery may actually improve control. Some theoretical and therapeutic work in the area of eating disorders has argued that by relinquishing control of food intake to parents and/or a health professional, patients with eating disorders may find that they develop an improved relationship with food (Dare & Eisler, 1995). The present study suggests that this paradoxical impact of imposed control may also be apparent in other areas of eating related problems. Too much choice may at times be disempowering, whereas the removal of choice may help a person to reestablish their sense of self-control.

In conclusion, although obesity is most commonly considered a behavioural problem that should be managed through behavioural interventions, the results from this study suggest that a non-behavioural solution to obesity may be effective in causing not only weight loss but also a multitude of shifts in the patient's psychological state. In particular, patients show changes in their eating behaviour, a less complex and damaging relationship with food and report improvements in their general quality of life. And central to all these psychological changes is control. Patients chose surgery through a sense of lack of control and a desire to hand over control to an external force. In turn, by imposing a reduction in food intake and taking choice away from the individual, surgery paradoxically results in an improved sense of control not only over what patients eat and how they feel about food but also over all other areas of their life.

Acknowledgements

The authors are grateful to the hospital for access to their patients and to the patients for speaking so openly to us.

References

Ajzen, I. (1988). *Attitudes, personality and behavior.* Milton Keynes: Open University Press.

Bandura, A. (1977). Self efficacy: Toward a unifying theory of behaviour change. *Psychological Review, 84,* 191–215.

Boan, J., Kolotkin, R. L., Westman, E. C., McMahon, R. L., & Grant, J. P. (2004). Binge eating, quality of life and physical activity improve after Rou en Y gastric bypass for morbid obesity. *Obesity Surgery, 14,* 341–348.

Bocchieri, L. E., Meana, M., & Fisher, B. L. (2002a). A review of psychosocial outcomes of surgery for morbid obesity. *Journal of Psychosomatic Research, 52,* 155–165.

Bocchieri, L. E., Meana, M., & Fisher, B. L. (2002b). Perceived psychosocial outcomes of gastric bypass surgery: A qualitative study. *Obesity Surgery, 12,* 781–788.

Brownell, K. D., & Wadden, T. A. (1992). Etiology and treatment of obesity: Understanding a serious, prevalent and refractory disorder. *Journal Consulting and Clinical Psychology, 60,* 435–442.

Coulter, A. (1999). Paternalism or partnership? Patients have grown up and there's no going back. *British Medical Journal, 319,* 719–720.

Dare, C., & Eisler, I. (1995). Family therapy. In G. Szmukler, C. Dare & J. Treasure (Eds), *Handbook of eating disorders: Theory, treatment and research* (pp. 333–349). London: Wiley.

De Zwann, M., Lancaster, K. L., Mitchell, J. E., Howell, L. M., Monson, N., & Roerig, J. L. (2002). Health related quality of life in morbidly obese patients: Effect of gastric bypass surgery. *Obesity Surgery, 12,* 773–780.

Garner, D. M., & Wooley, S. C. (1991). Confronting the failure of behavioral and dietary treatments of obesity. *Clinical Psychology Review, 6,* 58–137.

Garrow, J. (1997). Treatment of Obesity IV: Surgical treatments. In *Obesity.* Blackwell: British National Foundation.

Glinski, J., Wetzler, S., & Goodman, E. (2001). The psychology of gastric bypass surgery. *Obesity Surgery, 11,* 581–588.

Guadagnoli, E., & Ward, P. (1998). Patient participation in decision making. *Social Science and Medicine, 47,* 329–339.

Halmi, K. A., Mason, E., Falk, J. R., & Stunkard, A. (1981). Appetitive behaviour after gastric bypass for obesity. *International Journal of Obesity, 5,* 457–464.

Halmi, K. A., Stunkard, A. J., & Mason, E. E. (1980). Emotional responses to weight reduction by three methods: Diet, jejunoileal bypass, and gastric. *American Journal of Clinical Nutrition, 33,* 446–451.

Herman, C. P., & Polivy, J. A. (1984). A boundary model for the regulation of eating. In A. J. Stunkard & E. Stellar (Eds), *Eating and its disorders* (pp. 141–156). New York: Raven Press.

Holzwarth, R., Huber, D., Majkrazak, A., & Tareen, B. (2002). Outcome of gastric bypass patients. *Obesity Surgery, 12,* 261–264.

Horchner, R., Tuinebreijer, W., & Kelder, H. (2002). Eating patterns in morbidly obese patients before and after a gastric restrictive operation. *Obesity Surgery, 12,* 108–112.

Institute of Medicine (1995). Committee to develop criteria for evaluating the outcomes of approaches to prevent and treat obesity. In *Weighing the options – criteria for evaluating weight — management programmes.* Washington DC: National Academy Press.

Kalarchian, M. A., Marcus, M. D., Wilson, G. T., Labouvie, E. W., Brolin, R. E., & LaMarca, L. (2002). Binge eating among gastric bypass patients at long term follow up. *Obesity Surgery, 12,* 270–275.

Karlsson, J., Sjostrom, L., & Sullivan, M. (1998). Swedish Obesity Study (SOS) – and intervention study of obesity. Two year follow up of health related quality of life (HRQL) and eating behaviour after gastric surgery for severe obesity. *International Journal of Obesity, 22,* 113–126.

Kral, J. G. (1995). Surgical interventions for obesity. In K. D. Brownell & C. G. Fairburn (Eds), *Eating disorders and obesity* (pp. 510–515). New York: Guilford Press.

Lang, T., Hauser, R., Buddeberg, C., & Klaghofer, R. (2002). Impact of gastric banding on eating behaviour and weight. *Obesity Surgery, 12,* 100–107.

Leventhal, H., Benyamini, Y., & Brownlee, S. (1997). Illness representations: Theoretical foundations. In K. J. Petrie & J. A. Weinman (Eds), *Perceptions of health and illness* (pp. 1–18). Amsterdam: Harwood.

Lissner, L., & Brownell, K. D. (1992). Weight cycling, mortality and cardiovascular disease: A review of epidemiologic findings. In P. B. Bjorntorp & B. N. Brostoff (Eds), *Obesity* (pp. 653–661). Philadelphia: Lippincott.

Lukes, S. (1974). *Power: A radical view.* New York: Palgrave McMillan.

Mason, E. E. (1987). Morbid obesity: Use of vertical banded gastroplasty. *Surgical Clinics of North America, 67,* 521–537.

Mead, N., & Bower, P. (2000). Patient centredness: A conceptual framework and review of the empirical literature. *Social Science and Medicine, 51,* 1087–1110.

NHS Centre for Reviews and Dissemination (1997). *Systematic review of interventions in the treatment and prevention of obesity.* York: University of York.

Oakley, A. (1980). *Women confined: Towards a sociology of childbirth.* Oxford: Martin Robertson.

Ogden, J. (2000). The correlates of long term weight loss: A group comparison study of obesity. *International Journal of Obesity, 24,* 1018–1025.

Ogden, J. (2003). *The psychology of eating: From healthy to disordered behaviour.* Oxford: Blackwell.

Ogden, J., Bandara, I., Cohen, H., Farmer, D., Hardie, J., Minas, H., et al. (2001). GPs' and patients' models of obesity: Whose problem is it anyway? *Patient Education and Counselling, 40,* 227–233.

Ogden, J., Clementi, C., Aylwin, S., & Patel, A. (2005). Exploring the impact of obesity surgery on patient's health status: A quantitative and qualitative study. *Obesity Surgery, 15,* 266–272.

Perri, M. G., Nezu, A. M., McKelvey, W. F., Shermer, R. L., Renjilian, D. A., & Viegener, B. J. (2001). Relapse prevention training and problem solving therapy in the long term management of obesity. *Journal of Consulting and Clinical Psychology, 69,* 722–726.

Rand, C. S., Macgregor, A. M., & Hankins, G. C. (1987). Eating behaviour after gastric bypass surgery for obesity. *Southern Medical Journal, 80,* 961–964.

Saunders, R. (2001). Compulsive eating and gastric bypass surgery: What does hunger have to do with it? *Obesity Surgery, 11,* 757–761.

Saunders, R. (2004). Grazing: A high risk behaviour. *Obesity Surgery, 14,* 98–102.

Schwarzer, R. (1992). Self efficacy in the adoption and maintenance of health behaviors: Theoretical approaches and a new model. In R. Schwarzer (Ed.), *Self efficacy: Thought control of action* (pp. 217–243). Washington, DC: Hemisphere.

Shai, I., Henkin, Y., Weitzman, S., & Levi, I. (2002). Long term dietary changes after vertical banded gastroplasty: Is the trade off favourable? *Obesity Surgery, 12,* 805–811.

Smith, J. A. (1996). Beyond the divide between cognition and discourse: Using interpretative phenomenological analysis in Health Psychology. *Psychology and Health, 11,* 261–271.

Smith, J. A., & Osborn, M. (2003). Interpretative phenomonological analysis. In. J. A. Smith (Ed.), *Qualitative psychology* (pp. 51–80). London: Sage.

Stunkard, A. J. (1984). The current status of treatment for obesity in adults. In A. J. Stunkard & E. Stellar (Eds), *Eating and its disorders* (pp. 157–174). New York: Raven Press.

Stunkard, A. J., Stinnett, J. L., & Smoller, J. W. (1986). Psychological and social aspects of the surgical treatment of obesity. *American Journal of Psychiatry, 143,* 417–429.

Torgerson, J. S., & Sjostrom, L. (2001). The Swedish Obese Subjects (SOS) study – rationale and results. *International Journal of Obesity,* May 25 Suppl 1: S2–S4.

Vallis, T. M., Butler, G. S., Perey, B., Veldhuyzen va Zenten, S. J., & MacDonald, A. S. (2001). The role of psychological functioning in morbid obesity and its treatment with gastroplasty. *Obesity Surgery, 11,* 716–725.

van Gemert, W. G., Severeijns, R. M., Greve, J. W., Groenman, N., & Soeters, P. B. (1998). Psychological functioning of morbidly obese patients after surgical treatment. *International Journal of Obesity, 22,* 393–398.

Wadden, T. A. (1993). Treatment of obesity by moderate and severe calorie restriction: Results of clinical research trials. *Annals of Internal Medicine, 119,* 688–693.

Wallston, K. A., & Wallston, B. S. (1982). Who is responsible for your health? The construct of health locus of control. In G. S. Sanders & J. Suls (Eds), *Social psychology of health and illness* (pp. 65–95). Hillsdale, NJ: Erlbaum.

Wilson, G. T. (1995). Behavioral treatment of Obesity: Thirty years and counting. *Advances in Behavioural Research Therapy, 16,* 31–75.

Rapkin, B.D. and Schwartz, C.E. (2004) Toward a theoretical model of quality-of-life appraisal: implications of findings from studies of response shift, *Health and Quality of Life Outcomes*, 2: 14.

Toward a theoretical model of quality-of-life appraisal

Implications of findings from studies of response shift

Bruce D Rapkin*[1] and Carolyn E Schwartz[2,3,4,5]

Address: [1]Department of Psychiatry and the Behavioral Sciences, Memorial Sloan Kettering Cancer Center, New York, NY, USA, [2]QualityMetric Incorporated, Waltham, MA, USA, [3]Health Assessment Lab, Waltham, MA, USA, [4]Division of Preventive and Behavioral Medicine, Department of Medicine, University of Massachusetts Medical School, Worcester, MA, USA and [5]DeltaQuest Foundation, Concord, MA, USA

Email: Bruce D Rapkin* – rapkinb@mskcc.org; Carolyn E Schwartz – caroln.schwartz@deltaquest.org *Corresponding author

Abstract

Mounting evidence for response shifts in quality of life (QOL) appraisal indicates the need to include direct measurement of the appraisal process itself as a necessary part of QOL assessment. We propose that directly assessing QOL appraisal processes will not only improve our ability to interpret QOL scores in the traditional sense, but will also yield a deeper understanding of the appraisal process in the attribution of and divergence in meaning. The published evidence for response shift is reviewed, and an assessment paradigm is proposed that includes the explicit measurement of QOL appraisal process parameters: 1) induction of a frame of reference; 2) recall and sampling of salient experiences; 3) standards of comparison used to appraise experiences; and 4) subjective algorithm used to prioritize and combine appraisals to arrive at a QOL rating. A QOL Appraisal Profile, which measures key appraisal processes, is introduced as an adjunct to existing QOL scales. The proposed theoretical model, building on the Sprangers and Schwartz (1999) model and highlighting appraisal processes, provides a fully testable theoretical treatment of QOL and change in QOL, suggesting hypothesized causal relationships and explanatory pathways for both cross-sectional and longitudinal QOL research.

Quality of life (QOL) assessment involves a class of measurement fundamental to many aspects of health care planning and outcomes research. It is relevant for assessing symptoms, side effects of treatment, disease progression, satisfaction with care, quality of support services, unmet needs, and appraisal of health and health care options. Patient self-report is the most desirable, and often the only way to obtain this critical information. Thus, accurate and meaningful measures of the various dimensions of QOL are vitally important. Here, we 1) review evidence from the response shift literature regarding different cognitive processes that influence QOL appraisal; 2) build upon the Sprangers and Schwartz [1] model, to develop a theoretically grounded measurement model that addresses the phenomenology of QOL appraisal and suggest methods of assessing this phenomenology; and 3) discuss how appraisal assessment can be incorporated in statistical and clinical judgment models of QOL, to provide a coherent and empirically-testable definition of response shift.

Reconciling inconsistent findings in QOL research

The importance of QOL makes it critical to improve and refine measures to understand patients' experiences of health, illness, and treatment. Unfortunately, pervasive paradoxical and counterintuitive findings raise questions about what QOL measures actually assess and how scores should be interpreted: people with severe chronic illnesses report QOL equal or superior to less severely ill or healthy people [2–8], and consistent disparities arise between clinical measures of health and patients' own evaluations [9–11]. Indeed, several studies show that health care providers and significant others tend to underestimate patients QOL compared with patients' evaluations [12–15]. In short, QOL measures do not consistently distinguish known groups, are often only weakly related to objective criteria, and show little convergence across measurement perspectives.

These inconsistent findings support the notion of underlying differences in the phenomenology of QOL appraisal between people and are a function of coping with chronic or life-threatening illness and other sources of stress [16]. Rather than reflecting lack of validity, measurement bias, denial, or willful distortion, these phenomenological factors may reflect individual differences and intra-individual changes in internal standards, values, and meaning of QOL [1,17]. Differences in QOL appraisal are part of human adaptation and inherent in all QOL measurement.

QOL can mean different things to different people at different times [18,19]. Indeed, many QOL measures have been specifically crafted to be as generic as possible to circumvent such differences (as discussed by Stewart and Napoles-Springer [20]). In contrast, methods to detect response shift phenomena have assessed individual differences and intra-individual changes in the meaning of QOL. As we argue below, QOL research has much to gain by using methods that encompass these phenomena. Theoretical and empirical work on response shifts in QOL support the notion that differences in appraisal enter into all self-ratings of QOL and shed light on the nature of appraisal processes, demonstrating ways that appraisal might be directly assessed.

Background on response shift

The concept of response shift is grounded in research on educational training interventions [21–25] and organizational change [26]. The original definition of response shift specified recalibration of internal standards of measurement [21–24] and reconceptualization of the meaning of items [26]. Sprangers and Schwartz [1] added reprioritization of values as a third aspect of response shift phenomena and proposed a theoretical model (Figure 1), revised and updated here (Figures 2, 3), to clarify and predict changes over time in perceived QOL as a result of the interaction of catalysts, antecedents, mechanisms, and response shifts. **Catalysts** (a) refer to health states or changes in health states, as well as other health-related events, treatment interventions, the vicarious experience of such events, and other events hypothesized to have an impact upon QOL (life events). **Antecedents** (b) include characteristics of the person, culture, and environment hypothesized to influence the likelihood and type of catalysts and mechan-

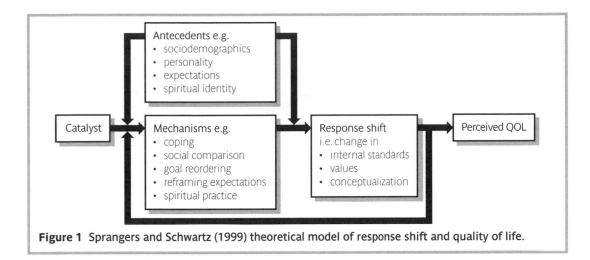

Figure 1 Sprangers and Schwartz (1999) theoretical model of response shift and quality of life.

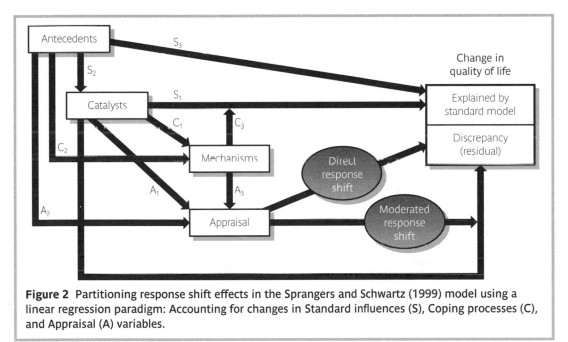

Figure 2 Partitioning response shift effects in the Sprangers and Schwartz (1999) model using a linear regression paradigm: Accounting for changes in Standard influences (S), Coping processes (C), and Appraisal (A) variables.

isms of appraisal. ***Mechanisms*** (c) encompass behavioral, cognitive, or affective processes to accommodate changes in catalysts (initiating social comparisons, reordering goals). **Response shift** (d) includes changes in the meaning of one's self-evaluation of QOL resulting from changes in internal standards, values, or conceptualization. This model posits a dynamic feedback loop to explain how quality of life scores can be stabilized despite changes in health status.

Although useful for hypothesizing relationships among key constructs relevant to QOL assessment, the model presents some problems of logical circularity as operationalizations of mechanisms or outcomes may be synonymous with operationalizations of response shift [27]. The model required expansion to distinguish these components from response shift and to differentiate response shift phenomena as initial responses to catalysts from those that reverberate or continue the process (feedback loop). Thus, in this paper, we attempt to resolve these problems by introducing new models incorporating constructs based on Schwartz and Sprangers'

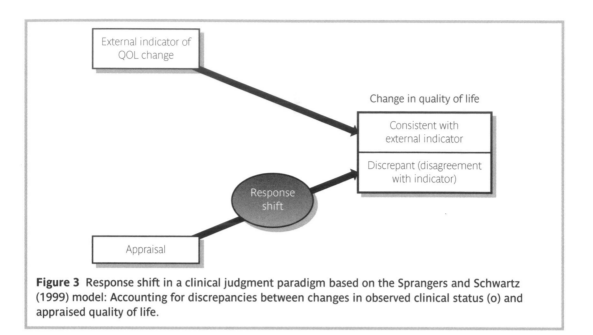

Figure 3 Response shift in a clinical judgment paradigm based on the Sprangers and Schwartz (1999) model: Accounting for discrepancies between changes in observed clinical status (o) and appraised quality of life.

work and direct measures of QOL appraisal processes to account for unexplained change in QOL ratings.

Recent empirical research documents the presence and importance of response shifts in both treatment outcome research and naturalistic longitudinal observations of QOL. Several studies suggest that patients make significant response shifts during treatment. Sprangers and colleagues [28] found changes in internal standards for fatigue in two subgroups of cancer patients undergoing radiotherapy: 1) patients experiencing diminishing levels of fatigue, and 2) patients facing early stages of adaptation to increased levels of fatigue. Jansen and colleagues [29] confirmed these changes in internal standards of fatigue and documented changes over time in patients' importance weights for one toxicity (skin reactions) associated with treatment. Multiple sclerosis patients receiving beta-interferon-1b demonstrated changes in the importance of various QOL dimensions over the course of treatment [30]. Adang and colleagues reported that pancreas-kidney transplant recipients retrospectively rate their pretransplant QOL lower when transplantation is successful [31]. Similary, Ahmed and colleagues reported that measures of improvement of health status differ in prospective versus retrospective assessment [32]. Hagedoorn and colleagues found that cancer patients who felt they were better off than others appeared to sustain their QOL under worsening physical condition [33]. Schwartz and colleagues [34] found that an apparently deleterious QOL effect of a psychosocial intervention was largely a function of response shifts in internal standards and conceptualization of QOL. Rees and colleagues found that recalibration response shifts are more likely in the first few months after a threatening event, that patients with more severe symptoms engage in recalibration response shifts longer than patients with milder symptoms [35], and that considering recalibration response shift produced a 10% increase in estimated QOL in prostate cancer patients [35]. Thus, intra-individual comparisons over time may not be comparable or sensitive to change unless they explicitly measure response shifts.

Response shift is also important for medical decision-making. Lenert, Treadwell, and Schwartz [36], using preference-assessment methods common in cost-effectiveness analysis to investigate interactions between preferences and health status, found that patients in poor health valued intermediate health states almost as much as near-normal states. Conversely, patients in good health valued intermediate states nearly as little as poor health states. Patients in poor physical and mental health tended to recalibrate their standards for comparing health states in a manner that downplayed current personal problems, and small gains were more valuable to disabled than to healthy persons. These findings are consistent with those of Cella and colleagues that, among cancer patients, relatively small gains in function and QOL have significant value, whereas comparable declines in status may be less meaningful [37]. Ultimately, cost-effectiveness of medical treatments may depend on the health status of persons rating preferences.

In addition to influencing our approach to outcomes measurement, response shift research also suggests reconsideration of standard QOL designs. Lepore and Eton [38] compared the fit of two theoretical models – suppressor and buffering models – for explaining the lack of association between physical health problems and reported QOL in men with prostate cancer. They used the then-test to operationalize recalibration response shift and a measure of primary life goal changes modeled after one used by Rapkin and Fischer [39] to assess reprioritization response shifts. The then-test, or retrospective-pre-test design, asks respondents to fill out the self-report measure in reference to how they perceive themselves to have been at the pretest [17]. Thus, the then-test asks for a renewed judgment about their pre-test level of functioning [17]. Suppressor analyses tested whether response shifts explained a null relation between negative health status changes and QOL. Buffering models examined whether the relation between changes in sexual/urinary problems and QOL was weaker among men who did or did not make response shifts. These linear regression analyses produced some evidence consistent with the buffering model. An interactive effect suggested that response shifts moderated the association between increases in urinary problems and changes in QOL. Specifically, response shifts appeared to buffer men from negative effects of declines in urinary function and QOL. They found no evidence for the suppressor model of response shifts. Thus, the response shift construct may help account for individual differences in QOL among prostate cancer patients who experience post-treatment complications.

Other recent research examines how an explicit consideration of response shifts might elucidate an understanding of QOL in various patient and caregiver populations. Richards and Folkman [40] examined response shifts among bereaved caregivers of men with AIDS from a coping perspective. Using qualitative data, they illustrated the processes through which response shift is achieved and maintained through meaning-based coping: marking loss, evolving new expectations with their own positive meanings, finding meaning in the ordinary, and creating global (deeply held core values) and situational (ordinary events of daily life) meaning for their caregiving experience.

Evidence for response shift has also been demonstrated in studies of the appraisal of health status. In a secondary analysis of cross-sectional data, Daltroy and colleagues [41] compared a measure of function based on observed performance (the Physical Capacity Evaluation, Daltroy et al., [42]) with a self-reported measure of disability (the Health Assessment Questionnaire, [43]) to test several response shift hypotheses, using stepwise linear regression and Fisher's Z transformation to compare correlation coefficients by type of recent loss (illness, fall, pain or stiffness, or perceived decline in function). Their data were consistent with response shift predictions. Specifically, people recalibrate their self-assessments of functional ability based on recent health problems. Additionally, physical performance testing provides salient information for subjects who have not experienced recent decline. Providing objective performance indicators can improve agreement between observed function and self-reported ability, perhaps by counteracting a response shift. They propose performance measures as a universal standard to correct for differential self-report of various subgroups. Further, patients might be reassured by a performance test that counteracts a response shift whereby they overestimate their disability, thereby possibly reducing health care expenditures by anxious patients seeking reassurance.

Finally, Rapkin [44] examined how the impact of life events on QOL were subject to reconceptualization and reprioritization response shifts associated with changes in personal goals in a longitudinal study of people with AIDS. Using idiographic assessment, people were asked to identify changes in personal goals most strongly associated with high life satisfaction. Individuals were free to mention any goals that mattered to them. Response shifts in self-appraised QOL were defined as discrepancies from some expected value that could be explained by direct measures of change in priorities associated with QOL (that is, change in personal goals). Expected QOL values in this study were operationalized using a regression model, taking into account initial QOL and changes in health status, stressful events, and coping resources. Rapkin's analysis attempted to explain discrepancies between observed and expected change in QOL by assessing whether people who changed their personal goals reacted to illness and events differently from those whose goals did not change. In statistical terms, QOL response shifts were operationalized as statistical interaction effects, with changes in goals amplifying or attenuating anticipated (main) effects of disease progression, life events, or treatments on QOL. Rapkin's findings suggested four distinct reprioritization response-shifts associated with changes in personal goals and concerns. People's reaction to life events and disease progression depended upon whether and how their goals changed. Perhaps more fundamentally, these findings provide direct evidence that people's goals and concerns continue to evolve during serious illness, perhaps up to death.

In summary, a variety of assessment methods of response shift confirms that QOL assessment involves a subjective process of appraisal, that individual differences in the appraisal process can affect observed QOL scores, and that individuals can change how they appraise QOL over time. Work on response shift phenomena is still at an early stage, but there is ample evidence to encourage investigators to include explicit methods for evaluating and integrating response shift phenomena in the next generation of QOL studies. Response shift findings point to the need for a broader QOL assessment paradigm that encompasses self-appraisal and meaning.

Definition of QOL based on appraisal

How then should one think about the appraisal of QOL? An individual's answer to any self-evaluative question depends upon this process. Individual differences or longitudinal changes in appraisal will affect how people respond to QOL items. Similarly, factors that correlate with QOL, including differences in personal circumstances, stressful events, disease progression, and interventions, also depend upon the criteria individuals use to evaluate QOL. Appraisal is a hidden facet in all measurement of QOL, and all studies involving self-reported QOL are influenced by appraisal.

In sum, any response to a QOL item can be understood as a function of an appraisal process. In other words, we view QOL scores as contingent upon several key variables related to appraisal. In order to describe QOL appraisal adequately, we posit at least four distinct cognitive processes suggested by research on QOL response shift and largely anticipated in Sprangers and Schwartz's original response shift model [1]. These four processes also relate to cognitive processes involved in formulating responses to surveys identified by Tourangeau, Rips and

Rasinski [45]. As Jobe [46] points out, there have been a number of variations on the four-process model. We have adopted our operational definitions of appraisal processes to correspond to psychological aspects of coping and adjustment intrinsically related to QOL appraisal. This is an important distinction: Tourangeau and colleagues emphasize psychological processes that arise in the survey situation [45]. Alternatively, we believe that cognitive aspects of quality of life appraisal are not merely a measurement issue, and may themselves become the focus of clinical interventions to help patients understand and think about their QOL in more adaptive ways.

First, QOL assessment induces a **frame of reference**, experiences individuals deem relevant to their response. This frame of reference depends upon the meanings the individual attaches to questions [47], as well as demand characteristics of the testing situation. This aspect of appraisal relates to the process of comprehension described by Tourangeau and colleagues [45]. Individuals implicitly understand that QOL items refer to certain aspects of their life, although what aspects are only partly determined by the overt item content. Questions about global well-being, general health, social functioning, or mood can each invoke a range of different issues and concerns idiosyncratic to the individual.

Second, in order to respond to any item, individuals necessarily sample specific experiences within their frame of reference. We posit a subjective **sampling strategy** that is at least in part determined by the item *per se* and the broader context of the QOL measure and the assessment situation [48–51]. Tourangeau and colleagues [45] discuss this in terms of retrieval of autobiographical information.

Third, each sampled experience is judged against relevant, subjective **standards of comparison**. This represents a special case of the answer-estimation heuristics discussed by Tourangeau and colleagues [45]. There has been considerable interest in how medical patients make comparisons to judge their health. Such comparisons may be based upon personal reference points [52], including prior functioning, lost capacities, and extreme experiences [53]. Observations of other patients, past encounters with illness, and communication from providers may also enter into appraisal [54,55]. Of course, individuals may select standards in a biased fashion, leading to criteria that are more or less demanding or strident, as Gruder [56] pointed out in the distinction between self-enhancing and self-evaluative comparisons.

Fourth, to arrive at a QOL score, individuals must apply some **combinatory algorithm** to summarize their evaluation of relevant experiences and formulate a response [45]. Individuals may combine their experiences in an additive and linear fashion, using subjective salience weights to increase or decrease the relative importance of different experiences [48,57,58]. However, the combinatory strategy may be more complicated. The significance of a particular experience may be determined only in contrast to other relevant experiences. Thus, individuals may place added emphasis on recent patterns or unusual events. Frequently repeated or continuous difficulties may be treated as a single experience and so receive less emphasis than if they were appraised as separate events.

It will be useful to depict these appraisal processes in more formal terms. As noted above, the prevailing assessment paradigm presumes that an observed QOL score at a specific time represents the sum of the latent true score plus random error, or $Q_t = q_t + e_t$. Although investigators rarely state this equation, this measurement model is the foundation for all research using QOL scales, including global well-being or life satisfaction and specific domains. It follows from our discussion of appraisal and response shift phenomena that there is much more to observed QOL scores than meets the eye. To understand better the nature of the latent variable q_t, the QOL true score at time t, we must we must "unpack" q_t to specify how different appraisal processes enter into QOL assessment. Given this formulation, a measurement model for q_t can be formally represented in terms of information about the appraisal processes that constrain and qualify QOL, as follows:

Equation I (induction): $\{FR_t\} \subset \{K_{kt}\}_{k=1 \to K}$

The induction of a frame of reference for QOL: A person's frame of reference for responding to a particular QOL scale or item is represented by the symbol $\{FR_t\}$, depicted as a set comprising one or more subsets $\{K_t\}$. These subsets can be understood as categories of experiences or events that the individual considers relevant to that QOL scale at that time. $\{K_{kt}\}$ stands for the $k^{\underline{th}}$-specific category at time t. In other words, Equation 1 states that the frame of reference may be understood as a set of categories of experience. Any individual's QOL rating is necessarily shaped and constrained by this frame of reference. A person thinking about QOL may consider a single category or multiple categories of concerns, including such areas as activities of daily living, emotional well-being, personal growth, social roles, and interpersonal relationships. If the frame of reference changes, we might expect the QOL score – or at least QOL correlates – to change. For example, if someone decides that work is no longer a priority, correlation between work-related events and QOL change should decrease correspondingly. Thus, the true QOL score at any given time is contingent upon $\{FR_t\}$, the person's frame of reference.

Equation 2 (identification): $x_{ikt} \in \{K_{kt}\} | S_{kt}$

Identification and sampling of specific experiences or events within that frame of reference in making QOL appraisals: The second equation indicates that QOL appraisal calls upon the individual to sample experiences from the various categories $\{K_{kt}\}$ that make up his/her frame of reference (from Equation 1). x_{ikt} represents the ith experience from the $k^{\underline{th}}$-category at time t. These experiences are sampled according to a strategy S_{kt}, represented as a constraint in this model. In other words, individuals consider specific experiences sampled from categories within their frames of reference and determined or constrained by some way of thinking that leads them to pay attention to some things and not others. Again, QOL true scores are contingent upon this identification process. Even if the frame of reference remains constant, sampling different experiences may lead to different ratings of QOL. Although the specific experiences individuals consider may change over assessment occasions, the strategy they use to recall or "sample" experiences must be articulated. For example, paying attention to "recent instances of pain" could lead to different ratings than considering "times when pain interfered with my activities".

Equation 3 (evaluation): $[A_t] = [X_t] - [O_t] | R_t$

Evaluation of sampled events or experiences against some standard of comparison: The third equation includes all the experiences an individual considers at time t (all of the x_{ikt} from Equation 2), arrayed in a one-dimensional vector [Xt]. Each experience is compared with some optimal situation or desired outcome according to the individual's standards of comparison at time t. These standards are represented as a vector $[O_t]$, which is the same dimension as $[X_t]$. Just as experiences are sampled according to a specific strategy (indicated by S_{kt} in Equation 2), standards for desired outcomes are derived relative to specific reference groups or external criteria, indicated as R_t. The difference between $[X_t]$ and $[O_t]$ yields a vector of appraisals of each experience under consideration at that time, $[A_t]$. Equation 3 makes it explicit that appraisal of the experiences related to QOL depends on standards that may be subject to change. For example, recent pain experiences might be compared to "the worst pain I ever had" or to "what my doctor told me to expect" or "how I wish things were". Clearly, QOL true scores are necessarily contingent on the standards an individual invokes.

Equation 4 (combination): $q_t = [W_t]'[A_t]$

Combination of evaluations into a summary appraisal of QOL: The fourth and final equation indicates that the QOL true score is the point product of the vector of appraisals $[A_t]$ premultiplied by a (transposed) vector of the same dimension $[W_t]'$. $[W_t]$ consists of the weights needed to combine appraisals across experiences. In other words, these weights represent a combinatory algorithm that dictates the relative impact or importance of specific experiences on QOL at time t. Equation 4 shows that any QOL rating is based on an amalgam of appraisals of different experiences that depends upon weights by their importance at a given time. For instance, a patient may give greater importance to recent instances when pain medications failed to provide relief, or on new sensations or locations.

In sum, this measurement model addresses the fact that QOL ratings are not intrinsically meaningful and can only be accurately understood through an underlying appraisal process. These four equations represent an attempt to identify and organize psychological processes involved in QOL appraisal to yield a definition of q_t as a contingent construct. The QOL true score is depicted as a direct function of weighted judgments of experiences in equation 4. This vector of experiences is identified according to equation 2 and evaluated according to equation 3. Available experiences are determined by the frame of reference in equation 1. This formulation allows us to specify this process in more precise terms. Thus, rather than speak of a true score in an absolute sense, QOL measures yield an estimation of $q_t|\{FR_t\}$, S_{kt}, R_t, $[W_t]$, or the true QOL score at a given point in time, contingent upon the individual's particular frame of reference, the ways that s/he identified and sampled relevant experiences, the reference groups and standards considered in evaluating those experiences, and the relative importance of each experience.

Measurement of appraisal constructs

As noted in our review of the response shift literature, many different approaches have been used to measure these appraisal constructs. This new measurement model conforms best with direct idiographic approaches that ask people to identify areas of concern, and then to sample, evaluate and prioritize salient experiences in those areas [59–61]. Such approaches literally ask individuals to "write" their own QOL items at each point of assessment. Although these techniques provide very rich data, they can be quite unwieldy to use and difficult to score. As an alternative, we have tried to develop more conventional self-report methods that directly assess parameters in the appraisal model. Such assessment is necessary to account for the effects of appraisal in QOL research, as we discuss below.

Appendix 1 (see Additional file: 1) provides the longitudinal version of the QOL Appraisal Profile (QOLAP) that we have developed to assess each of the appraisal parameters in this model. The QOLAP is designed to be used as an adjunct to standard QOL measures. Instructions presume that patients have just completed one or several such measures. The first item, based on questions used by Wernicke and colleagues [62], asks respondents to provide their perspective on quality of life. Items 2 through 7 are based on Rapkin and colleagues [44,61] assessment of personal goals. Item 8 asks people to highlight which of their personal goals (if any) were on their minds when they responded to QOL measures during the preceding portion of the interview. Together, these two sections provide a broad assay of an individual's frame of reference. Responses to these items are coded to identify the specific life domains and developmental themes of current concern to respondents. Occurrence of different codes can be tallied across different responses, to determine the range and variety of concerns mentioned. For example, an individual's goals may all pertain to health or family or mood, or they may pertain to multiple concerns.

Items 9a–9n are face valid questions, written to capture different implicit strategies people use to sample experiences. Items focus on the window of time patients may have considered, positive or negative aspects of experiences that may have made them stand out, clinically relevant features, as well as perceived demand characteristics of the interview situation. Similarly, Items 10a–10i provide a face valid assessment of possible comparison groups respondents may consider in rating their QOL. Following Suls and Miller's [63] classic work on social comparison theory, we tried to identify both historical and social reference groups that would provide for both self-critical and self-enhancing evaluations.

Item 11 provides a modified semantic differential to assess factors that respondents may use in weighing or prioritizing experience. Following Schwartz et al., [64] discussion of weights for individualized Quality-Adjusted Life Years (QALYs), we viewed the notion of "importance" as a multidimensional construct that may be related to several features of experience. For one individual, an unexpected event or experience may seem most important while others may be more concerned with typical or enduring problems. Importance may or may not be associated with other people's priorities. Positive events may receive greater, lesser or the same weight as negative events. This set of items tap these different possibilities by asking individuals to reflect on the factors that mattered most in their responses to the preceding QOL items.

Items 12a–12b represent a standard use of the retrospective pre-test [22,65,66]. This follow-up version of the QOLAP presumes that item 12a alone was asked at baseline. As we shall discuss below, studies of response shift have focused on the discrepancy between the original answer to 12a (QOL rating obtained at the time of prior assessment) and 12b (the retrospective rating of QOL at the time of prior assessment, obtained at the current assessment). Item 12c is included to help gauge, recall effects. Finally, item 12d gives respondent an opportunity to reflect on discrepancies in their answers, to provide insight into how their criteria for appraising QOL have changed over time. This is similar to approaches used in cognitive interviewing [46,67]. Although we expect that responses to item 12d will be particularly related to changes in standards of comparison, it is possible that the reasons given for discrepant ratings may reflect changes in the meaning of the term "overall health" (frame of reference) or the salience of different experiences.

Finally, items 13 and 14 of this follow-up measure ask people to consider their original verbatim responses to items 1–7 from the prior time of measurement. As item 13 demonstrates, it is entirely possible that people may use slightly different language to express similar concerns from time to time. People may also inadvertently omit concerns that were mentioned previously. We want to rule out these possibilities before assessing change in goal content. Finally, Item 14 asks people to reconcile earlier and later statements concerning QOL, as a way of assessing how their definitions may have changed over time.

At the present time, we are gathering QOLAP follow-up data from a cohort of Medicaid HIV/AIDS patients. This is an ideal sample to evaluate this measure, including an ethnically diverse mix of asymptomatic and symptomatic patients, all of whom are lower socioeconomic status, and approximately 50% with a significant history of substance use. Interviews are being administered in both English and Spanish. To date, over 200 patients have completed the base-line portion of the interview (Items 1–11 and 12a), in an average of 15–20 minutes. We anticipate reinterviewing 70–80% of this sample at six-month follow-up. Follow-up interviews are necessary to address our primary concern, the impact of response shift on the measurement of QOL outcomes.

Appraisal and response shift in the regression paradigm

In linear regression and all related approaches (e.g., SEM, HLM, GEE), the goal is to account for variance in change of QOL using a variety of different predictors. The model in Figure 2 includes several different families of hypothetical relationships that are frequently considered in QOL research, and shows how they are related to appraisal and response shift. It will be useful to consider each set of relationships in turn.

We refer to the first family of relationships as the "standard" QOL research model, whose primary hypothesis is that catalysts (e.g., changes in health, treatment, life events) are directly related to QOL (S_1). Negative catalysts are related to lower QOL and positive catalysts to higher QOL. The effects of antecedents (e.g., demographic factors, personality, cultural, and historical influences) on QOL are mediated through catalysts (S_2). For example, poverty may cause more negative life events leading to worse QOL. Antecedents may also be controlled as exogenous covariates (S_3).

The second family of hypotheses involves coping mechanisms. First, catalysts are hypothesized to encourage or disrupt coping mechanisms (C_1). There may also be hypothesized differences in coping associated with background variables (C_2). Mechanisms of problem-focused coping that reduce the impact of catalysts on QOL are included as moderators or buffering effects (C_3). Note that taking into account the direct, indirect, and moderator effects of catalysts, antecedents, and coping mechanisms on QOL effectively controls all of these variables, making it possible to isolate effects associated with appraisal in later steps of the model. For this reason, we have partitioned Change in QOL to distinguish variance associated with standard predictors such as overt health status and treatment from residual variance that remains after these familiar variables are controlled.

Our third family of hypothesized relationships concerns appraisal processes. The path from mechanisms to appraisal (A_3) indicates that coping mechanisms can lead to changes in the appraisal of QOL. However, catalysts (A_1) or antecedent variables (A_2) can also influence appraisal. Regardless of their cause, changes in appraisal may affect QOL ratings directly ("direct response shift" path) or by attenuating the impact of catalysts ("moderated response shift" path).

These different paths serve to demonstrate important distinctions and relationships among three broad constructs: coping, appraisal, and response shift. Emotion-focused coping represents cognitive behavior that individuals engage in intentionally, directed at changing the way that they understand QOL (or threats to QOL). Appraisal constructs represent the content of what an individual considers relevant to their QOL. For example, people may attempt to cope by reordering their goals. Appraisal assessment would explicitly describe how those goals have changed. However, changes in appraisal need not depend on intentional efforts to cope. Rather, such changes may be due to other mechanisms including habituation, trauma, or socialization to patient status.

In the context of a regression paradigm, response shift may be operationally defined in terms of residual variance in the QOL change score that can be explained by changes in appraisal, after taking into account standard influences. These changes in appraisal may be due to coping or other processes. Different appraisal parameters map to the different types of response shift identified by Schwartz and Sprangers [1]:

- changes in the frame of reference relate to *reconceptualization*;
- changes in strategies for sampling experience within one's frame of reference deemed relevant to rating QOL as well as changes in the factors that determine the relative salience of different experiences relate to *reprioritization*;
- changes in standards of comparison for evaluating one's experience relate to *recalibration*.

In the regression model, significant variance in QOL change associated with a given subset of appraisal measures would be taken as evidence for the corresponding type of response shift. In this sense, these response shifts may be considered "epiphenomena" that involve unexpected (e.g., unpredicted) or discrepant (e.g., residual) changes in QOL that can be explained by specific kinds of changes in the ways that individuals understand and appraise QOL.

Appraisal and response shift in clinical judgments and decision making

As noted above, measuring response shift involves accounting for changes in ratings of QOL that are discrepant from some expected value. In the regression model, the expected level of change in QOL is estimated statistically by adjusting observed QOL for catalysts and antecedents. Alternatively, investigators have also compared self-reported change in QOL to other external measures of QOL change that are independent of patient self-report – clinician judgment, performance tests, or family caregiver ratings. Even the popular retrospective-pretest approach [22] described above asks the individual to re-rate past QOL from an "independent" perspective. Discrepancies between self-reported and external criteria for QOL have also been used to identify response shifts. Figure 3 describes how measures of appraisal can be used in this context.

In this figure, as in the regression model, we have again partitioned change in QOL outcome variables. However, rather than using a residual score, the partition here may be derived by taking a simple difference score between observed and self-reported QOL (scaled using the same metric). The important feature in this model is that self-reported change in QOL is directly compared with an external measure of change. QOL discrepancy here reflects the difference between two different measurement perspectives.

Both external and self-reported measures of QOL are subject to the effects of catalysts, antecedents and coping constructs in the Sprangers and Schwartz [1] model. For the sake of clarity, we omit these paths from Figure 3. Figure 3 demonstrates that it is possible to determine whether discrepancies between external measures and self-reported QOL are explained by changes in the ways that individuals appraise QOL. If individuals' ratings of change in QOL closely map to the external measure, discrepancies would be small and there would be little variance left to explain. However, if a significant portion of variance in discrepancies can in fact be attributed to changes in appraisal, this effect would be evidence of response shift.

It is important to emphasize that the model presented in Figure 3 can be used to describe response shifts at the level of a single case. For example, a clinical interview may identify a patient who is very frustrated by a slow process of rehabilitation. Her rating of self-reported functioning may be very negative compared to an external performance measure. Over time, this patient's overt performance may change very gradually. However, this patient's subsequent ratings of QOL may improve as she adjusts her expectations of progress and begins to take satisfaction from small gains. This kind of change represents a (recalibration) response shift. As this example demonstrates, response shift cannot be considered merely a statistical artifact.

Conclusions

An adequate description of QOL appraisal is fundamental to our understanding of response shift phenomena. Findings from this proposed line of research should yield an approach to QOL assessment that surpasses the relatively superficial treatments of QOL currently available. Studies using comprehensive methodology to assess appraisal will help us to determine what should be included in briefer, more portable appraisal assessments. We envision studies of QOL outcomes designed according to the models presented in Figures 2 and 3, which use direct measures of appraisal to account for inter-individual and temporal differences in the meaning attributed to QOL scales.

This paper proposes that QOL response shift may best be understood as an epiphenomenon: individuals' ratings of QOL can respond to changes in illness, treatment and other life events in atypical (e.g., statistically different from some expected value) ways or in ways that do not gibe with external observation. Changes in QOL appraisal may be able to account for these discrepancies. This definition of response shift provides a way to unify and harmonize many of the different methods that have been used in the literature. Some studies have attempted to infer changes in appraisal parameters from changes in coping mechanisms. These are related but not identical (e.g., determining that one has coped by getting a better outlook does not, in and of itself, describe what that new outlook is). Other studies have used the retrospective pre-test to obtain a discrepancy score, but have not assessed the psychological reasons underlying this discrepancy. Still other studies have inferred changes in appraisal in a sample based on changes in the factor structure of items. Although such methods can be used to point to possible QOL response shifts, actual measurement of response shift per se requires direct assessment of changes in appraisal to account for discrepant changes in QOL ratings.

Elucidating QOL appraisal processes over time should lead to a more interpretable link between patient-reported indicators of QOL and external observers' (e.g., clinicians, caregivers) perspectives. Although we have focused this discussion around self-reported measures, this model of appraisal can readily be extended to clinician judgments, proxy ratings, and the like. The reason for discrepant scores between concurrent ratings of QOL measures from different perspectives ought to be explained by differences in perspective. Indeed, it would be interesting to observe whether discrepant scores between observers (e.g., patient and care giver) fall into line if they are first asked to come to consensus on what QOL appraisal criteria they will use.

Appraisal concepts and methods have bearing on the emerging interest in the use of cognitive assessment of survey methods applied to QOL research [46,67]. Cognitive methods attempt to determine the appraisal processes associated with a given item, scale or instructional set. Consistent with Sprangers and Schwartz' [1] original response shift model and the appraisal model presented here, cognitive techniques emphasize the assessment of psychological processes of comprehension, retrieval, judgment, and response. Cognitive methods have been used in a variety of research areas to arrive at self-report measures that have well-articulated, and widely shared meanings and to facilitate comparisons across individuals and over time.

However, there is an important tension between applications of cognitive methods to refine standard QOL measures and the methods presented here. Refinement of QOL measures to narrow the range of appraisals that they pull for may be quite valuable. Indeed, measures presented herein could be used as adjunct to cognitive interviews to determine how well this goal is achieved. For example, do most people answering a given QOL measure adopt the same frame of reference, rely on similar standards of comparison, or prioritize responses in the same (or at least, similar enough) ways?

There is a danger, however, that writing measures to constrict or constrain differences in QOL appraisals for the sake of comparability of ratings may obscure important aspects of individual experience. Methods discussed here and other cognitive methods provide a viable alternative to one-size-fits-all approaches. By including direct measures of appraisal parameters as an adjunct to standard QOL ratings, individual differences in cognitive processes can be detected and controlled in outcomes research. Indeed, in some studies, change in appraisal parameters themselves may be the main phenomenon of interest. In either case, both evidence and logic compel us to conclude that the study of change in QOL requires methodology to articulate the process of appraisal. By building on the Sprangers and Schwartz [1] model and explicitly integrating a formulation of QOL appraisal in both statistical and judgment models of QOL, we hope to pave the way for research that links response shift phenomena to other critical areas of research where self-evaluation comes into play.

Acknowledgements

We gratefully acknowledge Mirjam Sprangers, Ph.D. and Kathleen Wyrwich, Ph.D. for their helpful comments and discussions as the ideas in this manuscript evolved. We also want to acknowledge the participants in the University of Hull symposium on "Assessing Health-Related Quality of Life – What Can the Cognitive Sciences Contribute?" (December, 2000) and the subsequent special issue of *Quality of Life Research* (Volume 12, Number 3, May 2003), organized and edited by Ivan Barofsky, Ph.D., Keith Meadows, Ph.D. and Elaine McColl, Ph.D. These opportunities for scholarly exchange encouraged us to formulate the ideas in this paper in much greater depth.

References

1 Sprangers MAG, Schwartz CE: Integrating response shift into health-related quality-of-life research: A theoretical model. *Social Science and Medicine* 1999, 48:1507–1515.

2 Andrykowski MA, Brady MJ, Hunt JW: Positive psychosocial adjustment in potential bone marrow transplant recipients: cancer as a psychosocial transition. *Psycho-Oncology* 1993, 2:261–276.

3 Breetvelt IS, van Dam FSAM: Underreporting by cancer patients: the case of response shift. *Social Science & Medicine* 1991, 32:981–987.

4 Bach JR, Tilton MC: Life satisfaction and well-being measures in ventilator assisted individuals with traumatic tetraplegia. *Arch Phys Med Rehabil* 1994, 75:626–632.

5 Cassileth BR, Lusk EJ, Tenaglia AN: A psychological comparison of patients with malignant melanoma and other dermatologic disorders. *Am Acad Dermatol* 1982, 7:742–746.

6 Groenvold M, Fayers PM, Sprangers MAG, Bjorner JB, Klee MC, Aaronson NK, Bech P, Mouridsen HT: Anxiety and depression in breast cancer patients at low risk of recurrence compared with the general population – unexpected findings. *Journal of Clinical Epidemiology* 1999, 52:523–530.

7 Stensman R: Severely mobility-disabled people assess the quality of their lives. *Scandinavian Journal of Rehabilitation Medicine* 1985, 17:87–99.

8 Albrecht GL, Devlieger PJ: The disability paradox: high quality of life against all odds. *Social Science and Medicine* 1999, 48:977–988.

9 Kagawa-Singer M: Redefining health: living with cancer. *Social Science and Medicine* 1993, 37:295–304.

10 Padilla GV, Mishel MH, Grant MM: Uncertainty, appraisal and quality of life. *Quality of Life Research* 1992, 1:159–165.

11 Wilson IB, Cleary PD: Linking clinical variables with health-related quality of life: a conceptual model of patient outcomes. *JAMA* 1995, 273:59–65.

12 Friedland J, Renwick R, McColl M: Coping and social support as determinants of quality of life in HIV/AIDS. *AIDS Care* 1996, 8:15–31.

13 Sneeuw KC, Aaronson NK, Sprangers MA, Detmar SB, Wever LD, Schornagel JH: Value of care-giver ratings in evaluating the quality of life of patients with cancer. *J Clini Oncol* 1997, 15:1206–1217.

14 Sprangers MAG, Aaronson NK: The role of health care providers and significant others in evaluating the quality of life of patients with chronic disease: A review. *Journal of Clinical Epidemiology* 1992, 45:743–760.

15 Slevin ML, Stubbs L, Plant HJ, Wilson P, Gregory WM, Armes PJ, Downer SM: Attitudes to chemotherapy: comparing views of patients with cancer with those of doctors, nurses, and general public. *British Medical Journal* 1990, 300:1458–1460.

16 Leventhal H, Colman S: Quality of life: A process view. *Psychology and Health* 1997, 12:753–767.

17 Schwartz CE, Sprangers MAG: Methodological approaches for assessing response shift in longitudinal quality of life research. *Social Science and Medicine* 1999, 48:1531–1548.

18 Campbell A: Subjective measures of well-being. *American Psychologist* 1976, 31:117–124.

19 Cantril H: The pattern of human concerns. New Brunswick, NJ: Rutgers University Press; 1966.

20 Stewart AL, Napoles-Springer A: Health-related quality of life assessments in diverse population groups in the United States. *Med Care* 2000, 38(Review Suppl):11–102–11–124.

21 Howard GS, Ralph KM, Gulanick NA, Maxwell SE, Nance SW, Gerber SK: Internal invalidity in pre-test-posttest self-report evaluations and a re-evaluation of retrospective pre-tests. *Applied Psychological Measurement* 1979, 3:1–23.

22 Howard GS, Dailey PR, Gulanick NA: The feasibility of informed pre-tests in attenuating response-shift bias. *Applied Psychological Measurement* 1979, 3:481–494.

23 Howard GS, Millham J, Slaten S, O'Donnell L: Influence of subject response style effects on retrospective measures. *Applied Psychological Measurement* 1981, 5:89–100.

24 Howard GS, Schmeck RR, Bray JH: Internal invalidity in studies employing self-report instruments. A suggested remedy. *Journal of Educational Measurement* 1979, 16:129–135.

25 Howard GS, Dailey PR: Response shift bias: a source of contamination of self-report measures. *Journal of Applied Psychology* 1979, 64:144–150.

26 Golembiewski RT, Billingsley K, Yeager S: Measuring change and persistence in human affairs: Types of change generated by OLD designs. *J Applied Behavioral Science* 1976, 12:133–157.

27 Schwartz CE, Sprangers MAG, Eds: *Adaptation to changing health: Response shift in quality of life research* American Psychological Association: Washington DC; 2000.

28 Sprangers MAG, van Dam FSAM, Broersen J, Lodder L, Wever L, Visser MRM, Oosterveld P, Smets EMA: Revealing response shift in longitudinal research on fatigue: The use of the then-test approach. *Acta Oncologica* 1999, 38:709–718.

29 Jansen SJ, Stiggelbout AM, Nooij MA, Noordijk EM, Kievit J: Response shift in quality of life measurement in early-stage breast cancer patients undergoing radiotherapy. *Qual Life Res* 2000, 9:603–615.

30 Schwartz CE, Coulthard-Morris L, Cole B, Vollmer T: The quality-of-life effects of Interferon-Beta-1b in multiple sclerosis: An Extended Q-TWiST analysis. *Archives of Neurology* 1997, 54:1475–1480.

31 Adang EMM, Kootstra G, Engel GL, van Hooff JP, Merckelback HLGJ: Do retrospective and prospective quality of life assessments differ for pancreas-kidney transplant recipients? *Transpl Int* 1998, 11:11–15.

32 Ahmed S, Mayo NE, Wood-Dauphinee S, Hanley J: Response shift in the assessment of health-related quality of life (HRQL) post-stroke [Abstract]. *Quality of Life Research* 2001, 10:204.

33 Hagedoorn M, Sneeuw KC, Aaronson NK: Changes in physical functioning and quality of life in patients with cancer: Response shift and relative evaluation of one's condition. *J Clin Epidemiol* 2002, 55:176–183.

34 Schwartz CE, Feinberg RG, Jilinskaia E, Applegate JC: An evaluation of a psychosocial intervention for survivors of childhood cancer: Paradoxical effects of response shift over time. *PsychoOncology* 1999, 8:344–354.

35 Rees JE, Waldron D, O'Boyle CA, MacDonagh RP: Response shift in individualized quality of life in patients with advanced prostate cancer [abstract]. *Clinical Therapeutics* 2002, 24(Supplement B):33–34.

36 Lenert LA, Treadwell JR, Schwartz CE: Associations between health status and utilities: Implications for policy. *Medical Care* 1999, 37:479–489.

37 Cella D, Hahn EA, Dineen K: Meaningful change in cancer-specific quality of life scores: The direction of change matters. *Quality of Life Research* 2002, 11:207–221.

38 Lepore S, Eton D: Response Shifts in Prostate Cancer Patients: An Evaluation of Suppressor and Buffer Models. In: *Adaptation to changing health: Response shift in quality of life research* Edited by: Schwartz CE, Sprangers MAG. American Psychological Association: Washington DC; 2000.

39 Rapkin BD, Fischer K: Personal Goals of Older Adults: issues in Assessment and Prediction. *Psychology and Aging* 1992, 7:127–137.

40 Richards A, Folkman S: Response shift: A coping perspective. In: *Adaptation to changing health: Response shift in quality of life research* Edited by: Schwartz CE, Sprangers MAG. American Psychological Association, Washington D.C; 2000.

41 Daltroy LH, Larson MG, Eaton HM, Phillips CB, Liang MH: Discrepancies between self-reported and observed patient function in the elderly: the influence of response shift and other factors. *Social Science and Medicine* 1999, 48:1549–1561.

42 Daltroy LH, Phillips CB, Eaton HM, Larson MG, Partridge AJ, Logigian M, Liang MH: Objectively measuring physical ability in elderly persons: The Physical Capacity Evaluation. *American Journal of Public Health* 1995, 85:558–560.

43 Fries JF, Spitz P, Kraines RG, Holman HR: Measurement of patient outcome in arthritis. *Arthritis and Rheumatism* 1980, 23:137–145.

44 Rapkin B: Personal goals and response shifts: Understanding the impact of illness and events on the quality of life of people living with AIDS. In: *Adaptation to changing health: Response shift in quality of life research* Edited by: Schwartz CE, Sprangers MAG. American Psychological Association, Washington D.C; 2000.

45 Tourangeau R, Rips R, Rasinski K: *The Psychology of Survey Response* Cambridge: Cambridge University Press; 2000.

46 Jobe JB: Cognitive psychology and self-reports: models and methods. *Qual Life Res* 2003, 12(3):219–227.

47 Krause NM, Jay GM: What do global self-rated health items measure? *Medical Care* 1994, 32:930–942.

48 Wilson ME: A procedure for the determination of thresholds in impaired sensory fields. *J. Neurol. Neurosurg. Psychiat.* 1969, 32:419–422.

49 McGee H, O'Boyle CA, Hickey A, O'Malley K, Joyce CRB: Assessing the quality of life of the individual: the SEIQoL with a healthy and a gastroenterology unit population. *Psychological Medicine* 1991, 21:749–759.

50 Gonzalez-Calvo J, Gonzalez VM, Lorig K: Cultural diversity issues in the development of valid and reliable measures of health status. *Arthritis Care Res* 1997, 10:448–456.

51 McGraw SA, McKinlay JB, Crawford SA, Costa LA, Cohen DL: Health survey methods with minority populations: some lessons from recent experience. *Ethnicity & Disease* 1992, 2(3):273–287.

52 Allison PJ, Locker D, Feine JS: Quality of life: A dynamic construct. *Social Science and Medicine* 1997, 45:221–230.

53 Bernhard J, Hürny C, Maibach R, Herrmann R, Laffer U: Quality of life as subjective experience: Reframing of perception in patients with colon cancer undergoing radical resection with or without adjuvant chemotherapy. *Annals of Oncology.* 1999, 10:775–782.

54 Hoeymans N, Feskens EJM, Kromhout D, VanDenBos GAM: Ageing and the relationship between functional status and self-rated health in elderly men. *Social Science and Medicine.* 1997, 45:1527–1536.

55 Stanton AL, Danoff-Burg S, Cameron CL, Snider PR, Kirk SB: Social comparison and adjustment to breast cancer: An experimental examination of upward affiliation and downward evaluation. *Health Psychology* 1999, 18:151–158.

56 Gruder CL: Choice of comparison persons in evaluating oneself. In: *Social comparison processes: theoretical and empirical perspectives* Edited by: Suls JM, Miller RL. Hemisphere Publishing Corporation, Washington, D.C; 1977.

57 Blalock SJ, DeVellis BM, DeVellis RF, Giorgino KB, Sauter SVH, Jordan JM, Keefe FJ, Mutran EJ: Psychological well-being among people with recently diagnosed rheumatoid arthritis. *Arthritis and Rheumatism* 1992, 35:1267–1272.

58 Ramund B, Stensman R: Quality of life and evaluation of functions among people with severely impaired mobility and non-disabled controls. *Scandinavian Journal of Psychology.* 1988, 29(3–4):137–44.

59 Klinger E, Barta S, Maxeiner M: Current concerns: Assessing therapeutically relevant motivation. In *Assessment strategies for cognitive-behavioral intervention* Edited by: Kendall P, Holton S. New York: Academic Press; 1981:161–196.

60 Palys TS, Little BR: Perceived Life Satisfaction and the Organization of Personal Project Systems. *Journal of Personality and Social Psychology:* 1983, 44:1221–1230.

61 Rapkin BD, Smith MY, DuMont K, Correa A, Palmer S, Cohen S: Development of the ideographic functional status assessment: A measure of the personal goals and goal attainment activities of people with AIDS. *Psychology and Health* 1993, 9:111–129.

62 Warnecke RB, Ferrans CE, Johnson TP, Chapa-Resendez G, O'Rourke DP, Chavez N, Dudas S, Smith ED, Martinez Schallmoser L, Hand RP, Lad T: Measuring quality of life in culturally diverse populations. *J Nat Cancer Inst Monogr* 1996, 20:29–38.

63 Suls JM, Miller RL: *Social Comparison Processes: Theoretical and Empirical Perspectives* New York: John Wiley & Sons; 1977.

64 Schwartz CE, Mathias SD, Pasta DJ, Colwell HH, Rapkin BD, Genderson MW, Henning JM: A comparison of two approaches for assessing patient importance weights to conduct an Extended Q-TwiST analysis. *Quality of Life Research* 1999, 8(3):197–207.

65 Sprangers M, Hoogstraten J: Pretesting effects in retrospective pretest-posttest designs. *Journal of Applied Psychology.* 1989, 74:265–272.

66 Norman G: Hi! How are you? Response shift, implicit theories, and differing epistemologies. *Qual Life Res* 2003, 12(3):239–249.

67 Collins D: Pretesting survey instruments: an overview of cognitive methods. *Qual Life Res* 2003, 12(3):229–238.

Index